EVOLVING PERSPECTIVES ON THE HISTORY OF PSYCHOLOGY

EVOLVING PERSPECTIVES ON THE HISTORY OF PSYCHOLOGY

EDITED BY
WADE E. PICKREN AND DONALD A. DEWSBURY

AMERICAN PSYCHOLOGICAL ASSOCIATION
WASHINGTON, DC

Copyright © 2002 by the American Psychological Association. All rights reserved. Except as permitted under the United States Copyright Act of 1976, no part of this publication may be reproduced or distributed in any form or by any means, or stored in a database or retrieval system, without the prior written permission of the publisher.

Fourth Printing—February 2007

Published by
American Psychological Association
750 First Street, NE
Washington, DC 20002
www.apa.org

To order
APA Order Department
P.O. Box 92984
Washington, DC 20090-2984

Tel: (800) 374-2721; Direct: (202) 336-5510
Fax: (202) 336-5502; TDD/TTY: (202) 336-6123
Online: www.apa.org/books/
Email: order@apa.org

In the U.K., Europe, Africa, and the Middle East, copies may be ordered from
American Psychological Association
3 Henrietta Street
Covent Garden, London
WC2E 8LU England

Typeset in Goudy by EPS Group Inc., Easton, MD

Printer: Sheridan Books, Inc., Ann Arbor, MI
Cover Designer: NiDesign, Baltimore, MD
Technical/Production Editor: Casey Ann Reever

The opinions and statements published are the responsibility of the authors, and such opinions and statements do not necessarily represent the policies of the American Psychological Association.

Library of Congress Cataloging-in-Publication Data
Evolving perspectives on the history of psychology / edited by Wade Pickren & Donald Dewsbury.
    p. cm.
    Includes bibliographical references.
    ISBN 1-55798-882-X
    1. Psychology—History—20th century.   2. Psychology—History—19th century.
  I. Pickren, Wade.   II. Dewsbury, Donald A., 1939–

BF105 .E87 2001
150'.9—dc21

2001045909

British Library Cataloguing-in-Publication Data
A CIP record is available from the British Library.

Printed in the United States of America

CONTENTS

Contributors ix

Introduction 3

I. Methods of Historical Inquiry

Introduction 11

Chapter 1. History Without the Past 15
Thomas H. Leahey

Chapter 2. Epistemological Debates, Feminist Voices: Science, Social Values, and the Study of Women 21
Stephanie Riger

Chapter 3. The Crisis of Experimentalism in the 1920s: E. G. Boring and His Uses of History 45
John M. O'Donnell

II. Establishing the Discipline of Psychology

Introduction 59

Chapter 4. A Reappraisal of Wilhelm Wundt 65
Arthur L. Blumenthal

Chapter 5. Contributions of American Mental Philosophers to Psychology in the United States 79
Alfred H. Fuchs

Chapter 6. William James and the Art of Human Understanding 101
David E. Leary

Chapter 7. Testing the Limits of Sense and Science: American Experimental Psychologists Combat Spiritualism, 1880–1920 121
Deborah J. Coon

Chapter 8. Origins and Early Years of the American Psychological Association, 1890–1906 141
Michael M. Sokal

Chapter 9. The Origins of the Psychological Experiment as a Social Institution 169
Kurt Danziger

III. Psychology as a Natural Science

Introduction 187

Chapter 10. The Mythical Revolutions of American Psychology 191
Thomas H. Leahey

Chapter 11. From Machine to the Ghost Within: Pavlov's Transition From Digestive Physiology to Conditional Reflexes 217
Daniel P. Todes

Chapter 12. Whatever Happened to Little Albert? 237
Benjamin Harris

Chapter 13. On Prediction and Control: B. F. Skinner and the Technological Ideal of Science 255
Laurence D. Smith

IV. Psychology as a Social and Behavioral Science

Introduction 275

Chapter 14. G. Stanley Hall: From Philosophy to Developmental Psychology 279
Sheldon H. White

Chapter 15. The Mental Testing Community and Validity: A Prehistory 303
Richard T. Von Mayrhauser

Chapter 16. Gordon Allport, Character, and the "Culture of Personality" 325
Ian A. M. Nicholson

V. Psychology Between the World Wars

Introduction 349

Chapter 17. Unemployment, Politics, and the History of Organized Psychology 353
Lorenz J. Finison

Chapter 18. Organized Industrial Psychology before Division 14: The ACP and the AAAP 369
Ludy T. Benjamin, Jr.

Chapter 19. Cultural Contexts and Scientific Change in Psychology: Kurt Lewin in Iowa 385
Mitchell G. Ash

Chapter 20. On Publishing Controversy: Norman R. F. Maier and the Genesis of Seizures 407
Donald A. Dewsbury

VI. The Practices of Psychology

Introduction 429

Chapter 21. Clinical Psychology Seen Some 50 Years Later 433
David Shakow

Chapter 22. An Asocial Psychology and a Misdirected Clinical Psychology 453
Seymour B. Sarason

Chapter 23. The Return of the Repressed: Psychology's Problematic Relations With Psychoanalysis, 1909–1960 471
Gail A. Hornstein

VII. Psychology in the Public Interest

Introduction 495

Chapter 24. Assessing Psychology's Moral Heritage Through Our Neglected Utopias 499
Jill G. Morawski

Chapter 25. Placing Women in the History of Psychology: The First American Women Psychologists 527
Laurel Furumoto and E. Scarborough

Chapter 26. "The Defects of His Race": E. G. Boring and Antisemitism in American Psychology, 1923–1953 ... 545
Andrew S. Winston

Chapter 27. Recontextualizing Kenneth B. Clark: An Afrocentric Perspective on the Paradoxical Legacy of a Model Psychologist–Activist 575
Layli Phillips

Index 607

About the Editors 639

CONTRIBUTORS

Mitchell G. Ash
Ludy T. Benjamin, Jr.
Arthur L. Blumenthal
Deborah J. Coon
Kurt Danziger
Donald A. Dewsbury
Lorenz J. Finison
Alfred H. Fuchs
Laurel Furumoto
Benjamin Harris
Gail A. Hornstein
Thomas H. Leahey
David E. Leary
Jill G. Morawski

Ian A. M. Nicholson
John M. O'Donnell
Layli Phillips
Wade E. Pickren
Stephanie Riger
Seymour B. Sarason
E. Scarborough
David Shakow
Laurence D. Smith
Michael M. Sokal
Daniel P. Todes
Richard T. Von Mayrhauser
Sheldon H. White
Andrew S. Winston

EVOLVING PERSPECTIVES ON THE HISTORY OF PSYCHOLOGY

INTRODUCTION

WADE E. PICKREN AND DONALD A. DEWSBURY

The historical approach to the understanding of scientific fact is what differentiates the scholar in science from the mere experimenter. (Boring, 1961, p. 3)

The history of American psychology is embedded in the social and cultural history of the 20th century. For example, perhaps the most important Supreme Court decision of the past 100 years involved psychological research. On May 17, 1954, the U.S. Supreme Court ruled in *Brown v. Board of Education* that segregation in public schools was unconstitutional. As part of the supporting evidence, the justices cited the work of African American psychologist Kenneth B. Clark (1915–); he had indicated that both African American and White children suffered in segregated schools. Clark and his psychologist wife, Mamie Phipps Clark (1917–1983), asked children which of four dolls of various skin colors they preferred. Many African American children preferred the White doll. Clark's results suggested that there was a significant positive correlation between a child's racial self-identity and the degree of segregation in the school the child attended.

The implications of their findings for education were articulated by the Clarks in a series of publications and came to the attention of the attorneys of the National Association for the Advancement of Colored People (NAACP) in 1951. The Clarks were asked to assist the NAACP legal team in their court challenges to segregated school districts. The Supreme Court citation of the Clarks' work was the first time that psychological evidence had been used in the Court's decision. It remains one of the most important and controversial uses of psychology in American history.

The excitement and the importance of the history of psychology are exemplified in the story of Kenneth B. and Mamie Phipps Clark. You can read more about them later in this book. But theirs is not the only interesting, exciting, and important story in psychology. Like the best stories in any genre, good historical scholarship tells a great deal about the range of human experiences and the extent and uses of human knowledge. For example, at the end of the 20th century in the United States, most Americans assumed that the title "psychologist" referred to a mental health professional. Yet, the wholesale move of psychologists into the independent practice of clinical psychology did not begin until the 1950s and owed a great deal to the little-known efforts of two women, Leta Hollingworth (1886–1939) and Grace Kent (1875–1973). In 1917, Hollingworth organized the first professional association devoted to the needs and aims of psychological practitioners, the American Association of Clinical Psychology. However, she was not allowed to be its president because she was a woman. Kent developed in 1910 one of the first and most widely used psychological tests for the diagnosis of mental disorders, the Kent–Rosanoff Test. During her career she influenced many women and men who later were pioneers of the emerging field of modern clinical psychology, including David Shakow, whose account of his own career appears in Part VI on the practices of psychology.

The story of American psychology is not just about its triumphs; it is much richer than that. There are shameful episodes as well, whose telling allows us to see how psychological science and practice are best understood within a particular social and historical moment. Robert Yerkes (1876–1956) was one of the past century's most prominent scientists. His primate research and his role as science administrator stand as vital contributions to the development of American science. But Yerkes was a person of his time, as his interpretation of the psychological test data gathered from the mammoth testing of military personnel during World War I demonstrates. Results of the test data indicated significant differences among various ethnic and racial groups and an overall low average intelligence of American military recruits. As Yerkes saw it, the data were best understood as supporting a notion that intelligence was mainly due to inheritance (we would now say genetics). Overall, his interpretations reflected his belief in the heredity of intelligence and the superiority of some racial and ethnic groups over others. (To his credit, Yerkes did later recant some of these views.) Yerkes's beliefs were those of his same-race, same-social status peers and were unremarkable for their time as exemplified later in Part I's story of E. G. Boring's (1886–1968) delicate treatment of his students' Jewishness in his recommendation letters. These episodes indicate how the social and historical context influences science and practice.

As the stories told in this volume illustrate, American psychology has a rich and varied past that will, if we allow it, help us understand our complex present. Psychology circa 2001 nearly approximates the "blooming, buzzing confusion" that William James a century earlier claimed characterized the perceptual status of the newborn infant. There is a great diversity of approaches to both science and practice. The organization of psychology is also diverse, with three major organizations—the American Psychological Association (APA), the American Psychological Society, and the Association of Black Psychologists—representing well over 100,000 members. The APA is organized into 52 divisions that individually represent a broad range of interests across practice, science, and public interest domains. Such diversity makes it difficult to see the big picture of psychology and where and how it fits into the larger world.

The history of psychology, almost alone among current approaches, offers a comprehensive perspective on psychology as a science-based profession. The subdiscipline of the history of psychology is a relatively recent development, emerging in the mid- to late 1960s with the founding of two specialty societies, Division 26 of the APA, History of Psychology, and Cheiron, the International Society for the History of Behavioral and Social Sciences. Since that time, two graduate programs offering the PhD in the history of psychology have been founded, and various programs in the history of science have also graduated students who specialized in the area. Three journals devoted to historical scholarship in the social and behavioral sciences are thriving: the *Journal of the History of the Behavioral Sciences*, *History of Psychology*, and *History of the Human Sciences*. Along with attendant interest among psychologist–historians, the result has been an increasingly sophisticated corpus of scholarship in the history of psychology. This volume seeks to capture some of the excitement and depth in this new scholarship in the belief that it can help provide students and scholars with a historically informed perspective on both the science and practice of psychology.

A GUIDE TO THIS BOOK

While this book was being planned, we realized that there was significantly more quality scholarship than could be included. We take that as a marker of the health of the specialty. Because our primary aim is to provide students at the upper undergraduate and graduate level with information that will facilitate their understanding of the history of psychology, we chose to organize the volume into broad themes. The main criteria for selection of the articles for this book were quality and representativeness for each theme. It is hoped, as well, that our selection will prove a useful reference companion to scholars in the field.

This volume contains 27 chapters presented in seven sections. In Part I, we provide the reader with an introduction to historical methodology–historiography. Students in courses in the history of psychology often have no sense of how the methods of history differ from the methods of psychological research. Without at least a rudimentary grasp of these principles, students will not understand the basic premises or conclusions of the scholarship that follows. Failure to provide such an introduction would be comparable to neglecting to inform students in a course on basic learning theory about the research methods used to study learning.

The discipline of psychology emerged in a particular social and cultural context. It did not simply appear on the intellectual and institutional scene full-blown. To succeed, psychologists had to address critical issues of methodology, organization, and public relations and be able to differentiate their practices from those of neighboring approaches (e.g., philosophy, physiology, and psychical research). How were psychologists able to successfully find a niche for themselves in American scientific and professional life? What were their struggles, and with whom did they compete? In Part II, six chapters together offer substantive insight into how psychologists responded to these challenges.

The next three sections present historical scholarship focused on various aspects of psychological science and practice. The selection is meant to be representative, because a complete range of research and practice cannot be included due to space limitations. Learning theories have informed and guided much of 20th-century research in psychology. Ivan P. Pavlov (1849–1936), John B. Watson (1878–1958), and B. F. Skinner (1904–1990) remain important figures for psychologists today. The chapters in Part III offer historical insight into their lives and work.

Part IV offers examples of historical scholarship on psychology as a social and behavioral science. The three areas represented here are developmental psychology, psychometrics, and personality psychology. Although each of these areas would benefit from further historical research, these chapters indicate the rich potential of understanding psychology as a human science.

The period between the two world wars was one of great change and increasing social anxiety. Psychology in this period also experienced significant change. Standard textbook histories typically present the period as dominated by neobehaviorism and fail to address the heterogeneity of the discipline and the emerging professional practice of psychology. In Part V, four chapters illustrate psychology and psychologists in this period. The chapters provide nuanced histories that address issues of status, both personal and professional, among psychologists and their organizations, and we should note that the impact of the Great Depression on psychologists is an important text or subtext in these histories. The question of cultural style and its influence on psychological science is also addressed.

After World War II, clinical psychology emerged as the central professional practice of psychology and reshaped the public perception of the psychologist into that of a mental health professional. Of course, these changes have a historical context and have not gone undisputed within psychology. Psychoanalysis, although disparaged by many psychological scientists, proved to be an initially rich resource for the conceptualization and treatment of psychological disorders. The three chapters in Part VI provide a window into the development of clinical psychology and some of the controversy provoked by that development.

Since the late 1980s, the APA has had an entire directorate devoted to psychology in the public interest. Yet, American psychologists have a long history of interest in and devotion to social issues and causes. In Part VII are four representative examples of the history of psychology in the public interest: the moral project of psychology as represented by four psychologists' utopias; the struggle of women to find a place at the table of psychological science; the problem of anti-Semitism among psychologists until World War II; and a fresh perspective on Kenneth B. Clark, the only African American to ever serve as APA's president.

We envision various uses for this book. Most standard textbooks in the history of psychology present the accepted canon, or grand narrative, of the progress of psychological thought from philosophers to physiologists, to Wilhelm Wundt (1832–1920) and William James (1842–1910), the so-called schools of psychology, and post–World War II transformations of the field. There is much of value in this approach. However, recent scholars have pointed out that this oversimplifies the process and leaves much out. This has implications for the manner in which courses are taught and has resulted in some teachers of courses in history of psychology avoiding the use of textbooks in the course. This volume should prove useful to such instructors in organizing material and providing some structure without the constraints of traditional textbooks.

Other instructors feel responsible for making their students familiar with the prominent people and events in the field as portrayed in textbooks, although they recognize the constructed nature of this canon and want to enrich their courses to reveal for their students a hint of the complexity that exists at a deeper level. The present volume should be a useful supplement for such instructors. Of course, there are many instructors who are happy with standard textbooks but may want to enrich their own lectures or provide additional readings for students; this volume should be useful to them as well. Finally, we hope that there are readers with an intrinsic interest in the history of the field who will find pleasure and enlightenment in some of the best historical scholarship of recent years, even though they may have no courses about which to worry.

This volume is offered in the belief that the history of psychology is itself a viable and veridical way to understand psychological processes and phenomena. German philosopher–historian Wilhelm Dilthey (1833–1911) perhaps put it best a little over a century ago: "The totality of human nature is only to be found in history; the individual can only become conscious of it and enjoy it when he assembles the mind of the past within himself" (1976, p. 176).

REFERENCES

Boring, E. G. (1961). *Psychologist at large*. New York: Basic Books.

Dilthey, W. (1976). *Selected writings*. New York: Cambridge University Press.

I
METHODS OF HISTORICAL INQUIRY

INTRODUCTION: METHODS OF HISTORICAL INQUIRY

We begin this volume with a set of three readings dealing, in various ways, with issues of *historiography*—the methods used in the study of history. Like psychology, the study of history has a set of methods regarded as essential for solid work in the field. Although psychology students usually receive excellent training in experimental methods, they rarely gain comparable familiarity with the methodology of historical work. It is important for psychologists evaluating historical research or conducting studies of their own to gain at least some familiarity with these methods.

Although there are many individuals studying the history of psychology, it is possible to isolate three general types (Dewsbury, in press). The *dabbler* is a psychologist with a primary interest in some aspects of psychology and a secondary interest in history. The dabbler may teach a course in history and publish an occasional paper dealing with historical matters within his or her primary field but has only a limited commitment to history. The dabbler often publishes worthwhile summaries of historical facts but rarely asks significant historical questions. The dabbler becomes a *retread* upon becoming more interested in and committed to historical issues so that he or she makes historical work a primary focus, works to learn appropriate methodology, attends meetings of organizations devoted to the study of the history of psychology (e.g., Division 26, History of Psychology, of the American Psychological Association and the Cheiron Society), and publishes more substantial work in the field. The work of the retread is generally more analytical than is that of the dabbler. The *straight liner* does graduate study in a program in the history of psychology, the history of science, science and technology studies, or something similar and is committed to historical studies from the beginning. The straight liner often has a somewhat better grasp of methodology than even the retread and may be able to detect hidden aspects of the field that are so ingrained in the retread as to be unrecognized. The retread may detect subtle aspects of the discipline that are missed by the straight liner. All three can contribute to the field.

As the study of history became increasingly more sophisticated through the 20th century, the field that was dominated by dabblers early on has become dominated by retreads and straight liners. With this shift has come increased methodological sophistication. The so-called "new history" of psychology (Furumoto, 1989), in contrast to traditional approaches, has become quite influential in the field in recent years. The principles of the new history are illustrated in the first article, Thomas Leahey's "History Without the Past" (chapter 1, this volume). We were reluctant to include this article because it is so critical of one particular publication, which has many virtues, and because it refers to the work of several authors and two editors who have made many contributions to psychology. Nevertheless, this article was chosen because it is such a concise presentation of the principles of the new history. We know of no article in which these principles are stated as clearly and concisely as in this one. We hope that the reader can focus on the positive positions taken rather than on the criticisms of one work. Leahey levels six clearly labeled criticisms of the older approach as illustrated in this effort. The works of the dabbler are generally "Whig" histories, portraying the present as an inevitable consequence of progressive steps leading from the past. Related to this, they are "presentist," concerned with viewing history from the standpoint of the present, rather than "historicist," contextualizing events in the milieu in which they occurred (see Stocking, 1965). They tend to be "internalist," dealing only with events within the discipline rather than placing them in a broader context and often are "Great Man" studies, emphasizing the contributions of great people (who are generally male), great dates, and great ideas rather than dealing with influences of the zeitgeist. They tend to be historically ignorant, written by individuals who lack broad understanding of history. Finally, they tend to be historically shallow, dealing only with relatively recent history and then not digging beneath the surface of the major events in the field.

It should be noted that some historians working within "science studies" would go well beyond many new historians. Under the rubrics of a range of approaches from postmodernism to social constructionism, they would question the foundations of psychology, arguing against the idea of progress in science, emphasizing the complexities of analysis caused by our necessary reliance on our language, questioning the very idea of a human nature, emphasizing the extent to which science is culturally situated, and opposing realism and essentialism (e.g., Gergen, 1994).

Feminists have been both influential in and influenced by events in science studies. In chapter 2, "Epistemological Debates, Feminist Voices: Science, Social Values, and the Study of Women" (1992), Stephanie Riger explores these relationships. She adopts Sandra Harding's distinction among different kinds of feminism—feminist empiricism, feminist standpoint epistemologies, and feminist postmodernism—to illustrate the diversity of studies labeled as feminist. She explores the ways in which gender is a cultural product and places issues of power in sociocultural, historical, and political contexts.

Chapter 3, John M. O'Donnell's "The Crisis of Experimentalism in the 1920s: E. G. Boring and His Uses of History" (1979), provides an excellent case study of the way in which studies of history can be embedded within issues of scientific practice. At the same time that Edwin G. Boring (1886–1968) was becoming the most erudite and influential psychologist-historian of his generation, he was deeply embroiled in important debates concerning the conduct of scientific psychology. Boring supported pure, basic research in psychology at a time when there was growing pressure for the application of psychological knowledge after World War I. Boring's history was constructed with the purpose of demonstrating the value of his brand of pure psychology, untainted by applied concerns. Boring's was a history of *scientific* psychology written, as would be expected for his time, in a traditionalist mode, in support of a political agenda within psychology. His 1929 version of the history of *experimental* psychology became the primary history for the next 40 years or so and probably influenced at least some students toward basic and away from applied science interests.

Together, these three chapters provide a sample of some of the very complex issues of historiography that must be considered by students of the history of psychology.

REFERENCES

Dewsbury, D. A. (in press). Archival adventures in the history of comparative psychology. In D. Baker (Ed.). Akron, OH: University of Akron Press.

Furumoto, L. (1989). The new history of psychology. In I. S. Cohen (Ed.), *The G. Stanley Hall Lecture Series* (Vol. 9, pp. 9–34). Washington, DC: American Psychological Association.

Gergen, K. J. (1994). Exploring the postmodern: Perils or potentials? *American Psychologist, 49,* 412–416.

Stocking, G. W., Jr. (1965). On the limits of "presentism" and "historicism" in the historiography of the behavioral sciences. *Journal of the History of the Behavioral Sciences, 1,* 211–217.

1

HISTORY WITHOUT THE PAST

THOMAS H. LEAHEY

Traditionally, the history of science was written by scientists themselves. The tales they spun tended to be preoccupied with technical detail at the expense of setting scientific developments within larger social contexts. These works were smug and self-satisfied histories, viewing the past as a series of progressive steps leading to the supposed scientific wisdom of the present. Traditional histories of science thus congratulated the present at the expense of the past.

In the past three decades or so, however, historians have begun to write the history of science, painting a rather different picture of the scientific past than that found in scientists' histories. In the historian's view, science is a fallible human enterprise inextricable from the rest of human history. The new history of science has sometimes alarmed practicing scientists, who fear that nontraditional views of the history of their discipline will undermine their students' faith in science and destroy their scientific

Gregory A. Kimble and Kurt Schlesinger (Eds.) *Topics in the History of Psychology, Vol. 1.* Hillsdale, NJ: Erlbaum, 1985. 421 pp.
Gregory A. Kimble and Kurt Schlesinger (Eds.) *Topics in the History of Psychology, Vol. 2.* Hillsdale, NJ: Erlbaum, 1985. 441 pp.
Reprinted from *Contemporary Psychology*, 31, 648–650 (1986). Copyright © 1986 by the American Psychological Association. Reprinted with permission of the author.

talent (Brush, 1974). Nevertheless, the new history of science, including the history of psychology, has developed to a point where historians began to believe that the old scientists' tales had been eradicated, or at least confined to the first chapters of science textbooks, and that scientific history had been fully integrated with the other strands of the history of the world.

The two volumes of *Topics in the History of Psychology*, however, are here to remind the new historians of science that their battles are not yet won. Schlesinger states in the first chapter that "experts" in each field contributed chapters to these volumes, and with one exception, they commit every sin of the old, traditional history of science:

1. They are "Whig" histories. Just as the old Whig historians of the British constitution described the British past as a series of inevitable, progressive steps leading to the constitutional monarchy of the 19th century, so the contributors to *Topics* describe psychology's past as a set of inevitable, progressive steps leading to current scientific psychological wisdom. In the Whig view, the past is best seen as a series of "anticipations" of the present. In Matarazzo's chapter on the history of psychotherapy, for example, Maimonides and Shakespeare are congratulated for being "surprisingly modern-sounding" (Vol. 2, p. 240)—a truly ethnocentric, snobbish compliment.

2. They are presentist. Whig histories are always presentist, concerned with showing how the wisdom of the present was achieved; anything in the scientific past that does not conveniently fit into the present scientific canon is debunked as stupidity or pseudo-science or—as is frequently the case in *Topics*—is simply ignored. Diamond innocently expresses the presentist attitude of the Whig historian in his chapter, "A History of the Study of the Cortex": "In conclusion, if I have selected the pioneers wisely, then every research described here has made some lasting contribution" (Vol. 1, p. 382). He does not even mention Franz Joseph Gall and phrenology. Thus, a major event in neuroscience is overlooked, with the weird result of making Flourens's opposition to localization of brain function a reaction to Bell's hypothesis about nerve fiber specialization, not to Gall's advocacy of separate mental faculties located in distinct centers of the brain. In his introduction to Volume 1, Schlesinger tries to work the phrenologists in, but is led by Diamond's history to imply that Gall and phrenology *followed* Bell, whereas in fact Gall stated his basic ideas several years before Bell's work on the spinal nerves.

3. They are internalist. Virtually no attempt is made to place the history of psychology in any context larger than that of psychology's technical problems. The result is a tunnel vision of psychology's past, cutting it off completely from the rest of human history and ignoring the effects of social changes on the course of psychology's development. The new history of science is externalist, viewing scientific problem solving from the standpoint of cultural and social change.
4. They are "Great Man" histories. Throughout, we are told that some historical figure or other was a "giant," implying that he (there are no female "giants") stood apart from his times and single-handedly remade or created a field of psychology. The new history of science favors zeitgeist interpretations of history.
5. They are historically ignorant. In many chapters, for example, the hoary old notion of the Middle Ages as the "Dark Ages" is trotted out, and we are told that people were dirty, irrational, and ignorant in the centuries between Rome and the Renaissance. This picture has been thoroughly discredited for over half a century and has no place in any responsible history of the West. Even in the early Middle Ages, when, it must be acknowledged, philosophy and science were at a low ebb in Christendom, new technologies were invented. For example, the heavy plow and the shoulder harness for draught animals were invented, so that agriculture could spread from the light soils of the Mediterranean to the heavy soils of central Europe. The cathedrals of the high Middle Ages were not built by men and women ignorant of engineering principles. The works of the classical past began to be recovered centuries before the Renaissance. To say, as does Cooper in his chapter on comparative psychology and ethology, that Aristotle was one of the sources of the medieval church's "claim to infallibility" (Vol. 1, p. 139) is absurd. The introduction of Aristotle's naturalistic writings in the 13th century was a major reason for the dissolution of the medieval worldview, founded as it was on Christianized neo-Platonism. The Inquisition began in the postmedieval period. As for the contributors' vaunted classical philosophers and their beloved Renaissance, we must remember that the glory of Greece and the grandeur of Rome were built on slave economies and that the Renaissance was pervaded by Hermetic occultism of the most fantastic kind.

The new history of psychology is almost completely ignored by the authors assembled in *Topics*. Of 1,236 references (including duplications) in all of the chapters, only 119 (9.6%) are to works of history, and most of these are to Boring's traditional *History of Experimental Psychology* or to works like those in the present volumes. There are only 23 (1.9%) references to articles in history journals, including the *Journal of the History of the Behavioral Sciences*. Thirteen of the 19 chapters contain no such references at all.

6. They are historically shallow in two senses. The authors skate over the past before the 19th century, seeming to find before 1800 mostly ignorance worthy of ignoring, and began their stories about a century ago. At the same time, the authors do not dig beneath the surface of psychological discoveries and theories. They completely fail to seek out the hidden roots of psychological ideas in philosophies and social contexts taken for granted and fail to think seriously or reflect on psychology's intimate relations with society. So, in his chapter on the history of testing, Dahlstrom happily writes that "virtually every person in the Western world has by now had some contact with a psychological test" (Vol. 2, p. 107); Dahlstrom is an unintended ironist, because many people, such as high school seniors, feel terrified by tests (Owen, 1985).

Topics in the History of Psychology is history without the past. Not only is much of psychology's past ignored, but more important, the chapters provide no sense of the past, no sense of what it was like to be a philosopher, a physiologist, or a psychologist before the present. Thinkers and researchers of the past are treated as our contemporaries working on contemporary problems; the only way to tell these chapters apart from contemporary literature reviews such as the *Annual Review of Psychology* is that some of the references are a century or two old. The past does not live in these chapters; it is excluded from them.

The honorable exception to the dull and cramped histories that fill the two volumes are the two chapters on psychopathology by Winifred and Brendan Maher. If the other chapters are models of the old history of science, then these are models of the new. Presentism is eschewed and Whig notions, debunked. For example, the Mahers show that contrary to what psychologists' histories teach, ancient peoples practiced skull trephining not to release evil spirits but to remove bone particles from the brain resulting from depressed skull fractures. They point out that witchcraft persecutions should not be regarded as persecution of the mad and that they mostly occurred in the Renaissance, not the Middle Ages. They set the study of abnormal psychology squarely in the social history of the past. Of all of the chapters in the volumes under review, only these two represent history in any serious sense.

There are some remarkable omissions from the Whig histories, omissions of embarrassing moments or ideas that do not square with an author's sense of the field today. The chapter on behavior genetics (Schlesinger) says nothing about eugenics. The chapter on testing (Dahlstrom) contains only a cryptic allusion to the work and frauds of Sir Cyril Burt; he is not even named as the victim of "*ad hominem* attacks" (Vol. 2, p. 104, italics added). Dember and Bagwell forget Gibson in their chapter on perception. The chapter on psychotherapy (Matarazzo) fails to discuss Eysenck's famous psychotherapy outcome study or the resulting debate over the efficacy of psychotherapy, surely a major event in the history of that field.

Errors the new historians of psychology have corrected are repeated. The myth of a lineage of British Empiricism is told in several chapters, and Locke is consistently made out to be more radically empiricist and associationist than he in fact was. Several times—despite repeated publications showing the contrary—Wundt is described as an empiricist of the British mold, and the structuralism of Titchener is equated to Wundt's psychology. Watson and Rayner's Little Albert study is again misdescribed, despite prominent publications concerning textbook errors about the experiment. Kimble's introduction to Volume 2 asserts that Piaget was a maturationist, despite Piaget's well-known pleas to the contrary. Notwithstanding Smith's publications and presentations, the influence of logical positivism on Hull and Tolman is several times overstated. Perhaps the most curious error concerns Beach's well-known paper, "The Snark Was a Boojum." The reference is given correctly in Cooper's chapter on comparative psychology (i.e., *American Psychologist*, 1950, 5, 115–124), but in his introduction to Volume 1, Schlesinger twice lists the title as "The Snark Is a *Beejum*" and gives the reference as *American Psychologist*, 1960, 35 (which is the volume number for 1980), 1–18 (there is a Beach paper in the 1960 volume of these pages, on species-specific behavior), suggesting that Schlesinger has not read Lewis Carroll's *The Hunting of the Snark*, Beach's paper, or even the relevant chapter in his own edited volume!

The final puzzle of these two volumes is why they were written. Scientists who still want traditional histories of psychology in the Whig mold will find more convenient ones in the one volume collection edited by Hearst (1979), and also published by Erlbaum, *A Century of Experimental Psychology*. In their preface, Kimble and Schlesinger envision a "capstone course" for psychology majors, using *Topics*—at a cost of $80!—and a good introductory book as texts, which will give students "historical perspective" (Vol. 1, p. xii) on psychology. It should be obvious that historical perspective is exactly the thing students won't get from this two-volume set. At best, Kimble and Schlesinger's capstone course would be introductory psychology all over again with some old references thrown in. Gleitman's (1986) introductory *Psychology* would do a better job all by itself. Moreover, using *Topics* for such a course would be most difficult, because the chapters are written at wildly different levels. Matarazzo's chapter on psychotherapy could be read and understood by someone with little or no psychology background; Webb's chapter on sleep and dreaming is a useful summary for the undergraduate, whereas Riggs's chapter on vision is written at a professional level comprehensible only to near specialists in the field.

In sum, it is difficult to find any raison d'être for these two volumes. At best, they are a highly selective *Annual Review of Psychology* with old references. At worst they present a seriously distorted view of psychology's history, omitting or misrepresenting significant events and divorcing the history of psychology from the rest of the history of the world.

REFERENCES

Brush, S. G. (1974). Should the history of psychology be rated X? *Science, 183*, 1164–1172.

Gleitman, H. (1986). *Psychology* (2nd ed.). New York: Norton.

Hearst, E. (Ed.). (1979). *A century of experimental psychology*. Hillsdale, NJ: Erlbaum.

Owen, D. (1985). *None of the above: Behind the myth of scholastic aptitude*. Boston: Houghton Mifflin.

2

EPISTEMOLOGICAL DEBATES, FEMINIST VOICES: SCIENCE, SOCIAL VALUES, AND THE STUDY OF WOMEN

STEPHANIE RIGER

Modern scientific methods, invented in the 16th century, were not only a stunning technical innovation, but a moral and political one as well, replacing the sacred authority of the Church with science as the ultimate arbiter of truth (Grant, 1987). Unlike medieval inquiry, modern science conceives itself as a search for knowledge free of moral, political, and social values. The application of scientific methods to the study of

---

Michael S. Pallak served as action editor for this article.

The use of first names herein is intended to highlight the contributions of women to psychology. I am grateful to Dan A. Lewis for comments and discussion on numerous iterations of this article; to Marilyn Yalom, Karen Offen, and other members of the Affiliated and Visiting Scholars Seminar of the Institute for Research on Women and Gender of Stanford University; to Sandra Bartky, Cynthia Fuchs Epstein, Christopher Keys, Jane Mansbridge, and Shula Reinharz for helpful comments; and to Rondi Cartmill for outstanding research assistance. An extended version of this article will appear in *Psychology of Women: Biological, Psychological and Social Perspectives* (Riger, in preparation).

Reprinted from *American Psychologist*, 47, 730–740 (1992). Copyright © 1992 by the American Psychological Association. Reprinted with permission of the author.

human behavior distinguished American psychology from philosophy and enabled it to pursue the respect accorded the natural sciences (Sherif, 1979).

The use of "scientific methods" to study human beings rested on three assumptions:

> (1) Since the methodological procedures of natural science are used as a model, human values enter into the study of social phenomena and conduct only as objects; (2) the goal of social scientific investigation is to construct laws or lawlike generalizations like those of physics; (3) social science has a technical character, providing knowledge which is solely instrumental. (Sewart, 1979, p. 311)

Critics recently have challenged each of these assumptions. Some charge that social science reflects not only the values of individual scientists but also those of the political and cultural milieux in which science is done, and that there are no theory-neutral "facts" (e.g., Cook, 1985; Prilleltensky, 1989; Rabinow & Sullivan, 1979; Sampson, 1985; Shields, 1975). Others claim that there are no universal, ahistorical laws of human behavior, but only descriptions of how people act in certain places at certain times in history (e.g., K. J. Gergen, 1973; Manicas & Secord, 1983; Sampson, 1978). Still others contend that knowledge is not neutral; rather, it serves an ideological purpose, justifying power (e.g., Foucault, 1980, 1981). According to this view, versions of reality not only reflect but also legitimate particular forms of social organization and power asymmetries. The belief that knowledge is merely technical, having no ideological function, is refuted by the ways in which science has played handmaiden to social values, providing an aura of scientific authority to prejudicial beliefs about social groups and giving credibility to certain social policies (Degler, 1991; Shields, 1975; Wittig, 1985).

Within the context of these general criticisms, feminists have argued in particular that social science neglects and distorts the study of women in a systematic bias in favor of men. Some contend that the very processes of positivist science are inherently masculine, reflected even in the sexual metaphors used by the founders of modern science (Keller, 1985; Merchant, 1980). To Francis Bacon, for example, nature was female, and the goal of science was to "bind her to your service and make her your slave" (quoted in Keller, 1985, p. 36). As Sandra Harding (1986) summarized,

> Mind vs. nature and the body, reason vs. emotion and social commitment, subject vs. object and objectivity vs. subjectivity, the abstract and general vs. the concrete and particular—in each case we are told that the former must dominate the latter lest human life be overwhelmed by irrational and alien forces, forces symbolized in science as the feminine. (p. 125)

Critics see the insistence of modern science on control and distance of the knower from the known as a reflection of the desire for domination characteristic of a culture that subordinates women's interests to those of men (Hubbard, 1988; Reinharz, 1985). Some go so far as to claim that because traditional scientific methods inevitably distort women's experience, a new method based on feminist principles is needed (M. M. Gergen, 1988). Others disagree, claiming that the problem in science is not objectivity itself, but rather lack of objectivity that enables male bias to contaminate the scientific process (Epstein, 1988). The first part of this article summarizes feminist charges against standard versions of science; the second part explores three possibilities for a distinctly "feminist" response to those charges: *feminist empiricism, feminist standpoint epistemologies,* and *feminist postmodernism.* (By feminist, I refer to a system of values that challenges male dominance and advocates social, political, and economic equity of women and men in society.)

BIAS WITHIN PSYCHOLOGY IN THE STUDY OF WOMEN

Since Naomi Weisstein denounced much of psychology as the "fantasy life of the male psychologist" in 1971, numerous critics have identified the ways that gender bias permeates social science (summarized in Epstein, 1988, pp. 17–45; Frieze, Parsons, Johnson, Ruble, & Zellman, 1978, pp. 11–27; Hyde, 1991, pp. 7–15; Lips, 1988, pp. 64–75; Millman & Kanter, 1975; Wilkinson, 1986). For many years, subjects of relevance to women, such as rape or housework, have been considered either taboo topics or too trivial to study, marginal to more central and prestigious issues, such as leadership, achievement, and power (Epstein, 1988; McHugh, Koeske, & Frieze, 1986; Farberow, 1963; Smith, 1987). Women's invisibility as subjects of research extends to their role as researchers as well, with relatively few women in positions of power or prestige in science (Rix, 1990). Even today, women make up only 25% of the faculty in psychology departments and only 15% of editors of psychological journals (Walker, 1991). When women are studied, their actions often are interpreted as deficient compared with those of men. Even theories reflect a male standard (Gilligan, 1982). The classic example dates back to Freud's (1925/1961) formulation in 1925 of the theory of penis envy.

Over the last two decades, critics have compiled a long and continually growing list of threats to the validity of research on women and sex differences (see Jacklin, 1981). For example, a great many studies have included only male samples. Sometimes women are included only as the stimulus, not the subject of study—they are seen but not heard— but conclusions are generalized to everyone (Meyer, 1988). Sex-of-experimenter effects contaminate virtually every area of research (Lips, 1988), and field studies yield different findings than laboratory research on the same phenomenon (Unger, 1981). Multiple meanings of the term *sex* confound biological sex differences with factors that vary by sex (i.e., *sex-related* differences) and are more appropriately labeled *gender* (McHugh et al., 1986; Unger, 1979). Sex is treated an an independent variable in studies of gender difference, even though people cannot be randomly assigned to the "male" or "female" group (Unger, 1979). The emphasis on a "difference" model obscures gender similarities (Unger, 1979); this emphasis is built into the methods of science because experiments are formally designed to reject the null hypothesis that there is no difference between the experimental group and the control group. When a difference is found, it is usually small, but the small size is often overshadowed by the fact that a difference exists at all (Epstein, 1988). A focus on between-gender differences and a lack of attention to within-gender differences reflects a presupposition of gender polarity that frames this research (Fine & Gordon, 1989).

Findings of the magnitude of sex differences have diminished over time, perhaps because of an increasing willingness to publish results when such differences are not significant (Hyde, 1990), or perhaps because of a reduction in operative sex role stereotypes. For example, findings of differences in cognitive abilities appear to have declined precipitously over the past two decades (Feingold, 1988), and researchers have found greater influenceability among women in studies published prior to 1970 than in those published later (Eagley, 1978). Carol Jacklin (1981) pointed out that the more carefully a study is carried out, the less likely it is that gender differences will be found: "With fewer variables confounded with sex, sex will account for smaller percentages of variance. Thus, paradoxically, the better the sex-related research, the less useful sex is as an explanatory variable" (p. 271). The decline in findings of difference suggest either that increasing care in designing studies has eliminated differences that were artifacts of bias, or that historical factors, rather than ahistorical, universal laws, shape behavior, whether of subjects or experimenters. In fact, so many studies find no sex differences that this research might more appropriately be called the study of sex similarities (Connell, 1987).

Psychological research on women often contains another source of bias, the lack of attention to social context. The purpose of the laboratory experiment is to isolate the behavior under study from supposedly extraneous contaminants so that it is affected only by the experimental conditions. The experimental paradigm assumes that subjects leave their social status, history, beliefs, and values behind as they enter the laboratory, or that random assignment vitiates the effects of these factors. The result is to subtract people's action from social roles or institutions (Fine & Gordon, 1989; Parlee, 1979; Sherif, 1979). Instead of being contaminants, however, these factors may be critical determinants of behavior. By stripping behavior of its social context, psychologists rule out the study of sociocultural and historical factors, and implicitly attribute causes to factors inside the person. Moreover, an absence of consideration of the social context of people's actions is not limited to laboratory research (Fine, 1984). In an ironic reversal of the feminist dictum of the 1960s, when social context is ignored, the political is misinterpreted as personal (Kitzinger, 1987).

Ignoring social context may produce a reliance on presumed biological causes when other explanations of sex differences are not obvious, even when the biological mechanisms that might be involved are not apparent (Lips, 1988). Social explanations become residual, although sociocultural determinants may be just as robust and important as biological causes, if not more so (Connell, 1987). Although biological differences between the sexes are obviously important, it is critical to distinguish between biological difference and the social meaning attached to that difference (Rossi, 1979).

Alice Eagley (1987) raised a different objection to experimentation. She disagreed that the psychological experiment is context-stripped, and contended instead that it constitutes a particular context. An experiment typically consists of a brief encounter among strangers in an unfamiliar setting, often under the eye of a psychologist. The question is whether this limited situation is a valid one from which to make generalizations about behavior. To Eagley, the problem is that social roles (such as mother, doctor, or corporation president) lose their salience in this setting, bringing to the foreground gender-related expectations about behavior.

Cynthia Fuchs Epstein (1988) stated that "Much of the bias in social science reporting of gender issues comes from scientists' inability to capture the social context or their tendency to regard it as unnecessary to their inquiry—in a sense, their disdain for it" (p. 44). In psychology, this disdain has at least two sources (Kahn & Yoder, 1989; Prilleltensky, 1989). First, psychology focuses on the person as he or she exists at the moment. Such a focus leads the researcher away from the person's history or social circumstances. Second, the cultural context in which psychology is practiced (at least in the United States) is dominated by an individualistic philosophy (Kitzinger, 1987; Sampson, 1985). The prevailing beliefs assume that outcomes are due to choices made by free and self-determining individuals; the implication is that people get what they deserve (Kahn & Yoder, 1989). Not only assumptions of individualism, but also those of male dominance are often so taken for granted that we are not aware of them. Recognition that supposedly scientific assertions are permeated with ideological beliefs produces, in Shulamit Reinharz's (1985) words, a condition of "feminist distrust." Perhaps one of the most difficult challenges facing social scientists is to disengage themselves sufficiently from commonly shared beliefs so that those beliefs do not predetermine research findings (McHugh et al., 1986).

FEMINIST RESPONSES TO THE CRITICISMS OF SCIENCE

Challenges to the neutrality of science have long been a concern to those who study women, and have prompted three different reactions among feminists (Harding, 1986). Some remain loyal to scientific traditions, attempting to rise above the cultural embeddedness of these traditions by adhering more closely to the norms of science (e.g., Epstein, 1988; McHugh et al., 1986). Others seek to redress the male-centered bias in science by giving voice to women's experience and by viewing society from women's perspective (e.g., Belenky, Clinchy, Goldberger, & Tarule, 1986; Gilligan, 1982; Smith, 1987). Still others abandon traditional scientific methods entirely (e.g., Hare-Mustin, 1991). Philosopher of science Sandra Harding (1986) labeled these three approaches, respectively, feminist empiricism, feminist standpoint science, and postmodernism (see also Morgan's, 1983, distinction among positivist, phenomenological, and critical/praxis-oriented research paradigms). Next, I examine the manifestations of these three positions in the study of the psychology of women.

Feminist Empiricism

The psychologists who identified the problem of experimenter effects did not reject experimentation. Instead, they recommended strategies to minimize the impact of the experimenter (Rosenthal, 1966). Likewise, feminist empiricists advocate closer adherence to the tenets of science as the solution to the problem of bias. From this perspective, bias is considered error in a basically sound system, an outbreak of irrationality in a rational process. Scrupulous attention to scientific methods will eliminate error, or at least minimize its impact on research findings (Harding, 1986). Once neutrality is restored, scientific methods, grounded in rationality, will give access to the truth.

Maureen McHugh et al. (1986) presented a set of guidelines for eliminating bias. In addition to obvious corrections of the problems described earlier, other steps can be taken to ensure that the impact of the researcher's values is minimized, such as specifying the circumstances in which gender differences are found (because contexts tend to be deemed more appropriate for one sex than the other) and assessing experimental tasks for their sex neutrality (because many tasks are perceived to be sex linked; Deaux, 1984). The sex composition of the group of participants in research also may affect behavior because individuals act differently in the presence of females or males (Maccoby, 1990). Finally, attention ought to be paid to findings of sex similarities as well as sex differences, and the magnitude of such differences reported.

These suggestions are intended to produce gender-fair research using traditional scientific methods. The assumption is that a truly neutral science will produce unbiased knowledge, which in turn will serve as a basis for a more just social policy (Morawski, 1990). Yet the continuing identification of numerous instances of androcentric bias in research has led some to conclude that value-free research is impossible, even if it is done by those of good faith (Hare-Mustin & Maracek, 1990). Technical safeguards cannot completely rule out the influence of values; scientific rigor in testing hypotheses cannot eliminate bias in theories or in the selection of problems for inquiry (Harding, 1986, 1991). Hence critics assert that traditional methods do not reveal reality, but rather act as constraints that limit our understanding of women's experiences.

Feminist Standpoint Epistemologies

Feminist empiricism argues that the characteristics of the knower are irrelevant to the discovery process if the norms of science are followed. In contrast, feminist standpoint epistemologies claim that we should center our science on women because "what we know and how we know depend on who we are, that is, on the knower's historical locus and his or her position in the social hierarchy" (Maracek, 1989, p. 372). There are several justifications for this viewpoint (see Harding, 1986). First, some argue that women's cognitive processes and modes of research are different than men's. It has been suggested that a supposedly feminine communal style of research that emphasizes cooperation of the researcher and subjects, an appreciation of natural contexts, and the use of qualitative data contrasts with a supposedly masculine agentic orientation that places primacy on distance of the researcher from the subjects, manipulation of subjects and the environment, and the use of quantitative data (Carlson, 1972; cf. Peplau & Conrad, 1989). Evelyn Fox Keller (1985) attempted to provide grounds for this position in a psychoanalytic view of child development. She argued that the male child's need to differentiate himself from his mother leads him to equate autonomy with distance from others (see also Chodorow, 1978). The process of developing a masculine sense of self thus establishes in the male a style of thinking that both reflects and produces the emphasis in science on distance, power, and control. Keller identifies an alternative model of science based not on controlling but rather on "conversing" with nature.

Keller's (1985) argument that science need not be based on domination is salutary, but her explanation is problematic. She presumes, first, that male and female infants have quite different experiences and, second, that those early experiences shape the activities of adult scientists, but she does not substantiate these claims. The supposedly masculine emphasis on separation and autonomy may be a manifestation of Western mainstream culture rather than a universal distinction between women and men. Black men and women who returned from northern U.S. cities to live in the rural South manifest a relational as opposed to autonomous self-image (Stack, 1986), and both Eastern and African world views see individuals as interdependent and connected, in contrast to the Western emphasis on a bounded and independent self (Markus & Oyserman, 1989). Identifying a masculine cognitive style as the grounds for scientific methods seems to doom most women and perhaps non-White men to outsider status. Furthermore, an emphasis on cognitive style ignores the role played by social structure, economics, and politics in determining topics and methods of study (Harding, 1986). Experimental methods in psychology characterized by control and objectivity are accorded prestige partly because they emulate the highly valued physical sciences (Sherif, 1979). Within social science, the prestige of a study mirrors the prestige of its topic (Epstein, 1988). Sociocultural factors such as these seem more likely as determinants of the shape of science than individual psychology.

A more plausible basis for a feminist standpoint epistemology is the argument that women's life experiences are not fully captured in existing conceptual schemes. Research often equates *male* with the general, typical case, and considers *female* to be the particular—a subgroup demarcated by biology (Acker, 1978). Yet analytical categories appropriate for men may not fit women's experience. Dorothy Smith (1987) argues that women are alienated from their own experience by having to frame that experience in terms of men's conceptual schemes; in Smith's terms they have a "bifurcated consciousness"—daily life grounded in female experience but only male conceptual categories with which to interpret that experience. Starting our inquiries from a subordinate group's experience will uncover the limits of the dominant group's conceptual schemes where they do not fully fit the subordinates (see also Miller, 1986). Accordingly, a science based on women's traditional place in society not only would generate categories appropriate to women, but also would be a means of discovering the underlying organization of society as a whole (see also Code, 1981).

In contrast to traditional social science in which the researcher is the expert on assessing reality, an interpretive–phenomenological approach permits women to give their own conception of their experiences. Participants, not researchers, are considered the experts at making sense of their world (Cherryholmes, 1988). The shift in authority is striking. Yet phenomenological approaches are limited in at least two ways. First, they require that the subjects studied be verbal and reflective (Reinharz, 1992); second, they run the risk of psychological reductionism (attributing causation simply to internal, psychological factors; Morawski, 1988).

Carol Gilligan's (1982) theory of women's moral development is the most influential psychological study in this tradition. Her work asserting that women stress caring in the face of moral dilemmas in contrast to men's emphasis on justice has been criticized because other researchers have found no sex differences in moral reasoning using standardized scales (e.g.,

Greeno & Maccoby, 1986; Mednick, 1989). Gilligan (1986) retorted that women's responses on those scales are not relevant to her purposes:

> The fact that educated women are capable of high levels of justice reasoning has no bearing on the question of whether they would spontaneously choose to frame moral problems in this way. My interest in the way people *define* moral problems is reflected in my research methods, which have centered on first-person accounts of moral conflict. (p. 328)

Although standardized scales might tell us what women have in common with men, they will not reveal the way women would define their own experiences if given the opportunity to do so. The absence (and impossibility) of a comparison group of men in Gilligan's definitive study of 29 women considering abortions raises questions about whether moral orientations are sex linked, however (Crawford, 1989; Epstein, 1988, pp. 81–83).

The feminist standpoint epistemologies aim not simply to substitute "woman centered" for "man centered" gender loyalties, but rather to provide a basis for a more accurate understanding of the entire world. Howard Becker (1967) claimed that

> In any system of ranked groups, participants take it as given that members of the highest group have the right to define the way things really are.... Credibility and the right to be heard are differentially distributed through the ranks of the system. (p. 241)

Feminist standpoint epistemologies argue that traditional methods of science give credibility only to the dominant group's views. Listening to subordinates reveals the multifocal nature of reality (Riger, 1990). The term *subjugated knowledges* describes the perspectives of those sufficiently low on the hierarchy that their interpretations do not reflect the predominant modes of thought (Foucault, 1980, p. 81). Giving voice to women's perspective means identifying the ways in which women create meaning and experience life from their particular position in the social hierarchy.

Moreover, women (and minorities) sometimes have a better vantage point to view society than do majorities because minority status can render people socially invisible, thus permitting them access to the majority group that is not reciprocated (Merton, 1972). Accordingly, incorporating subordinates' experience will not only "add" women and minorities to existing understandings, it will add a more thorough understanding of the dominant group as well. For example, Bell Hooks (1984) described African Americans living in her small Kentucky hometown as having a double vision. They looked from the outside in at the more affluent White community across the railroad tracks, but their perspective shifted to inside out when they crossed those tracks to work for White employers. Movement across the tracks was regulated, however: Whites did not cross over to the Black community, and laws ensured that Blacks returned to it.

The arguments for feminist standpoint epistemologies have stimulated rich and valuable portrayals of women's experience. Yet there are problems with a feminist standpoint as the basis for science. First, assuming a commonality to all women's experience glosses over differences among women of various racial and ethnic groups and social classes (Spelman, 1988). The life experience of a woman wealthy enough to hire childcare and household help may have more in common with her spouse than with a poor woman trying to raise her children on a welfare budget. Standpoint epistemology can recognize multiple subjugated groups demarcated by gender, race, social class, sexual orientation, and so on. Yet carried to an extreme, this position seems to dissolve science into autobiography. A critical challenge for feminist standpoint epistemology is to identify the commonalities of subjugated experience among different groups of women without losing sight of their diversity. Moreover, those who are subjugated may still adhere to a dominant group's ideology.

Furthermore, we each have multiple status identities (Merton, 1972). The poet Audre Lorde (1984) described herself as "a forty-nine-year-old Black lesbian feminist socialist mother of two, including one boy, and a member of an interracial couple" (p. 114). Each of these identities becomes salient in a different situation; at times, they conflict within the same situation. The hyphenated identities that we all experience in different ways—Black feminist, lesbian mother, Asian American, and so on—call into question the unity of the category of woman, making it difficult to generalize about "women's experience" (Harding, 1987).

Nonetheless, feminist standpoint epistemologies do not claim that social status alone allows the viewer clarity. Reasonable judgments about whether views are empirically supported are still possible. Rather than proclaiming the one true story about the world, feminist standpoint epistemologies seek partial and less distorted views. These partial views, or situated knowledges, can be far less limited than the dominant view (Haraway, 1988).

Feminist Postmodernism

A number of perspectives, including Marxism, psychoanalysis, and postmodernism, share a challenge to the primacy of reason and the autonomy of the individual. Here I focus on postmodernism and, in particular, poststructuralism, because of its influence on an emerging stream of feminist psychology (e.g., Hare-Mustin & Maracek, 1990; Wilkinson, 1986). A traditional social scientist entering the terrain of poststructuralism at times feels a bit like Alice falling into a Wonderland of bewildering language and customs that look superficially like her own yet are not. Things that seem familiar and stable—the meaning of words, for example—become problematic. What once were nouns (e.g., privilege, valor, foreground) now are verbs. Even the landscape looks different, as words themselves are chopped up with parentheses and hyphens to make visible their multiple meanings. What is most unsettling, perhaps, is the fundamental poststructuralist assertion that science does not mirror reality, but rather creates it (i.e., making science a process of invention rather than discovery; Howard, 1991). Many scientists would agree that an unmediated perception of reality is impossible to obtain, and that research findings represent (rather than mirror) reality. However, they would maintain that some representations are better than others. The traditional scientific criteria of validity, generalizability, and so forth determine how close research findings come to actual truth. In contrast, poststructuralists reject traditional notions of truth and reality, and claim instead that power enables some to define what is or is not considered knowledge. Expressing our understanding of experience must be done through language, but language is not a neutral reflection of that experience because our linguistic categories are not neutral:

> If statements and not things are true or false, then truth is necessarily linguistic: if truth is linguistic, then it is relative to language use (words, concepts, statements, discourses) at a given time and place; therefore, ideology, interests, and power arrangements at a given time and place are implicated in the production of what counts as "true." (Cherryholmes, 1988, p. 439)

Or, as Humpty Dumpty said to Alice in *Through the Looking Glass*:

> "When I use a word," Humpty Dumpty said, in a rather scornful tone, "it means just what I choose it to mean—neither more or less."
> "The question is," said Alice, "whether you can make words mean so many different things."
> "The question is," said Humpty Dumpty, "which is to be master—that's all." (Carroll, 1872/1923, p. 246)

The central question in poststructuralism is not how well our theories fit the facts, or how well the facts produced by research fit what is real. Rather, the question is which values and social institutions are favored by each of multiple versions of reality (i.e., discourses). Of critical concern is whose interests are served by competing ways of giving meaning to the world (Weedon, 1987). Feminists of a postmodern bent claim that positivism's neutral and disinterested stance masks what is actually the male conception of reality; this conception reflects and maintains male power interests (Gavey, 1989). As legal scholar Catherine MacKinnon (1987) put it, "Objectivity—the nonsituated, universal standpoint, whether claimed or aspired to—is a denial of the existence of potency of sex inequality that tacitly participates in constructing reality from the dominant point of view" (p. 136). In MacKinnon's view, rather than being neutral, "the law sees and treats women the way men see and treat women" (p. 140). The same criticism can be made about traditional social science in its exclusion, distortion, and neglect of women.

The social constructionist stance, as poststructuralism is known within psychology (K. J. Gergen, 1985), offers a particular challenge to the psychology of women. In contrast to feminist empiricism, the central question no longer asks whether sex or gender differences exist. Knowing the truth about difference is impossible (Hare-Mustin & Maracek, 1990). Varying criteria of differentness can produce divergent findings, for example, when conclusions based on averages contradict those based on the amount of overlap or scores of men and women (Luria, 1986). When an assumed difference is not scientifically supported, the argument simply shifts to another variable (Unger, 1979), and similar findings can be interpreted in opposing ways. Given the impossibility of settling these questions, poststructuralism shifts the emphasis to the question of difference itself (Scott, 1988):

> What do we make of gender differences? What do they mean? Why are there so many? Why are there so few? Perhaps we should be asking: What is the point of differences? What lies beyond difference? Difference aside, what else is gender? The overarching question is choice of question. (Hare-Mustin & Maracek, 1990, pp. 1–2)

One goal of a feminist constructionist science is "disrupting and displacing dominant (oppressive) knowledges" in part by articulating the values supported by alternate conceptions of reality (Gavey, 1989, p. 462). An analysis of contrasting perspectives on sex differences demonstrates the relationship among values, assumptive frameworks, and social consequences. According to Rachel Hare-Mustin and Jeanne Maracek (1988), the received views of men and women tend either to exaggerate or to minimize the differences between them. On the one hand, the tendency to emphasize differences fosters an appreciation of supposedly feminine qualities, but it simultaneously justifies unequal treatment of women and ignores variability within each sex group. The consequence of emphasizing difference, then, is to support the status quo. On the other hand, the tendency to minimize differences justifies women's access to educational and job opportunities, but it simultaneously overlooks the fact that equal treatment is not always equitable, because of differences in men's and women's position in a social hierarchy. Gender-neutral grievance procedures in organizations, for example, do not apply equally to men and women if men are consistently in positions of greater power (Riger, 1991).

Researchers have widely different interpretations of the implications of poststructural critiques for social science methods. Some use empirical techniques for poststructuralist ends. Social constructionists see traditional research methods as a means of providing "objectifications" or illustrations, similar to vivid photographs, that are useful in making an argument persuasive rather than in validating truth claims (K. J. Gergen, 1985). Traditional methods can also help identify varying versions of reality. For example, Celia Kitzinger (1986, 1987) used Q-sort methodology to distinguish five separate accounts of lesbians' beliefs about the origin of their sexual orientation. Techniques of attitude measurement can also be used to assess the extent to which people share certain versions of reality. Rhoda Unger and her colleagues used surveys to assess belief in an objectivist or subjectivist epistemology, finding that adherence to a particular perspective varied with social status (Unger, Draper, & Pendergrass, 1986).

Others propose that we treat both psychological theories and people's actions and beliefs as texts (i.e., discursive productions located in a specific historical and cultural context and shaped by power), rather than as accounts, distorted or otherwise, of experience (Cherryholmes, 1988; Gavey, 1989). Methods developed in other disciplines, particularly literary criticism, can be used to analyze these texts. For example, through careful reading of an interview transcript with an eye to discerning "discursive patterns of meaning, contradictions, and inconsistencies," Nicola Gavey (p. 467) identified cultural themes of "permissive sexuality" and "male sexual needs" in statements by a woman about her experiences of heterosexual coercion (see also Hare-Mustin, 1991; Walkerdine, 1986). A particular technique of discourse analysis, deconstruction, can be used to expose ideological assumptions in written or spoken language, as Joanne Martin (1990) did to identify forces that suppress women's achievement within organizations. Deconstruction highlights the revealing quality not just of what is said, but rather of what is left out, contradictory, or inconsistent in the text. Deconstruction offers a provocative technique for analyzing hidden assumptions. Yet it is a potentially endless process, capable of an infinite regress, inasmuch as any deconstruction can itself be deconstructed (Martin, 1990).

The absence of any criteria for evaluation means that the success of accounts of social construction "depend primarily on the analyst's capacity to invite, compel, stimulate, or delight the audience, and not on criteria of veracity" (K. J. Gergen, 1985, p. 272). This raises the possibility that what Grant (1987) said in another context could apply here: "Such theories risk devolving into authoritarian non-theories more akin to religions" (p. 113). The relativism of poststructuralism can be countered, however, by the identification of moral criteria for evaluation (K. J. Gergen, 1985; Unger, 1983). Theory and research can be assessed in terms of their pragmatic utility in achieving certain social and political goals, rather than the allegedly neutral rules of science (Gavey, 1989). However, because feminists disagree about whether celebrating women's difference or emphasizing the similarity of the sexes is most likely to change women's basic condition of subordination (Snitow, 1990), agreement about criteria for evaluation seems unlikely.

What poses perhaps the greatest dilemma for feminists is the view of the subject advocated by poststructuralist theory. Poststructuralists consider the attribution of agency and intentionality to the subject to be part of a deluded liberal humanism, complicit with the status quo. The multiple discourses of selfhood, intentionality, and so forth that are present in our culture compete for dominance; those that prevail constitute individual subjectivity. Social cognition on the part of the individual is channeled into certain ways of thinking that dominate society (although resistance is possible). Those discourses antedate our consciousness and give meaning to our experience, which otherwise had no essential meaning (Weedon, 1987). In contrast, feminist standpoint epistemologies consider individuals to be the active construers of their reality; albeit within a particular social and historical context; women's subjectivity is considered an important source of information about their experience. Poststructuralism's rejection of intentionality on the part of the individual seems to deny the validity of women's voices, just at a time when women are beginning to be heard (see also Hartsock, 1987).

Poststructuralism offers a provocative critique of social science and makes us critically aware of the relationship of knowledge and power. Yet the focus on "problematizing the text" of our disciplines, although admirably self-reflexive, can lead to an inward emphasis that neglects the study of women in society. In a parallel manner, poststructuralism's emphasis on language as determining consciousness can lead to the disregard of other determinants, such as women's position in a social hierarchy (Segal, 1986). Furthermore, Rhoda Unger (1988) identified a dilemma for social scientists who reject traditional empirical methods:

> The attempt to infer cause-and-effect relationships about human behavior using the tools of empiricism is one of the few unique contributions that psychology as a discipline can offer to the rest of scholarship. If such tools may not be used by feminist psychologists there is little likelihood that their insights will be taken seriously by the rest of the discipline. (p. 137)

Feminist foremothers in psychology, such as Helen Thompson (Woolley) and her colleagues, at the turn of this century, used traditional scientific methods to contest social myths about women (Reinharz, 1992; Rosenberg, 1982); they may still serve that purpose today. Poststructuralists would likely retort that the fact that Thompson's insights have had to be repeatedly rediscovered (or, rather, reinvented) demonstrates that power, not truth, determines which version of reality will prevail.

IS THERE A FEMINIST METHOD?

On the basis of multiple critiques of the social sciences, some propose an alternative research method based on feminist values. The lack of consensus on what values are feminist makes this a daunting project, yet many would agree on the need for more interactive, contextualized methods in the service of emancipatory goals (cf. Peplau & Conrad, 1989). A feminist method should produce a study not just *of* women, but also *for* women, helping to change the world as well as to describe it (Acker, Barry, & Esseveld, 1983; Wittig, 1985). Mary Gergen (1988) advocated the following as central tenets of a feminist method (see also Wilkinson, 1986):

1. recognizing the interdependence of experimenter and subject;
2. avoiding the decontextualizing of the subject or experimenter from their social and historical surroundings;
3. recognizing and revealing the nature of one's values within the research context;
4. accepting that facts do not exist independently of their producers' linguistic codes;
5. demystifying the role of the scientists and establishing an egalitarian relationship between science makers and science consumers. (p. 47)

Joan Acker et al. (1983) attempted to implement some of these principles in a study of women who had primarily been wives and mothers and were starting to enter the labor market. Interviews became dialogues, a mutual attempt to clarify and expand understandings. Often friendships developed between researchers and the women in the study. Acker and her colleagues discovered that these methods are not without problems, however. The researcher's need to collect information can (perhaps inadvertently) lead to the manipulation of friendship in the service of the research. Methods that create trust between researchers and participants entail the risk of exploitation, betrayal, and abandonment by the researcher (Stacey, 1988). Acker's study took place over a number of years, and participant's interpretations of their lives were constantly changing in hindsight, raising problems of validity in the research. The desire to give participants an opportunity to comment on researchers' interpretations of the interviews became a source of tension when disagreements arose. The solution to these dilemmas reached by Acker and her colleagues—to report the women's lives in their own words as much as possible—was not satisfactory to the women in the study who wanted more analysis of their experience. Finally, it was difficult to determine if this research experience had an emancipatory effect on participants. Intending to create social change is no assurance of actually doing so.

The conflict between the researcher's perspective and that of the participants in this study raises a critical issue for those who reject positivism's belief in the scientist as expert. Because a feminist method (at least according to the principles listed) assumes that there is no neutral observer, whose interpretations should prevail when those of the researcher and the people under study conflict? Feminism places primacy on acknowledging and validating female experience (Wilkinson, 1986), yet postmodern perspectives challenge the authority of the individual (Gavey, 1989; Weedon, 1987). Consider, for example, Margaret Andersen's (1981) study of 20 corporate wives. She disbelieved their claims of contentment and attributed their lack of feminism to *false consciousness*, a Marxist term meaning that these women identified with (male) ruling class interests against their own (female) class interests. The women wrote a rebuttal rejecting Andersen's interpretation. In response, Andersen revised her position to accept the women's statements of satisfaction with their lives. Instead of treating them as deluded or insincere, she looked for sources of their contentment in their position in the social hierarchy. Lather (1986, 1988) recommended this kind of dialogic process to avoid imposing on research participants interpretations that disempower them (see also Kidder, 1982). Without it, we grant privilege to the authority of the researcher, even if on postmodern rather than positivist grounds.

CONCLUSION

Although the strategies intended as a feminist method overcome some of the objections to traditional social science, they raise as many problems as they solve (see Reinharz, 1992). No method or epistemology seems devoid of limitations or perfectly true to feminist values, which are themselves contested (e.g., Jaggar & Struhl, 1978). Feminism is most useful as a set of questions that challenge the prevailing asymmetries of power and androcentric assumptions in science and society, rather than as a basis for a unique method (Reinharz, 1992). Feminism thus identifies "patterns and interrelationships and causes and effects and implications of questions that nonfeminists have not seen and still do not see" (Lorber, 1988, p. 8).

The psychological study of women emerged from the field of individual differences. Dominated by the question of sex differences, this tradition assumes that an inner core of traits or abilities distinguishes women from men (Buss, 1976). Such a conceptualization no longer seems useful. Few gender differences in personality or abilities have been reliably demonstrated (Feingold, 1988; Hyde, 1990), and factors other than individual dispositions influence our behavior (Maccoby, 1990). A more appropriate strategy for the study of women would consider the ways in which gender is created and maintained through interpersonal processes (Deaux & Major, 1987).

From this perspective, gender does not reside within the person. Instead, it is constituted by the myriad ways in which we "do" rather than "have" gender; that is, we validate our membership in a particular gender category through interactional processes (West & Zimmerman, 1987). Gender is something we enact, not an inner core or constellation of traits that we express; it is a pattern of social organization that structures the relations, especially the power relations, between women and men (Connell, 1985, 1987; Crawford & Maracek, 1989): "In doing gender, men are also doing dominance and women are doing deference" (West & Zimmerman, 1987, p. 146). Transsexuals know well that merely altering one's sex organs does not change one's gender. Membership in the category of "male" or "female" must be affirmed continuously through social behavior (see, e.g., Morris, 1974).

Each of the epistemological positions described can contribute to this perspective, despite their contradictions. An interactional conceptualization of gender recognizes that the behavior and thoughts of men and women are channeled into certain sociocultural forms, as poststructuralism claims. As Peter Manicas and Paul Secord (1983) stated:

> Social structures (e.g., language) are reproduced and transformed by action, but they preexist for individuals. They enable persons to become persons and to act (meaningfully and intentionally), yet at the same time, they are "coercive," limiting the ways we can act. (p. 408)

The dominant ideology of a society is manifested in and reproduced by the social relations of its members (Unger, 1989). Unlike poststructuralism, however, an interactional view of gender also acknowledges individual agency in the production and transformation of social forms. Such a perspective would regard the person as an initiator of action and construer of meaning within a context composed not only of varying modes of interpreting the world but also of structural constraints and opportunities (see, e.g., Buss, 1978; Riegel, 1979; Sampson, 1978; Unger, 1983), as standpoint epistemologies claim.

Diverse methods, evaluated by reasonable criteria, are needed to capture the rich array of personal and structural factors that shape women and girls, and in turn are shaped by them. What is critical is that we are aware of the epistemological commitments—and value assumptions—we make when we adopt a particular research strategy (Unger, 1983). Moreover, rather than abandoning objectivity, systematic examination of assumptions and values in the social order that shape scientific practices can strengthen objectivity (Harding, 1991).

Epistemological debates in recent years have shattered the traditional picture of science as neutral, disinterested, and value free and have replaced it with a view of knowledge as socially constructed. Feminists' contributions to this debate highlight not only the androcentric nature of social science, but also its collusion in the perpetuation of male dominance in society. To assume that the multiple voices of women are not shaped by domination is to ignore social context and legitimate the status quo. On the other hand, to assume that women have no voice other than an echo of prevailing discourses is to deny them agency and, simultaneously, to repudiate the possibility of social change. The challenge to psychology is to link a vision of women's agency with an understanding of the shaping power of social context.

REFERENCES

Acker, J. (1978). Issues in the sociological study of women's work. In A. Stromberg & S. Harkness (Eds.), *Women working* (pp. 134–161). Palo Alto, CA: Mayfield.

Acker, J., Barry, K., & Esseveld, J. (1983). Objectivity and truth: Problems in doing feminist research. *Women's Studies International Forum, 6,* 423–435.

Andersen, M. (1981). Corporate wives: Longing for liberation or satisfied with the status quo? *Urban Life, 10,* 311–327.

Becker, H. S. (1967). Whose side are we on? *Social Problems, 14,* 239–247.

Belenky, M. F., Clinchy, B. M., Goldberger, N. R., & Tarule, J. M. (1986). *Women's ways of knowing: The development of self, voice, and mind.* New York: Basic Books.

Buss, A. R. (1976). Galton and sex differences: An historical note. *Journal of the History of the Behavioral Sciences, 12,* 283–285.

Buss, A. R. (1978). The structure of psychological revolutions. *Journal of the History of the Behavioral Sciences, 14,* 57–64.

Carlson, R. (1972). Understanding women: Implications for personality theory and research. *Journal of Social Issues, 28,* 17–32.

Carroll, L. (1923). *Alice's adventures in Wonderland; and Through the looking glass.* Philadelphia: Winston. (Original work published 1872)

Cherryholmes, C. H. (1988). Construct validity and the discourses of research. *American Journal of Education, 96,* 421–457.

Chodorow, N. (1978). *The reproduction of mothering.* Berkeley: University of California Press.

Code, L. B. (1981). Is the sex of the knower epistemologically significant? *Metaphilosophy, 12,* 267–276.

Connell, R. W. (1985). Theorizing gender. *Sociology, 19,* 260–272.

Connell, R. W. (1987). *Gender and power: Society, the person and sexual politics.* Stanford, CA: Stanford University Press.

Cook, T. D. (1985). Postpositivist critical multiplism. In L. Shotland & M. M. Mark (Eds.), *Social science and social policy* (pp. 21–62). Beverly Hills, CA. Sage.

Crawford, M. (1989). Agreeing to differ: Feminist epistemologies and women's ways of knowing. In M. Crawford & M. Gentry (Eds.), *Gender and thought: Psychological perspectives* (pp. 128–145). New York: Springer-Verlag.

Crawford, M., & Maracek, J. (1989). Psychology reconstructs the female, 1968–1988. *Psychology of Women Quarterly, 13,* 147–165.

Deaux, K. (1984). From individual differences to social categories. *American Psychologist, 39,* 105–116.

Deaux, K., & Major, B. (1987). Putting gender into context: An interactive model of gender-related behavior. *Psychological Review, 94,* 369–389.

Degler, C. (1991). *In search of human nature.* New York: Oxford University Press.

Eagley, A. H. (1978). Sex differences in influenceability. *Psychological Bulletin,* 1978, 85, 86–116.

Eagley, A. H. (1987). *Sex differences in social behavior: A social–role interpretation.* Hillsdale, NJ: Erlbaum.

Epstein, C. F. (1988). *Deceptive distinctions: Sex, gender, and the social order.* New Haven, CT: Yale University Press.

Farberow, N. L. (1963). *Taboo topics.* New York: Atherton Press.

Feingold, A. (1988). Cognitive gender differences are disappearing. *American Psychologist, 43,* 95–103.

Fine, M. (1984). Coping with rape: Critical perspectives on consciousness. *Imagination, Cognition, and Personality: The Scientific Study of Consciousness, 3,* 249–267.

Fine, M., & Gordon, S. M. (1989). Feminist transformations of/despite psychology. In M. Crawford & M. Gentry (Eds.), *Gender and thought: Psychological perspectives* (pp. 146–174). New York: Springer-Verlag.

Foucault, M. (1980). *Power/knowledge: Selected interviews and other writings, 1972–1977* (C. Gordon, Ed. and Trans.). New York: Pantheon Books.

Foucault, M. (1981). *The history of sexuality: Vol. 1. An introduction.* Harmondsworth, England: Viking.

Freud, S. (1961). Some psychical consequences of the anatomical distinctions between the sexes. In J. Strachey (Ed. and Trans.), *The complete psychological works of Sigmund Freud* (Vol. 19, pp. 248–258). London: Hogarth Press. (Original work published 1925)

Frieze, I. H., Parsons, J. E., Johnson, P. B., Ruble, D. N., & Zellman, G. L. (1978). *Women and sex roles: A social psychological perspective.* New York: Norton.

Gavey, N. (1989). Feminist poststructuralism and discourse analysis: Contributions to a feminist psychology. *Psychology of Women Quarterly, 13,* 459–476.

Gergen, K. J. (1973). Social psychology as history. *Journal of Personality and Social Psychology, 26,* 309–320.

Gergen, K. J. (1985). The social constructionist movement in modern psychology. *American Psychologist, 40,* 255–265.

Gergen, M. M. (1988). Building a feminist methodology. *Contemporary Social Psychology, 13,* 47–53.

Gilligan, C. (1982). *In a different voice.* Cambridge, MA: Harvard University Press.

Gilligan, C. (1986). Reply by Carol Gilligan. *Signs: Journal of Women in Culture and Society, 11,* 324–333.

Grant, J. (1987). I feel therefore I am: A critique of female experience as the basis for a feminist epistemology. In M. J. Falco (Ed.), *Feminism and epistemology: Approaches to research in women and politics* (pp. 99–114). Binghampton, NY: Haworth Press.

Greeno, C. G., & Maccoby, E. E. (1986). How different is the "different voice"? *Signs: Journal of Women in Culture and Society, 11,* 310–316.

Haraway, D. (1988). Situated knowledges: The science question in feminism and the privilege of partial perspective. *Feminist Studies, 14,* 575–599.

Harding, S. (1986). *The science question in feminism.* Ithaca, NY: Cornell University Press.

Harding, S. (1987). Introduction: Is there a feminist method? In S. Harding (Ed.), *Feminism and methodology: Social science issues* (pp. 1–14). Bloomington: Indiana University Press.

Harding, S. (1991). *Whose science? Whose knowledge?* Ithaca, NY: Cornell University Press.

Hare-Mustin, R. T. (1991). Sex, lies, and headaches: The problem is power. In T. J. Goodrich (Ed.), *Women and power: Perspectives for therapy.* New York: Norton.

Hare-Mustin, R. T., & Maracek, J. (1988). The meaning of difference: Gender theory, postmodernism, and psychology. *American Psychologist, 43,* 355–464.

Hare-Mustin, R. T., & Maracek, J. (1990). *Making a difference: Psychology and the construction of gender.* New Haven, CT: Yale University Press.

Hartsock, N. (1987). Epistemology and politics: Minority vs. majority theories. *Cultural Critique, 7,* 187–206.

Hooks, B. (1984). *Feminist theory: From margin to center.* Boston: South End Press.

Howard, G. S. (1991). Culture tales: Narrative approach to thinking, cross-cultural psychology, and psychotherapy. *American Psychologist, 46,* 187–197.

Hyde, J. (1990). Meta-analysis and the psychology of gender differences. *Signs: Journal of Women in Culture and Society, 16,* 55–73.

Hyde, J. (1991). *Half the human experience: The psychology of women* (4th ed.). Lexington, MA: Heath.

Hubbard, R. (1988). Some thoughts about the masculinity of the natural sciences. In M. M. Gergen, *Feminist thought and the structure of knowledge* (pp. 1–15). New York: New York University Press.

Jacklin, C. N. (1981). Methodological issues in the study of sex-related differences. *Developmental Review, 1,* 266–273.

Jaggar, A., & Struhl, P. R. (1978). *Feminist frameworks: Alternative theoretical accounts of the relations between women and men.* New York: McGraw-Hill.

Kahn, A. S., & Yoder, J. D. (1989). The psychology of women and conservatism: Rediscovering social change. *Psychology of Women Quarterly, 13,* 417–432.

Keller, E. F. (1985). *Reflections on gender and science*. New Haven, CT: Yale University Press.

Kidder, L. (1982). Face validity from multiple perspectives. In D. Brinberg & L. Kidder (Eds.), *Forms of validity in research* (pp. 41–58). San Francisco: Jossey-Bass.

Kitzinger, C. (1986). Introducing and developing Q as a feminist methodology: A study of accounts of lesbianism. In S. Wilkinson (Ed.), *Feminist social psychology: Developing theory and practice* (pp. 151–172). Milton Keynes, England: Open University Press.

Kitzinger, C. (1987). *The social construction of lesbianism*. London: Sage.

Lather, P. (1986). Research as praxis. *Harvard Educational Review, 56,* 257–277.

Lather, P. (1988). Feminist perspectives on empowering research methodologies. *Women's Studies International Forum, 11,* 569–581.

Lips, H. (1988). *Sex and gender: An introduction*. Mountain View, CA: Mayfield.

Lorber, J. (1988). From the editor. *Gender & Society, 1,* 5–8.

Lorde, A. (1984). *Sister outsider: Essays and speeches,* New York: Crossing.

Luria, Z. (1986). A methodological critique. *Signs: Journal of Women in Culture and Society, 11,* 316–320.

Maccoby, E. E. (1990). Gender and relationships: A developmental account. *American Psychologist, 43,* 513–520.

MacKinnon, C. A. (1987). Feminism, Marxism, method and the state: Toward feminist jurisprudence. In S. Harding (Ed.), *Feminism and methodology: Social science issues* (pp. 135–156). Bloomington: Indiana University Press.

Manicas, P. T., & Secord, P. F. (1983). Implications for psychology of the new philosophy of science. *American Psychologist, 38,* 399–413.

Maracek, J. (1989). Introduction: Theory and method in feminist psychology [Special issue]. *Psychology of Women Quarterly, 13,* 367–377.

Markus, H., & Oyserman, D. (1989). Gender and thought: The role of the self-concept. In M. Crawford & M. Gentry (Eds.), *Gender and thought: Psychological perspectives* (pp. 100–127). New York: Springer-Verlag.

Martin, J. (1990). Deconstructing organizational taboos: The suppression of gender conflict in organizations. *Organizational Science, 5,* 339–359.

McHugh, M., Koeske, R., & Frieze, I. (1986). Issues to consider in conducting nonsexist psychological research: A guide for researchers. *American Psychologist, 41,* 879–890.

Mednick, M. T. (1989). On the politics of psychological constructs: Stop the bandwagon, I want to get off. *American Psychologist, 44,* 1118–1123.

Merchant, C. (1980). *The death of nature: Women, ecology, and the scientific revolution*. New York: Harper & Row.

Merton, R. (1972). Insiders and outsiders: A chapter in the sociology of knowledge. *American Journal of Sociology, 78,* 9–47.

Meyer, J. (1988). Feminist thought and social psychology. In M. Gergen (Ed.),

Feminist thought and the structure of knowledge (pp. 105–123). New York: New York University Press.

Miller, J. B. (1986). *Toward a new psychology of women* (2nd ed.). Boston: Beacon.

Millman, M., & Kanter, R. (Eds.). (1975). *Another voice: Feminist perspectives on social life and social sciences.* Garden City, NY: Anchor Books.

Morawski, J. G. (1988). Impasse in feminist thought? In M. M. Gergen (Ed.), *Feminist thought and the structure of knowledge* (pp. 182–194). New York: New York University Press.

Morawski, J. G. (1990). Toward the unimagined: Feminism and epistemology in psychology. In R. L. Hare-Mustin & J. Maracek, *Making a difference: Psychology and the construction of gender* (pp. 150–183). New Haven, CT: Yale University Press.

Morgan, G. (Ed.). (1983). Toward a more reflective social science. In G. Morgan (Ed.), *Beyond method: Strategies for social research* (pp. 368–376). Beverly Hills, CA: Sage.

Morris, J. (1974). *Conundrum.* New York: Harcourt, Brace, Jovanovich.

Parlee, M. (1979). Psychology and women. *Signs: Journal of Women in Culture and Society, 5,* 121–133.

Peplau, L. A., & Conrad, E. (1989). Feminist methods in psychology. *Psychology of Women Quarterly, 13,* 379–400.

Prilleltensky, I. (1989). Psychology and the status quo. *American Psychologist, 44,* 795–802.

Rabinow, P., & Sullivan, W. M. (1979). The interpretive turn: Emergence of an approach. In P. Rabinow & W. M. Sullivan (Eds.), *Interpretive social science: A reader* (pp. 1–21). Berkeley: University of California Press.

Reinharz, S. (1985). Feminist distrust: Problems of context and context in sociological work. In D. N. Berg & K. K. Smith (Eds.), *The self in social inquiry: Researching methods* (pp. 153–172). Beverly Hills, CA: Sage.

Reinharz, S. (1992). *Feminist methods in social research.* New York: Oxford University Press.

Reigel, K. F. (1979). *Foundations of dialectical psychology.* San Diego, CA: Academic Press.

Riger, S. (1990). Ways of knowing and organizational approaches to community research. In P. Tolan, C. Keys, F. Chertok, & L. Jason (Eds.), *Researching community psychology* (pp. 42–50). Washington, DC: American Psychological Association.

Riger, S. (1991). Gender dilemmas in sexual harassment policies and procedures. *American Psychologist, 46,* 497–505.

Riger, S. (in preparation). *Psychology of women: Biological, psychological and social perspectives.* New York: Oxford University Press.

Rix, S. E. (Ed.). (1990). *The American woman, 1990–1991.* New York: Norton.

Rosenberg, R. (1982). *Beyond separate spheres.* New Haven, CT: Yale University Press.

Rosenthal, R. (1966). *Experimenter effects in behavioral research*. New York: Appleton-Century-Crofts.

Rossi, A. (1979). Reply by Alice Rossi. *Signs: Journal of Women in Culture and Society, 4*, 712–717.

Sampson, E. E. (1978). Scientific paradigms and social values: Wanted—A scientific revolution. *Journal of Personality and Social Psychology, 36*, 1332–1343.

Sampson, E. E. (1985). The decentralization of identity: Toward a revised concept of personal and social order. *American Psychologist, 40*, 1203–1211.

Scott, J. W. (1988). Deconstructing equality-versus-difference: Or, the uses of poststructuralist theory for feminism. *Feminist Studies, 14*, 33–50.

Segal, L. (1986). *Is the future female? Troubled thoughts on contemporary feminism*. London: Virago.

Sewart, J. J. (1979). Critical theory and the critique of conservative method: In S. G. McNall (Ed.), *Theoretical perspectives in sociology* (pp. 310–322). New York: St. Martin's Press.

Sherif, C. W. (1979). Bias in psychology. In J. A. Sherman & E. T. Beck (Eds.), *A prism of sex: Essays in the sociology of knowledge* (pp. 93–133). Madison: University of Wisconsin Press.

Shields, S. (1975). Functionalism, Darwinism, and the psychology of women: A study in social myth. *American Psychologist, 30*, 739–754.

Smith, D. (1987). *The everyday world as problematic*. Boston: Northeastern University Press.

Snitow, A. (1990). A gender diary. In M. Hirsch & E. F. Keller (Eds.), *Conflicts in feminism* (pp. 9–43). New York: Routledge.

Spelman, E. V. (1988). *Inessential woman: Problems of exclusion in feminist thought*. Boston: Beacon Press.

Stacey, J. (1988). Can there be a feminist ethnography? *Women's Studies International Forum, 11*, 21–27.

Stack, C. (1986). The culture of gender: Women and men of color. *Signs: Journal of Women in Culture and Society, 11*, 321–324.

Unger, R. K. (1979). Toward a redefinition of sex and gender. *American Psychologist, 34*, 1085–1094.

Unger, R. K. (1981). Sex as a social reality: Field and laboratory research. *Psychology of Women Quarterly, 5*, 645–653.

Unger, R. K. (1983). Through the looking glass: No wonderland yet! (The reciprocal relationship between methodology and models of reality). *Psychology of Women Quarterly, 8*, 9–32.

Unger, R. K. (1988). Psychological, feminist, and personal epistemology: Transcending contradiction. In M. M. Gergen (Ed.), *Feminist thought and the structure of knowledge* (pp. 124–141). New York: New York University Press.

Unger, R. K. (1989). Sex, gender, and epistemology. In M. Crawford & M. Gentry (Eds.), *Gender and thought: Psychological perspectives* (pp. 17–35). New York: Springer-Verlag.

Unger, R. K., Draper, R. D., & Pendergrass, M. L. (1986). Personal epistemology and personal experience. *Journal of Social Issues, 42,* 67–79.

Walker, L. (1991). The feminization of psychology. *Psychology of Women Newsletter of Division, 35, 18,* 1, 4.

Walkerdine, V. (1986). Post-structuralist theory and everyday social practices: The family and the school. In S. Wilkerson (Ed.), *Feminist social psychology: Developing theory and practice* (pp. 57–76). Milton Keynes, England: Open University Press.

Weedon, C. (1987). *Feminist practice and poststructuralist theory.* New York: Basil Blackwell.

Weisstein, N. (1971). *Psychology constructs the female: Or, the fantasy life of the male psychologist.* Boston: New England Free Press.

West, C., & Zimmerman, D. H. (1987). Doing gender. *Gender & Society, 1,* 125–151.

Wilkinson, S. (1986). Sighting possibilities: Diversity and commonality in feminist research. In S. Wilkinson (Ed.), *Feminist social psychology: Developing theory and practice* (pp. 7–24). Milton Keynes, England: Open University Press.

Wittig, M. A. (1985). Metatheoretical dilemmas in the psychology of gender. *American Psychologist, 40,* 800–811.

3

THE CRISIS OF EXPERIMENTALISM IN THE 1920s: E. G. BORING AND HIS USES OF HISTORY

JOHN M. O'DONNELL

Edwin G. Boring prefaced his *History of Experimental Psychology* with the assertion that sophisticated psychology requires a historical orientation (Boring, 1929, p. vii). Boring realized that the so-called lessons of history serve as powerful legitimators of contemporary psychological pursuits. The way in which a discipline views its past determines which ideas attain sanction and which invite suspicion, which professional styles are countenanced and which roles are contemned. Since our conceptions of a field's development are inevitably conditioned by the most influential historians of that development, Boring's axiom requires the following corollary: A sophisticated history demands historiographic perspective. Bereft of ex-

---

This article was presented as a paper at the Tenth Annual Meeting of Cheiron: The International Society for the History of the Behavioral and Social Sciences, Wellesley College, Wellesley, Massachusetts, June 1978.

Unless otherwise noted, all letters referenced in the article are located in the *Edwin G. Boring Papers* are are cited with permission of the Harvard University Archives, Cambridge, Massachusetts.

Reprinted from *American Psychologist, 34*, 289–295 (1979). Copyright © 1979 by the American Psychological Association. Reprinted with permission of the author.

perimental controls, the writing of history can easily become tendentious. It behooves us, therefore, to scrutinize the historian's preconceptions and to elicit his or her unstated purposes, for by examining the historian's biases we discover the roots of our own.

If Boring himself did not consider history a forceful persuader, it is doubtful that he, who often boasted of living in the laboratory, would have retreated to the study during what was potentially the most productive period of his life in order to write it.[1] Boring never construed the writing of his *History* as a genteel avocation but as an essential elaboration of his scientific ideology and as a polemic vehicle for his professional aspirations. Robert Young (1966) placed this monumental work "at the centre of both the achievements and the limitations of the history of psychology as a scholarly discipline" (p. 14). We can gain critical insight into both aspects of Boring's scholarly legacy by understanding the forces that prompted his historical engagement. What I wish to do, then, is to examine the intellectual and professional concerns of this staunch experimentalist as he attempted to cope with disturbing developments within his discipline during the 1920s. For Boring, history was not merely a matter of describing the past but of altering the future.

One of Boring's chief preoccupations during the 1920s involved the proscription of what he perceived to be a pernicious tendency toward applied psychology after World War I. His dedication to the ideal of pure research needs no verification here. He devotedly followed the lead of his mentor, E. B. Titchener, who, for example, had criticized behaviorism because he felt that J. B. Watson was asking psychologists to trade a science for a technology (Titchener, 1914, p. 14). At the 1917 Harvard meeting of the Experimentalists, when the dean of Cornell psychology stepped outside that fateful session in which Yerkes and his American associates were discussing how psychologists could assist the war effort, he did so not only because he was a British subject but because he sensed that his colleagues were about to make that trade. How right he was. After the Armistice, G. Stanley Hall (1919) had clucked that the "war has given applied psychology a tremendous impulse. This will, on the whole, do good, for psychology, which is the largest and last of the sciences, must not try to be too pure" (p. 48). George Daniels (1971) reminds us that "science is able to remain 'pure' only so long as it is without power" (p. 314).

Power had shifted significantly to the proponents of applied psychology after the war. Mobilization had invigorated the social ideals of service and efficiency and had stimulated the postwar demand for what was precipitately called psychotechnology. In the 1920s the business of psychology, like that of the country itself, was business. Psychologists had discovered

---

[1]Boring was sensitive to the disciplinary norms that identified historical pursuits with dysfunctional dilettantism. By his own admission, he never overcame his paranoia that "people were saying, 'But anyone can write history. Can he do research?'" (Boring, 1961, p. 15).

with Joseph Jastrow (1930) that applied psychology was "the pay vein that supports the mine" (p. 155), and with Watson (1936) that "it can be just as thrilling to watch the growth of a sales curve of a new product as to watch the learning curves of animals or men" (p. 280). Opportunity had knocked at the laboratory door and beckoned seductively to those inspired to do good while inclined to do well. Those who remained behind—the "experimentalizers," as Boring called them—watched with alarm as applied psychologists seemingly stretched their technologies beyond the sane boundaries of experimental verification and appeared to forget, when they did not repudiate, the traditional concerns that had guided psychological development.[2] When, for example, Jastrow (1930), of all people, declared that psychology was a "twentieth-century achievement" (p. 154), he was attempting to equate applied psychology with the discipline as a whole.

One defense against this short-sighted tendency was historical argumentation. It is no coincidence that only weeks after separating himself from the 1917 "war council" at Harvard, Titchener began writing the historical *Prolegomena* to his *Systematic Psychology* (Weld, 1929, p. xvii). Therein Titchener (1929, pp. 30, 32–33, 65–70, 78–79, 258–259, 266–270) crystallized the dichotomy between pure and applied psychology and argued that psychology's rush toward technology threatened scientific overreach. The most articulate and active disciple of Titchener's viewpoint was to become America's foremost historian of psychology. That too is no coincidence. Having staked his reputation on pure psychology's appeal, Boring sought to restore the research ideal through experimental studies, professional activity, and finally, through historical legitimation. Why he resorted to this final expedient at the expense of the first can be better comprehended by looking at the second.

No sooner had Boring arrived at Harvard in the fall of 1922 to assume an associate professorship than he received an apocalyptic epistle from Titchener (Note 1) warning that "there will have to be a breakdown, a bankruptcy, of common-sense psychologizing before we can get a serious hearing. I doubt if that comes before a century of mental tests." Interpreting Titchener's oracle as a mandate to raise the banner of Cornell psychology at Harvard, Boring apostolically resolved that pure psychology would make its comeback at Cambridge.

In vital respects this quest met little resistance, as Boring entered a psychological vacuum. Psychology at Harvard was a shambles. Functionalism, always uncomfortably close to practicality, was there defunct. Its sponsors were gone. William James had died in 1910, and Hugo Münster-

---

[2]This is, advisedly, an experimentalizer's interpretation of events. In many respects, both experimentalism and applied psychology benefited from the war experience, and the historian must attend to the realities as well as the rhetoric. But the rhetoric involved real apprehensions: Experimentalists reacted to applied psychology on the basis of their perceptions and self-interested calculations.

berg's popularizing and practicalizing of psychology had so disquieted the Harvard philosophers that his fatal collapse at the Radcliffe podium in December 1916 must have seemed to the New England mind downright providential. The promising E. C. Tolman left in 1915; Robert Yerkes, despairing of support for animal psychology, in 1917; and an embittered E. B. Holt, the following year. Within two years of his arrival Boring had forced a reluctant Langfeld to Princeton and by 1924 had become head of Harvard's psychological laboratory (Kuklick, 1977, pp. 413–414, 434, 459–461; Perry, 1930). Structural psychology, programmatically "pure," met little opposition within the Philosophy Department.

And yet it hardly commanded the philosophers' hearty support. Ralph Barton Perry and his colleagues gladly helped Boring keep psychology independent of practicalist alliances with the Medical Department and the Schools of Business and of Education, but they nevertheless considered psychology propaedeutic to philosophy. In this respect, Boring's ambitions for psychology were frustrated, and he spent the next decade struggling to secure psychology's independence from philosophy. As he himself acknowledged, the *History of Experimental Psychology* was written partly to show his philosophic brethren that philosophy had had an important historical role in psychology's development, a role that had served its purpose and had become anachronistic and obtrusive (Boring, Note 2, Note 3, Note 4).[3]

Boring might have tolerated psychology's administrative subordination to philosophy had that dependency involved satisfactory financial support. Finding Boring's laboratory concerns of little theoretical use, however, the philosophers matched the experimentalist's philosophic agnosticism with fiduciary austerity. Writing to James Rowland Angell a fortnight after Titchener's death, Boring (Note 5) described his dilemma:

> Psychology without T[itchener] will bob up and down as it's been doing. You think of all that applied stuff and groan. I am beautifully free of that here; the department would not stand for it.... But the other extreme is philosophy; and my good philosophical colleagues here ... doubt that experimental psychology has yet found anything worth doing.

Consequently, laboratory funding slowed to a trickle. When in 1924 Lewis Terman (Note 6) expressed his amazement that Harvard could possess such a "poverty stricken" laboratory while the memory of James remained, Boring (Note 7) replied caustically that James's speculative propensities precisely explained that indigence. In 1927, for example, the laboratory budget amounted to $148, $31 of which Boring (Note 8) supplied from his own pocket. This impoverished researcher repeatedly attempted to correct Pres-

---

[3]There are, of course, many personal, professional, and intellectual reasons that led Boring to reconstruct psychology's past. I have chosen, however, to concentrate on the single urging that in my opinion most severely affected his interpretation.

ident Lowell's misimpression "that there is no institution that could compete with Harvard" (Boring, Note 9).[4]

Indeed, psychology departments elsewhere could favorably compete with Harvard for faculty, funds, and pupils precisely because they catered to the tendency toward applied psychology that Boring resisted.[5] When, for example, Boring tried to induce Karl Lashley, then financially well endowed by the Behavior Research Fund at Chicago, to fill the vacancy created by McDougall's departure to a more lucrative position at Duke,[6] Lashley (Note 14) insisted that Harvard psychology must first develop "closer affiliations with the biology and medical groups" and recognize that recent trends toward application demanded that the department provide representation "of genetic, social, and personnel work." Boring (Note 15) curtly replied that

> the science, and not its applications should be our chief business.... Almost alone among the universities in America, H[arvard] stands as a place where it is possible to prosecute scientific work without the slightest pressure for application.

Not surprisingly, Lashley decided to remain at Chicago.

The story of Harvard psychology during the 1920s is a narrative of similar professional disappointments stemming from Boring's (Note 16) insistence that "anything that interfered at all with research had better give way at Harvard." Boring's correspondence chronicles his efforts to obtain funding without utilitarian strings attached (see, e.g., Franz, Note 17; Boring, Note 18), his rejection of candidates seeking to obtain degrees in applied fields (Boring, Note 19, Note 20, Note 21, Note 22), and his difficulties in placing those students whom he had trained as pure experimentalists. At both Clark and Harvard he was literally bombarded with requests from other institutions for promising PhDs who could conduct courses and investigations in industrial and educational psychology (Whipple, Note 23; Dashiell, Note 24, Note 25; Gault, Note 26; Boring, Note 27). Everyone but Boring, it seemed, was demanding mental testers. Having himself resisted professionally and financially tempting offers from Columbia, Minnesota, and the Carnegie Institute of Technology because these positions entailed applied work (Bingham, Note 28; Elliott, Note 29; Bor-

---

[4]In fact, six universities ranked ahead of Harvard in total expenditures for psychology (Boring, Note 10).

[5]Curriculum changes represent a sensitive indicator of social pressures on departmental programs. The earliest manifestations of academic responses to social demands are often concessions to undergraduates requiring nontraditional courses. For Boring's reaction to such pressures, see Boring (Note 11).

[6]Boring (Note 12, Note 13) petulantly referred to Duke as the "McDougall dukedumb," where "he will receive a fabulous salary in cash or cigaretts [sic] as compared with what Harvard can do in either medium."

ing, Note 30, Note 31; Thorndike, Note 32; Boring, Note 33),[7] Boring especially regretted the frequent news that colleagues and students had succumbed to what he ruefully called America's commercial democracy (Bingham, Note 36; Findley, Note 37; Anderson, Note 38). The psychologist's task was to cultivate the experimental garden, not to sell apples from the tree of psychological knowledge.

Impoverishment, inability to attract and to place future experimentalists, and the apostasy of established laboratory men fortified Boring's fears for the future of psychological research in America and fueled his resentment of applied psychology.[8] Space limitation proscribes the extensive documentation that can convey the texture of his apprehensions and the thrust of his animosities. Some attention, however, should be given to the strategies he employed to reestablish the experimentalist hegemony in the face of what he perceived to be a mounting crisis.

Boring realized that his mentor's elitist policies had become detrimental to experimentalists' professional aspirations. Titchener had not attended a meeting of the American Psychological Association since 1897 (Boring, 1961, p. 254). He had, in fact, created his Society of Experimentalists in the conviction that the APA as an inclusive and therefore pluralistic organization could not adequately represent the research ideal (Boring, 1967). The postwar growth and enhanced prestige of the APA, however, reinforced Boring's belief that experimentalists needed to reassert their influence within that body if they were to fulfill their mission.

One way of expediting that task was to attempt to make their pope their president. Together with his fellow experimentalizers Karl Dallenbach, Samuel W. Fernberger, and Langfeld, Boring quietly electioneered for Titchener's nomination as early as 1921. Titchener had let it be known in his modest way that he would accept the APA presidential nomination if it were unanimous and if that fact were published. Unanimity unattainable, the plot failed (Boring, Note 39, Note 40; Dallenbach, Note 41; Langfeld, Note 42).

If the experimentalizers could not elect a president; they could at least control the Council. While the presidency possessed symbolic significance, the secretariat had strategic value. The communications center of the APA, this office passed among the experimentalizers in apostolic succession from 1917 to 1928. In 1920 the incumbent Langfeld persuaded Boring to accept the position by convincing him of the need to keep the post in the family.

---

[7]Boring's (Note 33) letter, especially, illustrates his firm opposition to applied psychology (see also Boring, Note 34). Boring (Note 35) viewed Teachers College as "a big machine that would crush the life out of any one [sic] who wanted to do research."

[8]Impoverishment, of course, is a matter of relative deprivation. Historians of science must beware of rhetorical cries bemoaning America's "indifference to basic research." Nevertheless, delineation of the "real" state of experimentalism in the 1920s should be subordinated to a depiction of those imperfect apprehensions that motivated psychologists and that explain their professional strategies.

"I should much regret seeing things in the hands of an applied man," wrote Langfeld to his successor, "... you are keenly interested in the scientific aspects of psychology, and we must do all we can to keep up our standards" (Langfeld, Note 43, Note 44). Boring passed the torch in 1923 to John Anderson, an animal experimentalist who had studied with Yerkes. When Anderson was named Director of the Institute of Child Welfare in 1925, he apologized to Boring for betraying the experimental trust and tried to assure him: "I will not lose my present interest in the science of psychology, nor my feeling for research. I hope still to be an experimentalist" (Note 45). But not the APA's secretary. That job fell immediately to Fernberger, an intimate friend of Boring, whose self-ordained duty had been to serve as gadfly to the scientific consciences of his Pennsylvania colleagues, whom he condescendingly referred to as "the Witmerian applied bunch" (Fernberger, Note 46).[9]

Attempting to enhance the status of research at the expense of application, the experimentalizers used their positions on the Executive Council to accomplish two tactical objectives. The first involved criteria for association membership. A committee to revise membership requirements recommended in 1921 the discarding of nonacademic positions as a basis for belonging and prescribed published research and the PhD degree. A 1924 committee created the category of associate membership (Fernberger, 1932). Represented as efforts to uplift professional standards, these proposals served to suppress applied endeavor within the APA (Reisman, 1966, p. 185; Wallin, 1960). Even the associate membership—justified as a liberalization of the tendency toward restrictionism—represented a second-class, nonvoting citizenship, a badge of scientific inferiority (Fernberger, Note 48, Note 49; Anderson, Note 50). All of the members of the 1924 committee and all but one of the 1921 deputation were affiliates of Titchener's society. Both committees were chaired by E. G. Boring.

Circumscribing applied endeavor represented a defensive maneuver; offensively, Boring attempted to energize experimental activity by publicizing its worth. One way of increasing experimentalism's visibility was to inflate reports of its vitality. His "Statistics of the American Psychological Association in 1920," published in the *Psychological Bulletin*, tabulated research interests by fields and concluded that experimental research engaged the vast majority of laborers (Boring, 1920). Boring divided applied psychology into a multitude of disparate fields, thus fragmenting the opposition by making applied psychology appear as a narrow subspecialty. Yet his public stance belied his personal apprehension. While he was juggling labels in order to provide statistical "proof" of experimentalism's vigorous hegemony, he was privately bemoaning to Madison Bentley that "the test-

---

[9]When Fernberger left Clark for the University of Pennsylvania, his students (Note 47) expressed to him their hopes that he would "carry the only true Gospel to the unenlightened in the wilderness of Penn!"

ing sickens me more and more. Think of Germany going on as it is with Gestalt psychology, and the APA being able to find only 5 experimental papers, three of which are rather elementary (do not repeat this) ..." (Boring, Note 51). The situation, however, was hardly a secret. Lewis Terman (1921), the watchdog of applied psychology, immediately attacked Boring's methods in the *Journal of Applied Psychology*, using Boring's data to show that 51.5% of the APA membership was engaged in applied psychology, as opposed to 48.5% in experimental research.

If experimentalism were indeed as robust as Boring proclaimed, it is doubtful that he would have been campaigning for the expansion of experimental sessions at the annual meetings (Boring, Note 52). Boring (Note 53, Note 54) fought for a yearly conference dedicated to (1) improving communication between experimentalists, (2) dissolving links between experimental and applied psychologists, (3) publicizing experimental research, (4) engaging graduate students, (5) exhibiting the "laboratory atmosphere," and (6) abolishing "school prejudices." I have itemized his stated purposes because I wish to suggest that these exact intents likewise informed his writing of A *History of Experimental Psychology*. In short, Boring sought to make experimentalism more visible. If the experimentalists deprecated the uses of psychology in advertising, they never doubted the value of advertising for their psychology.

Boring's *History*, published in 1929 and dedicated to the recently deceased Titchener, "the historian *par excellence*," became not only experimentalism's consummate advertisement but also an intellectual apologia for the professional lives of embattled experimenters and a vital component of the disciplinary strategy thus far discussed. Boring arranged the history of modern psychological inquiry in terms of what it meant to experimentalism (and hence, in Boring's view, to science itself). He postulated a progressive consistency that could only be maintained by excising in Procrustean fashion a huge portion of psychological endeavor. He conspicuously ignored the impact of utilitarian concerns on psychological development.

Once again—this time privately—Terman protested Boring's experimentalist bias. Correctly claiming that Boring's magnum opus was more than the history of *experimental* psychology, Terman argued that a title which subsumed autonomous fields of research under experimentalism was invidious and ultimately misleading. "Concretely," replied Boring, "what title would you have given the book? You cannot say 'History of Psychology' because that is what the other histories have been, and Democritus and Aristotle come in. 'A History of Scientific Psychology' would have been just as offensive to you. I vote that we wait for history to change" (Boring, Note 55).

Ironically, Boring had prefatorily acknowledged in his *History* that psychologists caused as well as awaited change. In psychology's past, he wrote, "men have mattered much. Authority has again and again carried the day" (p. viii). The authoritative *History of Experimental Psychology* helped carry the day for proponents of the experimental ideal because it interpreted psychology's progress in terms of that ideal. It changed history by reorienting the way people conceived of it. But it did not do so without help from historical circumstance over which its author had no control.

Ten years after Titchener had warned of "the bankruptcy of common-sense psychologizing" even applied psychologists were persuaded to agree with him. During the 1920s applied psychologists had managed to convince themselves that their work had contributed to the country's thriving prosperity. But bullishness proved transient, and in the atmosphere of recrimination and accusation that followed the stock market crash and ushered in the Great Depression, psychology began, in the words of Charles Judd (1932), "paying the price of its popularity and of its intense human appeal" (p. 230).

The collapse of business prosperity helped to convince psychologists that their disciplinary stocks had been watered down by hasty application and by inflated promises of psychology's social value; that in their rush to supply the increasing demand for their services they had forsaken the broad theoretical foundations of their work. Boring's *History* appeared at precisely the time when disgruntled experimentalists were inclined to say "I told you so." Thus Bentley (1936), an ardent Titchenerian structuralist, praised that

> small number of psychologists who have built solidly outward from central and fundamental principles instead of merely translating situations which arise in business, advertising, ... and so on, into terms which possess the flavor instead of the essence of a well-integrated science. (pp. 63–64)

Judd (1932) agreed that "all of us who are at work in special fields suffer from the lack of well-grounded general doctrines" (p. 230). Even Jastrow (1930) urged "the psychologist of the future ... to acquire a sense of his antecedents" (p. 161). If doctrinal credos and historical antecedents were needed to secure scientific salvation after the fall, Boring could show the penitent psychologist where these could be found.

Boring had his axe to grind and I have mine. Jastrow (1930) knew that "to speak of the renaissance of psychology, especially in the American setting, without explicit recognition of the practical motive would be a glaring omission; for that renaissance found its momentum in the appeal for the regulation of human affairs" (p. 155). But Boring and his fellow puritans referred not to psychology's renaissance but to psychology's reformation. Embarrassed by the crass opportunism of applied psychology in the 1920s, he excised it from his historical vision as he sought to extirpate it from his professional environment. And the historiography of psychology has followed Boring's lead. To use a tempting analogy, he bequeathed to us a structuralist's interpretation of psychology's development: He delineated the intellectual *content* but not the social *function* of psychology in America. I hope this article has helped to explain why. The history of psychology will advance as a scholarly discipline in proportion to its attendance to both aspects of scientific development, to the interdependence of ideas and institutions. Beneficiaries of Boring's immense erudition, we must not remain prisoners of his perspective.

REFERENCE NOTES

1. Titchener, E. B. Letter to E. G. Boring, September 8, 1922.
2. Boring, E. G. Letter to E. B. Titchener, March 15, 1929.
3. Boring, E. G. Letter to J. G. Beebe-Center, November 27, 1926.
4. Boring, E. G. Letter to H. Langfeld, December 3, 1928.
5. Boring, E. G. Letter to J. R. Angell, August 17, 1927.
6. Terman, L. Letter to E. G. Boring, April 16, 1924.
7. Boring, E. G. Letter to L. Terman, April 23, 1924.
8. Boring, E. G. Letter to Wolfgang Köhler, June 4, 1925. *Wolfgang Köhler papers*, American Philosophical Society Library, Philadelphia, Pennsylvania.
9. Boring, E. G. Letter to H. Langfeld, March 15, 1922.
10. Boring, E. G. Letter to Members of Psychology and Philosophy, March 1, 1924. *Abbot Lawrence Lowell papers*, Harvard University Archives, Cambridge, Massachusetts.
11. Boring E. G. Letter to W. McDougall, April 16, 1923.
12. Boring E. G. Letter to H. Langfeld, December 13, 1922.
13. Boring, E. G. Letter to J. G. Beebe-Center, December 20, 1926.
14. Lashley, K. Letter to E. G. Boring, January 2, 1928.
15. Boring, E. G. Letter to K. Lashley, January 13, 1928.
16. Boring, E. G. Letter to H. Shapley, December 7, 1925.
17. Franz, S. I. Letter to E. G. Boring, May 29, 1921.
18. Boring, E. G. Letter to A. L. Lowell, March 24, 1927.
19. Boring, E. G. Letter to E. W. Smith, January 8, 1925.
20. Boring, E. G. Letter to C. W. Smith, October 1, 1925.
21. Boring, E. G. Letter to J. F. Sly, April 18, 1929.
22. Boring, E. G. Letter to "Miss Abbot," October 1, 1929.
23. Whipple, G. Letter to E. G. Boring, September 29, 1919.
24. Dashiell, J. F. Letter to E. G. Boring, February 3, 1921.
25. Dashiell, J. F. Letter to E. G. Boring, April 10, 1922.

26. Gault, R. H. Letter to E. G. Boring, July 26, 1921.
27. Boring, E. G. Letter to Mrs. C. W. Perky, January 23, 1924.
28. Bingham, W. V. Letter to E. G. Boring, May 9, 1916.
29. Elliot, R. M. Letter to E. G. Boring, March 7, 1921.
30. Boring, E. G. Letter to R. M. Elliott, March 14, 1921.
31. Boring, E. G. Letter to E. L. Thorndike, January 21, 1921.
32. Thorndike, E. L. Letter to E. G. Boring, January 31, 1921.
33. Boring, E. G. Letter to E. L. Thorndike, March 22, 1921.
34. Boring, E. G. Letter to C. M. Campbell, November 4, 1926.
35. Boring, E. G. Letter to R. M. Yerkes, February 4, 1921.
36. Bingham, H. C. Letter to E. G. Boring, January 3, 1921.
37. Findley, A. E. Letter to E. G. Boring, November 10, 1924.
38. Anderson, J. E. Letter to E. G. Boring, June 12, 1925.
39. Boring, E. G. Letter to R. M. Yerkes, January 18, 1921.
40. Boring, E. G. Letter to S. I. Franz, January 18, 1921.
41. Dallenbach, K. Letter to E. G. Boring, April 21, 1921.
42. Langfeld, H. Letter to E. G. Boring, November 28, 1921.
43. Langfeld, H. Letter to E. G. Boring, March 29, 1919.
44. Langfeld, H. Letter to E. G. Boring, November 27, 1919.
45. Anderson, J. E. Letter to E. G. Boring, June 12, 1925.
46. Fernberger, S. W. Letter to E. G. Boring, December 2, 1921.
47. Various students. Letter to S. W. Fernberger, December 23, 1920. *Samuel Weiller Fernberger correspondence*, University of Pennsylvania Biographical File, University of Pennsylvania Archives, Philadelphia, Pennsylvania.
48. Fernberger, S. W. Letter to E. G. Boring, February 5, 1923.
49. Fernberger, S. W. Letter to E. G. Boring, May 2, 1924.
50. Anderson, J. E. Letter to E. G. Boring, February 20, 1923.
51. Boring, E. G. Letter to M. Bentley, December 14, 1922.
52. Boring, E. G. Memo to directors of psychological laboratories from the APA. APA folder (1923–1924), *Edwin G. Boring papers*, Harvard University Archives, Cambridge, Massachusetts.
53. Boring, E. G. Letter to K. Lashley, March 14, 1924.
54. Boring, E. G. Letter to K. Lashley, May 27, 1924.
55. Boring, E. G. Letter to L. Terman, June 30, 1930.

REFERENCES

Bentley, M. Autobiography. In Carl Murchison (Ed.), *A history of psychology in autobiography* (Vol. 3). Worcester, Mass.: Clark University Press, 1936.

Boring, E. G. Statistics of the American Psychological Association in 1920. *Psychological Bulletin*, 1920, *17*, 271–278.

Boring, E. G. *A history of experimental psychology*. New York: Century, 1929.

Boring, E. G. *Psychologist at large: An autobiography and selected essays*. New York: Basic Books, 1961.

Boring, E. G. Titchener's Experimentalists. *Journal of the History of the Behavioral Sciences*, 1967, *3*, 315–325.

Daniels, G. H. *Science in American society: A social history*. New York: Knopf, 1971.

Fernberger, S. W. The American Psychological Association: A historical summary, 1892–1930. *Psychological Bulletin*, 1932, *29*, 1–89.

Hall, G. S. Some possible effects of the war on American psychology. *Psychological Bulletin*, 1919, *16*, 48–49.

Jastrow, J. Autobiography. In Carl Murchison (Ed.), *A history of psychology in autobiography* (Vol. 1). Worcester, Mass.: Clark University Press, 1930.

Judd, C. H. Autobiography. In Carl Murchison (Ed.), *A history of psychology in autobiography* (Vol. 2). Worcester, Mass.: Clark University Press, 1932.

Kuklick, B. *The rise of American philosophy: Cambridge, Massachusetts, 1860–1930*. New Haven, Conn.: Yale University Press, 1977.

Perry, R. B. Philosophy, 1870–1929. In S. E. Morison (Ed.), *The development of Harvard University since the inauguration of President Eliot, 1869–1929*, Cambridge, Mass.: Harvard University Press, 1930.

Reisman, J. M. *The development of clinical psychology*. New York: Appleton-Century-Crofts, 1966.

Terman, L. The status of applied psychology in the United States. *Journal of Applied Psychology*, 1921, *5*, 1–4.

Titchener, E. B. On "Psychology as the behaviorist views it." *Proceedings of the American Philosophical Society*, 1914, *53*, 1–17.

Titchener, E. B. *Systematic psychology: Prolegomena*. New York: Macmillan, 1929.

Wallin, J. E. W. History of the struggles within the American Psychological Association to attain membership requirements, test standardization, certification of psychological practitioners, and professionalization. *Journal of General Psychology*, 1960, *63*, 287–308.

Watson, J. G. Autobiography. In Carl Murchison (Ed.), *A history of psychology in autobiography* (Vol. 3). Worcester, Mass.: Clark University Press, 1936.

Weld, H. P. Preface. In E. B. Titchener, *Systematic psychology: Prolegomena*. New York: Macmillan, 1929.

Young, R. M. Scholarship and the history of the behavioral sciences. *History of Science*, 1966, *5*, 1–51.

II

ESTABLISHING THE DISCIPLINE OF PSYCHOLOGY

INTRODUCTION: ESTABLISHING THE DISCIPLINE OF PSYCHOLOGY

If there is one thing that most students recall from courses in the history of psychology, it is that experimental psychology began with the founding of Wilhelm Wundt's (1832–1920) laboratory at the University of Leipzig, Germany, in 1879. Although the event and date are somewhat arbitrary, they are probably as good as any and better than most. There was much other psychological thought and activity on the European continent, however. Eventually, Wundtian psychology, French clinical work, evolutionary theory, Scottish realism, and the incipient indigenous psychology blended near the end of the 19th century in the United States to form the "New Psychology," a psychology with a scientific foundation. This developed into a discipline with its own departments, courses, professional societies, journals, and meetings. Working within the framework of academic politics, the "New Psychologists" had to establish their place at the table. In general, they tried to do this by presenting the field as science, allied with physics, chemistry, astronomy, and physiology. Most worked hard to distance themselves from such "softer" topics as idealism, metaphysics, and spiritualism. This was to be an empirically and experimentally based discipline. With that approach, the New Psychologists hoped to establish the legitimacy of the New Psychology. The central theme of the chapters in this section concerns the nature of the science that would be developed and disagreements about the most effective course.

Although Wundt had important predecessors, we can begin with him. When many authors have described Wundt's psychology, they have presented misleading or erroneous pictures. The Wundt portrayed in many books and memorized by several generations of students is not the real Wilhelm Wundt of Leipzig. In the past quarter of a century, scholars, including Arthur L. Blumenthal, have re-evaluated Wundt's oeuvre and found a very different story. In chapter 4, "A Reappraisal of Wilhelm Wundt" (1975), Blumenthal brings out nicely the manner in which the popularity of various approaches ebbs and flows with broader cultural trends. During the first part of the 20th century, psychology was being established as a science. Those advocating this development battled to earn for psychology a place among the natural sciences. None was more active in this area than was Harvard psychologist Edwin G. Boring (1886–1968). When Boring, a student of Edward B. Titchener (1867–1927), wrote his famous *A History of Experimental Psychology* (1929), on which many psychologists cut their teeth, he presented a view of Wundt that justified the scientific approach but misrepresented Wundt's views. As Blumenthal shows, Wundt did not rely on introspection, did not use the model of chemistry with its elements as a model, and viewed mental activity as a process. He was a voluntarist, who believed that apperception, or focal attention, was an act of will. Although properly credited for his development of scientific psychology, Wundt opposed the movement to separate the New Psychology from philosophy. He developed a *Völkerpsychologie*, or cultural psychology, that dealt with language, myth, religion, art, law, culture, and society. This was not the narrow, scientific psychology that has been portrayed. Blumenthal concludes with a somewhat presentist analysis of the impact of Wundt's approach on recent cognitive psychology. We now have a more balanced understanding of Wundt's work. Still, we must remember that each generation treats Wundt's text in its own terms. Blumenthal's Wundt is the product of the cognitive psychology of his time; further revisions are to be expected, but future portrayals should be both more faithful to the original than have been those of the past and consistent with the dominant views of their times.

It is a mistake to think that American psychology began with William James (1842–1910). Prior to James there was a rich tradition of mental and moral philosophy that dealt with many of the focal problems of what would become psychology in the United States. In chapter 5, "Contributions of American Mental Philosophers to Psychology in the United States" (2000), Alfred H. Fuchs works to correct the long-standing view that American psychology began with James. He begins by tracing the origins of the tradition of neglect. He then discusses the work of some of the American mental philosophers, including Joseph Haven (1816–1874), Laurens Hickok (1798–1888), Thomas C. Upham (1799–1872), and Francis Wayland (1796–1865), and the context within which they taught and wrote. Fuchs completes the cycles with a discussion of the ascendancy of the New Psychology and the decline of the mental philosophy that preceded it. Nevertheless, the old psychology had an important role in shaping the New Psychology with regard to a home for the New Psychology, shaping its content, establishing a tradition of treating the mind scientifically, and establishing a tradition of functionalism, as Fuchs reveals.

It is fair to say that with James, and particularly with the publication of his 1890 *Principles of Psychology*, the traditional American psychology changed substantially, moved toward its status as a separate discipline, and began to merge as a force in American intellectual life. We know James, correctly, as the man most responsible for introducing the New Psychology to America. This picture is more complex than that, however. At the same time that he introduced the experimental approach, James was a dissenter from the hard-science view of psychology, favoring a psychology that was based on philosophical concerns and with personal experience. James was a master at reflecting on his mental life, his subjective experiences, and conveying them to the reader in ways that ring true (Bjork, 1988). In chapter 6, "William James and the Art of Human Understanding" (1992), David E. Leary shows that James's psychology and philosophy were based as much on his background as an artist as on science. For James, human understanding was the art of developing new perceptual patterns by detecting similarities among phenomena that were not previously obvious. He believed that we do this through analogy and metaphor. Leary shows how James repeatedly used metaphors from art in his efforts to present his versions of philosophy, especially pragmatism, and psychology. James was a dissenter from the hard-nosed scientific approach. He struggled with the materialistic implications of scientific psychology and sought a very different psychology than that which was emerging in his time.

Deborah J. Coon in chapter 7, "Testing the Limits of Sense and Science: American Experimental Psychologists Combat Spiritualism, 1880–1920" (1992), explores these themes further. While his students and colleagues were trying to establish the scientific nature of psychology by distancing it from spiritualism and psychic research, James was going the other way, trying to build bridges with spiritualistic endeavors. We thus have a fascinating tension in which most psychologists sought either to demonstrate the fraudulent nature of spiritualism or to analyze spiritualistic claims in terms of deception and belief while their acknowledged leader embarrassed them with his affinity to psychical research. The task of the scientific psychologists was difficult because of widespread public interest in spiritual phenomena and because the psychologists risked being branded as materialistic atheists in a deistic intellectual climate. Coon beautifully portrays these tensions, which were so critical for the science that was developing at the periphery of the scientific enterprise.

An emerging discipline must evolve a set of structures, journals, societies, departments, and the like to establish its legitimacy. In chapter 8, "Origins and Early Years of the American Psychological Association, 1890–1906" (1992), Michael M. Sokal reviews the work of G. Stanley Hall (1844–1924) in the founding of psychology's premier society, the American Psychological Association (APA). He traces the first 16 years of its history and shows how the organization was affected by personal struggles, academic politics, and the effort to become separate from philosophy. Hall was, in many respects, a difficult man with whom to work, and that complicated the development of the discipline. His autocratic approach to editing the *American Journal of Psychology*, which he founded, led to the founding of the *Psychological Review* in reaction. As part of academic politics, we see the APA aligning itself with the American Society of Naturalists and the American Association for the Advancement of Science and struggling with the role of philosophers in the organization as part of its efforts to develop its image as a science. Sokal shows how psychology in general and the APA in particular developed in the ecological context existing at the time of their emergence.

As psychology was emerging as a scientific discipline it was critical that standards of methodology be developed. Kurt Danziger traces the development of experimental methodology in chapter 9, "The Origins of the Psychological Experiment as a Social Institution" (1985). Psychology students today are socialized by their courses to accept certain ideas of what constitutes an experiment and the proper relationship between the experimenter and the subject. They often fail to realize that alternative models are possible and that the one that became dominant in American psychology has a history. Danziger focuses on the experiment as a social interaction and differentiates two primary models: the Leipzig and the Paris approaches.

In the Leipzig model, there was little differentiation between experimenter and subject. The participants often exchanged roles. The identity of the subjects, often trained observers who were coworkers, is usually indicated in the research report. With the Paris model, one that developed in the context of research on hypnosis, by contrast, the roles of experimenter and subject were rigidly differentiated. The Paris research was oriented more toward abnormal functioning, the Leipzig toward normal function. According to Danziger, when the Americans evolved a model of research, they stressed a short-term, one-on-one relationship between subject and experimenter. Hall's approach shifted the emphasis from the analysis of psychological processes to the distribution of psychological characteristics in populations. In later work, Danziger (1990) expanded on this article, developing more clearly the contrasts among the Leipzig and Paris models and the model of Sir Francis Galton (1822–1911) in England. Galton's approach was fee based, wherein there was a utilitarian contract between the subject and experimenter. We can see that there are alternate ways of structuring the experiment, and these alternatives merit recognition and exploration in contrast to the blind acceptance of received approaches.

Reading through these chapters we can see the struggles in which the early New Psychologists were engaged in their efforts to establish their science. They were generally successful in establishing their scientific approach, albeit one relevant to social problems such as those in education. By World War I they had in place all of the accoutrements of an established scientific discipline, if one near the boundaries of science.

REFERENCES

Bjork, D. W. (1988). *William James: The center of his vision*. New York: Columbia University Press.

Boring, E. G. (1929). *A history of experimental psychology*. New York: Century.

Danziger, K. (1990). *Constructing the subject: Historical origins of psychological research*. New York: Cambridge University Press.

James, W. (1890). *Principles of psychology*. New York: Henry Holt.

4

A REAPPRAISAL OF WILHELM WUNDT

ARTHUR L. BLUMENTHAL

Approximately 100 years ago, in an era of intellectual ferment, events of marked consequence took place in the history of psychology. It was in the decade of the 1870s that the first handbook of experimental psychology appeared, followed soon by the founding of the first formal laboratory of experimental psychology. Both were the achievements of Wilhelm Wundt, ever since recognized as experimental psychology's great patron, though later barred from any role that might remotely resemble sainthood. Soon after the wave of "new" psychologists spread out from Wundt's laboratory, a series of intellectual revolutions largely erased from memory the content of Wundtian psychological theory.

Now that the movement set in motion by Wundt has come through its first century, it would seem fitting to mark the centenary by briefly turning back, reexamining psychology's historical foundations, and paying homage to the founding father. There is, however, another reason for re-

---

This article is a revised and expanded version of a talk presented to the New York Academy of Sciences, New York City, October 19, 1974.
Reprinted from *American Psychologist*, 30, 1081–1088 (1975). Copyright © 1975 by the American Psychological Association. Reprinted with permission of the author.

view, being less ceremonial and clearly more interesting. To put it simply, the few current Wundt-scholars (and some do exist) are in fair agreement that Wundt as portrayed today in many texts and courses is largely fictional and often bears little resemblance to the actual historical figure (cf. Blumenthal, 1970; Bringmann, Balance, & Evans, 1975; Mischel, 1970).

Naturally, it might be suspected that the above radical statement is only the nit-picking of a few antiquarians obsessed with minor matters of interpretation. But alas, such is not the case. These are claims about the very fundamentals of Wundt's work, often asserting the opposite of what has been a standard description prevailing over much of the past century. Yet, if popular historical accounts of Wundt are in need of serious correction, then one might again ask whether Wundt still turns out to be irrelevant and of little interest. This article is addressed to that question, and its answers will, I suspect, contain some surprises for many readers.

There is another question that immediately follows upon these claims. It is, How could such historical misinterpretations have arisen? This is surely a fascinating question but one requiring separate treatment. For the moment merely take note that Wundtian anecdotes have long been passed down from author to author without worthy recourse to original sources, and, also, that it is common in intellectual history for later schools of thought to foster distortions and misinterpretations of earlier ones—psychology, of course, offering numerous opportunities. For now, let us examine the fundamentals of Wundt's psychology that have, for better or worse, been disguised or lost in the course of history's machinations.

WUNDT'S METHOD

The basic premise in Wundtian psychology is that the only certain reality is immediate experience. Proceeding from this premise, Wundt had accepted the following goals for all science: the construction of explanations of experience and the development of techniques for objectifying experience. By the latter, he meant that the scientist attempts to communicate and reproduce his experiences in others in standardized ways; thus it becomes possible to perform tests that lead to public agreement about phenomena and to agreement about their explanation. This was commonplace for Wundt and is found at the outset of many of his texts.

In the natural sciences, as Wundt continues, it is the attributes of experience derived from external objects and energies that are subjected to tests, explanations, and public agreement. But in the case of psychology, it is the attributes of experience derived from the processes of the experiencing subject that are made the object of tests, explanations, and public agreement. These psychological entities include experienced memory and perceptual capacities, fluctuations of attention or alertness, ranges of our sensitivities, etc. In the jargon of today, we would without hesitation say "human information-processing capacities."

Yet it is this subtle division between the physical and the psychological sciences that has led to innumerable textbook treatments of Wundt as a mind–body dualist, and that is one of history's glaring distortions. For if you read Wundt, in almost any of his texts, you will discover that his rejection of mind–body dualism is as emphatic a statement on the matter as you are likely ever to encounter. He often said that psychology cannot be defined as the science of the mind because there are no objects called "minds" that are distinct from objects called "bodies," a scenario that appears repeatedly in his works.

Although physiologists and psychologists study one and the same organism, Wundt viewed them as analyzing and objectifying different experiences derived from different vantage points. This is now usually called the "double-aspect" resolution of the mind–body problem. And Wundt's use of the phrase "psychophysical parallelism" referred to this same view, though again it unfortunately led many later reviewers to the mind–body-dualism interpretation. Rather, it referred to the separate orientations of physiology and psychology where it is separate *methodologies*, in the sense of separate types of observations, that here run in parallel.

Another serious problem of misinterpretation concerns Wundt and *introspection*. Contrary to frequent descriptions, Wundt was not an introspectionist as that term is popularly applied today. The thrust behind his entire experimental program was the claim that progress in psychology had been slow because of reliance on casual, unsystematic introspection, which had led invariably to unresolved debates. In several books and monographs (in particular, 1888 and 1907) Wundt argued that armchair introspection could, in principle, never succeed, being a logical impossibility as a scientific technique. The 1907 monograph was a severe critique of the Würzburg psychologists for their return to an earlier style of unverifiable introspection.

Wundt promoted the cause of experimental psychology more through accomplishments in his laboratory than through polemics. From its outset, the Wundtian program followed the general conceptions of experimental science and the requirement that private experience be made public and replicable, in this case for the study of perception, attention, memory, etc. To be sure, there were some disagreements, conflicting data, and unsupported speculations in those days, just as there are today.

Wundt's adherence to the canons of experimental procedure was so strict that, in fact, it sharply limited his use of experiments in psychology. Thus, in the case of most "higher" mental processes such as language or concept information, he felt that true experiments were not feasible. Instead these topics must, he argued, be studied through techniques of historical and naturalistic observation and also of logical analysis. This Wundt did by examining the social-cultural products of human mental activity, making logical inferences about the underlying processes. In the case of language, for example, he went deeply into the technical study of linguistics (Blumenthal, 1970). So in these ways, a large part of Wundt's psychological work is not experimental.

WUNDT'S THEORETICAL SYSTEM

But so far these are methodological matters and do not speak to the essence of Wundt's psychological theory. What emerged as the paradigm psychological phenomenon in his theoretical system would now be described as selective volitional attention. It is why he identified his psychology as "voluntaristic" to distinguish it from other schools (see especially Wundt, 1896b). He did not use the label "structuralist" which was proffered and perpetuated by Titchener and James.

Mischel (1970) has recently surveyed Wundt's writings, detailing Wundt's grounding in volitional-motivational processes. Yet it was with apparent forceful impact on later historical interpretation that Titchener (1908) had given short shrift to this theme, at the very heart of Wundtian psychology, because of the overtones of continental idealist philosophy in notions of volition. Titchener's longest period of formal education came at Oxford, and not surprisingly he maintained certain biases toward the British empiricist-sensationist tradition, even though that tradition was anathema to Wundt's views, and more than any other topic the brunt of Wundt's polemical writings.

Without giving supportive citation, Boring (1950) states that Wundt had opposed the implication of an active volitional agent in psychology. But now Mischel (1970) with extensive citation has shown, on the contrary, that volition-motivation is a central, primary theme in Wundt's psychology. Briefly, that theme runs as follows: To explain a volitional act on the basis of its motives is different from the explanation of occurrences in the physical sciences, and "volitional activities are the type in terms of which all other psychological phenomena are to be construed" (Wundt, 1908, Vol. 3, p. 162).

Wundt's studies of volition, in turn, amounted to an elaborate analysis of selective and constructive attentional processes (often summarized under the term *apperception*), which he localized in the brain's frontal lobes. Other psychological processes (perceptions, thoughts, memories) are, according to Wundt, generally under the control of the central attentional process.

It is on this basis that Wundt claimed another point of separation between psychology and physics—a difference between psychological and physical causality (see especially, Wundt, 1894). In the case of physics, actions and events obey inviolable laws; but in the case of psychosocial phenomena, actions are *made* by an active agent with reference to rule systems.

Wundt acknowledged the principle of the conservation of energy and, consequently, the theoretical possibility of reducing psychological observations to physiological or physical descriptions. Still, he argued, these physical sciences would then describe the act of greeting a friend, eating an apple, or writing a poem in terms of the laws of mechanics or in terms of physiology. And no matter how fine-grained and complicated we make such descriptions, they are not useful as descriptions of psychological events. Those events need be described in terms of intentions and goals, according to Wundt, because the actions, or physical forces, for a given psychological event may take an infinite variety of physical forms. In one notable example, he argued that human language cannot be described adequately in terms of its physical shape or of the segmentation of utterances, but rather must be described as well in terms of the rules and intentions underlying speech. For the ways of expressing a thought in language are infinitely variable, and language is governed by creative rules rather than fixed laws (Wundt, 1900–1920).

MECHANISM OR ORGANISM?

These distinctions lead to a related and consistent theme in Wundt's writings concerning what he called "the false materialization of mental processes," which he found prevalent in other schools of psychology, especially associationism. His reactions against associationism were directed mostly at the form it had assumed in mid-19th-century Germany in Herbart's psychology.

Herbart, you may recall, had atomized mental processes into elemental ideas that became associated into compounds according to classical associationist descriptions. Wundt considered that approach to be a mere primitive analogy to systems of physical mechanics, and he argued at length that those systems teach little about the interrelations of psychological processes (Wundt, 1894). For those systems were oblivious to what he felt was the essential distinction between psychological and physical causality; they portrayed mental processes as if they were a "mere field of billiard balls" colliding and interacting with each other, where central control processes are lacking.

Boring's widely repeated assertion that Wundt turned to chemistry for his model seems clearly inaccurate to the serious reader of Wundt. However, the Wundtian mental-chemistry cliché did become popular among later textbook writers. Wundt did in his early years make brief, passing references to J. S. Mill's use of a chemical analogy to describe certain perceptual processes, namely, that one cannot determine the quality of water (i.e., "wetness") from the separate qualities of oxygen and hydrogen. Similarly, the qualities of a perception are not directly given in its underlying elements.

But Wundt points out that this analogy does not go far enough, and by the end of the century he is describing it as a false analogy because the chemical synthesis is, in the final analysis, wholly determined by its elements while the psychological synthesis is "truly a new formation, not merely the result of a chemical-like formation." And, "J. S. Mill's discussion in which the mental formation is conceived as a 'psychic chemistry' leaves out its most significant aspect—the special creative character of psychic syntheses" (Wundt, 1902, p. 684). What the chemical analogy lacks is the independent, constructive, attentional process which in the psychological case is the source of the synthesis.

Wundt did, of course, write chapters on elementary sensory-perceptual processes and elemental affective processes, but with the emphasis on *process*. And he acknowledged that a major part of any scientific methodology involved analysis of a system into component processes. Further, he stressed that these elements were to be taken as hypothetical constructs. Such elemental processes would never actually be observed, he thought, in pure isolation but would always be aspects or features of larger images or configurations.

Here Wundt used the German word *Gebilde*. For a translation, the dictionary (*Cassell's*) gives us the following choices: either "creation," "product," "structure," "formation," "system," "organization," "image," "form," or "figure." But in the few English translations of Wundt, we find the word "compound," unfortunately again suggesting the analogy to chemistry. "Compound" is a conceivable choice, but in the context of Wundt's configurational system it seems not the best term. Another example: Wundt's "whole or unified mental impression" (*Gesamtvorstellung*) is unfortunately translated as "aggregate ideas."

In the following note in an obscure book, published in 1944, Wundt's own son, Max Wundt, rebutted the caricature of his father's work as a psychology of mental elements:

> One may follow the methodologically obvious principle of advancing from the simple to the complicated, indeed even employing the approach that would construct the mind from primitive mechanical elements (the so-called psychology of mental elements). In this case, however, method and phenomena can become grossly confused.... Whoever in particular ascribes to my father such a conception could not have read his books. In fact, he had formed his scientific views of mental processes in reaction against a true elementistic psychology, namely against that of Herbart, which was dominant in those days. (p. 15)

To confound matters further, the later movement toward holism in

Gestalt psychology placed Wundt in a contrastive position and again portrayed him as an elementalist and associationist in ways not characteristic of his intentions. True, there is always a chapter titled "Associations" in Wundt's texts—but it is a far cry from the serial linkages of atomistic ideas found among many associationists. Wundt's "associations" are "structural integrations," "creative syntheses," "fusions," and "perceptual patternings."

Wundt's later students, including Sander, Krueger, and Volkelt, renamed their school *Ganzheit* psychology or roughly "holistic psychology," and throughout the 1920s and 1930s the old Wundtian institute at Leipzig was a center for theorists with a holistic bent. Wundt's journal, the *Psychologische Studien*, which had ceased publication upon his retirement, was then reactivated with the title, *Neue Psychologische Studien*. It was the central organ of the *Ganzheit* psychologists; however, its articles primarily followed Wundt's interests in the "higher" mental processes and hence were mostly nonexperimental investigations.

Werner (1948) has written that Wundt represented the halfway mark in the transition from Herbart's atomism to the Gestaltist's holism. But from the point of view of Wundt's voluntaristic psychology, the essential central control processes were of no more primacy to the Gestaltists than to Herbart—both conceived a rather passive organism, one that is controlled by external or independent forces such as the a priori self-organizing qualities of sensory fields. Both, in sharp contrast to Wundt, appealed to physics for models and theories.

MODERN RECONSTRUCTIONS

Now to describe Wundt's psychology in more detail, and to consider its present relevance, I want to outline some six current trends that could be viewed as reconstructions of Wundtian psychology in modern clothing:

First, Wundt's central emphasis on volitional processes bears noteworthy resemblance to the modern work on "cognitive control" as found, for example, in extensive research by Gardner, Klein, Holzman, and their associates (cf. Gardner, Holzman, Klein, Linton, & Spence, 1959). Both traditions used notions of different styles of attention deployment to explain a variety of perceptual and thought processes (sometimes even involving the same materials, e.g., the Müller-Lyer illusion).

The recent research, employing factor analyses of a variety of performance tasks, has determined two independent variables of cognitive control, which Gardner et al. call "field-articulation" and "scanning." These can be defined, as well, simply by substituting a similar description found in Wundt's psychology texts, as follows: First, in corresponding order, is Wundt's mental "clearness" process that concerns the focusing or emphasizing of a single item of experience. Wundt described this as "apperceptive synthesis" where variations from broad to narrow syntheses may occur. The second variable is a mental "distinctiveness" process which is the marking off of an item of experience from all others. Wundt described this as "apperceptive analysis," a relating and comparing function. The discovery and testing of nearly identical attention-deployment factors in recent times occurred independently of the old Wundtian psychology. And too, the recent studies make frequent use of elaborate personality theories that were unavailable to Wundt.

Second, detailed comparisons have been made recently between the development of psycholinguistics in the 1960s and that of Wundtian psycholinguistics at the turn of the century (Blumenthal, 1970). Both the modern transformational grammarians after Chomsky and the Wundtian psycholinguists at the turn of the century trace their notions of language back to the same historical sources (e.g., to Humboldt). The psycholinguistic issues debated in the 1960s often parallel those debated at the turn of the century, such as the opposition between taxonomic and generative descriptions of language. Very briefly, Wundt's analysis of language usage depicts the transformation of simultaneous configurations of thought into sequential representations in language symbols by means of the scanning activities of attention (Wundt, 1900–1920, Vol. 1).

A *third* reconstruction concerns abnormal psychology. Among his students, the one who maintained the longest intellectual association with Wundt was the psychiatrist Emil Kraepelin (see Fischel, 1959). Kraepelin's (1919) attentional theory of schizophrenia is an application of Wundtian psychology, an explanation of schizophrenias as abnormalities of the attention-deployment (apperception) process. It conceives certain abnormalities of behavior as resulting from flaws in the central control process that may take the form of either highly reduced attentional scanning, or highly erratic scanning, or extremes of attention focusing. Kraepelin proposed that abnormalities in simple perceptual tests should show up in schizophrenic individuals corresponding to these particular control-process distortions.

The modern attentional theory of schizophrenia is a direct revival of the Kraepelinian analysis, as noted, for example, in an extensive review by Silverman (1964). As in the Kraepelinian descriptions, abnormalities of behavior result from disruptions of the central attentional processes where there is either highly reduced or highly erratic attentional scanning and focusing. And these mental changes, again, are indicated by divergent performances in simple perceptual tests.

Fourth is Wundt's three-factor theory of affect, which was developed by analogy to his formulations of multidimensional descriptions of certain areas of sensory experience. For the description of emotional experience, he used these three bipolar affective dimensions: *pleasant versus unpleasant, high arousal versus low arousal*, and *concentrated attention versus relaxed atten-*

tion. Wundt had adopted the first two dimensions from earlier writers on the topic of emotion. The third dimension reflects his characteristic emphasis on the process of attention.

Around the turn of the century, an intensive sequence of investigations to relate these dimensions to unique bodily response patterns did not meet with popular success. However, years later, when factor analysis became available, statistical studies of affective and attitudinal behavior again yielded factors that parallel those of Wundt rather closely (cf. Burt, 1950; Osgood, Suci, & Tannenbaum, 1957; Schlosberg, 1954; and several others reviewed by Strongman, 1973). Osgood's three dimensions are described as "good–bad," "active–passive," and "strong–weak." Schlosberg's dimensions are "pleasantness–unpleasantness," "high–low activation," and "attention–rejection."

Emotions and affects held an important place in Wundt's system because they were postulated as the constituents of volition. Further, Wundt suggested that almost every experience (perception, thought, or memory) has an affective component. Thus, affect became the basis for his explanation of pattern recognition: a melody, for instance, produces a very similar emotional configuration as it is transformed to other keys or played on other instruments. Wundt speculated that affect was the by-product of the act of apperceptive synthesis, and as such it was always on the periphery of consciousness. That is, we can never focus our attention upon an emotion, but can only focus on objects or memories that produce an emotional aura in immediate experience.

Fifth, the study of selective attention has been at the core of much of the recent work on human information processing (e.g., Broadbent, 1958; Kahneman, 1973; Moray, 1970; Neisser, 1967). It is impossible here to relate this highly complex field to the early Wundtian psychology other than to note the prominence of attention in both and that the time variable is central to both. Space permits mention of only two examples:

The seminal investigations of Sperling (1960) concerning perceptual masking are one example. Sperling took direct inspiration from Wundt's 1899 monograph on the use of tachistoscopes in psychological research in which Wundt came to the following three conclusions about the perception of extremely brief stimuli: (1) the effective duration of a percept is not identical with the duration of the stimulus—but rather reflects the duration of a psychological process; (2) the relation between accuracy of a perception and stimulus duration depends on pre- and postexposure fields (which may induce what we now call masking); and (3) central processes, rather than peripheral sense organ aftereffects, determine these critical times. Wundt's observations spurred a body of early research, and those early data are now relevant to a large body of similar modern investigations.

Perhaps the most frequently employed technique in Wundt's laboratory was that of reaction-time measurement. This was the direct adoption of a program suggested earlier by Donders (1868–1869). Essentially, inferences were made about human information-processing capacities on the basis of measured performance times under systematically varied performance conditions. This program has now, in post-mid-20th century, been widely and successfully revived. It is well illustrated, for instance, in the seminal studies of Sternberg (1970) on the attentional scanning of immediate-memory images, in which Sternberg draws the relation between his work and the earlier Donders program.

For a *sixth* and final comparison, I must refer to what Wundt called his deepest interest, which resulted in a 10-volume work titled *Völkerpsychologie: Eine Untersuchung der Entwicklungsgestze von Sprache, Mythus, und Sitte*. An English version of this title could be *Cultural Psychology: An Investigation of the Developmental Laws of Language, Myth, and Morality*.[1] Appearing from 1900 through 1920, this series contains two books on language, three on myth and religion, one on art, two on society, one on law, and one on culture and history. If there is a current work by another author that is conceptually close to these volumes, it is Werner's (1948) *Comparative Psychology of Mental Development*, today read in some circles of developmental psychologists.

Following Wundt, Werner described an *organismic* psychology that is in opposition to *mechanistic* psychologies. He also drew parallels, as did Wundt, between the development of individuals and of societies. And Werner acknowledged indebtedness to Wundt. But in Wundt's *Völkerpsychologie* there is, again, greater emphasis on volitional and attentional processes in the analysis of the development of human culture; he theorized that those central mental processes had emerged as the highest evolutionary development, and that they are the capacities that set men above other animals. It is the highly developed selective-attention capacities that, as he claimed, enabled mankind to make a consistent mental advance and to develop human culture. For without these capacities, men would forever be at the mercy of sporadic thoughts, memories, and perceptions.

WUNDT'S HISTORICAL CONTEXTS

Wundt was not a mere encyclopedist or compiler of volumes, contrary to many descriptions. It was typical of him, however, always to compare and to contrast his system with other schools of thought, ancient and

---

[1]*Völkerpsychologie* has also been translated as "folk psychology," "psychology of peoples," and "ethnic psychology." Wundt quite deliberately avoided the terms *sociology* and *anthropology* because they were then heavily identified with the mid-19th-century positivism of Auguste Comte and related Anglo-French trends, which Wundt opposed. Some later writers on the history of psychology erroneously stated that the *Völkerpsychologie* is available in English translation. They apparently mistook a different and simpler one-volume work that E. Schaub (1916) translated as *Elements of Folk Psychology*.

modern. Perhaps in that sense he could be considered an encyclopedist. True, most of his works begin with a long recital of his antecedents and the antecedents of rival positions.

Wundt's motivation for scholarly productivity should not be surprising, considering the strong family traditions that lay behind him (and that went unrecognized by most historical writers). Recent researchers (Bringmann et al., 1975) claim that no other German intellectual has a family tree containing as many ancestors engaged in intellectual pursuits. On his father's side were historians, theologians, economists, and geographers. On his mother's side were natural scientists and physicians. Two of his ancestors had been rectors of the University of Heidelberg.

To conclude, I wish to draw an outline of the streams of history in which Wundt lived and worked. Historians have often defined a few broad, alternating cultural epochs in the 19th century. At some risk in using a much-abused word, one might call each a "zeitgeist"—a time that favored a particular cultural style. These periods begin with the dominant romanticism and idealism early in the century, largely a German-inspired ethos shared by Kant, Humboldt, Schopenhauer, Goethe, Hegel, and Fichte, to mention a few. In that era, philosophy, science, religion, and art were often combined into something called "nature-philosophy." Such an integration was exemplified in the pantheistic writings of Gustav Fechner, an exotic latecomer to the romantic movement and an important source of inspiration for Wundt. (In several ways, Wundt's 10-volume *Völkerpsychologie* reflects the spirit of the old nature-philosophy.)

Around the mid-19th century, a positivist and materialist movement grew dominant by vigorously rejecting the previous idealism. There then appeared the influential Berlin Physical Society, the mechanistic psychology of Herbart, the behavioristic linguistics of the so-called *Junggrammatiker* linguistics, and Comtean positivist sociology, among other examples across the disciplines. At the peak of this movement, academicians became methodology conscious to the extreme. The taxonomic methods of biology were imported into the social sciences. There was often a downgrading of "mentalism" in favor of "physicalism" and "environmentalism."

Then, toward the end of the 19th century came a resurgence of the romanticist–idealist outlook, particularly in continental Europe. It has been described either as neoromanticism, neoidealism, or neo-Kantianism. H. Stuart Hughes (1958) has provided a summarization in his influential book, *Consciousness and Society: The Reorientation of European Social Thought 1890–1930*. At around the time of World War I, this movement went into sharp decline, being displaced by a rebirth and rise in popularity of positivism and behaviorism which subsequently dominated many intellectual circles well into the 20th century.

Wundt's psychology rose and fell with the late-19th-century neoidealism. His core emphasis on volition and apperception comes straight from the earlier German idealist philosophy. It is not surprising that this should be so, for as a youth he was deeply inspired by the romanticist–idealist literature and nature-philosophy (Wundt, 1920). Certainly his intellectual development also included the influence of mid-19th-century positivism, especially in his promotion of experimental psychology. Yet, during that positivist period, he had remained largely unrecognized as a psychological theorist. The popular success of his theoretical system seems coordinated with the beginnings of neoidealist reorientations, and his system became fully formed in the *Grundriss* of 1896 (and later editions; Wundt, 1896a).

But unfortunately for Wundt, zeitgeist support disappeared rapidly in the early 20th century; definitions of psychology were then changing, and his works were soon meaningless to a newer generation. Few, especially outside Germany, understood any more what the old term *apperception* had once referred to.

Strange as it may seem, Wundt may be more easily understood today than he could have been just a few years ago. This is because of the current milieu of modern cognitive psychology and of the recent research on human information processing. Yet this new understanding does require serious study of Wundt in the original German. Most current textbook summaries of Wundt grew out of a time when early behaviorist and positivist movements were eager to encourage a break with the past, hence giving understandably little effort to careful description of the enormous body of writings they were discarding. Simplistic historical accounts resulted.

Today much of the history of Wundt remains to be told, both of his personal development and of his psychological system. It is well worth telling.

REFERENCES

Blumemthal, A. L. *Language and psychology: Historical aspects of psycholinguistics.* New York: Wiley, 1970.

Boring, E. G. *A history of experimental psychology.* New York: Appleton-Century-Crofts, 1950.

Bringmann, W. G., Balance, W., & Evans, R. B. Wilhelm Wundt 1832–1920: A biographical sketch. *Journal of the History of the Behavioral Sciences,* 1975, *11,* 287–297.

Broadbent, D. *Perception and communication.* New York: Pergamon, 1958.

Burt, C. The factorial study of emotions. In M. Reymert (Ed.), *Feelings and emotions.* New York: McGraw-Hill, 1950.

Donders, F. Over de snelheid van psychische processen. *Tweede Reeks,* 1868–1869, II, 92–120. (Trans. by W. Koster as On the speed of mental processes, In *Acta Psychologica,* 1969, *30,* 412–431.)

Fischel, W. Wilhelm Wundt und Emil Kraepelin. *Karl Marx Universität Leipzig, Beiträge zur Universität Geschichte,* 1959, *1.*

Gardner, R. W., Holzman, P. S., Klein, G. S., Linton, H., & Spence, D. P. Cognitive control: A study of individual consistencies in cognitive behavior. *Psychological Issues,* 1959, Monograph 4.

Hughes, H. S. *Consciousness and society: The reorientation of European social thought 1890–1930.* New York: Knopf, 1958.

Kahneman, D. *Attention and effort.* Englewood Cliffs, N.J.: Prentice-Hall, 1973.

Kraepelin, E. *Dementia praecox and paraphrenia* (Trans. by M. Barclay from selected writings of Kraepelin). Chicago, Ill.: Chicago Medical Book, 1919.

Mischel, T. Wundt and the conceptual foundations of psychology. *Philosophical and Phenomenological Research,* 1970, *31,* 1–26.

Moray, N. *Attention.* New York: Academic Press, 1970.

Neisser, U. *Cognitive psychology.* New York: Appleton-Century-Crofts, 1967.

Osgood, C., Suci, G., & Tannenbaum, P. *The measurement of meaning.* Urbana: University of Illinois Press, 1957.

Schlosberg, H. Three dimensions of emotion. *Psychological Review,* 1954, *61,* 81–88.

Silverman, J. The problem of attention in research and theory in schizophrenia. *Psychological Review,* 1964, *71,* 352–379.

Sperling, G. The information available in brief visual presentations. *Psychological Monographs,* 1960, *74*(11, Whole No. 498).

Sternberg, S. Memory-scanning: Mental processes revealed by reaction-time experiments. In J. Antrobus (Ed.), *Cognition and affect.* Boston, Mass.: Little, Brown, 1970.

Strongman, K. T. *The psychology of emotion.* New York: Wiley, 1973.

Titchener, E. B. *The psychology of feeling and attention.* New York: Macmillan, 1908.

Werner, H. *The comparative psychology of mental development.* New York: Science Editions, 1948.

Wundt, M. *Die Wurzeln der deutschen Philosophie in Stamm und Rasse.* Berlin: Junker und Dunnhaupt, 1944.

Wundt, W. Selbstbeobachtung und innere Wahrnehmung. *Philosophische Studien,* 1888, *4,* 292–309.

Wundt, W. Ueber psychische Kausalität und das Prinzip des psychophysichen. Parallelismus. *Philosophische Studien,* 1894, *10,* 1–124.

Wundt, W. *Grundriss der Psychologie.* Leipzig: Engelmann, 1896 (10th ed., 1911). (Trans. by C. Judd of 1896 and 1907 editions as *Outlines of psychology.*) (a)

Wundt, W. Ueber die Definition der Psychologie. *Philosophische Studien,* 1896, *12,* 1–66. (b)

Wundt, W. Zur Kritik tachistokopischer Versuche. *Philosophische Studien,* 1899, *15,* 287–317.

Wundt, W. *Völkerpsychologie: Eine Untersuchung der Entwicklungsgesetze von Sprache, Mythus, und Sitte* (10 vols.). Leipzig: Engelmann, 1900–1920.

Wundt, W. *Grundzüge der physiologischen Psychologie* (Vol. 2). Leipzig: Engelmann, 1902 (5th ed.).

Wundt, W. Ueber Ausfrageexperimente und ueber Methoden zur Psychologie des Denkens. *Psychologische Studien*, 1907, 3, 301–360.

Wundt, W. *Logik* (3 vols.). Leipzig: Engelmann, 1908.

Wundt, W. *Erlebtes und Erkanntes*. Stuttgart: Krohner, 1920.

5

CONTRIBUTIONS OF AMERICAN MENTAL PHILOSOPHERS TO PSYCHOLOGY IN THE UNITED STATES

ALFRED H. FUCHS

The period of moral and mental philosophy in the United States from the colonial and early federal period to the Civil War is accorded little more than a footnote in most textbooks in the history of psychology. This period, if it is referred to at all, is usually characterized as a time when college courses in philosophy were dominated by the Scottish "common sense" school of Thomas Reid, Dugald Stewart, and Thomas Brown, with a strong contribution from John Locke. Stewart's *Elements of the Philosophy of the Human Mind* and Locke's *Essay Concerning Human Understanding* were the texts most commonly used as the basis for instruction in courses labeled *intellectual philosophy* or *mental philosophy*.[1]

This dominance was not absolute, however: Texts written by profes-

---

An earlier version of this article was presented at the 106th Annual Convention of the American Psychological Association, San Francisco, August 1998. I thank Wade Pickren, Program Chair of Division 26 (History of Psychology), for inviting me to present the article at the meeting.

Reprinted from *History of Psychology*, 3, 3–19 (2000). Copyright © 2000 by the American Psychological Association. Reprinted with permission of the author.

sors in American colleges before the Civil War were used in classrooms in addition to, or as a substitute for, the British texts.[2] These texts by American authors, the authors themselves, and the mental philosophy that preceded the new laboratory psychology in the United States have been neglected in accounts of the history of psychology in the United States. Those who went to Germany to study the new psychology and returned to the United States to establish the new discipline are those to whom the authors of textbooks of the history of psychology pay tribute as the founders of psychology in the United States. However, the psychology that evolved in the United States was indebted not only to the laboratories of Europe but also to the mental philosophy that the first generation of the new psychologists had learned from their college texts. James McKeen Cattell, for example, was not a psychological neophyte when he arrived in Wundt's laboratory. In addition to research and study at Johns Hopkins University, Cattell, as an undergraduate at Lafayette College, had studied *Mental Philosophy*, a textbook written by Joseph Haven of Amherst College.[3]

THE TRADITION OF NEGLECT

It was Cattell who, in 1929, began the tradition of describing the arrival of the new psychology in the United States as if America were a *tabula rasa* on which the new psychology could write—in German! Cattell characterized the period in America before 1879, as far as psychology was concerned, as "like Heaven, for there was not a damned soul there."[4] Nineteen twenty-nine was also the year in which E. G. Boring published the first edition of his influential *History of Experimental Psychology*.[5] Boring traced the beginning of psychology in the United States no farther back than to William James, which may be appropriate for a history of *experimental* psychology, but Boring's account became the standard for the history of *all* psychology for generations. Boring's 1929 text and its subsequent 1950 revised edition include no American mental philosophers. English and continental philosophers are treated at some length, but the Scottish school receives only brief mention as an influence on French associationism. There is no suggestion that the Scottish school had any influence on the development of psychology in the United States.

Cattell's speech and Boring's book set the pattern for the common understanding of the origins of psychology as a German import of the late 19th century. In doing so they, along with others of their generation, share responsibility for creating an "origin myth" by ignoring the mental philosophy that preceded the importation of German psychology by the first generation of post-Civil War psychologists.[6] Recent historians of psychology have demonstrated that psychology, as it developed in America, was not simply German psychology written on an American *tabula rasa*; neither was it the psychology of Wilhelm Wundt: "Virtually everything that happened in modern psychology was a repudiation of Wundt, explicitly or implicitly."[7]

The German psychology, still characterized as philosophy, that came to the United States after the Civil War was confronted by the philosophy taught in American colleges since colonial times. German and French philosophy were not unknown in the United States in the early decades of the 19th century, but continental philosophy was regarded with suspicion. French philosophy was often identified with the excesses of the French revolution, and German philosophy was viewed as tending toward pantheism, which was anathema to the prevailing Protestant religious views in American colleges.[8] Thus, in the early part of the century the philosophies of England and Scotland dominated courses in American colleges, with only modest European influences. At the same time, following the War of Independence, and especially in the aftermath of the War of 1812, Americans made a strong effort to create national independent traditions in politics, literature, the arts, and the sciences. Americans did not ignore British and European culture but were proud of their new republic and fervently tried to develop independent traditions, adapting their heritage to meet the needs of the new country.[9]

Attempts to recognize the role of the 19th-century mental philosophers and their forebears began a decade after the appearance of Boring's *History* and Cattell's welcoming address to the delegates to the International Congress. Jay Wharton Fay's *American Psychology Before William James*, published in 1939, provides an extensive treatment and appreciation of the mental philosophy of this period. A. A. Roback's *A History of American Psychology* appeared in 1952; Roback traced the development of American psychology from its beginnings in colonial times to the modern period and accorded the early textbook writers a place of significance in the history of psychology in the United States.[10] Although Boring found Roback's treatment "clearer and more sophisticated" than Fay's, he saw no connection between the early period of mental philosophy and the new psychology of the laboratory: "The ancients of American psychology were not the prophets."[11] Thus, even when the early period was described and its relation to later developments suggested, Boring (and the many historians of psychology who followed his lead) perceived a significant disjunction between the period of mental philosophy and the later period of the "new" psychology. The first generation of the new psychologists saw the discipline they established as revolutionary rather than an evolutionary development from the tradition of mental philosophy.

Boring's view, embodied in his popular text, dominated treatments of psychology's history for several decades. The contributions of Fay and Roback were cited in bibliographies, but the mental philosophers whose work they described were largely ignored in accounts of psychology's history, even in those texts devoted to psychology as it developed in the United States. Hilgard's 1978 historical survey devoted only approximately one and one half pages of its 806 pages of text to the pre-Civil War period, despite his acknowledgement that "It is unfair to the writers before Ladd and James to dismiss them abruptly, as having nothing to offer."[12]

The visibility of American professors of mental philosophy in the 19th century's "period of the texts" was raised more recently by Rand Evans in a 1984 essay on the origins of American academic psychology. The chapter on this period in Evan's revision of Robert I. Watson's text is unique among textbooks describing the history of psychology. It places the early textbook writers in the history of psychology in the United States and points to a greater continuity of subject matter between the mental philosophy of the early 19th century and that of contemporary psychology than is usually recognized.[13]

When German laboratory psychology was imported in the last quarter of the 19th century, it confronted the established British–American psychological tradition in what Blumenthal (1980) described as a "clash of cultures," a confrontation between the German tradition of Leibnitz and the British tradition that had descended from Locke.[14] That tradition had evolved from a British tradition into an American tradition, heavily indebted to its British origins but modified and adapted by the authors of textbooks written for undergraduates in colleges and universities in the United States. The "clash" was an accommodation in which American mental philosophy and German experimental psychology came together to produce the new discipline that became psychology in America.

THE EARLY AMERICAN MENTAL PHILOSOPHERS

The people who taught mental philosophy in the early to middle years of the 19th century were a generation who were educated at, and subsequently taught in, colleges founded in the colonial and federal periods of the history of the United States. Among those who wrote textbooks in intellectual or mental philosophy are Joseph Haven of Amherst College, Laurens Hickok of Union College, Thomas C. Upham of Bowdoin College, and Francis Wayland of Brown University.[15] Upham was the pioneer textbook writer in mental philosophy among his colleagues. His 1827 text led the other texts by several decades: Haven's text appeared in 1857, those by Hickok and Wayland in 1854.[16]

Hickok and Upham were born within a few weeks of each other at the end of the 18th century (December 1798 and January 1799, respectively); Wayland was older by a few years (born in 1796), and Haven was the youngest, born in 1816. All were educated for the ministry and served churches prior to a call to a professorship, a common pattern for professors of philosophy in the 19th century. All were born in the northeast part of the United States (Massachusetts, Connecticut, New Hampshire, and New York, respectively), and all were educated at small liberal arts colleges: Haven at Amherst College, Hickok and Wayland at Union College, and Upham at Dartmouth College. Hickok prepared for the ministry by studying with ministers near his home in Connecticut, but Haven and Upham graduated from the Andover Theological Seminary; Wayland studied there for 1 year.[17] Andover was the bastion of orthodox trinitarian Congregationalism, as opposed to Harvard's Unitarian theology.[18] At Andover, these future professors read Locke and Stewart, the staples of philosophy that they had read as undergraduates. Perhaps the additional indoctrination at Andover ensured that Haven, Upham, and Wayland would stay well within the Scottish tradition,[19] whereas Hickok's apprenticeship freed him to be influenced by Kant, as evidenced by his division of the discipline into rational and empirical psychology.[20]

Seminaries provided the only graduate education available in the pre-Civil War period. Those who attended seminaries were prepared and chosen not only for the ministry but also for college professorships. The curricula of seminaries provided, in addition to Biblical studies, an education in the classical languages and Hebrew as well as excellent training in rhetoric, logic, and philosophy. Learning German was encouraged so that German Biblical criticism and philosophy could be read and combated.[21] Awareness of continental philosophy did not undermine or seriously dilute American commitment to the Scots and Locke, but the ability to read German and keep abreast of developments in philosophy and theology in Germany paved the way for the increased influence of German scholarship in philosophy in the United States in the latter part of the 19th century.

The British enthusiasm for Baconian induction and empiricism in science, philosophy, and theology was a part of undergraduate and seminary education.[22] The method and content of philosophy were intertwined with theology; induction and empiricism were methodological constants in both. Natural philosophy, the source of the "natural" or physical sciences, was concerned with the study of nature and the natural world. The study of natural theology paralleled that of natural philosophy and complemented the study of revealed religion: "Revealed theology embraces those extraordinary discoveries which God has made to Mankind in the holy scriptures. Natural theology teaches what may be known of God, from the manifestations of his existence and perfections in the natural world."[23] William Paley, in *Natural Theology: Or Evidences of the Existence and Attributes of the Deity*, argued that, like a pocketwatch, the natural world implied both creation and a Creator, because both exhibited evidence of design. Paley's *View of the Evidences of Christianity* and Joseph Butler's *The Analogy of Religion to the Constitution and Course of Nature* offered similar arguments to support belief in Christianity.[24]

When seminary graduates became professors of mental philosophy they approached their subject with the same spirit of empirical inquiry and with the belief that the truths revealed by the study of the mind would reveal God's design and purpose for His creation. They prepared and delivered lectures that became textbooks[25] written to supplement or replace aging original sources not written for the youthful college senior or junior. Although some regretted this retreat from original sources, the textbook became a popular vehicle for instruction in colleges and universities.[26] Baconian in spirit, the texts summarized, organized, and attempted to find lawful relations among facts. Facts of mind came from introspective observations of conscious experience, anecdotal reports of human and animal behavior, observations from medical case histories, legal proceedings, literature, and the Bible. Although the mind was nonmaterial, and therefore indivisible, facts about the mind could be organized into distinct taxonomic categories corresponding to mental processes defined by conscious awareness, language, common understanding, and the philosophical tradition.

The content, as well as the scientific approach, of the British tradition became part of the textbooks of the first half of the 19th century. The senses, as the source of information about the external world, served as the starting point for the consideration of the mind. The senses and perception were part of the first category of mental processes typically designated *intellectual* (or *the intellect*), which included such cognitive processes as attention, memory, reasoning, imagination and, perhaps, even consciousness itself. Wayland's intellectual philosophy was confined to these cognitive categories, whereas Haven, Hickok, and Upham added the categories of "the sensibilities" (emotions, feelings and affections, motives and desires, instincts, appetites, and propensities) and the will, which was concerned with the question of how mental processes could result in action. Whether the will was free, or acted under the dominion of motives and was therefore governed by them, reflected the metaphysical past, as did the concern for ensuring that human beings were morally accountable for their actions.[27]

Mental processes were treated as functional properties of the mind. Their designation as faculties or powers (in the texts of Haven, Hickok, and Wayland) or states of mind (Upham) included discussions of their purpose or usefulness, the nature of their processes and, in some instances, their dependence on the physiological substrate. In this way the mental philosophers continued in the tradition of seeing the mind as comprising active powers, mind in use, as a defining characteristic of human existence.

THE REJECTION OF MENTAL PHILOSOPHY

G. Stanley Hall, writing from Berlin in 1878, described the "new Philosophy of the Future" and its origins in the physiological laboratory.[28]

The new philosophy had moved traditional topics of mental philosophy into the laboratory to establish an experimental psychology modeled on physiology. Laboratory work and the philosophy that inspired it was ascendent in Europe, while the teaching of philosophy in the United States was in the hands of college professors who were, in Hall's view, "philosophical indoctrinators," "the disciples of the disciples of Hopkins, Hickok, Wayland, Upham, Haven who still taught students from their mentors' texts." The result, as Hall lamented, was that "there are less than half a dozen colleges or universities in the United States where metaphysical thought is entirely freed from reference from theological formulae."[29] That mental philosophy still sought and found compatibility with the origins and operations of the mind as a reflection of God's creation seemed to Hall to evidence a lack of progress and an insularity from the new and advanced European scholarship.

The generation that emerged from the Civil War was ready for new challenges and change. The old systems and methods of mental philosophy became the catholicity against which the post-Civil War generation protested. They sailed to Europe, together with their colleagues in other branches of science, to find out what was new. They returned with the zeal of converts to replace the old with the new; to begin anew with fact gathering, this time in the laboratory; to understand the nature of the mind, in a new Darwinian world. The mental philosophers had taken the study of mind as far as the Baconian methods could take it. In their textbooks, the mind had been "neatly and carefully dissected, its parts labeled and stowed away in their proper pigeon holes, the inventory taken, and the whole stamped with the stamp of *un fait accompli*. Schematism was supreme, and the air of finality was over all."[30] That air of finality did not convey the sense of a job completed, but rather that of a dead end.

The textbooks of the mental philosophers of the pre-Civil War era were frozen in a pre-Darwinian time that viewed human beings and the human mind as a special creation of a Protestant God. After the Civil War, Darwin could no longer be ignored. Textbook writers in the last quarter of the 19th century wrestled with the challenge of writing a mental philosophy that continued to accord a place for the soul while incorporating the results of the new physiological psychology.[31] These late-19th century texts, while trying to incorporate evolution and the new laboratory results into more traditional mental philosophy, became defenders of traditional beliefs: "The mid-century tradition was a kind of Protestant scholasticism, deriving psychology from theological dogma."[32] Taking account of Darwin meant that

> the textbooks, ... from about 1870 to 1890, suffered as psychology from becoming more critically philosophical; and they became so obsessed with the mind–body problem that, when admitting any physi-

ological matter, they took time out to warn the student against any materialistic implications.[33]

The new beginning, stimulated by those who studied in the psychological laboratories of Germany and embodied in the *Principles of Psychology* of William James, was imbued with the spirit of evolutionary theory as Darwin's theories became the context for scientific pursuits and challenged the certainties of the first half of the century.[34]

As psychologists advocated the new psychology as a laboratory science they tried to both distance psychology from its religious ties while offering reassurance that they were not preaching materialism. Popular articles in magazines were designed to placate the public on this point.[35] The first generation of the new psychologists, such as G. Stanley Hall and George Trumbull Ladd, were themselves products of seminary training and were making a personal as well as a professional transition as the older religious tradition gave way in the post-Civil War crucible.[36] William James's *Psychology* effectively marked the end of the attempt to accommodate the soul in textbooks in the new psychology, which for James was a "superfluity for scientific purposes."[37] If psychology did not immediately adopt a materialistic stance, it gradually removed itself from concerns that were inherent in the old mental philosophy. Evolution replaced God as the extrapsychological explanation for the origins of the mind and its functions.[38]

The attack on the old psychology by the new was not entirely over issues of science and religion or the adequacy of the Baconian method. The new psychologists, with graduate educations from Europe, were beginning to see themselves as professionals specifically trained to teach the new philosophy and the methods of its laboratory. Their predecessors were prepared professionally for the ministry, but the credential now esteemed for teaching the new philosophy was a PhD from a German university, or at least a period of study there, preferably in a laboratory. Mental philosophers, with little or no education abroad, however well read in the new philosophy, were held in low esteem by the new generation. Mindful, perhaps, of his own seminary training, Ladd observed of the new psychologists, of whom he was one, "We are inclined to look too contemptuously upon the 'old' psychology and upon its teachers because mere schooling as a minister . . . was esteemed a sufficient test of fitness to exploit oneself as an authority in psychological science."[39]

The new psychologists had to contend for positions with the representatives of the old school, entrenched in professorships in colleges and universities; to find a place in departments of philosophy they needed to convince administrations and governing boards that they were indeed the philosophy of the future and deserved to supplement, if not replace, those who represented the philosophy of the past. The new generation, in short, argued for its place in the profession of philosophy as it worked its way toward the new professional role of psychology.

Cattell took issue with the statement by James that there was not a "new psychology" but simply "the old psychology which began in Locke's time, plus a little physiology of the brain and senses and theory of evolution, and a few refinements of introspective detail" by observing that "our leaders in psychology have become our leaders by belying such partial statements."[40] James may have been nearer the mark, but the banner of revolution is more likely to attract converts than the cloak of business as usual.[41] The relatively rapid attraction of individuals to pursue the new discipline, the founding of laboratories to train them, the establishment of journals to carry the results of their researches, and the increase in material support for laboratory apparatus attest to the success of the rhetoric of the new psychologists.[42] In their efforts to establish themselves, psychologists relegated the mental philosophy of the earlier generation to the long philosophical past and saw themselves as the founders of a new science with little debt, as a science, to the generation of mental philosophers, with consequences for the history of the discipline that their generation would write.

THE LEGACY OF MENTAL PHILOSOPHY AND THE MENTAL PHILOSOPHERS

A Home for the New Psychology

The place of mental philosophy in the college curricula was strengthened by the efforts of the textbook writers, a place that would later accommodate the new psychology. The study of the mind was important to the theologian–philosophers: The mind was a natural phenomenon that, like other objects of study in natural theology, could help to teach something of God; at the same time the mind was the medium through which the natural world was known and through which the Scriptures would be interpreted. If ministers were to influence members of their congregations and professors their students, an understanding of the mind was critical.

Colleges as well as seminaries accepted the importance of the study of the mind; the course in moral philosophy, and the course in intellectual or mental philosophy, was most often taught by the president of the college.[43] When they were not taught by the president, they were taught by a professor engaged principally for that purpose. However, the importance of the discipline had not always been universally accepted. For example, Upham, in 1827, argued that the study of mental philosophy was often denigrated through its prior association with metaphysical study, whose reputation for raising questions for which there were no answers had brought it into public disfavor, an argument similar to that advanced by Dugald Stewart.[44] In contrast, Upham pledged that mental philosophy was to be pursued on scientific principles—induction and empiricism—for its own sake and for its usefulness. Mental philosophy would pursue questions for which the Baconian empirical and inductive method could provide answers, not the metaphysical imponderable questions to which there were no answers. Mental philosophy, as Baconian science, would be useful to those who wanted to understand the mind as a natural phenomenon and to parents and educators responsible for the shaping of young minds.[45]

In establishing and defending the place of mental philosophy in college and university curricula throughout the 19th century, and by making the study of mental philosophy an essential part of the curricula, the pre-Civil War generation provided a home for the new psychologists who succeeded in making themselves the anointed successors of their forebears. The mental philosophers and the new psychologists shared a rhetoric that proclaimed the discipline a science of value for its own sake and capable of application to important social problems as a means of seeking public acceptance and support.[46]

The Shaping of the Content of Psychology in the United States

The content of Upham's *Elements of Mental Philosophy* "defined the course of psychology as it finally evolved" and "did much to standardize the form of the mental philosophy and finally the psychology course."[47] Upham's enthusiasm for the subject and for "a robust interest in everything and anything"[48] may be seen to anticipate Cattell's definition of psychology as "anything a psychologist is interested *qua* psychologist."[49] Both Upham and Cattell represent a Baconian faith in empiricism and distrust of preconceptions or hypotheses that might hinder or limit observations.

R. S. Woodworth observed the similarity of content between the textbooks of 1842 and 1942: "The old mental philosophy course continued without break into the elementary course of today"; after all, the new psychologists were the new instructors or assistant professors in the departments of philosophy in which the old guard was well entrenched. Even when they did get to teach the introductory course,

> they could not remodel it suddenly and completely, for they did not possess the experimental data for tackling all the questions that were traditionally and quite properly taken up in the psychology course. ... New material has been introduced bit by bit and some of the older discussional material has been eliminated, but we of the present day cannot, and need not, deny our academic ancestry of a hundred years ago.[50]

The early generation not only established an academic home for the new psychologists but they also furnished it with the course content that the new psychology could refurbish and modernize.

A Tradition of Treating the Mind Scientifically

As Evans observed, a funny thing happened to the German psychology that returned with the Leipzig PhDs: That which survived the trans-Atlantic crossing was a method that came to be used in the service of the content of the old psychology.[51] The revolution that the new psychologists saw in the change from mental philosophy to the study of psychology consisted in the method of experiment that "supplemented and corrected the old method of introspection."[52] Moreover, the new method was extended to realms outside the academic laboratory and to regions in which introspection as a method was severely limited or impossible: "The cradle and the asylum are becoming the laboratory of the psychologist in the latter half of the nineteenth century."[53]

The romance with the laboratory and the fascination with brass instruments and the measurements they made possible were perhaps the most salient characteristics of the new psychology, but the adoption of the laboratory experiment as the hallmark of the new science was not so much a sharp break with the past as it was an extension of it. Scottish philosophy had adopted inductive, empirical Baconian science as the appropriate means of study in both science and religion. John Dewey welcomed the laboratory method to psychology as "the least developed of the *sciences*" (italics added): Physiological psychology produced "a revolution in psychology" because "it has given a new instrument, introduced a new *method* —that of experiment, which has supplemented and corrected the old method of introspection."[54]

In fostering the conception of a mental philosophy that was to be pursued as a science, the mental philosophers facilitated the adoption of experimental methods in the service of a new mental philosophy. Although the experimental psychologists thought of themselves as replacing a philosophical discipline with a science, they could be more accurately characterized as adding laboratory experimental procedures to what was already defined as an empirical, inductive science. Research in contemporary psychology is not all experimental, but it is inductive and empirical. Experiment came to psychology as it came to other sciences: after a period of Baconian fact gathering and a gradual shedding of Bacon's proscription against speculative hypotheses. The process was more evolutionary than revolutionary.

A Tradition of Functionalism

In 1907, James Rowland Angell felt called on to delineate a system of psychology that he labeled *Functionalism*, in contrast to E.B. Titchener's 1898 description of his system of *structuralism*.[55] Titchener advocated the analysis of the mind into structural, mental elements as the primary task of the new scientific psychology, in contrast to the traditional functional descriptive psychology, which he identified with a metaphysical and unscientific faculty psychology. Titchener argued that for psychology to become a science, its "problems should be formulated, explicitly or implicitly, as static rather than dynamic, structural rather than functional."[56]

Titchener, the Oxford undergraduate with a graduate degree from Leipzig, reflected the British tradition that fostered a faith in the capability of the mind to analyze itself. "English psychology," James Mark Baldwin wrote in 1894, "was a detailed analysis of the experiences of the individual consciousness."[57] The German laboratory method that emphasized introspective judgments under laboratory conditions provided Titchener with a method with which to attempt to delineate the structural elements of the normal, adult human consciousness.

Angell defended the functional approach as less narrow than a structural approach and equally appropriate to the new science. That Angell's approach was rooted in the mental philosophy of the past is embodied in the criticism that his functionalism was "a bastard offspring of the faculty psychology masquerading in biological plumage."[58] Angell aligned his approach with descriptions and theories of mental action and identified a functional approach "with the effort to discern and portray the typical operations of consciousness under actual life conditions."[59] Although Angell did not cite the mental philosophers, his psychology followed in their tradition.

Angell's formal school of "functionalism" legitimized observations of behavior and inferences made from them, in addition to introspective reports, structural or functional. The mental philosophers also had adopted a functional approach to the mind, emphasizing process over content within the several meanings of mental function: What was mind for (what was its purpose or "function"), how did it work (what were the mechanisms of mind, and how did they operate or "function"), and of what were mental processes a function (did mental events depend on experience or native endowment, and how were these processes a "function of," or related to, the underlying physiology of the organism)? These functions were presumed to be a product of evolution in the new psychology rather than a product of a deity's design as in the earlier mental philosophy, but they were functional properties of mind nevertheless.

The Darwinian attire that functionalism acquired made it seem modern, with origins in Darwinian biology and 19th-century advances in physiology[60] but, as Angell acknowledged, the philosophical analysis of mind in use is even older. In any case, functionalism (with a small f) was well developed in America when Titchener arrived at Cornell; it was left to Angell to give it formal definition as a system of psychology, prompted only by Titchener's attempt to replace a functionalist approach to mind with a restrictive structural approach.

SUMMARY AND CONCLUSION

The new psychology was marked by the celebration of laboratory foundings well into the 20th century.[61] The laboratories came to be part of departments of psychology but were initially, of course, part of departments of philosophy to which the new psychologists were appointed. Puzzled as philosophers might have been by the brass instruments of the laboratories, and their budgetary demands, departments made room for the new breed of philosophers and their courses.[62] Mental philosophy, empirical and inductive, had made a secure place for itself in the curricula. In addition, there was continuity in course content; in a functionalist approach; in using experimental methods for gathering facts on topics that were, perhaps, as Wundt said of Cattell's research, "ganz Ameikanisch."

Grace Adams, a student of Titchener's, wrote in 1931, as she surveyed the systems of psychology vying for supremacy: "Many European countries have their own national brands of psychology, but America has had all brands."[63] The importation of systems of thought began with British colonization. The Scottish, English, and German and other philosophical and psychological imports have become an American psychology, with roots that extend farther back than the new psychologists were prone to credit. Histories of psychology, especially those that emphasize the history of psychology in America, need to assess the influence of those roots and to reconsider the myths of the origins of the discipline in the United States. If the early mental philosophers were not, in Cattell's words, "damned souls," they also have not been souls accorded a place in psychology's heaven. Further efforts may help to rescue them from the limbo to which they have been consigned and enable them to find their place in the heaven of psychology's history.

NOTES

1. Dugald Stewart, *Elements of the Philosophy of the Human Mind*, vol. 1 (Brattleborough, VT: William Fessenden, 1808). The first volume of Stewart's book was first published in Edinburgh in 1792, the second volume in 1813; both volumes were published in New York in 1814 by Eastburn, Kirk, & Co. John Locke's *Essay Concerning Human Understanding*, first published in 1690, was revised and has been reprinted many times; see, for example, John Locke, *Essay Concerning Human Understanding*, ed. Peter H. Niddich (Oxford, England: Clarendon Press, 1975).

2. Harvard and Yale provide two examples. At Harvard, Locke's *Essay* and Stewart's *Elements* were the texts for the course in intellectual philosophy in the academic years 1840–1841 and 1841–1842; Thomas C. Upham's *Elements of Mental Philosophy* was assigned for the next 2 years, after which there was a return to Stewart's text. At Yale, Upham's *Elements of Intellectual Philosophy* (Portland, ME: William Hyde, 1827) and his *Elements of Mental Philosophy* (Boston: William Hyde,

1832) were used by Noah Porter in 1838–1839 and in 1854–1855, respectively, interspersed with other texts. Noah Porter later published his own influential text, *The Human Intellect* (New York: Scribner's, 1868).

3. James McKeen Cattell was the first individual in the United States to have the title "Professor of Psychology" (University of Pennsylvania, 1888); he later founded the psychological laboratory at Columbia University. The text he read as an undergraduate was that of Joseph Haven, *Mental Philosophy* (New York: Sheldon, 1878), first published in 1857. For this early influence on Cattell, see Michael Sokal, ed., *James McKeen Cattell's Journal and Letters from Germany and England, 1880–1888* (Cambridge, MA: MIT Press, 1981), 13–17.

4. James McKeen Cattell, "Address of the President," in *Ninth International Congress of Psychology, Proceedings and Papers* (Princeton, NJ: Psychological Review, 1930), 12. This was the first international congress to be held in the United States.

5. E. G. Boring, *A History of Experimental Psychology* (New York: Century, 1929); the influential second edition was published by Appleton-Century-Crofts in 1950. Boring's approach may have been conditioned in part by his attempt to represent experimental scientific psychology with its roots in physiology as the only psychology worthy of the name and to promote the separation of psychology from the Department of Philosophy at Harvard. See Mitchell G. Ash, "The self presentation of a discipline," in *Functional Uses of Disciplinary Histories*, vol. 8, eds. Loren Graham, Wolf Lepennies, and Peter Weingart (Boston: Reidell, 1983), 143–189, esp. 148–155; and John M. O'Donnell, "The Crisis of Experimentation in the 1920s: E. G. Boring and His Uses of History," *American Psychologist* 34 (1979): 289–295.

6. Franz Samelson, "History, Origin Myth, and Ideology: 'Discovery' of Social Psychology," *Journal for the Theory of Social Behaviour*, 4 (1974): 217–231; see also Laurel Furumoto, "The New History of Psychology," in *The G. Stanley Hall Lecture Series*, vol. 9, ed. Ira S. Cohen (Washington, DC: American Psychological Association, 1989), 5–34, for an account of some of the consequences of recent historiographic research in the history of psychology.

7. Kurt Danziger, *Constructing the Subject* (Cambridge, England: Cambridge University Press, 1990), 34; Arthur Blumenthal, "Wilhelm Wundt and the Two Traditions in Psychology," in *Wilhelm Wundt and the Making of a Scientific Psychology*, ed. R. W. Rieber (New York: Plenum, 1980), 117–135; Rand Evans, "The Origins of American Academic Psychology," in *Explorations in the History of Psychology in the United States*, ed. J. Brozek (Lewisburg, PA: Bucknell University Press, 1984).

8. Before, and especially after, the Civil War, the German idealist philosophy of Hegel made some inroads in philosophy in the United States prior to the influence of the new psychology. For the Hegelian influence, and its relation to a more general interest in German idealist philosophy, such as New England transcendentalism, see Elizabeth Flowers and Murray G. Murphey, *A History of Philosophy in America*, vol. 2 (New York: Capricorn Books and G. P. Putnam, 1977), Ch. 8, 463–514, and, for an account of the history of the St. Louis school in particular, see William Schuyler, "The St. Louis Philosophical Movement," *Educational Review* 29 (1905):450–467.

9. In the period after the Revolutionary War and the War of 1812, Amer-

icans were particularly conscious of the fact that the United States was now an independent republican nation: "With respect to science, this meant two things: as the example par excellence of useful knowledge, science must be cultivated to promote the interests, prosperity, and power of the rising American nation; and as the supreme example of the powers of the human mind, the successes of sciences challenged Americans to prove to the world that republican institutions were as favorable to intellectual achievement as they were to liberty": John C. Greene, *American Science in the Age of Jefferson* (Ames: Iowa State University Press, 1984), 5–6. The case was made for the arts and literature by a youthful Thomas Upham who, in the preface to a volume of his poetry, called for America "to nourish in her bosom a succession of scholars as eminent in the departments of literature, as her statesmen are in the cabinet and her soldiers in the field": Thomas C. Upham, *American Sketches* (New York: David Longworth, 1819), 7–8.

10. Jay Wharton Fay, *American Psychology Before William James* (New Brunswick, NJ: Rutgers University Press, 1939); A. A. Roback, *History of American Psychology* (New York: Library, 1952).

11. E. G. Boring, review of *History of American Psychology*, by A. A. Roback, *American Journal of Psychology* 4(1953): 651–654; the quotation is from p. 652.

12. Ernest R. Hilgard, *Psychology in America* (San Diego, CA: Harcourt Brace Jovanovich, 1978), 6.

13. Evans, "The Origins": R. I. Watson and Rand Evans, *The Great Psychologists* (New York: HarperCollins, 1991).

14. Blumenthal, "Wilhelm Wundt."

15. The first textbook published in the United States to use the term *psychology* in the title is that of Frederick Rauch, *Psychology or a View of the Human Soul, Including Anthropology* (New York: M. W. Dodd, 1840); a second, posthumous edition appeared in 1841; for the use of the term *psychology* in book titles before Rauch, see Hendrika Vande Kemp, "A Note on the term 'Psychology' in English Titles: Predecessors of Rauch," *Journal of the History of the Behavioral Sciences*, 19 (1983): 185. Trained in Germany, Rauch attempted a synthesis of German and American mental philosophy. Perhaps because of his early death, the influence of his text "was slight, and it soon passed into an unfortunate oblivion, giving place to the more popular texts of Upham, Wayland, and Haven" (Fay, *American Psychology*, 114). For a brief summary of Rauch's psychology, see Roback, *History of American Psychology*, 55–59.

16. The texts of these professors were the major texts of the pre-Civil War period. The first to appear was that of Thomas Cogswell Upham, *Elements of Intellectual Philosophy* (Portland, ME: William Hyde, 1827). The other texts were first published in the 1850s: Laurens Perseus Hickok, *Empirical Psychology* (New York: Ivison and Phinney, 1862), first published in 1854; Francis Wayland, *The Elements of Intellectual Philosophy* (New York: Sheldon, 1872), first published in 1854; and Joseph Haven, *Mental Philosophy* (New York: Sheldon, 1878), first published in 1857. Hickok's book, edited and revised by his nephew Julius Seelye, was in print until 1893; Upham's text was expanded and revised as *Elements of Mental Philosophy* in 1832 and continued in print in multivolume and abridged editions until its last printing in 1886, although it was still being advertised as late as 1892 by Harper's in John Dewey's *Psychology*, 3rd ed. (New York: Harper, 1892). The

last edition of Haven's text appeared in 1886, and Wayland's text was last published in 1896. Haven's text was translated into Chinese in 1888 and introduced western psychology to China; Seiji Kodama, "Life and Work of Y. K. Yen, the First Person to Introduce Western Psychology to China," *Psychologia—An International Journal of Psychology in the Orient* 34 (1991): 213–226. Upham's two-volume *Elements of Mental Philosophy* and his treatise on the will was translated into Armenian by Cyrus Hamlin: "As there was no work on mental philosophy, I proposed the translation of Upham. I considered it the best to begin with. President Porter, of Yale, when I asked him what work he would advise for a beginning, replied at once: 'Upham'." Cyrus Hamlin, *My Life and Times*, 2nd ed. (Boston: Congregational Sunday School and Publishing Society, 1893), 254. The copy of the Armenian translation of Upham's *Elements of Mental Philosophy* in the Special Collections of the Bowdoin College Library is a revised Armenian edition, translated by Ghazaros Boghossian and published by K. Polis in Constantinople in 1870.

17. Biographical information for Joseph Haven, Laurens Perseus Hickok, Francis Wayland, and Thomas Cogswell Upham may be found in the following sources: for Haven, see Claude Moore Fuess, *Amherst: The Story of a New England College* (Boston: Little, Brown, 1935), 210, and William J. Newlin (Ed.), *Amherst College: Biographical Record of the Graduates and Non-Graduates* (rev. ed.) (Amherst, MA: The Trustees of Amherst College, 1939); for Hickok, see John Bascom, "Laurens Perseus Hickok," *American Journal of Psychology* 19 (1908): 359–373; for Upham, see Alfred H. Fuchs, "Thomas Cogswell Upham," in *American National Biography*, eds. John H. Garraty and Mark C. Carnes, vol. 22 (New York: Oxford University Press, 1999); for Wayland, see Francis Wayland and H. L. Wayland, *A Memoir of the Life and Labors of Francis Wayland D.D., L.L.D.* (vol. 1) (New York: Sheldon, 1868).

18. Jerry Wayne Brown, *The Rise of Biblical Criticism* (Middletown, CT: Wesleyan University Press, 1969).

19. Moral, as well as intellectual or mental philosophy, was included in the titles and teaching of Haven, Hickok, Upham, and Wayland; all except Upham published texts in moral philosophy; Joseph Haven, *Moral Philosophy* (Boston: Gould and Lincoln, 1859); Laurens P. Hickok, *A System of Moral Science* (New York: Ivison, Blakeman, Taylor, 1853); Francis Wayland, *Elements of Moral Science* (Boston: Gould, Kendall, & Lincoln, 1835). For the origins of the social sciences from moral philosophy, see Gladys Bryson, "The Comparable Interests of the Old Moral Philosophy and the Modern Social Sciences," *Social Forces* 11 (1932): 19–27, and Gladys Bryson, "The Emergence of the Social Sciences From Moral Philosophy," *International Journal of Ethics* 42 (1932): 304–323. For an extended assessment, particularly for the indebtedness of the social sciences to Scottish philosophy, see Gladys Bryson, *Man and Society: The Scottish Inquiry of the Eighteenth Century* (Princeton, NJ: Princeton University Press, 1945). Dorothy Ross, *The Origins of American Social Science* (Cambridge, England: Cambridge University Press, 1991) concerns the development of the social sciences from the period after the Civil War and specifically excludes psychology from its account.

20. Laurens P. Hickok, *Rational Psychology* (Auburn, NY: Derby, Miller & Company, 1849); his *Empirical Psychology* was in accord with the mental philosophy of Haven, Upham, and Wayland in its goal of determining the facts of mind

and organizing them systematically. Rational psychology is a prerequisite to empirical psychology and proceeds deductively from general principles. For a description and assessment of Hickok's psychology, see John K. Bare, "Laurens Perseus Hickok: Philosopher, Theologian, and Psychologist," in *Portraits of Pioneers in Psychology* vol. 3, eds. Gregory A. Kimble and Michael Wertheimer (Washington, DC, and Mahwah, NJ: American Psychological Association and Erlbaum, 1998).

21. Brown, *The Rise of Biblical Criticism*; Van Wyck Brooks, *Flowering of New England 1815–1865* (New York: The Modern Library, 1941), noted that "Although German was so little known in Boston, there were a few students of the language elsewhere in New England. Dr. Bentley of Salem and Professor Moses Stuart of Andover both owned collections of German books" (fn. 76).

22. Ross, *The Origins*, noted: "In the American colleges commonsense realism encouraged the belief in Baconian empiricism as the proper method of all the sciences; indeed Newton's method was assimilated to this trust that empirical observation would yield, through rational reflection upon its evidence, the highest truths of science. It also supported belief in the harmony between science and religion, keeping the advance of science within the Christian purview" (p. 37). The relation between religion and science in the period of the mental philosophers was addressed by Bernard Spilka, "Religion and Science in Early American Psychology," *Journal of Psychology and Theology* 15 (1987): 3–9.

23. I. Nichols, *A Catechism of Natural Philosophy* (Portland, ME: Shirley and Hyde, 1829), 1. The Bible, as well as the natural world, could be studied empirically. Upham, in a junior-year paper at Andover, counted the frequency of occurrence of the number 7 in the Bible as approximately 500 and classified the different senses in which 7 was used (e.g., as a specific quantity, to indicate several or many, or in some figurative sense): Thomas C. Upham, "The Use of the Number Seven in Prophecy." Collections of the Franklin Trask Library, Andover Newton Theological School. Empirical, inductive approaches to truth were assumed to be but a parallel path to the same immutable truth that rational, deductive approaches would reveal; thus, the results of one method would, it was assumed, confirm the truth revealed by the other. A conflict between Biblical truth and empirical observation, as, for example, in the time specified for creation, created crises in the beliefs about the immutability of truth. See Paul Jerome Croce, *Science and Religion in the Age of William James*, vol. 1, *Eclipse of Certainty 1820–1880* (Chapel Hill: University of North Carolina Press, 1995).

24. William Paley, *Natural Theology: Or Evidences of the Existence and Attributes of the Deity, Collected From the Appearances of Nature* (New York: Evart Duyckinck, 1814); William Paley, *View of the Evidences of Christianity* (Hallowell, ME: C. Spaulding, 1826); Joseph Butler, *The Analogy of Religion to the Constitution and Course of Nature* (1736; reprint, Philadelphia: Lippincott, 1881).

25. Wayland, *The Elements*: "The following pages contain the substance of the Lectures which, for several years, have been delivered to the classes in Intellectual Philosophy at Brown University" (Preface, iii).

26. Thomas Upham, in the second edition (1828) of his *Elements of Intellectual Philosophy*, offered several reasons for publishing a textbook: the scarcity, and potential high cost, of primary texts, which made them inaccessible to students; the desire to spare students from the complex and lengthy discussions from many

different sources that supported accepted principles; the need to present students with basic elements and thus to avoid the confusion that could arise from conflicting and contradictory statements; the recognition that students have not the time in their course of study to consult the many possible sources of relevant scientific information; that the responsibility for assessing the observations and theories of others lies with professionals who present students with the results of their research. In 1840, an anonymous reviewer of Upham's *Elements of Mental Philosophy* lamented the growing use of textbooks and the diminishing reliance on primary contributors, although he exempted Upham's book from the faults of most texts; Anonymous Reviewer, "Elements of Mental Philosophy . . . ," *North American Review* 51 (1840): 240.

27. Upham did not consider his mental philosophy complete until he added the will to the intellect and sensibilities; in *A Philosophical and Practical Treatise on the Will* (Portland, ME: William Hyde, 1834) he concluded that the will was both free and operated under laws; the former allowed for individuals to be held accountable, whereas the latter acknowledged uniformities and lawfulness in human behavior. How both could be true, however, Upham was content to leave as a mystery.

28. G. Stanley Hall, "The Philosophy of the Future," *The Nation*, 7 November 1878, p. 283.

29. G. Stanley Hall, "Philosophy in the United States," *Mind* 4 (1879): 89–105, quotation from p. 90. "Hopkins" was Mark Hopkins of Williams College, renowned for his teaching and known for his textbook in moral philosophy. Not only were the disciples teaching, but also it was still possible for them to be using the master's texts: see note 14 of the present article.

30. John Dewey, "The New Psychology," *Andover Review* 2 (1884): 278–289.

31. The new psychologists faced the same choices as had the biologists of the 1850s when confronted with Darwin: fight the new ideas, as Louis Agassiz did, succumb to materialism and reject religion, separate the realms of religious belief from scientific practice, or continue to try to integrate evolution and theology. George T. Ladd, the second president of the American Psychological Association, after G. Stanley Hall and before William James, saw his task as that of forming a bridge between the old psychology and the new; see Eugene S. Mills, *George Trumbull Ladd Pioneer American Psychologist* (Cleveland, OH: The Press of Case Western Reserve University, 1969). John Dewey wrestled with the question of whether a textbook of scientific psychology could ignore philosophical issues because "it is the practice of our colleges to make psychology the path by which to enter the fields of philosophy," Dewey, *Psychology*, iv. Theologians, too, had to confront evolutionary theory, and their response was also part of the context in which psychologists responded to Darwinian theory; see Frederick Gregory, "The Impact of Darwinian Evolution on Protestant Theology in the Nineteenth Century," in *God and Nature*, eds. David C. Lindberg and Ronald L. Numbers (Berkeley and Los Angeles: University of California Press, 1986).

32. R. C. Davis, "American Psychology, 1800–1885," *Psychological Review* 43 (1936): 471–493; quotation is from pp. 480–481.

33. R. S. Woodworth, "The Adolescence of American Psychology," *Psycho-

logical Review 20 (1943): 10–32; quotation is from p. 14. The textbooks that represented the old mental philosophy while wrestling with evolution and the results of research from psychological laboratories include, for example, Dewey, *Psychology*, and Porter, *The Human Intellect*.

34. Darwin's theory raised doubts about the compatibility of science and religion, questioned the assumption that science could lead to certain truth, and ultimately led to the doubt that even religion could provide certain truth. That change, from the early belief that certainty was possible to an acceptance of probability and uncertainty, first in science and later in theology, is part of the context in which the new psychology replaced the old. See Croce, *Science and Religion*.

35. Wade Pickren, "A Lamp Unto Our Feet, a Light Unto Our Way: The New Psychology and Religion in Popular Periodicals" (paper presented at the annual meeting of Cheiron, the International Society for the History of the Behavioral Sciences, Windsor, Ontario, Canada, June 1992).

36. See David Leary, "Telling Likely Stories: The Rhetoric of the New Psychology, 1880–1920," *Journal of the History of the Behavioral Sciences* 23 (1987): 315–331; Leary suggests (p. 316) that for Hall, James, and Cattell "the New Psychology offered them an opportunity to resolve personal conflicts concerning science and religion, materialism and spiritualism, determinism and free will."

37. William James, *The Principles of Psychology*, vol. 1 (New York: Henry Holt, 1890), 350. Textbook authors after James followed his lead, and the remaining texts of the "old psychology" soon disappeared.

38. For example, the organization of the eye and its role in receiving visual patterns as an example of the foresight of the Creator gave way to accounts of how the eye might have evolved through natural selection.

39. George Trumbull Ladd, "On Certain Hindrances to the Progress of Psychology in America," *Psychological Review* 6 (1899):121–133.

40. James McKeen Cattell, "The Conceptions and Methods of Psychology," *Popular Science Monthly* 66 (1904): 176–186; reprinted in *James McKeen Cattell, Man of Science* (Lancaster, PA: Science Press, 1947), 197–207; quotation is from p. 201.

41. On the issue of revolutions in psychology, see Thomas H. Leahey, "The Mythical Revolutions of American Psychology," *American Psychologist* 47 (1992): 308–318.

42. The rise of the acceptance of psychology by colleges and universities was chronicled by Burt G. Miner, "The Changing Attitude of American Universities Toward Psychology," *Science* 20 (1904): 299–307.

43. Robert S. Woodworth, "The Adolescence of American Psychology," *Psychological Review* 50 (1943): 10–32.

44. Upham, *Elements of Intellectual Philosophy* (2nd ed., 1828); Stewart began his *Elements of the Philosophy of the Human Mind* with the following: "The prejudice which is commonly entertained against metaphysical speculations, seems to arise chiefly from two causes: First, from an apprehension, that the subjects about which they are employed, are placed beyond the reach of the human faculties; and, secondly, from a belief, that these subjects have no relation to the business of life" (vol. 1, p. 1). He subsequently argued that, like the natural philosophers, the philosophers of mind could avoid metaphysical speculation and confine themselves to observing phenomena and determining the general laws that govern them.

45. These arguments by Upham, omitted from later editions of his text, were not so different from those used by the new psychologists to gain acceptance for their discipline in the academic world. The new psychology proclaimed itself a science, a study worthy in its own right, and useful in education and child rearing. In 1904, for example, President Hyde of Bowdoin College, in his annual report to the Governing Boards, celebrated the "dignifying of Psychology in the curriculum" when laboratory courses in psychology were added to the college's offerings. He emphasized the usefulness of psychology for the teacher, the parent, the physician, the lawyer, the preacher, the social worker, and in world affairs. The college, by extending the offerings of the Department of Philosophy in this way, was able to make available to students "the means of becoming versed in a science of such wide and intimate social application." Hyde appointed an Amherst graduate with a new PhD from Harvard, Charles T. Burnett (1873–1946), to teach laboratory courses; Burnett taught at Bowdoin from 1904–1944.

46. Leary, "Telling Likely Stories." Faith in the ability of science to address social problems grew throughout the 19th century; see, for example, George H. Daniels, *American Science in the Age of Jackson* (New York: Columbia University Press, 1968) and John Burnham, *How Superstition Won and Science Lost: Popularizing Science and Health in the United States* (New Brunswick, NJ: Rutgers University Press, 1987).

47. Watson and Evans, *The Great Psychologists*, 341–342.

48. R. Davis, "American Psychology," 477. An example of Upham's inclusiveness are his chapters on disorders of mental functions, a concern that was a departure from the Scottish philosophy; see Marian C. Madden and Edward H. Madden, "Thomas Upham on Relations and Alienation," *Transactions of the Charles S. Pierce Society* 19 (1983): 227–253. Upham's sections on abnormal mental functioning were expanded into a book for Harpers. Thomas C. Upham's *Outlines of Imperfect and Disordered Mental Action* (New York: Harper and Bros., 1840) was arguably the first textbook in abnormal psychology to appear in America, just as his 1827 text is considered to be the first textbook in psychology in America.

49. Catell, "The Methods and Conceptions," 200.

50. Woodworth, "The Adolescence," 15.

51. Evans, "The Origins," 55.

52. Dewey, "The New Psychology," 282.

53. Ibid., 286.

54. Ibid., 278, 282.

55. For the initial statements of structuralism and functionalism, see E. B. Titchener, "The Postulates of a Structural Psychology," *Philosophical Review* 7 (1898): 449–465, and James R. Angell, "The Province of a Functional Psychology," *Psychological Review* 14 (1907): 61–91. Both articles are reprinted in Wayne Dennis, *Readings in the History of Psychology* (New York: Appleton-Century-Crofts, 1948); page references in subsequent notes refer to the pages in Dennis's *Readings*. The era of the "schools" of psychology that these articles helped launch is depicted in C. Murchison, ed., *Psychologies of 1925* (Worcester, MA: Clark University, 1926) and C. Murchison, ed., *Psychologies of 1930* (Worcester, MA: Clark University Press, 1930). Classic texts on schools and systems include those by Edna Heidbreder, *Seven Psychologies* (New York: Century, 1933), and R. S. Woodworth, *Con-*

temporary Schools of Psychology rev. ed. (New York: Ronald Press, 1948). For comparisons among the schools, see Alfred H. Fuchs and George F. Kawash, "Prescriptive Dimensions for Five Schools of Psychology," *Journal of the History of the Behavioral Sciences* 10 (1974): 355–366, and George F. Kawash and Alfred H. Fuchs, "A Factor Analysis of Ratings of Five Schools of Psychology," *Journal of the History of the Behavioral Sciences* 10 (1974): 426–437.

56. Titchener, "The Postulates," 369.

57. James Mark Baldwin, "Psychology Past and Present," *Psychological Review* 1 (1894): 363–391. Conscious experience was the primary criterion for accepting mental facts in Upham's psychology: Was the distinction, for example, between perception and sensation intelligible on the basis of one's own conscious experience? E. B. Titchener represents an even purer marriage of English psychology with German method, as he strove valiantly to use the analysis of consciousness under laboratory conditions to arrive at an understanding of the content of the normal, adult, human generalized mind.

58. Angell, "The Province," 441.

59. Ibid., 440.

60. Alison Turtle, "Mind as Function: An Aspect of Nineteenth Century British Psychology," in *Conceptual Analysis and Method in Psychology, Essays in Honor of W. M. O'Neil*, ed. J. P. Sutcliffe (Sydney, Australia: Sydney University Press, 1978).

61. The symbolic and practical importance of the laboratory to the new psychology has been described by James Capshew, "Psychologists on Site," *American Psychologist* 47 (1992): 132–142.

62. Miner, "The Changing Attitude."

63. Grace Adams, *Psychology: Science or Superstition?* (New York: Covici-Friede, 1931), 10.

6

WILLIAM JAMES AND THE ART OF HUMAN UNDERSTANDING

DAVID E. LEARY

It has long been noted that William James, one of the founders of philosophical pragmatism as well as psychological science, had the sensibility of an artist. It has also been suggested that his artistic sensibility made a tangible difference in the crafting of his thought, both in philosophy and in psychology. G. Stanley Hall (1891), for instance, said that James was "an impressionist in psychology" whose "portfolio" (*The Principles of Psychology*, W. James, 1890/1983c) contained many stimulating and even brilliant "sketches" (Hall, 1891, p. 585). Later, James Jackson Putnam (1910) averred that James was "through and through an artist" (p. 842),

---

Preliminary versions of this article were presented at Brock University, Carleton College, and the University of New Hampshire. A penultimate version was presented in August 1990 as an invited address at the 98th Annual Convention of the American Psychological Association in Boston.

The thesis of this article supplements my earlier argument that poetry influenced the development of James's thought (Leary, 1988), and its explication expands the outline of James's theory of human understanding presented in the introductory chapter of *Metaphors in the History of Psychology* (Leary, 1990a). Material from James (ca. 1894) is quoted by permission of Alexander R. James and the Houghton Library of Harvard University.
Reprinted from *American Psychologist, 47,* 152–160. Copyright © 1992 by the American Psychological Association. Reprinted with permission of the author.

and John Dewey (1910) stated that he was "an artist who gave philosophical expression to the artist's sense of the unique" (p. 507). Still later, George Santayana (1930) referred to James's "pictorial cosmology" (p. 252), and Ralph Barton Perry (1935) wrote about his "pictorial manner of philosophizing" (Vol. 2, p. 684).

It may surprise some to learn that James not only had the sensibility of an artist, but that his first vocation (as he himself called it) was to be an artist. This was no whimsical aspiration. From a young age, James drew very capably and persistently, he studied art in American and European museums with great avidity and insight, and at the age of 18, he committed himself to an apprenticeship with William Morris Hunt, one of the major painters in America. As testimony to his ability, the well-known artist John La Farge, who had been an apprentice to Hunt at the same time as James, asserted that James "had the promise of being a remarkable, perhaps a great, painter" (La Farge, 1910, p. 8).

Recently, Jacques Barzun (1983, 1985), Daniel Bjork (1983, 1988), and Howard Feinstein (1984) have suggested some of the possible consequences of James's artistic ability, aesthetic interests, and abbreviated artistic career for his subsequent work in psychology and philosophy. Their scholarship is extremely valuable, but it has left many unresolved questions and issues to be explored. For instance, Barzun (1985) argued that "the Jamesian mind is artist first and last" (p. 909), but he did not articulate in concrete detail what this meant, nor did he relate his thesis to James's own particular artistic experiences. Feinstein (1984), whose detailed and fascinating research has provided grist for many mills (including my own), was primarily concerned with the emotional antecedents and consequences of James's turn away from his early artistic vocation and with the effects of these emotional factors (rather than artistic factors per se) on the development of James's thought. Even Bjork, who has examined the extent to which James, the psychologist, was a "compromised artist" (Bjork, 1983, pp. 15–36) and has portrayed the center of James's subsequent vision (Bjork, 1988), has not analyzed many of the tangible ways in which James's artistic background and sensitivities affected the development of his specific premises and doctrines. Nor has he pursued his insight that James often articulated his thought in terms of metaphors drawn from the arts.

Through the aid of such metaphors, drawn by James from the realm of the arts, I will introduce and illustrate my thesis in the next section. This thesis is simply that James's artistic sensibility and experience were critically important in the development of his psychological and philosophical thought and, more particularly, in the articulation of a view of human understanding that was fundamental to his psychology and philosophy. This view of human understanding, I will argue, underlay how James characterized all thought, ranging from the philosophical and psychological through the common-sensical and scientific. It also influenced the way in which he thought about and formulated his own specific psychological and philosophical doctrines. To underscore its centrality as a fundamental motif throughout all his work, I shall begin by reviewing the ways in which— and the artistic metaphors through which—James characterized philosophy and philosophizing over the course of his career. Subsequently, I shall turn my attention to James's view of human understanding, its development, and its further articulation and application in his psychology.

JAMES'S PORTRAIT OF PHILOSOPHY

The heuristic goal of philosophy, according to James, is to achieve the most all-encompassing view, or perspective, possible. In practice, however, "no philosophy can ever be anything but a summary sketch, a picture of the world in abridgment, a foreshortened bird's-eye view of the perspective of events" (James, 1909/1977, p. 9). Because no single person or group can achieve a view that is all-inclusive, James (1876/1978b) defined philosophical study as "the habit of always seeing an alternative," of gaining and changing "mental perspective," like a connoisseur walking around a three-dimensional statue (p. 4).

Just as Plato once described science as the search for likely stories, James (1905/1978a) said that the philosopher searches for "more or less plausible pictures" (p. 143). Concepts are "views taken on reality," he suggested (James, 1910/1979, p. 200), and "philosophies are only pictures of the world which have grown up in the minds of different individuals" (quoted in Myers, 1986, p. 570). If you want to understand anyone's philosophical system, James argued, you should "place yourself ... at the centre of [that person's] philosophic vision." When you do, "you understand at once all the different things it makes [that person] write or say. But keep outside [that vision] ... and of course you fail" (James, 1909/1977, p. 117). For "philosophy is more a matter of passionate vision than of logic.... Logic only find[s] reasons for the vision afterwards" (p. 81). Given this conviction, it is not surprising that James felt that "a man's vision is the great fact about him" (p. 14).

Although James had a special affinity for the notion that philosophers "paint" their views (see, e.g., James, 1907/1975b, p. 275; 1903–1904/1988), he was not indelibly wedded to the painting metaphor. On occasion he characterized his system of thought, instead, as a "mosaic philosophy" in which the picture of reality was composed of myriad little pieces or aspects of reality (James, 1912/1976, pp. 22, 42). The mosaic, James said, would never be completed, for "every hour of human life" can add a new aspect, achieved from a novel perspective, guided by a distinctive interest, thus enlarging the "picture gallery" of human life (p. 83). Because "of no concrete bit of experience was an exact duplicate ever framed" (James, 1910/1979, p. 76), he insisted that truth should be conceptualized "to mean everywhere, not duplication, but addition" (James, 1909/1975a, p. 41). The full truth about the universe, which includes the experiences and conceptual constructions of humans within it, cannot possibly be known—it will not even exist—until all its aspects have been created.

JAMES'S PORTRAIT OF HUMAN UNDERSTANDING

The preceding review of James's metaphorical descriptions of philosophy and philosophizing should serve as an apt introduction to his view of human understanding in general. This view was solidly grounded in the analyses presented in his masterpiece, *The Principles of Psychology* (1890/1983c), and these psychological analyses were based, in turn, on insights gained or corroborated through his experiences as a fledgling artist and artist's apprentice and through his reading of Ralph Waldo Emerson, William Wordsworth, and others.

Before discussing their experiences, I want to provide a "charcoal sketch" (to use a Jamesian term) of two major features in James's portrait of human understanding. Stated most simply, these features (or claims) are (a) that all knowledge, including science, is ultimately based on the finding of analogy, which is to say, on the finding of an appropriate, enlightening comparison or metaphor; and (b) that the analogies or metaphors in any field of knowledge, including science, are (or should be) always changing rather than fixed. In the words of his much-beloved Emerson, they should be "fluxional" rather than "frozen" (Emerson, 1837/1983a, p. 55; 1844/1983c, p. 463; on these important points, see James, 1890/1983c, pp. 500, 753–754, 984; Leary, 1987, pp. 326–327; 1988; 1990a, pp. 19–20, 45–47). In other words, James felt that the analogies, comparisons, or metaphors that provide the means of human understanding are partial and temporary in their utility, and that they should be changed as newer aspects of reality come to the fore in the stream of experience. For James, a staunch empiricist, there was always a new way to experience any reality and a new way to categorize any experience. Although a given analogy may provide useful insight into experience and reality, it can never provide a truly definitive and final view of it. His convictions in this regard pertained perforce to his philosophy of science. "Any bit of scientific research," he wrote, "becomes an angle and place of vantage from which arguments are brought to bear" (James, 1885/1987b, pp. 383–384). Whenever a scientific theory is taken as "definitive," it cuts off other vantage points and hence becomes "perspectiveless and short" (James, 1896/1986a, p. 136).

For example, if one wishes to understand the nature of the mind, it might be helpful to note that the mind is like a machine in a number of regards, and it may prove fruitful to explicate the ways in which, and the degrees to which, this is the case. But James would insist that the mind is not identical, structurally or functionally, with any known machine, including the most sophisticated computer of our own day. The use of other analogies will be necessary to elucidate the mind's other, perhaps neglected aspects.

Another way to express James's belief—a belief that he began to articulate in the 1870s—is to say that we humans can understand things, events, and experiences only from and through the viewpoint of other things, events, and experiences. This belief or thesis by no means rules out valid and reliable human understanding. On the contrary, if in addition to noting parallels among a variety of phenomena, we abstract and name the specific similarities that account for these parallels, we can develop reasonable and coherent arguments regarding the aptness of particular analogies and of the theories based on them. Such arguments will sometimes result in quite reliable inferences. Crafting such arguments, James pointed out, is something that occupies both scientists and philosophers: Disconfirming or verifying them is something at which scientists excel, and leaving analogical or metaphorical insights in their more complex, "unresolved," but highly suggestive form accounts for the genius and fertile works of poets, artists, and others (see James, 1890/1983c, pp. 984–988). Whatever the various uses to which analogies and metaphors can be put, James emphasized that the offering of what he called "similar instances," far from being "a perverse act of thought," is "the necessary first step" in any type of human understanding, whether scientific or nonscientific (p. 987).

It should also be noted, because it will underscore the *art* involved (according to James) in creative cognition, that the conjuring of "similar instances" was, for him, a very subtle affair. Some individuals, and not others, are unusually adept at this task. As he stated in *The Principles of Psychology*, "*some people are far more sensitive to resemblances, and far more ready to point out wherein they consist, than others are*" (James, 1890/1983c, p. 500). Indeed, he was convinced that "*a native talent for perceiving analogies is ... the leading fact in genius of every order*" (p. 500). For whereas most people "have no eyes but for those aspects of things which [they] have already been taught to discern," creative individuals are precisely those who further human understanding by noting analogies that others "could never cogitate alone," although they may recognize and appreciate them once they are pointed out, whether by Shakespeare, Newton, Darwin, Tolstoy, or some other genius (p. 420). (The persons I have just named were some of James's favorite examples of genius. See James, 1890/1983c, pp. 984–988.)

DEVELOPMENT OF JAMES'S PORTRAIT OF HUMAN UNDERSTANDING

James's theory of what I shall call the *art of human understanding*—the art of grasping similarities among phenomena and of thus forging perceptual patterns and conceptual categories out of the flux or chaos of experience—evolved in the 1870s from a very rich mixture of his own reading and experience. The reading, as I have argued elsewhere (Leary, 1988), included especially the work and thought of Ralph Waldo Emerson and William Wordsworth—for instance, Emerson's essays on "The American Scholar" (1837/1983a), "Art" (1841/1983b), and "The Poet" (1844/1983c), and Wordworth's long poem, "The Excursion" (1814/1977). It also included works by Robert Browning, Johann Wolfgang von Goethe, and Nathaniel Hawthorne. The experience, as opposed to the reading, that formed the basis for James's insight and belief had more to do with his efforts and encounters with art, and it started long before his time as a painter and artist's apprentice. Here is the way that his brother, the novelist Henry James (1913/1983b), subsequently described the youthful William: "As I catch W. J.'s image, from far back, at its most characteristic, he sits drawing and drawing, always drawing ... and not as with a plodding patience ... but easily, freely and ... infallibly" (p. 118). This image is repeated in Henry's various reminiscences, and it is a picture that emerges from other sources as well, not least from William's own drawing notebooks (many fine examples of James's drawings are reproduced in Feinstein, 1984). From early in life, James showed a remarkable aptitude with a pencil and a strong inclination to give free rein to it. In addition, first in New York City, then in Europe, and finally in Newport, Rhode Island, James took lessons and developed the obvious abilities that he had. Supplementing the exercise and development of his own talent, he also showed a distinctive interest and an unusual sensitivity as an observer of art. Throughout his life he was a curious and omnivorous museum visitor, often attracted to what was new and experimental.[1]

---

[1] James's fascination with, and close study of, the paintings of Eugène Delacroix in Paris—at thirteen years of age—is a relevant example (see Bjork, 1988, pp. 14–19). There is good reason to suppose that his ruminations on the works of Delacroix stimulated his thinking about the lack of any clear distinction between the subjective and objective poles in experience. This was an important concern of his later work. At the other end of his life, perhaps the best example of his continuing openness to novelty in art was his joyful astonishment at the work of Matisse and Picasso (see Stein, 1933/1960, p. 80). Clearly, his awareness that modes of representation and understanding are liable to change was nurtured and sustained by his familiarity with art. If he sometimes expressed regret about his lack of formal education, he could nonetheless have agreed with his brother Henry that, for them, "the great rooms of the Louvre" were "educative, formative, fertilizing, in a degree which no other 'intellectual experience' ... could pretend ... to rival" (H. James, 1913/1983b, p. 197). My argument here is that James's shortcomings in terms of mathematics and logic, which formal education would have corrected, were more than counterbalanced by the insights he gained from art. As his "master" William Morris Hunt (1875–1883/1976) said with

In this context, James was persuaded at the age of 18 to become an artist, and he committed himself whole-heartedly to an apprenticeship in Newport, Rhode Island, with the highly regarded painter, William Morris Hunt (on this period of James's life, see Bjork, 1988, pp. 22–36; Feinstein, 1984, pp. 103–145; Perry, 1935, Vol. 1, pp. 190–201). Significantly, this was James's first commitment to any field of study or potential career. In explaining his decision to his father, he said that he continually received from his "intercourse with art ... spiritual impressions the intensest and purest I know." Not only was he inclined toward art, he said, but life "would be embittered if I were kept from it." With foresight he added, "That is the way I feel *at present*. Of course I may change" (quoted in Perry, 1935, Vol. 1, pp. 199–200).

The following year was full of the explorations, discoveries, and trials of apprenticeship, enhanced in significant ways by the friendship and ideas of his fellow apprentice, John La Farge. La Farge was seven years older than William and much more experienced than either William or William's younger brother Henry, who often accompanied him to Hunt's studio. As Henry (1914/1983a) later recalled, La Farge quickly became "quite the most interesting person we knew" (p. 287). Although Hunt was clearly "a figure unmistakable" (p. 279) from whom William learned a great deal, La Farge became "the figure of figures" for both William and Henry (p. 289). "An embodiment of the gospel of aesthetics" (p. 290), La Farge "opened up ... prospects and possibilities that made the future flush and swarm" (p. 287). Besides introducing them to Browning and Balzac, who were to influence William and Henry respectively, he represented for William a continuation of the visual and intellectual challenges presented earlier by Delacroix. He also encouraged Henry to turn from dabbling in art to committing himself seriously to writing. As La Farge's Newport paintings show, he was already guided by his later-renowned proposition that, in human consciousness or experience, subjectivity is intertwined with the supposedly objective, material world. One critic who has speculated on La Farge's influence on William and Henry (Adams, 1985) expressed it this way:

> La Farge's paintings created a new relation between the artist and his subject. His paintings unite the external world with subjective inner experience to the point where subject and object, the viewer and the thing seen, merge into one. Perception ceases to lead to solid, substantive qualities but culminates instead in feelings of transition and relation—in ever-changing gradations of light, focus, interest, and emotion, in continually fluctuating perceptual nuances, which never become fixed or solid. (Adams, 1987, p. 30)

---

considerable foresight, at least as regards James, "mathematics ... don't develop a person like painting" (p. 86).

William was so struck by the technical and conceptual issues with which La Farge was struggling at that time that he remembered and discussed them with La Farge—to La Farge's amazement—almost 50 years later (La Farge, 1910). Although James's subsequent "psychology of consciousness" was no doubt multiply determined, Gay Wilson Allen (1967) had good reason to suggest that La Farge was among those who influenced its development (p. 69).[2]

Despite the creative energy and growth produced during this apprenticeship, by the fall of 1861 James had left Hunt's studio, given up his aspiration to an artistic career, and moved with his family to Cambridge, Massachusetts. He entered Lawrence Scientific School at Harvard University, thus starting down the path that led to his accomplishments and renown in psychology and philosophy.

Much has been written about James's one-year apprenticeship. In particular, there has been a great deal of speculation about James's motives for giving up his calling to become an artist, despite plentiful evidence of his interest and ability; but in fact, little is known for certain. That his father was not happy about his choice of vocation is abundantly clear, and this almost certainly played a role in James's decision (see especially Feinstein, 1984, pp. 140–145). However, it is also plausible, as Perry (1935, Vol. 1, p. 200) and Bjork (1988, pp. 30–31) have suggested, that James simply concluded that he could not become a painter of the very first rank, and hence turned to science, another of his (and his father's) many interests. In any case, as his brother Henry (1914/1983a) put it, "nothing ... could have been less logical, yet at the same time more natural, than that William's interest in the practice of painting should have suddenly and abruptly ceased" (p. 300). There was in the event "no repining at proved waste" on William's part (pp. 300–301), perhaps because on a deeper level there was no waste. As Henry (1913/1983b) had noted earlier, William "flowered in every [seeming] waste" (p. 117). And indeed, with hindsight, I would argue that his year-long stay in Newport was a tutorial for his later philosophical and scientific work, not a detour on the way to it.

Whatever factors were involved, the motives and rationale for James's turn from art to science are less important than the fact that he had such a formative exposure to art and painting.[3] This experience, building on his

---

[2] Allen (1967) also claimed that "it would be futile to attempt to trace any lasting influence of William Hunt on his life," although Hunt's school of painting was consonant with James's later insights (p. 69). Without asserting any singularity of influence, I think that Allen's claim is exaggerated. Hunt's (1875–1883/1976) repeated admonishments to his students contained many hints of James's later doctrines (e.g., regarding the centrality of experience and the primacy of action), and James himself suggested how sensitive and retentive he was with regard to these hints by periodically referring to "the endless advice of every [art] teacher to his pupil" (James, 1890/1983c, p. 875). Indeed, James's portrait of philosophy echoed his teacher's dictum that painting is "the *only universal language*! All nature is creation's picture-book!" (Hunt, 1875–1883/1976, p. 73).

[3] After leaving Newport, James kept his drawing alive for another decade before he claimed to

native artistic aptitude, prepared him to be sympathetic and responsive, in the 1860s and 1870s, to Emerson's and Wordsworth's ideas regarding the nature of human thought. In James's own rendition, as in Emerson's and Wordworth's, the notion that human understanding is basically analogical or metaphorical was often expressed with visual imagery. It wasn't simply that humans can apply different analogies or metaphors; rather, humans can assume different viewpoints and achieve new perspectives. As a former artist, James felt the rightness of Emerson's and Wordsworth's claims. He was deeply and intimately aware that one can come to see things anew, to notice fresh aspects, and to create novel possibilities in reality. As Wordsworth put it in "The Excursion," which James read and reread in the early 1870s much as Charles Darwin had done to similar effect in the early 1840s (see Perry, 1935, Vol. 1, pp. 338–339, 355), the mind has an "excursive power" to "wander about" the world, viewing it from this and now that vantage point, thus shaping its "prospects" (Wordsworth, 1814/1977, pp. 155, 173). Even what is taken to be normal reality needs to be learned, as James came to realize. As he put it quite tellingly in *The Principles of Psychology* (1890/1983c), just as "in poetry and the arts, someone has to come and tell us what aspects we may single out" (p. 420), so too all humans "must go through a long education of the eye and ear before they can perceive the realities which adults perceive" (p. 724). Ideally, the labels for reality that are thus stamped in our mind through this long education will be fluxional rather than frozen. Unfortunately, this proves often not to be the case, so that we become all too conventional or literal in our mentality. As a result, James said, "if we lost our stock of labels we should be intellectually lost in the midst of the world" (p. 420). Human understanding, he realized, depends on such labels, whose meanings are derived (or were derived long ago) from their analogical relations. It can be advanced, however, only with the exchange of these labels for new concepts and terms, grounded in new views of reality.

FURTHER ARTICULATION AND APPLICATION OF JAMES'S VIEW OF HUMAN UNDERSTANDING IN PSYCHOLOGY

James's belief in the analogical or metaphorical foundations of knowledge is richly illustrated in his psychological writings. His treatment of

---

have let it "die out" (quoted in Perry, 1935, Vol. 1, p. 330). He regretted this loss of serious drawing, but he maintained his interest in art, with some fluctuations, throughout his life. As he told his brother in 1872, he envied Henry's belonging to "the world of art" because "away from it, as we live, we sink into a flatter, blanker kind of consciousness, and indulge in an ostrich-like forgetfulness of all our richest potentialities." These potentialities, he said, "startle us now and then when by accident some rich human product, pictorial, literary, or architectural slaps us with its tail" (quoted in Perry, 1935, Vol. 1, p. 327). At critical points in 1868, 1873–1874, 1882, and 1892, art "slapped" him into important meditations. This remains a largely untold story.

thought or consciousness as a stream instead of a chain or train is well-known (see James, 1890/1983c, chap. 9), and his discussion of other psychological topics is similarly informed by underlying analogies and metaphors. The ultimate metaphors that founded and framed his psychological thinking, and that came to undergird his philosophical pragmatism, pluralism, and radical empiricism, were the Darwinian metaphors of variation, selection, and function. All psychological states and actions, according to James, are products of spontaneous variation or selection in terms of their consequential utility. This functionalist orientation has influenced many other American psychologists and has structured much of the theoretical argumentation in modern psychology. Unfortunately, it has in some respects become frozen, despite James's advocacy of a fluxional approach to human and scientific understanding, and it is often taken (in one or another of its contemporary versions) as a definitively authoritative portrait of human nature.

I have discussed this elsewhere (Leary, 1990a, pp. 20–21, 47–49). The point here is that James's own psychology (not to mention his philosophy) reflected and reinforced his view of human understanding. James used analogies and metaphors throughout his works, not simply as ways of expressing his ideas, but as ways of constructing them. He often drew on his artistic experiences in his attempt to understand and explain psychological phenomena as well as in his attempt to pursue philosophical reflection. In fact, the frequency with which he drew on his artistic experience in important, often critical, passages is noteworthy. Insofar as these passages often have to do with the nature of human cognition and understanding, which he conceived from the start on the model of artistic experience, this is not surprising. But his use of artistic experience as a source of metaphorical referents suggests a basic principle of human cognition—that humans tend, naturally enough, to draw their most telling analogies from their own experience. In other words, they use what is familiar to understand the less familiar.

In this section I quote at length from various passages in *The Principles of Psychology* (1890/1983c) to demonstrate sufficiently how James often used a transparently artistic analogy to reach, explicate, and defend a point. In these passages, note how often the notion of *perspective*, of seeing from a different angle or within a different context, was crucial for James, and attend to his frequent references to what he had learned as an artist. For instance, looking forward to his chapter on perception, James wrote,

> We shall see how inveterate is our habit of not attending to sensations as subjective facts, but of simply using them as stepping-stones to pass over to the recognition of the realities whose presence they reveal. The grass out of the window now looks to me of the same green in the sun as in the shade, and yet a painter would have to paint one part of it dark brown, another part bright yellow, to give its real sen-

sational effect. We take no heed, as a rule, of the different way in which the same things look and sound and smell at different distances and under different circumstances. The sameness of the *things* is what we are concerned to ascertain; and any sensations that assure us of that will probably be considered in a rough way to be the same with each other.... What appeals to our attention far more than the absolute quality or quantity of a given sensation is its *ratio* to whatever other sensations we may have at the same time. When everything is dark a somewhat less dark sensation makes us see an object white. (pp. 225–226)

Further on:

> If the assumption of "simple ideas of sensation" recurring in immutable shape is so easily shown to be baseless, how much more baseless is the assumption of immutability in the larger masses of our thought! For there it is obvious and palpable that our state of mind is never precisely the same. Every thought we have of a given fact is, strictly speaking, unique, and only bears a resemblance of kind with our other thoughts of the same fact. When the identical fact recurs, we *must* think of it in a fresh manner, see it under a somewhat different angle, apprehend it in different relations from those in which it last appeared.... From one year to another we see things in new lights. What was unreal has grown real, and what was exciting is insipid. (p. 227)

In summing up at the end of his critical "Stream of Thought" chapter, in a famous passage that articulated his view of human understanding as well as anything he ever wrote, James wrote,

> Looking back, then, over this review, we see that the mind is at every stage a theatre of simultaneous possibilities. Consciousness consists in the comparison of these with each other, the selection of some, and the suppression of the rest by the reinforcing and inhibiting agency of attention.... The mind, in short, works on the data it receives very much as a sculptor works on his block of stone. In a sense the statue stood there from eternity. But there were a thousand different ones beside it [within the same block of stone], and the sculptor alone is to thank for having extricated this one from the rest. Just so the world of each of us, howsoever different our several views of it may be, all lay embedded in the primordial chaos of sensations, which gave the mere *matter* to the thought of all of us indifferently.... Other sculptors, other statues from the same stone! Other minds, other worlds from the same monotonous and inexpressive chaos! My world is but one in a million alike embedded, alike real to those who may abstract them. How different must be the worlds in the consciousness of ant, cuttle-fish, or crab! (p. 277)

The selection of one possible statue, of one possible view of the world, rather than another was intricately and deeply related, for James, to the interests of each person. The concept of *interest* is thus fundamental to James's psychology and philosophy, and in particular to his view of human understanding. The next passage provides James's definition of interest. It should be clear that the artistic analogies that he used in this passage are not secondary; rather, they reflect the most fundamental way in which he conceived this important concept.

> Millions of items of the outward order are present to my senses which never properly enter into my experience. Why? Because they have no *interest* for me. *My experience is what I agree to attend to.* Only those items which I *notice* shape my mind—without selective interest, experience is an utter chaos. Interest alone gives accent and emphasis, light and shade, background and foreground—intelligible perspective, in a word. It varies in every creature, but without it the consciousness of every creature would be a gray chaotic indiscriminateness, impossible for us even to conceive ... The interest itself, though its genesis is doubtless perfectly *natural, makes* experience more than it is made by it. (pp. 380–381)

To underscore how fundamental this concept of interest is, recall that in James's psychology, interest directs attention, attention directs selection, and selection confers coherence on each level of psychological functioning—the perceptual, the conceptual, the practical, the aesthetic, and the moral (see James, 1890/1983c, pp. 273–278).[4] Interest, then, defined as "intelligible perspective," underlies the art of human understanding.

James supplied a nice example of the application of this art:

> Let four men make a tour in Europe. One will bring home only picturesque impressions—costumes and colors, parks and views and works of architecture, pictures and statues. To another all this will be non-existent; and distances and prices, populations and drainage-arrangements, door- and window-fastenings, and other useful statistics will take their place. A third will give a rich account of the theatres, restaurants, and public balls, and naught beside; whilst the fourth will perhaps have been so wrapped in his own subjective broodings as to tell little more than a few names of places through which he passed. Each has selected, out the same mass of presented objects, those which suited his private interest and has made his experience thereby. (pp. 275–276)

---

[4]James's critical concept of selection was not drawn solely from Darwinian thought. Rather, his artistic experience prepared the way for his acceptance of this Darwinian principle and its application on all levels of psychological phenomena. As he wrote in an unpublished manuscript on the psychology of aesthetics, there is an "analogy between art and life in that by both, results are reached only by selection & elimination." Quoting Robert Louis Stevenson, he went on to say that "there is but one art—to omit" (James, ca. 1894). The importance of selection in James's psychology was unambiguously expressed when he asserted that "selection is the very keel on which our mental ship is built" (James, 1890/1983c, p. 640).

Many other passages could be cited, making the same point. For instance, in a passage already quoted in part, James wrote,

> Men have no eyes but for those aspects of things which they have already been taught to discern. Any one of us can notice a phenomenon after it has once been pointed out, which not one in ten thousand could ever have discovered for himself.... *The only things which we commonly see are those which we preperceive* [those for which we are on the lookout], *and the only things which we preperceive are those which have been labelled for us, and the labels stamped into our mind.* (p. 420)[5]

After discussing the perception of likeness, which is to say, the perception of analogies or metaphors, James said,

> If the reader feels that this faculty [of perceiving similarities] is having small justice done it ... I think I emphasize it enough when I call it one of the ultimate foundation-pillars of the intellectual life. (p. 500)

Not surprisingly, James drew on his sensibilities and experience as an artist and artist's apprentice throughout his chapter on perception, pointing out (for instance) that the "eye-picture" created by stimuli impinging on the optic nerve is quite different from the mind-picture that is produced, the mind somehow correcting for the angle of vision and substituting a concept of the object as it would appear from a hypothetically ideal vantage point (James, 1890/1983c, p. 724). Similarly, in the chapter on space perception, James discussed what is now called brightness and size constancy. In one passage he explicitly referred to the training that underlay his psychological insights:

> Usually we see a sheet of paper as uniformly white, although a part of it may be in shadow. But we can in an instant, if we please, notice the shadow as local color. A man walking towards us does not usually seem to alter his size; but we can, by setting our attention in a peculiar way, make him appear to do so. The whole education of the artist consists in his learning to see the presented signs as well as the represented things. No matter what the field of view *means*, he sees it also as it *feels*—that is, as a collection of patches of color bounded by lines—the whole forming an optical diagram of whose intrinsic proportions one who is not an artist has hardly a conscious inkling. The ordinary man's attention passes *over* them to their import; the artist's turns back and dwells *upon* them for their own sake. "Don't draw the thing as it *is*, but as it *looks*!" is the endless advice of every [art] teacher to his pupil; forgetting that what "is" is what it would also "look," provided

---

[5] James articulated a version of this principle in his first psychological essay, in which he pointed out that "a layman present at a shipwreck, a battle, or a fire is helpless.... But the sailor, the fireman, and the general know directly at what point to take up the business. They 'see into the situation' ... with their first glance" (James, 1878/1983a, p. 15).

it were placed in what we have called the "normal" [that is, the ideal] situation for vision. (pp. 874–875)[6]

In his chapter on the perception of reality, in which the psychology of belief was his central concern, James went beyond the usual focus on things and distinguished very effectively among a number of different worlds—the world of sensory things, the world of scientific qualities and forces, the world of ideal relations and abstract truths, the world of "idols of the tribe," the various supernatural worlds of religious belief, the innumerable worlds of individual opinion, and the worlds of "sheer madness and vagary" (pp. 920–922). "*Every object we think of gets at last referred to one world or another of this or of some similar list*," he wrote (p. 922).

> Propositions concerning the different worlds are made from "different points of view"; and in this more or less chaotic state the consciousness of most thinkers remains to the end. Each world *whilst it is attended to* is real after its own fashion; [but] the reality lapses with the attention. (p. 923)

I need not remind you that attention is directed by interest, which for James is a natural, individuating factor. Thus, he said,

> *The fons et origo [the starting point and foundation] of all reality, whether from the absolute or the practical point of view, is . . . subjective, is ourselves.* . . . Reality, starting from our Ego, thus sheds itself from point to point. . . . It only fails when the connecting thread is lost. A whole system may be real, if it only hang to our Ego by one immediately *stinging* term. (pp. 925–926)

What is felt and understood to be real, then, is what is of "stinging" interest, which according to James's definition of interest is whatever is linked to a compelling intelligible perspective.[7]

As the fundamental role of perspective in James's thought becomes clearer, his later reduction of the self or ego to a point of view or field of vision, in the years after the publication of *The Principles of Psychology*,

---

[6] This "endless advice" about drawing a thing as it looks was obviously given to James by his art teacher. In the very first of his published talks on painting and drawing, Hunt (1875–1883/1976) proclaimed, "You are to draw *not reality, but the appearance of reality*!" (p. 3).

[7] Not only reality, but also its meaning and worth are a matter of perspective. As James (1899/1983b) wrote in an essay that expressed the heart of his thought: "Some years ago, whilst journeying in the mountains of North Carolina, I passed by a large number of 'coves'. . . . The impression on my mind was one of unmitigated squalor. . . . I said to the mountaineer who was driving me: 'What sort of people are they who have to make these new clearings?' 'All of us,' he replied; 'why, we ain't happy here unless we are getting one of these coves under cultivation.' I instantly felt that I had been losing the whole inward significance of the situation. . . . When *they* looked on the hideous stumps, what they thought of was personal victory. . . . I had been as blind to the peculiar ideality of their conditions as they certainly would also have been to the ideality of mine, had they had a peep at my strange indoor academic ways of life at Cambridge" (pp. 133–134). "Neither the whole of truth, nor the whole of good, is revealed to any single observer, although each observer gains a partial superiority of insight from the peculiar position in which he stands" (p. 149).

begins to make increasing sense (see Leary, 1990b, pp. 116–117).[8] In this little-known development of his thought, James came to depict the individual ego, not human understanding alone, in terms of the fundamental artistic concept of perspective. From the present historical vantage point, one can see how this largely unexplored extension of his thought was consistent with his career-long reliance on the concept of perspective. Starting from his earliest definition of philosophy as "the possession of mental perspective" (James, 1876/1978b, p. 4), James had infused his principles of psychology with his perspectivalist vision, and he went on subsequently to develop versions of philosophical pragmatism, pluralism, and radical empiricism that were equally premised on the assumption that there is always another view to be had. Together with many other artistic insights and metaphors, this belief in the fundamental reality of alternative and supplemental perspectives permeated James's entire system of thought.

CONCLUSION

I have argued that William James's portrait of human understanding was influenced, as he put it, by "the whole drift of my education" (James, 1902/1985, p. 408). In particular, it was influenced in a deep and lasting way by his artistic sensitivity, experience, and training. On the basis of this view of human understanding, James felt that it was perfectly legitimate—even necessary—to use analogies and metaphors, often from the realm of the arts, in the development of his psychological and philosophical doctrines. It also led him to organize his major psychological work in a very distinctive manner.[9]

Given this background and orientation, it is not surprising that James came to understand the place and type of his psychology and philosophy,

---

[8] Having extended perspectivism to his treatment of the self or ego, James came to understand personal identity and religious conversion as involving, respectively, a centering or changing of one's perspective (James, 1902/1985, pp. 161–162). Beyond that, he came to understand "the Absolute" as the sum of all actual perspectives, nonhuman as well as human, and thus to suggest that even the Absolute is open to continual development, as more pictures of reality are created by its constituent points of view (1909/1977, pp. 130–131, 139–144; 1899/1983d, p. 4; 1902/1985, pp. 409–414). This led Santayana (1913/1940) to comment, with perhaps more justification than he knew, that James's God was "a sort of ... struggling artist" (p. 210).
[9] The organization of *The Principles of Psychology* (James, 1890/1983c) has baffled many psychologists and critics. In fact, this organization makes reasonably good sense if one assumes James's artistic point of view. After getting preliminary discussions out of the way in the first eight chapters, James provided an overview of his psychology of consciousness (or "our study of the mind from within," as he called it on p. 219) in the "Stream of Thought" chapter. This chapter, James said, is "like a painter's first charcoal sketch upon his canvas, in which no niceties appear" (p. 220). Then, after reviewing the various levels of psychological functioning in this chapter, James went on in subsequent chapters to fill in his charcoal sketch with more detailed treatments of the various aspects of his system, proceeding from the most general (consciousness of self) to the most circumscribed (the will) of the mind's experiences. Although this scheme does not account completely for the placement of each chapter, it makes sense of the book's overall organization.

in relation to previous and alternative modes of thought, in explicitly artistic terminology. His system of thought, he said, was "romantic" rather than "classic" (James, 1901/1986b, pp. 193–194). His views, he explained, were concrete, uncouth, complex, overflowing, open-ended, and incomplete. On the one hand, they lacked the "clean pure lines and noble simplicity" typical of the abstract constructions of the "classic-academic" approach, but on the other, they were consonant with the art of human understanding as he comprehended it (see James, 1907/1975b, pp. 16–17; 1910/1979, pp. 76–79).

The fact that his view of human understanding was based on his experience as an artist may help explain why James's psychology and philosophy, grounded as they are on this view of human understanding, have attracted the attention and respect of so many artists and humanists—not to mention scientists and psychologists—to the present day.[10] As James (1897/1987a) once said of someone else's work, his own works do not "violate" the "deepest instincts" of artists (p. 536).

Perhaps the leading artist in James's life was his brother Henry James, Jr., the novelist. It is interesting to note that Henry published a novel, *The Tragic Muse* (1890/1988), in the same year that William published *The Principles of Psychology*. William himself suggested that this concurrence made 1890 a banner year for American literature (James, 1920, p. 299). Not purely by chance, Henry's novel dealt with the world of art.[11] In his own inimitable language (H. James, 1906–1908/1934), the "pictorial fusion" of the novel brings together a "multiplication of aspects" (p. 85) that denies any "usurping [specially privileged] consciousness" (p. 90). The overlap of Henry's and William's motifs has often been noted. I use Henry's quotation here simply to provide a context for saying that I do not intend my view of William James's art of human understanding, and of its impact on his system of thought, to have any undue privilege over other perspectives on the development of his thought. Both James and his work are

---

[10]Besides the various roles that he played in establishing the physiological, behavioral, cognitive, and therapeutic traditions in contemporary psychology, James profoundly influenced individuals all across the cultural landscape—individuals as disparate as Bernard Berenson, Niels Bohr, Jorge Luis Borges, John Dewey, W. E. B. DuBois, Nelson Goodman, Helen Keller, Walter Lippmann, Stephen Pepper, Oliver Sacks, Gertrude Stein, and Wallace Stevens. Another such person, Alfred North Whitehead, the great mathematician, philosopher, and historian of science, considered James to be one of the four major thinkers in the entire Western tradition, along with Plato, Aristotle, and Leibniz (see Whitehead, 1938, pp. 3–4). Whitehead (1956) noted that when the foundations of the modern worldview were blown apart by various discoveries at the turn of this century, William James was one of the few intellectuals prepared and able to windstand the blow (p. 272), and James withstood it without having to change his way of thinking.

[11]Art and artists in modern society—especially painting and painters—provided frequent topics, themes, motifs, and devices in Henry's work (e.g., H. James, 1868–1897/1956; 1874–1909/1984; see also Bowden, 1956; Holland, 1964; Hopkins, 1961; Ward, 1965; Winner, 1967, 1970). The importance of art, particularly painting, in Henry's conceptual scheme is strongly suggested by his assertion that "the analogy between the art of the painter and the art of the novelist is, so far as I am able to see, complete" (H. James, 1884/1987, p. 188).

incredibly rich and overdetermined. But I do believe that the particular aspect of William James's life and work that I have pointed out in this article is important and needs to be fused into our picture of this remarkable and influential person.

REFERENCES

Adams, H. (1985). William James, John La Farge, and the foundations of radical empiricism. *American Art Journal, 17*, 60–67.

Adams, H. (1987). The mind of John La Farge. In H. Adams, (Ed.), *John La Farge* (pp. 11–77). New York: Abbeville Press.

Allen, G. W. (1967). *William James: A biography*. New York: Viking Press.

Barzun, J. (1983). *A stroll with William James*. New York: Harper & Row.

Barzun, J. (1985). William James: The mind as artist. In S. Koch & D. E. Leary (Eds.), *A century of psychology as science* (pp. 904–910). New York: McGraw-Hill.

Bjork, D. W. (1983). *The compromised scientist: William James in the development of American psychology*. New York: Columbia University Press.

Bjork, D. W. (1988). *William James: The center of his vision*. New York: Columbia University Press.

Bowden, E. T. (1956). *The themes of Henry James: A system of observation through the visual arts*. New Haven, CT: Yale University Press.

Dewey, J. (1910). William James. *Journal of Philosophy, Psychology and Scientific Methods, 7*, 505–508.

Emerson, R. W. (1983a). The American scholar. In J. Porte (Ed.), *Essays and lectures* (pp. 51–71). New York: Library of America. (Original work published 1837)

Emerson, R. W. (1983b). Art. In J. Porte (Ed.), *Essays and lectures* (pp. 429–440). New York: Library of America. (Original work published 1841)

Emerson, R. W. (1983c). The poet. In J. Porte (Ed.), *Essays and lectures* (pp. 445–468). New York: Library of America. (Original work published 1844)

Feinstein, H. M. (1984). *Becoming William James*. Ithaca, NY: Cornell University Press.

Hall, G. S. (1891). Review of William James's *Principles of psychology*. *American Journal of Psychology, 3*, 578–591.

Holland, L. B. (1964). *The expense of vision: Essays on the craft of Henry James*. Princeton, NJ: Princeton University Press.

Hopkins, V. (1961). Visual art devices and parallels in the fiction of Henry James. *Modern Language Association Publications, 76*, 561–574.

Hunt, W. M. (1976). *On painting and drawing* (H. M. Knowlton, Ed.). New York: Dover. (Original two-volume work published 1875–1883)

James, H., Jr. (1934). *The art of the novel: Critical prefaces* (R. P. Blackmur, Ed.). New York: Scribner. (Original works published 1906–1908)

James, H., Jr. (1956). *The painter's eye* (J. L. Sweeney, Ed.). Cambridge, MA: Harvard University Press. (Original works published 1868–1897)

James, H., Jr. (1983a). Notes of a son and brother. In F. W. Dupee (Ed.), *Autobiography* (pp. 237–544). Princeton, NJ: Princeton University Press. (Original work published 1914)

James, H., Jr. (1983b). A small boy and others. In F. W. Dupee (Ed.), *Autobiography* (pp. 1–236). Princeton, NJ: Princeton University Press. (Original work published 1913)

James, H., Jr. (1984). *Tales of art and life* (H. Terrie, Ed.). Schenectady, NY: Union College Press. (Original works published 1874–1909)

James, H., Jr. (1987). The art of fiction. In R. Gard (Ed.), *The critical muse: Selected literary criticism* (pp. 186–206). London: Penguin Books. (Original work published 1884)

James, H., Jr. (1988). *The tragic muse*. New York: Viking Penguin. (Original work published 1890)

James, W. (ca. 1894). *Manuscript on psychology of aesthetics*. In William James Papers, File 4393, Houghton Library, Harvard University, Cambridge, MA.

James, W. (1920). *The letters of William James* (Vol. 1; Henry James III, Ed.). Boston: Atlantic Monthly Press.

James, W. (1975a). *The meaning of truth: A sequel to "pragmatism."* Cambridge, MA: Harvard University Press. (Original work published 1909)

James, W. (1975b). *Pragmatism: A new name for some old ways of thinking*. Cambridge, MA: Harvard University Press. (Original work published 1907)

James, W. (1976). *Essays in radical empiricism*. Cambridge, MA: Harvard University Press. (Original work published 1912)

James, W. (1977). *A pluralistic universe*. Cambridge, MA: Harvard University Press. (Original work published 1909)

James, W. (1978a). Preface to Harald Höffding's *Problems of philosophy*. In *Essays in philosophy* (pp. 140–143). Cambridge, MA: Harvard University Press. (Original work published 1905)

James, W. (1978b). The teaching of philosophy in our colleges. In *Essays in philosophy* (pp. 3–6). Cambridge, MA: Harvard University Press. (Original work published 1876)

James, W. (1979). *Some problems of philosophy*. Cambridge, MA: Harvard University Press. (Original manuscript incomplete and unpublished at James's death in 1910)

James, W. (1983a). Brute and human intellect. In *Essays in psychology* (pp. 1–37). Cambridge, MA: Harvard University Press. (Original work published 1878)

James, W. (1983b). On a certain blindness in human beings. In *Talks to teachers on psychology and to students on some of life's ideals* (pp. 132–149). Cambridge, MA: Harvard University Press. (Original work published 1899)

James, W. (1983c). *The principles of psychology*. Cambridge, MA: Harvard University Press. (Original work published 1890)

James, W. (1983d). *Talks to teachers on psychology and to students on some of life's ideals*. Cambridge, MA: Harvard University Press. (Original work published 1899)

James, W. (1985). *The varieties of religious experience*. Cambridge, MA: Harvard University Press. (Original work published 1902)

James, W. (1986a). Address of the president before the Society for Psychical Research. In *Essays in psychical research* (pp. 127–137). Cambridge, MA: Harvard University Press. (Original work presented 1896)

James, W. (1986b). Frederic Myers's service to psychology. In *Essays in psychical research* (pp. 192–202). Cambridge, MA: Harvard University Press. (Original work published 1901)

James, W. (1987a). Review of George Santayana's *The sense of beauty*. In *Essays, comments, and reviews* (pp. 536–539). Cambridge, MA: Harvard University Press. (Original work published 1897)

James, W. (1987b). Review of Josiah Royce's *The religious aspect of philosophy*. In *Essays, comments, and reviews* (pp. 383–388). Cambridge, MA: Harvard University Press. (Original work published 1885)

James, W. (1988). Introduction: Philosophies paint pictures. In *Manuscript essays and notes* (pp. 3–6). Cambridge, MA: Harvard University Press. (Original work written 1903–1904)

La Farge, J. (1910, September 2). A new side of Prof. James. *The New York Times*, p. 8.

Leary, D. E. (1987). Telling likely stories: The rhetoric of the New Psychology, 1880–1920. *Journal of the History of the Behavioral Sciences, 23*, 315–331.

Leary, D. E. (1988, August). *Poetry and science: Wordsworth's influence on Darwin and James*. Paper presented at the 96th Annual Convention of the American Psychological Association, Atlanta, GA.

Leary, D. E. (1990a). Psyche's muse: The role of metaphor in the history of psychology. In D. E. Leary (Ed.), *Metaphors in the history of psychology* (pp. 1–78). New York: Cambridge University Press.

Leary, D. E. (1990b). William James on the self and personality: Clearing the ground for subsequent theorists, researchers, and practitioners. In M. G. Johnson & T. B. Henley (Eds.), *Reflections on The Principles of Psychology: William James after a century* (pp. 101–137). Hillsdale, NJ: Erlbaum.

Myers, G. E. (1986). *William James: His life and thought*. New Haven, CT: Yale University Press.

Perry, R. B. (1935). *The thought and character of William James* (Vols. 1 and 2). Boston: Little, Brown.

Putnam, J. J. (1910). William James. *Atlantic Monthly, 106*, 835–848.

Santayana, G. (1930). Brief history of my opinions. In G. P. Adams & W. P. Montague (Eds.), *Contemporary American philosophy* (Vol. 2, pp. 239–257). New York: Scribner.

Santayana, G. (1940). The genteel tradition in American philosophy. In *Winds of doctrine: Studies in contemporary opinion* (pp. 186–215). New York: Scribner. (Original work published 1913)

Stein, G. (1960). *The autobiography of Alice B. Toklas.* New York: Vintage Books. (Original work published 1933)

Ward, J. A. (1965). Picture and action: The problem of narration in James's fiction. *Rice University Studies, 51,* 109–123.

Whitehead, A. N. (1938). *Modes of thought.* New York: Macmillan.

Whitehead, A. N. (1956). *Dialogues of Alfred North Whitehead* (L. Price, Ed.). New York: New American Library.

Winner, V. H. (1967). Pictorialism in Henry James's theory of the novel. *Criticism, 9,* 1–21.

Winner, V. H. (1970). *Henry James and the visual arts.* Charlottesville: University Press of Virginia.

Wordsworth, W. (1977). The excursion. In J. O. Hayden (Ed.), *The poems* (Vol. 2, pp. 35–289). Harmondsworth, Middlesex, England: Penguin. (Original work published 1814)

7

TESTING THE LIMITS OF SENSE AND SCIENCE: AMERICAN EXPERIMENTAL PSYCHOLOGISTS COMBAT SPIRITUALISM, 1880–1920

DEBORAH J. COON

Since its inception, experimental psychology has occupied a precarious place in the hierarchy of the sciences. It is well-known that whereas sociology sat at the peak of the Comtian hierarchy, psychology was not even on the pyramid, having been deemed incapable of becoming a science because its subject matter was unquantifiable and its methods mired in a metaphysical morass. Psychology has never quite lived this down and, as

---

Portions of the research for this article were funded by a Hodgson Grant from the Psychology Department at Harvard University, a Whiting Fellowship in the Humanities at Harvard, a Smithsonian Fellowship at the Museum of American History, and a Paul S. Beer Trust Minigrant from Rensselaer Polytechnic Institute. I thank Clark University (where Stuart Campbell was especially helpful), the Houghton library of Harvard University, Alexander R. James, and the State Historical Society of Wisconsin Library for permission to cite unpublished sources. I am especially grateful to David Hess, Jon Roberts, and two anonymous reviewers for critical readings of the manuscript.
Reprinted from *American Psychologist, 47,* 143–151 (1992). Copyright © 1992 by the American Psychological Association. Reprinted with permission of the author.

psychologists themselves like to say, has never recovered from its adolescent physics envy.

Precisely because psychology's place within the sciences has traditionally been so insecure, it can be useful to the historian as a sort of litmus test for what a given era deemed "scientific." Throughout its brief history, I would argue, psychology has been a magnet for cultural anxieties about the hazy borderline between science and pseudoscience, between the natural and the supernatural.

At the turn of the century, while humanity witnessed the death throes of the religious worldview among intellectuals, the cultural anxiety was particularly acute. Many psychologists gave voice to that anxiety by articulating their scientific worldview as they attempted to establish experimental psychology as a legitimate science. They attempted to set themselves up as arbiters of what would be considered "scientific," as keepers of the scientific light (Burnham, 1987).

This article discusses the battle American psychologists waged against spiritualism and psychic research between 1880 and 1920, as they attempted to establish and maintain the boundaries of their new scientific discipline. That psychologists were never able to present a united front and were forced to confront the differences within their own ranks only makes the tale all the more telling.

SPIRITUALISM

Although spiritualism would eventually achieve a groundswell of popular interest throughout the world in the late 19th century, it began quite modestly in 1848 in a small town near Rochester, New York (Braude, 1989; Moore, 1977). The young adolescents Kate and Margaret Fox began to hear rapping sounds that they believed to be the messages of a dead peddler, murdered and buried in the basement of their farmhouse. The youngsters were related to prominent Rochester Quaker abolitionists, who investigated the mystery and decided it was not a fraud. With their help, the girls quickly became a cause célèbre in radical reform circles and from there moved into public lecture halls and private parlors.

Interest in and enthusiasm for spiritualism spread rapidly in the 1850s and 1860s, not only in rural areas, but in urban elite circles as well. The wildfire of interest in spiritualism was given additional fuel by the staggering death toll of the Civil War, because large numbers of people hoped to communicate with their lost sons and husbands (Brown, 1983). In addition, the advent of the telegraph and later the wireless telegraph sparked people's imaginations about the possibilities of spiritualistic communication —there might be a sort of "celestial wireless" through which people could communicate with the living and the dead. The discovery of roentgen rays in the 1890s had a similar effect by showing that science could discover hitherto unknown forms of energy; might it not eventually find types of mental and spiritual energy even more subtle (Sibley, 1898; but see Münsterberg, 1899)?

Spiritualism did not require belief in the Christian God, but provided its own proofs of spiritual immortality and its own forms and rituals of spiritual union with beings beyond the veil (Cerullo, 1982; Moore, 1977; Oppenheim, 1985; Turner, 1974). It straddled the arenas of science and religion, requiring empirical evidence to prove the existence of its spiritual phenomena. Among those who developed an interest in spiritualism were a broad range of thinkers, including a number of scientists whose names are well-known: William B. Carpenter, Simon Newcomb, Alfred Russel Wallace, William Crookes, Oliver Lodge, Gustav Theodor Fechner, and, most important for our present concern, the American psychologist and philosopher William James (1842–1910).

James's public interest in spiritualism and psychic research in the 1880s and 1890s is well-known and well documented (Gauld, 1968; James, 1986; Leary, 1980; Murphy & Ballou, 1960; Myers, 1986; Perry, 1935; E. Taylor, 1982). Less well-known is a fascinating private exchange regarding spiritualism between James and Thomas Davidson, a lifelong friend of James's and an independent philosopher. Davidson wrote James in 1883 that

> Nothing can save Europe but a complete social regeneration.... Moreover no social regeneration is possible without a moral regeneration, & no moral regeneration is possible without a scientific insight into the eternity of the individual, such as no philosophy now in vogue is able to give. (T. Davidson to W. James, March 1883, James Papers)[1]

Scientific proof of the afterlife would be put to no meaner purpose than the complete moral and social regeneration of Western civilization.

In subsequent letters, James and Davidson discussed the possibility of new forms of secular religion, Davidson having founded one such in 1883 in his London-based Fellowship of the New Life (McBriar, 1962). In a letter of 1884, James confirmed the goals underlying his lasting interest in spiritualism and psychic research. He believed that in order for some new "popular religion [to be] raised on the ruins of the old Christianity" there would have to be a renewed "belief in new *physical* facts & possibilities" (W. James to T. Davidson, March 30, 1884, James Papers). He continued,

> Abstract considerations about the soul & the reality of a moral order will not do in a year, what the glimpse into a world of new phenomenal possibilities ... would do in an instant. Are the much despised "spiritualism" & the "Society for Psychical Research" to be the chosen in-

---

[1] For the source of the James correspondence cited throughout this article, see "James Papers" in the reference list.

struments for a new era of faith? It would surely be strange if they were, but if they are not, I see no other agency that can do the work. (W. James to T. Davidson, March 30, 1884, James Papers)

Both Davidson and James were eager to see the moral and social regeneration of society through a new secular faith, but James made explicit to Davidson that he thought such faith would come about only through phenomenal proof of an afterlife. In a subsequent letter to Davidson, after James had helped found the American Society for Psychical Research (ASPR) in 1884, he reiterated his belief that "the urgent thing" was to gather convincing evidence about the conditions under which spiritualistic phenomena occurred: "Not till that is done can spiritualistic or antispiritualistic theories be even mooted" (W. James to T. Davidson, February 1, 1885, James Papers). He then made clear that the most credible judges of spiritualistic phenomena in the modern age would be scientists:

> The choice of officers [of the ASPR] was largely dictated by motives of policy. Not that scientific men are necessarily better judges of all truth than others, but that their adhesion would popularly seem better evidence than the adhesion of others, in this matter. And what we want is not only truth, but evidence. (W. James to T. Davidson, February 1, 1885, James Papers)

James was quite explicit that scientists would be best not because they were intrinsically better judges than others, but because they would be publicly perceived as such. The prestige and authority of science and the perceived objectivity of scientists would make them the most powerful witnesses to call in the trial of spiritualistic phenomena. He briefly wondered more prophetically whether "our scientific names [would] grow discredited the instant they subscribe to any 'spiritual' manifestations" (W. James to T. Davidson, February 1, 1885, James Papers)

James's continuing interest in spiritualism and psychic research set him apart from the majority of his professional colleagues, especially in the United States. (There was somewhat more support for psychical research among his British and European colleagues in psychology and philosophy, e.g., Charles Richet, Pierre Janet, F. W. H. Myers, and Henry Sidgwick.) Although a few American psychologists and philosophers such as G. Stanley Hall, James Mark Baldwin, Joseph Jastrow, Christine Ladd-Franklin, and George Fullerton were founding members of the ASPR, virtually all had dropped out by 1890 (Albrecht, 1961). James H. Hyslop, a philosopher at Columbia University, was a notable exception, continuing to do active research and writing on psychic research until his death. Hall and Jastrow became avid opponents of spiritualism and psychic phenomena and used their attacks on "pseudoscience" as a foil against which to bolster the scientific status of psychology. Especially because of James's world fame and reputation, his continuing interest in the paranormal would become a major source of contention for psychologists eager to differentiate their science from spiritualism.

A NEW SCIENCE OF PSYCHOLOGY

Even as spiritualism was gaining a hold on the popular imagination in the 1860s through 1880s, a new academic discipline was slowly emerging that would enter into a kind of *immortal* combat with the spiritualism for the public's mind and soul.

The beginnings of psychology as an experimental science, like the first stirrings of spiritualism, occurred roughly in the middle of the 19th century, with the psychophysical experiments of the German scientist Gustav Theodor Fechner and the timing of nervous transmission by Hermann von Helmholtz. As a result of these experiments, perception, sensation, and the temporal extension of thought (if not thought itself) were believed to be measurable (Boring, 1950; Danziger, 1990; Davis & Merzbach, 1975; Hornstein, 1988; Sokal, 1980, 1987; Zupan, 1976).

The psychophysical methods derived from Fechner and reaction time methods developed after Helmholtz's work were revolutionary and enabled psychology to become a quantifiable, laboratory-based science. Psychologists increasingly realized that goal in the late 19th century, especially in the United States, where experimental psychology took off with a vigor unmatched elsewhere.

In many respects, psychology at the end of the 19th century followed the pattern of professionalizing common to other scientific specialties, with the establishment of journals, laboratories, and a national organization (Camfield, 1973; Danziger, 1979; O'Donnell, 1985). Use of laboratory methodology in psychology proliferated rapidly, from two rudimentary laboratories in 1881 (if one includes James's early laboratory) to at least 27 laboratories at the leading private and state universities in 1894 (Delabarre, 1894).

Scientific psychologists hoped that this "New Psychology," as they called it, would place the study of the mind on equal scientific footing with the more established sciences of physics, chemistry, astronomy, and the newly emerging science of physiology. They placed articles in which they praised the "New Psychology," defined its subject matter, and proclaimed its scientific promise in journals such as *Science, Nature,* and *Popular Scientific Monthly* and in broader popular magazines such as *Harper's, Atlantic Monthly, The Nation,* and *North American Review.* They wrote hundreds of articles about psychology's status among the sciences and its relations to various sciences, education, logic, medicine, industry, and advertising (e.g., see Fullerton, 1896; Griffing, 1896; Hall, 1906b; Mills, 1908–1909; Pace, 1902; Sanford, 1903; A. E. Taylor, 1906; Yerkes, 1910). It is not overdramatizing to say that they were self-consciously engaged in a battle for intellectual and disciplinary survival.

PROBLEMATIC BOUNDARIES

Psychology had a critical problem in the process of its professionalization and conceptualization, however. It was haunted by a public and by some members of its own ranks who thought that the most interesting questions about the mind concerned not the range of perception and the timing of thought, but whether or not people could communicate with each other by direct thought transference, whether gifted individuals could foretell the future, or whether the living could communicate with the dead. When people began to hear and read about the "New Psychology" in the popular and literary magazines of the late 19th century, they turned to this new breed of mental experts to answer their innermost questions about the more mysterious powers of the mind and spirit.

Harvard psychologist Hugo Münsterberg (1863–1916) claimed that since he had arrived in the United States from Germany in 1893, he was asked weekly to explore or comment on some mystical or spiritualistic phenomenon. He generally refused, he wrote, because it was "not . . . a part of scientific psychology to examine the so-called mystical occurrences" (Münsterberg, 1910, p. 119). Yet he did not always refuse and eventually wrote several articles on mystics, mediums, and the psychically sensitive. Münsterberg's case is but one example of psychologists' ambivalence toward paranormal topics in the turn-of-the-century decades.

The problem was that much of psychology's popular appeal lay in precisely those topics of its possible subject matter that many psychologists wanted to shed as pseudoscience—topics such as mental telepathy, clairvoyance, and spiritistic communication with the dead. Psychologists already had enough trouble trying to prove their investigations of normal mental phenomena were scientific and not subjective (Burnham, 1987; Coon, in press; Danziger, 1990). Investigating the supernatural and supernormal seemed to many psychologists simply to be courting disaster for the budding discipline.

Psychology's boundaries with spiritualism and psychic research were ill defined, as evidenced in the terminology of the period. For example, in the scientific literature the term *psychical* was often used interchangeably with the term *psychological*. Unlike its meanings today, *psychical* simply referred to phenomena that were mental as opposed to physical. Physicists would study the physical realm and psychologists would study the psychical. *Psychical* began to acquire its specific association with mental telepathy, clairvoyance, and spiritualistic phenomena after the founding in 1882 in England of the Society for Psychical Research (SPR) and the American branch (ASPR) in 1884. But the term was still occasionally used in its broader signification—meaning "psychological"—for at least two decades after the turn of the century.

To add to the confusion, the term *psychological* was occasionally used to refer specifically to paranormal phenomena. In 1881, Wundt named his journal *Psychologische Studien* but changed the name within months to *Philosophische Studien*, most likely because there was already a journal of spiritism and parapsychology published under the former name (Bringmann, Bringmann, & Ungerer, 1980). Ten years before the founding in 1893 of the American experimental psychology journal, the *Psychological Review*, a British *Psychological Review* existed as a "journal of spiritualism." Dorothy Ross (1972) recounted how Hall (1844–1924) actually took advantage of this sort of confusion when establishing his *American Journal of Psychology*: Several of his benefactors believed they were contributing to a journal of psychic phenomena, and he did not correct their misimpression.

As late as 1918, a National Psychological Institute was founded for the purpose of "'experimental research in ... demonology ..., [and] to develop and instruct psychic-sensitives'" (Ruckmich, 1918, p. 193). Christian A. Ruckmich, a psychologist at the University of Illinois, publicly denounced the institute for using the label *psychological*. He argued that there was too great a danger of the public's associating the discipline of psychology with "pseudo-psychologists," thereby damaging the reputation of "so youthful a scientific discipline as psychology" (Ruckmich, 1918, p. 193).

It is clear that many psychologists felt a threat to their discipline's scientific status because of its fuzzy boundary with spiritualism and psychic research. Joseph Jastrow (1863–1944), an experimental psychologist at the University of Wisconsin, published popular articles and books throughout his career in which he condemned psychic research and occult phenomena. He attacked the SPR for harming the fledgling science of psychology by lending a "protective authority" to all sorts of occult phenomena, credulity, and superstition (Jastrow, 1900). As a result, Jastrow said, "the status of that science has suffered" (1900, p. 75). Jastrow argued that although psychology needed popular interest and support in order to advance as a science, the type of popular interest was crucial. In his opinion, the popular interest in mystical phenomena did far more harm than good for psychology's scientific reputation.

Thus at the turn of the century, we find the scientific community using the terms *psychical* and *psychological* interchangeably, the public conflating spiritualism and psychology, and experimental psychologists concerned with the scientific status of their discipline having to state repeatedly that they did not deal with mystical phenomena (e.g., Scripture, 1895, 1897; Titchener, 1901).

RELUCTANT WITNESSES

Psychologists at the turn of the century might have decided that it was important for the sake of their science to establish clear boundaries between psychology and what they perceived as its pseudoscientific counterparts (Gieryn, 1983). Then they could have refused any attempt to discuss pseudoscientific problems and could have proceeded with what they took to be their real scientific subject matter.

This is not what happened, however. Despite their professed reluctance to investigate spiritualism, after 1900 many of those who had previously remained aloof, such as Jastrow, Münsterberg, and Titchener, began to investigate mediums and psychic sensitives. Psychologists conducted such research partly because they could not afford to ignore the public's interests. Their new place within the universities depended in part on public interest for filling their lecture halls and lobbying their administrators for funding (O'Donnell, 1985). Despite their protestations to the contrary, they may have privately understood that in the early stages of disciplinary development any sort of attention was better than no attention at all.

Furthermore, some of the early funding for psychology laboratories was provided by citizens interested in supporting psychic research. At Clark University, Hall was embarrassed when the first major bequest—some $5,000—given to the university for psychological research in 1906 was specifically tagged for research into spiritualism. The archival correspondence between Hall and the estate's lawyer reveals Hall delicately asking if the term "spiritualism" could be left out of the wording of the bequest (G. S. Hall to H. A. Willis, January 13, 1906, Hall Papers).[2] They compromised on the terms "spiritism" and "psychical research," which had marginally more scientific connotations. Hall was again chagrined, however, when the Massachusetts Institute of Technology (MIT) called attention to the spiritualism fund at Clark in a 1916 survey on resources for academic research. Hall asked MIT to substitute "psychological research" for "psychical research," inasmuch as "we do not indulge in what is generally known as psychic research here" (G. S. Hall to C. R. Cross, June 24, 1915; Cross to Hall, May 22, 1916; Hall to Cross, May 24, 1916; Hall Papers). By 1913, both Harvard University and Stanford University had also received handsome bequests for similar purposes of psychic research (Hyslop, 1917; Mauskopf & McVaugh, 1980).

If psychologists at these universities wanted to use the money, they had to devote it to psychic research or spiritualism. So, despite Hall's disclaimer, they did. At Clark, Hall and psychologist Amy Tanner conducted

---

[2]For the source of the Hall correspondence cited throughout this article, see "Hall Papers" in the reference list.

experiments (see the Modes of Combat section) on the medium Mrs. Piper. The Hodgson fund at Harvard supported psychic research by a specialist in physiological optics, Leonard Thompson Troland, and the bequest at Stanford funded psychic research by psychologist John E. Coover. Both Troland and Coover published initial reports in 1917 (Mauskopf & McVaugh, 1980).

Another crucial reason that psychologists did not simply drop discussion of these topics as pseudoscience was that they could not agree among themselves about what constituted science and what constituted pseudoscience. All agreed, as University of Chicago psychologist James R. Angell (1869–1949) reported in *The Chautauquan* in 1905, that most of the table rappings and physical manifestations at séances were sheer fraud, but beyond that there was little consensus.

Some of those who thought spiritualism clearly unscientific, for instance, believed that mental telepathy could be studied scientifically. Logically speaking, mental telepathy had no necessary connection with spiritualism. Spiritualism entailed a belief in life after death, whereas mental telepathy, if it existed, was a type of communication between living persons and could conceivably have been based on some special sort of mental energy present only in living organisms.

Angell (1905) remarked that "the camp of psychologists is bitterly divided against itself" (p. 457) on the questions of telepathy, clairvoyance, and spirit communication. "By far the larger contingent regard the alleged evidence for these unusual modes of communication between minds as puerile and inconclusive. A few hardy souls, however, keep up the fight" (Angell, p. 457). Although the "larger contingent" of psychologists opposed the possibility of psychic and spiritistic phenomena, it was difficult for the public or the profession to consider the matter settled when among those "few hardy souls" keeping up the fight on behalf of psychic research was the most popular and influential American psychologist of his day, William James.

THE NEMESIS

James's (1890) notion of experimentalism as he defined it in his *Principles of Psychology* was extremely broad, broader than the subsequent orthodoxy of the field would allow. He believed that psychologists should make use of a plurality of methods, in order to cast a net as broadly as possible over the subject matter of psychology (James, 1890). When he established the official laboratory at Harvard in 1890, he stocked it not only with the usual scientific apparatus such as chronoscopes, kymographs, tuning forks, and physiological models, but also with a hypnotizer and a Ouija board (*Account Book, 1890–c.1920*). He had been involved with the

English SPR since its founding and, as already mentioned, helped establish the ASPR.

James argued that because the psychological realm had never been studied scientifically before the mid-19th century, little was known about the actual laws and conditions governing it. Therefore, his argument continued, it was too early in the course of the young science to rule out some phenomena as impossible a priori (James, 1890; W. James to C. Stumpf, December 20, 1892, James Papers). For example, James was not convinced that mental telepathy really took place, but thought that psychologists, as scientists, ought to study reported instances of it as they would any other psychological phenomena—impartially attempting to specify the conditions under which the phenomena occurred.

James (1890) argued in *Principles* that in order to be a natural science, psychology had to remain completely positivistic and not inquire into metaphysical matters of causality and ontology. [James violated these pronouncements at various points throughout *Principles*, and indeed, his interest in spiritualism and psychic research was more deeply rooted than he publicly admitted, as shown earlier. But he strategically used the positivistic argument to justify inclusion of psychic phenomena within scientific psychology.]

The appeal to positivism enabled James to dismiss concerns about psychophysical causality, that is, how the mental could possibly induce other mental (or even physical) consequences, as spiritualists claimed. All that any positivistic science could study was the functional relationships among its special phenomena. James argued that just as the physical sciences had abandoned worries about how mechanical causality worked, so psychology should abandon worries about how psychological causality and psychophysical causality worked. They should simply study phenomena presented to them—which included telepathy and spiritistic phenomena—and describe the functional relationships among them.

As the discipline of psychology gained more of an institutional base in the 1890s, it began to establish its own sort of orthodoxy, which did not include James's sympathy toward spiritualism. James argued that his colleagues would stunt psychology's growth by refusing to explore the fertile field of psychic phenomena, and he included defenses of psychic research and spiritualism in his public lectures and in the essays "The Will to Believe" (James, 1897/1979) and "Pragmatism" (James, 1907/1975). He railed against "authoritative scientism" for dictating what people should believe (W. James to J. M. Baldwin, January 1899, James Papers). He engaged in blistering correspondence over psychic research with colleagues Titchener and Cattell in private and in the pages of *Science* (Cattell, 1898a, 1898b; James, 1898a, 1898b, 1899a, 1899b; Titchener, 1898, 1899a, 1899b, 1899c). His activities with the ASPR were daily newspaper fare. He therefore became a formidable opponent of those psychologists who were trying to dismiss psychic research as sheer fraud or as otherwise outside the scope of psychological inquiry.

Because psychic research was being promoted by such a prominent figure as James, along with noted physical scientists such as Oliver Lodge, William Crookes, and numerous other public figures, psychologists were forced to offer alternative explanations for spiritistic and psychic phenomena. These phenomena, if real, seemed to fall within the realm of psychological science, and refusal to address them made the science look inadequate.

There is no question that psychologists viewed James as their private nemesis. Even 10 years after James's death, Hall made the point when writing to encourage Jastrow in an antispiritualist book he was writing. Hall wrote,

> The "medium-mad" Bostonians . . . all point to James and say with him that there is a germ of truth in all the bosh and dross. It is James who laid the foundations of all this credulity. . . . The first thing I shall look for in your [new] book is whether you have had the courage and insight to deal with James' responsibility in this matter as it ought to be dealt with. (G. S. Hall to J. Jastrow, February 9, 1920, Hall Papers)

AUTHORITY

Finally, psychologists could not ignore the public's interest in spiritualism because to do so was to leave in doubt the authority of the psychologist as scientist. Psychologists, trying to assert their claim as scientific experts of the mental realm, found their authority challenged by the public's interest in alternative, nonscientific explanations of mental phenomena. Psychologists either had to prove that spiritualistic phenomena were fraudulent or offer naturalistic explanations to account for them.

As early as 1879, neurologist George M. Beard had written that spiritualistic phenomena would eventually be seen to be due to psychological and physiological causes, because "spirits only dwell in the cerebral cells. . . . not our houses but our brains are haunted" (p. 67). He argued that psychologists, physiologists, and physicians expert in neurology ought to investigate these phenomena and not relegate their study to the lay public. He summarized, "The rejection of non-expert human testimony is and has ever been, the first step in the development of a science; it is only by rejecting or ignoring all testimony save that of experts that any science is possible" (Beard, 1879, p. 70).

Jastrow (1889a) likewise argued in *Harper's* that the layperson was a mere child in the hands of a medium and therefore the layperson's account was not trustworthy. According to Jastrow, properly trained scientists were needed to "record their observations and draw their conclusions with all the caution and deliberation characteristic of solid scientific advance" (1889a, p. 82).

However, by 1900, Jastrow made explicit that not only were laypersons inadequate judges, but even scientists from sciences other than psychology should not be trusted: "If the problems of Psychical Research . . . are ever to be illuminated . . . it will only come about when they are investigated by the same methods and in the same [scientific] spirit as are other psychological problems" (Jastrow, 1900, p. 54). These remarks are striking because they call for defense of territory that relatively few psychologists wanted to inhabit. Even Jastrow, several pages later, argued that although psychologists were the only ones qualified to investigate psychical phenomena, they were under no necessary obligation to do so.

Whether or not they chose to study psychic phenomena, psychologists wanted the authority to dictate who could. In the 1880s psychologists had welcomed the help of the more established physical sciences in debunking psychic claims. By 1900, with growing confidence in the institutionalization of their own science, they were ready to reserve such territory as their exclusive property. However, this still left them with believers in their midst. Hence Jastrow narrowed the term even further so that the "experts" qualified to investigate spiritualism did not include all psychologists—for this would include James—but only individuals of a certain "general logical attitude in the smaller affairs of life" (Jastrow, 1910, p. 83). From scientist, to psychologist, to only those psychologists predisposed not to believe, psychologists progressively shrunk the definition of the term *expert* as they anxiously tried to establish and maintain scientific credibility for their discipline.

MODES OF COMBAT

Psychologists used a variety of means to address the public's interest in spiritualism while countering the topic as pseudoscience. Some orthodox psychologists like Hall and Münsterberg eventually performed psychological tests on mediums and others thought to be psychically sensitive. They had the explicit aim of proving that the individuals were either frauds or naïfs who were unaware that their "powers" were the result of natural causes. Pursuing another tack, Jastrow and others used the issue to pioneer a new field—the psychology of deception and belief.

One instance of the testing approach is Münsterberg's examination of a young Rhode Island girl named Beulah Miller who was alleged to be psychic. As Münsterberg (1913) reported in *The Metropolitan*, he did some mind-reading experiments with her in her home, using playing cards and squares of cardboard with single letters on each, and "treated the case with the same carefulness with which I am accustomed to carry on the experiments in the Harvard Psychological Laboratory" (p. 18).

Münsterberg (1913) concluded that Beulah Miller was not a fraud, but she was not clairvoyant either. She did have "supernormal sensitiveness" to the minute muscular movements made by the person concentrating on the cards, but if she was not allowed to see that person, her abilities failed. Münsterberg (1913) asserted that all people made these minute muscular movements when thinking, a fact that "we can easily show with delicate instruments in the psychological laboratory" (p. 17). Her "mind-reading" was thus a thoroughly natural process, he explained, although at the outer limits of human sensitivity. Cases like Beulah's were fairly straightforward for scientific psychologists and were ones in which they were able rhetorically to wield the authority of the laboratory and its instruments—in short, the authority of science—even when they could not actually bring the accouterments along.

A more difficult case was that of Mrs. Leonora Piper, a trance medium who had the endorsement of the SPR and James. These were impressive credentials. The ASPR studied few mediums because members had learned from long experience that many mediums were outright frauds. They had established a rule that they would examine only nonprofessional mediums, and even then they were careful before placing trust. When Mrs. Piper was discovered by James in the mid-1880s, the ASPR had her and her husband shadowed by a detective to make sure that she wasn't getting information on the sly (Moore, 1977).

When Mrs. Piper was in trance, her spirit controls [the spirits that allegedly communicated through her] would apparently offer astonishingly private information about séance attendees. Once assured that she was not cheating, members of the ASPR were convinced that they had found a valuable object of study, someone who was truly a vessel of the spirits, or at least had extraordinary telepathic abilities, reading the minds of the sitters and then telling them their own deepest secrets. James claimed that he had been a sceptic about séances until attending one of Mrs. Piper's in the 1880s. For at least the next 25 years, she became virtually the scientific instrument of the ASPR, working exclusively for them and occasionally for the SPR (Moore, 1977).

Therefore, when Hall financed several sittings with Mrs. Piper in 1909 under the auspices of Clark University's spiritualist bequest, it was neither a fraud nor a 13-year-old Beulah Miller that he took on. He was battling the accumulated prestige, credibility, and authority of the leading lights of the ASPR—including James—and their primary subject of study.

In the course of six sittings with Mrs. Piper in her home, Hall and research associate Amy Tanner performed a number of psychological and physiological tests on her (Tanner, 1910). When she was deep in trance, they used the new Freud–Jung word association tests on her. They were unable to draw any conclusions from these except that Mrs. Piper's associations while in trance were generally different from those out of trance.

Hall and Tanner also performed various crude sensory tests on Mrs. Piper while she was in trance. It was alleged by spiritualists that the spirits who spoke through mediums had no connection to the mediums' bodies. If this were true, then the spirit should not be able to experience Mrs. Piper's sensations. Tanner and Hall hoped that if they could get Mrs. Piper to respond to stimulation while in trance, they might be able to convince her that the spirit voice was a part of her own psyche.

Hall and Tanner therefore performed various routine sensory tests for vision, taste, odor, pressure, and pain. The spirit reported no sensations, although Mrs. Piper did draw back at the smell of ether. Only when the maximum pressure of 25 pounds was applied during the pressure test did the spirit voice finally respond, asking them to stop. Hall and Tanner were able to conclude that the spirit could feel Mrs. Piper's pain after all, although they could not convince either Mrs. Piper or the spirit of that.

For all their efforts, Hall and Tanner proved little with their tests except that they could do physical damage to Mrs. Piper. Her daughter wrote to protest her mother's sore palms, blistered lips, and numb fingers (A. L. Piper to G. B. Dorr, enclosed in G. B. Dorr to G. S. Hall, May 16, 1909, Hall Papers). Hall and Tanner went into the tests with an alternative explanation of Mrs. Piper's phenomena and came out with their explanation intact. Mrs. Piper was "impulsive," "impressionable," "hysterical," and "neurotic." She was a clear case, Hall declared, of divided personality (Tanner, 1910).

In short, Hall, Münsterberg, and other psychologists studied mediums and sensitives in order to expose them as frauds or to reinterpret their abilities with naturalistic explanations. Another way of combatting spiritualism lay in developing a new field of psychology—the psychology of deception and belief. Many experimentalists were loath to study the psychic and spiritistic phenomena per se, which they assumed were fraudulent, so they took the lead of Jastrow (1888) and studied how people could possibly believe in these phenomena. Armed with their knowledge of hypnosis and suggestion, expectation, illusion, perception, and attention, orthodox experimentalists, including Chicago's Angell (1905), Wisconsin's Jastrow (1888, 1889b, 1911, no date), Harvard's Münsterberg (1899, 1910), Cornell's Titchener (1898), and Yale's Scripture (1908), argued that people could be duped into belief in the supernatural by their own natural, psychological limitations. In articles, books, and lectures, they argued that the limits of attention, the limits of the senses, and the desire to communicate with lost loved ones all conspired to make believers out of otherwise sensible people.

This particular defensive maneuver enabled psychologists to address the public's interests, while still attempting to maintain the boundaries between their own scientific enterprise and its "pseudoscientific" analogues, and to assert their authority as experts scientifically trained to rout out the forces of deception. Spiritualism and other pseudoscientific belief systems were "of direct interest to psychology," Jastrow (no date) wrote, "because they represent untrained modes of thought and belief. Thinking is natural but right thinking is an art, difficultly and slowly acquired" (p. 1). Psychologists would provide the antidote: "With a knowledge of the possibilities of deception and of the psychological processes by which error is propagated, the soil upon which spiritualism and kindred delusions can flourish will be rendered unfit" (Jastrow, 1888, p. 157). Psychologists would preserve the scientific worldview by exposing and correcting wrong thinking, superstition, and credulity.

KEEPERS OF THE SCIENTIFIC LIGHT

In an era of increasing skepticism about God, scientific naturalism offered the latest and best substitute providing order and reason in the universe. In this worldview, espoused by the majority of experimental psychologists, psychophysical parallelism held sway. Physical phenomena could only occur as the result of physical causes. Psychological phenomena might bear a one-to-one correspondence to physical phenomena but could not cause or be caused by them.

Spiritualists and psychic researchers, on the other hand, were demanding that a different order of facts be considered possible—that nonphysical forces, mental and spiritual forces, could cause other mental and even physical events. Most psychologists saw this possibility as little short of miraculous. They retorted that if it were true, the whole structure of modern science would collapse. Münsterberg (1910) wrote,

> Let us at least understand clearly that if we accept this revised universe, then really nothing of value remains in the poor sham edition of the world with which science and scholarship have wasted their efforts so far.... From the standpoint of natural science we have to begin anew. ... Can we really be blamed if before this death sentence on the scientific reason is fulfilled ... we cry out, "Fraud!" (pp. 130–131)

Experimental psychologists studied the mind, its limitations and its capabilities. Many perceived their own science as the most fundamental of the sciences because it was only through the mind that knowledge was possible. Belief in spiritual and psychic phenomena was to these psychologists not only the secular ghost of a religious past, but a malevolent ghost preventing public confidence in scientific naturalism. Psychologists, as experts of the mental realm, would therefore expose fraud, credulity, and deception in matters psychic and spiritualistic. They would offer alternative naturalistic explanations and would be the self-appointed guardians of the scientific light.

Angell (1901) voiced the anxieties of an era when he wrote in *The Dial,*

> If spirits can lift tables and hold them suspended in the air, in spite of the operation of gravity, then knowledge is at an end, the whole fabric of science deliquesces into a mere logomachy, ... and man himself becomes the plaything of every eddy that may happen to roil the waters of his ignorance. (p. 264)

Psychologists were stationed at the periphery of science, and therefore they were the most threatened by challenges to the boundary and the most susceptible to cultural anxieties about what it meant to be "scientific." Although many psychologists had begun their careers by testing the limits of the senses, in their battle against spiritualism they embraced the mission of surveying and defending the limits of science itself.

REFERENCES

Account book [of the Psychological Laboratory], *1890–c.1920.* Harvard University Archives, Nathan Marsh Pusey Library, Harvard University, Cambridge, MA.

Albrecht, F. M. (1961). *The new psychology in America: 1880–1895.* Unpublished doctoral dissertation, Johns Hopkins University, Baltimore.

Angell, J. R. (1901). Fact and fable in psychology. *The Dial, 30,* 264–266.

Angell, J. R. (1905). Contemporary psychology. *The Chautauquan, 40,* 453–459.

Beard, G. M. (1879). The psychology of spiritism. *North American Review, 129,* 65–80.

Boring, E. G. (1950). *A history of experimental psychology* (2nd ed.). New York: Appleton-Century-Crofts.

Braude, A. (1989). *Radical spirits: Spiritualism and women's rights in nineteenth-century America.* Boston: Beacon Press.

Bringmann, W. G., Bringmann, N., & Ungerer, G. (1980). The establishment of Wundt's laboratory: An archival and documentary study. In W. G. Bringmann & R. D. Tweney (Eds.), *Wundt studies: A centennial collection* (pp. 123–157). Toronto, Ontario, Canada: Hogrefe.

Brown, E. M. (1983). Neurology and spiritualism in the 1870s. *Bulletin of the History of Medicine, 57,* 563–577.

Burnham, J. C. (1987). *How superstition won and science lost: Popularizing science and health in the United States.* New Brunswick, NJ: Rutgers University Press.

Camfield, T. M. (1973). The professionalization of American psychology, 1870–1917. *Journal of the History of the Behavioral Sciences, 9,* 66–75.

Cattell, J. M. (1898a). Mrs. Piper, the medium. *Science, 7*(new series), 534–535.

Cattell, J. M. (1898b). Untitled. *Science, 7*(new series), 641–642.

Cerullo, J. (1982). *Secularization of the soul: Psychical research in modern Britain.* Philadelphia: Institute for the Study of Human Issues.

Coon, D. J. (in press). Standardizing the subject: Experimental psychologists, introspection, and the quest for a technoscientific ideal. *Technology and Culture.*

Danziger, K. (1979). The social origins of modern psychology. In A. R. Buss (Ed.), *Psychology in social context* (pp. 27–45). New York: Irvington.

Danziger, K. (1990). *Constructing the subject: Historical origins of psychological research.* Cambridge, England: Cambridge University Press.

Davis, A. B., & Merzbach, U. C. (1975). *Early auditory studies: Activities in the psychology laboratories of American universities.* Washington, DC: Smithsonian Institution Press.

Delabarre, E. B. (1894). Les laboratoires de psychologie en Amérique [Psychological laboratories in America]. *L'annèe psychologique, 1,* 209–255.

Fullerton, G. S. (1896). Psychology and physiology. *Psychological Review, 3,* 1–20.

Gauld, A. (1968). *The founders of psychical research.* New York: Schocken Books.

Gieryn, T. (1983). Boundary-work and the demarcation of science from non-science: Strains and interests in professional ideologies of scientists. *American Sociological Review, 48,* 781–795.

Griffing, H. (1896). On the relations of psychology to other sciences. *Philosophical Review, 5,* 489–501.

Hall, G. S. (1906b). The affiliation of psychology with philosophy and the natural sciences. *Science, 23,* 297–301.

Hall papers, Robert Hutchings Goddard Library, Clark University, Worcester, MA.

Hornstein, G. (1988). Quantifying psychological phenomena. In J. Morawski (Ed.), *The rise of experimentation in American psychology* (pp. 1–34). New Haven, CT: Yale University Press.

Hyslop, J. H. (1917). Psychic research in American universities. *Journal of the American Society for Psychical Research, 11,* 444–458.

James papers, Houghton Library, Harvard University, Cambridge, MA.

James, W. (1890). *The principles of psychology* (2 vols.). New York: Holt.

James, W. (1898a). Mrs. Piper, "the medium." *Science, 7*(new series), 640–641.

James, W. (1898b). Lehmann and Hansen "on the telepathic problem." *Science, 8*(new series), 956.

James, W. (1899a). Messrs. Lehmann and Hansen on telepathy. *Science, 9*(new series), 654–655.

James, W. (1899b). Telepathy once more. *Science, 9*(new series), 752–753.

James, W. (1975). *Pragmatism: A new name for some old ways of thinking.* In F. H. Burkhardt (Gen. ed.), *The Works of William James.* Cambridge, MA: Harvard University Press. (Original work published 1907)

James, W. (1979). *The will to believe and other essays in popular philosophy.* In F. H.

Burkhardt (Gen. ed.), *The works of William James*. Cambridge, MA: Harvard University Press. (Original work published 1897)

James, W. (1986). *Essays in psychical research*. In F. H. Burkhardt (Gen. ed.), *The works of William James*. Cambridge, MA: Harvard University Press.

Jastrow, J. (1888). The psychology of deception. *Popular Science Monthly, 34,* 145–157.

Jastrow, J. (1889a). The problems of "psychic research." *Harper's New Monthly Magazine, 79,* 76–82.

Jastrow, J. (1889b). The psychology of spiritualism. *Popular Science Monthly, 34,* 721–732.

Jastrow, J. (1900). *Fact and fable in psychology*. Boston: Houghton Mifflin.

Jastrow, J. (1910). The case of Paladino. *American Monthly Review of Reviews, 42,* 74–84.

Jastrow, J. (1911). The will to believe in the supernatural. *Nineteenth Century, 69,* 471–486.

Jastrow, J. (no date). *Pseudology*. Unpublished manuscript, Jastrow papers, State Historical Society of Wisconsin Library, Madison, WI.

Leary, D. E. (1980, September). *William James, psychical research, and the origins of American psychology*. Paper presented at the 88th Annual Convention of the American Psychological Association, Montreal, Quebec, Canada.

Mauskopf, S. H., & McVaugh, M. R. (1980). *The elusive science: Origins of experimental psychical research*. Baltimore: Johns Hopkins University Press.

McBriar, A. M. (1962). *Fabian socialism and English politics: 1884–1918*. Cambridge, England: Cambridge University Press.

Mills, W. (1908–1909). Psychology in relation to physiology, psychiatry and general medicine. *American Journal of Insanity, 65,* 25–38.

Moore, R. L. (1977). *In search of white crows: Spiritualism, parapsychology, and American culture*. New York: Oxford University Press.

Münsterberg, H. (1899). Psychology and mysticism. *Atlantic Monthly, 83,* 67–85.

Münsterberg, H. (1910). *American problems from the point of view of a psychologist*. New York: Moffat, Yard.

Münsterberg, H. (1913). The case of Beulah Miller: An investigation of the new psychical mystery. *The Metropolitan, 16–18,* 61–62.

Murphy, G., & Ballou, R. O. (Eds.). (1960). *William James on psychical research*. New York: Viking Press.

Myers, G. E. (1986). *William James: His life and thought*. New Haven, CT: Yale University Press.

O'Donnell, J. M. (1985). *The origins of behaviorism: American psychology, 1870–1920*. New York: New York University Press.

Oppenheim, J. (1985). *The other world: Spiritualism and psychical research in England, 1850–1914*. Cambridge, England: Cambridge University Press.

Pace, E. A. (1902). On the definition of some modern sciences: Psychology. *Popular Science Monthly, 61*, 110–113.

Perry, R. B. (1935). *The thought and character of William James* (2 vols.). Boston: Little, Brown.

Ross, D. (1972). *G. Stanley Hall: The psychologist as prophet.* Chicago: University of Chicago Press.

Ruckmich, C. A. (1918). Pseudo-psychology. *Science, 48*(new series), 191–193.

Sanford, E. C. (1903). Psychology and physics. *Psychological Review, 10*, 105–119.

Scripture, E. W. (1895). *Thinking, feeling, doing.* Meadville, PA: Chautauqua-Century Press.

Scripture, E. W. (1897). *The new psychology.* New York: Scribner.

Scripture, E. W. (1908). The professor and the medium. *The Independent, 64,* 96–98.

Sibley, N. W. (1898). Psychical research and the roentgen and other X rays. *The Westminster Review, 49,* 211–213.

Sokal, M. M. (Ed.). (1981). *An education in psychology: James McKeen Cattell's journal and letters from Germany and England, 1880–1888.* Cambridge, MA: MIT Press.

Sokal, M. M. (Ed.). (1987). *Psychological testing and American society, 1890–1930.* New Brunswick, NJ: Rutgers University Press.

Tanner, A. (1910). *Studies in spiritism.* New York: Appleton.

Taylor, A. E. (1906). The place of psychology in the classification of the sciences. *Philosophical Review, 15,* 380–386.

Taylor, E. (1982). *William James on exceptional mental states: The 1896 Lowell lectures.* New York: Scribner.

Titchener, E. B. (1898). The "feeling of being stared at." *Science, 8*(new series), 895–897.

Titchener, E. B. (1899a). Lehmann and Hansen on "the telepathic problem." *Science, 9*(new series), 36.

Titchener, E. B. (1899b). Professor James on telepathy. *Science, 9*(new series), 686–687.

Titchener, E. B. (1899c). The telepathic question. *Science, 9*(new series), 787.

Titchener, E. B. (1901). *Experimental psychology: A manual of laboratory practice* (Vol. 1). New York: Macmillan.

Turner, F. M. (1974). *Between science and religion: The reaction to scientific naturalism in late Victorian England.* New Haven, CT: Yale University Press.

Yerkes, R. M. (1910). Psychology in its relation to biology. *Journal of Philosophy, Psychology and Scientific Methods, 7,* 113–124.

Zupan, M. L. (1976). The conceptual development of quantification in experimental psychology. *Journal of the History of the Behavioral Sciences, 12,* 145–158.

8

ORIGINS AND EARLY YEARS OF THE AMERICAN PSYCHOLOGICAL ASSOCIATION, 1890–1906

MICHAEL M. SOKAL

The American Psychological Association (APA) emerged at a particular time, in a unique social and institutional environment, and as the result of actions of specific individuals. Like any organism suddenly appearing in a given environment, it had to adapt to its ecological setting and find itself an ecological niche in which it could thrive, or at least survive. The course of events surrounding its establishment reflected America in the late Gilded Age, its emerging university system, the organizational precedents set by other American scientists of the period, and the personal interplay between G. Stanley Hall and his contemporaries. These factors did more to shape the course of events surrounding its establishment —and its character during its earliest years—than did any of the intellectual and scientific issues to which psychologists devoted their attention during that period.

From the start, APA was explicitly the *American* Psychological As-

Reprinted from *American Psychologist*, 47, 111–122 (1992). Copyright © 1992 by the American Psychological Association. Reprinted with permission of the author.

sociation; although its membership always included Canadians, its character has always reflected its U.S. base. In particular, through the Gilded Age, the nation's intellectual life gradually coalesced around America's newly emerging universities. As the institutional builders of the period looked to Europe and adopted (in large part) the German research ideal as the basis for new universities in Ithaca, New York (Cornell, founded in 1865); Baltimore (Johns Hopkins, 1876); Worcester, Massachusetts (Clark, 1887); Chicago, Illinois (University of Chicago, 1891); and Palo Alto, California (Stanford, 1892), the older colleges—which an earlier society had charged with instilling discipline and piety in its professional leaders —began converting into universities that emphasized graduate education. (In short, they adapted, and even mutated, in response to changes in their immediate environment; see Veysey, 1965.) So, too, did many state universities; by 1890, those in California, Indiana, Michigan, and Wisconsin, for example, had more in common with the private universities than with most other public universities. In all of these institutions, the educational magnates adopted the principle of division of labor that their industrial counterparts had found so successful; thus, highly specialized departments thrived. These usually focused on one of the research-based academic disciplines that had emerged in the 19th-century German universities. Johns Hopkins and others, for example, bragged regularly about their seminar-based instruction in classical philology (Hawkins, 1960). Physics, too, emerged from natural philosophy, as for the first time large numbers of Americans began to call themselves scientists and practice research (Kevles, 1978).

Meanwhile, through the 1880s, research-oriented scientists based in universities and in federal scientific agencies grew dissatisfied with the older scientific organizations, such as the American Association for the Advancement of Science (AAAS), founded in 1848. The AAAS opened its membership to all who paid its dues, published only summary proceedings of its peripatetic summer meetings, and comprised only two general sections, which limited program time for any one discipline. In 1882, responding to the interests of researchers, the AAAS adapted itself by establishing nine slightly more specialized programs. But this halfway move did little to satisfy these special interests and led instead to further adaptation by promoting further discussion that led to the formation of disciplinary societies with restricted membership (Appel, 1988).

In 1883, biologists and geologists founded the Society of Naturalists of the Eastern United States (soon renamed the American Society of Naturalists) that "encouraged the formation of disciplinary societies"—including, eventually, the APA—"and enabled them to survive their early years when there were still few prospective members with the desired training and attainment" (Appel, 1988, p. 90). In many ways, it represented a transitional form between the AAAS and the highly specialized and limited-membership organizations of research scientists that soon emerged. The earliest of these, the American Physiological Society, appeared in 1887 and restricted its membership to those who had "conducted and published an original research" (Appel, p. 94) in physiology. When its organizers invited only 28 researchers to join as charter members, they deliberately excluded many who taught physiology at American medical schools and all whose interests were solely clinical. Within the decade, other specialists founded the Association of American Anatomists (also in 1887; renamed the American Association of Anatomists in 1909), the Geological Society of America (1888), the American Morphological Society (1890; renamed the American Zoological Society in 1902), and the Botanical Society of America (1892). Through the 1890s and even afterward, the American Society of Naturalists provided an infrastructure that provided a nurturing environment for these new societies. As the "Affiliated Societies," they usually met together for three days between Christmas and New Years Day. The American Society of Naturalists scheduled only a presidential address and a symposium, with speakers from all of the organizations present, on a topic of general interest. Its secretary took charge of all local arrangements, including reduced-rate rail fares and an extensive social program. Then as now, the societies' members all enjoyed and often profited more from these less structured sessions and informal discussions in the halls than they did from any formal presentations, and these meetings did much to promote the growth of research-oriented science in late 19th-century America (Appel).

PSYCHOLOGY SLOWLY EMERGES

In many ways, however, philosophy and its subdiscipline, psychology, lagged behind their cohort. Through the 1880s, conventional mental and moral philosophy, rooted in the Scottish realism of the late 18th century, continued to serve the needs of many colleges, which saw no reason to change. The new universities, however, often sought to move beyond this tradition and establish research-based philosophy departments alongside those in the sciences. But their founders often found German Idealism uncongenial, or at least they projected their own concerns on their institutions' trustees. By the mid-1880s, then, at least some of them began considering the newly emerging discipline of experimental psychology as a substitute (Ross, 1972). After all, psychology had always been a part of philosophy, and even those who taught mental philosophy in American colleges had long since begun to bring German physiological psychology into their texts and classes.

By 1892, American universities had established about 20 psychological laboratories, and at some of them, psychology dominated philosophy

(Garvey, 1929; Murray & Rowe, 1979). These laboratories taught a science that had already begun to adapt to the new environment in which its practitioners found themselves. Their psychology moved away from Germany's, with its focus on the working of the normal, healthy, adult male mind in laboratory conditions; American psychologists began quite early to assimilate evolutionary, primarily Darwinian, principles into their science. American psychology also retained from its mid 19th-century phrenological tradition, and to some degree from the earlier Scottish realism, an interest in life in the real world. From the start, then, this science was functionally oriented and deeply concerned with development—especially with individual differences (i.e., the variation that made natural selection possible). Americans were also more interested in the latent practicality of their science; therefore, although little pre-1900 psychology focused directly on applied problems, much was at least potentially applicable, as it often dealt with the "real world" outside the laboratory (O'Donnell, 1985).

The new science had also begun to adapt to its professional environment and develop its own infrastructure, as G. Stanley Hall established the *American Journal of Psychology* (the *Journal*) in 1887 (Dallenbach, 1937; Hall, 1923; Ross, 1972). Like most late 19th-century American scientific periodicals, it was privately owned, and despite its title, it played for Clark University the house-organ role played by Wilhelm Wundt's *Philosophische Studien* for Leipzig students. Although it drew submissions from around the country, it often had more in common with Columbia's *Contributions to Philosophy and Psychology*, Harvard's *Psychological Studies*, Iowa's *Studies in Psychology*, the *Publications of the University of Pennsylvania*, and other locally oriented and sporadically issued university series, many of which were later subsumed in *Psychological Monographs*. No wonder, then, that in 1889, when European psychologists organizing the first International Congress of Psychology (in conjunction with the Paris Universal Exposition) tried to identify a national organization of psychologists in North America, they could find only the American Society for Psychical Research (ASPR; Wetmore, 1992). The two Americans attending the international congress, William James and Joseph Jastrow, knew the ASPR's limitations. Despite its name, it was as locally oriented as the different university publication series, and the Europeans even wrote of it as the "Boston Society." Although some evidence suggests that ASPR sought to move beyond the narrow focus its name implied (Mauskopf, 1989), Jastrow strongly opposed any attempt to link psychical research to the new psychology and could argue, at least, that most American psychologists disparaged the organization and its interests. Thus, later international congresses ignored the ASPR. On their return to America, James and Jastrow probably reported these events to their colleagues, including G. Stanley Hall, who earned his Harvard PhD with James in 1878 and who directed Jastrow's Johns Hopkins dissertation in 1886.

Although these developments shaped the environment and formed the context within which APA emerged, its particular form and initial character derived largely from the temperament of one individual, G. Stanley Hall. Unfortunately for APA—which Hall founded in 1892—his disposition prevented all of the institutions he led from thriving under his leadership. Fortunately, however, within 18 months, the association established an identity of its own, and by the mid-1890s Hall had little to say about the course of APA affairs.

THE AMBITIOUS G. S. HALL

Hall was strongly ambitious, and the opportunities for personal advancement he saw in the new psychology attracted him as much as any of the intellectual questions its practitioners asked (Koelsch, 1987). In 1884, he gained his Johns Hopkins professorship in competition with two of American's leading philosophers, largely because Daniel Coit Gilman, the university's president, found him fittest for the environment of Baltimore. Gilman preferred Hall's laboratory-based psychology to George Sylvester Morris's Idealism and Charles Sanders Peirce's marital uncertainties (Ross, 1972). He also appreciated Hall's interest in child study and pedagogy, in part because he could cite its implied practicality, and (especially) Hall's status as an ordained Congregational minister, to defend the university against charges of religious irregularity. But the negative aspects of Hall's temperament emerged even before he assumed his professorship, and in 1883 he went out of his way to rid the university of those who might challenge his intellectual leadership (Ross, 1972; Sokal, 1981). Throughout his career, Hall often seemed to deal loosely with the truth. For example, in 1887, he obtained funds to start the *American Journal of Psychology* from Robert Pearsall Smith, a spiritualist active in ASPR, who had expected the new journal to share his interests. As Hall's biographer (Ross, 1972) concluded, "to what extent Hall tacitly encouraged that assumption is unknown" (p. 170; cf. Dallenbach, 1937; Hall, 1923). Later that year, he became founding president of Clark University in Worcester, Massachusetts, and through the next half-decade continually misled the institution's principal benefactor, Jonas Clark, as to his educational policies and goals. Once Clark realized just how seriously Hall had deceived him, he withdrew his support from the university, and Hall, in turn, blamed this action for all of the trouble that followed. In building Clark University, Hall gathered a world-renown faculty with "extravagant promises" (Koelsch, p. 35) he could never fulfill and, in the years that followed, dealt with its members as he had dealt with Smith and Clark. By January 1892, these scholars and scientists had grown tired of Hall's "arbitrary ways, his double-dealing, and his constant attempts to blame either the trustees or Jonas Clark" (Koelsch,

p. 35) for his own troubles (see also Ross, 1972). Finally, in April 1892, William Rainey Harper, president of the University of Chicago (which would open the following fall) came to Worcester and hired most of Clark's faculty for his institution. Hall's colleagues in psychology, notably Edmund C. Sanford, stuck by him, but his hopes for Clark had collapsed.

Defeat rarely daunted Hall. During the previous summer (1891) he had renewed ties with the National Educational Association (NEA)—which had not yet evolved into a labor union—whose members had continually called for a more "scientific pedagogy." In response, Hall founded the *Pedagogical Seminary* (which after 1925 became the *Journal of Genetic Psychology*), and at the NEA's annual summer meeting in Toronto, Hall's informal discussions of "The Study of Children" attracted more attendees than did most official programs. In July 1892, Hall held a two-week summer school at Clark on "the higher pedagogy and psychology" that attracted dozens of school teachers, principals, and superintendents. NEA's conservative leadership, however, fearing both Hall's innovations and his approach to others, put off pressures to establish an NEA child study department. (One finally emerged in 1894, with Hall as its first president; see Ross, 1972.) In the meantime, Joseph Jastrow, by then professor of psychology at the University of Wisconsin, began organizing a section of psychology for the World Columbian Exposition, planned for Chicago for the summer of 1893, and told Hall of his plans to visit eastern colleagues. Hall likely saw Jastrow's eastern trip as an opportunity to reassert himself. His Clark colleagues had deserted him, and NEA's leadership proved unresponsive to his wiles, but he knew the specialized biological societies organized under the aegis of the American Society of Naturalists; he was a charter member of the American Physiological Society. Hall thus refocused his attention on his colleagues in psychology.

APA's "PRELIMINARY MEETING": JULY 1892

Sometime late in the spring of 1892, Hall invited many of these colleagues to join in forming an American psychological association, and on July 8, 1892, he gathered in his Worcester study a small group for that explicit purpose (see Cattell, 1917, 1929, 1943; Jastrow, 1943). A report on this "preliminary meeting" published only six weeks later emphasized an otherwise unspecified "general expression of opinion as to the form of the organization" ("The American Psychological Association," 1892, p. 104) and the decision to refer details to a seven-member committee, charged to organize the association's first annual meeting, "to report a plan of organization," and "to act as Council" (p. 104). Despite decades of speculation, no precise roll exists (Dennis & Boring, 1952; Fernberger, 1932,

1943); however, those attending heard papers by Clark professors, instructors, and alumni, and "Professor Jastrow asked the cooperation of all members for the section of psychology at the World's Fair, and invited correspondence upon the matter" (Cattell, 1894b, pp. 1–2). Most notably, the group learned that 26 men (including those present) had accepted membership in the new organization and had agreed to elect to membership 5 others, including 2 whom Hall had neglected to invite and 3 recent Leipzig PhDs—Hugo Münsterberg, Edward A. Pace, and Edward B. Titchener—who were about to assume professorships at Harvard, Catholic, and Cornell universities, respectively, and had not yet arrived in (or returned to) America.

Although 6 of the 31 original APA members taught at Clark (and another 4 had earned their PhDs with Hall in Worcester or in Baltimore), they formed a diverse lot. By including several Canadians, at least 2 identifiable Jews (Jastrow and Münsterberg, although the latter had earlier converted to Lutheranism; see Hale, 1980), and a Roman Catholic priest (Pacer; see Sexton, 1980), the early APA showed a greater openness than did many organizations of that time. Hall had always opened Clark to "outsiders," and this "patronage" contributed much to his academic success (Sokal, 1990). The professional interests in psychology of the charter members also varied greatly, and the group included psychiatrists (Edward Cowles and William Noyes of the McLean Hospital outside Boston), philosophers (e.g., John Dewey of Michigan, George S. Fullerton of Pennsylvania, James H. Hyslop of Columbia, and Josiah Royce of Harvard), pedagogists (e.g., William H. Burnham and Benjamin I. Gilman of Clark), as well as Leipzig- (or Clark- or Johns Hopkins-) trained experimentalists. Indeed, of late 19th-century approaches to psychology, Hall omitted only psychical research. To be sure, Hyslop and William James shared an interest in the subject, and James (at least) could not have been omitted. But if Hall had included ASPR activist Richard Hodgson among the initial members, many others—such as Jastrow (1900) and Columbia University's James McKeen Cattell (1893a)—would likely have declined from membership.

In their diversity, however, these 31 men shared at least two other significant traits (besides their sex). First, they were all quite young. Aside from Cowles (aged 54), James and George T. Ladd of Yale (both 50) were the oldest, and Hall himself was only 48. At least 6 were in their 20s, and their average age was about 35. Like most of the university-based research-oriented fields of the late 19th century, psychology was a young man's science. And like most young men, its practitioners shared an enthusiasm for their science that infused their work. For its first few years, then, the American Psychological Association reflected an enthusiasm that did much to shape its character.

APA's FIRST ANNUAL MEETING: DECEMBER 1892

The enthusiasm and breadth of interest of its first members emerged clearly at the association's first regular meeting, held at the University of Pennsylvania the following December (Cattell, 1894b). Of the 31 members, 18 attended the meeting and heard a dozen papers, many illustrating ways in which American psychology had evolved beyond the narrowly focused experimental tradition in which many of its members had been trained. For example, Jastrow's paper, "Experimental Psychology at the World's Fair," emphasized the kinds of anthropometric tests he planned to give the following summer to visitors to the section of psychology; William L. Bryan (1892) of Indiana University reported on his "Psychological Tests in the Schools of Springfield;" and Lightner Witmer of the University of Pennsylvania described the "Chronoscopic Measurement of Simple Reactions on All Classes of Persons." Even Cattell's detailed report of his massive reevaluation of classical psychophysical methods (Cattell, 1893b; Fullerton & Cattell, 1892) served primarily—or so one observer (O'Donnell, 1985) later claimed—"to demolish one of the cornerstones of traditional physiological psychology (p. 144)." In the program's final paper, Münsterberg attacked his colleagues' work as "rich in decimals but poor in ideas" (Cattell, 1894b, p. 11) and called for closer ties with philosophy (see also Münsterberg, 1898b). As the events of this first annual meeting illustrate, psychologists have never shied away from intellectual controversy.

In their enthusiasm for their new science the psychologists worked together effectively to reach important professional goals. For example, they considered calls for cooperation from anthropologists, philosophers, and educators organizing symposia in connection with the Chicago World's Fair, but declined all of these invitations in order to "leave the members free to place their allegiance where they thought best" (Cattell, 1894b, p. 13). Their new association gave other scholars the point of contact with psychology that they had sought and thus helped them claim their place in the late 19th-century scientific community. They elected Hall as president; heard his presidential address, "History and Prospects of Experimental Psychology in America;" and made plans to publish the proceedings of the meeting in his *American Journal of Psychology*. The first council did not propose a constitution, but recommended the adoption of several "regulations ... to be regarded as in effect in so far as the continuance of the Association depended upon them" (Cattell, 1894b, p. 13). Annual dues were set at $3, but unlike other organizations at the time, APA did not spell out membership criteria. The regulations assigned "the right of nomination for membership [to] the Council," but stipulated that "the election [was] to be made by the Association" (Cattell, 1894b, p. 13). During APA's first years, members applied their relatively loose standard rather strictly; although two recent Clark PhDs presented papers at this first annual meeting, they were not elected to membership. The association did elect (on council nomination) 11 new members. Significantly, none had been trained in experimental psychology, and although most worked at the intersection of psychology and traditional philosophy, at least two—Nicholas Murray Butler of Columbia and Jacob Gould Schurman of Cornell—were philosophers, with little real interest in psychology as such. The new association thus reaffirmed its commitment to inclusiveness and worked to extend its influence more broadly. Cowles and Noyes—the psychiatrists who had accepted election the previous summer—did not attend and never participated actively in the association's affairs; however, within six months of its founding, APA could boast of 42 members and recognition from other learned societies.

Unfortunately, tensions within the psychological community soon diluted the good feelings that pervaded this meeting. As usual, most derived from Hall's behavior and the "personal and professional antagonism [he] aroused" (Ross, 1972, p. 235), which soon focused on his dictatorial editorship of the *American Journal of Psychology* (which, to be sure, he owned). American psychologists came to distrust his "capricious taste" and never knew what criteria he used in accepting or rejecting submissions. Dissatisfaction grew through 1892, and Hall's biographer (Ross, 1972) has speculated that support emerging at an informal gathering at the December 1892 APA meeting led Cattell and James Mark Baldwin of Princeton to approach Hall with several schemes to help make the *Journal* more responsive to them and the colleagues they represented. Negotiations led nowhere, however, and by late 1893, Baldwin and Cattell had made plans to establish the *Psychological Review* (*Review*), which first appeared in January 1894. Hall did not attend APA's second annual meeting, held in December 1893 at Columbia, and the association dropped its plan to publish its proceedings in his journal.

LEADERSHIP CHANGES

Hall's detractors assumed leading roles in the association; George T. Ladd served as president at the meeting, James was elected president for the following year, and Cattell was elected secretary (Cattell, 1894a). As host, Cattell had begun acting as secretary in the months before the meeting (Cattell, 1893–1894), arranging the program (he invited Hall to speak as former president and expressed regret when Hall decided not to attend), and dealing with local arrangements. He did so well that James (1893) praised his "tact, good humor, and flexibility of intellect." Through December 1893, Cattell also collected names of potential new members. He nominated for membership Mary Whiton Calkins of Wellesley College and Christine Ladd-Franklin of Baltimore, both of whom had already published extensively in the *American Journal of Psychology* and other journals. His letters on the subject argued that "we psychologists ought not to draw a sex-line" (Cattell, 1893–1894, pp. 5–7), and his colleagues agreed. Aside from several anthropological groups, which recognized that women could do kinds of fieldwork that no man could do, no other society had women members earlier in its development (Rossiter, 1982). Other experimentally trained psychologists, such as James R. Angell of Minnesota and Howard C. Warren of Princeton, also became members. However, as in 1892, at least four new members were more interested in philosophy than psychology, and several papers—such as "A Note on Anaximander" by Butler (Cattell, 1894a, p. 21) and "The Case of John Bunyan" by Royce (Cattell, 1894a, pp. 17–18)—seemed out of place to many. But philosophers at late 19th-century American universities lacked their own learned society to turn to, and through its first decade APA served philosophy as much as it did psychology, a fact that had many implications for the association.

In many ways, through the mid-1890s, and even afterward, the APA's development and adaptation to its changing environment articulated many of the patterns its members established during the first two years. As secretary, Cattell edited and published (in an edition of 300) the proceedings of the first meetings (Cattell, 1894a). From 1894 on, however, the association published its annual proceedings in the *Psychological Review*, and at the annual meeting in 1894, the association finally adopted its first formal constitution. It emphasized "the object of the Association [as] the advancement of Psychology as a science" and that "those are eligible for membership who are engaged in this work" (Cattell, 1895, p. 150). The constitution kept the council's authority to nominate new members, but reaffirmed procedures that called for a vote of the membership on all new members. Through the next decade, successive councils interpreted these newly stringent criteria rather loosely, and the 1906 council explicitly noted that its predecessors had "historically and consistently recognized two sorts of qualifications: professional occupation in psychology and research" (Davis, 1907, p. 203). Despite attempts to tighten the nomination process, which called for nominators to list the publications of those who they proposed, the association's membership policies remained inclusive through about 1905, when councils openly began interpreting these criteria much more strictly. Membership reached 101 in 1898 and 127 in 1900 (Cattell, 1929).

CONNECTIONS WITH OTHER ORGANIZATIONS

From 1895, APA met regularly with the other "Affiliated Societies" promoted by the American Society of Naturalists. Doing so had many practical benefits, as (like the other societies) the association profited from the larger group's local arrangements ("Scientific Notes and News," 1895). Meeting formally and informally with other scientists and participating in the society's annual symposium helped psychologists gain status for their science. In 1896, for example, William James represented the association effectively in a symposium that focused on "The Inheritance of Acquired Characteristics" (Farrand, 1897). Through these early years the association's annual programs included many philosophical papers, but many others illustrated American psychology's functional, developmental, and differential concerns. Many psychologists seemed to cluster around what was gradually becoming known as mental testing, and the collection of mental and physical statistics of large numbers of individuals. Scientifically, this concern for individual differences derived from an interest in the variation that made natural selection possible, and as Jastrow's plans for the World Columbian Exposition exemplified this tradition, the association had promoted work along these lines from the start (Sokal, 1987). As noted earlier, even at the first annual meeting, others presented results of similar kinds of studies, and through the mid 1890s, Arthur MacDonald of the U. S. Bureau of Education regularly presented "Neuro–Social Data" of, for example, the "Sensibility to Pain by Pressure in the Hands of Individuals of Different Classes, Sexes, and Nationalities." More notably, in 1895, Livingston Farrand of Columbia described the "Series of Physical and Mental Tests on the Students of Columbia College" (see Cattell & Farrand, 1896) that he and Cattell had undertaken

> to obtain a record for comparative purposes of certain mental and physical characteristics of the students at different times during a period of rather active intellectual growth and at the same time to furnish material for a statistical study of the particular points examined. (Farrand, 1896, p. 124)

This presentation stimulated excited discussion that led the association, on Baldwin's motion, to establish a committee "to consider the feasibility of cooperation among the various psychological laboratories in the collection of mental and physical statistics" (Sanford, 1896b, p. 122). This committee was APA's first venture beyond the sponsorship of meetings, and its activities deserve further attention.

APA COMMITTEE ON PHYSICAL AND MENTAL TESTS

In gathering what soon became known as the APA Committee on Physical and Mental Tests, the association's leadership—President Cattell, Secretary–Treasurer Sanford, and council members Baldwin, Dewey, Fullerton, James, and G. Ladd—sought both to ensure their control of the group and to involve those APA members who had experience with this type of work. Ignoring MacDonald, who had a well-deserved reputation as a crank (Gilbert, 1977), they named three of their own—Baldwin, Sanford, and Cattell (as chair)—to the committee, illustrating the centrality of the issue for the association. Both Cattell and Sanford had sponsored testing programs in their laboratories, as had Jastrow and Witmer, the other two members of the committee, and Witmer soon began using these tests in an informal psychological clinic at the University of Pennsylvania. The testing programs concerned themselves primarily with sensory and motor capacities—for example, most measured different kinds of reaction times under varying conditions—and none reflected any overarching view of "the mind," or human ability or function. Despite the name the committee assumed and the goals of later tests, committee members were primarily concerned with the collection of mental and physical statistics. This interest had its roots in physical anthropometry, especially as practiced in England by Francis Galton, who had earlier done much to shape both Cattell's and Jastrow's scientific agendas and views on human variation (Sokal, 1987). Throughout the 1890s, the growing physical education movement reinforced this tradition, and the committee's work reflected its members' experience (e.g., Hartwell, 1893–1894).

Through 1896, the committee did most of its work through correspondence, which peaked only a month before the December meeting. Its preliminary report, presented at the meeting, listed "a series of physical and mental tests[,] . . . especially appropriate for college students . . . the general public and, with . . . modifications, school children[,] . . . which seemed most likely to reveal individual differences and development" (Baldwin, Cattell, Jastrow, Sanford, & Witmer, 1897, p. 132). It urged the association's members to use a "variety" of such tests on students at their home institutions "so that the best ones may be determined." But it offered no criteria for "best" and never established a goal beyond the collection of statistics. Unfortunately, a crowded agenda prevented the association at large from discussing the issues that were raised, and even in their letters to each other, its members seemed unsure about how they should proceed.

At the 1897 APA meeting, however, members began to address these issues, even as Jastrow (for example) emphasized the measurement of "the normal capacity of simple and typical sensory, motor and intellectual endowments" (Baldwin, Cattell, & Jastrow, 1898, p. 172). He also mentioned interests in "the distribution of such powers, their development in child growth, their relation to practical and daily pursuits, and their correlation with one another" (p. 172; i.e., just the kinds of issues to which functional psychologists of the late 19th and early 20th century devoted themselves). But these were clearly subsidiary to his (and the colleagues') primary goals, and although he reviewed "the selection of the capacities to be tested" (p. 172) and spoke of "(a) the senses, (b) the motor capacities, and (c) the more complex mental processes" (p. 173), his remarks focused on the first two and slighted the third. For his part, Cattell argued that tests should be easy to administer and emphasized the constraints that testers faced. Only Baldwin, whose concurrent studies of *Mental Development in the Child and the Race* (1895) helped set an agenda for 20th-century developmental psychology (Cahan, 1984), claimed that tests should be given "as psychological a character as possible" (Baldwin et al., p. 175). Thus, Baldwin disparaged many of the procedures suggested by his colleagues and even cited contemporaneous work by Alfred Binet on tests of memory. In reply, committee chair Cattell noted that the concerns Baldwin recommended "seem . . . rather a subject for research than for anthropometric tests" and admitted that "the tests most interesting to the psychologist are those most difficult to make in three minutes" (Baldwin et al., p. 176). He thus confirmed the committee's limited view of testing, which dominated its activities until it passed out of existence sometime in the late 1890s. However, in 1897, the association appropriated $100 for the committee's use—its first expenditure for anything beyond administrative expenses—which its members used to purchase apparatus and have test forms printed.

Three years later, in 1900, MacDonald asked the association (and others) to endorse his call for "the establishment in the Department of the Interior of the Psycho–Physical Laboratory [for] . . . the collection of sociological, anthropological, abnormal and pathological data [for] the study of criminal, pauper and defective classes" (cited in Gilbert, 1977, p. 183). But MacDonald's contentiousness had grown since 1895—one APA member called him "too disgusting a person for self-respecting people to have anything to do with" (Franklin, 1900)—and again the association did nothing (Farrand, 1901). Even in the short run, the Committee on Physical and Mental Tests had no real impact on psychology's evolution. Most significant developments emerged elsewhere—notably at what were then known as "schools for the feebleminded"—without the APA's support or imprimatur. In 1906, the association again discussed "the question of Organized Cooperation in Standardizing Psychologists Tests" (Davis, 1907, p. 202), and although many members doubted the propriety of organizing it at all, the council appointed a Committee on Measurements. But like its predecessor it did little and had negligible influence on the practice of psychology. In many ways, then, the association's first efforts to shape its members' science proved unsuccessful.

APA proved equally uninfluential in other areas of concern. For example, in 1898, at Baldwin's instigation, it organized a Standing Committee on Psychological and Philosophical Terminology, charged it broadly to deal with "new terms" in these fields in both English and other languages and urged its members to collaborate actively with psychologists from other countries. But aside from Baldwin's brief remarks in 1900, the committee never reported (Farrand, 1899, 1901). In 1897, Cattell urged APA to hold an informal meeting that August in conjunction with the American Association for the Advancement of Science's (AAAS's) annual meeting, then being planned for Boston (Farrand, 1898). In July, *Science* even announced the time of the meeting ("Scientific notes and news," 1898), but the following September, *Psychological Review* noted that the "summer meeting ... was given up owing to the small number of papers offered" ("Notes," 1898). In a similar action in 1900, APA voted to allow members to organize "local sections" of the association and immediately authorized "branches" in Cambridge, Massachusetts; Chicago; and New York (Farrand, 1901). In New York, the branch grew out of earlier meetings sponsored by the section for anthropology and psychology of the New York Academy of Sciences and met regularly through 1935, eventually leading to the formation of the Eastern Psychological Association in the 1930s (Benjamin, 1991). The branch centered in Chicago—known at various times as the Western Branch, the Northwestern Branch, and the North Central Branch —sponsored and reported on several meetings through 1908 (Gore, 1905a, 1905b; "Notes," 1902, 1903; "Notes and News," 1904). But it then passed into oblivion, and direct antecedents of what emerged in 1928 as the Midwestern Psychological Association did not appear until 1926 (Benjamin, 1979).

PUBLICATION POSSIBILITIES CONSIDERED AND ABANDONED

Another potentially useful initiative emerged in 1900, when James H. Leuba, a Hall PhD who had taught at Bryn Mawr since 1898 (McBride, 1947), asked the association "for financial support in publishing his catalogue of psychological literature" (Farrand, 1901, p. 159), a bibliography and card index of older and more recent publications in the field. Since 1894, however, the *Psychological Review* had annually issued a *Psychological Index*, a bibliography of current work in the field, so many members believed that Leuba's work was redundant, at least in part. But many members also shared Leuba's interests in earlier psychological literature (Leuba, 1900; Sanford, 1902a, 1902b) and one or two, perhaps, may have seen in his request an opportunity to challenge Baldwin's and Cattell's prominent positions within the field. As a result, the association created a Committee on Bibliography "to take the whole matter under consideration." Its first report was tabled in 1901 (Farrand, 1902), but the following year the committee urged the association to purchase "Prof. Leuba's collection belonging to the years prior to January 1, 1894" (Farrand, 1903, p. 151), to charge it with expanding the card index, and to begin plans to publish the bibliography. After a long discussion of the detailed report, the association accepted this recommendation, but in 1903 the committee went further and urged APA to hire an "executive agent who could carry on the correspondence necessary to secure the cooperation in this undertaking of the members of the association, and others" (Farrand, 1904, p. 35) and to assume general charge of the project. This recommendation would have had APA employ its first staff member, and spend more in one year than it had in the previous five years. The association's "accumulated fund" could have supported this expenditure, and many members saw great value in the project. But many did not, and the Council urged its tabling. The committee still endorsed the plan at the association's next two meetings, presenting detailed budgets that demonstrated how APA could afford it. But consensus eluded continued discussion until the middle of the decade, when the association at large learned that Benjamin Rand, a librarian working at Harvard, would publish a 1,200-page, two-volume *Bibliography of Philosophy, Psychology, and Cognate Subjects* (Rand, 1905a, 1905b) as part of the *Dictionary of Philosophy and Psychology* that Baldwin (1901–1905) was editing. In 1906, the committee concluded, with some embarrassment, that "after an examination of the bibliography of Dr. Rand, it was regarded as injudicious that anything further be done in the matter" (Davis, 1907, p. 203).

Leuba's bibliography was not the only publication opportunity that the APA managed to avoid, and indeed, it never embarked on any publications program in its early years. In 1893, one option Baldwin and Cattell offered Hall in their attempts to broaden the *American Journal of Psychology* was to have it become—although still privately owned—the association's official journal (Ross, 1972). Other societies benefited from similar contracts with other journals, as they guaranteed an outlet for reports of their meetings and the journals' owners could be sure of larger circulations. Some made large profits from such arrangements, even when the societies paid them less for each subscription than nonmembers paid, as wider distribution allowed them to sell additional advertising at higher rates. For example, Cattell did quite well financially when *Science* (which he owned and edited) became in 1900 the official journal of the AAAS (Sokal, 1980). Even earlier, the American Society of Naturalists adopted the *American Naturalist*, founded privately in 1867, as its official journal (Nyhart, 1979), and Baldwin and Cattell probably cited this example in their talks with Hall. But Hall proved intransigent; the association issued its first volume of *Proceedings* in 1894 (at a cost of $55.93), and later that year it "resolved that the minutes should be printed in such journals as were prepared to print them in full" (Cattell, 1895, p. 151). Through the 1890s, most scientific periodicals had to spend more time soliciting submissions than screening them, and from 1895 Baldwin and Cattell's *Psychological Review* regularly published each meeting's full proceedings, thus serving the association and its members well throughout the decade.

PSYCHOLOGICAL REVIEW EDITORS SPLIT

Later in 1895, Cattell urged the council to arrange for APA members to have their $3 annual dues credited toward annual subscriptions to his and Baldwin's *Review* (which then cost $4) or Hall's *Journal* (then $5). The journals' owners would have then had to provide subscriptions at effective rates of $1 and $2, respectively, but would have benefited from the increased circulation that Cattell projected. The council, however, declined his proposal, as Sanford (representing Hall and by then, himself, an editor of the *Journal*) spoke against it (Sanford, 1896a). Unlike the *Review*—which regularly ran advertisements for typewriters and bicycles, as well as books and graduate programs—the *Journal* refused to carry such notices, in order (so it claimed) to keep its reviews "more impartial" (Hall, 1895, p. 5). Hall, thus, would have earned less from this arrangement than would Baldwin and Cattell. In any event, the association again refrained from taking the initiative, and the *Psychological Review* continued to publish detailed reports on APA meetings through 1904. During these years, the relations between the *Review*'s two owner-editors grew progressively worse, and they soon began alternating (rather than sharing) editorial control, with Baldwin having responsibility for odd-numbered years ("Notes," 1896). By April 1904, their differences had become irreconcilable, and Cattell suggested (perhaps as a ploy) that APA take charge of the *Review*, the *Psychological Index*, and the series of *Psychological Review Monographs* that had appeared during the preceding decade. But the association's leaders again avoided taking action, and late that year, after a bitter and divisive public debate,[1] Cattell sold his share of the *Review* to Baldwin (1926, Vol. 1).

In 1905, as Baldwin continued the *Review*, he established the *Psychological Bulletin*, which began that year to carry the association's proceedings. Cattell meanwhile had founded the *Journal of Philosophy, Psychology and Scientific Methods*, whose control he soon yielded to his philosopher colleagues at Columbia, and which in 1920 dropped the final four words of its title. In the early 1910s, soon after a sex scandal forced Baldwin from Johns Hopkins, he had to yield control of the *Psychological Bulletin*, *Index*, *Monographs*, and *Review* to his junior colleague, Howard C. Warren, of Princeton. Warren retained private ownership through the mid-1920s, when he sold them to the association at prices far below their assessed values (Fernberger, 1932).

The association's sluggish response to initiatives and its seeming inability to capitalize on opportunities did not stem from any financial con-

---

[1]Historians have yet to publish an account of this episode, which the papers of those who were actively involved richly document (e.g., see Cattell, 1904a, 1904b; Judd, 1904; Münsterberg, 1904).

straints. After all, the first council had set annual dues at $3 in 1892—a level confirmed in the first constitution of 1894—and an inclusive membership policy combined with a lack of serious expenses led to an unchecked growth for the association's "accumulated fund." It opened at $50.30 in 1892, reached $800.88 in 1898, jumped to $1,585.78 at the association's 10th meeting in 1901, and reached $2,770.17 five years later (Buchner, 1903; Davis, 1906). (During APA's first decade, the Consumer Price Index remained at just about one quarter of its 1967 level; through the 1890s, nonfarm employees earned, on the average, $455 annually; and Cattell's $5,000 salary in 1905 probably made him one of the highest paid APA members [U.S. Bureau of the Census, 1975].) The association did make several grants to support its members' research—most notably, that for the Committee on Physical and Mental Tests (Farrand, 1898, 1899; "Notes," 1898)—but for the most part its only expenses were secretarial. In 1895, the council discussed reducing annual dues to $1, but Cattell's argument against the move—that "it would be very difficult to raise them if they were once put down" (Sanford, 1896a)—prevailed. Seven years later, the council first formally recommended a constitutional amendment that would have decreased dues, but the association at large tabled the motion (Farrand, 1905). The rapidly growing accumulated fund, however, led to renewed calls for decreases. In 1904, the council recommended a decrease in dues, to $1 annually, and a remission of two thirds of the dues paid for the previous year. As the constitution required, the 1905 annual meeting reaffirmed the dues decrease and instructed the council "to consider the whole question of the guardianship and utilization of the Association's accumulated fund, and to report upon the same at the next annual meeting" (Davis, 1906, p. 39). In doing so, the council realized the rashness of its act and attempted to double dues to $2, a proposal that the association at large quickly stifled (see Davis, 1907). (Dues again reached $2 only in 1919 [see Fernberger, 1932].) With its final report on the accumulated fund, which finally appeared in 1907, the council reaffirmed the early APA's apparent inability to act. It found "at present no special activity of the association which requires the expenditure of any money which might be properly drawn from this fund" and thus urged its preservation "till such time as the association shall formulate special work which will require its use in whole or in part" (Woodworth, 1908, p. 35).

Ironically, in its early years the association achieved perhaps its greatest success by promoting the development of philosophy, its parent discipline, in a way that encouraged it to be professional and grow through the early 20th century as other disciplines had done in the late 19th century. In doing so, the APA alienated many of those psychologists who had campaigned most strongly for psychology's independence from philosophy, a group of experimentalists that included both those with functional concerns and those whose work continued the traditional research fostered since the late 1870s by German psychological laboratories. In several ways, this second group seemed to many to be APA's natural constituency. After all, the physiologists and others had founded their scientific societies to promote basic research, and the membership criteria their societies adopted decried the kinds of practical issues that interested many American psychologists. But just about all up-to-date life science after Darwin, whether physiological or psychological, was functional, and "functional" in psychology typically implied a concern for life in the real world, not necessarily implied by "functional" in physiology. As John O'Donnell (1985) has shown, functional concerns led American psychology to evolve toward behavioristic perspectives typically unsympathetic with traditional experimental psychology. Those APA members with these concerns thus felt slighted on two accounts: that is, by the association's support for philosophy and by their psychological colleagues' interest in practicable problems. As early as 1896, an *American Journal of Psychology* comment—almost surely written by Titchener, who (with Sanford) had joined G. Stanley Hall as editor the previous year—complained about "the retirement of the experimentalists" from the association. Although Titchener overstated the case, he did emphasize another reason for his dissatisfaction (i.e., the form of presentation demanded by the format of the association's annual meeting). He thus claimed that

> Unless the meetings are allowed to take the form of a conversazione, the apparatus employed shown in their working, and the results made to speak for themselves in charts and diagrams near the apparatus, it would seem that the drift of the Association must continue in the non-experimental direction. ("The American Psychological Association," 1896, p. 448)

In 1904, Titchener self-assuredly invited both kinds of experimentalists to meet and focus on just these kinds of presentations, which APA meetings continued to ignore. This group soon took on a life of its own, evolving eventually into the Society of Experimental Psychologists. It has its own history, which others have dealt with effectively (Boring, 1938; Goodwin, 1985). But as these historians have made clear, few of its members, besides Titchener, ever felt the need to withdraw from APA. Psychologists can thus learn much by tracing the course of APA's inclusive policy as an adaptive response to developments in its intellectual and professional environment and by following its influence on the association's development.

GRADUAL INDEPENDENCE FOR PHILOSOPHY

Although APA's early support for philosophy may seem out of place to at least some late 20th-century psychologists, through the century's first half decade, at least, psychology's position as a newly scientific offspring of philosophy made ties between the disciplines seem quite appropriate. Even as it complained about the retirement of the experimentalists and decried the format of APA annual meetings, the *American Journal of Psychology* noted that "the plan and restrictions of the meetings are of a kind to favor" the philosophers, and admitted that "it is not that the systematic psychologists are forcing their way unduly to the front" ("The American Psychological Association," 1896, p. 448). Other more general factors also shaped these developments, as many late 19th-century philosophers tried to help their discipline evolve in its new intellectual environment. In particular, as they worked to adapt their field for the new universities' hierarchy, they sought to follow their specialized siblings, and inasmuch as they lacked their own national society, they flocked to APA (Veysey, 1979; Wilson, 1979). At times their presentations seemed to dominate the association's meetings, as interpretations of "The Freedom of the Will" (Chrysostom, 1895) and similar topics provoked much discussion. An early 20th-century statistical analysis concluded that only about 12% of the papers presented at annual meetings during APA's first decade focused on philosophical issues (Buchner, 1903). Only one other subject, experimental psychology, commanded more attention, and at several meetings—notably those of 1896 at Harvard, under the presidency of Mary W. Calkins, and 1898 at Columbia—APA members actually heard more philosophical papers than papers on any other single topic. Furthermore, as soon became clear, Titchener was not the only psychologist who found this trend displeasing.

As a result, in 1895, "the question of the formation of a philosophical society or a philosophical section within the present Association was ... referred to the Council with full power to act" (Sanford, 1896b, p. 122). Thus, at the 1896 meeting most of the large cluster of "papers of a distinctly philosophical character" were scheduled on one morning (Farrand, 1897, p. 107). But this action did not satisfy all psychologists, and some seemed particularly disturbed that many newly elected members had stronger credentials in philosophy than psychology. Witmer thus proposed formally (a) that APA "select only such papers and contributions to the program of the annual meeting as are psychological in subject matter"; (b) that the council begin to "plan for the formation of an American Philosophical or Metaphysical Association" as one of the "present Affiliated Societies"; and, going still further, (c) that the council post, for all nominees for membership, "a statement of the[ir] contribution or contributions to psychology" (cited in Farrand, 1897, p. 109). Although many APA members shared some of Witmer's concerns, they knew him as one of the association's most contentious members, and few wanted to restrict membership. But in 1897, the council did ask nominators to list the publications of the new members they proposed, and for the first time, the association held parallel sessions,

"Section A ... for the discussion of physical and mental tests, and Section B ... for the reading of psychological papers" (Farrand, 1898, p. 145).

Despite this compromise, many psychologists still perceived problems with the philosophers' large presence, and at the 1898 meeting—when philosophical papers again dominated the program—they took action. Led this time by Sanford, one of APA's best-liked members, the association resolved to instruct council to consider and report on "the organization of the Association with reference to a possible philosophical section," to poll its members on their opinion about this matter, and to arrange "the programme for the next meeting to gather philosophical papers ... into ... one session" (Farrand, 1899, pp. 147–148). During the following 12 months, psychologists debated the issue, notes on it appeared in the *Psychological Review* and elsewhere (e.g., Bliss, 1899), and at the 1899 meeting, although the parallel sessions appeared to "work satisfactorily, ... many members would have been glad to have been present in both sections at the same time" ("Notes and News," 1900, p. 280). In an editorial note written, perhaps, by Sanford, the *American Journal of Psychology* thus claimed that "there seemed little desire to take any action that might lead to an actual division of the Association" ("Notes and News," 1900, p. 280). But others disagreed, and psychologists and philosophers both continued working toward that end.

Only two days after the end of the 1899 APA meeting, philosophers meeting in Kansas City on January 1, 1900 organized the Western Philosophical Association, "to stimulate an interest in philosophy in all its branches and to encourage original investigation" ("Notes," 1900, p. 104). Two of the five members of its first Executive Committee, including its president, Frank Thilly of the University of Missouri, were active APA members, and the organizers clearly profited from APA's example and, indeed, from that set by the other "Affiliated Societies." About 20 months later, philosophers in the East, led by Cornell professor J. E. Creighton (who had served on the APA Council from 1898), followed the lead of their western colleagues and founded an American Philosophical Association ("Notes," 1902; cf. Creighton, 1902; and Gardiner, 1926). These organizers were again among the many who had spoken at APA meetings as members during the preceding half decade, and the first president of the American Philosophical Association after Creighton was A. T. Ormond of Princeton, who had been a charter member of APA. As these new organizations appeared, fewer individuals sought APA membership. But all three societies grew through the early 1900s, and APA met jointly with the Western Philosophical Association in 1902 and 1907, and with the American Philosophical Association in 1904, 1905, and 1906 (see "The American Philosophical Society," 1902). These philosophical societies thrived and finally amalgamated in the late 1910s. Today's American Philosophical Association comprises three divisions: Eastern, Central, and Pacific.

CONSOLIDATING CHANGE

By 1905, the APA could put aside its fears of being dominated by philosophers and resume its growth, which had been slowed only by the withdrawal of philosophers from the association in 1902. American universities boomed through the 20th century's first decade, and psychology grew along with its host campuses. Perhaps more importantly, other institutions, such as psychiatric hospitals and schools for the feebleminded, began hiring psychologists, and this development had many longer term implications for psychology's evolution (Napoli, 1981). During APA's first decade, these universities and other institutions established 30 new psychological laboratories, and by 1910 about 70 U.S. institutions supported such facilities (Garvey, 1929). In 1906, the association elected 19 new members, bringing its membership to about 181. The council announced plans to tighten its application of the membership criteria—"engage[ment] in the advancement of Psychology as a science" (Davis, 1907, p. 203)—that had been in effect since 1894. As noted earlier, it explicitly recognized that its predecessors had "historically and consistently recognized two sorts of qualifications: professional occupation in psychology and research" (Davis, 1907, p. 203). With continued growth of psychology, however, the council decided that it would strictly interpret the first of these criteria, "so that, in the absence of research, positions held in related branches, such as philosophy and education, or temporary positions, such as assistantships in psychology, are not regarded as qualifying a candidate for membership" (p. 203). It even went so far as to propose a constitutional amendment that would have allowed the council, by unanimous vote, to "drop any member of the Association who has not been engaged in the advancement of Psychology for a period of five or more years" (Davis, 1907, p. 203). The association at large, however, referred this amendment back to council, which tabled it the following year. APA may have decided to adopt a more exclusive membership policy, but it was not about to dismiss its long-term members (Woodworth, 1908).

But why did psychologists continue to join the American Psychological Association through its early years, even as it failed in its attempts to develop a range of programs in support of its members' research and other professional interests? More particularly, why did experimentalists retain their APA membership, even as from 1904 they annually met together separately to discuss their scientific research?

An early *American Journal of Psychology* editorial (Hall, 1895), which inflated Hall's role in the origins of American psychology, emphasized the association's role in encouraging cooperation among the country's psychological laboratories and in promoting a psychological "esprit de corps." Through its first years, the association did foster enthusiasm and good feeling that meant much to those who had previously worked in isolation. But this good feeling began to break down by the end of the decade, when several members stopped attending APA meetings lest they run into those with whom they felt antipathy (Münsterberg, 1898; Scripture, 1899). More seriously, the association's record after 1895 belies any claim that it actually promoted psychological cooperation. A deeper answer to these questions lies in recognizing the ecological niche that the association filled for its members in the scientific environment of early 20th-century America. On one level, it supplemented the journals that published their research by fostering, through its annual meetings, the rapid exchange of ideas and information. The experimentalists, of course, found this function of lesser importance than did most other psychologists of the period. But even they found in APA an informal forum in which they could discuss their professional concerns and through which they could follow their colleagues' gossip. Then, as now, the passing hallway conversations and spontaneous discussions over meals that these meetings fostered often meant more to those attending than did any formal sessions.

On another, more significant level, the APA gave its members a conduit that allowed them to communicate with the larger American scientific community and, even more important, one through which others could recognize their discipline. After all, in establishing a new science, psychologists of a century ago faced (or believed they faced) much opposition (or at least ignorance) from their scientific contemporaries. The association's continued ties with the American Society of Naturalists thus meant much to APA's first members, and a 1902 invitation to affiliate with the AAAS and send a delegate to the AAAS council meant even more (Farrand, 1903). From the following year, APA met regularly with the AAAS and took part in the Convocation Week programs that the larger association, following the naturalists' lead, organized annually from 1903 on, during the week between Christmas and New Years Day. To be sure, some psychologists took greater pride that the National Academy of Science elected several of their colleagues to membership, recognizing Cattell in 1901, James in 1903, and Royce in 1906 (Cattell, 1929). But such recognition was beyond most psychologists, and they looked to the American Psychological Association for a sense of legitimacy.

By 1906, then, the American Psychological Association had established itself as an important feature in the environment in which psychology in America thrived. If it could not point to an unblemished record of success during the preceding dozen years, neither could any other contemporaneous scientific organization. More important, during its early years, APA members established a firm foundation on which their successors could build a highly effective institution. This achievement, then, was APA's first real success.

REFERENCES

The American Philosophical Society and the American Philosophical Association. (1902). *Popular Science Monthly, 61*, 91–92.

The American Psychological Association. (1892). *Science, 20* (old series), 104.

The American Psychological Association. (1896). *American Journal of Psychology, 7*, 448–449.

Appel, T. A. (1988). Organizing biology: The American Society of Naturalists and its "Affiliated Societies," 1883–1923. In R. Rainger, K. R. Benson, & J. Maienschein (Eds.), *The American development of biology* (pp. 87–120). Philadelphia: University of Pennsylvania Press.

Baldwin, J. M. (1895). *Mental development in the child and the race: Methods and processes*. New York: Macmillan.

Baldwin, J. M. (Ed.). (1901–1905). *Dictionary of philosophy and psychology* (3 vols. in 4 books). New York: Macmillan.

Baldwin, J. M. (1926). *Between two wars (1861–1921)* (Vol. 1). Boston: Stratford.

Baldwin, J. M., Cattell, J. M., & Jastrow, J. (1898). Physical and mental tests. *Psychological Review, 5*, 172–179.

Baldwin, J. M., Cattell, J. M., Jastrow, J., Sanford, E. C., & Witmer, L. (1897). Preliminary report of the Committee on Physical and Mental Tests. *Psychological Review, 4*, 132–138.

Benjamin, L. T., Jr. (1979). The Midwestern Psychological Association: A history of the organization and its antecedents. *American Psychologist, 34*, 201–213.

Benjamin, L. T., Jr. (1991). A history of the New York Branch of the American Psychological Association, 1903–1935. *American Psychologist, 46*, 1003–1011.

Bliss, C. B. (1899). Proposed changes in the American Psychological Association. *Psychological Review, 6*, 237–238.

Boring, E. G. (1938). The Society of Experimental Psychologists: 1904–1938. *American Journal of Psychology, 51*, 410–423.

Bryan, W. L. (1892). On the development of voluntary motor ability. *American Journal of Psychology, 5*, 125–204.

Buchner, E. F. (1903). Ten years of American Psychology: 1892–1902. *Science, 18*, 193–204, 233–241.

Cahan, E. D. (1984). The genetic psychologies of James Mark Baldwin and Jean Piaget. *Developmental Psychology, 20*, 128–135.

Cattell, J. M. (1893a). Esoteric psychology. *The Independent, 45*, 316–317.

Cattell, J. M. (1893b). On errors of observation. *American Journal of Psychology, 5*, 285–293.

Cattell, J. M. (1893-1894). [Unpublished letter book] In J. M. Cattell papers, Library of Congress, Washington, DC.

Catell, J. M. (1894a). The American Psychological Association. *Psychological Review, 1*, 214-215.

Cattell, J. M. (Ed.). (1894b). *Proceedings of the American Psychological Association*. New York: Macmillan.

Cattell, J. M. (1895). Report of the secretary and treasurer for 1894. *Psychological Review, 2*, 149-152.

Cattell, J. M. (1904a, April 16). *Letter to H. Münsterberg*. In H. Münsterberg papers, Boston Public Library, Boston, MA.

Cattell, J. M. (1904a, May 9). *Letter to H. Münsterberg*. In H. Münsterberg papers, Boston Public Library, Boston, MA.

Cattell, J. M. (1917). Our psychological association and research, *Science, 45*, 275-284.

Cattell, J. M. (1929). Psychology in America. *Science, 70*, 335-347.

Cattell, J. M. (1943). The founding of the association and the Hopkins and Clark laboratories. *Psychological Review, 50*, 61-64.

Cattell, J. M., & Farrand, L. (1896). Physical and mental measurements of students of Columbia University. *Psychological Review, 3*, 618-648.

Chrysostom, B. (1895). The freedom of the will. *Psychological Review, 2*, 157-158.

Creighton, J. E. (1902). The purposes of a philosophical association. *Philosophical Review, 11*, 219-237.

Dallenbach, K. M. (1937). The American Journal of Psychology: 1887-1937. *American Journal of Psychology, 50*, 489-506.

Davis, W. H. (1906). Report of the secretary for 1905. *Psychological Bulletin, 3*, 37-41.

Davis, W. H. (1907). Report of the secretary for 1906. *Psychological Bulletin, 4*, 201-205.

Dennis, W., & Boring, E. G. (1952). The founding of the APA. *American Psychologist, 7*, 95-97.

Farrand, L. (1896). Series of physical and mental tests on the students of Columbia College. *Psychological Review, 3*, 124.

Farrand, L. (1897). Report of the secretary and treasurer for 1896. *Psychological Review, 4*, 107-110.

Farrand, L. (1898). Report of the secretary and treasurer for 1897. *Psychological Review, 5*, 145-147.

Farrand, L. (1899). Report of the secretary for 1898. *Psychological Review, 6*, 146-148.

Farrand, L. (1901). Report of the secretary for 1900. *Psychological Review, 8*, 158-160.

Farrand, L. (1902). Report of the secretary for 1901. *Psychological Review, 9*, 134-136.

Farrand, L. (1903). Report of the secretary for 1902. *Psychological Review, 10,* 150–153.

Farrand, L. (1904). Report of the secretary for 1903. *Psychological Bulletin, 1,* 33–36.

Farrand, L. (1905). Report of the secretary for 1904. *Psychological Bulletin, 2,* 37–38.

Fernberger, S. W. (1932). The American Psychological Association: A historical summary, 1892–1930. *Psychological Bulletin, 29,* 1–89.

Fernberger, S. W. (1943). The American Psychological Association, 1892–1942. *Psychological Review, 50,* 33–60.

Franklin, C. L. (1900, December 21). *Letter to J. M. Cattell.* In J. M. Cattell papers, Library of Congress, Washington, DC.

Fullerton, G. S., & Cattell, J. M. (1892). On the perception of small differences, with special reference of the extent, force, and time of movement. *Publications of the University of Pennsylvania* (Philosophical Series No. 2).

Gardiner, H. N. (1926). The first twenty-five years of the American Philosophical Association. *Philosophical Review, 35,* 145–158.

Garvey, C. R. (1929). List of American psychological laboratories. *Psychological Bulletin, 26,* 652–660.

Gilbert, J. B. (1977). Anthropometrics in the U.S. Bureau of Education: The case of Arthur MacDonald's "laboratory." *History of Educatoin Quarterly, 17,* 169–195.

Goodwin, C. J. (1985). On the origins of Titchener's experimentalists. *Journal of the History of the Behavioral Sciences, 21,* 383–389.

Gore, W. G. (1905a). Meeting of the north central section of the American Psychological Association. *Psychological Bulletin, 2,* 6–10.

Gore, W. G. (1905b). Proceedings of the meeting of the north central section of the American Psychological Association. *Psychological Bulletin, 2,* 200–203.

Hale, M., Jr. (1980). *Human science and social order: Hugo Münsterberg and the origins of applied psychology.* Philadelphia, PA: Temple University Press.

Hall, G. S. (1895). Editorial. *American Journal of Psychology, 7,* 3–8.

Hall, G. S. (1923). *Life and confessions of a psychologist.* New York: Appleton.

Hartwell, E. M. (1893–1894). Interrelation of mental, moral, and physical training. In *Report of the Commissioner of Education* (pp. 458–459). Washington, DC: U.S. Government Printing Office.

Hawkins, H. (1960). *Pioneer: A history of the Johns Hopkins University, 1874–1889.* Ithaca, NY: Cornell University Press.

James, W. (1893, December 30). *Letter to J. M. Cattell.* In J. M. Cattell papers, Library of Congress, Washington, DC.

Jastrow, J. (1900). The modern occult. *Popular Science Monthly, 57,* 449–472.

Jastrow, J. (1943). American psychology in the '80's and '90's. *Psychological Review, 50,* 65–67.

Judd, C. H. (1904, March 29). *Letter to H. Münsterberg.* In H. Münsterberg papers, Boston Public Library, Boston, MA.

Kevles, D. J. (1978). *The physicists: The history of a scientific community in modern America.* New York: Knopf.

Koelsch, W. A. (1987). *Clark University, 1887–1987: A narrative history.* Worcester, MA: Clark University Press.

Leuba, J. H. (1900, May 23). *Letter to J. M. Cattell.* In J. M. Cattell papers, Library of Congress, Washington, DC.

MacDonald, A. (1900, July 6). *Letter to J. M. Cattell.* In J. M. Cattell papers, Library of Congress, Washington, DC.

Mauskopf, S. H. (1989). The history of the American Society for Psychical Research: An interpretation. *Journal of the American Society for Psychical Research, 83,* 7–29.

McBride, K. E. (1947). James H. Leuba: 1867–1946. *American Journal of Psychology, 60,* 645–646.

Münsterberg, H. (1898a). *Letter to J. M. Cattell.* In J. M. Cattell papers, Library of Congress, Washington, DC.

Münsterberg, H. (1898b). The danger from experimental psychology. *Atlantic Monthly, 81,* 159–167.

Münsterberg, H. (1904, May 28). *Letter to J. M. Cattell.* In H. Münsterberg papers, Boston Public Library, Boston, MA.

Murray, F. S., & Rowe, F. B. (1979). Psychology laboratories in the United States prior to 1900. *Teaching of Psychology, 6,* 19–21.

Napoli, D. S. (1981). *Architects of adjustment: The history of the psychological profession in the United States.* Port Washington, NY: Kennikat Press.

Notes. (1896). *Psychological Review, 3,* 705.

Notes. (1898). *Psychological Review, 5,* 344–346, 554, 677.

Notes. (1900). *Psychological Review, 7,* 104, 323–324.

Notes. (1902). *Psychological Review, 9,* 103, 216, 327–328, 431–432.

Notes. (1903). *Psychological Review, 10,* 223–224.

Notes and news. (1900). *American Journal of Psychology, 11,* 280–281.

Notes and news. (1904). *Psychological Bulletin, 1,* 45, 133–135, 291–292.

Nyhart, L. K. (1979). *The American Naturalist, 1867–1886: A case study of the relationship between amateur and professional naturalists in nineteenth-century America* (Senior thesis), Princeton University.

O'Donnell, J. M. (1985). *The origins of behaviorism: American psychology, 1870–1920.* New York: New York University Press.

Rand, B. (1905a). *Bibliography of philosophy, psychology, and cognate subjects* (Vol. 1). New York: Macmillan.

Rand, B. (1905b). *Bibliography of philosophy, psychology, and cognate subjects* (Vol. 2). New York: Macmillan.

Ross, D. (1972). *G. Stanley Hall: The psychologist as prophet*. Chicago: University of Chicago Press.

Rossiter, M. W. (1982). *Women scientists in America: Struggles and strategies to 1940*. Baltimore: John Hopkins University Press.

Sanford, E. C. (1896a, January 10). *Letter to E. B. Titchener*. In E. B. Titchener papers, Cornell University Archives, Ithaca, NY.

Sanford, E. C. (1896b). Report of the secretary and treasurer for 1895. *Psychological Review, 3*, 121–123.

Sanford, E. C. (1902a, May 24). *Letter to J. M. Cattell*. In J. M. Cattell papers, Library of Congress, Washington, DC.

Sanford, E. C. (1902b, December 1). *Letter to J. M. Cattell*. In J. M. Cattell papers, Library of Congress, Washington, DC.

Scientific notes and news. (1895). *Science, 2*, 803.

Scientific notes and news. (1898). *Science, 8*, 73.

Scripture, E. W. (1899, November 29). *Letter to J. M. Cattell*. In J. M. Cattell papers, Library of Congress, Washington, DC.

Sexton, V. S. (1980). Edward Aloysius Pace. *Psychological Research, 42*, 39–47.

Sokal, M. M. (1980). Science and James McKeen Cattell, 1894–1945. *Science, 209*, 43–52.

Sokal, M. M. (Ed.). (1981). *An education in psychology: James McKeen Cattell's journal and letters from Germany and England, 1880–1888*. Cambridge, MA: MIT Press.

Sokal, M. M. (1987). James McKeen Cattell and mental anthropometry: Nineteenth-century science and reform and the origins of psychological testing. In M. Sokal (Ed.), *Psychological testing and American society, 1890–1930* (pp. 21–45). New Brunswick, NJ: Rutgers University Press.

Sokal, M. M. (1990). G. Stanley Hall and the institutional character of psychology at Clark, 1889–1920. *Journal of the History of the Behavioral Sciences, 26*, 114–124.

U.S. Bureau of the Census. (1975). *Historical statistics of the United States: Colonial times to 1970* (Vol. 1). Washington, DC: U.S. Government Printing Office.

Veysey, L. (1965). *The emergence of the American university*. Chicago: University of Chicago Press.

Veysey, L. (1979). The plural organized worlds of the humanities. In A. Oleson & J. Voss (Eds.), *The organization of knowledge in modern America, 1860–1920* (pp. 51–106). Baltimore: Johns Hopkins University Press.

Wetmore, K. (1992). *A note on the founding of the American Psychological Association*. Unpublished manuscript, Harvard Medical School.

Wilson, D. J. (1979). Professionalization and organized discussion in the American Philosophical Association, 1900–1902. *Journal of the History of Philosophy, 17*, 53–69.

Woodworth, R. S. (1908). Report of the secretary for 1907. *Psychological Bulletin, 5*, 33–37.

9

THE ORIGINS OF THE PSYCHOLOGICAL EXPERIMENT AS A SOCIAL INSTITUTION

KURT DANZIGER

Whatever else it may be, the psychological experiment is clearly a social institution that has flourished in certain societies and that implies patterns of social regulations that closely circumscribe the relationships of those who participate in it. The investigative situations in which knowledge about human psychology is gathered are highly institutionalized and involve a generally accepted distribution of role expectations among the participants, a clearly understood status differential, and an elaborate set of rules governing the permissible interactions among the role incumbents.

The sizable literature devoted to various aspects of the social psychology of the psychological experiment (e.g., Adair, 1973; Jung, 1982; Rosenthal & Rosnow, 1975; Silverman, 1977) has paid virtually no attention to the history of the social features of the psychological experiment. Apart from Schultz's (1970) recognition of the fact that there *is* a history

---

Reprinted from *American Psychologist, 40*, 133–140 (1985). Copyright © 1985 by the American Psychological Association. Reprinted with permission of the author.

to the use of human subjects in psychological research, there has been no systematic attempt to uncover this history.

Because the rules of scientific experimentation prescribe the preparation of a formal account of the proceedings for publication, the literature in psychological journals contains much material that throws light on historically changing social practices. Of course, published experimental articles mainly contain information on the public and formal aspects of the experimental situation, but it is precisely these aspects that are of interest in tracing historical changes in institutionalized patterns.

In pursuing this kind of analysis the wisest course is to pay special attention to historical beginnings. It is in the early stages of the growth of a field that fundamental directions of development are laid down and that traditions are established that become implicit models for later generations. Historians and philosophers of science have long recognized this by paying an extraordinary amount of attention to those 17th century developments that mark the beginning of modern physical science, even though the scientific production of that period represents only a tiny fraction of what was accomplished later. In the case of experimental psychology, the last two decades of the 19th and the first two decades of the 20th century occupy a similar position.

The material that provides the basis for the present discussion is drawn from the first half of this period, a time when the practice of psychological experimentation was in the process of becoming institutionalized. It involves an analysis of the procedures reported in all empirical studies published in the major relevant journals for the period from 1879 to 1898. This includes two German-language journals (*Philosophische Studien* and *Zeitschrift für Psychologie und Physiologie der Sinnesorgane*), two French language journals (*Revue philosophique* and *Anneé psychologique*), and four English-language journals (*Mind, Pedagogical Seminary, American Journal of Psychology,* and *Psychological Review*).

INCIPIENT INSTITUTIONALIZATION

One striking feature that characterized the first half of this period is the absence of an agreed-upon uniform nomenclature for identifying the participants in a psychological experiment. Although in the case of Wundt and his first group of students we are dealing with a research community that was quite sharply defined in terms of goals, methods, and knowledge of each other's work, there are clearly no strong conventions about the identification of experimenter and subject roles. In their published reports, different members of the Leipzig group used different terms to refer to experimenters and subjects in their experimental studies. The terms *experimenter* and *subject* (*Versuchperson*) do occur in several of the experimental reports, but their usage is far from general, and they are also used interchangeably with other terms. Some of these other terms were to have a more extended life, but others hardly survived this early period.

Not only are there several alternative labels for the experimental subject, but there is also no uniformity of usage within the research community. This becomes particularly striking when two investigators are concerned with the same type of experimentally established phenomena but use different terms to refer to their experimental subjects. For example, in an early investigation of the "time sense," Kollert (1883) referred to his subjects as *reactors*, whereas Estel (1885), whose study followed directly from Kollert's, switched to the term *observers*. This lack of semantic uniformity is also reflected in the fact that some investigators used two or three terms interchangeably within the same experimental report to refer to their experimental subjects (e.g., Merkel, 1885).

Echoes of the Leipzig pattern during this early period are to be found in scattered experimental psychological reports published in English. Thus G. Stanley Hall variously referred to the experimenter as the *operator* or the *attendant*, and to the subject as the *observer, percipient,* or *subject* (Hall & Donaldson, 1885; Hall & Jastrow, 1886; Hall & Motora, 1887). One early report from the Johns Hopkins laboratory used the awkward formulation *the individual under experiment* (Stevens, 1886), but not surprisingly, this did not catch on. Among these early experimenters Cattell was relatively consistent in his use of the term *subject*, but even he used it interchangeably with *observer* (Cattell, 1888; Cattell & Bryant, 1889) at times, and in his pioneering article on mental tests he introduced the unsuccessful term *experimentee* (Cattell, 1890).

The original terminological chaos soon yielded to a very limited number of accepted terms, as the practice of psychological experimentation established its own recognized models and institutionalized patterns. By the mid-1890s, half of the experimental reports in the *American Journal of Psychology* and *Psychological Review* used the term *subject*, and a quarter preferred *observer*. *Reagent* was a distant third, and all other terms have remained purely idiosyncratic. However, it is worth noting that the crystallization of routine practice did not involve the adoption of a *single* model of usage but of a small number of alternative models. It took virtually another half century for one model to achieve overwhelming preponderance. As late as 1930 there was heated discussion about the rival claims of *observer* and *subject* (Bentley, 1929; Dashiell, 1930). The establishment of alternative terminologies was only a sign of the multimodal development of early experimental practice that needs to be examined.

ROLE STRUCTURE OF THE WUNDTIAN EXPERIMENT

In the social system of the contemporary mainstream experiment the function of serving as a data source is confined to the subject role, and this function cannot be combined with theoretical conceptualization, task administration, or publishing. No such segregation existed in the early stages of psychological experimentation. Wundt's students frequently alternated with one another as stimulus administrators and sources of data within the same experiment. The case of Cattell and Berger has been documented in some detail (Sokal, 1980); another early instance is provided by Lorenz and Merkel (Lorenz, 1885). Moreover, the person under whose name the published account of the experiment appeared was not necessarily the one who had played the experimenter role. For instance, Mehner (1885) published an article on an experiment in which he had functioned solely as the subject although two other persons had functioned as experimenters at various times.

Nor was the role of functioning as a data source considered incompatible with the function of theoretical conceptualization. Wundt, who generally shouldered much of this latter function himself in the Leipzig experiments, also featured quite regularly as a subject or data source in these experiments, especially in the early days of his laboratory (e.g., Dietze, 1885; Estel, 1885; Friedrich, 1883; Kollert, 1883; Tischer, 1883; Trautscholdt, 1883). The experimental reports, however, were published under the names of his students. It is perfectly clear that the role of data source, or subject, was considered to be of higher or more important status than the role of experimenter. The role of experimental subject was quite compatible with Wundt's exalted status, but once his laboratory got under way, none of the experimental reports mention him as having actually functioned in the role of experimenter.

We might also note that the participants in these early psychological experiments were never strangers to one another. They interacted outside the laboratory as professor and student, as fellow students, and often as friends. They clearly saw themselves as engaged in a common enterprise in which all the participants were regarded as collaborators, including the person who happened to be functioning as the experimental subject at any particular time. In fact, when introducing the experimental subjects in their published reports, authors would sometimes do so not by saying that the observers (or subjects) were so and so, but by saying "my co-workers (*Mitarbeiter*) were," followed by the names (Lange, 1888; Titchener, 1893). This involved a complex set of reciprocal obligations and services, such as functioning as experimenter and subject for each other.

Although we may analyze the psychological experiment as a miniature social system, it is far from being hermetically sealed off from broader institutional and cultural contexts. The social structure of a psychological research situation cannot be created in a cultural and institutional vacuum but must make use of whatever material happens to be available at a particular time and place. The Wundtian program of systematic psychological research constituted a genuine innovation, but its social features clearly carried the mark of the institutional context in which it arose. That context was, of course, the late 19th century German university with its elitism and its emphasis on active involvement in research for both faculty and students. Thus, its basic organizational units were not teaching departments, as in America, but research institutes, of which Wundt's laboratory was an example, even though it did not gain formal recognition for a few years. Admittance to these institutes and research seminars was restricted, but once students were accepted they became involved in a collaborative enterprise; although the direction was determined by the professor, there was also a basic demand that students involve themselves actively in the material under investigation. Where that material was defined in terms of Wundtian concepts of psychic causality, the structure of the investigative situation followed as a matter of course (Danziger, 1980). The collaborative interchange of roles and the high status of the observer or subject role were a natural consequence of extending an existing social pattern of academic research to a subject matter that the investigators carried around in their heads instead of finding it spread out before them.

EXPERIMENTAL HYPNOSIS AS THE ALTERNATIVE

At exactly the same time that Wundt's Leipzig laboratory was getting under way, a group of French investigators embarked on the systematic use of experimental hypnosis as a tool of psychological research. First on the scene was Richet (1879, 1880), soon followed by Beaunis (1885, 1886), Binet and Féré (Binet, 1886; Binet & Féré, 1885) and the Belgian, Delboeuf (1886a, 1886b). In their studies, various psychological functions were investigated under conditions of experimentally induced hypnosis. Contrary to the practice in Leipzig, there was no interchange of experimental roles among the participants in these French studies. There was a clear and permanent distinction between experimenters and individuals experimented on. Experimenters remained experimenters, and hypnotic subjects remained hypnotic subjects. Moreover, there was a glaring status difference between these male scientists and their lay subjects, who were generally female. The distribution of social functions approximated the pattern in the typical modern experiment, with the function of providing the data source being strictly segregated in an experimental subject role.

The link made between role-playing in hypnosis and role-playing in the psychological experiment, which ushered in the period of contemporary concern with the social psychology of the psychological experiment (Orne,

1962), turns out to be more than just an analogy. From the point of view of its social psychology it is the hypnosis experiment rather than the Wundtian experiment that constitutes the historical prototype of the modern psychology experiment. By 1890, Binet had turned from experiments on hypnotized subjects to experiments on infants (Binet, 1890). This was possible without altering the essential social structure of the experimental situation. For the Wundtian experiment, on the other hand, this kind of extension of scope was not possible, and in due course it paid for this limitation by becoming virtually extinct.

As we have seen, the hypnosis experiment of the 1880s involved a rigid and well-defined role and status structure from the beginning. What was the origin of this instant social structure? Very likely, it was the medical context in which these experiments were carried out. The subjects in these experiments were essentially a clinical population of hysterics and "somnambulists," and the experimenters were for the most part strongly identified with the medical profession. The experiments themselves arose directly out of ongoing medical research into the nature of hysteria and hypnosis. Before experimental sessions began, the experimenter and the subject were already linked in a doctor–patient relationship, and the essential features of this relationship were simply continued into the experimental situation. The whole situation was defined in medical terms. A crucial feature of this definition was the understanding that the psychological states and phenomena under study were something that the subject or patient underwent or suffered. This contrasted quite sharply with the Wundtian experiment in which most of the phenomena studied were understood as the products of the individual's activity.

The much less fluid social structure of the hypnosis experiment is reflected in a high degree of linguistic uniformity in referring to the participants in the experimental situation. It is in this context that we find the first consistent usage of the term *subject* in experimental psychology. These medically oriented experimenters quite spontaneously referred to a case they experimented on as a *subject* (*sujet*), because that term had long been in use to designate a living being who was the object of medical care or naturalistic observation. This usage goes back at least to Buffon in the 18th century. Before that a *subject* was a corpse used for purposes of anatomical dissection, and by the early 19th century people spoke of patients as being good or bad subjects for surgery (*Grand Larousse*, 1973; Littré, 1968). When hypnosis came to be seen as an essentially medical matter, which was certainly the case in Paris in the 1880s, there was nothing more natural than to extend an already established linguistic usage to yet another object of medical scrutiny. However, within the medical context we immediately get the formulation *healthy subject* (*sujet sains*) (Féré, 1885, and in the titles of studies by Bremaud and by Bottey cited in Dessoir, 1888) when it is a matter of comparing the performance of normal and abnormal individuals. From this it is a very short step to the generalized use of the term *subject* to refer to any individual under psychological investigation. This step was quickly taken by Binet and others.

Thus, in the earliest years of experimental psychology there simultaneously emerged two very different models of the psychological experiment as a social situation. These can be called the Leipzig model and the Paris model. The Leipzig model involved a high degree of fluidity in the allocation of social functions in the experimental situation, reflected in the lack of a uniform terminology to refer to experimenter and subject roles as such. Persons playing these roles at any particular time were more likely to be defined in terms of their relationship to the physical apparatus than in terms of their relationship to each other. At the same time, the subject function had a higher status than the experimenter function, though these functions could be assumed by any participant in the experimental situation. In the Paris model, by contrast, experimenter and subject roles were rigidly segregated, with the experimenter clearly being in charge and the subject serving as an object of study who underwent certain manipulative interventions on the part of the experimenter. With this went a more uniform terminology that unambiguously identified the subject as such. The two models were typically employed to investigate different aspects of psychological functioning: the Leipzig model to study aspects of normal cognition and the Paris model to study abnormal functioning.

The occasional English-language studies of this early period were not the product of a research community as well defined as the Leipzig and Paris groups but were rather in the nature of relatively isolated individual contributions. Accordingly, we find that in this period British and American contributors to the experimental literature tended to follow French and German models. This is reflected in their use of terminology. The first uses of the term *subject* occurred in the context of experiments involving the hypnotic state (Gurney, 1884; Hall, 1883). It is interesting to note that at this time G. Stanley Hall used the term *subject* in the context of his work in the area of experimental hypnosis but switched to the terms *percipient* (Hall & Donaldson, 1885) and *observer* (Hall & Jastrow, 1886) when reporting on his experimental work with normal individuals.

Cattell appears to have been the first to use the English term *subject* in describing a psychological experiment involving a normal adult human data source (Cattell, 1886). However, he was by no means sure of his ground, for in an 1889 paper coauthored by him we find the formulation *an observer or subject* (Cattell & Bryant, 1889), with *subject* in inverted commas. Putting the term *subject* in inverted commas, when used in this context, was quite common in the English literature of this time (Gurney, 1884, 1887; Gurney, Myers, & Podmore, 1886, pp. 330–331; Jacobs, 1887), indicating that this usage was of recent origin, possibly influenced by French models. The English term *subject* had acquired similar medical connotations as its French equivalent. In the 18th century it was used to refer to a corpse employed for anatomical dissection, and by the middle of the 19th century it could also mean "a person who presents himself for or undergoes medical or surgical treatment" (*Oxford English Dictionary*, 1933, Vol. 10). Hence its use in the context of hypnosis. It was already used occasionally by James Braid (e.g., Braid, 1960, p. 209).

AMERICAN INNOVATIONS

By the turn of the century there were clear signs that American psychology would develop a style of research that differed in certain fundamental ways from either of the European models. The most striking feature of this style was the introduction of a new object of psychological investigation, that of a *population* of individuals.

In the forms in which it was first established, the psychological experiment involved strictly one-to-one relationships among the participants. However, there was another possibility. The recently expanded and bureaucratized educational systems of the economically advanced countries had produced large captive groups of young people who were not only a source of new psychological problems but who could also be seen as a potential source of psychological data. Although there were a few isolated and sporadic European moves in this direction, the systematic pursuit of this new style of psychological investigation was initially an American phenomenon.

A primitive form of the new style was promoted with considerable early success by G. Stanley Hall. The research reported in his journal *Pedagogical Seminary* (founded only 4 years after the *American Journal of Psychology*) differs from other psychological research of the time in several interesting ways, not the least of which is its predominant focus on psychological characteristics of populations rather than individuals. Studies are commonly based on data from hundreds of subjects, and investigations involving thousands of children are by no means rare (e.g., Barnes, 1895; Kratz, 1896; Schallenberger, 1894).

Obviously, this kind of research involved a very different set of social relationships than those that characterized the academic laboratories of the time. The contrast with the Leipzig model was total, with the Paris model, somewhat less so. As in the latter, the asymmetry between investigators and the human objects of investigation was clearly established and fixed. Also, in both cases the human data source was categorized as something less than a normally responsible and enlightened adult. However, the novel features of Hall's research situations are so profound that one cannot possibly regard them simply as a replication of the Paris model. There is a fundamental shift of interest from the *analysis* of psychological processes, necessarily manifested in specific individuals, to the *distribution* of psychological characteristics in populations. Age and sex differences, as well as differences among various educationally or clinically defined populations, are the bread and butter of this research. This means that individual subjects become totally anonymous, and their specific contributions to the research enterprise remain unidentified and unreported. The research contact between investigator and subject becomes much less intense and extends over much shorter periods of time. Psychological tasks are administered in group sessions, and instead of an extended sequence of interactions between investigator and subjects, there is generally a one-shot episode of instruction followed by response. Paper and pencil instruments are the favored medium for this exchange.

Although the research sponsored by Hall could find much common ground with emerging work on mental tests, it could be called *experimental* only within the loosest definition of that term. Nevertheless, some of the American experimental literature of the time bears the marks of a similar style (e.g., Baldwin, Shaw, & Warren, 1895; Griffing, 1895; Jastrow, 1894; Kirkpatrick, 1894). Here the experimental tasks were administered to children and college students in group sessions, and the results were presented simply as group averages without any analysis of the response patterns of individual subjects. This was a striking departure from the then-established practice of attributing all experimental results to specific individuals. What emerged was an impersonal style of research in which experimental subjects played an anonymous role, experimenter–subject contacts were relatively brief, and the experimenter was interested in the aggregate data to be obtained from many subjects.

What would be an appropriate label for this model of experimentation, which clearly differed in important ways from the other two models? The early investigators themselves sometimes referred to these as *statistical* studies. But one hesitates to follow them because within the Leipzig model the statistics of error were employed quite widely. It was more a matter of the function of statistics being different in the two cases. The third model could be referred to as "Galtonian," but in the present context that might be misleading because the application of Galtonian statistics to studies of this type effectively belongs to a later period. Some early studies sponsored by Franz Boas at Clark (Bolton, 1891; Bryan, 1892) were exceptional in their statistical sophistication. Most of these early "statistical" studies were statistical only in the crude sense that they were trying to obtain averages and percentages. The application of Galtonian, or more accurately Pearsonian, techniques to studies of this type did not really develop until after the turn of the century, with Boas's expupil, Thorndike, playing a key role.

Both conceptually and historically it makes for greater clarity to distinguish between the forms of statistical technology and the research practices that provide the context for the application of this technology. This is not to deny the development of intimate ties between the two aspects, as indeed happened in the 20th century history of the Galtonian paradigm. But in terms of the emergence of certain patterns of social practice in psychological research, we have to consider the research community most closely identified with this historical process. Pinpointing such a community in early American psychology is a little more doubtful than in the European cases that have been discussed. Many American psychologists engaged in a mixture of practices at that time. However, one major center clearly overshadowed all others in its systematic employment of new research practices, not sanctioned by the accepted European models. This was Hall's little empire at Clark, and so it does not seem inappropriate to refer to this third pattern of research practice as the Clark model.

It seems, then, that psychology entered the 20th century with three different models for structuring the social interactions that are a necessary part of its research enterprise. For a few years these models coexisted relatively peacefully, and occasionally two of them would even appear side by side in the same research report. But this was not a stable situation. Social relations in the laboratory were not hermetically sealed off from social relations outside. The demands of a wider social practice brought changes to investigative practices and favored some at the expense of others. New forms of older models and composite models appeared. Sometimes these were associated with monopolistic claims regarding their ability to provide the only guaranteed framework for the generation of true and worthwhile psychological knowledge. However, detailed consideration of these later developments lies outside the scope of this article.

IMPLICATIONS AND QUESTIONS

The distinctions among the patterns of investigative social practice discussed here show that from its earliest beginnings experimental psychology involved a structuring of social interaction and that alternative ways of accomplishing this were always available. An analysis of these original cases suggests certain general implications.

One of these implications concerns the embeddedness of social psychological aspects of experimentation in a historically limited normative framework. For instance, it is not plausible to assume that generalizations about the social psychology of the subject role in any one of these models would hold for the other two. Yet, virtually all of the existing empirical work in this area tends to take a certain social structure of experimentation for granted. Although this has some practical justification, the principle of the historicity of social psychological generalizations (Gergen & Gergen, 1984) needs to be applied also to the social psychology of the psychological experiment.

Discussions about the pros and cons of experimentation in psychology represent another area that might well benefit from a more historically informed perspective. Such discussions are apt to revolve around something that is identified as *the* psychological experiment (e.g., Gadlin & Ingle, 1975; Kruglanski, 1976). But the definite article can be misleading in this context. From its beginnings experimental psychology used more than a single model of the experiment, and the differences among these models may be of more profound significance than their similarities. It is true that at certain times and in certain locations a particular model of experimentation achieved an overwhelming predominance, but this does not establish the existence of the psychological experiment as an ahistorical entity. Instead of equating a particular form of experimentation with experimentation as such, we should be asking questions about the scope and limits of different social patterns of experimentation (Hendrick, 1977).

Another implication concerns the social contextualization of psychology. We know that the historical development of psychology cannot be divorced from characteristics of the culture and from structural features of the wider society within which psychology exists (e.g., Buss, 1979). Usually these influences are thought to operate on the level of conceptual preferences and theoretical biases. But if psychological ideas are not produced in a social vacuum, the same holds true of the psychological experiment as a miniature social system. The social interactions that are necessary for psychological experimentation were not designed from scratch on the basis of purely rational considerations but simply grew out of patterns of interaction that were already familiar to the participants. Medical and educational institutions provided the original forms of these patterns, just as medical and educational theories provided the sources of many psychological concepts. Other social institutions probably became relevant at a later stage. The point is that methodology is no more free of the influence of social contextual factors than is the formation of theoretical concepts.

This leads to a third implication, which concerns the need to relate differences in theoretical position to differences in the social practice of investigation. We get a one-sided, idealized picture of the development of psychology if we see it only in terms of changes in theoretical orientation. Where theoretical differences have been profound, they have generally been linked to different investigative practices (for an example from the history of psychology, see Böhme, 1977). This is true of the cases examined here, but it is equally true of 20th century cases like psychoanalysis, Gestalt psychology, and behaviorism. Once we have recognized this we have to resist the temptation of engaging in fruitless speculation about the chicken and egg problem of the priority of theoretical orientation and the social practices involved in investigation. What is important is the recognition that psychological theorizing is not an activity totally divorced from the social relationships that psychologists establish with those who are the source of their data.

The social situations that characterize psychological experiments are explicitly designed to function as knowledge-generating situations. Interactions that lead to the production of data that count as psychological knowledge are part of what have been called "social proof structures" (White, 1977). In the examples discussed here, different patterns of interaction were associated with the production of different kinds of knowledge. Insofar as this can be generalized, it leads to a relativization of questions about experimentation in psychology. As long as such questions are framed in terms of experimentation in general and knowledge in the abstract, they are likely to remain sterile. A more promising approach would involve raising questions about relationships between the social structure of knowledge-generating situations and the nature of their products. In addressing such questions it would be as well not to ignore the potentially rich source of evidence buried in the published record of psychologists' past practices.

REFERENCES

Adair, J. G. (1973). *The human subject: The psychology of the psychology experiment.* Boston: Little, Brown.

Baldwin, J. M., Shaw, W. J., & Warren, H. C. (1895). Memory for square size. *Psychological Review, 2,* 236–244.

Barnes, E. (1895). Punishment as seen by children. *Pedagogical Seminary, 3,* 235–245.

Beaunis, H. (1885). L'expérimentation en psychologie par le somnambulisme provoqué [Psychological experimentation by induced somnambulism]. *Revue philosophique, 20,* 1–36.

Beaunis, H. (1886). *Études physiologiques et psychologiques sur le somnambulsime provoqué* [Physiological and psychological studies on induced somnambulism]. Paris: Alcan.

Bentley, M. (1929). "Observer" and "subject." *American Journal of Psychology, 41,* 682–683.

Binet, A. (1886). *La psychologie du raisonnement: Recherches experimentales par l'hypnotisme* [The psychology of reasoning: Experimental investigations by means of hypnotism]. Paris: Alcan.

Binet, A. (1890). Recherches sur les movements chez quelques jeunes enfants [Investigations of the motor activity of young children]. *Revue philosophique, 29,* 297–309.

Binet, A., & Féré, C. (1885). L'hypnotisme chez les hysteriques: Le transfert psychique [Hypnotism with hysterics: Mental transfer]. *Revue philosophique, 19,* 1–25.

Böhme, G. (1977). Cognitive norms, knowledge-interests and the constitution of the scientific object: A case study in the functioning of rules for experimentation. In E. Mendelsohn, P. Weingart, & R. Whitley (Eds.), *The social production of scientific knowledge* (pp. 129–141). Dordrecht, The Netherlands: Reidel.

Bolton, T. L. (1891). The growth of memory in school children. *American Journal of Psychology, 4*, 362–380.

Braid, J. (1960). *Braid on hypnotism: The beginnings of modern hypnosis.* New York: Julian Press. (Original work published 1843)

Bryan, W. L. (1892). The development of voluntary motor ability. *American Journal of Psychology, 5*, 123–204.

Buss, A. R. (Ed.). (1979). *Psychology in social context.* New York: Irvington.

Cattell, J. M. (1886). The time taken up by cerebral operations. *Mind, 11*, 220–242.

Cattell, J. M. (1888). Psychometrische Untersuchungen III [Psychometric investigations]. *Philosophische Studien, 4*, 241–250.

Cattell, J. M. (1890). Mental tests and measurements. *Mind, 15*, 373–380.

Cattell, J. M., & Bryant, S. (1889). Mental association investigated by experiment. *Mind, 14*, 230–250.

Dashiell, J. F. (1930). A reply to Professor Bentley. *Psychological Review, 37*, 183–185.

Danziger, K. (1980). Wundt's psychological experiment in the light of his philosophy of science. *Psychological Research, 42*, 109–122.

Delboeuf, J. (1886a). La memoire chez les hypnotisés [Memory in the hypnotized]. *Revue philosophique, 21*, 441–472.

Delboeuf, J. (1886b). De l'influence de l'education et de l'imitation dans le somnambulisme provoqué [The influence of education and of imitation in induced somnambulism]. *Revue philosophique, 22*, 146–171.

Dessoir, M. (1888). *Bibliographie des Hypnotismus* [Bibliography of hypnotism]. Berlin: Duncker.

Dietze, G. (1885). Untersuchungen über den Umfang des Bewusstseins bei regelmassig auf einander folgenden Schalleindrücken [Investigations on the range of consciousness with auditory sensations in regular sequence]. *Philosophische Studien, 2*, 362–393.

Estel, V. (1885). Neue Versuche über den Zeitsinn [New experiments on the time sense]. *Philosophische Studien, 2*, 37–65.

Féré, C. (1885). Sensation et mouvement [Sensation and movement]. *Revue philosophique, 20*, 337–368.

Friedrich, M. (1883). Über die Apperceptionsdauer bei einfachen und zusammengesetzten Vorstellungen [On the duration of apperception with simple and compound ideas]. *Philosophische Studien, 1*, 39–77.

Gadlin, H., & Ingle, G. (1975). Through the one-way mirror: The limits of experimental self reflection. *American Psychologist, 30*, 1003–1009.

Gergen, K. J., & Gergen, M. (Eds.). (1984). *Historical social psychology*. Hillsdale, NJ: Erlbaum.

Grand Larousse de la langue Française. (1973). (vol. 6). Paris: Librairie Larousse.

Griffing, H. (1895). On the development of visual perception and attention. *American Journal of Psychology, 7*, 227–236.

Gurney, E. (1884). The stages of hypnotism. *Mind, 9*, 110–121.

Gurney, E. (1887). Further problems of hypnotism. *Mind, 12*, 212–222.

Gurney, E., Myers, F. W. H., & Podmore, F. (1886). *Phantasms of the living* (2 vols). London: Trübner.

Hall, G. S. (1883). Reaction time and attention in the hypnotic state. *Mind, 8*, 170–182.

Hall, G. S., & Donaldson, H. H. (1885). Motor sensations on the skin. *Mind, 10*, 557–572.

Hall, G. S., & Jastrow, J. (1886). Studies of rhythm. *Mind, 11*, 55–62.

Hall, G. S., & Motora, Y. (1887). Dermal sensitiveness to gradual pressure changes. *American Journal of Psychology, 1*, 72–98.

Hendrick, C. (1977). Role-taking, role playing and the laboratory experiment. *Personality and Social Psychology Bulletin, 3*, 467–478.

Jacobs, J. (1887). Experiments on "prehension." *Mind, 12*, 75–79.

Jastrow, J. (1894). Community and association of ideas: A statistical study. *Psychological Review, 1*, 152–158.

Jung, J. (1982). *The experimenter's challenge: Methods and issues in psychological research*. New York: Macmillan.

Kirkpatrick, E. A. (1894). An experimental study of memory. *Psychological Review, 1*, 602–609.

Kollert, J. (1883). Untersuchungen über den Zeitsinn [Investigations on the time sense]. *Philosophische Studien, 1*, 78–89.

Kratz, H. C. (1896). Characteristics of the best teacher as recognized by children. *Pedagogical Seminary, 3*, 413–418.

Kruglanski, A. W. (1976). On the paradigmatic objections to experimental psychology. *American Psychologist, 31*, 655–663.

Lange, L. (1888). Neue Experimente über den Vorgang der einfachen Reaction auf Sinneseindrücke [New experiments on the process of simple reaction to sensory impressions]. *Philosophische Studien, 4*, 497–510.

Littré, E. (1968). *Dictionnaire de la langue Française* [Dictionary of the French language, vol. 7]. Paris: Gallimard/Hachette.

Lorenz, G. (1885). Die Methode der richtigen und falschen Fälle in ihrer Anwendung auf Schallempfindungen [The method of right and wrong cases applied to auditory sensations]. *Philosophische Studien, 2*, 394–474.

Mehner, M. (1885). Zur Lehre vom Zeitsinn [On the doctrine of the time sense]. *Philosophische Studien, 2*, 546–602.

Merkel, J. (1885). Die Zeitlichen Verhältnisse der Willensthätigkeit [Temporal relationships of volitional activity]. *Philosophische Studien, 2*, 73–127.

Orne, M. T. (1962). On the social psychology of the psychological experiment: With particular reference to demand characteristics and their implications. *American Psychologist, 17*, 776–783.

Oxford English Dictionary. (1933). Oxford, England: Clarendon Press.

Richet, C. (1879). De l'influence des mouvements sur les idées [On the influence of movements on ideas]. *Revue philosophique, 8*, 610–615.

Richet, C. (1880). Du somnambulisme provoqué [On induced somnambulism]. *Revue philosophique, 10*, 337–374; 462–493.

Rosenthal, R., & Rosnow, R. L. (Eds.). (1975). *The volunteer subject*. New York: Wiley.

Schallenberger, M. (1894). A study of children's rights as seen by themselves. *Pedagogical Seminary, 3*, 87–96.

Schultz, D. P. (1970). The nature of the human data source in psychology. In D. P. Schultz (Ed.), *The science of psychology: Critical reflections* (pp. 77–86). New York: Appleton-Century-Crofts.

Silverman, I. (1977). *The human subject in the psychological laboratory*. New York: Pergamon.

Sokal, M. (Ed.). (1980). *An education in psychology: James McKeen Cattell's journal and letters from Germany and England, 1880–1888*. Cambridge, MA: MIT Press.

Stevens, L. T. (1886). On the time sense. *Mind, 11*, 393–404.

Tischer, E. (1883). Ueber die Unterscheidung von Schallstärken [On the discrimination of auditory volume]. *Philosophische Studien, 1*, 495–542.

Titchener, E. B. (1893). Zur Chronometrie des Erkennensactes [The chronometry of the act of recognition]. *Philosophische Studien, 8*, 138–144.

Trautscholdt, M. (1883). Experimentelle Untersuchungen über die Association der Vorstellungen [Experimental investigations on the association of ideas]. *Philosophische Studien, 1*, 213–250.

White, S. (1977). Social proof structures: The dialectic of method and theory in the work of psychology. In N. Datan & H. W. Reese (Eds.), *Life-span developmental psychology: Dialectical perspectives on experimental research* (pp. 59–92). New York: Academic Press.

III

PSYCHOLOGY AS A NATURAL SCIENCE

INTRODUCTION: PSYCHOLOGY AS A NATURAL SCIENCE

Psychology has had and continues to have many faces. One that is present today, but that was essentially prominent prior to World War II, is the natural-science approach. Following on the work of the New Psychologists around the turn of the 20th century, some psychologists continue to model their approaches after the physical and biological sciences and to claim their primary affinities to be with them. In this section we discuss four chapters dealing with psychology as a natural science written by four leading historians of psychology. The first provides an overview that challenges traditional presentations of the material covered. The final three are excellent studies of particular aspects of the more general story. A secondary theme in this section, as elsewhere in this book, concerns the care that readers must exercise in accepting secondary presentations of the received histories of the field.

A reading of most presentations of the history of psychology will reveal the putative occurrence of two major revolutions in the history of experimental psychology in the 20th century. The first was the "behaviorist revolution" in which, during the 1910s, John B. Watson (1878–1958) swept the field clean of mentalistic constructs, such as consciousness, and focused the field on the study of behavior rather than on mind. The second was the "cognitive revolution" of the 1950s and 1960s, in which there was a retreat from strictly behavioristic approaches as mental processes became focal. In chapter 10 "The Mythical Revolutions of American Psychology" (1992), Thomas Hardy Leahey challenges this neat story. He first examines carefully the very concept of *revolution*; he considers what that concept entails and how we can determine whether or not a revolution has occurred. Using this rigorous measuring stick, Leahey admits only one true revolution in the history of psychology, that of Wilhelm Wundt (1832–1920).

Where others see revolution, Leahey sees gradual change and evolution. He points out that throughout this period, alternative research traditions generally existed side by side with the tradition that is generally viewed as dominant. It may be true that one or the other was better presented and publicized at a particular time, but evidence of the domination and sudden sweeping change that characterize revolutions is lacking. For example, he shows that many of the features of Watson's "behavioristic revolution" were already prominent and widely accepted before Watson's so-called manifesto of 1913. Leahey views the appearance of cognitive psychology not as a revolution but as the appearance of a new form of behavioralism stimulated by developments in computer science. It should be noted that interest in issues of an essentially cognitive nature continued, although in new guises, during the period of apparent domination of behaviorism (see Dewsbury, 2000; Lovie, 1983). Leahey's article provides a worthwhile opportunity for students to question the stories presented in their textbooks—a prospect most unsettling for many students.

Three of the key figures in the natural-science/behavioristic approach to psychology during the 20th century were Ivan P. Pavlov (1849–1936), John B. Watson, and B. F. Skinner (1904–1990). Pavlov was not a psychologist; he was a Russian physiologist. He was first noted for his work on the digestive system and won a Nobel Prize for that work. In chapter 11, "From Machine to the Ghost Within: Pavlov's Transition from Digestive Physiology to Conditional Reflexes" (1997), Daniel P. Todes explores Pavlov's shift from work on digestion to an emphasis on *conditional reflexes* (a term preferable to *conditioned reflexes*, as Todes shows). Pavlov told this story on a number of occasions. Using the documents of the time, however, Todes's careful analysis reveals that Pavlov distorted the tale. Todes shows that to undertake this transition Pavlov needed to make two major departures from the procedures that had previously characterized his large and complex laboratory. First, he had to develop a new approach, because he and his associates found that the approach previously applied so fruitfully in the study of the gastric and pancreatic glands was ineffective in the study of the salivary glands. The second departure was that, faced with what was essentially a psychological problem, Pavlov recruited outside experts to participate in the development of the new methodology. Todes concludes that Pavlov's distortion of this story served the end of helping to legitimate his new endeavor. This story shows again the importance of careful study of documents of the time in evaluating received views of the history of the field.

Yet another story of misrepresentation can be found in presentations of one of the most famous experiments in the history of psychology, Watson and Rayner's (1920) study of conditioned fear in "Little Albert." In chapter 12, "Whatever Happened to Little Albert?" (1979), Benjamin Harris summarizes this classic experiment and the ways that it has been distorted by subsequent authors. Watson and Rayner found that Albert B., approximately age 9 months at the start of testing, did not fear several kinds of animals but did fear the noise from a long steel bar struck behind his head. When a rat was later presented followed by the noise whenever Albert touched the animal, Albert's behavior changed so that he showed responses associated with fear on presentation of the rat alone. The responsiveness generalized to several, but not all, other stimuli tested 5 days later. After another 5 days, additional conditioning was attempted. Some evidence of fearful responses to some of the stimuli was apparent for at least 31 days beyond that. Testing ended when Albert's mother removed him from the hospital in which he had been living, as Watson and Rayner knew she would.

Harris reviews the presentations of this experiment in introductory-level textbooks, writings in behavior therapy, and in presentations of preparedness theory. He finds a pattern of misrepresentation of the experiment with regard to Albert's age, the spelling of Rayner's name, whether Albert was initially conditioned to a rat or rabbit, and stimuli used in generalization tests. According to some accounts, Little Albert was later reconditioned; that did not happen. Watson himself was responsible for some of these distortions. Harris goes on to explore the function of such "origin myths" in the history of psychology. It should come as no surprise that this article, and the phenomenon in general, has proved to be quite controversial (Church, 1980; Cornwell, Hobbs, & Prytula, 1980; Harris, 1980; Prytula, Oster, & Davis, 1977; Samelson, 1980; Seligman, 1980). Once more, we see the importance of going to the original source for an accurate presentation of research. Those who wish to do so can find the article in most university libraries or on-line at http://www.yorku.ca/dept/psych/classics/Watson/emotion.htm.

The final chapter concerns one of the best known of the experimental psychologists, B. F. Skinner. In chapter 13, "On Prediction and Control: B. F. Skinner and the Technological Ideal of Science" (1992), Laurence D. Smith addresses a very basic issue at stake: the fundamental objective of scientific research. Smith distinguishes between research oriented toward *understanding* and that aimed at the *prediction and control* of natural phenomena; the latter is essentially a technological rather than a scientific goal. The stated goals of the behaviorisms of both Watson and Skinner are prediction and control. Smith looks both backward and forward for the implications of this approach. Looking backward, he traces this approach directly to Sir Francis Bacon (1561–1626) and his influence on Skinner. It is interesting that both Bacon and Skinner chose to demonstrate the possible benefits of their technological approaches through utopian novels. Looking forward, Smith questions the long-term viability of the approach. Smith sees an unprecedented decline of interest in technologically oriented research in recent postmodern culture. He wonders how Skinnerian operant conditioning will survive in this general intellectual climate. Smith suggests that there has been a shift from the "golden age of technological ebullience" to the present concern that an experimental, interventionist approach might cause more harm for nature than can be justified by potential benefits. Smith questions the long-term future of the present approach and suggests the possibility that operant psychologists might return to a contemplative model of knowledge.

With these four chapters we gain a view of the history of psychology as a natural science in general and behaviorism in particular that is both more accurate and more nuanced than what is presented in many traditional sources.

REFERENCES

Church, R. M. (1980). The Albert study: Illustration vs. evidence. *American Psychologist, 35,* 215–216.

Cornwell, D., Hobbs, S., & Prytula, R. (1980). Little Albert rides again. *American Psychologist, 35,* 216–217.

Dewsbury, D. A. (2000). Comparative cognition in the 1930s. *Psychonomic Bulletin & Review, 7,* 267–283.

Harris, B. (1980). Ceremonial versus critical history of psychology. *American Psychologist, 35,* 218–219.

Prytula, R., Oster, G. D., & Davis, S. F. (1977). The rat rabbit problem: What did John B. Watson really do? *Teaching of Psychology, 4,* 44–46.

Lovie, A. D. (1983). Attention and behaviourism: Fact and fiction. *British Journal of Psychology, 74,* 301–310.

Samelson, F. (1980). J. B. Watson's Little Albert, Cyril Burt's twins, and the need for a critical science. *American Psychologist, 35,* 619–625.

Seligman, M. E. P. (1980). Harris on selective misrepresentation: A selective misrepresentation of Seligman. *American Psychologist, 35,* 214–215.

Watson, J. B. (1913). Psychology as the behaviorist views it. *Psychological Review, 20,* 158–177.

Watson, J. B., & Rayner, R. (1920). Conditioned emotional reactions. *Journal of Experimental Psychology, 3,* 1–14.

10

THE MYTHICAL REVOLUTIONS OF AMERICAN PSYCHOLOGY

THOMAS H. LEAHEY

How shall the story of psychology be told? At the centennial of the American Psychological Association (APA), American psychology finds itself divided into bitterly quarreling factions exchanging charges of bad faith. The way our history is told has helped create and maintain divisions within our discipline. For the guiding myth of American psychology is a story of conflict and struggle, dominance and revolution.

There is a story of the development of American psychology widely told and widely repeated. In the beginning—1879—psychology was born as the science of mental life, studying consciousness with introspection. Then, in 1913, the dominance of mentalism was challenged and shattered by the rude and simplistic behaviorists, who made a revolution against the ancien régime mentalists. They slew the science of mental life and replaced it with the science of behavior, creating a decades-long rule of behavior study and behavior theory. However, in 1956, a new revolution began, its makers waving the banner of cognition, aided by outside forces from linguistics and artificial intelligence. After two decades of struggle, the ancien

Reprinted from *American Psychologist, 47*, 308–318 (1992). Copyright © 1992 by the American Psychological Association. Reprinted with permission of the author.

régime of behaviorism was defeated, or at least repressed, and the rule of information-processing cognitive psychology began. Today, we stand perhaps on the threshold of a new revolution, as the young warriors of connectionism challenge the aging stalwarts of information processing (Bechtel & Abrahamsen, 1990; Schneider, 1987; Tienson, 1991).

It is an exciting story, full of sound and fury, but what does it signify? Is it true? I hope to show that the romantic drama of revolution in the history of American psychology is a plausible but dangerous myth, and to suggest a better story, of developing traditions.

REVOLUTIONS

> Despite its dubious ancestry, the word "revolution" by now has a Pavlovian effect on some historians: applied to any event, it leads at once to eager expectations of radical structural change, profound discontinuity, a sweeping away of the old order. (Clark, 1986, p. 38)

The Concept of Revolution

The nature of revolutions has received a great deal of attention over the last few decades in history and political science (Brinton, 1952; Clark, 1986; Porter & Teich, 1986; Paynton & Blackey, 1971) and more recently in history of science (Cohen, 1985; Kuhn, 1957, 1962/1970; Porter, 1986). Although revolutions were once seen as rare interruptions in the natural course of human history, they have come to be regarded as frequent, even commonplace, events (Clark, 1986; Porter, 1986).

It is interesting that the term *revolution* did not originate in politics, but in science (Griewank, 1969/1971). The term arose in astronomy to describe the circular movement of objects through the heavens, and via astrology came to be applied to history. Galileo wrote, "The revolutions of the globe we inhabit give rise to the mishaps and accidents in human existence" (cited in Griewank, p. 17). The new image of celestial rotations reinforced older beliefs in the wheel of fortune governing human lives, raising them up to power, fame, and fortune, and then inevitably smashing them down again (Cohen, 1985).

The first metaphorical application of the concept of astronomical revolution to political revolution was expressed by Polybius (200–118 B.C.): "Such is the cycle of political revolutions, the course appointed by nature in which constitutions change, disappear and finally return to the point from which they started" (cited in Cohen, 1985, p. 54). Polybius's conception of revolutions was conservative, a circular movement of return rather than a forward leap in linear progress. Thus, into the early modern period, the term *revolution* was generally applied to restorations of an older order that had been disturbed by rebellion or corruption.

Nevertheless, the circular concept of historical revolutions also contained the idea of a revolution as a violent overturning (Cohen, 1985), and during the 17th century, the meaning of *revolution* gradually lost its cyclic component and acquired its now-familiar sense of a sharp, fundamental, and improving break with the past (Griewank, 1969/1971).

The first political change to be described by contemporaries in this new sense was the Glorious Revolution of 1688, and during the 18th century, the idea of revolutions as decisively progressive leaps permanently replaced the older conservative notion (Cohen, 1985; Porter, 1986). Behind the changing conception of political revolutions from cyclic to progressive overturnings lay the concept of revolutions in science (Porter, 1986).

Revolutions in Science

In the first declaration of revolution in the history of science, Bernard de Fontenelle (1657–1757) declared in the early 1700s that the invention of the calculus had constituted a revolution in mathematics. A little later, Antoine Lavoisier (1743–1794) declared in 1733 that his research constituted a revolution in chemistry (Cohen, 1985). The view of revolutions advanced by Fontenelle and Lavoisier developed the idea that revolutions were progressive breaks with the past, a view advanced with fervor by the Enlightenment philosophies, who linked their French Revolution—and revolutions yet to come—to progressive leaps in science (Porter, 1986). Because they are at once romantically dramatic and daringly progressive, many scientists (and historians) have dubbed as *revolutionary* almost any new idea, until "our dominant image of the history of science [and history *tout court*; (Clark, 1986)] is bursting at the seams with revolutions" (Porter, p. 291).

Not all change or even innovation is revolutionary, no matter that revolutionary talk satisfies our eager expectations. If one is to weigh properly the thesis that psychology has experienced revolutions, one must be guided by models of revolution and criteria of revolutionary change.

MODELS OF REVOLUTION IN SCIENCE

Thomas S. Kuhn

Thomas S. Kuhn, through his study of the Copernican Revolution (Kuhn, 1957) and his subsequent general analysis of revolutions in science, *The Structure of Scientific Revolutions* (Kuhn, 1962/1970), has done more than anyone else to popularize the idea of scientific revolution. Kuhn's *The Structure of Scientific Revolutions* has been widely influential not only in history and philosophy of science (Gutting, 1980; Hacking, 1981), but also in psychology (Coleman & Salamon, 1988).

Kuhn is heir to a tradition in history of science begun by Alexander Koyré, which created the idea of scientific eras controlled by guiding weltanschauungen (Kuhn's paradigms) and, in consequence, the idea of scientific change as involving changes in weltanschauungen, as "putting on a new pair of spectacles" (Kuhn's gestalt switch). Koyré and his followers also created the historiographical event of the Scientific Revolution itself (Porter, 1986). Although Fontenelle and Lavoisier (and others since) had spoken of revolutions *in* science, it was not until 1939 that, beginning with Koyré, anyone spoke of *the* Scientific Revolution. Once minted, the term became common currency and now seems as old as the Scientific Revolution itself.

Kuhn (1962/1970) brought the Koyréan lineaments of the Scientific Revolution to his picture of later revolutions in science. The Scientific Revolution was an event of high drama, in which great thinkers had great thoughts and defeated the entrenched forces of superstition and ignorance. It "outshines everything since the rise of Christianity and reduces the Renaissance and Reformation to the rank of mere episodes" (Butterfield, 1949/1957, p. 7). Similarly, Kuhn depicted revolutions in science as smaller dramas with crisis and conflict, the clash of ideas, and the overturning of one worldview by another. It is hardly surprising that, to Kuhn's own chagrin, most of the attention his book received focused on revolutionary change, not normal science. Next to the revolution makers, normal scientists seem pathetic, puny souls (Lakatos & Musgrave, 1970). And it is no wonder that, after 1962, scientists should want to make (and see) revolutions in their own work and time.

Kuhn (1962/1970) proposed that any particular science begins in a preparadigm stage, during which several weltanschauungen attempt to define and dominate the field. At some point, one weltanschauung's way of conducting the science becomes definitive, and it becomes a controlling paradigm, as the other soi-disant paradigms fall into desuetude or are stigmatized as pseudoscientific. Thus, in the Scientific Revolution, Newton's achievement in the *Principia* defined classical physics, and the rival Cartesian viewpoint faded away. Control of a field by a single paradigm marks the maturing of a field into a genuine science, and the cycle of normal science and revolutionary science begins.

Kuhn (1962/1970) described scientific revolutions as passing through four stages.

1. *Normal science*. During this phase, ordinary scientific research and scientific progress take place. The dominant paradigm

establishes a research agenda, in which explanatory puzzles are solved by empirical research and theorizing within the framework established by the paradigm. When a paradigm becomes dominant it operates rather like a large-scale schema as understood in cognitive psychology (Brewer & Nakamura, 1984). Its network of beliefs fades into the background but, like a schema, continues to shape the thinking and behavior of the scientists who hold it. Clearly, as Kuhn's analysis implies, the creation and imposition of a paradigm are more glorious things than is operating mindlessly within one.

2. *Appearance of anomaly.* Inevitably, some puzzles prove harder to solve than others, and these are anomalies. Solving the hard ones wins Nobel prizes, but some puzzles continue to resist solution. Sometimes, recalcitrant puzzles are shelved, set aside for another day. But others, especially if they are seen as fundamental, may greatly disturb the scientific community and induce a period of crisis.

3. *Crisis.* If an important anomaly provokes a crisis, the grip of the paradigm on scientists weakens. Its hold will be especially weak on young scientists, as the crisis undermines the normal dogmatism of scientific training. The more brilliant among them—the Einsteins and Heisenbergs—break out of the confines of the paradigm altogether, rejecting one or more of its defining tenets, proposing new ones in their stead. If a new viewpoint is persuasive—clearing up the anomalies and suggesting fresh lines of investigation—the ancien régime is imperiled.

4. *Revolution.* Crisis becomes revolution if the adherents of the emerging paradigm gain control of the levers of power in science: journal editorships; textbooks; and, today, granting agencies. Followers of the old paradigm may in some cases be able to convert to the new, but often they abandon research to become chairpersons and deans. The old paradigm is replaced by the new, beginning again the cycle of normal science, anomaly, crisis, and revolution.

It would be profitless to rehearse the many complaints made about Kuhn's (1962/1970) picture of science and scientific change (Gutting, 1980; Hacking, 1981; Lakatos & Musgrave, 1970). Whatever its faults, it is undoubtedly appealing, if not always compelling, as in Kuhn's hands science becomes an intellectual adventure, paradigm making being human creativity at its highest pitch and greatest influence. Perhaps the chief failing of Kuhn's account was that it offered sketchy examples of revolutions fit to Kuhn's Procrustean model. To remedy this defect, I. Bernard

Cohen (1985) proposed a more empirically based model of scientific revolutions.

Bernard Cohen

Like Kuhn, Cohen (1985) saw revolutions as passing through distinct stages, but unlike Kuhn's stages, Cohen's are more precisely defined in terms of ascertainable historical occurrences.

1. *The revolution in itself*. The revolution in itself is the creative phase, in which a scientist or group of scientists proposes a radically new solution to a problem or a radically new theory, sets forth a new framework, or finds a new method of using existing information.
2. *Private commitment*. The innovative ideas are committed to paper in notes, diary entries, research logbooks, or some other nonpublic form.
3. *The revolution on paper*. The new ideas are circulated among the members of the scientific community, beginning informally, proceeding to oral presentations, and culminating in publication. During this phase, revolutionary ideas are criticized, improved, and polished.
4. *Conversion*. If it passes the gauntlet of "brutal insistence on demonstration" (Cohen, 1985, p. 35), a revolution becomes a success, converting the majority of scientists in a field to its ideas.

More important than his model of stages is Cohen's (1985) proposal of precise criteria by which to evaluate the claim that an episode in science constituted a revolution. Cohen set out four tests:

1. *Contemporary testimony*. How was the event regarded by those who experienced it? Scientists must describe experiencing a revolutionary change to their discipline. Cohen regarded this as the major criterion, to be supplemented—but never overridden—by the remaining three.
2. *Later documentary history*. How was the event treated by later writings in the field? Texts, treatises, and articles must regard the event as revolutionary.
3. *Historian's judgment*. How is the event treated by competent historians of the field? To count as a revolution, historians must consider it to have been one.
4. *Opinion of working scientists*. Is the event regarded by modern scientists as a revolution? Cohen argued that myths of rev-

olution provide important clues to the existence of major changes in science.

It is important to bear in mind the supplementary nature of the final three criteria of revolution. Cohen (1985) refused to recognize as a revolution any event that was not recognized as revolutionary by those who lived through it, regardless of later opinion. Texts, histories, and scientific folklore can only support a claim of revolution, but cannot establish one. I apply Cohen's criteria to claims for revolutions in the brief history of psychology. However, in the case of putative revolutions in psychology, the second and fourth criteria blur together. Too little time has passed since the beginning of psychology to distinguish them, and by and large, the historians of psychology have been psychologists themselves.

Roy Porter

In a brief but insightful analysis of revolutions in science, Porter (1986) offered a model of and criteria for evaluating scientific revolutions that distills the essence of Kuhn's and Cohen's schemes and emphasizes the parallel to political revolutions. First, "a revolution in science requires overthrow of an entrenched orthodoxy; challenge, resistance, struggle and conquest are essentials . . . a new order must be established, a break visible" (p. 300). Second, "revolutions presuppose both grandeur of scale and urgency of tempo" (p. 300). Third, "it is vital that, at some stage, consciousness should dawn of revolution afoot. The notion of silent or unconscious revolution is next door to nonsense" (p. 300). Finally, "surely *scientific* revolutions at least must be international" (p. 308).

Conclusion

The models of Kuhn, Cohen, and Porter suggest a series of questions to frame our inquiry into the existence of revolutions in the history of psychology. (a) Was there an old regime of normal science dominated by an "entrenched orthodoxy"—Kuhn's paradigm—to be overthrown? (b) Was the existing paradigm experiencing difficulties brought on by empirical anomalies demanding solution by radical innovation and the creation of a new worldview? (c) Was there a brief period of intense and acute struggle between proponents of the old regime and the new, and a "break visible" between the old order and the new? (d) Was the alleged revolution international? (e) Was a new regime—paradigm—established?

In answering each question, I apply the empirical criteria for revolutions laid down by Cohen (1985) and Porter (1986), emphasizing, with Cohen, perceptions of revolution by the psychologists involved.

REVOLUTIONS IN PSYCHOLOGY

Although a number of revolutions in psychology have been proposed, including the foundings of experimental psychology by Wundt (Cohen, 1985), of psychoanalysis (Buss, 1978; Michels, 1986), and of humanistic psychology (Buss), I will restrict myself to consideration of the main story, told earlier, concerning the behaviorist and cognitivist revolutions.

The Behaviorist Revolution

> There is unquestionably a widespread movement on foot in which interest is centered in the *results* of conscious process, rather than in the *processes* themselves. This is peculiarly true in animal psychology; it is only less true in human psychology. In these cases interest in what may for lack of a better term be called "behavior"; and the analysis of consciousness is primarily justified by the light it throws on behavior, rather than *vice versa*. (Angell, 1911, p. 47)

According to our reigning mythology, psychology's first revolution took place when John B. Watson's behaviorism overthrew the established paradigm of mentalism. During this revolution, psychology abandoned its first (and traditional) definition as the science of mental life, or consciousness as such, along with its method of introspection, replacing them with a definition of psychology as the science of behavior and implementation of its methods of behavior study. I argue that although the changes in psychology that took place in the first decades of APA's life were deep and profound, it is more useful to look on the changes as gradual rather than revolutionary.

Did Mentalism Constitute a Paradigm Dominating Psychology Before 1913?

Certainly there was general agreement that psychology was primarily the science of consciousness and that its method was introspection, but beyond these very general points there was serious disagreement over fundamental, foundational issues.

Consider, first, psychology's method: introspection. Wundt (1907) was highly critical of the traditional armchair introspection used by the philosophers of psychology's prescientific past. Essential to his founding of scientific psychology was the repudiation of ordinary self-introspection, and its replacement by a new method of experimental introspection (Blumenthal, 1975; Bringmann & Tweney, 1980; Rieber, 1980). Wundt's procedures involved immediate reports of consciousness under carefully controlled standardized conditions, and Wundt rigorously insisted on control, replicability, and systematic variability as criteria to be met by any valid experimental procedure. Indeed, many of his techniques would not be regarded today as introspective at all, such as the tachistoscopic method used to study span of apprehension, later modified by Sperling (1960) in his studies of iconic memory (Leahey, 1981).

William James (1890), on the other hand, insisted that ordinary self-introspection—the very method rejected by Wundt—was psychology's essential method for probing consciousness. Although he respected experimental results and incorporated them into his *Principles of Psychology*, it is clear that he found experimentation boring, and in *Principles of Psychology* he mostly supported his theoretical positions with vivid examples of everyday introspection. Meanwhile, the Würzburg psychologists, and the later E. B. Titchener (1901–1905), developed a form of experimental introspection involving the retrospective analysis of remembered consciousness and the generation of long descriptive protocols (Leahey, 1992). Their methods deviated from Wundt's (1907) criteria of strict control and systematic variability, producing eccentric and unrepeatable results, most famously in the imageless thought controversy of the 1910s (Ogden, 1911a, 1911b). There was, in conclusion, no precise agreement among psychologists concerning their scientific method, introspection.

There was also significant disagreement over how psychology should explain its findings. The deepest division concerned the principles governing conscious events. Although Wundt (1896) called the experimental branch of his science "physiological psychology," he nevertheless proposed that mental events were shaped by mental processes governed by mental laws. On the other hand, James (1890) rejected the "Kantian machine-shop" (Vol. 2, p. 275) of the unconscious and the existence of mental forces such as association of ideas. He insisted psychology should be cerebralist and traced conscious events directly to their causes in the nervous system, without postulating intervening mental way stations. Similarly, Titchener (1972) derided Wundt's hypothesizing of mental forces and laws, preferring to replace them with motor sensations, and in his last years, he moved to a purely descriptive phenomenology.

These differences over methodology and theory are as deep as any in later psychology. Beyond an agreed-upon definition of psychology as the study of consciousness, perforce relying on introspection, everything was disputed. But debates over basic foundational issues characterize preparadigm, not normal science. Had the term been available, it seems likely contemporary psychologists would have recognized the presence of competing would-be paradigms. In 1898, Titchener distinguished two approaches to psychology, structural psychology and functional psychology, and the ensuing years saw structuralists and functionalists argue for the preeminence of their point of view (Leahey, 1992). Given the nature and depth of the disputes among the founders of psychology, there was no single paradigmatic ancien régime of mentalism for behaviorism to overthrow revolutionarily.

Was Mentalism Experiencing Difficulties Brought on by Anomalies Shortly Before 1913?

There can be no doubt that the period 1892–1912, especially 1910–1912, was a difficult one for psychology, well attested to by contemporary witnesses. In his annual report, "Psychological Progress in 1906" in the *Psychological Bulletin*, E. F. Buchner (1907) noted a "rising tide of dissatisfaction" (p. 1), and in 1911 confessed that many psychologists had become unclear as to what their field was about. The 1910 meeting of the APA (at which Angell delivered the paragraph quoted at the beginning of this section) was dominated by sessions rethinking the definition of psychology (Haggerty, 1911). However, the uncertainties of the period 1910–1912 may be viewed not as a prerevolutionary crisis, indicating psychology was *about* to change, but as a dawning consciousness that psychology had *already* changed.

Anomalies in Kuhn's (1962/1970) sense of troubling recalcitrant puzzles are hard to find. The imageless thought controversy comes closest to filling the bill, as the tone of the controversy was often sharp and occasionally was used to raise basic issues, such as the validity of introspection (Ogden, 1911a, 1911b). However, most articles involved in the debate treated it as a difficult but soluble problem (e.g., Titchener, 1904), and, in any event, behaviorism did not solve the problem of imageless thought, as should happen in a Kuhnian revolution. Instead, behaviorism declared the problem of imageless thought irrelevant. Psychology's real anomalies were not Kuhnian empirical puzzles, but difficulties created by broadening psychology to include—in addition to the study of adult human consciousness—animal, child, abnormal, and clinical psychology.

Was There a Brief Period of Intense Crisis and Struggle Leading to a Break Visible?

Here is the key question, and I will try to show that the important relevant changes in psychology occurred before 1913 and took place in a gradual and largely unnoticed way. The years 1892–1912 defined American psychology as it transformed continuously and without break from the study of consciousness to the study of behavior. Space precludes full discussion (see Leahey, 1991, or 1992), but I will sketch as a series of narrowing circles the main forces acting on psychology, showing how the changeover from consciousness to behavior occurred.

The largest circle of influence came from American society as it was transforming from an agricultural sea of island communities to an industrial nation state with international influence (Wiebe, 1967). People migrated from rural communities, ruled by tradition and social control by kith and kin, to industrializing cities that were collections of strangers. New ways of life had to be learned, new skills taught to urban migrants. Led by John Dewey (1900), psychologists recognized the value their discipline might have for creating new means of social adjustment. Focusing on social adjustment meant focusing on behavior—most important, learning—and so American social conditions drew psychologists' attention away from consciousness and toward adjustive behavior.

In the next circle of influence, developments in psychology's intellectual neighbors reinforced a focus on behavior. In Darwinian evolution, thoughts not acted on are as of little consequence as thoughts not thought. Psychologists, such as Thaddeus Bolton (1902) and H. Heath Bawden (1903, 1904, 1910), argued that perception and consciousness had survival value only if they produced adaptive behavior. Inevitably, the focus of a biologically informed psychology (Angell, 1907) shifted from consciousness itself to the fruits of consciousness—behavior. In philosophy, Jamesian pragmatism helped shift psychology from concern with consciousness to concern with behavior. Pragmatism—itself a product of Darwinian influence—valued ideas by their concrete consequences, their Jamesian "cash value"; in short, ideas were valued by their effects on behavior.

Finally, within psychology itself, research problems and theoretical issues undercut the primacy of consciousness. The research problem leading the way to behavior study involved comparative psychology. Animal psychology had begun as the study of animal mind, but became bogged down on the question of what behaviors permitted one to attribute mental events and processes to animals, because they are incapable of introspection. Various criteria of mentality were offered, but none seemed adequate (Watson, 1907). Merely raising the question shifted attention to behavior from the consciousness lurking ghostlike behind it, and at least one animal psychologist had concluded by 1908 that behavior could be studied independently of any translation into mentalese (Swartz, 1908; Watson, 1909). Similar developments took place in abnormal and child psychology (Sanford, 1903) and in clinical psychology, whose main tool, the mental test, was not introspective (Cattell, 1904).

On the theoretical side, it was becoming unclear what, if anything, consciousness contributes to motor response. Specifically, building on Jamesian foundations, the motor theory of consciousness moved consciousness to a peripheral position in the work of behavior adjustment. The motor theory of consciousness began with James's observations on the determination of conscious content by one's responses to stimuli, most familiarly expressed in the James–Lange theory of emotion. As John Dewey (1896), and even the arch introspectionist Hugo Münsterberg (Hale, 1980), developed the theory, consciousness was increasingly seen as an observer of behavior, rather than as an actor that causes behavior. The motor theory of consciousness implied that study of consciousness was something of an intellectual luxury, because what counted in Darwinian evolution and social change was how organisms adjust their behavior to changing circumstances.

The upshot of all of these developments was the situation described by Angell (1911) at the 1910 meeting of the APA. Reporting to philosophers, M. E. Haggerty (1911) noted that at the 1910 meeting no one defended the traditional definition of psychology as the study of consciousness. For a host of reasons psychologists had moved in the direction of studying behavior, although Angell's phrase "for lack of a better word" suggests how difficult it was for psychologists to recognize and label the change their field had undergone.

Psychology, then, moved almost without notice from the science of mental life to the science of behavior in the two decades preceding 1913. No innovation or cluster of innovations caused the change. Instead, one finds the gradual shaping of a field by a combination of social, intellectual, and indigenous forces. Never was there a break visible, an awareness of making a revolution. Even in his behaviorist manifesto, Watson (1913) does not use the term *revolution*, although the word had been applied to science by Fontenelle, Lavoisier, and by Darwinians (Cohen, 1985) well before 1913. Nor was the response to Watson's article one of rejection and resistance (Samelson, 1981). Nor, in the aftermath, did Watson in his autobiography (Watson, 1936/1961) boast of making a revolution. Contemporary observers, such as Jastrow (1927), Woodworth (1924), and Williams (1931) said Watson's angry rhetoric and extreme muscle twitchism created but the illusion of novelty; only compared with the subjective introspective techniques of the Würzburgers and Titchener—which the founding introspectionist, Wundt (1907), excoriated—did behaviorism seem new. As a psychologist, Watson was as good at public relations as he would be later as an ad man. He created smoke, but there was no fire.

Was Behaviorism an International Revolution?

Science is supposed to constitute an international community, so revolutions in science, because they change the field, should be international in scope. However, even proponents of the concept of a behavioral revolution concede that behaviorism was largely an American phenomenon (Baars, 1986).

Conclusion

The conclusion best supported by the evidence is that psychology experienced no behaviorist revolution in 1913. Introspective psychology did not constitute a paradigm to be overthrown, and although psychology did change in the years before 1913, the changes were gradual and only dimly perceived and did not occur in response to empirical anomalies demanding radical solution. Behavioral psychology emerged continuously—if rapidly—out of introspective psychology, and the so-called revolution constituted recognition of change rather than making change. The last question, whether behaviorism constituted a new paradigm, is the first question to ask of the "cognitive revolution."

The Cognitive Revolution

> Le thème d'une révolution cognitive en psychologie, qui emprunte sa terminologie a la théorie des révolutions scientifiques de Kuhn, est aujourd'hui devenu banal [The theme of a cognitive revolution in psychology, which borrows its terminology from the theory of scientific revolutions of Kuhn, has today become banal]. (Legrand, 1990, p. 248).

Belief in a cognitive revolution is an entrenched part of modern psychology's form of life. However, I will press the case that there is even less to the alleged cognitive revolution than to the alleged behaviorist revolution. By 1913, psychology had indeed changed deeply, albeit not in a revolutionary fashion. The very subject matter of psychology had changed from the description and explanation of consciousness to the description, prediction, control, and explanation of behavior, as Angell appears to have been the first to notice. I shall call the psychology described by Angell *behavioralism* (Leahey, 1992), to distinguish it from the introspective mentalism, reserving *behaviorism* to refer to the specific schools of behavior study that flourished from about 1930 to 1960. My central arguments will be that these various behaviorisms did not constitute a paradigm and that cognitive psychology represents the continued development of behavioralist psychology.

Did Behaviorism Constitute a Paradigm Dominating Psychology After 1913?

Certainly behaviorism brought an end to the lush excesses of Würzburg and late Titchenerian introspection, but it did not expunge the experimental psychology of consciousness. Practically speaking, what Wundt inaugurated was the scientific study of sensation and perception, including processes such as attention. Although after 1910 such studies no longer occupied center stage in psychology—being overshadowed by research on behavior, especially learning—they did not disappear (Davis & Gould, 1929; Lovie 1983). The central work of mentalistic psychology continued, but it was no longer thought of as the study of consciousness.

Psychology after 1913 still looked preparadigmatic. As the behavioral movement proceeded, contemporary observers, such as Hunter (1922) and Woodworth (1924), recognized that there was no single enterprise called behaviorism beyond the general commitment to behavior study. Although the definition of psychology had changed from the study of consciousness to the study of behavior, psychologists remained as divided as ever over the foundations of their field.

For example, consider a metatheoretical issue as foundational as any a science might debate: What should be the fundamental explanatory terms in its theoretical vocabulary? Should psychology regard consciousness as outside the scope of psychology because it is private (the view of methodological behaviorism), or should it be included in scientific psychology because science must explain everything (the view of Lashley's, 1923, strict behaviorism) and because consciousness can influence behavior (the view of radical behaviorism; Skinner, 1957)? Should we look to neurophysiology for our theoretical framework (Lashley, 1923)? Should we postulate intervening variables coming between stimulus and response (the view of Tolman, Hull, and mediational psychology; Leahey, 1991, 1992), or should they be shunned as invitations to pseudoscientific myth making (Skinner, 1953). If we do allow intervening variables, how should we construe them? Should we regard them as placeholders for physiological processes, as Hull did (Smith, 1986)? Should they be interpreted realistically (Leahey, 1992) as referents to real but unconscious mental states, as Tolman did (Smith)? Or, finally, should they be construed instrumentalistically (Leahey 1992) as fictions operationally defined, having no surplus meaning beyond the observations they organize, as argued by MacCorquodale and Meehl (1948) and Kendler (1952)?

Because fighting over such issues has seldom, if ever, ceased in psychology, psychologists may take it to be part of "normal" science. However, according to Kuhn (1962/1970), it is precisely these kinds of debates that acceptance of a paradigm is supposed to settle. If a discipline, such as psychology, debates foundational questions, it is not in a period of normal science; if a movement, such as behaviorism, debates foundational questions, it is not a paradigm. There was, therefore, no paradigmatic ancien régime of behaviorism for cognitive psychology to overthrow revolutionarily.

Was Behaviorism Experiencing Difficulties Brought on by Anomalies in 1951–1956?

Writing in 1971, David Palermo, participant writing as historian, said that psychology was only "ripe" for revolution. But 15 years later, Baars (1986) and Gardner (1985) in their books on the cognitive revolution located its metaphorical conception in 1948 at the Hixon Symposium on Cerebral Mechanisms in Behavior (Jeffress, 1951), and its metaphorical birthdate at September 11, 1956 (G. Miller, 1979) during the Symposium on Information Theory at the Massachusetts Institute of Technology

(MIT). The Hixon symposium is best known for Lashley's famous paper on the problem of serial order in behavior (Lashley, 1951); at MIT, the key presentations were by Newell and Simon on their pioneering work building a thinking computer program and by Chomsky on the inadequacy of existing theories of language (Gardner, 1985).

It is not obvious, however, that the birth of cognitive psychology owed anything to empirical anomalies demanding innovation in order to solve them. Under the influence of Kuhn, Palermo (1971), writing when the question was still "*Is* [italics added] a scientific revolution taking place" (p. 135), proposed a list of anomalies, beginning with the finding that children's discrimination learning differed from that of animals (Kuenne, 1946). But the anomalies listed by Palermo had already aided the creation of "liberalized S–R [stimulus–response] theory" (N. Miller, 1959), in which chains of covert stimulus–response connections were said to mediate between external stimuli and overt responses, especially in humans, and mediational theories were going strong in the early 1960s. Although Palmero tried to find in mediational theories—especially Kendler and Kendler (1962)—cracks in behaviorism, they are not readily apparent in the articles themselves or in the statements of the mediational theorists (including Kendler, 1952) interviewed by Baars (1986).

Moreover, neither Baars (1986) nor Gardner (1985)—the leading historiographical advocates of the cognitive revolution—discussed any supposed anomalies. Baars interviewed many participants in the "revolution," from old-line behaviorists to young, iconoclastic, cognitive scientists. Almost all of them discussed how good experiments and solid data advanced the cause of cognitive psychology, but none drew attention to Kuhnian anomalies. The pattern that emerges from the interviews is not one of insoluble anomalies stumbled on by behaviorists and triumphantly solved by cognitivists, but of experiments invented by psychologists already committed to cognitivism and used rhetorically to persuade others.

To the degree that malaise and unhappiness existed during the critical years of cognitivism's gestation and infancy—and one cannot deny that they existed—they involved amorphous disquiet about psychological theory and a vague worry that S–R theories possessed serious shortcomings, especially with regard to human behavior. Certainly, some psychologists were eager to proclaim a crisis (Koch, 1951), but others—perhaps most—thought that a reformed S–R theory (N. Miller, 1959; Osgood, 1956) or a purified behaviorism (Skinner, 1950) would carry the behavioral movement progressively forward.

Indeed, the major causes and supports of the revival of cognitive psychology came from outside psychology itself. Although Lashley (1951) was a psychologist, he spoke as a physiologist in his Hixon symposium paper. Newell (1973) and Simon (1990) pursued and originally published their work outside psychology, in economics and computer science. Chomsky was a linguist who had happened to encounter psychologists. Psychology did not get its own influential statement of cognitive science until Neisser's 1967 text, *Cognitive Psychology*. Most important, the leading theory in cognitive psychology, information processing, was taken over from computer science. As in the period 1892–1912, the pressures making for change in psychology between 1948 and 1956 arose not from internal, technical failures of psychological research, but were conceptual, primarily driven by forces outside psychology.

Was There a Brief Period of Intense Crisis and Struggle Leading to a Break Visible?

The evidence here is conflicting, but adds up to an interesting although not prerevolutionary picture. Gardner (1985) never advanced a case for revolution, but calmly narrated the continuous development of cognitive psychology from its Cartesian roots to the present, with remarkably little reference to behaviorism or conflict between it and cognitivism. Baars (1986) wrote, "Between 1955 and 1965 a quiet revolution in thought took place in scientific psychology ... the cognitive shift was not self-conscious. ... Experimental psychologists did not set out to make a revolution" (p. 141). Nor was the existence of a revolution acknowledged by most of those he interviewed. If we accept his (and Gardner's) dates for the revolution, it fails the key evidentiary test of recognition by contemporaries.

On the other hand, in 1971, Palermo sensed crisis and incipient revolution. In 1968, Horton and Dixon, too, felt a "revolution is certainly in the making" (p. 580). Robert E. Shaw (1986) described the Center for Human Learning at the University of Minnesota as a center of revolution after 1965. Baars (1986) wrote, "The understanding of the cognitive revolution followed the event" (p. 141).

What accounts for these differences of opinion? There are various possible explanations, of course, but I think the right one is suggested by James J. Jenkins, who ran the Center for Learning at the University of Minnesota in the years of supposed revolution. Jenkins told Baars (1986), "And, of course, everybody toted around their little copy of Kuhn's *The structure of scientific revolutions*" (p. 249).

Jenkin's testimony suggested that *there was no awareness of revolution until Kuhn's book suggested it*. Its publication in 1962 colored an era (Coleman & Salamon, 1988) and itself provided a justification for the "revolution" (Peterson, 1981). Especially for graduate students learning the (boring) tools of their profession, the high romantic drama and intellectual adventure of revolution making and the joy of breaking behaviorist crockery must have been much more appealing than the day-to-day mundaneness of normal science. I was in graduate school at the University of Illinois from 1970 to 1974 and was always told by William F. Brewer that a revolution was going on. The present article started as a dissenting class paper that I wrote for him.

In the period after 1965, as in the period 1892–1912, the larger social environment played an important role. The 1960s were the days of drugs and protest and of the revolution smashing the intellectual crockery of Western civilization and the actual glass of the ruling class (Collier & Horowitz, 1989). Participating in a scientific revolution at the same time as a political one unified personal and professional lives, heightened the romantic sense of making epochal change, and made the changing times that much more exciting. Surely, it was satisfying to attack tenured old fogies, supported by a scholarly reference to "Kuhn, 1962."

Thus, there was no experienced disciplinary struggle in the revolutionary era identified by Baars (1986) and Gardner (1985), but there was after 1965, created by Kuhn's (1962/1970) book in a sort of self-fulfilling prophecy. It is also hard to identify any moment of a break visible between behaviorism and cognitivism. If G. Miller (1979) is right that cognitive science was born September 11, 1956, it is a break visible only with 20–20 hindsight. In any event, a revolution drawn out from 1948 to at least 1971 is no revolution; as Porter (1986) wrote, "Long revolutions are terminological abuses" (p. 300).

Was the Cognitive Revolution International?

George Miller told Baars (1986) about a talk he gave at Oxford University in 1963, in which he "lambasted the hell out of the behaviorists" (p. 212) to a puzzled audience, because, as he found later that there were only three behaviorists in England, none of whom were present. Because behaviorism was not international, the cognitive revolution could not have been international. It must be acknowledged, though, that information-processing psychology has had world-wide influence, perhaps because of the international influence of its metaphorical base, the computer.

Did the Cognitive Revolution Create a New Paradigm and Inaugurate an Era of Normal Science?

In 1971, Palermo did not correctly foresee the direction psychology would take. He thought that Chomsky's revolution in linguistics would bequeath a rationalist paradigm to psycholinguistics and thence to experimental psychology as a whole. Instead, the main form taken by cognitive science was the information-processing paradigm, rooted in the computer metaphor. It was introduced to psychology mainly by Neisser (1967) in his *Cognitive Psychology*, and then self-consciously enshrined as the new Kuhnian paradigm for psychology by Lachman, Lachman, and Butterfield (1979).

Although some psychologists today, such as Neisser (1976) himself, wish it were not so, information-processing psychology is the mainstream in experimental psychology. Two questions then pose themselves: Is information processing a Kuhnian paradigm, and is information processing a form of behavioralism or genuinely something new?

A paradigm, in Kuhn's (1962/1970) revised scheme has two components, the shared exemplar and the disciplinary matrix. The shared exemplar is close to what scientists call a paradigm, being an ideal model of research. In the case of information processing, however, a recognized problem has been the proliferation of research paradigms. It is virtually the case that small research teams each have their own experimental paradigm, making it very difficult to assemble a general picture of the human cognitive architecture (Estes, 1991; Newell, 1973; Simon, 1990).

The disciplinary matrix consists of a shared set of metatheoretical, philosophical, and metaphysical beliefs that determine a normal science community's form of life. As I have tried to show, psychology has had a difficult time establishing agreement on foundational issues. Both introspective psychology and the behaviorism that followed were defined by only the vaguest commitments to the nature of psychological science. So it remains with information-processing psychology. It is agreed that organisms take in information from the environment; process it internally, creating representations; make decisions based on represented information; and in consequence, behave.

Such a characterization would not exclude Tolman (1932) from a cognitive science. Nor would it necessarily exclude the mediational S–R theorists of liberalized S–R theory, if covert responses are counted as representations and the formation of mediating connections is counted as processing. Indeed, it was from the ranks of mediational psychologists and their students that many of the early cognitivists sprang (Baars, 1986; Kessel, 1986; Leahey, 1992). Moreover, there is good reason to regard cognitivism as a new form of behavioralism that is based on the computer metaphor but aimed at the description, prediction, and control of behavior.

For example, Ericsson and Simon (1980) wanted to achieve "processing models so explicit that they could actually produce the predicted behavior from the information in the stimulus" (p. 215), which perfectly echoed Watson's (1913) goal for psychology: "In a system of psychology completely worked out, given the response the stimuli can be predicted; given the stimuli the response can be predicted" (p. 167). Or consider cognitive psychology's attitude toward consciousness. Nisbett and Wilson (1977) dismissed introspective reports as of essentially no value in constructing and testing theories of cognitive processes, nor do they even entertain the notion—central to psychology's founders—that cognitive psychology ought to attempt to explain why people have the experiences they do, even apart from their possible causal effects, or lack thereof, on behavior (Tulving, 1989). George Mandler is often considered one of cognitive psychology's more radical thinkers, but in conversation with Baars (1986) he defined modern psychology as any methodological behaviorist would:

> Psychology must talk *about* people. *Your* private experience is a theoretical construct to me. I have no direct access to your private experience. I do have direct access to your behavior. In that sense I'm a behaviorist. In that sense, *everybody* is a behaviorist today. (p. 256)

And that sense of psychology is behavioralism, as defined by Angell in 1910.

Conclusion

The coming of cognitive psychology is best regarded, not as the revolutionary creation of a new paradigm slaying the older one of behaviorism, but as the appearance of a new form of behavioralism based on a new technology, the computer. By the 1950s, mediational S–R behaviorists were already looking for ways to represent internal processing of stimuli, and the computer metaphor provided a better language than mediational r–s notation did. Moreover, the existence of artificial intelligence—the manufacture of information-processing devices behaving intelligently and purposively—bolstered faith in mediating mental processes by showing they could be embodied in material devices rather than immaterial souls (J. Miller, 1983). Information-processing psychology, no less than any form of historical behaviorism, aims at the description, prediction, control, and explanation of behavior, without any special attention being given to conscious experience (Tulving, 1989). Perhaps during the feverish days of the 1960s, another, less behavioral, road might have been taken—but it was not taken, at least not by the main body of experimental psychologists. The mainstream of psychology in 1992 remains as firmly behavioralistic as it was in 1910.

CONCLUSION: WHO NEEDS REVOLUTIONS?

In the 1930s, psychologists, ever uncertain about their status as scientists, adopted logical positivism's philosophy of science as a recipe for making psychological science. Doing so, they distorted their perceptions of their own leading theorists, Hull and Tolman (Smith, 1986), and forced psychology onto the Procrustean bed of logical positivism (Leahey, 1980, 1983). Later on, it emerged that logical positivism was bad philosophy of science (Suppe, 1977), but the damage was done. If I am right about psychology's history, then we might conclude, assuming that Kuhn's (1962/1970) analysis is correct, that psychology is not a science, because it has had no normal science and hence no revolutions. But we need not assume that Kuhn is good philosophy of science, and instead rescue psychology from the Procrustean bed of Kuhnianism. His various theses have been roundly criticized (Suppe, 1977), and the trend in history and philosophy of science today, excepting Cohen, is toward emphasizing continuity and development instead of revolution. In the revised edition of *The Structure of Scientific Revolutions* (1962/1970), Kuhn retracted many of his more controversial and radical proposals, although many psychologists remain unaware of it (Coleman & Salamon, 1988). Moreover, Cohen's account of revolutions is less philosophical and more empirical than Kuhn's, and the revolution he assigns to psychology is plausibly genuine: its innovative founding by Wundt and James. Moving away from Kuhn, some historians (e.g., Hull, 1988a, 1988b; Shrader, 1980) want to impose on history of science a model based on biological evolution extending the Darwinian process of mutation and natural selection from organisms to ideas. However, having rescued psychology from positivism and Kuhn, I do not want to force it onto the bed of evolutionary epistemology.

In place of a story of revolutions, one can tell psychology's story as a narrative of research traditions (Laudan, 1977; MacIntyre, 1977, 1981), changing over time in a framework of pairs of metatheoretical commitments called *themata* (Holton, 1973). Some of the important psychological themata would be molar–molecular, representationalism–realism, mentalism–reductionism, and rules–connections. Some of the developing traditions would be representational psychology, running from Locke through Tolman to information-processing psychology; realist psychology, running from the Scottish realists through the American neo-realists, to the early Tolman, Gibson, and radical behaviorism; connectionist psychology, running from the British associationists through Titchener, Thorndike, Hull, neo-Hullians, and today's connectionists; and reductive psychology, running from La Mettrie (fitfully) through parts of Wundt, Titchener, James, and Freud, briefly emerging aggressively in Lashley, and reviving today with Churchland (1987).

Each tradition has progressed. The representations posited by cognitive science are more sophisticated than Locke's *idea* or Tolman's cognitive map. The analyses of behavior by contemporary radical behaviorists are more precise and robust than Skinner's own. The neural networks of contemporary connectionism have advanced past traditional laws of association or S–R bonds to mathematically characterized state spaces. In the decade of the brain, of course, neurophysiological research is quantum leaps ahead of Lashley's pioneering search for the engram. Save for Wundt's founding of psychology, revolution in psychology is a myth.

REFERENCES

Angell, J. R. (1907). The province of functional psychology. *Psychological Review, 14,* 61–91.

Angell, J. R. (1911). Philosophical and psychological usage of the terms mind, consciousness, and soul. *Psychological Bulletin, 8,* 46–47.

Baars, B. J. (1986). *The cognitive revolution in psychology.* New York: Guilford Press.

Bawden, H. H. (1903). The functional theory of parallelism. *Philosophical Review, 12,* 299–319.

Bawden, H. H. (1904). The meaning of the psychical in functional psychology. *Philosophical Review, 13,* 298–319.

Bawden, H. H. (1910). Mind as a category of psychology. *Psychological Bulletin, 7,* 221–225.

Bechtel, W., & Abrahamsen, A. (1990). *Connectionism and the mind.* Cambridge, MA: Blackwell.

Blumenthal, A. (1975). A reappraisal of Wilhelm Wundt. *American Psychologist, 30,* 1081–1088.

Bolton, T. (1902). A biological view of perception. *Psychological Review, 9,* 537–548.

Brewer, W. F., & Nakamura, G. V. (1984). The nature and function of schemas. In R. S. Wyer & T. K. Srull (Eds.), *Handbook of social cognition* (Vol. 1, pp. 119–160). Hillsdale, NJ: Erlbaum.

Bringmann, W. G., & Tweney, R. D. (1980). (Eds.). *Wundt studies.* Toronto, Canada: Hogrefe.

Brinton, C. (1952). *The anatomy of revolution.* New York: Vintage.

Buchner, E. F. (1907). Psychological progress in 1906. *Psychological Bulletin, 4,* 1–9.

Buchner, E. F. (1911). Psychological progress in 1910. *Psychological Bulletin, 8,* 1–10.

Buss, A. R. (1978). The structure of psychological revolutions. *Journal of the History of the Behavioral Sciences, 14,* 57–64.

Butterfield, H. (1957). *The origins of modern science, 1300–1800* (rev. ed.) New York: Free Press. (Original work published 1949)

Cattell, J. M. (1904). The conceptions and methods of psychology. *Popular Science Monthly, 66,* 176–186.

Churchland, P. S. (1987). *Neurophilosophy.* Cambridge, MA: MIT Press.

Clark, J. C. D. (1986). *Revolution and rebellion, state and society in England in the seventeenth and eighteenth centuries.* Cambridge, England: Cambridge University Press.

Cohen, I. B. (1985). *Revolution in science.* Cambridge, MA: Belknap Press.

Coleman, S. R., & Salamon, R. (1988). Kuhn's *Structure of scientific revolutions* in the psychological journal literature, 1969-1983: A descriptive study. *Journal of Mind and Behavior, 9,* 415-445.

Collier, P., & Horowitz, D. (1989). *Destructive generation: Second thoughts about the sixties.* New York: Summit.

Davis, R., & Gould, S. E. (1929). Changing tendencies in general psychology. *Psychological Review, 36,* 320-331.

Dewey, J. (1896). The reflex-arc concept in psychology. *Psychological Review, 3,* 357-370.

Dewey, J. (1900). Psychology and social practice. *Psychological Review, 4,* 27-53.

Ericsson, K. A., & Simon, H. A. (1980). Verbal reports as data. *Psychological Review, 87,* 215-251.

Estes, W. K. (1991). Cognitive architectures from the standpoint of an experimental psychologist. *Annual Review of Psychology, 42,* 1-28.

Gardner, H. (1985). *The mind's new science: A history of the cognitive revolution.* New York: Basic Books.

Griewank, K. (1969/1971). Emergence of the concept of revolution. In C. Paynton & R. Blackey (Eds.), *Why revolutions? Theories and analyses* (pp. 16-22). Cambridge, MA: Schenkman.

Gutting, G. (1980). (Ed.). *Paradigms and revolutions: Applications and appraisals of Thomas Kuhn's philosophy of science.* Notre Dame, IN: University of Notre Dame Press.

Hacking, I. (1981). (Ed.). *Scientific revolutions.* Oxford, England: Oxford University Press.

Haggerty, M. E. (1911). The nineteenth annual meeting of the A.P.A. *Journal of Philosophy, 8,* 204-217.

Hale, M. (1980). *Human science and social order.* Philadelphia: Temple University Press.

Holton, G. (1973). *Thematic origins of scientific thought, Kepler to Einstein.* Cambridge, MA: Harvard University Press.

Horton, D. L., & Dixon, T. R. (1968). Tradition, trends, and innovations. In T. R. Dixon & D. L. Horton (Eds.), *Verbal behavior and general behavior theory* (pp. 572-580). Englewood Cliffs, NJ: Prentice-Hall.

Hull, D. (1988a). A mechanism and its metaphysics: An evolutionary account of the social and conceptual development of science. *Biology and Philosophy, 3,* 123-155.

Hull, D. (1988b). *Science as a process: An evolutionary account of the social and conceptual development of science.* Chicago: University of Chicago Press.

Hunter, W. S. (1922). An open letter to the anti-behaviorists. *Journal of Philosophy, 19,* 307-308.

James, W. (1890). *Principles of psychology.* New York: Holt.

Jastrow, J. (1927). The reconstruction of psychology. *Psychological Review, 34,* 169-195.

Jeffress, L. A. (1951). (Ed.). *Cerebral mechanisms in behavior.* New York: Wiley.

Kendler, H. H. (1952). "What is learned?"—A theoretical blind alley. *Psychological Review, 59,* 269–277.

Kendler, H. H., & Kendler, T. S. (1962). Horizontal and vertical processes in problem solving. *Psychological Review, 36,* 471–490.

Kessel, F. (1986, August). *Cognitive psychology reconsidered: What happened to the revolution?* Symposium presented at the 94th Annual Convention of the American Psychological Association, Washington, DC.

Koch, S. (1951). Theoretical psychology, 1950: An overview. *Psychological Review, 58,* 295–301.

Kuenne, M. R. (1946). Experimental investigation of the relation of language to transposition behavior in young children. *Journal of Experimental Psychology, 36,* 471–490.

Kuhn, T. S. (1957). *The Copernican revolution.* New York: Vintage.

Kuhn, T. S. (1970). *The structure of scientific revolutions* (Rev. ed.). Chicago: University of Chicago Press. (Original work published 1962)

Lachman, R., Lachman, J., & Butterfield, E. (1979). *Cognitive psychology and information processing.* Hillsdale, NJ: Erlbaum.

Lakatos, I., & Musgrave, A. (1970). (Eds.). *Criticism and the growth of knowledge.* Cambridge, England: Cambridge University Press.

Lashley, K. S. (1923). The behavioristic interpretation of consciousness. *Psychological Review, 30,* 237–272, 329–353.

Lashley, K. S. (1951). The problem of serial order in behavior. In L. A. Jeffress (Ed.), *Cerebral mechanisms in behavior* (pp. 112–136). New York: Wiley.

Laudan, L. (1977). *Progress and its problems.* Berkeley: University of California Press.

Leahey, T. H. (1980). The myth of operationism. *Journal of Mind and Behavior, 1,* 127–143.

Leahey, T. H. (1981). The mistaken mirror: On Wundt's and Titchener's psychologies. *Journal of the History of the Behavioral Sciences, 17,* 273–282.

Leahey, T. H. (1983). Operationism and ideology: Reply to Kendler. *Journal of Mind and Behavior, 4,* 81–90.

Leahey, T. H. (1991). *A history of modern psychology.* Englewood Cliffs, NJ: Prentice Hall.

Leahey, T. H. (1992). *A history of psychology* (3rd ed.). Englewood Cliffs, NJ: Prentice-Hall.

Legrand, M. (1990). Du behaviorisme au cognitivisme [From behaviorism to cognitivism]. *L'Annee Psychologique, 90,* 247–286.

Lovie, A. D. (1983). Attention and behaviourism: Fact and fiction. *British Journal of Psychology, 74,* 301–310.

MacCorquodale, K., & Meehl, P. (1948). On a distinction between hypothetical constructs and intervening variables. *Psychological Review, 55,* 95–107.

MacIntyre, A. (1977). Epistemological crises, dramatic narrative, and the philosophy of science. *The Monist, 60,* 453-471.

MacIntyre, A. (1981). *After virtue.* Notre Dame, IN: University of Notre Dame Press.

Michels, R. (1986). How psychoanalysis changes. *Journal of the American Academy of Psychoanalysis, 14,* 285-295.

Miller, G. (1979, June 1). *A very personal history.* Talk presented at the Cognitive Science Workshop, MIT, Cambridge, MA.

Miller, J. (1983). *States of mind.* New York: Pantheon.

Miller, N. (1959). Liberalization of basic S-R concepts. In S. Koch (Ed.), *Psychology: Study of a science* (Vol. 2, pp. 196-292). New York: McGraw-Hill.

Neisser, U. (1967). *Cognitive psychology.* New York: Appleton-Century-Crofts.

Neisser, U. (1976). *Cognition and reality.* San Francisco: Freeman.

Newell, A. (1973). You can't play 20 questions with nature and win. In W. G. Chase (Ed.), *Visual information processing* (pp. 283-308). San Diego, CA: Academic Press.

Nisbett, R. E., & Wilson, T. D. (1977). Telling more than we can know: Verbal reports on mental processes. *Psychological Review, 84,* 231-259.

Ogden, R. M. (1911a). Imageless thought. *Psychological Bulletin, 8,* 183-197.

Ogden, R. M. (1911b). The unconscious biases of laboratories. *Psychological Bulletin, 8,* 330-331.

Osgood, C. E. (1956). Behavior theory and the social sciences. *Behavioral Science, 1,* 167-185.

Palermo, D. (1971). Is a scientific revolution taking place in psychology? *Science Studies, 1,* 135-155.

Peterson, G. L. (1981). Historical self-understanding in the social sciences. The use of Thomas Kuhn in psychology. *Journal for the Theory of Social Behaviour, 11,* 1-30.

Paynton, C. T., & Blackey, R. (1971). (Eds.). *Why revolution? Theories and analyses.* Cambridge, MA: Schenkman.

Porter, R. (1986). The scientific revolution, a spoke in the wheel? In R. Porter & M. Teich (Eds.), *Revolutions in history* (pp. 290-316). Cambridge, England: Cambridge University Press.

Porter, R., & Teich, M. (1986). (Eds.). *Revolutions in history.* Cambridge, England: Cambridge University Press.

Rieber, R. W. (1980). (Ed.). *Wilhelm Wundt and the making of a scientific psychology.* New York: Plenum.

Samelson, F. (1981). Struggle for scientific authority: The reception of Watson's behaviorism, 1913-1920. *Journal of the History of the Behavioral Sciences, 17,* 399-425.

Sanford, E. C. (1903). Psychology and physics. *Psychological Review, 10,* 105-119.

Schneider, W. (1987). Connectionism: Is a paradigm shift taking place? *Behavior Research Methods, Instruments, and Computers, 19,* 73–83.

Shaw, R. E. (1986, August). *The cognitive psychology revolution: A personal perspective.* Paper presented at the 94th Annual Convention of the American Psychological Association, Washington, DC.

Shrader, D. (1980). The evolutionary development of science. *Review of Metaphysics, 34,* 273–296.

Simon, H. A. (1990). Invariants of human behavior. *Annual Review of Psychology, 41,* 1–20.

Skinner, B. F. (1950). Are theories of learning necessary? *Psychological Review, 57,* 196–215.

Skinner, B. F. (1953). *Science and human behavior.* New York: Macmillan.

Skinner, B. F. (1957). *Verbal behavior.* New York: Appleton-Century-Crofts.

Smith, L. S. (1986). *Behaviorism and logical positivism: A revised account of the alliance.* Stanford, CA: Stanford University Press.

Sperling, G. (1960). The information available in brief visual presentations. *Psychological Monographs, 74* (11, Whole No. 498).

Suppe, F. (1977). (Ed.). *The structure of scientific theories.* Urbana: University of Illinois Press.

Swartz, C. K. (1908). The scientific association of Johns Hopkins University. *Science, 28,* 814–815.

Tienson, J. (1991). An introduction to connectionism. In J. L. Garfield (Ed.), *Foundations of cognitive science: The essential readings* (pp. 381–397). New York: Paragon House.

Titchener, E. B. (1901–1905). *Experimental psychology: A manual of laboratory practice* (4 vols.). New York: Macmillan.

Titchener, E. B. (1904). *Lectures on the experimental psychology of the thought processes.* New York: Macmillan.

Titchener, E. B. (1972). *Systematic psychology: Prolegomena.* Ithaca, NY: Cornell University Press.

Tolman, E. C. (1932). *Purposive behavior in animals and men.* New York: Century.

Tulving, E. (1989). Memory, performance, knowledge, and experience. *European Journal of Psychology, 1,* 3–26.

Watson, J. B. (1907). Comparative psychology. *Psychological Bulletin, 4,* 288–302.

Watson, J. B. (1909). A point of view in comparative psychology. *Psychological Bulletin, 6,* 57–58.

Watson, J. B. (1913). Psychology as the behaviorist views it. *Psychological Review, 20,* 158–177.

Watson, J. B. (1961). John Broadus Watson. In C. Murchison (Ed.), *History of psychology in autobiography* (Vol. 3, pp. 271–281). New York: Russell & Russell. (Original work published 1936)

Wiebe, R. (1967). *The search for order, 1877–1920.* New York: Hill & Wang.

Williams, K. (1931). Five behaviorisms. *American Journal of Psychology, 43*, 337–361.

Woodworth, R. S. (1924). Four varieties of behaviorism. *Psychological Review, 31*, 257–264.

Wundt, W. M. (1896). *Lectures on human and animal psychology.* New York: Macmillan.

Wundt, W. M. (1907). Über Ausfrageexperimente und über die Methoden zur Psychologie des Denkens [Concerning interrogation—Experiments and methods for the psychology of thought]. *Psychologische Studien, 3*, 301–360.

11

FROM THE MACHINE TO THE GHOST WITHIN: PAVLOV'S TRANSITION FROM DIGESTIVE PHYSIOLOGY TO CONDITIONAL REFLEXES

DANIEL P. TODES

Ivan Pavlov is best known today for his research on conditional reflexes, which captured the attention of physiologists, psychologists, and the general public, for whom he (and his salivating dogs) became a symbol of the power of experimental biology to explain, and perhaps even control, human behavior.

Relatively few people are aware that Pavlov won the Nobel Prize in 1904 for contributions to digestive physiology, and fewer still recognize in today's cultural icon the scientist who, in the 1890s, insisted that an idio-

---

This article draws on research for a larger project, a modern biography of Pavlov, that has been funded by the National Endowment for the Humanities, the John Simon Guggenheim Memorial Foundation, Fulbright-Hays, and the International Research and Exchanges Board. I am also grateful to Eleonora Filippova for research assistance and helpful criticism of successive drafts and to Raymond Fancher, Karen Hollis, and George Windholz for suggestions that improved the final article.

Reprinted from *American Psychologist, 52,* 947–955 (1997). Copyright © 1997 by the American Psychological Association. Reprinted with permission of the author.

syncratic psyche played a central role in glandular responses to food. Pavlov's vigorous experimental argumentation for this point, however, was widely recognized by contemporaries as an important scientific contribution. In a 1901 report supporting Pavlov's candidacy for a Nobel Prize, Finnish physiologist Robert Tigerstedt emphasized the nominee's

> assertion of the influence of the psychic moment upon the secretions of certain digestive glands. We have here an extremely obvious example of how organs that are definitely not under the influence of our will can also, in their activity, be rather closely dependent on our mental state—and we have thereby acquired a new intimation of the close dependence in which mind and body stand in relation to one another. (Tigerstedt, 1901)

The transformation of Pavlov's research interests and approach to the psyche involved related departures from two firmly established traditions in his laboratory. One was conceptual: The standardized line of investigation that Pavlov had applied fruitfully to the gastric and pancreatic glands proved inapplicable to the salivary glands, leading him to reevaluate his approach to "psychic secretion." The dynamics and nature of this reevaluation owed much to a second departure, this one from a standard laboratory practice: Confronted with a conceptual problem that he recognized as psychological and, therefore, beyond his expertise, Pavlov recruited outside experts to help him resolve it, thus importing perspectives from contemporary psychology and psychiatry. The important role of insights from these two disciplines in the birth of research on conditional reflexes has been obscured, I think, by Pavlov's tale about this episode—a tale repeated uncritically by subsequent commentators.[1]

PAVLOV'S LABORATORY AND RESEARCH IN THE 1890s

The terms of Pavlov's transition were set by the scientific and managerial style that he developed in the 1890s and by his laboratory's approach to "psychic secretion" in those years. Pavlov's scientific style—his notion of "good physiology" and his related practices—owed much to the French physiologist Claude Bernard. Like Bernard, Pavlov viewed the organism as a purposeful, complex, specifically biological machine governed by deterministic relations. Physiology's task was to uncover these unvarying relations, to control experimentally, or otherwise to account for the "numberless factors" (Bernard, 1865/1957, p. 122) that concealed them behind

---

[1]For an exception, and a substantially different interpretation than the one I offer here, see Joravsky (1989, pp. 134–148).

a veil of apparent spontaneity (Bernard, 1865/1957; Pavlov, 1897/1951c, 1923/1951a). For Pavlov, the physiologist demonstrated conceptual control over these determined relations by expressing experimental results quantitatively and explaining the similarities and differences between them in terms of underlying regularities. He always insisted on results that were "*pravil'nye*," a Russian word that means both "*regular*" and "*correct*"—capturing his conviction that, in physiological experiments, these were one and the same. In this spirit, the centerpiece of Pavlov's *Lectures on the Work of the Principal Digestive Glands* (1897/1951c) is a series of "characteristic secretory curves" through which Pavlov described quantitatively the responses of the gastric, pancreatic, and salivary glands to various foodstuffs.

The great majority of the experiments referenced in this work were conducted by Pavlov's coworkers. These were usually physicians who, with only the most superficial knowledge of physiology, were seeking a quick doctoral degree to advance their career.[2] These physicians usually had a maximum of two years to choose a research topic, research it, write a doctoral thesis, and defend it. Pavlov incorporated them into a factory-like system that, essentially, used them as his own hands and eyes: He assigned them a specific topic, provided them with a suitably equipped dog technology, supervised (together with the laboratory's assistants and attendants) their research, interpreted their results, and closely edited their written products. In the years 1891–1904, about 100 of these coworkers passed through the laboratory; about 75% successfully completed their thesis and received their doctoral degree (Todes, 1997; Windholz, 1990).

Throughout the 1890s, Pavlov deployed these coworkers along standardized lines of investigation for each digestive gland. He first sought to establish nervous control over each gland; then to devise a dog technology for the precise quantitative measurement of its secretory products during normal digestion; then to establish the specific exciters for each gland; and, finally, to describe quantitatively the gland's secretory patterns. Laboratory research in these years concentrated on the gastric and pancreatic glands, because Pavlov considered these most important for digestion. The salivary glands received comparatively little attention until the latter part of the decade.

Beginning in 1894—and most famously in his *Lectures on the Work of the Principal Digestive Glands* (1897/1951c)—Pavlov described the digestive system as a "chemical factory." For him, the digestive glands responded

---

[2]Russian medical students took only a single short course in physiology, and the nature and quality of this course varied widely among medical schools. In 1895, Pavlov became professor of physiology at St. Petersburg's Military–Medical Academy, and the course he delivered to medical students there was devoted almost entirely to digestive physiology and based largely on his own work. Even in this course, however, instruction was based entirely on lectures and did not involve laboratory exercises.

purposefully, precisely, and regularly to different foods, producing secretions of the necessary quantity and proteolytic power for optimal digestion of an ingested foodstuff (Pavlov, 1897/1902, p. 2; 1897/1951c, p. 20).[3]

This digestive machine, however, was inhabited by a "ghost"—by the psyche and its capricious, highly individualized manifestations in the secretory responses of laboratory dogs. For Pavlov, digestive secretion normally occurred in two phases: The first, psychic phase was excited by appetite (through the vagus nerves) during the act of eating, and the second, nervous–chemical phase was excited by the products created when this initial "psychic secretion" acted on the food in the stomach. These products, in turn, excited the nervous mechanisms of the glands. Throughout the 1890s, Pavlov and his coworkers struggled experimentally and interpretively to separate these psychic and nervous–chemical phases and to define their different qualities.

Three points about these efforts are important here. First, the dogs used in "chronic experiments" lived much longer than those consumed in "acute experiments," enabling experimenters to identify in each a distinct personality (*lichnost'*) or character (*kharakter*). In 1896, for example, one coworker noted the following:

> Dogs exhibit a great variety of characters, which it is well to observe in their relation to food and manner of eating. There are passionate dogs, especially young ones, who are easily excited by the sight of food and are easily subject to teasing; others, to the contrary, have great self-possession and respond with great restraint to teasing with food. Finally, with certain dogs it is as if they understand the deceit being perpetrated upon them and turn their back on the proferred food, apparently from a sense of insult. These dogs only react to food when it falls into their mouth. ... Certain dogs are distinguished by a very suspicious or fearful character and only little-by-little adapt to the laboratory setting and the procedures performed upon them—it stands to reason that their depressed state does not facilitate the success of experiments. The age of dogs is also important in determining their character: the older the dog the more restrained and peaceful it is, and vice versa. (Lobasov, 1896, pp. 30–31)

Second, this assessment of a laboratory dog's psychological particularities played an important role in the interpretation of experimental results. As one coworker put it, "Professor Pavlov has many times told those working in his laboratory that knowledge of the individual qualities of the experimental dog has important significance for a correct understanding of many phenomena elicited by the experiment. During the conduct of our experiments we always kept this in view" (Kazanskii, 1901, p. 22). Judg-

---

[3] All translations in this article are my own. Where available, I also give page references to the standard English-language translation.

ments about these individual qualities shaped decisions about "good" and "bad" experiments and laboratory animals and, so, played an important role in the shaping of much-varied experimental results into "characteristic secretory curves" (Todes, 1997).

Third, throughout the 1890s, Pavlov treated the psyche as a "black box." That is, although the psyche (and, therefore, the dogs' individual personalities) was a constant presence in digestive processes, and was constantly invoked in explanations of experimental results, Pavlov did not systematically address its nature or the mechanisms behind it. For his purposes, it was sufficient to separate "psychic" from "nervous–chemical" mechanisms and to use the features of each to interpret the secretory reactions of his dogs to various foods.

PAVLOV, VUL'FSON, AND THE PSYCHE'S CHOICES

By late 1896, laboratory research on the salivary glands had reached the point where, according to Pavlov's standardized path of investigation, the next step was to determine the specific excitants of salivation. He entrusted this task to S. G. Vul'fson, who fit the typical profile of a laboratory coworker. A physiologically untrained physician, Vul'fson required only a quick thesis to complete his requirements for a doctorate of medicine. Pavlov assigned him "to establish precisely the exciters of salivation and to confirm their specificity and purposiveness" (Vul'fson, 1898, p. 15). From March 1897 through February 1898, Vul'fson experimented on four dogs with various salivary fistulas, analyzing the quantity and quality of glandular reactions to a variety of edible and inedible substances.

As had the coworkers who worked previously on the gastric and pancreatic glands, Vul'fson identified a "strict purposefulness" in the work of the salivary glands. The salivary response to edible substances varied in quantity according to the food's dryness and was uniformly rich in mucin. The response to inedible substances, on the other hand, was uniformly low in mucin and varied little from one inedible substance to another. This, Vul'fson observed, made good "sense": Mucin served to lubricate a foodstuff for its passage down the digestive canal. Since the dog did not swallow inedible substances, but rather ejected them from its mouth, a watery saliva low in mucin was secreted to rinse out any remnants of the ejected substance remaining in the mouth (Vul'fson, 1898, pp. 53–55).

Vul'fson also discovered, however, a fundamental difference between salivary secretion and that of other glands: In the salivary glands,

> psychic secretion is a complete reflection of the direct, purely physiological secretion, differing only in amount. ... The very same results regarding quantity and quality of saliva that are acquired when substances come into direct contact with the roof of the mouth occur also

when [these substances] are used for teasing alone. (Vul'fson, 1898, p. 56)

In other words, and in contrast to gastric and pancreatic secretion, the "psychic secretion" from the salivary glands was essentially identical to secretion during the second, nervous–chemical phase of digestion. This "psychic secretion" manifested the same ability to differentiate among substances that, in the gastric and pancreatic glands, occurred only in the nervous–chemical phase of digestion, when, according to laboratory doctrine, the specific excitability of nerve endings generated various "characteristic secretory curves" for different foods.

For Vul'fson, the specificity (or "adaptation") that was evident in "psychic secretion" from the salivary glands reflected not only "emotion, but also an element of thought—a representation [predstavleniia] about the nature of the external substances falling into the roof of the mouth" (Vul'fson, 1897, p. 113). Since this "adaptation" of salivary reactions to specific substances was "almost entirely of a psychic nature" (Vul'fson, 1898, p. 53), the usual Pavlovian program for glandular physiology seemed to lead directly into the psychology of the salivary glands.

Vul'fson, then, ascribed to the psyche a property that the laboratory had previously reserved for the nervous system: the ability to distinguish between different substances and to generate an appropriate secretory response to each. "The task of the psyche," he wrote, is "to sort out" substances, "to divide" them into two groups—accepted and rejected substances—in order to respond to each appropriately. The psyche exhibited great "scrupulousness," an unerring "judgment of particular circumstances," and the ability to "generalize" (Vul'fson, 1898, pp. 43, 53, 56).

This discovery supported Pavlov's long-standing insistence on the importance of appetite and the psyche, and he enthusiastically endorsed Vul'fson's conclusions. Lauding Vul'fson's report (which he had closely edited) for demonstrating the "subtle and sharp adaptation of the salivary glands," Pavlov emphasized that in salivation "the participation of the psyche emerges clearly, so psychology almost entirely overshadows physiology." This "dominance of psychology" was clear from "the fact that appropriate types of saliva are secreted both when a tested substance is put into the mouth and when it is only used to tease the dog." He added, "If in other cases we speak in jest, metaphorically, about 'the mind' of the glands, then in this case we should understand the term 'the mind of the glands' literally" (Pavlov, 1898, pp. 458–459).

The qualities of this "mind," however, presented an obstacle to Pavlov's standardized investigatory path. For years, he and his coworkers had recognized the importance of the psyche but had simply black-boxed it. In analyses of the gastric glands, for example, a dog's initial secretory reaction to foodstuffs was simply attributed to the influence of appetite or the psyche. This "psychic secretion" gave way, in the second phase of the digestive process, to the specific nervous mechanisms that produced the "characteristic secretory curves" elicited by particular foods. Vul'fson's research, however, demonstrated the inapplicability of this scheme to the salivary glands. Here, "psychic secretion" was essentially identical to the nervous–chemical secretion. The purposeful, precise, and specific reactions of the salivary glands to different foods resulted, then, not from the specific excitability of the nervous system (as was the case with the gastric and pancreatic glands) but rather from the psyche's ability to, as Vul'fson put it, "sort out," "arrange," and "judge."

Recognizing that here "psychology almost entirely overshadows physiology," and conceding his own lack of expertise in this area, Pavlov turned, uncharacteristically, to an outside expert.

PSYCHOLOGY TO THE RESCUE: SNARSKII OPENS THE BLACK BOX

A. T. Snarskii was an atypical coworker. Holding both university and medical degrees, he entered Pavlov's laboratory to study a subject about which he possessed greater expertise than the chief. Snarskii had worked both in neurologist–psychiatrist V. M. Bekhterev's clinic for mental and nervous illnesses and, shortly thereafter, in the Alexander III Charity Home for the Mentally Ill (which was directed by Pavlov's longtime friend, A. V. Timofeev). Pavlov usually assigned an incoming coworker to an ongoing line of investigation without respect to that coworker's background. In 1900, however, and despite the fact that five other new coworkers arrived at the laboratory that year, he recruited Snarskii to study the "mind of the glands."

The doctoral thesis (Snarskii, 1901) that resulted was also atypical. Most important, unlike the vast majority of coworkers' theses, Snarskii's thesis made extensive use of scientific authorities from outside the laboratory: He cited physiologists who had addressed the biology of purposeful behavior (including Jacques Loeb and I. M. Sechenov), the Russian zoopsychologist V. A. Vagner, and a range of Russian and Western European psychologists (including G. I. Chelpanov, William James, and Wilhelm Wundt).

Snarskii mobilized these authorities to criticize Vul'fson's (and, implicitly, Pavlov's) conclusion that the psyche actively "chooses," "sorts out," "arranges," and "judges." By the standards of contemporary psychology, Snarskii insisted, Pavlov's "mind of the glands" did not deserve the word "mind." Like the contemporary psychologists whom he cited, Snarskii distinguished among a wide variety of mental qualities that involved a broad range of different capacities. He concluded that "psychic secretion" reflected not high-level processes such as will, choice, and judgment, but rather the relatively low-level process of "visual associations." Citing Wundt and other "authoritative teachers of psychology," Snarskii argued that "psychic secretion" resulted from "the simplest process that united new impressions with preceding ones: elementary memory." This process of recognition by means of "newly-established associations"—which Wundt termed "recognition anew"—was devoid of the higher rung psychological qualities that Vul'fson and Pavlov had attributed to it:

> To conclude from this entirely elementary act that the dog makes a "choice" about what kind of saliva to secrete in the given case is to make an unfounded logical leap. Direct recognition does not rise even to [the level of] a free representation, to say nothing of the long chain of psychic acts—such as the formation of concepts, judgments and conclusions—that must precede a conscious choice and decision. (Snarskii, 1901, p. 9)

Snarskii offered a different explanation, which he developed through a polemic against Vul'fson's conclusions:

> When the dog recognizes a previous irritant ... it repeats a habitual reflex; but repeats it automatically, without any participation of conscious, active will. Schematically, this would be expressed as follows: a common reflexive arc is established between the direct irritant and the act of salivation. We can imagine that the centripetal end of this arc is ... split, and therefore the very same salivary reflex can be received by the representations associated directly with the irritation.... This act is accomplished entirely stereotypically, automatically, through a well-trod path. The consciousness of the dog plays no "important" role; it "chooses" nothing and in itself does not "determine" the activity of the salivary glands. (Snarskii, 1901, pp. 9–10)

For Snarskii, then, the "psychic secretion" of the salivary glands was an "association" or "habitual reflex" that was accomplished in the subcortical region of the brain, entirely outside of the brain's conscious centers in the cortex (Snarskii, 1901, p. 50).

In Snarskii's person, contemporary psychology had challenged the lay, black-boxed notion of the psyche that had governed laboratory discourse throughout the 1890s. One could argue that Snarskii's approach to "psychic secretion" was both truer to contemporary trends in psychology and "more physiological" than that previously propounded by Vul'fson and Pavlov. Snarskii's new perspective did not, however, reveal a means by which "psychic secretion" could be addressed in a manner consistent with Pavlov's notion of "good physiology." The chief again looked outside his laboratory for "a person with whom one could go further" (Pavlov, 1926).

A KEY ANALOGY FROM PSYCHIATRY: TOLOCHINOV ON THE EYE AND KNEE REFLEXES

Pavlov settled on a second atypical coworker, I. F. Tolochinov. Like Snarskii, Tolochinov was a veteran of Bekhterev's laboratory who worked at the Alexander III Charity Home for the Mentally Ill. Unlike Snarskii, Tolochinov had already received his doctoral degree for a thesis completed under Bekhterev on changes in the nerve fibers of the brain during paralytic imbecility (Tolochinov, 1900). From November 1901 until about April 1902, Tolochinov left his job at the Charity Home several afternoons a week to conduct experiments in Pavlov's laboratory.

In this article, I can only touch on some key aspects of Tolochinov's research. First, his initial trials were oriented toward acquiring consistent results with "psychic secretion" under varying conditions—in other words, toward making the "ghost" behave as regularly as the machine it inhabited. Tolochinov's first success, from which Pavlov later dated the beginnings of research on conditional reflexes, occurred in February 1902, when he discovered the phenomenon that would later be termed "extinction." ("Extinction" was the term soon applied to the disappearance of a conditional response after the conditional stimulus had been repeated several times without repetition of the unconditional stimulus.)

Second, according to Tolochinov's later account, his interpretation of this phenomenon drew on his experience in psychiatry with the knee and eyelid reflexes. Tolochinov recalled that he had initially used the lexicon prevailing in the laboratory after Snarskii's work: "'representation,' 'association,' and so forth" (Tolochinov, 1912, p. 1278). Explaining his subsequent decision to abandon such psychological terms, Tolochinov wrote:

> It had been noticed long ago that in several patients knee reflexes sometimes result, not only from the blow of a hammer, but even when this instrument is merely waved with the intention to strike the lig. patel. propr. ... It is also remarkable that this phenomenon is to a certain degree involuntary; therefore it is most easily understood as a reflexive act from the brain cortex by means of waves of light, just as the reflexive response of the knee to a blow is the result of mechanical waves. This is the same type of phenomenon as the nictating reflex of the eyelid, which occurs, not only when the eyelid is touched, but also when any object, or the investigator's fingers, make a more or less rapid approach to the eye.
>
> On these foundations I proposed that the phenomena of salivation during irritation of the dogs at a distance by foodstuffs be considered a *reflex* at a distance, which was accepted by *prof. I. P. Pavlov*, who termed it a *conditional reflex*, as distinct from the *unconditional* reflex received when the mucous membrane of the roof of the mouth is irritated directly by edible and inedible substances.

> My conviction of the truth of this new view ... was further strengthened by the circumstance that the salivary reflex elicited at a distance obeyed the same basic physiological law as the nictating reflex of the eyelid or the knee reflex elicited at a distance. That is, it obeyed the law of extinction or decline of the reflex, and, mainly, when certain conditions were observed, it was distinguished by an involuntary, fatal character. (pp. 1281–1282)

As had Snarskii, then, Tolochinov brought to Pavlov's laboratory professional experiences and expertise critical to the reevaluation of "psychic secretion" and foreign to Pavlov himself. For Tolochinov, the extinction of "psychic secretion" was reminiscent of his recent experiences in Bekhterev's clinic with the knee and eyelid reflexes. Bekhterev had devoted special attention to these reflexes and regularly demonstrated to physicians like Tolochinov the usefulness of the knee reflex as a diagnostic tool for nervous and mental diseases (see Bekhterev, 1896, 1901). Just as Snarskii had drawn on authorities in psychology to strip the "mind of the glands" of will and judgment, to portray "psychic secretion" as a simple "association" or "habitual reflex"; so did Tolochinov draw on clinical psychiatry to establish that "psychic secretion" behaved similarly to other "reflexes from a distance" that were "distinguished by an involuntary, fatal character." This rendered it, at least in principle, accessible to physiological investigation.

PAVLOV'S DIFFICULT TRANSITION

These developments did not in themselves determine Pavlov's decision to shift investigations from digestion to the psyche. The laboratory, after all, was constantly uncovering new phenomena and investigatory possibilities, many of which were never pursued. Pavlov was both an experimental physiologist and the manager of a large laboratory enterprise; so, his evaluation of this new line of research necessarily involved both scientific and managerial decisions. Given Pavlov's notion of "good physiology," the key scientific question was as follows: Could investigations of the psyche, like his research on digestion, generate precise, repeatable patterns that could be expressed quantitatively and interpreted according to their purposefulness? Given the institutional imperatives of his laboratory, the key managerial question was as follows: Could this line of research consistently generate fresh dissertation topics that could be satisfactorily completed by physiologically untrained physicians within two years? Only when Pavlov decided that both questions could be answered affirmatively did he shift the focus of laboratory research.

His decision was also influenced by a series of other considerations. First, the discovery of secretin by Bayliss and Starling (1902) undermined

Pavlov's nervist portrayal of digestive processes, reopening and complicating questions that he had considered closed. As one coworker (Tsitovich, n.d.) recalled, this introduced a certain "dissonance" in the laboratory. As a theorist, Pavlov could accommodate himself, however reluctantly, to the existence of humoral mechanisms; but, as an experimentalist, he found this more difficult. Furthermore, Pavlov simply found nervous mechanisms more aesthetically pleasing and, thoroughout the 1890s, had consistently avoided topics that forced him to confront humoral ones. Second, developments in Russian psychology and psychiatry had normalized the previously controversial view that psychological phenomena might be explicable physiologically. By 1900–1901, Pavlov found himself taking a considerably "less physiological" position toward "psychic secretion" than did a number of his medical students, who "often asked: but can't this be explained as a reflex, just one from another sensory organ?" (Orbeli, 1967, p. 172). Studies of brain localization in Bekhterev's laboratory also portrayed psychic secretion as "nothing other than a reflex transmitted to the gastric glands through the central nervous system" (Gerver, 1900, p. 142; see also Bekhterev, 1902; Gorshkov, 1900). Finally, Pavlov had always been interested in the mysteries of the human mind and human behavior and had imbibed in the 1860s a positivist faith that a scientific understanding of these subjects was the surest path to improving human society.

The complexity of the scientific and managerial issues at stake made Pavlov's decision-making process slow and contradictory. As one longtime coworker later recalled, "Of course, I[van] P[etrovich] expected attacks on his new child and suffered through a great series of doubts and vacillations" (Savich, 1924, p. 18). In July 1902, after Tolochinov delivered a short paper on his research to the Northern Congress of Physiologists in Helsingfors (i.e., Helsinki), Pavlov reportedly spoke animatedly to scientists in the corridor about the potential of this new line of investigation and about his plans to pursue it single-mindedly. Yet, the response was apparently "restrained" (Samoilov, 1925, p. 214), and Pavlov himself, in his lectures to medical students some months later, analyzed "psychic secretion" precisely as he had before Tolochinov's (and even Snarskii's) work. Explaining the dog's secretory reactions to teasing experiments, he noted that it "can think, desire, and express its feelings. It follows instructions, guesses, shows what is pleasant and unpleasant to it" (Pavlov, 1902–1903, p. 18). One searches in vain for a crucial experiment that convinced Pavlov that "psychic secretion" was a reflex or launched his new line of investigation.

We can, however, track Pavlov's transition through the scientific products of his laboratory, the changing pattern of coworker assignments, and his annual reports to his patron, Prince Ol'denburgskii. In February 1903, Pavlov's comments about one coworker's paper on the nerves of the salivary glands indicated a significant, public shift in his interpretation of "psychic secretion" (Pavlov, 1952b), and two months later he delivered his first public address on the new line of investigation to the XIV International Congress of Physiologists in Madrid, Spain (Pavlov, 1923/1951a, pp. 23–39). The pattern of coworker assignments highlights this same period: In 1902, only Tolochinov was assigned to research on "psychic secretion"; when he departed the following year, only one of five new coworkers was assigned to continue this work. It is significant, however, that in October 1903 Pavlov pulled a favorite coworker, Boris Babkin, off a developed investigation of the pancreas and assigned him instead to the new subject. In 1904, one of two new coworkers was assigned to the new line of investigation; in 1905, two of three; in 1906, three of four; and, in 1907, all new coworkers. Pavlov's annual reports to Ol'denburgskii fit the same basic chronology. He first mentioned the new line of investigation in his report of December 1903. He listed it last among the laboratory's research topics from 1903 to 1906 and as the only topic in his report of 1907 (Pavlov, 1903–1907).

ARE CONDITIONAL REFLEXES CONDITIONED?

The conceptual dynamics of Pavlov's transition can be appreciated by considering the term that he chose to replace "psychic secretion"—"*uslovnyi refleks*," which has become known to English speakers as "*conditioned reflex*." The Russian phrase, however, can be translated as either "conditioned reflex" or "conditional reflex." The latter is much closer to Pavlov's original meaning. It is significant that in the French abstract of the report in which Tolochinov first used this term—an abstract edited by Pavlov—the term "*uslovnyi refleks*" is translated, not as "le reflex conditionné," but precisely as "le reflexe conditionnel" (Tolotschinoff, 1902).

What, exactly, did Pavlov mean by "conditional reflex" in the years that are covered here? Why did he use this term to replace Snarskii's "association, or habitual reflex" and Tolochinov's "reflex at a distance?" According to L. A. Orbeli, who worked in the laboratory from 1901 to 1917, Pavlov used the term "conditional reflexes" "in part because their very inclusion as reflexes then had for him a conditional character" (Orbeli, 1967, p. 172). This fits Pavlov's common usage of the word *uslovyni*, which he employed as a synonym for "tentative" or "hypothetical" (see, e.g., Pavlov, 1901/1952a, p. 164). For Pavlov, I think, the term "conditional reflex" reflected not only whatever ontological reservations he may have had but, more important, the test that this potential new line of investigation had to pass to qualify as good physiology.

The promise and the peril of research on "psychic secretion" both resided in the apparent "conditionality" of the relationship between stimulus and response. On the one hand, this conditionality perhaps represented the animal's complex but determined adaptation to the subtlest change in its conditions—to changing signals about available food or an approaching predator (Pavlov, 1903/1951a, pp. 29–30; also in 1923/1928, p. 52). On the other hand, this conditionality might represent either the indeterminacy of psychological phenomena or a determinacy that is inaccessible to physiological methods. In either case, conditionality would deprive experiments on this subject of the determinedness that constituted the sine qua non of "good physiology." As Pavlov put the central question in 1903 (answering it, perhaps, with a bit more conviction that he actually felt),

> The center of gravity in our subject lies, then, in this: is it possible to include all this apparent chaos of relations within certain bounds, to make these phenomena constant, to discover their rules and mechanism? It seems to me that the several examples which I shall now present give me the right to respond to these questions with a categorical "yes" and to find at the basis of all psychic experiments always the very same special reflex as a fundamental and most common mechanism. True, our experiment in physiological form always gives one and the very same result, excluding, of course, any extraordinary conditions—this is an unconditional reflex; the basic characteristic of the psychic experiment, on the other hand, is its inconstancy, its apparent capriciousness. Nevertheless, the result of the psychic experiment also recurs, otherwise we could not even speak about it. Consequently, the entire matter is only in the great number of conditions influencing the result of the psychic experiment as compared with the physiological experiment. This will be, then, a conditional reflex. (Pavlov, 1923/1951a, p. 30; also in Pavlov, 1923/1928, pp. 52–53)

For Pavlov, the "conditional reflex" was a suitable subject for physiological research only if it was, in the final analysis, a fully determined "conditioned reflex." As an experimentalist and laboratory manager, he defined the question operationally: "To what extent can regular, quantitative, determined results be acquired in the laboratory?" This is what made Tolochinov's discovery of extinction so important to Pavlov: It represented the first case in which conditional reflexes behaved in a quantifiably repeatable, orderly fashion. After his report in Helsinki, Tolochinov conducted a number of experiments—from August 1902 to April 1903—that gradually reinforced Pavlov's intuition that research on conditional reflexes could reveal "firm lawfulness, ... constantly recurring facts" (Pavlov, 1923/1951a, p. 33). For example, conditional reflexes diminished and disappeared if conditional stimuli were repeated without repetition of the unconditional reflex on which they were based, they were renewed by a strong unconditional irritation, and they were stronger when an object irritated several sensory organs rather than just one. Babkin's (1904) research further buttressed Pavlov's growing confidence that the conditional reflex would, with sufficient research, prove to be fully determined.

Once Tolochinov's and Babkin's experiments had established a few basic, repeatable patterns, Pavlov could address the "conditional reflex" in precisely the same manner as he had addressed digestive physiology. Feeding the same dog the same quantity of the same food in two different experiments had never, after all, yielded exactly the same secretory results. The differences were explained by reference to the dog's personality, mood, and so forth, and varying results were thereby contained within "characteristic secretory curves." Similarly, differing results in two apparently identical experiments with conditional reflexes could be contained within a few basic patterns by invoking numerous uncontrolled variables (what Bernard had termed the "numberless factors" in any complex organic machine), allowing Pavlov to interpret the "conditional reflex" as a "conditioned reflex."[4]

Confidence in the ability of experiments on the conditional reflex to generate relatively regular, quantifiable results was also critical to Pavlov's concerns as manager of a large laboratory. Regardless of its scientific promise, the new line of investigation was only feasible if it could be pursued by the physiologically untrained physicians who performed the vast majority of experiments in his laboratory. Pavlov could not sit on the bench beside each of these coworkers, who usually numbered about 15 at a time. For him to adequately supervise their work and interpret their results—to exercise "quality control"—Pavlov required that experiments be of relatively simple design and, most important, that their results be expressible quantitatively. This was not only necessary to Pavlov's notion of good physiology, it also provided a simple language in which his coworkers could gather results and communicate them to the chief for final interpretation. Pavlov trusted numbers both as a reflection of physiological reality and as a managerial tool (Porter, 1995). By 1903–1904, he was confident that the investigation of conditional reflexes could generate reasonably regular, repeatable numbers in the same way as had investigations of digestive physiology over the previous 15 years and, so, that it met the scientific and managerial criteria for a new focus of laboratory research.

---

[4]In my opinion, the nature of this interpretive process—in which a constantly increasing number of new variables and laws was invoked to contain a constantly increasing amount of varying data within a mechanistic framework—was the main reason that Pavlov, for all his public confidence, suffered privately, at least through the mid-1920s, from grave doubts about his research on conditional reflexes. For example, in 1926—after some 25 years of experimental work—he oscillated between confession and self-congratulation in comments to a small gathering of coworkers:

> I must thank you for all your work, for the mass of collected facts—for having superbly subdued this beast of doubt. And now—when the book [*Lectures on the Work of the Large Hemispheres of the Brain*, 1926/1951b] is appearing—now, I hope, this beast will retreat from me. And my greatest gratitude for liberating me from torment is to you. On the other hand, you have taken part in the creation of a new chapter of science. For this I congratulate you. (Pavlov, 1926)

PAVLOV'S TALE

Pavlov related several times the story of his transition to research on conditional reflexes—always with the story line first presented in a speech of 1906 at a London ceremony honoring T. H. Huxley. Space limitations permit me to analyze only one aspect of this tale, which I present in the version that Pavlov offered in the preface to *Lectures on Conditioned Reflexes: Twenty-Five Years of Objective Study of the Higher Nervous Activity (Behaviour) of Animals* (1923/1928):

> I began to investigate the question of this [psychic] secretion with my collaborators, Drs. Vul'fson and Snarskii. While Vul'fson collected new and important material regarding the details of the psychic excitation of the salivary glands, Snarskii undertook an analysis of the internal mechanism of this excitation from the subjective point of view; that is, considering the imagined internal world of the dogs (upon whom our experiments were conducted) by analogy with our own thoughts, feelings, and desires. There then occurred an event unprecedented in the laboratory. We differed sharply from each other in our interpretations of this world and could not by any further experiments come to agreement on any general conclusion, despite the laboratory's consistent practice by which new experiments undertaken by mutual agreement usually resolved any disagreements and arguments.
>
> Dr. Snarskii held to his subjective explanation of the phenomena, but I, struck by the fantastic nature and barrenness for science of such an approach to the problem, began to seek another exit from this difficult position. After persistent deliberation, after a difficult intellectual struggle, I decided, finally, in the face of the so-called psychic excitation, to remain in the role of a pure physiologist, that is, of an objective external observer and experimenter, dealing exclusively with external phenomena and their relations. For implementation of this decision I also began with a new co-worker, Dr. I. F. Tolochinov, and there subsequently followed twenty years of work with the participation of many tens of my dear coworkers. (Pavlov, 1923/1928, pp. 38–39)

According to Pavlov, a distant influence from his youth gave him the courage to address psychological phenomena "objectively":

> I think that . . . the most important impetus for my decision, although at the time an unconscious one, was the influence, from the long distant years of my youth, of the talented brochure of Ivan Mikhailovich Sechenov, the father of Russian physiology, entitled *Reflexes of the Brain* (1863[/1866]). You know, the influence of an idea that is powerful by virtue of its novelty and truthfulness to reality, especially in one's younger years, is so profound, so enduring, and, one must add again, often concealed. In this brochure, a brilliant attempt was made—a truly extraordinary attempt for that time (of course theoretically, in the form of a physiological scheme) to represent our subjective world

in a purely physiological manner. (Pavlov, 1923/1928, p. 39; 1923/1951a, p. 14)

The reader, I hope, has noticed that Pavlov's version of his conflict with Snarskii corresponds neither to the content of Snarskii's thesis nor to Pavlov's actual position on "psychic secretion" in the years immediately before and after Snarskii's research. Pavlov and Snarskii clearly differed about something, and perhaps their disagreement indeed concerned differing estimations of contemporary psychology. As the reader has seen, however, far from "holding to a subjective explanation of the phenomena," Snarskii was the first laboratory coworker to insist that "psychic secretion" was "an association" or "habitual reflex" and that "the consciousness of the dog plays no important role." Furthermore, he developed this idea in a polemic against Vul'fson's view that the psyche actively "chooses" and "judges"—a view that Pavlov had enthusiastically endorsed and continued to propound in his lectures through at least the fall of 1902. As for the "unconscious" influence of Sechenov's *Reflexes of the Brain*—this tract, published in 1863 and unmentioned by Pavlov until his tale of 1906, was cited, for the first time in any laboratory publication, by Snarskii in his doctoral thesis.

Why—if my own account of the transition is correct—would Pavlov have told such a tale? This is especially puzzling because he was usually scrupulous, even generous, in crediting coworkers for their contributions. I suggest two reasons. First, in his tale, Pavlov cast himself as a committed struggler for the scientific worldview in the spirit of Darwin, Huxley, and other such heroes. Snarskii (as the subjective psychologist) served him well here as a villain. Second, Pavlov's tale established a reputable physiological paternity for a line of research that he regarded, in Savich's words, as a vulnerable "child." Dismissed by many as speculative and ridiculed by others as "spitting science," the study of conditional reflexes was a risky endeavor for a basically conservative man who treasured the respect of his colleagues. In Pavlov's tale, this line of investigation was born through a combination of Vul'fson's and Tolochinov's experiments, the conceptual influence of "the father of Russian physiology," and his own courage and faith in the scientific worldview. It was, in other words, respectably modern and objective; it was "good physiology," untainted by influences from psychology, a discipline that had been associated in Pavlov's formative intellectual years with barren, reactionary metaphysics. In this same spirit, as Pavlov embraced his new line of investigation with growing enthusiasm and confidence, he redefined it in increasingly physiological terms. In his annual reports of 1903–1905 he termed it "the study of questions of experimental psychology on animals," in 1906 he renamed it "the objective investigation of the higher divisions of the central nervous system," and in 1907 finally settled upon "the investigation of the activity of the large hemispheres and sense organs" (Pavlov, 1903–1907).

Pavlov's tale, then, was a part of this changing lexicon, this redefinition and legitimization of his new endeavor. In this sense, it was a final step in his transition to research on conditional reflexes.

REFERENCES

Babkin, B. P. (1904). *Opyt sistematicheskago izucheniia slozhno-nervnykh (psikhicheskikh) iavlenii u sobaki* [An attempt at the systematic study of complex-nervous (psychic) phenomena in the dog]. St. Petersburg, Russia: Military–Medical Academy.

Bayliss, W. M., & Starling, E. H. (1902). The mechanism of pancreatic secretion. *The Journal of Physiology, 28,* 325–353.

Bekhterev, V. M. (1896). O fenomene kolennoi chashki, kak raspoznavatel'nom priznake nervnykh boleznei, i o drugikh srodnykh iavleniiakh [On the kneecap phenomenon as a diagnostic sign of nervous illnesses, and on other similar phenomena]. *Obozrenie Psikhiatrii, Nevrologii i Eksperimental'noi Psikhologii, 3,* 171–176.

Bekhterev, V. M. (1901). O refleksakh v oblasti litsa i golovy [On the reflexes of the face and head]. *Otchety nauchnogo sobraniia vrachei S. Peterburgskoi kliniki dushevnykh i nervnykh boleznei.* St. Petersburg, Russia.

Bekhterev, V. M. (1902). *Psikhika i zhizn'* [The psyche and life]. St. Petersburg, Russia.

Bernard, C. (1957). *An introduction to the study of experimental medicine* (H. C. Greene, Trans.). New York: Dover. (Original work published 1865)

Gerver, A. V. (1900). O vlianii golovnogo mozga na otdelenie zheludochnago soka [On the influence of the brain on the secretion of gastric juice]. *Trudy obshchestva russkikh vrachei, 67,* 142–143, 153–156, 158–162, 165–168.

Gorshkov, Ia. P. (1900). O lokalizatsii tsentrov vkusa v mozgovi kore [On the localization of taste centers in the cerebral cortex]. *Obozrenie Psikhiatrii, Nevrologii i Eksperimental'noi Psikhologii, 10,* 737–742.

Joravsky, D. (1989). *Russian psychology: A critical history.* Oxford, England: Basil Blackwell.

Kazanskii, N. P. (1901). *Materialy k eksperimental'noi patologii i eksperimental'noi terapii zheludochnykh zhelez sobaki* [Material toward the experimental pathology and experimental therapeutics of the gastric glands of the dog]. St. Petersburg, Russia: Military–Medical Academy.

Lobasov, I. O. (1896). *Otdelitel'naia rabota zheludka sobaki* [The secretory work of the stomach of the dog]. St. Petersburg, Russia: Military–Medical Academy.

Orbeli, L. A. (1967). Pamiati Ivana Petrovicha Pavlova [Recollections of Ivan Petrovich Pavlov]. In E. M. Kreps (Ed.), *Pavlov v vospominaniiakh sovremennikov* (pp. 162–175). Leningrad, Russia: Nauka.

Pavlov, I. P. (1898). Remarks during discussion of Vul'fson 1898b. *Trudy russkikh vrachei, 65,* 458–459.

Pavlov, I. P. (1902). *The work of the digestive glands* (W. H. Thompson, Trans.). London: Griffin. (Original work published 1897)

Pavlov, I. (1902–1903). Zapisi lektsii po fiziologii pishchevareniia prochitannykh Ivana Petrovicha Pavlova v 1902–1903 gg [Transcription of lectures on digestive physiology delivered by Ivan Petrovich Pavlov in 1902–1903]. Archive of the Russian Academy of Sciences (St. Petersburg), *fond* 259 *opis'* 1 *delo* 78.

Pavlov, I. P. (1903–1907). *Annual reports to Prince A. P. Ol'denburgskii on laboratory activities*. Central State Archive of Scientific–Technical Documentation (St. Petersburg), *fond* 2282 *opis'* 1 *dela* 201 (1903), 222 (1904), 239 (1905), 252 (1906), and 263 (1907).

Pavlov, I. P. (1926). *Stenographed remarks of December 27, 1926 to a group of coworkers*. Archive of the Russian Academy of Sciences (St. Petersburg), *fond* 259 *opis'* 1 *delo* 203.

Pavlov, I. P. (1928). *Lectures on conditioned reflexes: Twenty-five years of objective study of the higher nervous activity (behaviour) of animals* (W. H. Gantt, Trans.). New York: International Publishers. (Original work published 1923; includes original works published from 1903–1922)

Pavlov, I. P. (1951a). Dvadtsatiletnii opyt ob"ektivnogo izucheniia vysshei nervnoi deiatel'nosti zhivotnykh [Twenty years of the objective study of the higher nervous activity of animals]. In *Polnoe sobranie sochinenii* (Vol. 3, Pt. 1). Moscow, Russia: Akademiia Nauk SSSR. (Original work published 1923; includes original works published from 1903–1922)

Pavlov, I. P. (1951b). Lektsii o rabote bol'shikh polusharii golovnogo mozga [Lectures on the work of the large hemispheres of the brain]. In *Polnoe sobranie sochinenii* (Vol. 4). Moscow, Russia: Akademiia Nauk SSSR. (Original work published 1926)

Pavlov, I. P. (1951c). Lektsii o rabote glavnykh pishchevaritel'nykh zhelez [Lectures on the work of the principal digestive glands]. In *Polnoe sobranie sochinenii* (Vol. 2, Pt. 2). Moscow, Russia: Akademiia Nauk SSSR. (Original work published 1897)

Pavlov, I. P. (1952a). Predislovie k perevodu knigi R. Tigershtedta "Uchebnik fiziologii cheloveka" [Introduction to the translation of R. Tigerstedt's "Textbook of human physiology"]. In *Polnoe sobranie sochinenii* (Vol. 6, pp. 163–171). Leningrad, Russia: Akademiia Nauk SSSR. (Original work published 1901)

Pavlov, I. P. (1952b). Remarks during discussion of N. M. Geiman's report to the Society of Russian Physicians. In *Polnoe sobranie sochinenii* (Vol. 6, p. 201). Leningrad, Russia: Akademiia Nauk SSSR.

Porter, T. (1995). *Trust in numbers: The pursuit of objectivity in science and public life*. Princeton, NJ: Princeton University Press.

Samoilov, A. F. (1925). Obshchaia kharakteristika issledovatel'skogo oblika I. P. Pavlova [A general characterization of the investigative profile of I. P. Pavlov]. In E. M. Kreps (Ed.), *Pavlov v vospominaniiakh sovremennikov* (pp. 203–218). Leningrad, Russia: Nauka.

Savich, V. V. (1924). Ivan Petrovich Pavlov: Biograficheskii ocherk [Ivan Petrovich Pavlov: A biographical essay]. In *Sbornik posviashchennyi 75-letiiu akademika I. P. Pavlova* (pp. 3–31). Leningrad, Russia: Institut Eksperimental'noi Meditsiny.

Sechenov, I. M. (1866). *Refleksy golovnogo mozga* [Reflexes of the brain]. St. Petersburg, Russia. (Original work published 1863)

Snarskii, A. T. (1901). *Analiz normal'nykh uslovii raboty sliunnykh zhelez u sobaki* [Analysis of the normal conditions of the work of the salivary glands in the dog]. St. Petersburg, Russia: Military–Medical Academy.

Tigerstedt, R. (1901). Memo of 10 July 1901 to Nobel Prize Committee. In *P. M. Forsandelser och Betankanden 1901*. Stockholm, Sweden: Nobel Archives, Karolinska Institutet.

Todes, D. (1997). Pavlov's physiology factory, 1891–1904. *Isis, 88*, 1–42.

Tolochinov, I. F. (1900). *O patologo—anatomicheskikh izmeneniiakh cherepnykh nervov i otnosiashchikhsia k nim nervnykh volokon mozgovogo stvola pri narastaiushchem paralichnom slaboumii* [On pathological–anatomical changes in the cranial nerves and the related nervous fibers of the brain stem during progressive paralytic imbecility]. St. Petersburg, Russia: Military–Medical Academy.

Tolochinov, I. F. (1912). Pervonachal'naia razrabotka sposoba uslovnykh refleksov i obosnovanie termina "uslovnyi refleks" [The original development of the conditional reflexes method and the basis of the term "conditional reflex"]. *Russkii vrach, 11*, 1277–1282.

Tolotschinoff, I. F. (1902). Contribution a l'etude de la physiologie et de la psychologie des glandes salivaries [Contribution to the study of the physiology and psychology of the salivary glands]. In *Forhandlingar vid Nordiska naturforskare och lakermotet* (pp. 42–46). Helsinki, Finland.

Tsitovich, I. S. (n.d.). *Vospominaniia ob akademike Ivane Petroviche Pavlove* [Reminiscences about academician Ivan Petrovich Pavlov]. Archive of the Russian Academy of Sciences (St. Petersburg), *fond* 259 *opis'* 7 *delo* 77.

Vul'fson, S. G. (1897). O psikhicheskom vliianii v rabote sliunnykh zhelez [On psychic influence in the work of the salivary glands]. *Trudy obshchestva russkikh vrachei, 65*, 110–113.

Vul'fson, S. G. (1898). *Rabota sliunnykh zhelez* [The work of the salivary glands]. St. Petersburg, Russia: Military–Medical Academy.

Windholz, G. (1990). Pavlov and the Pavlovians in the laboratory. *Journal of the History of the Behavioral Sciences, 2*, 64–74.

12

WHATEVER HAPPENED TO LITTLE ALBERT?

BENJAMIN HARRIS

Almost 60 years after it was first reported, Watson and Rayner's (1920) attempted conditioning of the infant Albert B. is one of the most widely cited experiments in textbook psychology. Undergraduate textbooks of general, developmental, and abnormal psychology use Albert's conditioning to illustrate the applicability of classical conditioning to the development and modification of human emotional behavior. More specialized books focusing on psychopathology and behavior therapy (e.g., Eysenck, 1960) cite Albert's conditioning as an experimental model of psychopathology (i.e., a rat phobia) and often use Albert to introduce a discussion of systematic desensitization as a treatment of phobic anxiety.

Unfortunately, most accounts of Watson and Rayner's research with Albert feature as much fabrication and distortion as they do fact. From information about Albert himself to the basic experimental methods and

---

Preparation of this article was aided by the textbook and literature searches of Nancy Kinsey, the helpful comments of Mike Wessels, and the bibliographic assistance of Cedric Larson. The author also thanks Bill Woodward and Ernest Hilgard for their comments on earlier versions of this work.
Reprinted from *American Psychologist*, 34, 151–160 (1979). Copyright © 1979 by the American Psychological Association. Reprinted with permission of the author.

results, no detail of the original study has escaped misrepresentation in the telling and retelling of this bit of social science folklore.

There has recently been a revival of interest in Watson's conditioning research and theorizing (e.g., MacKenzie, 1972; Seligman, 1971; Weimer & Palermo, 1973; Samelson, Note 1), and in the mythology of little Albert (Cornwell & Hobbs, 1976; Larson, 1978; Prytula, Oster, & Davis, 1977). However, there has yet to be a complete examination of the methodology and results of the Albert study and of the process by which the study's details have been altered over the years. In the spirit of other investigations of classic studies in psychology (e.g., Ellenberger, 1972; Parsons, 1974) it is time to examine Albert's conditioning in light of current theories of learning. It is also time to examine how the Albert study has been portrayed over the years, in the hope of discovering how changes in psychological theory have affected what generations of psychologists have told each other about Albert.

THE EXPERIMENT

As described by Watson and Rayner (1920), an experimental study was undertaken to answer three questions: (1) Can an infant be conditioned to fear an animal that appears simultaneously with a loud, fear-arousing sound? (2) Would such fear transfer to other animals or to inanimate objects? (3) How long would such fears persist? In attempting to answer these questions, Watson and Rayner selected an infant named Albert B., whom they described as "healthy," and "stolid and unemotional" (p. 1). At approximately 9 months of age, Albert was tested and was judged to show no fear when successively observing a number of live animals (e.g., a rat, a rabbit, a dog, and a monkey), and various inanimate objects (e.g., cotton, human masks, a burning newspaper). He was, however, judged to show fear whenever a long steel bar was unexpectedly struck with a claw hammer just behind his back.

Two months after testing Albert's apparently unconditioned reactions to various stimuli, Watson and Rayner attempted to condition him to fear a white rat. This was done by presenting a white rat to Albert, followed by a loud clanging sound (of the hammer and steel bar) whenever Albert touched the animal. After seven pairings of the rat and noise (in two sessions, one week apart), Albert reacted with crying and avoidance when the rat was presented without the loud noise.

In order to test the generalization of Albert's fear response, 5 days later he was presented with a rat, a set of familiar wooden blocks, a rabbit, a short-haired dog, a sealskin coat, a package of white cotton, the heads of Watson and two assistants (inverted so that Albert could touch their hair), and a bearded Santa Claus mask. Albert seemed to show a strong fear response to the rat, the rabbit, the dog, and the sealskin coat; a "negative" response to the mask and Watson's hair; and a mild response to the cotton. Also, Albert played freely with the wooden blocks and the hair of Watson's assistants.

After an additional 5 days, Watson reconditioned Albert to the rat (one trial, rat paired with noise) and also attempted to condition Albert directly to fear the previously presented rabbit (one trial) and dog (one trial). When the effects of this procedure were tested in a different, larger room, it was found that Albert showed only a slight reaction to the rat, the dog, and the rabbit. Consequently, Watson attempted to "freshen the reaction to the rat" (p. 9) by presenting it with the loud noise. Soon after this, the dog began to bark loudly at Albert, scaring him and the experimenters and further confounding the experiment.

To answer their third question concerning the permanence of conditioned responses over time, Watson and Rayner conducted a final series of tests on Albert after 31 days of neither conditioning nor extinction trials. In these tests, Albert showed fear when touching the Santa Claus mask, the sealskin coat, the rat, the rabbit, and the dog. At the same time, however, he initiated contact with the coat and the rabbit, showing "strife between withdrawal and the tendency to manipulate" (Watson & Rayner, 1920, p. 10). Following these final tests, Albert's mother removed him from the hospital where the experiment had been conducted. (According to their own account, Watson and Rayner knew a month in advance the day that Albert would no longer be available to them.)

THE CONTEXT OF WATSON AND RAYNER'S STUDY

What was the relationship of the Albert experiment to the rest of Watson's work? On a personal level, this work was the final published project of Watson's academic career, although he supervised a subsequent, related study of the deconditioning of young children's fears (M. C. Jones, 1924a, 1924b). From a theoretical perspective, the Albert study provided an empirical test of a theory of behavior and emotional development that Watson had constructed over a number of years.

Although Watson had publicly declared himself a "behaviorist" in early 1913, he apparently did not become interested in the conditioning of motor and autonomic responses until late 1914, when he read a French edition of Bekhterev's *Objective Psychology* (see Hilgard & Marquis, 1940). By 1915, Watson's experience with conditioning research was limited to this reading and his collaboration with his student Karl Lashley in a few simple studies. Nevertheless, Watson's APA Presidential Address of that year made conditioned responses a key aspect of his outline of behaviorism and seems to have been one of the first American references to Bekhterev's work (Hilgard & Marquis, 1940, p. 24; Koch, 1964, p. 9; Watson, 1916b). Less than a year after his APA address, two articles by Watson (1916a, 1916c) were published in which he hypothesized that both normal defense mechanisms and psychiatric disorders (e.g., phobias, tics, hysterical symptoms) could be understood on the basis of conditioning theory.

Six months later, the *American Journal of Psychology* featured a more extensive article by Watson and J. J. B. Morgan (1917) that formulated a theory of emotion, intended to serve both experimentalists and clinicians. Its authors hypothesized that the fundamental (unlearned) human emotions were fear, rage, and love; these emotions were said to be first evoked by simple physical manipulations of infants, such as exposing them to loud sounds (fear) or restricting their movements (rage). Concurrently, they hypothesized that "the method of conditioned reflexes" could explain how these basic three emotions become transformed and transferred to many objects, eventually resulting in the wide range of adult emotions that is evoked by everyday combinations of events, persons, and objects. In support of these theoretical ideas, Watson and Morgan began to test whether infants' fears could be experimentally conditioned, using laboratory analogues of thunder and lightning. In the description of this work and the related theory, a strong appeal was made for its practical importance, stating that it could lead to a standard experimental procedure for "bringing the human emotions under experimental control" (p. 174).

By the early months of 1919, Watson appears not yet to have found a reliable method for experimentally eliciting and extinguishing new emotional reactions in humans. However, by this time he had developed a program of research with infants to verify the existence of his hypothesized three fundamental emotions. Some early results of this work were described in May 1919, as part of a lengthy treatise on both infant and adult emotions. Anticipating his work with Albert,[1] Watson (1919b) for the first time applied his earlier principles of emotional conditioning to children's fears of animals. Based on a case of a child frightened by a dog that he had observed, Watson hypothesized that although infants do not naturally fear animals, if "one animal succeeds in arousing fear, any moving furry animal thereafter may arouse it" (p. 182). Consistent with this hypothesis,

---

[1] In tracing the development of Watson's ideas about conditioning, it would be helpful to know whether the experiments with Albert had already begun when Watson wrote his 1919 *Psychological Review* article. Unfortunately, there is no hard evidence of exactly when the Albert study was completed. Watson and Rayner's original report was published in the February 1920 *Journal of Experimental Psychology*, suggesting that the research was completed in 1919. Also, M. C. Jones (1975, Note 2) remembers that Watson lectured about Albert as early as the spring of 1919 and showed a film of his work with infants at the Johns Hopkins University (Watson, 1919a). Individual frames of this film published later ("Behaviorist Babies," 1928; "Can Science Determine Your Baby's Career Before It Can Talk?," 1922; Watson, 1927, 1928a) suggest that at some date this film contained footage of Albert's conditioning. Since the work with Albert lasted for approximately 4 months, there seems to be a strong possibility that Watson's 1919 prediction was not entirely based on theoretical speculation.

the results of Watson and Rayner's experiments with Albert were reported 9 months later.

Although Watson's departure from Johns Hopkins prematurely ended his own research in 1920, he continued to write about his earlier findings, including his work with Albert. In 1921, he and Rayner (then Rosalie Rayner Watson) summarized the results of their interrupted infant research program, concluding with a summary of their experience with Albert. Although this was a less complete account than their 1920 article, it was the version that was always referenced in Watson's later writings. These writings included dozens of articles in the popular press (e.g., Watson, 1928b, 1928c), the books *Behaviorism* (1924) and *Psychological Care of Infant and Child* (1928a), and a series of articles in *Pedagogical Seminary* (Watson, 1925a, 1925b, 1925c). Many of these articles retold the Albert story, often with photographs and with added comments elaborating on the lessons of this study.

INTRODUCTORY-LEVEL TEXTBOOK VERSIONS OF ALBERT

A selective survey of textbooks[2] used to introduce students to general, developmental, and abnormal psychology revealed that few books fail to refer to Watson and Rayner's (1920) study in some manner. Some of these accounts are completely accurate (e.g., Kennedy, 1975; Page, 1975; Whitehurst & Vasta, 1977). However, most textbook versions of Albert's conditioning suffer from inaccuracies of various degrees. Relatively minor details that are misrepresented include Albert's age (Calhoun, 1977; Johnson & Medinnus, 1974), his name (Galanter, 1966), the spelling of Rosalie Rayner's name (e.g., Biehler, 1976; Helms & Turner, 1976; McCandless & Trotter, 1977; Papalia & Olds, 1975), and whether Albert was initially conditioned to fear a rat or a rabbit (CRM Books, 1971; Staats, 1968).

Of more significance are texts' misrepresentations of the range of Albert's postconditioning fears and of the postexperimental fate of Albert. The list of spurious stimuli to which Albert's fear response is claimed to have generalized is rather extensive. It includes a fur pelt (CRM Books, 1971), a man's beard (Helms & Turner, 1976), a cat, a pup, a fur muff (Telford & Sawrey, 1968), a white furry glove (Whittaker, 1965), Albert's aunt, who supposedly wore fur (Bernhardt, 1953), either the fur coat or the fur neckpiece of Albert's mother (Hilgard, Atkinson, & Atkinson, 1975; Kisker, 1977; Weiner, 1977), and even a teddy bear (Boring, Langfeld, & Weld, 1948). In a number of texts, a happy ending has been added to the story by the assertion that Watson removed (or "reconditioned")

---

[2]After this survey of texts was completed, similar reviews by Cornwell and Hobbs (1976) and by Prytula et al. (1977) were discovered. Interested readers should consult these articles for lists of additional textbook errors.

Albert's fear, with his process sometimes described in detail (Engle & Snellgrove, 1969; Gardiner, 1970; Whittaker, 1965).

What are the causes of these frequent errors by the authors of undergraduate textbooks? Prytula et al. (1977) catalogued similar mistakes but offered little explanation of their source. Cornwell and Hobbs (1976) suggested that such distortions, if not simply due to overreliance on secondary sources, can be generally seen as authors' attempts to paint the Albert study (and Watson) in a more favorable light and to make it believable to undergraduates. Certainly, many of the common errors *are* consistent with a brushed-up image of Watson and his work. For example, not one text mentions that Watson knew when Albert would leave his control —a detail that might make Watson and Rayner's failure to recondition Albert seem callous to some modern readers.

However, there are other reasons for such errors besides textbooks' tendencies to tell ethically pleasing stores that are consistent with students' common sense. One major source of confusion about the Albert story is Watson himself, who altered and deleted important aspects of the study in his many descriptions of it. For example, in the *Scientific Monthly* description of the study (Watson & Watson, 1921), there is no mention of the conditioning of Albert to the dog, the rabbit, and the rat that occurred at 11 months 20 days; thus Albert's subsequent responses to these stimuli can be mistaken for a strong generalization effect (for which there is little evidence). A complementary and equally confusing omission occurs in *Psychological Care of Infant and Child* (Watson, 1928a). There, Watson begins his description of the Albert study with Albert's being conditioned to a rabbit (apparently the session occurring at 11 months 20 days). As a result, the reader is led to believe that Albert's fear of a rat (a month later) was the product of generalization rather than the initial conditioning trials. Besides these omissions, Watson and Rayner (1920) also made frequent editorial comments, such as the assertion that fears such as Albert's were "likely to persist indefinitely, unless an accidental method for removing them is hit upon" (p. 12). Given such comments, it is understandable that one recent text overestimates the duration of the Albert experiment by 300% (Goldenberg, 1977), and another states that Albert's "phobia became resistant to extinction" (Kleinmuntz, 1974, p. 130).

A second reason for textbook authors' errors, it seems, is the desire of many of us to make experimental evidence consistent with textbook theories of how organisms should act. According to popular versions of learning theory (as described by Herrnstein, 1977), organisms' conditioning should generalize along simple stimulus dimensions; many textbooks list spurious fear-arousing stimuli (for Albert) that correspond to such dimensions. To illustrate the process of stimulus generalization, Albert is often said to have feared every white, furry object—although he actually showed fear mostly of nonwhite objects (the rabbit, the dog, the sealskin coat,

Watson's hair), and did not even fear everything with hair (the observers). But to fit a more simplified view of learning, either new stimuli appear in some texts (e.g., a *white* rabbit, a white glove) or it is simply asserted that Albert's conditioning generalized to all white and furry (or hairy) stimuli (see Biehler, 1976; Craig, 1976; Helms & Turner, 1976). Though it might seem as if Albert's fear did generalize to the category of all animate objects with fur (e.g., the rabbit) or short hair (e.g., Watson's head), this is impossible to show conclusively. The only experimental stimuli not fitting this category were the blocks and the observers' hair. Apparently the blocks were a familiar toy (thus not a proper stimulus), and Albert's familiarity with the observers is not known (although we may guess that one might have been his mother).

BEHAVIOR THERAPISTS' VIEWS OF ALBERT

Unfortunately, misrepresentations of Watson and Rayner's (1920) work are not confined to introductory-level texts. For proponents of behavioral therapies, Albert's conditioning has been a frequently cited reference, although its details have often become altered or misinterpreted. Joseph Wolpe, for example, is well known for his conditioning-anxiety model of phobias and his treatment of various neurotic disorders by what was originally termed "reciprocal inhibition" (Wolpe, 1958). According to Wolpe and Rachman (1960):

> Phobias are regarded as conditioned anxiety (fear) reactions. Any "neutral" stimulus, simple or complex, that happens to make an impact on an individual at about the time that a fear reaction is evoked acquires the ability to evoke fear subsequently. (p. 145)

In support of this model Wolpe and Rachman cited the Albert study to "indicate that it is quite possible for one experience to induce a phobia" (p. 146). Also, Eysenck (1960) asserted that "Albert developed a phobia for white rats and indeed for all furry animals" (p. 5). Similar interpretations of Watson and Rayner's (1920) experiment were found in subsequent writings by Wolpe and other behavior therapists (e.g., Rachman, 1964; Sandler & Davidson, 1971; Ullman & Krasner, 1965; Wolpe, 1973).

Critical reading of Watson and Rayner's (1920) report reveals little evidence either that Albert developed a rat phobia or even that animals consistently evoked his fear (or anxiety) during Watson and Rayner's (1920) experiment. For example, 10 days after the completion of the initial (seven-trial) conditioning to a white rat, Albert received an additional trial of conditioning to the same rat. Immediately following this, his reaction to the rat was described as: "Fell over to the left side, got up on all fours and started to crawl away. On this occasion there was no crying, but strange to say, as he started away he began to gurgle and coo, even while leaning far over to the left side to avoid the rat" (p. 7).

On the same day as this, Albert received a trial of conditioning to the rabbit he had seen previously (using the clanging steel bar). When shown the rabbit twice again, he whimpered but did not cry. Immediately after this, his reactions were tested in a different (larger) room. When shown the rabbit, Albert's response was described as: "Fear reaction slight. Turned to left and kept face away from the animal but the reaction was never pronounced" (p. 9).

Finally, 31 days later and after having received an additional conditioning trial to the rat at the end of the preceding session, Albert's reactions to the (same) rat were:

> He allowed the rat to crawl towards him without withdrawing. He sat very still and fixated intently. Rat then touched his hand. Albert withdrew it immediately, then leaned back as far as possible but did not cry. When the rat was placed on his arm he withdrew his body and began to fret, nodding his head. The rat was then allowed to crawl against his chest. He first began to fret and then covered his eyes with both hands. (p. 11)

Not only does Albert's response seem lacking in the strength that we associate with phobia (possibly due to Watson's alternation of acquisition and extinction trials) but on a qualitative basis it seems unlike the classically conditioned anxiety on which some behavior therapists base their theoretical models of phobias.

Of course, it might be argued by proponents of a two-factor theory of phobias that Albert's reactions to the rat and the rabbit were successful escape responses from the anxiety-arousing stimuli, thus explaining Albert's relative calm (no rapid breathing, crying, etc.). However, Albert did not consistently avoid the animals to which he was conditioned. On his final day of testing, for example, Albert initially did not avoid the rabbit to which he had been conditioned; he then attempted to avoid it, but then "after about a minute he reached out tentatively and slowly and touched the rabbit's ear with his right hand, finally manipulating it" (Watson & Rayner, 1920, p. 11).[3]

---

[3] Another model that has been applied to the Albert study is that of operant or instrumental conditioning. For example, Larson (1978) and Reese and Lipsitt (1970) cited a paper by R. M. Church (Note 3) on this point (see also Kazdin, 1978). Such an interpretation is apparently based on Watson's notes indicating that at least for the first two trials, the loud noise was contingent on Albert's active response (i.e., touching the rat). Also, the one trial of conditioning to the rabbit occurred when Albert had begun "to reach out and manipulate its fur with forefingers" (Watson & Rayner, 1920, p. 8). The attractiveness of an (aversive) instrumental model of Albert's conditioning is that it would not necessarily predict any emotional reaction by Albert and would help explain his reluctance to touch the experimental animals. Strong support for this model is lacking, however, with Watson and Rayner describing at least four conditioning trials on which the loud sound was not contingent on Albert's instrumental response, and a number of trials the character of which is uncertain.

A more serious problem with clinicians' citing of the Albert study is the failure of Watson's contemporaries to replicate his work. Although H. E. Jones (1930) subsequently demonstrated persistent galvanic skin response (GSR) conditioning with an infant (using a mild electric current as an unconditioned stimulus, and a light and various sounds as conditioned stimuli), attempts to replicate the Albert study using variations of Watson's own method were unsuccessful. Valentine (1930), for example, used extensive naturalistic observation and failed to find conditioned fear of infants to loud noises; he criticized both Watson's methodology and his simplistic theory of emotional development. Bregman (1934) was also unsuccessful in her attempts to condition even 1 of 15 infants to fear wooden and cloth objects, using a disagreeable noise as an unconditioned stimulus (see Thorndike, 1935). Finally, whatever our retrospective view of Albert's conditioned reactions, a conditioned-avoidance model of phobias (with fear as a necessary component) is not consistent with more recent experimental and clinical literature (see Costello, 1970; Hineline, 1977; Marks, 1969, 1977).

ALBERT AND PREPAREDNESS THEORY

One of the reasons that Albert is so well known is that he is rediscovered every 5 or 10 years by a new group of psychologists. In the early 1960s, Wolpe and Eysenck were the curators and analysts of the Albert myth. Ten years later, Wolpe and Eysenck were supplanted by M. E. P. Seligman, who has seized control of the Albert story and uses it (in slightly revised form) to attack the views of its former proponents. At the same time, Seligman both challenges traditional theories of learning and proposes his own reformulation, known as "preparedness theory."

Briefly stated, preparedness theory (Seligman, 1970, 1971; see also Schwartz, 1974) posits that traditionally held laws of learning cannot be uniformly applied to all stimuli interacting with all organisms. In a classical conditioning paradigm, organisms may be physiologically or cognitively "prepared" to form certain conditioned stimulus–unconditioned stimulus associations and "contraprepared" to develop others. In the former case (e.g., rats learning taste aversion to food causing illness) the association is easily formed, but in the latter case (e.g., rats learning taste aversion to food prepared with footshock) it is difficult if not impossible to form. Similarly, Seligman (1970) summarized evidence from instrumental-learning paradigms to suggest that for a particular organism, certain behaviors differ in their potential to be successfully conditioned (see Shettleworth, 1973).

Relevant to Albert, Seligman (1971) hypothesized that the strength of human phobic reactions (i.e., their resistance to extinction) is due to the high degree of preparedness of certain stimuli (e.g., snakes). This conditioning to phobic objects occurs very quickly, whereas conditioning to other stimuli (assumed to be of low preparedness or contraprepared) results in fear reactions that are less intense, take longer to establish, and extinguish more quickly. As Marks (1977) noted, there is some evidence that objects differ in their ability to produce conditioned GSR in humans over time (e.g., Öhman, Erixon, & Löfberg, 1975). It also makes sense that evolution may have made it easier for humans to learn some responses than others (see Herrnstein, 1977). However, much of Seligman's (1971) discussion of human phobias is based on an erroneous interpretation of Watson and Rayner's (1920) work.

As described in his article "Phobias and preparedness," Seligman's version of Albert's conditioning is generally consistent with the exaggerated claims for the study made by Watson (e.g., Watson, 1924). According to preparedness theory, the existence of strong animal phobias in the human clinical literature is evidence that "furry things" (Seligman, 1971, p. 315) are strongly prepared phobic stimuli for humans. If furry things are highly prepared and Watson and Rayner (1920) used furry things in their study, then Albert must have quickly developed a strong fear of animals and other furry things. Consistent with this logic is Seligman's (1971) assertion that "Albert became afraid of rats, rabbits, and other furry objects" (p. 308, italics added) and that Watson "probably did not" become an aversive stimulus to Albert. In fact, Albert was "completely negative" to Watson's hair (Watson & Rayner, 1920, p. 7), and of course, Albert's fear was only tested to a single rat, a single rabbit, and to no previously neutral, nonfurry objects.

In addition to presenting this inaccurate picture of how Albert's fear initially generalized, Seligman's account also misrepresents the ease with which Albert was conditioned, the durability of his reactions, and the details of an attempt to replicate the Albert study. According to Seligman (1971), Albert's "conditioning occurred in two trials" and this "prepared fear conditioning [did] not extinguish readily" (p. 315). In fact, "seven joint stimulations were given [to Albert] to bring about the complete reaction" (Watson & Rayner, 1920, p. 5), and there is little if any evidence either that the reactions of Albert were resistant to a formal extinction procedure (or to the passage of time) or that he was tested with valid contraprepared stimuli. Further, in describing a similar study that actually used a contraprepared stimulus (a wooden duck), Seligman erred in his statement that the experimenter "did not get fear conditioning to a wooden duck, even after many pairings with a startling noise" (1971, p. 315). In fact, the experimenter himself admitted that his failure was due to the inadequacy of his unconditioned stimulus, not to the inappropriateness of a wooden duck as a phobic stimulus:

> We did not succeed in establishing a conditional fear response to the duck for the simple reason that the noise failed to evoke fear. Once

only in something over fifty trials did the child exhibit what might be called a worried look. (English, 1929, p. 222)

One can understand how the Albert study could be selectively misperceived by Seligman, since the errors that he committed result in a historical account that provides more support for the predictions of his preparedness theory than does (subsequent) clinical observation (DeSilva, Rachman, & Seligman, 1977; Rachman & Seligman, 1976). It seems ironic that in making his case for the new theory of preparedness, Seligman first had to strengthen the old Watsonian interpretation of the Albert study: that it was a successful laboratory demonstration of fear conditioning, its generalization, and resistance to extinction.

CONCLUSIONS

What can be deduced from reviewing the many versions of Watson and Rayner's study of Albert? One somewhat obvious conclusion is that we should be extremely wary of secondhand (and more remote) accounts of psychological research. As Cornwell and Hobbs (1976) suggested, this may be most relevant to often-cited studies in psychology, since we may be more likely to overestimate our knowledge of such bulwarks of textbook knowledge.

What about the process by which secondary sources themselves come to err in their description of classic studies? A simple explanation might assume that more recent authors, like any recipients of secondhand information (e.g., gossip), are more likely to present an account of much-cited research that has "drifted well away from the original" (Cornwell and Hobbs, 1976, p. 9). For the Albert study at least, this relatively passive model of communication is an oversimplified view. Not only was Watson quick to *actively* revise his own description of his research (e.g., Watson, 1928a; Watson & Watson, 1921) but it took little time for textbook authors to alter the details of Albert's conditioning. For example, within a year after Watson's original article, one text (Smith & Guthrie, 1921) had already invented spurious stimuli to which Albert's initial fear generalized; such errors were also contained in early texts by H. L. Hollingworth (1928) and J. W. Bridges (1930).

There has undoubtedly been some distortion due to the simple retelling of the Watson and Rayner study, but a more dynamic influence on textbook accounts seems to have been the authors' opinions of behaviorism as a valid theoretical viewpoint. For example, the agreement of Harvey Carr's (1925) text with Watson's overgeneralizations about Albert was consistent with Carr's (1915) relatively favorable review of Watson's early work. Similarly, as behaviorism's influence grew, even relative skeptics seem to have been willing to devote more attention to the Albert study. For example, the fourth edition of Robert S. Woodworth's (1940) text, *Psychology*, mentioned that Albert's "conditioned fear was 'transferred' from the rat to similar objects" (p. 379), though the previous edition of the text (Woodworth, 1934) did not mention this generalization and was more critical of Watson's theory of emotional development. Woodworth's 1934 text also had Albert initially conditioned to a rabbit, while the 1940 one correctly described the conditioned stimulus of a rat. This greater accuracy in Woodworth's later account is an indication of at least one author's ability to resist any general drift toward increasing misinformation.

Any attempted explanation of textbook errors concerning Albert raises the question of the role of classic studies and the nature of historical changes in psychology. As discussed by Samelson (1974) and Baumgardner (1977), modern citations of classic studies can often be seen as attempts by current theorists to build a false sense of continuity into the history of psychology. In social psychology, for example, claiming Auguste Comte as a founder of the field (see Allport, 1968) gives the impression that our contemporary motives (especially the wish for a well-developed behavioral science) have directed the field's progress for almost a century (Samelson, 1974). To cite another classic "origin," the Army's psychological testing program during World War I is taken by some clinical psychologists as an early example of how the profession of psychology has always grown in relation to its increased usefulness. However, it has recently been shown that World War I intelligence testing was of little practical use at the time (Samelson, 1977).

In reviewing these classic studies or *origin myths* in psychology, it should be emphasized that this myth-making process is not anyone's attempt to defraud the public. Instead, it arises "as largely a byproduct of pedagogy: as a means to elucidate the *concepts* of a scientific specialty, to establish its *tradition*, and to attract students" (Samelson, 1974, p. 223).[4] This seems a fair explanation of the Albert case—one that casts the frequent "rediscoverers" of Watson and Rayner (Garrett, 1941; Harlow, 1949; Salter, 1949; Seligman, 1971; Watson, 1928a; Wolpe, 1958) as participants in the process of building historical support for new theoretical perspectives (e.g., preparedness theory).

As Samelson (1974) noted, the major difficulty with such reevaluations of classic studies is that they obscure the actual factors that determine the course of scientific research. In the case of the Albert study, debate still surrounds the question, How did behaviorism become a dominant force in American psychology (MacKenzie, 1972, 1977; Weimer & Palermo, 1973)? The answer is beyond the scope of this study, since it involves much more than an evaluation of the Albert study.[5] However, it is now possible

---

[4]Samelson noted that he was paraphrasing T. S. Kuhn (1968) here.
[5]Other relevant factors include the relation of Watson's theory to psychoanalysis (Bakan,

to assert that by itself the Albert study was not very convincing proof of the correctness of Watson's general view of personality and emotions. In addition to the study's reliance on only one subject, the experimental stimuli were sufficient to test for generalization effects, the observers' accounts were too subjective, and the technology did not exist to permit reliable assessment of emotional responses (see Sherman, 1927); there was insufficient follow-up and there was a confounding of instrumental and classical conditioning paradigms (see Footnote 3). These methodological flaws were also apparent to critical reviewers of the day (e.g., English, 1929; Valentine, 1930) and surely to Watson and Rayner themselves. However, they are worth emphasizing here because of continuing attempts to integrate the study into the early conditioning literature (e.g., Seligman, 1971). It may be useful for modern learning theorists to see how the Albert study prompted subsequent research (i.e., Bregman, 1934), but it seems time, finally, to place the Watson and Rayner data in the category of "interesting but uninterpretable results."

REFERENCE NOTES

1. Samelson, F. *Reactions to Watson's behaviorism: The early years*. Paper presented at the meeting of the Cheiron Society, Wellesley, Massachusetts, June 1978.
2. Jones, M. C. Personal communication, April 1, 1978.
3. Church, R. M. The role of fear in punishment. In J. R. Braun (Chair), *The effects of punishment on behavior*. Symposium presented at the meeting of the American Psychological Association, New York, September 1966.
4. Buckley, K. W. *Behaviorism and the professionalization of American psychology: A study of John Broadus Watson (1878–1958)*. Doctoral dissertation in preparation, University of Massachusetts—Amherst, 1979.
5. Harris, B., & Morawski, J. *John B. Watson's predictions for 1979*. Unpublished manuscript, Vassar College, 1978.

REFERENCES

Allport, G. The historical background of modern social psychology. In G. Lindzey & E. Aronson (Eds.), *The handbook of social psychology* (2nd ed., Vol. 1). Reading, Mass.: Addison-Wesley, 1968.

Bakan, D. Behaviorism and American urbanization. *Journal of the History of the Behavioral Sciences*, 1966, 2, 5–28.

Baumgardner, S. R. Critical studies in the history of social psychology. *Personality and Social Psychology Bulletin*, 1977, 3, 681–687.

1966), the state in 1920 of other theories of emotion, the impact of Watson's popular writing (Buckley, Note 4; Harris & Morawski, Note 5), and Watson's national reputation.

Behaviorist babies. *Review of Reviews*, November 1928, pp. 548–549.

Bernhardt, K. S. *Practical psychology* (2nd ed.). New York: McGraw-Hill, 1953.

Biehler, R. F. *Child development: An introduction.* Boston: Houghton Mifflin, 1976.

Boring, E. G., Langfeld, H. S., & Weld, H. P. (Eds). *Foundations of psychology.* New York: Wiley, 1948.

Bregman, E. O. An attempt to modify the emotional attitudes of infants by the conditioned response technique. *Journal of Genetic Psychology*, 1934, *45*, 169–198.

Bridges, J. W. *Psychology: Normal and abnormal.* New York: Appleton, 1930.

Calhoun, J. F. *Abnormal psychology* (2nd ed.). New York: CRM Books, 1977.

Can science determine your baby's career before it can talk? *New York American Sunday Magazine*, January 8, 1922.

Carr, H. A. Review of *Behavior, an introduction to comparative psychology* by J. B. Watson. *Psychological Bulletin*, 1915, *12*, 308–312.

Carr, H. A. *Psychology: A study of mental activity.* New York: Longmans, Green, 1925.

Cornwell, D., & Hobbs, S. The strange saga of little Albert. *New Society*, March 18, 1976, pp. 602–604.

Costello, C. G. Dissimilarities between conditioned avoidance responses and phobias. *Psychological Review*, 1970, *77*, 250–254.

Craig, G. J. *Human development.* Englewood Cliffs, N.J.: Prentice-Hall, 1976.

CRM Books. *Developmental psychology today.* Del Mar, Calif.: Author, 1971.

DeSilva, P., Rachman, S., & Seligman, M. E. P. Prepared phobias and obsessions: Therapeutic outcome. *Behavior Research and Therapy*, 1977, *15*, 65–77.

Ellenberger, H. F. The story of "Anna O": A critical review with new data. *Journal of the History of the Behavioral Sciences*, 1972, *8*, 267–279.

Engle, T. L., & Snellgrove, L. *Psychology: Its principles and applications* (5th ed.). New York: Harcourt, Brace & World, 1969.

English, H. B. Three cases of the "conditioned fear response." *Journal of Abnormal and Social Psychology*, 1929, *34*, 221–225.

Eysenck, H. J. Learning theory and behaviour therapy. In H. J. Eysenck (Ed.), *Behaviour therapy and the neuroses: Readings in modern methods of treatment derived from learning theory.* Oxford, England: Pergamon Press, 1960.

Galanter, E. *Textbook of elementary psychology.* San Francisco: Holden-Day, 1966.

Gardiner, W. L. *Psychology: A story of a search.* Belmont, Calif.: Brooks/Cole, 1970.

Garrett, H. E. *Great experiments in psychology.* New York: Appleton-Century-Crofts, 1941.

Goldenberg, H. *Abnormal psychology.* Monterey, Calif: Brooks/Cole, 1977.

Harlow, H. F. The formation of learning sets. *Psychological Review*, 1949, *56*, 51–65.

Helms, D. B., & Turner, J. S. *Exploring child behavior.* Philadelphia, Pa.: Saunders, 1976.

Herrnstein, R. J. The evolution of behaviorism. *American Psychologist*, 1977, *32*, 593–603.

Hilgard, E. R., Atkinson, R. C., & Atkinson, R. L. *Psychology* (6th ed.). New York: Harcourt Brace Jovanovich, 1975.

Hilgard, E. R., & Marquis, D. G. *Conditioning and learning*. New York: Appleton-Century, 1940.

Hineline, P. N. Negative reinforcement and avoidance. In W. K. Honig & J. E. R. Staddon (Eds.), *Handbook of operant behavior* (Vol. 2). Englewood Cliffs, N.J.: Prentice-Hall, 1977.

Hollingworth, H. L. *Mental growth and decline*. New York: Appleton, 1928.

Johnson, R. C., & Medinnus, G. R. *Child psychology: Behavior and development* (3rd ed.). New York: Wiley, 1974.

Jones, H. E. The retention of conditioned emotional reactions in infancy. *Journal of Genetic Psychology*, 1930, *37*, 485–497.

Jones, M. C. The elimination of children's fears. *Journal of Experimental Psychology*, 1924, *7*, 383–390. (a)

Jones, M. C. A laboratory study of fear: The case of Peter. *Pedagogical Seminary*, 1924, *31*, 308–315. (b)

Jones, M. C. A 1924 pioneer looks at behavior therapy. *Journal of Behavior Therapy and Experimental Psychiatry*, 1975, *6*, 181–187.

Kazdin, A. E. *History of behavior modification: Experimental foundations of contemporary research*. Baltimore, Md.: University Park Press, 1978.

Kennedy, W. A. *Child psychology* (2nd ed.). Englewood Cliffs, N.J.: Prentice-Hall, 1975.

Kisker, G. W. *The disorganized personality* (3rd ed.). New York: McGraw-Hill, 1977.

Kleinmuntz, B. *Essentials of abnormal psychology*. New York: Harper & Row, 1974.

Koch, S. Psychology and emerging conceptions of knowledge as unitary. In T. Wann (Ed.), *Behaviorism and phenomenology: Contrasting bases for modern psychology*. Chicago: University of Chicago Press, 1964.

Kuhn, T. S. Science: I. The history of science. In D. L. Sills (Ed.), *International encyclopedia of the social sciences* (Vol. 14). New York: Macmillan, 1968.

Larson, C. Some further notes on the "rat rabbit" problem and John B. Watson. *Teaching of Psychology*, 1978, *5*, 35.

MacKenzie, B. D. Behaviourism and positivism. *Journal of the History of the Behavioral Sciences*, 1972, *8*, 222–231.

MacKenzie, B. D. *Behaviourism and the limits of scientific method*. Atlantic Highlands, N.J.: Humanities Press, 1977.

Marks, I. *Fears and phobias*. New York: Academic Press, 1969.

Marks, I. Phobias and obsessions: Clinical phenomena in search of a laboratory model. In J. D. Maser & M. E. P. Seligman (Eds.), *Psychopathology: Experimental models*. San Francisco: Freeman, 1977.

McCandless, B. R., & Trotter, R. J. *Children: Behavior and development* (3rd ed.). New York: Holt, Rinehart & Winston, 1977.

Öhman, A., Erixon, G., & Löfberg, I. Phobias and preparedness: Phobic versus neutral pictures as conditioned stimuli for human autonomic responses. *Journal of Abnormal Psychology*, 1975, *84*, 41–45.

Page, J. D. *Psychopathology: The science of understanding deviance* (2nd ed.). Chicago: Aldine, 1975.

Papalia, D. E., & Olds, S. W. *A child's world: Infancy through adolescence*. New York: McGraw-Hill, 1975.

Parsons, H. M. What happened at Hawthorne? *Science*, 1974, *183*, 922–932.

Prytula, R. E., Oster, G. D., & Davis, S. F. The "rat rabbit" problem: What did John B. Watson really do? *Teaching of Psychology*, 1977, *4*, 44–46.

Rachman, S. Learning theory and child psychology: Therapeutic possibilities. In H. J. Eysenck (Ed.), *Experiments in behaviour therapy*. Oxford, England: Pergamon Press, 1964.

Rachman, S., & Seligman, M. E. P. Unprepared phobias: "Be prepared." *Behaviour Research and Therapy*, 1976, *14*, 333–338.

Reese, H. W., & Lipsitt, L. P. *Experimental child psychology*. New York: Academic Press, 1970.

Salter, A. *Conditioned reflex therapy*. New York: Creative Age Press, 1949.

Samelson, F. History, origin myth and ideology: "Discovery" of social psychology. *Journal for the Theory of Social Behavior*, 1974, *4*, 217–231.

Samelson, F. World War I intelligence testing and the development of psychology. *Journal of the History of the Behavioral Sciences*, 1977, *13*, 274–282.

Sandler, J., & Davidson, R. S. Psychopathology: An analysis of response consequences. In H. D. Kimmel (Ed.), *Experimental psychopathology: Recent research and theory*. New York: Academic Press, 1971.

Schwartz, B. On going back to nature. *Journal of the Experimental Analysis of Behavior*, 1974, *21*, 183–198.

Seligman, M. E. P. On the generality of the laws of learning. *Psychological Review*, 1970, *77*, 406–418.

Seligman, M. E. P. Phobias and preparedness. *Behavior Therapy*, 1971, *2*, 307–320.

Sherman, M. The differentiation of emotional responses in infants: I. Judgments of emotional responses from motion picture views and from actual observation. *Journal of Comparative Psychology*, 1927, *7*, 265–284.

Shettleworth, S. J. Food reinforcement and the organization of behaviour in golden hamsters. In R. A. Hinde & J. Stevenson-Hinde (Eds.), *Constraints on learning*. London: Academic Press, 1973.

Smith, S., & Guthrie, E. R. *General psychology in terms of behavior*. New York: Appleton, 1921.

Staats, A. W. *Learning, language and cognition*. New York: Holt, Rinehart & Winston, 1968.

Telford, C. W., & Sawrey, J. M. *Psychology*. Belmont, Calif.: Brooks/Cole, 1968.

Thorndike, E. L. *The psychology of wants, interests, and attitudes*. New York: Appleton-Century, 1935.

Ullman, L. P., & Krasner, L. Introduction. In L. P. Ullman & L. Krasner (Eds.), *Case studies in behavior modification*. New York: Holt, Rinehart & Winston, 1965.

Valentine, C. W. The innate bases of fear. *Journal of Genetic Psychology*, 1930, *37*, 394–420.

Watson, J. B. Behavior and the concept of mental disease. *Journal of Philosophy*, 1916, *13*, 589–597. (a)

Watson, J. B. The place of the conditioned reflex in psychology. *Psychological Review*, 1916, *23*, 89–116. (b)

Watson, J. B. The psychology of wish fulfillment. *Scientific Monthly*, 1916, *3*, 479–487. (c)

Watson, J. B. *Experimental investigation of babies* (Film). Chicago: Stoelting, 1919. (a) (*Psychological Abstracts*, 1937, *11*, No. 6061.)

Watson, J. B. A schematic outline of the emotions. *Psychological Review*, 1919, *26*, 165–196. (b)

Watson, J. B. *Behaviorism*. New York: Norton, 1924.

Watson, J. B. Experimental studies on the growth of the emotions. *Pedagogical Seminary*, 1925, *32*, 328–348. (a)

Watson, J. B. Recent experiments on how we lose and change our emotions. *Pedagogical Seminary*, 1925, *32*, 349–371. (b)

Watson, J. B. What the nursery has to say about instincts. *Pedagogical Seminary*, 1925, *32*, 293–327. (c)

Watson, J. B. Can psychology help me rear my child? *McCall's*, September 1927, pp. 44; 72.

Watson, J. B. *Psychological care of infant and child*. New York: Norton, 1928. (a)

Watson, J. B. The heart or the intellect. *Harper's Magazine*, February 1928, pp. 345–352. (b)

Watson, J. B. What about your child? *Cosmopolitan*, October 1928, pp. 76–77; 108; 110; 112. (c)

Watson, J. B., & Morgan, J. J. B. Emotional reactions and psychological experimentation. *American Journal of Psychology*, 1917, *28*, 163–174.

Watson, J. B., & Rayner, R. Conditioned emotional reactions. *Journal of Experimental Psychology*, 1920, *3*, 1–14.

Watson, J. B., & Watson, R. R. Studies in infant psychology. *Scientific Monthly*, 1921, *13*, 493–515.

Weimer, W. B., & Palermo, D. S. Paradigms and normal science in psychology. *Science Studies*, 1973, *3*, 211–244.

Weiner, B. (Ed.). *Discovering psychology*. Chicago: Science Research Associates, 1977.

Whitehurst, G. J., & Vasta, R. F. *Child behavior.* Boston: Houghton Mifflin, 1977.

Whittaker, J. O. Introduction to Psychology. Philadelphia, Pa.: Saunders, 1965.

Wolpe, J. *Psychotherapy by reciprocal inhibition.* Stanford, Calif.: Stanford University Press, 1958.

Wolpe, J. *The practice of behavior therapy* (2nd ed.). New York: Pergamon Press, 1973.

Wolpe, J., & Rachman, S. Psychoanalytic "evidence": A critique based on Freud's case of Little Hans. *Journal of Nervous and Mental Disease,* 1960, *130,* 135–148.

Woodworth, R. S. *Psychology* (3rd ed.). New York: Holt, 1934.

Woodworth, R. S. *Psychology* (4th ed.). New York: Holt, 1940.

13

ON PREDICTION AND CONTROL: B. F. SKINNER AND THE TECHNOLOGICAL IDEAL OF SCIENCE

LAURENCE D. SMITH

Like John B. Watson before him, B. F. Skinner declared that the aim of behavioral science is the prediction and control of behavior. As behaviorism rose to prominence in the 20th century, this way of characterizing the aims of science became so commonplace in the ideology of American psychology that few psychologists stopped to reflect on it. For example, it was often forgotten that the *control* of phenomena as an explicit aim of science is of relatively recent origin and is far from ubiquitous even now. For centuries, the aim of science was taken to be the *understanding* of

---

Parts of this article are based on my paper "Operant Psychology and the Technological Ideal of Science: An Historical Perspective," presented in the symposium "Perspectives on Behaviorism" at the 98th Annual Convention of the American Psychological Association, Boston, MA, on August 11, 1990.

I am grateful to David Boynton, Donald Dewsbury, Laurel Furumoto, Linda Silka, and Alan Stubbs for their helpful commentaries on the manuscript.

Reprinted from *American Psychologist*, 47, 216–223 (1992). Copyright © 1992 by the American Psychological Association. Reprinted with permission of the author.

natural phenomena (or perhaps of the causal structure of the world), and fields such as astronomy and anthropology have never shown much concern for control per se. The concern with the capacity of science to yield control over nature is often traced to 17th-century England—where technological advances inspired science advocates such as Francis Bacon—and it has remained more characteristic of scientific thinking in England and America than on the Continent to this day. In 20th-century psychology, those who have drawn chiefly on Continental science—for example, Chomsky and Piaget—have retained the goal of understanding natural phenomena, whereas those whose roots lie in Anglo-American culture—such as Watson and Skinner—have upheld the Baconian goal of controlling nature.

A number of historians of science (Kuhn, 1977; Pauly, 1987; Perez-Ramos, 1988; Toulmin, 1975) have distinguished between two broad ideal-types of science: the contemplative ideal, originating with Aristotle, which seeks to understand the natural world and its causes, and the technological ideal, originating with Bacon, which seeks means of controlling, making, and remaking the world. The former is based largely on passive observation, emphasizing classification of natural phenomena and systematic description. The latter is grounded in active experimentation, emphasizing hands-on manipulation of natural materials as well as experimental variables. Intervention in the course of nature is held to be especially revealing of natural processes, and the reformist bent implicit in the technological ideal has had a strong appeal in American culture (Burnham, 1988; Segal, 1985).

It is no coincidence, of course, that behaviorism, with its avowed aim of controlling behavior, arose in America. At a general level, behaviorism's alliance with the technological ideal is well understood (Bakan, 1966; Buckley, 1989; O'Donnell, 1985). What has not always been fully grasped is the depth of behaviorism's commitment to that ideal and the implications of that commitment for the fate of modern behaviorism, both as a scientific research tradition and as a movement for the reform of culture. The first aim of this article is to illuminate the technological orientation of behaviorism by tracing its leading modern version—the operant psychology of B. F. Skinner—directly to its source in none other than Francis Bacon himself. The second aim is to raise questions about the long-term viability of a movement whose orientation is inherently technological, at a time when the prestige of technology and the technological ideal is suffering an unprecedented decline in postmodern culture. The question that will emerge is this: Can a movement that has so wholeheartedly embraced the technological ideal, and that has drawn on the general prestige accorded technology in our culture, escape the devastating critiques of technology that have arisen in the last half of this century (critiques that, in fact, have often cast Bacon in the role of the central villain)? In particular, what are the prospects for the large-scale employment of behavioral technologies at a time when skepticism about technology in general is widespread?

BACONIAN ROOTS

The connecting of a uniquely 20th-century figure, such as Skinner, with an antiquated figure, such as Bacon, may seem odd, especially given that behaviorists have usually been eager to sever connections with the past. Yet the clues are there throughout Skinner's writings. In the first volume of his autobiography, Skinner reported having immersed himself in the works of Francis Bacon while in the eighth grade, reading not only Bacon's *Essays, New Organon,* and *Advancement of Learning* but also biographies of Bacon and books on his philosophy. He said that he became an "ardent Baconian" in the process and that Bacon would serve him "in serious pursuits" later on (Skinner, 1976, pp. 128–129). It is with a tone of reverence that Skinner (1983) told of picking up a book on Bacon later in his life, of its deeply calming and inspirational effect on him, and of being reminded how "thoroughly Baconian" he is (p. 406). Reflecting on his life at the end of his three-volume autobiography, Skinner (1983) spoke explicitly of the Baconian themes that had governed his life and work. His books, especially the more philosophical works, are sprinkled with references to Bacon, and many parts of his controversial novel *Walden Two* are patterned directly after Bacon's *New Atlantis,* which was the first utopian work that Skinner read.

What, then, did Skinner find in his reading of Bacon, and how were these Baconian ideas woven into the fabric of operant psychology? To answer these questions requires some understanding of Bacon's historical context. Living at the turn of the 17th century, Bacon and his contemporaries were faced with a perplexing situation in regard to the remarkable technological creations of the time and their implications for the nature of science (Perez-Ramos, 1988). The reigning Aristotelian philosophy drew a sharp distinction between theoretical (or contemplative) knowledge and the lower forms of knowledge that Aristotle called *practical* and *productive* knowledge. For Aristotle, productive knowledge—knowledge of how to make things—was inferior because it involved mere imitations of nature, and such imitations could never fully reproduce the effects of nature, much less supersede them. The full understanding of nature was, for him, attainable only through theoretical knowledge. Yet, by Bacon's time, a series of profound technological innovations—the compass, gunpowder, and the printing press—had made it clear that human artifacts, at least the more radically innovative ones, could not be construed as mere imitations of nature or even completions of nature's work. Citing the biblical sanction of Adam's dominion over nature, Bacon (1623/1937, 1620/1960; see Whitney, 1986) seized every opportunity to exalt technological innovation, not only for the power of its concrete products to relieve human sufferings but, more important, as a new model of the knowing process. Bacon's epistemology elevated the role of the artisan above that of the theoretician, and he repeatedly contrasted the steady piecemeal progress exhibited by the technical arts (what we would now call *technology*) with what he saw as the stagnant and fruitless speculations of the Aristotelian tradition.

The kernel of Bacon's new conception of knowledge is that we know best what we can ourselves make; to know nature, for Bacon, is to be able to produce and reproduce its effects at will (Perez-Ramos, 1988). Yet to understand nature, in this strictly operative sense of understanding, is also to be able to bend the ways of nature to the production of novel effects. The creation of novelties, however unnatural they may appear in the Aristotelian scheme, thus becomes the surest test of knowledge. Bacon's (1620/1960) epochal declaration that "human knowledge and human power meet in one" (p. 39)—one of the Baconian principles that Skinner (1983) said governed his own life—is no mere claim that contemplative knowledge can be put to human uses; rather it is the declaration of a different kind of knowing, in which the power of producing effects is not simply the by-product of knowledge, but rather the criterion of its soundness. With this declaration, the age-old distinction of fact and artifact is broken down, and the artificial assumes, in a sense, more value than the natural. Facts, the traditional objects of knowledge in the Aristotelian scheme of natural science, are still valued in the Baconian scheme, but artifacts are preferred as being especially revealing of nature's ways. And because they can be freely produced and reproduced and are thus ready at hand, artifacts constitute the most convenient objects of investigation. Let all humans "be surely persuaded of this," Bacon (1623/1937) wrote, "that the artificial does not differ from the natural in form or essence but only in the efficient" (p. 380).[1]

The human powers of creation are not, however, infinite or unfettered for Bacon. Human dominion over nature is constrained by nature's own

---

[1] This statement, variants of which occur repeatedly in Bacon's writings (see Anderson, 1948), alludes to the well-known Aristotelian distinction between formal and efficient causes, a distinction fundamental to the scholastic philosophy that Bacon was opposing. In the statement, Bacon proclaimed that human artifacts—whether experimental outcomes or technological products—differ from their naturally occurring counterparts not in their essences (or formal causes) but in their means of production (or efficient causes). Given Bacon's other views about the relative expedience of creating human artifacts (as compared with waiting for nature to yield accidentally useful results), the statement also connotes that the artificial is more efficient in the modern sense of "efficiency." Skinner (e.g., 1955/1961c) often made similar points, citing (for example) the case of modern synthetic fibers: Synthetics share the beneficial formal properties of cotton or wool but differ from natural fibers in the means and efficiency of their production, and the synthetics obviate the need to await the natural emergence of improved variants of cotton or wool. (Whether synthetic materials are actually equivalent in utility and superior in efficiency to their natural analogues is of course debatable, particularly when the relative environmental costs are factored in.)

ways. Nature is malleable, but not infinitely so; natural objects can be transformed but nature has its preferences for the forms that its objects can assume. To understand nature's preferred forms, says Bacon (1602/1960), requires "a very diligent dissection and anatomy of the world" (p. 113) in order to reveal those "true and exquisite lines" by which underlying order is expressed in nature (p. 114). Human power over nature thus depends crucially on due regard for its inherent causal structure. Bacon expressed this idea in another of his well-known aphorisms, and again one that Skinner cited as having governed his own life: "Nature to be commanded must be obeyed" (Bacon, 1620/1960, pp. 39, 119; Skinner, 1983, p. 407).

For Bacon, to know a cause is to have the ability to produce an effect. As he put it, "that which in contemplation is as the cause is in operation as the rule" (1620/1960, p. 39). In this regard, Bacon spoke of two aspects of natural science. The first is what Bacon (1623/1937) called the "Inquisition of Causes," which involves "searching into the bowels of nature" to learn of its causal structure and preferred forms. The second is what Bacon called the "Production of Effects"—also referred to by him as "the Operative" aspect of science—which involves "shaping nature as on an anvil" (p. 413). But just as knowledge and power are ultimately one for Bacon, so too the inquisition of causes is fused with the production of effects. In Bacon's view, the search for causes, although sometimes aided by naturalistic observation, is best pursued through the experimental method—that is, the production and reproduction of effects. If we are to learn efficiently from nature, wrote Bacon (1620/1960), nature must be "forced out of her natural state, and squeezed and moulded," because "the nature of things betrays itself more readily under the vexations of art [i.e., experiments] than in its natural freedom" (p. 25). For Bacon, the power to manipulate nature is thus the beginning and end of science: the beginning when nature is "squeezed and moulded" by experiments to reveal its order, and the end when scientific laws, construed as rules of operation, permit the "shaping" of nature "as on an anvil" for the improvement of the human condition. In taking the artisan as the model knower, Bacon elevated homo faber (the making human) over homo sapiens (the knowing human); just as the anthropologists give homo faber temporal priority over homo sapiens in the development of the species, so Bacon gave the human maker epistemological priority over the human knower (Perez-Ramos, 1988).

OPERANT PSYCHOLOGY AND THE TECHNOLOGICAL IDEAL OF SCIENCE

Skinner and Bacon

The connection between Baconian thought and Skinner's operant psychology is not difficult to discern, if only because it is revealed, in part, in the very language used by Bacon—such language as the "production of effects," the "shaping" of nature, and the "operative" side of science with its "rules of operation." In his writings, Skinner (1953, 1974) repeatedly attributed the origins of science to the skilled performances of artisans and craftsworkers, and to the rules used by them in constructing artifacts. He long held that knowledge in general is simply effective behavior and that the vaunted laws of science are really just rules for successful action (Skinner, 1969, 1974; see Zuriff, 1980). He also, of course, spoke of the "shaping" of that part of nature called behavior, and even explicitly likened the shaping of behavior to the molding of clay by a sculptor (1951/1961d, p. 413).

These similarities are, of course, reflections of Skinner's underlying adherence to the technological ideal of science. Operant psychology is deeply and inherently technological, and in a twofold sense: It depicts both the subject and the investigator as technological creatures, as inherently manipulators and controllers of their environments. Just as the rat operates a lever to produce effects on the environment, so the scientist operates on the environment, manipulating variables and shaping the behavior of organisms in it. Both are interveners in the world, or, as Skinner (1957, 1947/1961b) sometimes put it, both are loci of variables defined by their *effects on* the environment. In discussing Bacon's equation of knowledge with power, Skinner (1974) characterized operant behavior in the following terms:

> Operant behavior is essentially the exercise of power: it has an effect on the environment.... That an organism should act to control the world around it is as characteristic of life as breathing or reproduction ... we can no more stop controlling nature than we can stop breathing or digesting food. (pp. 144, 194, 195)

In view of Skinner's allegiance to the technological ideal of science and his Baconian reverence for the tradition of the manual arts, it is no coincidence that Skinner himself was the consummate builder of laboratory artifacts, renowned for his fabrication of such instruments as the Skinner box and the cumulative recorder. Nor is it coincidence that Skinner often preoccupied himself with the construction of novel behaviors, shaped by hand, as a way to demonstrate his knowledge of the causes of behavior. One need only think of the trained rat Pliny, the pigeons who played ping-pong or performed on a toy piano, or the more recent Columban simulations in which pigeons were trained to "talk" to one another in a contrived language (Epstein, Lanza, & Skinner, 1980). Unless the Baconian roots of operant psychology are understood, these demonstrations may strike us as trivial or merely amusing; their scientific value seems questionable, in part, because none of the behaviors involved is natural in a rat or pigeon. But to a Baconian scientist, their significance is enhanced rather than diminished by their artificiality, for in the Baconian scheme the production of novel effects at will is the surest proof of the producer's knowledge of causes. It is not surprising that Skinner often invoked the language of technology in describing his work, as when he spoke of behavior as being a "product" that can be "constructed" to "specification" (1953, p. 427). Echoing the Baconian priority of productive knowledge over contemplative knowledge, Skinner stated outright that "science is not concerned with contemplation" (1953, p. 14) and asserted in particular that operant psychology "is not concerned with testing theories but with directly modifying behavior" (1969, p. 97).

The Interventionist Impulse and the Discovery of the Operant

The hands-on, interventionist style of science practiced by Skinner was intimately tied to his strict adherence to the experimental method. When Bacon wanted to discover those "true and exquisite lines" of division by which order is expressed in nature, he advocated the use of experimental manipulations to force nature out of its usual course. Skinner's early laboratory research—the research of the 1930s that led to the formulation of the operant concept—relied on experimental manipulations to test the stability of the response unit. The so-called *third variables* were changed, and the particular sequence of stimulus–response–reinforcer that exhibited orderly variation as a result would emerge as the genuine unit of behavior (Coleman, 1987). The now-familiar, three-term operant contingency was, in effect, nature's preferred form. When it came to delineating natural units of behavior, Skinner (1938) used Baconian language in introducing the definition of the operant:

> The analysis of behavior is not an act of arbitrary subdividing. We cannot define the concepts of stimulus and response quite as simply as "parts of behavior and environment" without taking account of the natural lines of fracture along which behavior and environment actually break. (p. 33)

Recapitulating the Baconian idiom, Skinner was reporting that the order of nature—its lines of fracture—had revealed itself, and it had done so, not in its natural freedom, but only when forced out of its natural course by the experimenter's hand. The resulting natural unit of behavior consisted of those parts of behavior and environment that had what Skinner (1938) called "experimental reality" (p. 41). For him, as for Bacon, experiment was the royal road to reality because it is the manipulator, not the contemplator, who can best know reality. The very phrase *experimental reality* is one that neatly captures the intrinsic connection postulated by Baconians between the natural order and the human capacity to manipulate the world. For a Baconian, the reproducibility of experimental results

—so often touted as their chief virtue—is not a matter of mere statistical reliability; rather it is the power to produce and reproduce effects at will (Skinner, 1956/1961a). It is the control, not of statistical sources of error, but of nature itself—the sort of control that led Bacon to revere productive knowledge above all other forms.

The Reformist Impulse and Walden Two

The close link between the experimental method and the power to produce effects is also the key to understanding the reformist impulse inherent in the Baconian tradition. Bacon himself felt that a proper understanding of the value of the technical arts and the acceptance of the manual arts as a new model of knowing would bring about unprecedented changes in society, leading steadily to the satisfaction of all human wants and the emergence of a harmonious society. This vision of the future was portrayed by Bacon (1624/1942) in his utopian book *The New Atlantis*. In the advanced technological culture described by Bacon, productive knowledge is given full respect; nature is experimented with and remade with an eye toward human benefit. There are synthetic dyes, artificial gemstones, newly compounded metals, engines for the multiplication of physical force, and perpetual motion machines; there are submarines, methods of flight, telephones, and means of artificially synthesizing and reproducing human speech; there are synthetic foods and drink, including novel milks and wines; and there are new medicines, methods of surgically transplanting organs, and artificial means of extending the life span. Significantly, the technology of the New Atlantis is not restricted to the physical and medical realms. There are also laboratories for the study of plants and animals, in which new creatures are produced through "commixtures and copulations of divers kinds." The animals there, related Bacon (1624/1942), are made to differ in "color, shape, and activity . . . neither do we do this by chance, but we know beforehand of what matter and commixture, what kind of those creatures will arise" (p. 292).

The citizens of New Atlantis are depicted as placid, productive, and happy. At the core of the society is a scientific institute called *Solomon's House* (an institute that would later serve as the model for the Royal Society of London). Research teams in Solomon's House work in an intricate division of labor to fathom the ways of nature and remake it, producing effects for the common good. The goal of the institute, we are told, is nothing less than the "enlarging of the bounds of human empire, to the effecting of all things possible" (Bacon, 1624/1942, p. 288).

The New Atlantis reveals in dramatic form the Baconian license to intervene in the world, to actively rework nature's materials—both physical matter and biological species—toward human ends. It is, as Bacon himself understood, the license for humans to play God in their earthly domain. No less dramatic a feature of the New Atlantis is the assumption that human benefits will *automatically* ensue from technological progress. Like his utopian predecessor Thomas More, Bacon was concerned about rising poverty in England, and he followed More in assuming that social strife could be attributed to the shortage of material goods (Farrington, 1963). If the control of nature could be turned to the "relief of man's estate," the resulting material well-being would be the sufficient condition for the benevolent reform of society. The salvation of humankind would come from the rightful exercise of godlike control over nature. For Bacon, the interventionism of the experimental method thus translated readily into the reform of society through remaking the world.

The salvation of humans from social ills by means of the experimental method and remaking the world was, of course, the dominant theme of Skinner's writings after the 1940s. At the end of his autobiography, Skinner himself traced that theme to Bacon:

> A third Baconian theme completes [my] story. The *New Atlantis* was the first utopia I read. A better world was possible, but it would not come about by accident. It must be planned and built, and with the help of science.... By its very nature an experimental analysis of behavior spawns a technology because it points to conditions which can be changed to change behavior. I said as much in my own *New Atlantis, Walden Two*. (1983, p. 412)

As depicted in Skinner's (1948) novel, the Walden Two community was a technological utopia, much like that of the New Atlantis. The use of behavioral technology in designing the culture had produced inhabitants who were happy, productive, and well cared for. As with Bacon, there was a division of labor (into workers, planners, managers, and scientists), but, in a fitting tribute to the value of the manual arts, even the scientists were required to devote part of each workday to manual labor. The experimental method was applied to the design of every aspect of life, down to the minutia of domestic chores, and the resulting efficiency had reduced the average workday to four hours. Moreover, experimentalism was promoted as an ongoing way of life, and the assumption that human benefits would ensue was a conspicuous article of faith. As Frazier, the community's designer and Skinner's alter ego, put it:

> The main thing is, we encourage our people to view every habit and custom with an eye to possible improvement. A constantly experimental attitude toward everything—that's all we need. Solutions to problems of every sort follow almost miraculously. (Skinner, 1948, pp. 29–30)

The underlying principle of Walden Two was that because people are products of their environment, the remaking of the environment would mean the remaking of humans. As Bacon was aware of playing God in the creation of new species, so too Frazier was aware of the powers of creation yielded by a behavioral technology. "I like to play God," he said. "Who wouldn't, under the circumstances?" (Skinner, 1948, p. 299). By the time Skinner wrote *Walden Two*, he had learned in the laboratory that behavior could be shaped by hand to specification, and his wartime experience with Project Pigeon had convinced him that even highly precise specifications could be met (Skinner, 1960). But the mass production of desirable behavior would require the large-scale design of a new social environment —the production of a culture to specification. This too was viewed as a hands-on exercise in productive knowledge. In his notebooks, Skinner (1980) analogized the creation of a culture to the turning of a physical artifact on a lathe, resulting in a "smoothly turned" society (p. 199); this metaphor, along with his earlier metaphor of the shaping of behavior as the sculptor shapes a lump of clay, serves as a striking reminder of Skinner's roots in the Baconian glorification of the manual arts.

In part because of its hands-on character, the design and production of a better culture was viewed by Skinner as well within reach. In his writings that followed *Walden Two*, he took pains to point out that although the book was a utopian novel, the term *utopian* need not connote the impossible. As the reaction to the book showed, however, the deliberate design of a culture raised deep concerns among his readers. Not only did it offend the political sensibilities of many, but the deliberate, artificial control of culture somehow seemed unnatural, and even dangerously so (e.g., Krutch, 1953; Viteles, 1955).

In *Beyond Freedom and Dignity* and other works, Skinner (1971) responded with a sustained argument that, in cultural design as elsewhere, the natural is no better than the artificial. The argument consisted of four points, each with a distinctly Baconian flavor. The first was that a designed culture would be easier to control and hence would operate more efficiently. If culture could be remade as a human artifact it would share in that Baconian attribute of all artifacts, namely, being better understood and better controlled than its naturally occurring counterpart (Skinner, 1955/1961c). Second, Skinner (1971) argued that when it comes to the provenance of cultures there is no virtue in accident. The historical process of cultural evolution by which extant cultures had been produced had been due to a series of accidents, and humans could do better. Bacon had argued similarly that the products of unconstrained natural processes (the "births of time") were less noble that those of human art (the "births of wit"; see Farrington, 1964). Third, an artifactual culture would not differ from a naturally evolved one in the degree of control its members were subjected to, simply because all behavior is controlled anyway. To leave culture undesigned was to leave the control of behavior to other, largely accidental, sources (Skinner, 1953, 1969, 1971). Fourth, Skinner undercut the artificial–natural distinction by claiming that *all* cultures are experiments. Cultures, whether or not designed, are simply ways of living that are being tried out, subject to selection by consequences in competition with other extant cultural patterns. Utopias, in particular, are a special type of cultural experiment, but only in the sense that they are better-controlled experiments by virtue of their smaller size and their isolation from the larger culture. As experiments in living, cultural reforms are to be encouraged because they represent mutations in cultural evolution, and to increase the rate of mutations is to augment the possibilities for progress (Skinner, 1953). In sum, human salvation would come from applying the Baconian experimental attitude, not only as a prevailing ethos *within* a culture, but to the overall design and production of the culture. A willingness to experiment was required, and fears that engineered cultures were somehow unnatural could be dismissed on Baconian grounds as simply unwarranted.

THE FALL OF THE TECHNOLOGICAL IDEAL

Skinner's enthusiastic defense of behavioral technology stemmed directly from his Baconian worldview, but it came at an ironic time when viewed from the larger perspective of the history of technology. Skinner was writing at the end of what has been called the "golden age of technological ebullience" (Slade, 1989). America's great century of invention had come to a close (Hughes, 1989), and it was already clear that the blessings of technological innovation were far from unmixed. The once-burgeoning genre of technological utopias was being replaced by a new genre of technological *dystopias* (Segal, 1985). *Walden Two* itself was written in the summer of 1945 and completed shortly before the bombing of Hiroshima, an event from which the prestige of technology has never fully recovered. It would not be long before Rachel Carson's (1962) landmark *Silent Spring* was drawing attention to the damaging environmental effects of modern systems of production, citing the very industries whose existence had been forecast in Bacon's *New Atlantis*. The criticism has continued to the present. Skinner's own city of Cambridge, in Massachusetts, has passed ordinances against genetic engineering, and more than one city has debated legislation restricting the use of behavioral technology. The "technological imperative"—classically embodied in the Baconian urge for "the effecting of all things possible"—has been rejected in favor of the sharply restricted use of technology in small-scale systems of so-called "appropriate technology" (Schumacher, 1979; see discussion in Segal, 1985). Scholarly analyses of the modern technological dilemma have repeatedly identified Bacon as a chief culprit in bringing about the dilemma (Leiss, 1972; Merchant, 1989;

Winner, 1977). Yet, through it all, Skinner never wavered from his talk of a "technology of behavior" or even evinced any weakening of his Baconian commitments.

The questions being asked by the critics of technology have gone to the root of the Baconian ideology. Is it true that the human estate is best served by the constant adoption of the experimental attitude toward nature? Does the artificial differ from the natural only in the efficient? Perhaps most crucially, is it true that what we know best are the objects of our own creation, that to control phenomena in the sense of being able to produce and reproduce them is to understand them? These have become pressing questions in the postmodern era, and they are increasingly being answered in the negative, as the implications of the technological ideal are being realized.

The unexpected and unfortunate consequences of widespread interventions in nature that are now being discovered at a disturbing pace suggest that human welfare is often not served by the Baconian experimental attitude, and certainly not invariably so (as Bacon and Frazier had hoped). It is now clear that in producing our works we are protected neither by the divine license of Bacon's God nor by the long-held faith in the inevitability of scientific and technological progress (Basalla, 1988; Rescher, 1980). We are discovering in many cases that the artificial does, after all, differ from the natural—that synthetic artifacts do not always have the same consequences as their natural counterparts, even though the two may be equivalent in terms of those narrower ends for which the synthetic version was designed. As for the cherished value of experimental method, we have learned that the same elimination (or control) of variables in laboratory experiments that favors the creation of novel effects can also prevent the detection of unforeseen consequences of those creations; variables that are "extraneous" in the laboratory may well be intrinsic to, and uncontrollable in, the larger systems into which the novel artifact is introduced.

Above all, we seem to be learning that we do not always understand that which we can reliably produce and reproduce at will. There is a world of difference, as it turns out, between predicting that the intended effect of an operation will occur and predicting that no other effects, say, of a deleterious nature, will occur. The former has turned out to be so easy as to now appear routine; the latter has proved to be enormously difficult. If the glory of technology has been its provision of recipes for the creation of novel artifacts, its liability has been the neglect of contemplative understanding of the natural systems that are perturbed by those artifacts. A given, naturally evolved state of affairs may not be to our liking, but it may possess a kind of stability and equilibrium that we do not know how to recreate in the wake of interventions.

THE SURVIVAL OF OPERANT PSYCHOLOGY

Postmodern criticism of the technological ideal has indeed been severe, and Baconian principles, including the ones that Skinner embraced wholeheartedly, have been chief among its targets. But granting that operant psychology is historically rooted in the beleaguered Baconian ideology and that it still shares many of its assumptions, does the critique of the Baconian tradition really apply also to the operant movement? After all, part of Skinner's motivation in advocating the large-scale adoption of behavioral technology was to create a world in which the self-control of humans would allow the previous excesses of physical technology to be remedied. As Skinner recognized, the salvation to be gained through technology is no longer salvation from material want but salvation primarily from technology itself. But even on Skinner's own terms his proposals amount to an effort to solve technology's problems with technology, and the burden of proof now seems to be on technology's advocates. In the realm of physical technology, the track record of technological interventions to solve technology's problems has been scarcely less uneven than that of the original technology. The opposition to large-scale implementation of behavioral technology may stem not so much from simple neophobia, benighted obscurantism, or stubborn allegiance to the literature of freedom and dignity as from a skepticism, not wholly unjustified, about the prospects for solving technologically generated problems with further technology of any sort.[2]

It is doubtful whether skepticism about the technological imperative can be allayed by claiming that implementations of technology are inevitable because "we can no more stop controlling nature than we can stop breathing or digesting food"; such a blanket statement, even if accepted as a truism, obscures rather than enlightens important distinctions between types of control, the very distinctions that are at issue. Nor is it likely that skepticism will be allayed by divorcing behavioral technology from physical technology in an effort to rescue it from the declining prestige of the latter. According to Skinner (1974),

> When we say that science and technology have created more problems than they have solved, we mean physical and biological science and

---

[2]This skepticism can even be formulated in Skinner's (1953) own idiom. Suppose that cultures *are* subject to evolution, that they represent highly evolved systems, and that to advocate the "experimental attitude" toward cultural practices is to urge an increase in the rate of mutations (see discussion in Creel, 1987). What, then, does one make of the biologists' finding that the vast majority of mutations in highly evolved systems are deleterious? Cultural reforms are not simply "blind variation," of course, as long as we have the advantage of predicting their consequences. But the blindness of deliberately induced cultural mutations can be overcome only to the extent that unintended consequences are predicted as thoroughly and accurately as the intended ones; and this is precisely where the narrow Baconian focus on the reliable production of works has so often failed us.

> technology. It does not follow that a technology of behavior will mean further trouble.... We cannot say that a science of behavior has failed, for it has scarcely been tried. (p. 258)

Nonetheless, if operant psychology has emulated physical technology and appealed to its prestige to further its own cause, then it can hardly avoid careful attention to the lessons learned from the fate of physical technology. It would now seem incumbent on the advocates of large-scale applications of technology to undertake the difficult task of risk assessment. The research literature has not been silent on the potential risks of behavioral interventions (e.g., Lepper & Greene, 1978; Schwartz, 1982), but such studies have tended to come from critics of the operant movement, not its proponents. Those who would propose technological interventions (whether physical or behavioral) can ill afford to ignore the wish of those who would live with the interventions to have a reasonably comprehensive understanding of their consequences, and not simply demonstrations of their immediate effectiveness.

If the operant movement is in fact deeply wedded to the Baconian ideology that has fallen from grace, then it is not easy to see how it can escape the consequences of that affiliation. However, such matters are rarely black and white. Given that the death of behaviorism has been announced with somewhat greater frequency than the actual event has taken place (Zuriff, 1979), it is worth considering three facets of the operant tradition that could mitigate the damaging force of its Baconian affiliation and, perhaps, brighten its prospects. First, by its very nature, operant conditioning focuses on the consequences of action. With a suitably broadened concept of consequences, the operant tradition may yet contribute to clarifying the relationship between human technological action and its overall consequences. Indeed, Skinner's later writings (e.g., 1987) showed a marked concern with *long-term* consequences, and they included a thoughtful analysis, at least at a general level, of how prevailing short-term contingencies with dangerous consequences might be rearranged to produce desirable remote outcomes—in effect, a sort of behavioral analysis of the tragedy of the common (see Hardin, 1968; Mazur, 1986; Nevin, 1982; Platt, 1973). The growing research literature on the problem of self-control (e.g., Grosch & Neuringer, 1981), along with quantitative models of relevant phenomena (Rachlin, 1989), substantiates this concern. What remains is for the operant tradition to show an equally serious concern with the possible unintended, long-term consequences of its own behavior-technological recommendations.

Second, operant psychology offers possibilities for *local* applications of behavioral technology to pressing problems (e.g., Geller, 1989). Often lost in the controversy generated by *Walden Two* is the recognition that the Walden Two community itself embodied many practices that would qualify as appropriate technology by the standards of contemporary critics of technology. It was a small community characterized by harmony with the natural environment, modest use of resources, and planned abstinence from conspicuous consumption. It is well to remember that the creation of artificial markets for consumer products that John B. Watson helped engineer *into* American culture during the 1920s and 1930s (Buckley, 1989) was deliberately engineered *out* of Walden Two. For this and other reasons, the operant tradition would seem well-suited to contribute to designing the behavioral components of effective, small-scale systems of appropriate technology.

Finally, there is the possibility of the operant tradition moving back toward a contemplative model of knowledge. Operant psychologists have long scorned branches of psychology that by their very nature have little to say about how behavior can be directly changed—for example, the nativist traditions of ethology, developmental psychology, and Chomskian psycholinguistics (Skinner, 1969). But it is just such fields that have enjoyed a resurgence as the technological model of science has fallen from grace. The interest in naturalistic behavior in (relatively) naturalistic settings with the aim of understanding behavior as part of a larger system (rather than manufacturing novel forms of it) has not gone unrepresented in the operant tradition. One thinks, for example, of recent work on behavior in open versus closed economies (Collier, 1983) and efforts to relate the matching law to foraging behavior in natural ecosystems (see Robinson & Woodward, 1989). Perhaps more important, some members of the operant tradition (e.g., Killeen, 1978; Staddon, 1983) have shown a renewed interest in the sort of mathematical models characteristic of contemplative science, models that by virtue of their relative comprehensiveness hold the promise of underwriting technologies whose short- *and* long-term consequences are well understood. Even Bacon (1620/1960) himself warned scientists not to "reap the green corn" (p. 24)—that is, not to jump too quickly from knowledge of causes to production of effects. This is a warning that has become ever more pertinent with the growing realization that we do not always understand that which we can make, and it is one Baconian principle that can profitably be heeded even as we grow increasingly wary of Bacon's other tenets.

REFERENCES

Anderson, F. H. (1948). *The philosophy of Francis Bacon.* Chicago: University of Chicago Press.

Bacon, F. (1937). De dignitate et augmentis scientiarum. In R. F. Jones (Ed. and Trans.), *Essays, Advancement of Learning, New Atlantis, and other pieces* (pp.

377–438). Garden City, NY: Doubleday, Doran. (Original work published 1623)

Bacon, F. (1942). New Atlantis. In G. S. Haight (Ed.), *Essays and New Atlantis* (pp. 243–302). New York: Black. (Original work published 1624)

Bacon, F. (1960). *The New organon* (F. H. Anderson, Ed.). Indianapolis, IN: Bobbs-Merrill. (Original work published 1620)

Bakan, D. (1966). Behaviorism and American urbanization. *Journal of the History of the Behavioral Sciences, 2,* 5–28.

Basalla, G. (1988). *The evolution of technology.* Cambridge, England: Cambridge University Press.

Buckley, K. W. (1989). *Mechanical man: John Broadus Watson and the beginnings of behaviorism.* New York: Guilford Press.

Burnham, J. C. (1988). *Paths into American Culture: Psychology, medicine, and morals.* Philadelphia: Temple University Press.

Carson, R. (1962). *Silent spring.* Boston: Houghton Mifflin.

Coleman, S. R. (1987). Quantitative order in B. F. Skinner's early research program, 1928–1931. *Behavior Analyst, 10,* 47–65.

Collier, G. H. (1983). Life in a closed economy: The ecology of learning and motivation. In M. D. Zeiler & P. Harzem (Eds.), *Advances in analysis of behavior; Vol. 3. Biological factors in learning* (pp. 223–274). Chichester, England: Wiley.

Creel, R. (1987). Skinner on science. In S. Modgil & C. Modgil (Eds.), *B. F. Skinner: Consensus and controversy* (pp. 103–111). New York: Falmer.

Epstein, R., Lanza, R. P., & Skinner, B. F. (1980). Symbolic communication between two pigeons (*Columba livia domestica*). *Science, 207,* 543–545.

Farrington, B. (1963). *Francis Bacon: Pioneer of planned science.* New York: Praeger.

Farrington, B. (1964). *The philosophy of Francis Bacon.* Chicago: University of Chicago Press.

Geller, E. S. (1989). Applied behavior analysis and social marketing: An integration for environmental preservation. *Journal of Social Issues, 45,* 17–36.

Grosch, J., & Neuringer, A. (1981). Self-control in pigeons under the Mischel paradigm. *Journal of the Experimental Analysis of Behavior, 35,* 3–22.

Hardin, G. (1968). The tragedy of the commons. *Science, 162,* 1243–1248.

Hughes, T. P. (1989). *American genesis: A century of invention and technological enthusiasm, 1870–1970.* New York: Viking.

Killeen, P. R. (1978). The reflex reserve. *Journal of the Experimental Analysis of Behavior, 50,* 319–331.

Krutch, J. W. (1953). *The measure of man.* Indianapolis, IN: Bobbs-Merrill.

Kuhn, T. S. (1977). Mathematical versus experimental traditions in the development of physical science. In *The essential tension: Selected studies in scientific tradition and change* (pp. 31–65). Chicago: University of Chicago Press.

Leiss, W. (1972). *The domination of nature.* New York: Braziller.

Lepper, M. R., & Greene, D. (Eds.). (1978). *The hidden costs of reward.* Hillsdale, NJ: Erlbaum.

Mazur, J. E. (1986). *Learning and behavior.* Englewood Cliffs, NJ: Prentice-Hall.

Merchant, C. (1989). *The death of nature: Women, ecology and the scientific revolution.* New York: Harper & Row.

Nevin, J. A. (1982). On resisting extinction [Review of *The fate of the earth*]. *Journal of the Experimental Analysis of Behavior, 38,* 349–353.

O'Donnell, J. M. (1985). *The origins of behaviorism: American psychology, 1870–1920.* New York: New York University Press.

Pauly, P. J. (1987). *Controlling life: Jacques Loeb and the engineering ideal in biology.* New York: Oxford University Press.

Perez-Ramos, A. (1988). *Francis Bacon's idea of science and the maker's knowledge tradition.* Oxford, England: Oxford University Press.

Platt, J. (1973). Social traps. *American Psychologist, 28,* 641–651.

Rachlin, H. (1989). *Judgment, decision, and choice: A cognitive/behavioral synthesis.* New York: Freeman.

Rescher, N. (1980). *Unpopular essays on technological progress.* Pittsburgh, PA: University of Pittsburgh Press.

Robinson, J. K., & Woodward, W. R. (1989). The convergence of behavioral biology and operant psychology: Toward an interlevel and intertheory science. *Behavior Analyst, 12,* 131–141.

Schumacher, E. F. (1979). *Small is beautiful: Economics as if people mattered.* New York: Harper & Row.

Schwartz, B. (1982). Reinforcement induced behavioral stereotypy: How not to teach people to discover rules. *Journal of Experimental Psychology: General, 111,* 23–59.

Segal, H. P. (1985). *Technological utopianism in American culture.* Chicago: University of Chicago Press.

Skinner, B. F. (1938). *The behavior of organisms: An experimental analysis.* New York: Appleton-Century-Crofts.

Skinner, B. F. (1948). *Walden Two.* New York: Macmillan.

Skinner, B. F. (1953). *Science and human behavior.* New York: Free Press.

Skinner, B. F. (1957). *Verbal behavior.* New York: Appleton-Century-Crofts.

Skinner, B. F. (1960). Pigeons in a pelican. *American Psychologist, 15,* 28–37.

Skinner, B. F. (1961a). A case history in scientific method. In *Cumulative record* (enlarged ed., pp. 76–100). New York: Appleton-Century-Crofts. (Original work published 1956)

Skinner, B. F. (1961b). Current trends in experimental psychology. In *Cumulative record* (enlarged ed., pp. 223–241). New York: Appleton-Century-Crofts. (Original work published 1947)

Skinner, B. F. (1961c). Freedom and the control of men. In *Cumulative record* (enlarged ed., pp. 3–18). New York: Appleton-Century-Crofts. (Original work published 1955)

Skinner, B. F. (1961d). How to teach animals. In *Cumulative record* (enlarged ed., pp. 412–419). New York: Appleton-Century-Crofts. (Original work published 1951)

Skinner, B. F. (1969). *Contingencies of reinforcement: A theoretical analysis.* New York: Appleton-Century-Crofts.

Skinner, B. F. (1971). *Beyond freedom and dignity.* New York: Knopf.

Skinner, B. F. (1974). *About behaviorism.* New York: Knopf.

Skinner, B. F. (1976). *Particulars of my life.* New York: Knopf.

Skinner, B. F. (1980). *Notebooks* (R. Epstein, Ed.). Englewood Cliffs, NJ: Prentice-Hall.

Skinner, B. F. (1983). *A matter of consequences.* New York: Knopf.

Skinner, B. F. (1987). *Upon further reflection.* Englewood Cliffs, NJ: Prentice-Hall.

Slade, J. W. (1989). Review of *Imagining tomorrow: History, technology, and the American future. Technology and Culture, 30,* 459–460.

Staddon, J. E. R. (1983). *Adaptive behavior and learning.* Cambridge, England: Cambridge University Press.

Toulmin, S. E. (1975). The twin moralities of science. In N. H. Steneck (Ed.), *Science and society: Past, present, and future* (pp. 111–124). Ann Arbor: University of Michigan Press.

Viteles, M. (1955). Review of *Walden Two. Science, 122,* 1167.

Whitney, C. (1986). *Francis Bacon and modernity.* New Haven, CT: Yale University Press.

Winner, L. (1977). *Autonomous technology: Technics-out-of-control as a theme in political thought.* Cambridge, MA: MIT Press.

Zuriff, G. E. (1979). The demise of behaviorism—exaggerated rumor? [Review of Mackenzie's *Behaviourism and the limits of scientific method*]. *Journal of the Experimental Analysis of Behavior, 32,* 129–136.

Zuriff, G. E. (1980). Radical behaviorist epistemology. *Psychological Bulletin, 87,* 337–350.

IV

PSYCHOLOGY AS A SOCIAL AND BEHAVIORAL SCIENCE

INTRODUCTION: PSYCHOLOGY AS A SOCIAL AND BEHAVIORAL SCIENCE

One of the most important individuals in the development of American psychology as a science-based profession was G. Stanley Hall (1844–1924). Hall has become such an icon of psychology that, for the centennial of its founding in 1992, the American Psychological Association (APA) proposed the issuance of a new stamp to feature Hall and William James (1842–1910; the move was rejected by the U.S. Postal Service). Hall was arguably Wilhelm Wundt's (1832–1920) first American student, the first American professor of psychology, the founder of psychology's first American laboratory, and the founder of the APA. In chapter 14, "G. Stanley Hall: From Philosophy to Developmental Psychology" (1992), Sheldon H. White contextualizes Hall's career and efforts in the establishment of the "New Psychology."

Educated at Williams College, Hall learned the older psychology that was rooted in moral philosophy. Later, he adopted the New Psychology, but, as White shows, remnants of the older approaches were still present in his approaches. Hall was an early professor at Johns Hopkins University and the first president of Clark University, the first two universities in the United States oriented primarily to research and graduate education. As such, he occupied a pivotal position in academic politics and was in an ideal position to shape the emerging discipline and the perceptions thereof. White is especially interested in Hall's role in shaping developmental psychology. His development of the child study movement helped secure popular support for psychology at Clark but necessitated the use of questionnaire methods that could not be as methodologically sound as the laboratory approaches that were then popular. White brings out the story of Hall's struggles in shaping psychology, both within the academy and within himself. He also examines some core principles in the kind of psychology that Hall favored. Late in his career, Hall returned to an interest in religion, a focal concern from his earlier days, reflecting his internal struggles.

Testing has become the stock-in-trade of psychologists in the 20th century. As the profession of psychology developed in America, it was increasingly drawn toward practical application and away from the study of the generalized adult (usually White) mind (Danziger, 1990). A territorial struggle ensued over which profession owned testing. Physicians, especially psychiatrists, were resentful of the success of psychologists in this new arena and railed against the perceived intrusion into what they perceived as their professional domain (Sokal, 1987). In the middle of these professional battles, psychologists developed a variety of approaches to intelligence and its testing.

In chapter 15, "The Mental Testing Community and Validity: A Prehistory" (1992), Richard T. von Mayrhauser delineates the competing explanations for intelligence and methods for measuring it that emerged among the first generation of American intelligence testers. Those who favored a "pure" science approach viewed mind as unitary and preferred explanations and methods that revealed a common intellective factor. Those psychologists who were committed to a psychology oriented toward application preferred explanations and methods that revealed the diversity of intellectual ability. These differences created problems when American psychologists were called on to provide service during World War I. A major issue was the validity of the tests. In particular, methods did not exist to ensure that the tests had construct validity. The very particular and practical demands of the military forced psychologists to address and, at least temporarily, to resolve this most basic problem. One result of the struggle was the development of the field of psychometrics and the expansion of testing into a vast intellectual and commercial enterprise.

Gordon Allport (1897–1967) remains a figure of enduring interest in the history of American psychology. He was key to the development of personality as a legitimate subfield of psychological research (see, e.g., Allport, 1921, 1930). In 1939, Allport was elected president of the APA, two years after the publication of his influential text, *Personality: A Psychological Interpretation* (1937). But the history of personality psychology is more complex than just an interesting story about one man. In chapter 16, "Gordon Allport, Character, and the 'Culture of Personality'" (1998), Ian A. M. Nicholson situates Allport's work on personality within the matrix of changing ideas about the person in the field of psychology, as well as in the larger society. The precursor term for personality was *character*. Yet, character carried a heavy religious and moral baggage that placed unbearable weight on its possible use as a scientific term. Nicholson shows how character was abandoned in favor of *personality*, a term far more suitable for its moment in culture. This is an important example of the cultural approach to understanding the history of psychology.

These three chapters form a brief introduction to an area ripe for further investigation. What we hope is clear from these chapters is that psychology is not only a social and behavioral science, it is also embedded in social and behavioral matrices that create its possibility as a science.

REFERENCES

Allport, G. (1921). Personality and character. *Psychological Bulletin, 18*, 441–455.

Allport, G. (1930). The field of personality. *Psychological Bulletin, 27*, 677–730.

Allport, G. (1937). *Personality: A psychological interpretation.* New York: Henry Holt.

Danziger, K. (1990). *Constructing the subject: Historical origins of psychological research.* New York: Cambridge University Press.

Sokal, M. M. (1987). *Psychological testing and American society, 1890–1930.* New Brunswick, NJ: Rutgers University Press.

14

G. STANLEY HALL: FROM PHILOSOPHY TO DEVELOPMENTAL PSYCHOLOGY

SHELDON H. WHITE

In 1884, G. Stanley Hall was appointed professor of psychology and pedagogics at Johns Hopkins University. Today, when we have come to see psychology as distinct from philosophy, the appointment is generally referred to as the first professorship in psychology in the United States. Hall and Daniel Coit Gilman, president of Johns Hopkins, saw the appointment as a strategic new professorship in philosophy (O'Donnell, 1985; Wilson, 1990).

Hall (1876, 1879) had examined the teaching of philosophy in 300 American colleges, and he saw psychology as vital to the regeneration of that teaching. Gilman was building the first successful graduate university in America and wanted a reconstructed philosophy, but he had to be careful. Johns Hopkins had been criticized when opening-day ceremonies opened and closed without prayer and Thomas Huxley, the notorious Darwinian, had been brought in to give an invited address. Many people in

---

Reprinted from *Developmental Psychology*, 28, 25–34 (1992). Copyright © 1992 by the American Psychological Association. Reprinted with permission of the author.

Baltimore considered Johns Hopkins to be a center of godless materialism. The new philosophy professor had to be "safe." Three potential philosophy professors held half-time lectureships. Charles Sanders Peirce held a lectureship in logic. What he taught was not controversial, but his name came to be linked with divorce and scandal. George Sylvester Morris was a brilliant lecturer and a man who had been a mentor to G. Stanley Hall and would be one to John Dewey, but Morris had once turned down a chair at Bowdoin rather than give assurances about his orthodoxy. Hall was the third half-time lecturer. There was evidence that he was a fine teacher, and William James had told Gilman that Hall was the only man in America other than himself qualified to teach the new physiological psychology. Hall had reassured Gilman that he was a Christian believer.

> I am as far as *possible* from materialism in every form. My physiological studies of the nervous system bring me incessantly before the question of the identity of thought and matter, and I can only say that my deepest private feeling ... is that materialism is simply want of education. As to my religious sentiments. I am a graduate of divinity, and without agreeing entirely with all that I hear, am in the habit of church going, and indeed am still a nominal church member I believe. (Quoted in Albrecht, 1960, p. 112)

In 1884, Hall was given the Johns Hopkins chair. In an introductory lecture on October 6 of that year, he mapped out the new psychology he would teach. It had three branches—comparative, experimental, and historical—and it was fundamentally and profoundly religious.

> This whole field of psychology is connected in the most vital way with the future of religious belief in our land.... The new psychology, which brings simply a new method and a new standpoint to philosophy, is, I believe, Christian to its root and center; and its final mission in the world is ... to flood and transfuse the new and vaster conceptions of the universe and of man's place in it ... with the old Scriptural sense of unity, rationality, and love.... The Bible is being slowly re-revealed as man's great text book in psychology—dealing with him as a whole, his body, mind, and will, in all the larger relations to nature, society,—which has been misappreciated simply because it is so deeply divine. That something may be done here to aid this development is my strongest hope and belief. (Hall, 1885, pp. 247–248)

Hall would hold true to his religious conception of psychology until the end of his life (Hall, 1917; Rodkin, 1990).

Beginning with his new position in Johns Hopkins, Hall would become a leader in the building of the modern research university, the establishment of psychology in that university, and diverse outreach efforts to create philosophies of social practice for individuals reconstructing American institutions for education, welfare, and health. Hall was one of a new class of Americans in the late 19th century—people whose work stitched thousands of localities and "island communities" together into a national political order (Wiebe, 1967).

THE OLD PSYCHOLOGY IN AN OLDER COLLEGE SYSTEM

What was G. Stanley Hall like as a person? Various shorter or longer, warmer or cooler, literary snapshots of him exist. In Hall's (1923) *Life and confessions*, he talks about himself in his own voice. There are warm accounts of him by colleagues and former students (Burnham, 1925; Pruett, 1926; Sanford, 1924; Starbuck, 1925; Wilson, 1914); a mixed estimation offered in a superb full-length biography (Ross, 1972); and an unfriendly sketch in a recent book by Karier (1986).

Hall was born in 1844 in Ashfield, a village in western Massachusetts. His father farmed, but his father and his mother had some education and had once been schoolteachers. Both parents were pious Congregationalists, with ambitions for their son to become a minister. When G. Stanley Hall got older, he would look back on his country boyhood with warmth and nostalgia (e.g., Hall, 1907), although his student, Pruett (1926, p. 35), saw that early life as hard.

> There is a bareness, a lack of softness, about his early life, a sense of angles and harsh lines, which is a little painful to contemplate, although in his last years Hall himself declared that he would not have had it otherwise.

Hall went to Williston Seminary in 1862 for 1 year and then to Williams College, where he took the classical curriculum of the old-time American college. For the first 2 years, there was an obligatory sequence of Greek, Latin, and intermediate mathematics, with recitations in each subject every day. There were no electives. As a junior, Hall got a little leeway, but not much. Almost no science was taught, but then there was almost no literature, modern languages, or philosophy, as we now teach those subjects. In his senior year, Hall took moral philosophy with Mark Hopkins, president of the college, and in the course he met an older, theistic developmental psychology.

MARK HOPKINS AND WILLIAMS COLLEGE

Mark Hopkins had studied a little law and had completed medical training, but he presented himself to his undergraduates as an ordained minister full of the dignity and authority of an old-time college president. He was not learned nor did he aspire to be. "It is now long since I have read anything but newspaper," he wrote in 1862. He had never read Kant or Hume. He attacked Darwin and Huxley but had not read them (Rudolph, 1956, p. 28). He saw himself as an inspirational teacher whose goal was to make men.

Hopkins is remembered today largely because of a flight of oratory by President James Garfield, who once said, "Give me a log hut with only a simple bench, Mark Hopkins on one end and I on the other, and you may have all the buildings, apparatus and libraries without him." Four years before Garfield's speech, young Hall experienced the reality of Hopkins's teaching. Fifty-eight years later, he would recollect it in four pages of his *Life and Confessions*. The moral philosophy Hall studied was written out in Hopkins's *Lectures on Moral Science* in 1865 and elaborated 20 years later (Hopkins, 1885). We have a reasonably good picture of Hopkins's course.

Mark Hopkins's teaching was designed to turn the minds of Williams seniors towards contemporary human affairs, to help them grasp the ways of people and politics, and to explain the moral basis of civil society. The course was part of an older tradition of college education. Other presidents in other American colleges taught senior-year courses in which an older psychology that listed the faculties, powers, and motives of the human mind was put together with other precursors of the behavioral and social sciences to offer spiritual and moral guidance (Hall, 1879; Wetmore, 1991).

Moral Science of Conditionality

> Hopkins's declared goal was to treat morality scientifically: Moral science has usually been studied as isolated. My wish is to connect it with the laws of that physical system which not only supports man, but has its culmination in him. I wish to show that there runs through both one principal of gradation and one law for the limitation of forces and activities, and so of the forms of good resulting from them. (Hopkins, 1865, p. 63)

Psychology was fundamental for Hopkins's moral science but subordinate to it. Because psychology is conditional for moral philosophy, the moral philosopher stands above the psychologist:

> The moral philosopher is, therefore, not excluded from the domain of the psychologist. It is *his* domain. It is the soil into which his science strikes its roots ... and if the psychologist does not do his work in those portions as he thinks it ought to be done, he has a right to revise it, and do it for himself. It is not to be allowed that the mere psychologist may lay down such doctrines as he pleases regarding the moral nature. (Hopkins, 1865, p. 80)

Conditionality was an important tool of Hopkins's analysis. It is a relationship between entities that allows them to be ordered. Hopkins analyzed physical objects, people, mental faculties, and social institutions to determine which are conditional for, and therefore subordinate to, others.

> The forces that are at work around us and the faculties within us, from the lowest to the highest, may be ranked as higher and lower as they are or are not a condition for one another. That which is a condition for another is always the lower. (Hopkins, 1865, pp. 63–64)

Orders of Physical Matter

All physical things are ordered in a pyramid of six planes of organization. At the bottom there is rudimentary matter massed by gravitation. Matter aggregated by cohesion or crystallization stands on a second plane. Chemically bound molecules stand on a third plane, vegetable life on a fourth, animal life on a fifth, and humankind on the sixth and topmost plane. Higher order entities are built from lower level entities by the method of addition. At each higher plane we meet more complex forms of matter that link with others of its kind in more complex ways. Man stands at the top of the pyramid of creation, incorporating all its levels.

> Hence, the plan of the creation may be compared to a pyramid, growing narrower by successive platforms. It is to be noticed, however, that while the field of each added and superior force is narrowed, yet nothing is dropped. Each lower force shoots through and combines itself with all that is higher. Because he is rational, man is not the less subject to gravitation, and cohesion, and chemical affinity. He has also the organic life that belongs to the plant, and the sensitive and instinctive life that belongs to the animal. In him none of these are dropped; but the rational life is united with and superinduced upon all these, so that man is not only a microcosm, but is the natural head and ruler of the world. (Hopkins, 1865, p. 67)

Hopkins's moral reasoning linked formal properties of conditionality with human relations of authority and submission. Ultimately, such linkages enabled him to find sermons in nature.

Law of Limitation

Because the human body embodies lower levels of physical organization, it has lower level needs that the individual should meet but in a measured way respecting the law of limitation.

> Hence the law of limitation will be, that every activity may be put forth, and so every good be enjoyed, up to the point when it is most perfectly conditional for a higher good. Anything beyond that will be excess and evil.... Here, then, is our model and law. Have we a lower sensitive and animal nature? Let that nature be cherished and expanded for all its innocent and legitimate enjoyments, for it is an end. But—and here we find the limit,—let it be cherished only as subser-

vient to the higher intellectual life, for it is also a means. (Hopkins, 1865, pp. 72–73)

Man must satisfy his natural desires, but to give the lower levels of his being more than they need is excess and evil. Hopkins (1865) gave his law of limitation wide application. We should care for a child's bodily development to set the stage for the higher planes of the child's development (p. 76). We should care for the body while aiming for the mind, care for people while aiming to elevate and educate them, cherish woman and give her "her true place" while aiming for perfect social organization. Similarly, we should care for children, servants, slaves, and criminals (p. 76). In politics, the law of limitation teaches us that we should give the lower sectors of government their due and try to harmonize their requirements with those of higher sectors (p. 253).

Orders of Psychological Faculties

Turning to mind, Hopkins discerned a second pyramid of psychological faculties. The intellect and the cognitive faculties are conditional for the feelings and the emotions; these in turn are conditional for the faculties of desire and of will. Now, however, we leave the material world and entities built by the method of addition. Psychological faculties are built stratum on stratum by a method of development. Hopkins said that development is the uniquely human principle. There were other 19th-century writers who said development is a unique principle of living things. Robert Chambers (1853) made the same argument in his book *Vestiges of the Natural History of Creation*, a widely read popular precursor of Darwinian theory.

Powers of the Mind

Hopkins's psychology set forth a hierarchical analysis of human goalfulness and purposefulness. The lower strata of the mind are spontaneous, and the higher are voluntary. Arising spontaneously are the instrumental powers in thought—mechanical, unconscious, and unwilled (the instincts, appetites, desires, and affections). The higher, voluntary powers of the mind are directive. With them, the human declares ends to himself and becomes self-motivated, autonomous, and responsible. Three classes of these higher powers complete the second pyramid: reason, the rational will or will in freedom, and finally man's knowledge of his own ends (p. 166).

Two Orders of Governance

In the end, Hopkins moved to declarations of what is ethical and right. A former student, writing to Hopkins in 1859, recalled a moment of academic dramaturgy:

> After you had . . . given us somewhat in detail the great principles that underlie all reasoning . . . you laid aside your glasses, passed your hand slowly over your forehead, bowed your head amid the reigning silence for a few seconds, then slowly uttered the words 'But—Nature . . . [is] moral' and the class dismissed. (Rudolph, 1956, p. 52)

Hopkins defined the rights of authority—the parent, guardian, teacher, magistrate, and government—as the ability to declare motives or ends to subordinates. The authority of the governing over the governed is legitimately directed toward certain ends and is not unlimited. It imposes duties on the governing and the governed. Hopkins wrote, "Government has no right *to be*, except as it is necessary to secure the ends of the individual in his social capacity; and it must, therefore, be found *so to be* as to secure these ends in the best manner" (Hopkins, 1865, p. 266).

In the physical world, lower forms are independent of and unmodified by the higher forms that they constitute. In the living world, lower forms and higher forms act on one another. There are two orders of governance.

> At first, and in mere organizations, the lower builds up the higher, and sustains it, and is wholly for that. Any action from the higher to the lower is simply to sustain the lower in its own place and function as tributary, but never to elevate it out of that sphere. But when we reach the sphere of intelligence the object of the action from above is to elevate the lower. (Hopkins, 1865, p. 264)

The higher sphere brings forth growth and righteousness. The highest form of governance is that which leads to development in which the high help the low to become higher.

CHANGES AT WILLIAMS COLLEGE

The Williams College that Hall attended was a country college slowly becoming more citified and sophisticated. Nathaniel Hawthorne attended the Williams commencement in 1838 and described the students as "great unpolished bumpkins . . . rough, brown-featured, schoolmaster looking, half-bumpkin, half scholar figures, in black ill-cut broadcloth;—their manners quite spoilt by what little of the gentleman there was in them" (Rudolph, 1956, p. 65). But Williams's undergraduates were changing. Fewer were going into the ministry—28% between 1836 and 1845, 22% between 1846 and 1865, 13% between 1866 and 1872—and more were turning towards law, business, and medicine. (Bledstein, 1976, p. 198, has noted a similar trend away from the ministry among the graduates of Yale, Bowdoin, Brown, and Dartmouth at that time.)

Hall studied with Mark Hopkins when the older man was nearing the end of a 36-year presidency. Hopkins was a stalwart of an older tradition, standing his ground against winds of change that in a few years would begin to transform small old-time colleges into large modern universities. Twenty-five years later, G. Stanley Hall—now himself a college president—would call the year 1870 "almost the Anno Domini of educational history" (Veysey, 1965, p. 1). The winds of change could be felt in Hall's time; Williams's students supplemented their official coursework with a substantial amount of student-run education.

Students' Curriculum

Students at Williams had established two literary societies, one of them the one the young Hall attended that by 1861 owned over 8,000 books to supplement the Williams College collection (Rudolph, 1956, pp. 74-76). (Williams's library, like its courses, was classical and religious; it was open one afternoon a week for juniors and seniors and one afternoon a week for freshmen and sophomores.) Hall met with a Saturday night club to talk about Emerson, Carlyle, Coleridge, Lamb, Wordsworth, the Lake Poets, Tennyson, Shakespeare, Dante, Goethe, Schiller, and Lessing. These authors were presumably too frivolous to be represented in the regular curriculum. Other philosophical and scientific writers were held to be harmful because they "taught men to hold no opinions." It would take the young Hall years after Williams to read Darwin, Spencer, Tyndall, Renan, Strauss, Emerson, Feuerbach, Comte, Tom Paine, Charles Kingsley, Canon Farrar, Matthew Arnold, G. H. Lewes, John Stuart Mill, and John Smith (Hall, 1923, pp. 184-185).

A Lyceum of Natural History, founded by eight Williams students in 1835, was the scientific counterpart of the student literary societies. Lyceum members studied flying machines, the dyes used in the manufacture of cotton cloth, the usefulness of spiders in the manufacture of raw silk, cotton culture and industry, artesian wells, the mechanics of nest building, natural resources, coal beds, whale fisheries, oil wells, iron ores, gold mining, volcanoes, giraffes, condor hunting, icebergs, entrances to the Sphinx, etc. The Lyceum offered courses in botany in 1836. It laid the foundation for a science library in 1839, raised money and constructed a building of its own in 1855, and hired an assistant of Louis Agassiz to aid in the classification of its fishes in 1863. The Lyceum was in communication with leading scientists of the United States. It sent expeditions to Nova Scotia in 1835, Florida in 1857, Greenland in 1860, South America in 1867, and Honduras in 1871. Finally, between 1868 and 1871, Williams College absorbed the Lyceum and in effect made the Lyceum's mission its own. The second scientific curriculum that Hall found available to him at Williams could be found in other old-time colleges. Kohlstedt (1988) notes that student natural history societies providing courses in science and putting together study collections were established between 1822 and 1848 at Amherst, Brown, Williams, Rutgers, Yale, Wesleyan, Harvard, Geneva, Pennsylvania, Marshall, and Haverford.

Hall did not turn towards science at Williams; he was a romantic at this stage of his life. Ross (1972) remarks:

> His classmates said that "when Stan gets to thinking clearly, he will think greatly," and they considered him "the smartest man" in their class. Hall's persistent effort to give intellectual form to the full range of his emotional experience was the chief source of both the insight and confusion he would display in his intellectual career. (pp. 28–29)

Hall was class poet. He graduated Phi Beta Kappa in 1867 and went on to Union Theological Seminary to become a divinity student. He took a time-out and went to Europe to study philosophy and theology but came back reluctantly because his parents would support him no further in Europe. He became an ordained minister, and for a short time he preached and might have gotten stuck in a country parish for life, "out of place, a misfit, restless and unhappy" (Hall, 1923, p. 183). Fate helped him take a doctorate at Harvard with James and Bowditch and then to go to Europe again, this time for scientific training.

In the introduction of his *Founders of Modern Psychology*, Hall (1912) would later summarize all his German education. Between 1870 and 1882 he spent nearly 6 years as a student in Germany. In his first 3-year visit, ending in 1873, he concentrated on philosophy and attended lectures on theology, Aristotle, biblical psychology, logic, recent psychology, comparative religions, Hegel, and Herbart. In his second 3-year stay, he took courses in chemistry, biology, physiology, anatomy, neurology, psychopathology, and anthropology. Hall returned from his studies in Germany equipped to work in a new kind of college that, in a sense, he had no choice but to help to establish.

NEW PSYCHOLOGY IN A NEW UNIVERSITY

Hall's professorship at Johns Hopkins placed him in the vanguard of what Jencks & Riesman (1968) call an academic revolution—when the American college "ceased to be a marginal, backward-looking enterprise shunned by the bulk of the citizenry" and became instead a "major growth industry." The new American college was larger, governed by a faculty of arts and sciences, and offered electives and lectures rather than textbooks and recitations. Jencks & Riesman (1968, p. 13) say, "Perhaps the most important breakthroughs were the founding of Johns Hopkins and Clark as primarily graduate universities." After establishing the new psychology at Hopkins, Hall would carry the torch from Hopkins to Clark.

The new psychology Hall taught at Hopkins took three years to deliver. He gave 1 year to sensation, half of the second year to perception and psychophysics, and half to association, memory, habit, attention, and the will. His third year was spent on "the topics of instinct in animals, psychogenesis in children, the psychological parts of anthropology (including animism, the chief mythic cycles, traditions, rites and ceremonies), and morbid psychology (especially aphasia, hypnotic and allied states, paranoia, epilepsy, hysteria, paralysis, etc.) . . ." (Evans, 1984, p. 54).

Hall established a brass-instruments laboratory at Johns Hopkins. He had done his thesis research in Henry Pickering Bowditch's physiology laboratory at Harvard Medical School (Hall, 1878) and he cared about physiology, but he was not completely committed to experimental psychology and he would do only a limited amount of work in it (Miles & Miles, 1929; Ross, 1972, pp. 155–157). His major research program would be the questionnaire studies of child development he would undertake with his students at Clark University.

FIRST "NORMAL SCIENCE" OF DEVELOPMENTAL PSYCHOLOGY

In the spring of 1888, Hall left Johns Hopkins and moved to Worcester, Massachusetts, to live as a guest in Jonas Clark's home while Clark built the university that Hall would take over as president. Hall planned to build a set of graduate departments—psychology, biology, chemistry, physics, and mathematics—to create first a graduate school and then in time an undergraduate college. Hall toured Europe gathering ideas. He put together a faculty that was by all accounts distinguished. Clark University opened in 1889 with 18 faculty and 34 students. Hall had a special vision of what a university ought to be like and for 2 or 3 years the vision lived. Then there were personal and professional tragedies. Hall's wife and daughter were accidentally killed in 1890. There were town–gown problems in Worcester, and Jonas Clark, sole financial supporter of the university, began to withdraw his support. In one of the famous raids of academic history, William Rainey Harper, president of the new University of Chicago, swooped down on Clark and made off with two thirds of the faculty and 70% of the students.

In 1891, Hall turned towards child study, at first probably because he needed an activity at Clark that would win some popular support in the city of Worcester and later because he saw it as an activity that might help him sustain his university. He founded the *Pedagogical Seminary* (now the *Journal of Genetic Psychology*), and he began a program of questionnaire studies of child development that had to be for a time a prominent force in psychology. It must be remembered that as late as 1898, 30 of the 54 doctorates in psychology awarded in the United States had been awarded by Hall. A science has to have some form of cooperative empirical inquiry, and Hall's "Clark method" is one of the three forms of psychological research identified by Danziger (1985, 1990) in his content analyses of the early psychological journals.

Hall had done some preliminary questionnaire studies of children in the 1880s, extending prior German work. He could find scientific precedents for questionnaire inquires in antecedent work of Darwin, Fechner, and Calton (While, 1990). On the one side, questionnaire studies of childhood seemed feasible and reasonable; on the other, a grass roots movement called for scientific child study. The movement reflected the rise of the "whole child professions" and the turn-of-the-century renegotiation of American social contracts distributing responsibilities for the socialization of children among families, professionals, and governmental institutions (Siegel & White, 1982).

Hall's (1923) autobiography lists the titles, dates, and authors of 194 topical syllabi (questionnaires) published at Clark between October 1894 and February 1915. He was personally most involved in the questionnaire work between 1894 and 1903, and this is when the work of the program looked most like early developmental psychology. Students and associates have left us descriptions of the child study work (Monroe, 1899; Sheldon, 1946; Smith, 1905; Wiltse, 1895, 1896–97). Near the end of his active period, Hall (1903) offered a summary of what in his estimation the contribution of the research program had been. Wilson's (1975) bibliographies list over 4,000 entries and give a useful sense of the larger social movement toward child study.

Hall's questionnaire studies were rather vigorously denounced within a few years after they were begun. Some of the denunciation was probably politically motivated. Hall had been a powerful figure, but he had been high-handed in his dealings and now personal and political troubles made him vulnerable. Opponents happily pointed out scientific shortcomings of the questionnaire studies. These were real problems but, nonetheless, those studies sketched a picture of child development not dissimilar to the picture we hold today (White, 1990).

The questionnaire inquiries dealt with (a) simple automatisms, instincts, and attitudes, (b) the small child's activities and feelings, (c) control of emotions and will, (d) development of the higher faculties, (e) individual differences, (f) school processes and practices, and (g) church processes and practices.

Simple Automatisms, Instincts, and Attitudes

Many of the questionnaires sought for the inborn predispositions of childhood (*Early Forms of Vocal Expression; Some Common Traits and Habits; Tickling, Fun, Wit, Humor, Laughing*) and belief and habits of the small child (*Migrations, Tramps, Truancy, Running Away, Etc., vs. Love of Home;*

Affection and its Opposite States in Children). Such questionnaires generally tried to trace the movement of the developing child from the spontaneous to the voluntary, from instinct to reason, and from simple sociality to the development of scientific and ethical reasoning.

Nowadays, much research on infancy and toddlerhood tends to be upward seeking, looking for early signs of reason, language, numerical understanding, morality, self-awareness, altruism, etc. Hall, because of his great concern about the dangers of precocity, looked for the simplest and crudest organizations of children's behavior, the unique and the non-adultlike characteristics of children. It has taken us much serious effort to come to terms with the fact that the playful in children is serious. Hall's questionnaires again and again sought out mannered, stylized, playful, theatrical facets of children's behavior, taking for granted that these were important organizers of childhood behavior. A questionnaire on *Early Forms of Vocal Expression* in January, 1895 asks the following:

> Describe any expressive gesture or attitude, whether of hands, body or face, and note rhythm, stress, inflection and especially spontaneous singing. Describe every trace of pantomime, special gesture with a speech value, buffoonery, mimicry, love of acting.

In February 1895, *Some Common Traits and Habits* invited respondents to write about teasing, bullying, showing off, mimicry and imitation, bashfulness, awkwardness and boldness, and curiosity.

> SHOWING OFF . . . Describe mincing, acting a part, putting on airs, acts or words thought to show superfine manners or breeding, playing the role of another self. How far is this due to vivid imagination, how long kept up, is it sustained or practiced when alone, or only before others, and are the traits assumed systematized or incoherent.

Small Child's Activities and Feelings

A second group of questionnaires asked about the objects children care about and like to deal with—*Dolls, Toys and Playthings*—and the rhythmic, ritualistic, or superstitious aspects of children's behavior. For Hall, mind is built on feelings, and many of the questionnaires tried to get at children's feelings about themselves and things about them—*The Early Sense of Self, Feeling for Objects of Inanimate Nature, Feelings for Objects of Animate Nature, Children's Thoughts, Reactions, and Feelings to Animals*—and to pursue the idea that such feelings are the foundation for later, more rational understandings.

Control of Emotions and Will

There were questionnaire inquiries into children's outbursts of emotionality. Generally, the questions on these moved towards questions about when and by whom the emotions were eventually controlled. Question sequences like this are found in *Anger, Crying and Laughing, Fears in Childhood and Youth,* and *Affection and Its Opposite States in Children.* It was assumed that at first parents and other adults regulated and controlled a child's outbursts, but later the child gradually came to exert self-control and self-regulation. Very important for the latter were the growth of higher faculties.

Development of the Higher Faculties

Hall and his students were keenly interested in the development of moral and religious sentiments in children—through growth and through moral education. There were early questionnaires entitled *Moral and Religious Experiences, Moral Education,* and *Confession.* Increases in cognitive capacity were thought to be essential for participation in complex forms of human society, and so there was a questionnaire on *Memory,* and numerous inquiries into children's capacities to think in symbolic and ideal terms. The questionnaires asked about more humane and altruistic sentiments: *Pity, The Sense of Honor Among Children, Unselfishness in Children.*

Individual Differences

The four groups of questionnaires so far described explored general processes of child development. A fifth group explored dysfunction. A 1901 questionnaire entitled *Sub-normal Normal Children and Youth* by Arthur R. T. Wylie opens with the following text:

> It is desired by means of this syllabus to gain material for the study of the bad and troublesome children of school and family life, those who have reached their limit in only one line, the runaways, the vagrants, spendthrifts, dudes, hoboes, hoodlums, religious fanatics, sensualists, sentimentalists, vicious and impulsive characters, impulsive masturbators, the ne'er-do-wells, the gilded youth and those who gave early promise but dropped into a humble station which they just managed to fill.

Nowadays, inquiries into individual differences are usually directed towards continuous, normally distributed individual differences in cognition or personality. Hall's inquires into individual differences explored the boundaries of psychopathology and sociopathology. Many in the late 19th century were concerned about degeneracy as a source of crime, anarchism, vagrancy, social disorder, mental disease, and various human dysfunctions. Clark questionnaires such as *Peculiar and Exceptional Children, Moral Defects and Perversions, Signs of Nervousness,* and *Precocity and Tardiness of Development* were directed towards exploring early signs of such characteristics in children.

School Processes and Practices

Many of the Clark questionnaires, particularly in the later years of the program, were directly oriented to problems of schools and professional educators. These questionnaires were one point of beginning of an applied child study. Some were directed at curriculum, some at methods, some at professional and political issues in teaching (e.g., *The Beginnings of Reading and Writing, Kindergarten, Number and Mathematics, Examinations and Recitations, Local Voluntary Association among Teachers, Examinations, Differences Between Old and Young Teachers*).

Church Processes and Practices

As in the case of schools, there were Clark questionnaires directed toward a mixture of psychological and service-oriented issues confronting members of the ministry. Psychological questionnaires were directed toward *Religious Experiences, Immortality, Questionnaire on the Soul,* and *Questionnaire on Children's Prayers*. More institutional questionnaires were directed towards *Sabbath and Worship in General, Questions for the Essential Features of Public Worship,* and *Hymns and Sacred Music,* or *The Sermon*.

G. STANLEY HALL'S SCHEME OF CHILD AND ADOLESCENT DEVELOPMENT

Hall's developmental psychology was spelled out in his two-volume *Adolescence: Its Psychology and its Relations to Physiology, Anthropology, Sociology, Sex, Crime, Religion, and Education* (Hall, 1904). The volumes are unread today. They are mentioned from time to time as (a) an argument for recapitulationism, (b) a source of the Sturm und Drang view of adolescence, or (c) occasionally, as a source for what some claim is 20th-century society's invention of adolescence. There is more to the volumes than their condensation into a few slogans would suggest.

The first volume of *Adolescence* gives extended reviews of (a) anthropometric and body–organ studies of growth in size and weight, (b) studies of the growth of motor power and functional abilities and of various training schemes designed to foster that growth, (c) physical and mental diseases associated with adolescence; (d) sociological, criminological, and cross-cultural studies of adolescent crimes and antisocial behavior; (e) physical and psychological phenomena of sexual development; (f) phenomena of animal and human sexual periodicity, and (g) literary, biographical, and historical writings about adolescence.

The second volume discusses (a) sensory and voice changes in adolescents; (b) evolution of the feelings and instincts; (c) adolescent feelings about nature and their response to science; (d) cross-cultural and cross-religious practices in the initiation and education of adolescents; (12) phenomena of adolescent religious conversion; (e) social instincts and institutions among adolescents; (f) intellectual development and education; (g) adolescent girls and their capabilities for and response to education; and (h) the possibility of an ethnic psychology and of a pedagogy missionaries might use for "adolescent races."

Some Suggested Patterns of Human Development

The two *Adolescence* volumes are huge, and Hall is prodigious in the scholarly detail that he presents and the variety of practical issues that he takes up for discussion. It seems worthwhile to present here a very rudimentary sketch of Hall's scheme of human development. The following are some of his principal theses:

1. People, human faculties, social institutions, societies may be ordered on an evolutionary line, with the order reflecting not only the historic time at which they came into existence but their relative state of perfection
2. Child development recapitulates human evolution:

   Holding that the child and the race are each keys to the other, I have constantly suggested phyletic explanations of all degrees of probability.... Realizing the limitations and qualifications of the recapitulation theory in the biologic field, I am now convinced that its psychogenetic applications can have a method of their own, and although the time has not yet come when any formulation of these can have much value I have done the best I could with each instance as it arose. Along with the sense of the extreme importance of further coordinating childhood and youth with the development of their race, has grown the conviction that only here can we hope to find true norms against the tendency to precocity in home, school, church, and civilization generally, and also to establish criteria by which to both diagnose and measure arrest and retardation in the individual and in the race." (Hall, 1904, Vol. 1, p. viii)

3. What mediates this recapitulation is biology—the fact that evolutionarily older areas of the brain mature before evolutionarily newer areas. Work of John Hughlings Jackson, Flechsig, Kaes, Vulpius, and others has shown that the central nervous system "is made up of three superposed levels closely correlated" (Hall, 1904, Vol. 1, p. 110) and that the lower levels mature before the higher ones.

   Certain types of insanity are rare before puberty, because the child cannot reason according to adult standards until fourteen, the age at which Aristotle would begin the education of reason. Before this comes the age of the spinal reflex and automatic nascency of the later prenatal life and the early months of infancy. Then comes the stage of controlled muscular actions—walking, plays—when drill, habituation, memory, and instinct culminate, which is associated with the mid-level regions of the brain. Lastly comes the age of rational thought, higher logical correlation, personal opinion and conviction, higher esthetic enjoyments, deliberate choice, and willed action. . . . Each lower level, however, must have its full development, for it is a necessary condition for the unfoldment of the higher. Logical methods, on the other hand, if too early, tend to stultify and violate the law that fundamental must always precede accessory structures and functions. (Hall, 1904, Vol. 1, p. 111)

4. There are "nascent stages." The child grows towards not one but a series of perfections. The stages do not center on feelings and motives as in Freud's theory, nor on cognition as in Piaget's theory. Each stage is the attainment of a mode of social existence or a way of life. As children get older, feelings, sentiments, attitudes, motives, and abilities change so that they become capable of participating in ever more complex and sophisticated societies.
5. In very small children you find many automatisms, fidgets, nonvolitional movements, "motor odds and ends." They increase in the kindergarten years, diminishing in the primary years. They are associated with fatigue, task difficulty, the need to maintain fixed attention. They are mostly in the accessory muscles; those in the fundamental muscles disappear rapidly with age. The automatisms diminish as the will grows in force. They are (Hall, 1904, Vol. 1, p. 160) "paleopsychic."
6. Ages 6 or 7 represent an old time of human maturity, the "shores of an ancient pubic sea."

After the critical transition age of six or seven, when the brain has achieved its adult size and weight and teething has reduced the chewing surface to its least extent, begins an unique stage of life marked by reduced growth and increased activity and power to resist both disease and fatigue which . . . suggests what was, in some just post-simian age of our race, its period of maturity. Here belong discipline in writing, reading, spelling, verbal memory, manual training, practice of instrumental technique, proper names, drawing, drill in arithmetic, foreign languages by oral methods, the correct pronunciation of which is far harder if acquired later, etc. The hand is never so near the brain. Most of the content of the mind has entered it through the senses, and the eye- and ear-gates should be open at their widest. Authority should now take precedence of reason. Children comprehend much and very rapidly if we can only refrain from explaining, but this slows down intuition, tends to make casuists and prigs and to unfeeble the ultimate vigor of reason. It is the age of little method and much matter ...

[By the end of this preadolescent era] Morally he should have been through many if not most forms of what parents and teachers commonly call badness and Professor Yoder even calls meanness. He should have fought, whipped and been whipped, used language offensive to the prude and to the prim precisian, been in some scrapes, had something to do with bad, if more with good associates, and been exposed to and already recovering from ... many forms of ethical mumps and measles.... Something is amiss with the lad of ten who is very good, studious, industrious, thoughtful, altruistic, quiet, polite, respectful, obedient, gentlemanly, orderly, always in good toilet, docile to reason, who turns away from stories that reek with gore, prefers adult companionship to that of his mates, refuses all low associates, speaks standard English, or is pious and deeply in love with religious services ... (Hall, 1904, Vol. 2, pp. 451–453)

7. Motor activity and education are essential for child development, Hall says, and he gives extended arguments for industrial education, manual training, gymnastics, and sports. "Motor specialties requiring exactness and grace like piano-playing, drawing, writing, pronunciation of a foreign tongue, dancing, acting, singing, and a host of virtuosities" should be begun before adolescence (Hall, 1904, Vol. 1, p. 164)." However, from ages 4 to age 8, overexercising the accessory muscles may "sow the seeds of chorea." From age 8 to age 12, overprecision, especially if fundamental activities are neglected, will bring nervous strain and stunting precocity.

8. Adolescence is a second point of initiation for socialization and education. Early adolescence, age 8 to age 12, constitutes a "unique period in human life." The child develops a life of its own outside the home; it is "never so independent of adult influence"; it has acute perception, immunity to exposure, danger, accident, as well as temptation. In short, the child is independently viable but capable of participating in a very simple sort of society. "Reason, true morality, religion, sympathy, love, and esthetic enjoyment are but slightly developed" (Hall, 1904, Vol. 1, p. *ix*). Hall conveys an image of the early adolescent prepared for a Lord-of-the-Flies kind of social life, and somewhere in his writings he regrets the fact that we have to coop youths of that age

in middle schools, when they would be happiest in simple self-run societies. The tendency of adolescents to form a great number and variety of clubs reflects this natural development.

9. Adolescence is a time of oscillations and oppositions, between inertness and excitement, pleasure and pain, self-confidence and humility, selfishness and altruism, society and solitude, sensitiveness and dullness, knowing and doing, conservatism and iconoclasm, sense and intellect.
10. One can introduce science at adolescence, slowly. A need to explain the world arises at the very beginning as a feeling that the mysteries of nature must be looked at and addressed. The youth responds to nature sentimentally and is drawn towards mythic or poetic formulations or the religions of nature. Next in the genetic order comes an interest in popular science.

> Here ... belongs every contact which science can suggest with the daily life of the pupil at home or school, at play or resting, in dress and regimen, and here, too begins the need of abundant apparatus, models, diagrams, collections, and all aids that eye or hand can give the mind. A science building or course without these is a soulless corpse.
>
> Then comes an interest in the practical, technological side of science. Last and highest comes an interest in pure science freed from all alloy of myth, genetic stage, or utility, and cultivated for its own sake, with no motive but love of truth (Hall, 1904, Vol. 2, pp. 153–154).

11. At adolescence, one can begin to teach a higher morality. Hall (1904, Vol. 2, pp. 433–448) proposes a radical change in the pedagogy of the vernacular language, literature, and history. The prime purpose would be moral—so to determine intelligence and will to secure the largest increase of social service, advance altruism, and reduce selfishness through (a) oratory and debates; (b) drama; (c) reading, particularly myths; (d) the Bible; and (e) history and literature.

From the very beginning of his child study work, Hall had challenged the American kindergarten movement and had a very substantial impact on it (Shapiro, 1983; White & Buka, 1987). The *Adolescence* volumes represented for Hall the culmination of his child study interests. There are many and various practical suggestions scattered through the volumes; both the suggestions and the question of their possible impacts on American social practices deserve more serious examination than they have so far had. It seems most likely that Hall, along with Edward L. Thorndike and John Dewey, had a very substantial impact on American educational and social institutions at a historic time of great flux and change (White, 1991).

Echoes of Mark Hopkins's Developmental Psychology

Buried beneath the wealth of new scientific work and scholarly detail, Hall's developmental analysis in *Adolescence* carried forward some of the developmental themes presented to him out of an older philosophy by Mark Hopkins. In Hall's concern about the dangers of precocity, a concern about bringing children too rapidly into adulthood that he would express again and again in *Adolescence*, Hall echoed Hopkins's law of limitation, a principle that he appealed to again and again in his moral philosophy. Like Hopkins, Hall argued the following:

1. The human mind and human nature may be understood by a developmental analysis.
2. People, human faculties, social institutions, and societies may be ordered genetically, with the order reflecting not only the historic time at which they came into existence but their relative state of perfection.
3. Lower order mental faculties are mechanical, unwilled and animal-like; higher order faculties are self-motivated, autonomous, and responsible.
4. Human relationships of authority and subordination may be derived from the developmental analysis as well as some human responsibilities.
5. Ultimately, the mental science that gives the developmental analysis forms the ground on which a moral philosophy—a set of ethical prescriptions—may be built.
6. Recall Mark Hopkins's pyramid of ever more complex and perfect entities, each aggregating with its kind in ever more complex and perfect ways. As Hall's children get older they become capable of participating in ever more complex and sophisticated societies.

LATER INTERESTS: HALL'S RETURN TO RELIGION: THE CHILDREN'S INSTITUTE

With the completion of his *Adolescence*, Hall's personal interests turned away from child study. He said in his *Life and Confessions*:

> In 1904, when I printed my two volumes on adolescence, that subject became thereafter more or less of a closed one to me. As usual, having

printed, I never read it again and avoided the subject in my courses of instruction, and in 1911 I closed my account with child study as applied to education by publishing my two volumes, *Educational Problems* and thereafter ceased to lecture on education." (Hall, 1923, p. 405)

In his last years, Hall turned back to religion. The last chapter of *Adolescence* proposes that genetic psychology be made the basis for a "science of missions." In the same year in which he published *Adolescence*, Hall founded the *American Journal of Religious Psychology and Education*. He had largely drafted his two-volume *Jesus, the Christ, in the Light of Psychology* in 1900, but he held off publication until 1917 (Hall, 1917; Ross, 1972, p. 418). Hall was not completely finished with genetic psychology, however. He turned toward the exploration of old age and what we call lifespan development, writing a book on *Senescence* (Hall, 1922).

Hall tried to give Clark University a continuing position in child study. Suddenly, the children's cause was beginning to win ground in American politics. The first White House Conference was convened in 1909, and the Children's Bureau was established in 1912. In 1910, Hall persuaded the Clark trustees to appropriate $5,000—no small sum in those days—to establish a Children's Institute to serve as a center for research on childhood (Burnham & Fitzsimmons, 1912; Hall, 1910; Wilson, 1910). Hall hoped that Clark would become the partner and research arm of the forthcoming Children's Bureau. Hall's vision of the future was accurate, but he could not consolidate Clark's place in that future. A few years later, in 1917, Cora Bussey Hillis succeeded in establishing the Iowa Child Welfare Research Station, and it was at Iowa that the second growth wave of developmental psychology began.

G. STANLEY HALL'S CONTRIBUTION: A REAPPRAISAL

G. Stanley Hall's psychological work deserves more direct examination than it has recently received. Because Hall was active and influential at just the right time, he compiled many firsts and foundings—as Wundt's first American student, first American professor of psychology, founder of what some say was the first American psychology laboratory, founder of the *American Journal of Psychology*, first president of Clark University, founder and first president of the American Psychological Association, leader of the child study movement, founder of the *Pedagogical Seminary*, and so on. Hall invited Freud to Clark University in 1909 and thus helped psychoanalysis get international recognition. Recent writings usually picture Hall as a functionary and figurehead, condense his ideas into a few slogans, quote criticisms of his work by his often-rivalrous peers, and effectively concede Hall his administrative trophies while ignoring most of what he had to say. What Hall had to say about developmental psychology is worth some contemporary examination.

1. Through his questionnaire program, Hall set up a first cooperative "normal science" of child development. The findings obtained through that work suggested local patterns and orderlinesses and a larger movement that is quite consistent with our view of child development today. The questionnaire work was methodologically weak, to be sure, but the methodological regulations psychology subsequently put into place have probably been excessively restrictive. Hall's questionnaires asked people to give narrative accounts of children's behaviors in everyday situations, and this kind of approach is becoming more popular nowadays.
2. Hall elaborated a social–biological conception of childhood. As children grow, they develop capacities that enable them to participate in more and more complex kinds of social organization. Growth brings changes in cognition, memory, feelings, emotions, symbolization, and social behaviors, but what orchestrates all the changes and brings them toward a unity is the movement of the child toward different forms of social participation. Contemporary research and theory is reviving Hall's vision and moving away from the view that cognitive development should be taken as synonymous with child development, the faster the better (e.g., Elkind, 1981).
3. Hall wrote a massive account of adolescence, looking across the work of different disciplines, examining social practices, and trying to arrive at scientific syntheses on the one side and practical recommendations on the other. We need to trace the influence of Hall's ideas and recommendations as they entered the complex infrastructure of American professional and social services for children. By looking at such influences, we may better understand when and how and to what extent the work of developmental psychology can be meaningful and useful for society.

REFERENCES

Albrecht, F. M., Jr. (1960). *The new psychology in America: 1880–1895.* Unpublished doctoral dissertation, Johns Hopkins University, Baltimore, MD.

Bledstein, B. J. (1976). *The culture of professionalism: The middle class and the development of higher education in America.* New York: Norton.

Burnham, W. H. (1925). The man, G. Stanley Hall. *Psychological Review, 32,* 89–102.

Burnham, W. H., & Fitzsimmons, M. E. (1912). The educational museum at Clark University: Catalogue of the department of school hygiene. *Pedagogical Seminary, 19,* 526–552.

Chambers, R. (1853). *Vestiges of the natural history of creation* (10th ed.). London: John Churchill.

Danziger, K. (1985). The origins of the psychological experiment as a social institution. *American Psychologist, 40,* 133–140.

Danziger, K. (1990). *Constructing the subject: Historical origins of psychological research.* Cambridge, England: Cambridge University Press.

Elkind, D. (1981). *The hurried child: Growing up too fast too soon.* Reading, MA: Addison-Wesley.

Evans, R. B. (1984). The origins of American academic psychology. In J. Brozek (Ed.), *Explorations in the history of psychology in the United States* (pp. 17–60). Lewisburg, PA: Bucknell University Press.

Hall, G. S. (1876). College instruction in philosophy. *Nation, 23,* 180.

Hall, G. S. (1878). The muscular perception of space. *Mind, 3,* 433–450.

Hall, G. S. (1879). Philosophy in the United States. *Mind, 4,* 89–105.

Hall, G. S. (1885). The new psychology. *Andover Review, III,* 120–135, 239–248.

Hall, G. S. (1903). Child study at Clark University: An impending new step. *American Journal of Psychology, XIV,* 96–106.

Hall, G. S. (1904). *Adolescence: Its psychology and its relations to physiology, anthropology, sociology, sex, crime, religion, and education* (2 vols.). New York: Appleton-Century-Crofts.

Hall, G. S. (1907). Boy life in a Massachusetts country town forty years ago. In T. L. Smith (Ed.), *Aspects of child life and education* (pp. 300–322). Lexington, MA: Ginn Press.

Hall, G. S. (1910). General outline of the new child study work at Clark University. *Pedagogical Seminary, 17,* 160–165.

Hall, G. S. (1912). *Founders of modern psychology.* New York: Appleton-Century-Crofts.

Hall, G. S. (1917). *Jesus, the Christ, in the light of psychology* (2 vols.). Garden City, NY: Doubleday.

Hall, G. S. (1922). *Senescence: The last half of life.* New York: Appleton.

Hall, G. S. (1923). *Life and confessions of a psychologist.* New York: Appleton-Century-Crofts.

Hopkins, M. (1865). *Lectures on moral science.* Boston, MA: Gould and Lincoln.

Hopkins, H. (1885). *The law of love and love as a law: Or, Christian ethics* (rev. ed.). New York: Scribner.

Jencks, C., & Riesman, D. (1968). *The academic revolution.* Garden City, NY: Doubleday.

Karier, C. J. (1986). *Scientists of the mind: Intellectual founders of modern psychology.* Urbana: University of Illinois Press.

Kohlstedt, S. C. (1988). Curiosities and cabinets: Natural history museums and education on the antebellum campus. *Isis, 79,* 405–426.

Miles, W., & Miles, C. (1929). Eight letters from G. Stanley Hall to Henry Pickering Bowditch, with introduction and notes. *American Journal of Psychology, 41,* 326–336.

Monroe, W. S. (1899). Status of child study in Europe. *Pedagogical Seminary, 6,* 372–381.

O'Donnell, J. M. (1985). *The origins of behaviorism: American psychology, 1870–1920.* New York: New York University Press.

Pruett, L. (1926). *G. Stanley Hall: A biography of a mind.* New York: Appleton-Century-Crofts.

Rodkin, P. C. (1990, June). Blasphemers of method: How G. Stanley Hall and William James undertook to reconcile their psychology and their religion. Paper presented at the annual meeting of the Cherion Society, Westfield, MA.

Ross, D. (1972). *G. Stanley Hall: The psychologist as prophet.* Chicago, IL: University of Chicago Press.

Rudolph, F. (1956). *Mark Hopkins and the log: Williams College, 1836–1872.* New Haven, CT: Yale University Press.

Sanford, E. C. (1924). Granville Stanley Hall, 1846–1924. *American Journal of Psychology, 35,* 313–321.

Shapiro, M. S. (1983). *Child's garden: The kindergarten movement from Proebel to Dewey.* University Park, PA: Pennsylvania State University Press.

Sheldon, H. D. (1946). Clark University, 1897–1900. *Journal of Social Psychology, 24,* 227–247.

Siegel, A. W., & White, S. H. (1982). The child study movement: Early growth and development of the symbolized child. *Advances in Child Development and Behavior, 17,* 233–285.

Smith, T. L. (1905). Child study at Clark University. *Pedagogical Seminary, 12,* 93–96.

Starbuck, E. D. (1925). G. Stanley Hall as a psychologist. *Psychological Review, 32,* 89–102.

Veysey, L. R. (1965). *The emergence of the American university.* Chicago, IL: University of Chicago Press.

Wetmore, K. E. (1991). The evolution of psychology from moral philosophy in the nineteenth century American college curriculum. Unpublished doctoral dissertation, University of Chicago, Chicago, IL.

White, S. H. (1990). Child study at Clark University: 1894–1904. *Journal of the History of the Behavioral Sciences, 26,* 131–150.

White, S. H. (1991). Three visions of educational psychology. In L. Tolchinsky-Landsmann (Ed.), *Culture, schooling, and psychological development* (pp. 1–38). Norwood, NJ: Ablex.

White, S. H., & Buka, S. (1987). Early education: Programs, traditions, and policies. *Review of Research in Education, 14,* 43–91.

Wiebe, R. H. (1967). *The search for order: 1877–1920*. Westport, CT: Greenwood Press.

Wilson, D. J. (1990). *Science, community, and the transformation of American philosophy, 1860–1930*. Chicago, IL: University of Chicago Press.

Wilson, L. N. (1910). Library facilities for the work of the Children's Institute and the new building for this work. *Pedagogical Seminary, 17*, 166–175.

Wilson, L. N. (1914). *G. Stanley Hall: A sketch*. New York: Stechart & Co.

Wilson, L. N. (1975). *Bibliography of child study: 1898–1912*. New York: Arno Press.

Wiltse, S. E. (1895). A preliminary sketch of the history of child study in America. *Pedagogical Seminary, 3*, 189–212.

Wiltse, S. E. (1896–97). A preliminary sketch of the history of child study, for the year ending September, 1896. *Pedagogical Seminary, 4*, 111–125.

15

THE MENTAL TESTING COMMUNITY AND VALIDITY: A PREHISTORY

RICHARD T. VON MAYRHAUSER

American readers of the *Journal of Educational Psychology* had three good reasons to feel glad in the summer of 1916. First, there was at least one professional journal devoted to applied psychology in the United States, and they were reading it. Second, for a few months, the journal had been running a lively symposium ("Mentality Tests," 1916) in which numerous experts reported on intriguing new measures of "general intelligence" and special mental abilities. And last but not least, their country was *not* in the terrible European war.

Readers who were interested in the testing method of Alfred Binet (1857–1911) took special notice of the criticism that occasioned the symposium. Robert M. Yerkes (cited in "Mentality Tests," 1916) had challenged the "correctness" and ultimate usefulness of age scaling, which was the hallmark of tests that bore Binet's name. Arguing a pure scientific position, Yerkes held that such scales were "violating the laws of mental development" (p. 163). He recently had published *A Point Scale for Measuring Mental Ability* (Yerkes, Bridges, & Hardwick, 1915), which he con-

Reprinted from *American Psychologist, 47*, 244–253 (1992). Copyright © 1992 by the American Psychological Association. Reprinted with permission of the author.

sidered more correct, or accurate, and for this reason "universally applicable" (Yerkes, 1917a).

The journal's editor, Carl E. Seashore, published Yerkes's purist critique as a model report on current research. Hoping its controversial recommendations would provoke discussion, he called for responses from all mental test researchers, however pure or practical:

> Let the criticism be direct and frank with due regard to present needs and the necessity of temporizing; let each one say what he is actually doing in the use or the improvement of the tests without fear of losing caste or priority. ("Mentality Tests," 1916, pp. 164–165)

Seashore requested discussion of what to name the common apparatus in addition to 10 more substantive issues. Of these topics, 6 dealt with experimental procedure, one pertained to adaptability to social needs, and one touched on accuracy: "What sort of co-operation for the development and standardizing of mental tests is now most needed?" ("Mentality Tests," p. 166).

"GATHERING OF THE CLAN": MOST OF IT, ANYWAY

Because Seashore (1911) had promoted "applied" psychology well before the verbal became professionally correct, Yerkes's peremptory view of cooperation concerned him (Seashore, 1916). Yerkes hoped that a testing committee would "abandon" or "ignore" Binet testing, thus excluding researchers who placed social priorities ahead of scientific ones. Yerkes (cited in "Mentality Tests," 1916) also announced intentions for a book in which he planned "to set forth principles and to call attention to the dangerous developments in so-called mental testing" (p. 164).

After reading the first batch of responses, Seashore recognized that consensus was a long way off. The "heart to heart" ("Mentality Tests," 1916, p. 229) quality of the communications lowered his expectations for any quick standardization of methods and content, let alone quick cooperation on an issue as ticklish as accuracy. It was enough of a task at the moment just to sort through the apples and oranges that came raining in from diverse experimental sites. Each contained diverse experimental treatments of whom to test (e.g., individuals with mental deficiencies and students), how to test (e.g., Binet vs. point scales and individual vs. group tests), what to test (e.g., "general intelligence," special intellectual abilities, and conative abilities), and why to test (to diagnose or to predict). Regarding Yerkes's views on a committee of standardization, some supported, some criticized, and others ignored them. Nonetheless, Yerkes's challenge had stirred a sense of community among testers of complex mental ability. Seashore (cited in "Mentality Tests," 1916) called it a "gathering of the clan . . . a fireside chat at a gathering of the leaders in this most promising field of work" (p. 229).

Still, some readers, of the symposium may have noticed the absence of two important chiefs from the "clanvocation." Edward L. Thorndike and Walter D. Scott, two of the most prominent names in the educational and business applications of mental testing, did not appear. The pair did show up at another fireside a few months later. As contributing editors to the new *Journal of Applied Psychology*, a forum that encouraged research relevant to a broad range of social needs, they endorsed the welcoming appeals of the first issue:

> The problem which is here concerned is one which must appeal to the interest of every psychologist who besides being a "pure scientist" also cherishes the hope that in addition to throwing light upon the theoretical problems of his science, his findings may also contribute their quota to the sum-total of human happiness; and it must appeal to every human being who is interested in increasing human efficiency and human happiness by the more direct method of decreasing the number of cases where a square peg is condemned to a life of fruitless endeavor to fit itself comfortably into a round hole. (Hall, Baird, & Geissler, 1917, p. 6)

Scott's (1917) research on methods of checking intelligence and special ability tests appeared in the premier issue and would have fit in at the summer roundtable except for the squareness of Scott's objective. He was certifying accuracy for the sake of a specific application (vocational selection), not for the sake of improving the accuracy of mental testing in general.

Although Scott was speaking to the question of accuracy, Yerkes was not listening. Yerkes paid no heed to such expedient research, not just because it was uninformed by "the laws of mental development" ("Mentality Tests," 1916, p. 163), but, much worse, it enlisted untutored outsiders —*businesspersons*—to judge the tests! Yerkes was not a contributing editor of the new applied journal. The appeals of the foreword did not entice him. The art of fitting persons into appropriate vocational slots held no interest; he would *never* "cherish the hope" of service. When his point scale became universally applied, he would be happy, no doubt. But for this positivist, what was true would be used of course.

Moreover, for Yerkes, there could be no question of scientists giving over their methods to others for social use. Scientists must do the testing, as experts in other areas were expected to wield their precision tools. There would be no division of labor between test creators and implementers because, for him, psychologists needed to execute the entire process: The administration of scientific tests required as much empirical rigor as their invention and refinement (von Mayrhauser, 1987).

Yerkes's prescription for purism presupposed a social environment that valued a large measure of scientific freedom, not an environment that might dictate usefulness or even science itself. The latter was virtually inconceivable in the United States and in most peace-loving nations. In November 1916, U.S. voters re-elected the President who "kept us out of war." A month later, the American Psychological Association (APA) elected Yerkes to its presidency, which presented him with a grand opportunity to redirect the profession toward experimental purity. By contrast, the coincidental inauguration of the *Journal of Applied Psychology* signaled a wrong direction. Although the name of the APA's new president was unlikely ever to appear among its authors, it did appear twice, in 1917, and for unusual reasons.

First, the new journal's chief editor, G. Stanley Hall, chose to publish Yerkes's critique of an applied psychological program that one of Hall's most prominent students had recently authored. In Hall's seminar at Clark University in March (Reed, 1987; Yerkes, 1917a), Yerkes had attacked Lewis M. Terman's Stanford Revision of the Binet Scale (1916), which had upstaged Yerkes's point scale. Yerkes dismissed the Stanford-Binet as "technologically useful, but possess[ing] little research value" and "exhibit[ing] ... the lack of any scientific principle, so far as the placing of a test in particular groups is concerned" (1917a, pp. 115, 121). So much for applied psychology.

Second, American entry into World War I led to Yerkes's only other publication in the *Journal of Applied Psychology*. This article, a report on the mobilization of psychologists to serve in the national emergency, appeared 5 months after the APA president had learned of the Congressional War Declaration (April 6). Given Yerkes's unwillingness to consider his "universally applicable" research as "applied" (von Mayrhauser, 1987), it seems fitting that news of the Declaration reached Yerkes as he was hosting a conference of E. B. Titchener's Experimentalists (Yerkes, 1921). Despite this fraternity's collective aversion to technological distortions of psychology, Yerkes redirected the discussion toward war preparation. Under the circumstances, this clan was very pleased to have one of their own members leading psychology, carefully, into wartime. Over the next few hectic months, Yerkes was indefatigable in mobilizing and advocating the profession, partly for patriotism, but especially for the research opportunity that now presented itself (Camfield, 1969; Kevles, 1968). His second publication in the *Journal of Applied Psychology*, written for the September 1917 issue, displayed an attitude that was more appropriate to a forum that encouraged serviceable research. Reporting the wartime activities of psychologists, Yerkes conceded that the cause of purism had encountered difficulties: "It is no longer a matter, as at first appeared to be the case, of inducing military authorities to accept methods of psychological measurement, but instead primarily one of meeting their expressed needs and requests for assistance" (Yerkes, 1917b, p. 304).

Military authorities induced a willingness to compromise that Yerkes previously would not have countenanced. They strongly encouraged the mental testers to combine their efforts, and in August Yerkes joined with Terman, Thorndike, and Scott to create the Committee on the Classification of Personnel in the Army. The military sought new techniques of managing officers and recruits that would surpass the efficiency and accuracy of traditional methods. The demands of this client not only drove the mental testers together but also drove them to produce and to integrate efficiency and accuracy.

The emergence of this community—and modern validity—has received little attention because of its origins, which lie both in the uneasy development of a mental testing community and in negotiations between the mental testers and their clients. Because pure and practical psychologists were little inclined to discuss their differences explicitly or to discuss client negotiations directly with one another, they left few explicit records about how they reached consensus. This article reviews how mental testers checked the "value" of their methods before there was a psychometric research community and before they would have to achieve consensus on how to make mental tests accurate.

RESEARCH COMMUNITY AS MEDIATOR AND LEGITIMATOR

The modern standard of validity requires corroboration of a given test's results with an external criterion. Correlation with alternative evaluations, including subjective evaluations and other more objective tests, allows a check on how well a test measures what it purports to measure (Cronbach, 1970). Although this standard may seem empirically basic or commonsensical in the present, it was not available to the first generation of professional psychological testers. Validity did not itself become legitimated, or canonized, until the mid-1920s (Rogers & Rogers, 1990), about the same time the term *psychometrics* first designated (1923) the theory and technique of mental measurement (*Webster's Ninth*, 1985). This is not to say that the psychologists who participated in military personnel management or earlier innovators did not practice aspects of modern validity before 1917. They were developing what later would become canonized as "concurrent" and "predictive" validities (Cronbach & Meehl, 1955), and a few were discussing accuracy checking, as we have seen.

Understanding how consensus emerged in a time of nonstandard and diverse practices can be made easier by performing a social analysis of this very social activity. Danziger's (1990, p. 7) graphing of psychology's social contexts in concentric spheres is very helpful here. The core circle, called "experimental situation," encloses an area that represents the relationships between psychologists and their subjects, psychological objects, and techniques. The first circle outside the core, called "research community," encloses an area that represents intraprofessional relations and consensus formation. The ultimate circle, called "[extra]professional environment," encloses an area that represents interaction between psychologists and their clients or patrons. As Danziger has shown, each of the areas has influenced the others in the early history of professional psychology: For example, the psychological objects studied in the profession's first laboratory, or experimental situation, impeded development of a Wundtian school, or research community; disdain for extraprofessional application limited the influence of Titchener's experimentalist research community in America.

Because our present concern is the research community of mental testers, not psychology as a whole, we shall consider the function of this specialized community in mediating differences between experimental situations, between extraprofessional environments, and between the internal and external influences of these two contexts, taken as opposite orientations. Before 1917, mental testers lacked the social cohesion, first, to integrate their various experimental styles and extraprofessional concerns and, second, to manage the opposing impulses of the internal and external contexts. Such integration and management were necessary steps to the formation of consensus on test legitimation. After 1917, and through events that space precludes description of here, the mental testers combined, determined conjointly what was valid, and soon became a leading counselor to the marriage that defines modern psychology—the marriage of scientific experimentation and social service.

The lack of psychometric community before World War I stems from a divergence in 19th century conceptions of mind and social order. This divergence continued in the first testing projects designed to isolate intellectual (as opposed to simpler psychophysical) abilities. Both of these projects, which Charles Spearman and Alfred Binet began in Europe, addressed scientific standards and attempted to demonstrate methodological accuracy. Yet their methods of test assessment did not comport with one another because they designed their tests for different experimental situations and different extraprofessional environments. I will examine these differences, and then I will consider the parallels among Terman, Yerkes, Thorndike, and Scott, the leading American mental testers of 1917.

THEORETICAL UNIFIERS AND PRACTICAL PLURALISTS

Rapid social change invigorates the ancient psychological debate about one or many sources of mentality. With the extension of suffrage to all white males in mid-19th century America, the upper and middle classes adopted refashioned arguments of one or many minds as principles on which they based their respective ideologies of social order.

The premier articulators of unitary mind in the new democracy were the ministerially trained college presidents (Meyer, 1972). These mental philosophers rejected the materialistic and disunifying drift of British associationism in favor of Scottish realism. The latter school rationalized a "common sense" that was universal in humankind and served to unify the mind's rational faculties, classified under reason, with its nonrational faculties, classified under will and emotions. Its pedagogical system of mental discipline trained the diverse facultative "desires" of their students and served as a model for the rational stabilization of society. A unified soul–mind and a unifying pedagogy reenforced the social dominance of the tiny elite who received a college education. If Enlightenment-era revolutions destroyed the organic metaphor underpinning monarchical order (Tillyard, 1944), Scottish realism supplied a psychological prop for the traditional unified concept of social hierarchy, which presumed horizontal equivalence between degrees of intellect, virtue, wealth, and beauty at each social stratum (Bushman, 1967; Cmiel, 1990; Veysey, 1965).

Meanwhile, in attempting to serve the vast majority of Americans who did not attend even a secondary school, popular phrenologists charted a diverse arrangement of mental abilities according to a normative cranial map. Their diversified concept of mentality, which derived from 18th century materialism, imaged special mental strengths and weaknesses for middle-class individuals. The phrenologists chose qualities with wide social relevance, clothed them in the vocabulary of education (such as "philoprogenitiveness"), and localized them in parts of the brain. In this way they offered a predictive classification of the mentality and character of the strangers the middle class was meeting more frequently in a more mobile society (Cooter, 1984; Davies, 1955).

After the Civil War, industrial capitalists dominated government and the economy and strove to gain acceptance in elite social confines; for the less well off, the growth of secondary education and other popular institutions increased democratic opportunities and diversions. As the middle class and its goal-oriented values traveled upward and outward, leaders of the educated elite turned inward. They protected their value orientation by forming exclusive communities committed to the intrinsically satisfying endeavors of arts and sciences.

The upper and middle classes converged in the modern university, and, after a generation, the unifying and diversifying traditions became espoused by colleagues in the same psychology departments of several universities. At first, though, the unifiers were more influential in constructing the new higher education, which can be considered a tower in more than the ivory sense. The early philanthropy of wealthy (and usually non-college-educated) industrialists financed the modern university and its capstone value, scientific research, as a quick means of gaining social legitimacy. The industrialists knew the limits of their largesse, however, and proposed the democratic expansion of college enrollment and curricula to ensure future support of the new capstone with a broad base of tuitions. The tower, which grew straight up from the college in the early years, would have to form a pyramid sooner or later.

American psychologists who established their profession during the seed-money era tended to emphasize the unity of mental ability in early testing, despite, or perhaps on account of, the very evident contrast between their own intellectual values and those of higher education's new patrons and students. Becoming ensconced at the top of a temporary tower, psychologists developed empirical methods and evolutionary concepts beyond the comprehension of most laypersons. They delineated a professional status by distinguishing their concepts, methods, and objectives at a vertical distance from conventional practical concerns (Danziger, 1979).

The experimental context of early professional psychology also inspired the tendency to unify mental ability. American psychologists misinterpreted Wundt's philosophically generalized mind as a quantifiable object (Danziger, 1990). Explanation of mentality by Darwinian theories and objective methods allowed psychologists to supplant the old-time college president as the arbiter of the the academic curriculum. Faith in the positivist continuity of quantitative measurement encouraged psychologists to merge the nonrational and moral aspects of human behavior with rational mentality as a whole. Faith in positivism itself led experimental psychologists to expose phrenology and other pseudosciences as detours from the progress of human knowledge.

Social change continued, however, and the practical reality of diversity started filling the classrooms down the hall. Undergraduate colleges began to accept increasing numbers of students whose parents did not have a collegiate or traditional ethnic background. The liberal arts tradition of training the desires of the WASP gentleman scholar began to give way to a pluralist liberal style: Harvard University President Charles Eliot advanced the elective system and research (Veysey, 1965) as opportunities that liberated students and scholars from the disciplinary program of the old-time college's unified mentality.

University psychologists, increasingly the beneficiaries of practical-minded businesspersons and teachers of practical-minded students, began to conceptualize mentality in ways that protected the disinterest of theoretical activity as it comprehended the needs of a mobile and goal-oriented middle class. The diversifying tradition was apparent in the early profession, and not just on the phrenological margins. The most substantive influence was the pluralist effect of Darwinian functionalism on psychologists trained in the faculty psychology tradition. The theory of natural selection dispatched the unity of soul–mind and transmuted the faculties into activities or abilities.

The cohabitation of traditions is apparent in the first mental testing project of professional American psychology, conducted by the psychology department at Columbia University. Although this project's definition of mentality was monistic, its prospective goal was to manage the diversity of students at Columbia. The pluralist style is even more apparent in an influential attack on the old unifying program of mental discipline that came from the same psychology department in the nation's largest and most diverse city.

James McKeen Cattell, who coined the term *mental test* in 1890, applied the psychophysical tests of Wundt's laboratory to the discovery of individual differences in "mental energy." Extending the anthropometric tests of Francis Galton to a wider range of mental ability (including memory as well as dermal sensation), Cattell advanced the core assumption of modern mental testing. This holds that the relationship of individual test performance to the performance of large populations on the same test (distributed on a normal curve) is indicative of individual mental inheritance. The compilation of test scores was thus to bridge a part of mentality with the whole nature of mentality.

A large part of Cattell's purpose was to record individual differences for the curiosity of individuals. This objective, which resembled that of the popular phrenologists, did not lend itself to easy systematization. Cattell hoped the records would serve to counsel undergraduates on their choice of career. He believed the science of psychology could thus make a very practical contribution to the American university environment, in assessing the varied physical and mental qualities of its increasingly diverse population (Sokal, 1982). Because Cattell was unfamiliar with the regression method of comparing variables that Galton had developed, he defined the accuracy of the tests in relation to other tests and, through his assumption of a "mental energy" underlying all mentality, hinted that they were predictive of academic abilities:

> The repetition of the tests will be one of the best criteria of their validity, and we hope the results will be of interest in showing the development of the student during his college course, more especially when taken in connection with the nature of his course, his standing in his studies, etc. (Cattell & Farrand, 1896, p. 624)

Although Cattell suggested it was possible to build a bridge to the other "criteria" of "validity," his ignorance of a method to link, say, class standing with his tests forced him to fall back on experimental repetition as the best criterion of "validity." Ironically, the linking method he might have implemented for validation was used by his own student to invalidate the predictiveness Cattell hoped the psychophysical tests would show. As is well known, Clark Wissler made one of the first American psychological uses of correlation to demonstrate the tests' negative and low correlation with academic performance in 1901.

That same year at Columbia, two other students of Cattell challenged the abiding pedagogy of mental discipline. Thorndike and Woodworth (1901a, 1901b, 1901c) demonstrated the lack of a bridge, or "transfer," between training in a specific area and performance in an unrelated field of mental activity. While interring the key pedagogical assumption of faculty psychology, the critique of transfer vindicated the new undergraduate elective system, which allowed students to pursue their own course of study in a curriculum that was expanding to meet middle-class interests. It also helped deliver the research professor from the character-shaping responsibilities of the old-time college. The disproof appeared the year after Columbia dropped Latin as an admissions requirement and joined the American Association of Universities, which instituted research scholarship as its primary criterion for membership (Veysey, 1965).

After 1901 the theortical–unifying and practical–diversifying traditions of psychology diverged again within early mental testing. Adherents to the monistic tradition turned inward to the formalism of statistical method in order to demonstrate an objectively real relationship between the experimentally controlled mental performance of an individual and the unity of intellect. Their means of measuring this relationship allowed them to rationalize an evolutionary essence that determined rational and nonrational abilities, if not class, race, and gender as well. In contrast, adherents to the pluralistic tradition turned outward and ad hoc, toward the needs of school boards and business employers, to advance the pursuit of happiness as middle-class managers defined it.

ACCURACY FOR SPEARMAN AND BINET

Partly in reaction to Wissler's invalidation of Cattell's research, Spearman refined the use of correlation statistics in 1904 and thereby reified the unity of mentality. Spearman enhanced mental test reliability through the use of the probable error equation (Fancher, 1985). This accounted for the difference or "attenuation" between two "factors" (e.g., measures of intellect gained from school grades and teachers' judgments) and the "true" relationship between the factors. Because the "true" relationship could only become known after an infinite series of correlations, Spearman implemented a correction formula to overcome the accidental errors of a finite set of observations, which he believed obscured the "common intellective factor." This he called "general intelligence" or "g."

Here was the "connection" of the whole with the parts that eluded Cattell. Spearman believed the connection would continue to elude psychological testers on the continent and in America who were too concerned with the trees to notice the forest. Concern for the practicality of particular mental abilities, which he believed was "urged on" by a desire to be useful and please the masses ("*ad captandum vulgus*"), had prevented the emergence of a method that revealed the "functional uniformity" beneath the diverse phenomena of mentality (Spearman, 1904).

Spearman used the term *validity* to mean *reliability* and believed the predictiveness of any intelligence tests would follow on experimental consistency. In choosing tests, Spearman (1904) believed psychologists should consider reliability and an unnamed quality, which referred to the use to which a test would be put:

> Two points must always be carefully kept asunder: first the *reliability* with which any system of measurement represents any particular form of intelligence; and secondly, the claims of the said form of intelligence to merit the name. The former point must be definitely ascertained in the course of the experiments, while the latter, though a very desirable piece of information, may or may not be eventually elucidated by the whole investigation. (p. 238)

Spearman's indifference to the predictive "claims" of a test was rooted in a distrust of extraprofessional practicality that was social as well as scientific. Written after 20 years of universal male suffrage in England, and 7 years before Lloyd George destroyed the authority of the House of Lords, Spearman's purification of testing reliability and his reification of *g* defended the traditional unification of social hierarchy and its current method of academic testing. Like the old-time college presidents in America, Spearman took moral offense with associationism (Fancher, 1985) and would attempt to preserve the dominance of the upper class. Spearman did have a practical purpose, at least in the long term, which would update the conventional methods of training and selecting the leaders of the British Empire. After discovering a hierarchy of *g* in the curriculum, with classics at the top (which Spearman claimed was "no small surprise"), Spearman (1904) revealed how intelligence testing could augment social abilities in the selection of leaders:

> Here would seem to lie the long wanted general rational basis for public examinations. Instead of continuing ineffectively to protest that high marks in Greek syntax are no test as to the capacity of men to command troops or to administer provinces, we shall at last actually determine the precise *accuracy* [italics added] of the various means of measuring General Intelligence, and then we shall in an equally positive objective manner ascertain the exact relative importance of this General Intelligence as compared with the other characteristics desirable for the particular post which the candidate is to assume. (p. 277)

One of the reasons why performance in Greek would no longer serve to certify the social elite was Thorndike's transfer critique, which Spearman (1904) cited as a "vigorous onslaught" on the "dynamical correlation" (p. 216). Spearman marveled at the practical predictiveness of correlation with training in the classics and felt relieved that g testing would bring order to the diverse and vulgar concerns of personnel management.

Spearman's correction method allowed him to avoid Cattell's problem of lacking criteria beyond test repetition, because it obviated demonstrations of how measures of "general intelligence" might predict an individual's ability to perform special mental tasks. Whereas Cattell hoped for but lacked the tools to connect the tested parts of mentality to the whole, Spearman claimed to have built the bridge, by constructing the connection of accuracy out of improved reliability. The bridge was in the bridge-building equipment.

As Americans enjoyed a greater range of educational and job opportunities, they needed more concrete and predictive connections than the Spearman formula per se. The Binet age scale soon appeared to link the tested parts and theoretical utility of mind, even though all Binet (and his associate, Theodore Simon) discovered was a pragmatic set of bridges, arranged by age level for educational convenience. Binet systematized the connection of "mental [grade] level" with chronological age, but extraprofessional setting defined the objective of his intelligence tests. The purpose of the scale was to discover individual schoolchildren who could not perform tasks that society expected the majority of schoolchildren of the same chronological age to perform. Why those who compared poorly were deficient Binet did not attempt to solve (Wolf, 1973). For the practical purposes of school administration in the democratic era, however, his age-level scale served as a helpful, and ad hoc selection tool.

Practical purposes also helped define Binet's experimental object (von Mayrhauser, 1989). The age scale included a diverse collection of tests, such as "counting backwards" and "writing from dictation," because Binet's intention was to classify individuals according to "intelligence in general" (Wolf, 1973). The rationale for this scattershot approach was to neutralize an individual's mental strengths and weaknesses. Binet refused to define the "intelligence" his scale measured as other than adaptability to normatively measured levels on criteria that were socially relevant. He believed that tests of single faculties or g encouraged testers to entify what they tested.

The scattershot approach also allowed the age scale to succeed in measuring what it purported to measure. Because school administrators' conventions of performance expectations helped select the component tests, the normal distributions of answers "standardized" (Wolf, 1973), or showed the accuracy of, the component tests in conforming to the conventions. For the sake of consistency, the fixing of standard questions on paper regularized the examination. This did not replace the examiner, however, who was expected to maintain strict clinical control over the individualized testing of the child (Wolf, 1973).

The program reenforced the middle-class morality of the administrators. Binet's intelligence combined cognitive and volitional abilities not to rationalize unitary mind, but to enlist self-help as a criterion:

> An individual is normal when he can conduct himself without having need of tutelage of others, when he earns sufficient income for his needs, and finally, when his intelligence does not take him into work of a lower classification than that of his parents. (Wolf, 1973, p. 194)

Binet seemed to move toward a unitary explanation of mentality shortly before his death in 1911. Whereas earlier he believed an unevenness in mental strengths and weaknesses had caused low scores, by 1909 he perceived a "harmony" (Wolf, 1973) between the diverse abilities the age scale tested. The previous year he had proposed another method of demonstrating the accuracy of the age scale: a longitudinal study in which the earlier scores of subjects would be compared with their later development. That an interest in this kind of test checking arose as Binet was moving in a more theoretical direction underscores the source of validity in a bifurcation of social contexts.

ACCURACY FOR TERMAN, YERKES, THORNDIKE, AND SCOTT

The first American to translate Binet, H. H. Goddard, construed Binet's scale of mental level as one of mental age. This made unified g theory practicable in America, as the age scale came to measure mentality with reference to the phenomena of (a) educational fitness and (b) the deeper reality of recapitulationism, which theory held that the individual's development retraced the evolution of the animal kingdom. Goddard and Terman brought Spearman's g down to the "earth" of recapitulation theory, which both had learned from Hall. Possessing backgrounds in teacher training, Goddard and Terman resonated to Binet's reform goals for education, even as they misinterpreted him. After Terman implemented William Stern's ratio of an individual's mental age to his or her chronological age and called it the "Intelligence Quotient" (IQ), he lent numerical authority to the misbelief that Binet had discovered a real bridge between partial and whole mentality.

Terman (1916) assessed accuracy against normative distributions of various component tests that were, like Binet's, relevant to school administrators, but he further assessed accuracy against recapitulationist expectations and the consistency of the scale:

> The validity of each test was checked up by measuring it against the scale as a whole ... if ten-year-old children having 11-year intelligence succeed with a given test decidedly better than 10-year children who have 9-year intelligence, then either this test must be accepted as valid

> or the scale as a whole must be rejected. Since we know, however, that the scale as a whole has at least a reasonably high degree of reliability, this method becomes a sure and ready means of judging the worth of a test. (p. 76)

Experimental consistency was again the bridge, at least for the time being. For the future, and as Cattell, Spearman, and Binet had suggested for their own programs, Terman proposed that the IQ test would help sort individuals for vocational placement, although he did not explain how this would come about:

> When thousands of children who have been tested by the Binet scale have been followed out into the industrial world, and their success in various occupations noted, we shall know fairly definitely the vocational significance of any given degree of mental inferiority or superiority. (p. 17)

Terman's social agenda was more elite oriented than Binet's, but more democratic and practical than Spearman's. Whereas Binet was helping administrators discover the "unintelligent," Terman wanted to select the gifted. Terman and Spearman both wanted to discover the students most capable of a traditional higher education, which trained theoretical as opposed to practical abilities. In contrast to Spearman's defense of the social status quo, however, Terman wanted to help teachers identify the gifted student whose talents were hidden by a nonprivileged social background (Minton, 1988). Terman did not unify intellect with all the other qualities of social hierarchy at that time, but like Jefferson separated "genius and virtue" from wealth, class, and beauty to "rake from the rubbish" a "natural aristocracy" (Jefferson, 1984, pp. 272, 365, 1304–1310).

Yerkes (1917a) exposed the educational and majority-group bias of Terman's democratic IQ testing 5 years before Walter Lippmann alerted the public at large. Yerkes's purpose was hardly a liberal one, however, as he sought to throw over "mental age" for a more scientific "physiological age." His "laws of mental development" differed from recapitulationism and supported a more unified concept of social Darwinian hierarchy.

Yerkes believed g was the essence of evolution that transcended the animal kingdom. Earlier in his career, he attempted to demonstrate that the lower animal species possessed the complex mental abilities of humans, albeit in smaller degrees (Yerkes, 1905). Yerkes's classification of species mentality according to discrete quantitative ranges led him to measure human intelligence according to the "varied measures of efficiency in living" (1917a, p. 122) that he believed different racial, social, and gender groups possessed. For him, the age scale method ignored the physiological unity underlying psychological and sociological qualities because it was directed too narrowly toward the practical interests of school administrators.

In contrast with the age scale, which offered tests of different abilities for different ages, Yerkes advocated that a single scale (collection of tests) would be much more scientific and statistically convenient. Believing that all intellectual functions appeared in humans by age three, he held that a single scale for everyone over this age would allow standardization by "vertical" comparisons of individual scores with the norms of the social class, race, or gender group to which the individual belonged. Because the Stanford-Binet collected "horizontal" data, creating distributions by age and without regard for race, class, and so on, Yerkes correctly detected cross-group bias (Reed, 1987). He attributed this to "internally standardized" norms that were, for him, "violating the laws of mental development" (Yerkes, 1917a, p. 114) and concealing inaccuracy under experimental reliability. Yerkes (1917a) claimed his point scale was "externally standardized because the selection and arrangement of the tests have nothing to do with the norms which as standards of judgment are used in the evaluation of results" (p. 114). Yet the object of his pursuit, unitary g, got the better of the pursuing, as Yerkes (1917a) proceeded to unify "accuracy and reliability":

> With the application of the Point Scale to increasing numbers of individuals, the norms, whether for age, sex, race, educational or social status, become increasingly numerous and *reliable*, and the *value* of the method correspondingly increases. In order to use the Point Scale profitably for a new race, or social group, it is necessary only to make a sufficient number of examinations to yield *reliable* norms. They *immediately* become standards of judgment. The method does not have to be revised. Thus it is evident that where the Binet Scale is inflexible, the Point Scale is flexible and universally applicable. (pp. 114–115, italics added)

Moreover, after criticizing Binet and Terman for weighting the component tests of their scales equally, Yerkes's "more scientific" method was to add extra weight to the component tests that correlated higher "with general intelligence, or rather with the point-scale score" (1917a, p. 116). The whole defined the parts.

The universal applicability Yerkes promised for his point scale protected both the social status quo and the intrinsic value system of scientific research. In his Spearmanlike view, psychologists should serve society according to the true needs of society, which scientists were uniquely able to discern. Unlike Terman, who accommodated the goals of middle-class educators in order to cull the gifted from all classes, Yerkes (1918) proposed a radical overhaul. His blueprint for education would redirect student attention from the trees to the forest, from short-term practical concerns with vocation to the long-term practicality of the racial "tasks of parenthood." To "guarantee that posterity shall be well-born and well-reared," he believed, teachers "should educate to an appreciation of the values of research" (pp. 248–249).

The two most practical-minded American mental testers on the eve of America's entry into World War I also tested for innate mentality, but with a scale considered much more blunt than those of Yerkes and Terman. These were Thorndike and Scott, who, like Binet, defined "intelligence" as a complex of diverse capacities. They preferred more practical methods than Binet's, because the Binet scale had become associated with g in America and because they stressed environmental adjustments of mental qualities as functions.

A justification for this approach might be gathered from Thorndike's (1915) theory of utility, but an other-directed (1930/1961) research style required no theory. This pragmatic style shaped the experimental situation (e.g., methods and choice of psychological objects) to meet the needs of clients. Whereas the theoretical unifiers stood apart from the world they brought their research to and identified accuracy as consistent experimentation, the practical diversifiers accommodated the world too readily to make experimental consistency a priority.

Thorndike and Scott's rating scale adapted flexibly to various clients' needs: to evaluate the rational and nonrational abilities that clients valued in their students or employees. Galton, Cattell, and others had originated this system for surveying laypersons' judgments about others' qualities (Guilford, 1936/1942). Spearman averaged teachers' and students' judgments about other students' intelligence as factors to be correlated and statistically corrected. His objectification of subjective ratings as preliminary criteria provided the rough materials for his bridge between partial mentality, shown on tests, and the whole of g.

Thorndike's skepticism of "intelligence" theories was no less acute when dealing with the human "general" kind than when he critiqued the "animal" kind in his dissertation. In 1909, Thorndike, Lay, and Dean inspected Spearman's bridge and discovered that, as the correction equipment, it produced a poor correlation (.23) between tests of "general discrimination" and ratings of "general intelligence." After watching the bridge collapse under the weight of its own construction, Thorndike gathered up the crude building materials and initiated a multiple-bridge project, to link mentality as various practical environments defined it with assessments of particular mental abilities that addressed those definitions.

The rating scale was, for Thorndike, the best method available for helping teachers evaluate the special kinds of intelligence that were relevant to education, such as the ability "complex" of handwriting. Until physiologists mapped the neuronal interaction of the myriad mental "capacities" (that were his "intelligence"), Thorndike knew teachers would rely on relative measurements of individual performance. As a positivist who valued experimental rigor, Thorndike (Strayer & Thorndike, 1917) chafed at the quality of subjective comparisons, which were "essentially inferior" to absolute assessments of "an amount of some thing or quality or power" (pp. 207–208). As an optimistic positivist, he felt certain that crude evaluations could approximate the reality that physiologists would discover someday.

Thorndike (1910) developed and marketed a very influential handwriting scale between 1910 and 1914. The lack of a defined psychological object is striking, but because Thorndike believed environmental selection of inherited abilities was tantamount to definition of those abilities, a precise definition was unnecessary. The practical need for good handwriting existed, and, as Thorndike later stated, "Whatever exists, exists in some amount" (1923, p. 9). After explaining the method for objectifying evaluations of "competent judges," Thorndike (Strayer & Thorndike, 1917) revealed that no standard criterion for evaluation had been used or was necessary:

> It is true that some judges find it hard to judge handwriting for the complex of legibility, beauty, ease, "character," etc., into which "quality" or "goodness" or "merit" resolves itself. But none of them found it impossible to do so, and most of them rated the writing for the complex—"merit or goodness in your opinion," as readily as an appraiser would rank articles of sale by money price. (pp. 228–229)

What did this mean for the advance of professional psychology if it took "competent judges," presumably teachers, to call good handwriting as they saw it, from one school to another?

Thorndike (1910) here encountered a problem that was the obverse of the accuracy problem facing the g testers. After tailoring an assessment to make it predict a student's ability in a special practical area, Thorndike avoided concern for reliability by suggesting that a consensus of competent opinions could operationalize the meaning of a student's inherited and trained ability in this area. Although the practical predictiveness of g testing was subordinate to its consistency, the reliability of the subjective rating scale was secondary to its practical predictiveness.

Between 1915 and 1917, Thorndike applied the scalar technique to quantify judgments of clerical ability complexes. He advised Scott and his colleagues at the first American department of applied psychology, at the Carnegie Institute of Technology, as they developed a "Rating Scale for Selecting Salesmen" (Baritz, 1960; Jonçich, 1968). Scott had a lengthy background in applying psychology to meet the needs of advertisers and employment managers, but little knowledge of scientific testing techniques, as he began adapting Thorndike's scalar method to personal as well as mental characteristics.

Despite his technical unsophistication, Scott's promotion of psychology in business led him to discuss test checking for the first issue of the *Journal of Applied Psychology*. While reviewing three methods and describing a fourth he had innovated, Scott alluded to well-known practices. His objective for testing differed from most other mental testers, however, in his desire to help employers decide whether tests of general mental ability or tests of special mental ability were accurate in their particular workplace.

The ringer and applicants–experts procedures disqualified tests that failed to give high scores to those with job experience and low ones to newcomers. Scott did not offer normal distributions to demonstrate reliability for these methods of (what would later be called) concurrent validation. Tests of g would not have been impressed.

Scott's firm rank method called for the correlation of "dependable" —reliable—tests against a distribution of employees ranked by three persons' judgments. This (concurrent) check resembled the g testers' system of constructing tests through comparison with outside judgments. But because Scott was checking general intelligence (and other) tests against specific needs, he was selling Spearman's bridge promiscuously, in any number of practical environments. As opposed to Thorndike, who destroyed the Spearman span and took the raw judgment materials to build widely, if less elegantly, Scott accepted the "dependable" legitimation of g testing and offered it for the consideration of employers who wanted to select personnel with special abilities. Social criteria would, for Scott, legitimate the use of g testing.

The vocational accomplishments method compared test results with later employment success. As we have seen, Cattell, Spearman, Binet, and Terman had proposed this technique, a form of (what would later be called) predictive validation. Scott (1915) had been researching this method for at least 2 years. Scott advised that "No man engaged in vocational selection should rest content in giving any tests that are not being constantly approved by this most crucial of all checks" (1917, p. 62), but each workplace had to check tests of its own choosing against the accomplishments of its personnel. Although Scott (1917) touted this method as "the most dependable of all" (p. 62), he conceded that it was "not available until after the tests have been put into operation" (p. 62).

THE PRACTICAL TRUTH(S) ABOUT VALIDITY

As the military required mental testers to consolidate their research community in World War I, a funny thing happened on the way to proving the value of the first national mass test, known later as the "Army alpha." During the summer of 1917, after Yerkes and Terman could not agree on whether to use the Stanford-Binet or the Yerkes point scale to demonstrate the reliability of alpha, Yerkes asked Thorndike and a statistical unit to settle the issue. Thorndike delivered two reports on August 15, which set the precedent for separating experimental reliability from a method of legitimation that required a criterion extrinsic to test construction. For his colleagues he demonstrated the consistency between alpha's component tests and previous test results. For the military, he correlated alpha's components with the officer ratings of "intelligence" that Scott had collected with his "Rating Scale for Selecting Captains." That scale sold the military on approving a Committee on Classification of Personnel in the Army (von Mayrhauser, 1991). Although the check against concurrent judgments did not impress Yerkes and Terman, it salvaged development of the instrument that would become the profession's most influential contribution to American society.

Taken in perspective, it should not be a surprise that innovations in general and special mental ability testing preceded methods of verifying the accuracy of these tests' claims. Elsewhere in the history of American technology, such as in mass production by interchangeable parts, theories and grandiose claims have run far ahead of actual demonstration (Marcus & Segal, 1989; Smith, 1977). Also, considering the context of a utilitarian culture, it is no surprise that the unitary conception of "intelligence" got "lost" (McNemar, 1964). What is surprising is the lingering commitment of modern psychometricians, testing services, educators, and even social critics to a bridge that was jerry-built by testers who did not agree on what they were bridging.

For some of those so committed, further consideration of the wartime testing activities of the nonintelligence testers, who initially made "intelligence" workable and much less than "general" in the process, may help signal BRIDGE OUT AHEAD. One suspects this will not be enough for the true believers, however, which raises the question of why they believe so strongly in something that is so illogical, let alone unhistorical.

The myth of the common intellective factor endures by assuaging the status anxieties that are chronic in a mobile society (e.g., Seligman, 1991). It also simplifies the messy reality of social justice by appearing to connect the tested part of an individual's mentality to the whole of concepts, which help us make sense of the world as well as the workplace. A more effective explanation for the myth's appeal awaits discussion of how the method of finding truth in testing became a professional standard. In a future article, I demonstrate how the formation of consensus on validity entailed the concealment of the procrustean quality of modern mass intelligence testing, which resuscitated the unified theory of mentality on a higher level of practicality.

REFERENCES

Baritz, L. (1960). *The servants of power*. Middletown, CT: Wesleyan University Press.

Bushman, R. L. (1967). *From puritan to yankee: Character and social order in Connecticut, 1690–1765*. Cambridge, MA: Harvard University Press.

Camfield, T. M. (1969). *Psychologists at war: The history of American psychology and the First World War*. Unpublished doctoral dissertation, University of Texas at Austin.

Cattell, J. M., & Farrand, L. (1896). Physical and mental measurements of the students of Columbia University. *Psychological Review, 3*, 618–648.

Cmiel, K. (1990). *Democratic eloquence: The fight over popular speech in nineteenth-century America*. New York: William Morrow.

Cooter, R. (1984). *The cultural meaning of popular science: Phrenology and the organization of consent in nineteenth-century Britain*. New York: Cambridge University Press.

Cronbach, L. J. (1970). *Essentials of psychological testing* (3rd ed.). New York: Harper & Row.

Cronbach, L. J., & Meehl, P. E. (1955). Construct validity in psychological tests. *Psychological Bulletin, 52*, 281–302.

Danziger, K. (1979). The social origins of modern psychology. In A. R. Buss (Ed.), *Psychology and social context* (pp. 27–45). New York: Irvington.

Danziger, K. (1990). *Constructing the subject: Historical origins of modern psychology*. New York: Cambridge University Press.

Davies, J. D. (1955). *Phrenology: Fad and science, a nineteenth century crusade*. New Haven, CT: Yale University Press.

Fancher, R. E. (1985). *The intelligence men: Makers of the IQ controversy*. New York: Norton.

Guilford, J. P. (1942). *Fundamental statistics in psychology and education*. New York: McGraw-Hill. (Original work published 1936)

Hall, G. S., Baird, J. W., & Geissler, L. R. (1917). Foreword. *Journal of Applied Psychology, 1*, 5–7.

Jefferson, T. (1984). *Writings*. New York: Library of America.

Jonçich, G. (1968). *The sane positivist: A biography of Edward L. Thorndike*. Middletown, CT: Wesleyan University Press.

Kevles, D. J. (1968). Testing the Army's intelligence: Psychologists and the military in World War I. *Journal of American History, 55*, 565–581.

Marcus, A. I., & Segal, H. P. (1989). *Technology in America: A brief history*. New York: Harcourt Brace Jovanovich.

McNemar, Q. (1964). Lost: Our intelligence? Why? *American Psychologist, 19*, 871–882.

Mentality tests. (1916) *Journal of Educational Psychology, 7*, 163–166, 229–240, 278–286, 348–360, 427–433.

Meyer, D. H. (1972). *The instructed conscience: The shaping of the American national ethic*. Philadelphia: University of Pennsylvania Press.

Minton, H. (1988). *Lewis M. Terman: Pioneer in psychological testing*. New York: New York University Press.

Reed, J. (1987). Robert M. Yerkes and the mental testing movement. In M. M. Sokal (Ed.), *Psychological testing and American society: 1890–1930* (pp. 75–94). New Brunswick, NJ: Rutgers University Press.

Rogers, T., & Rogers, P. (1990). *The origin of validity in psychological testing: Doing some historical homework*. Unpublished manuscript.

Scott, W. D. (1915, December). The scientific selection of salesmen: III. Testing the tests: *Advertising and Selling*, pp. 11, 69–70.

Scott, W. D. (1917). A fourth method of checking results in vocational selection. *Journal of Applied Psychology, 1*, 61–66.

Seashore, C. (1911). The consulting psychologist. *Psychological Bulletin, 8*, 46.

Seashore, C. (1916, February 23). *Letter to R. M. Yerkes*. Robert M. Yerkes papers, Yale University Library, New Haven, CT.

Seligman, D. (1991, April 15). Is America smart enough? *National Review*, pp. 24–31.

Smith, M. R. (1977). *Harpers Ferry armory and the new technology: The challenge of change*. Ithaca, NY: Cornell University Press.

Sokal, M. M. (1982). James McKeen Cattell and the failure of anthropometric mental testing, 1890–1901. In W. Woodward & M. Ash (Eds.), *The problematic science: Psychology in nineteenth century thought* (pp. 322–345). New York: Praeger.

Spearman, C. (1904). "General intelligence": Objectively determined and measured. *American Journal of Psychology, 15*, 201–293.

Strayer, G. D., & Thorndike, E. L. (1917). *Educational administration: Quantitative studies*. New York: Macmillan.

Terman, L. M. (1916). *The measurement of intelligence: An explanation of and a complete guide for the use of the Stanford revision and extension of the Binet-Simon intelligence scale*. Boston: Houghton Mifflin.

Thorndike, E. L. (1910). Handwriting. *Teachers College Record, 11*, 1–81.

Thorndike, E. L. (1915). *Educational psychology: Briefer course*. New York: Teachers College.

Thorndike, E. L. (1923). Measurement in education. In G. M. Whipple (Ed.), *Intelligence tests and their use: Part 1. The nature, history, and general principles of intelligence testing* (pp. 1–9). Bloomington, IL: Public School.

Thorndike, E. L. (1961). Edward Lee Thorndike. In *A history of psychology in autobiography* (Vol. 3, pp. 263–270). New York: Russell & Russell. (Original work published 1930)

Thorndike, E. L., Lay, W., & Dean, P. R. (1909). The relation of accuracy in sensory discrimination to general intelligence. *American Journal of Psychology, 20*, 364–369.

Thorndike, E. L., & Woodworth, R. S. (1901a). The influence of improvement in one mental function upon the efficiency of other functions: I. *Psychological Review, 8,* 247–261.

Thorndike, E. L., & Woodworth, R. S. (1901b). The influence of improvement in one mental function upon the efficiency of other functions: II. The estimation of magnitudes. *Psychological Review, 8,* 384–395.

Thorndike, E. L., & Woodworth, R. S. (1901c). The influence of improvement in one mental function upon the efficiency of other functions: III. Functions involving attention, observation, and discrimination. *Psychological Review, 8,* 553–564.

Tillyard, E. M. W. (1944). *The Elizabethan world picture.* New York: Random House.

Veysey, L. (1965). *The emergence of the American university.* Chicago: University of Chicago Press.

von Mayrhauser, R. T. (1987). The manager, the medic, and the mediator: The clash of professional psychological styles and the wartime origins of group mental testing. In M. M. Sokal (Ed.), *Psychological testing and American society: 1890–1930* (pp. 128–157). New Brunswick, NJ: Rutgers University Press.

von Mayrhauser, R. T. (1989). Making intelligence functional: Walter Dill Scott and applied psychological testing in World War I. *Journal of the History of the Behavioral Sciences, 25,* 60–72.

von Mayrhauser, R. T. (1991). The practical language of American intellect. *History of the Human Sciences, 4,* 371–393.

Webster's ninth collegiate dictionary. (1985). Springfield, MA: Merriam–Webster.

Wolf, T. H. (1973). *Alfred Binet.* Chicago: University of Chicago Press.

Yerkes, R. M. (1905). Animal psychology and the criteria of the psychic. *Journal of Philosophy, Psychology and Scientific Methods, 2,* 141–149.

Yerkes, R. M. (1917a). The Binet versus the point scale method of measuring intelligence. *Journal of Applied Psychology, 1,* 111–122.

Yerkes, R. M. (1917b). Psychology and national service. *Journal of Applied Psychology, 1,* 301–304.

Yerkes, R. M. (1918). Educational and psychological aspects of racial well-being. *National Education Association,* 248–252.

Yerkes, R. M. (Ed.). (1921). *Memoirs of the National Academy of Sciences: Vol. 15. Psychological examining in the United States Army.* Washington, DC: U.S. Government Printing Office.

Yerkes, R. M., Bridges, J. W., & Hardwick, R. S. (1915). *A point scale for measuring mental ability.* Baltimore: Warwick & York.

16

GORDON ALLPORT, CHARACTER, AND THE "CULTURE OF PERSONALITY," 1897–1937

IAN A. M. NICHOLSON

In recent years, a number of historians have documented a pronounced change in the language of American selfhood.[1] Beginning in the late 19th century and continuing into the 1920s, Americans moved from a language of "character" to a language of "personality." According to most historians, this shift was no linguistic trifle: The emergence of personality and the decline of character signaled the development of a new kind of American self. This was a self for an industrialized and urbanized age: expressive, adaptable, and morally unencumbered. The cultural shift from character to personality coincided with the emergence of a new object of psychological investigation: personality. Starting in the early teens and continuing into the 1920s, psychologists devoted increasing attention to measuring personality, documenting its component parts and theorizing about the form a mature personality might take. By 1940, personality had become an entrenched category of psychological investigation.

Reprinted from *History of Psychology*, 1, 52–68 (1998). Copyright © 1998 by the American Psychological Association. Reprinted with permission of the author.

Several scholars have studied the emergence of personality as a research category in American psychology.[2] Most of these investigations have been oriented primarily around issues of methodology and marketability. For instance, in his illuminating discussion of early American personality psychology, Kurt Danziger highlighted the links between (a) personality as an object of research, (b) the methodological conventions of intelligence testing, and (c) the practical need for measures of nonintellectual traits.[3] According to Danziger, the technology of mental testing helped shape the "model of the human person" that personality psychologists adopted. In this measurement-driven vision, the individual was viewed as a collection of "discrete, stable, and general qualities" or "traits," the sum total of which equaled his or her personality. The choice of categories for personality measurement was driven largely by the demands of the marketplace. "There appear to be no grounds intrinsic to the subject matter for this constantly shifting empirical basis of trait psychology," Danziger argued. "It is much more likely that these changes represent the coming and going of research fads, but in this case [personality] the fads are directly related to events in the social environment of the discipline."[4]

Although recent studies in the history of personality psychology have underscored the pragmatic origins of this form of research, relatively little attention has been paid to the cultural context in which this work was situated. More specifically, few scholars have devoted any sustained attention to the relationship between personality's emergence as a research category in academic psychology and the larger cultural shift in the language of American selfhood. The goal of this article is to explore the often-neglected cultural landscape of personality psychology. My focal point is the early career and thought of Gordon Allport (1897–1967). Although Allport is frequently discussed in relation to his work in the field of social psychology, his early career was oriented largely around personality. Allport was devoted to the category, and in the 1920s and 1930s he spent most of his time campaigning on its behalf. His efforts were truly extensive, ranging from literature reviews and theoretical articles to semipopular articles, radio appearances, and a highly influential textbook. By 1937 Allport was widely acknowledged as personality's leading spokesman in American psychology. In 1939 he was elected president of the American Psychological Association (APA). With the exception of John Watson, Allport was the youngest person to have ever held the office and the first APA president clearly identified with the field of personality.[5]

Allport's tireless promotion of personality and the remarkable success he attained make him an instructive case study in the cultural politics of personality psychology. As we shall see, his career dramatizes the pragmatic and methodological themes that often feature in historical discussions of the field. At the same time, however, Allport's experience helps clarify the various ways in which the new field of personality was informed by transformations in the moral economy and discursive practices of American society. Although this relationship might initially appear to be relatively straightforward—a case of psychologists mirroring the moral codes and categories of popular culture—Allport's advocacy on behalf of personality reveals a dynamic of much greater complexity. Far from being a conduit for the morally unencumbered self, Allport used psychology to hold the line on human nature. By embracing the new category of personality, and scientifically calculating its nature, he strove to safeguard a vision of the self grounded more in the agrarian world of Victorian America than in the increasingly industrialized, urbanized nation of the 1920s.

A MAN OF CHARACTER

In an 1891 diary entry, Gordon Allport's mother Nellie wrote of the hopes she harbored for one of her newborn sons' future:

> Many important things have come to my life of which the most important is the life of another precious boy to train for God.... This event stirred my soul more than tongue can express with the great responsibility of three previous souls to train for him. I have no thought to train them for wordly praise, fame, or honor. One thought surpasses all others—to train them to be for Christ and His work. As this little one was given me I had one wish, one desire, that he would be worthy to be called to labor for him in dark heathen lands.[6]

Nellie's choice of missionary as a vocation for her son reveals a great deal about the moral landscape in which Gordon Allport grew up. In the 19th century mind, missionaries were the consummate "characters." They had sacrificed all of the comforts of western civilization in order to save "heathen" souls. Moreover, by venturing into inhospitable climes they demonstrated their bravery and piety, and in so doing they deflected charges of effeminacy that were sometimes leveled against American-based churchmen. Kind, brave, pious, and self-sacrificing, the missionary embodied all the virtues that Nellie endeavored to instill in her young sons.

In a strict sense, Nellie's late Victorian missionary aspirations went unrealized. Her sons did not devote their careers to laboring in "dark, heathen lands." However, a more figurative reading of Gordon Allport's career reveals several distinct points of connection between the missionary character for whom Nellie hoped and the personality psychologist that Allport became.

Born in Montezuma, Indiana, in 1897, Allport was the youngest son of John Allport, a traveling salesman turned physician, and Nellie Wise Allport, a homemaker.[7] Although both parents were spiritually minded, the Allport family subscribed to the conventional division of labor of the day. John Allport was the practical man of affairs, and his wife oversaw the family's spiritual development.[8] Gordon Allport assimilated his father's reverence for hard work, but as a child he identified particularly strongly with his mother's religious interest and refined manner. Nellie was a devout Methodist from the famous "burned over district" of upstate New York.[9] As a student at Falley Seminary in Fulton, New York, she was well known for her "self chosen path of personal service to a religious ideal."[10] Self-sacrificing, hard working, and strict in her moral ideals, Nellie construed human nature through the language of character, and she actively strove to raise her sons to be men of character.

Most cultural historians agree that character was a dominant part of the cultural landscape of Victorian America. Susman noted that "the word character became fundamental in sustaining and even in shaping the significant forms of culture."[11] *Character* usually referred to the nature of the internal qualities of an individual. To have character, a person's traits had to have substance, durability, and integrity. Traits had to come together in an enduring, cohesive, and morally uplifting totality. The moral dimension was particularly important. The character ideal was all about realizing selfhood by internalizing the values of a supposedly permanent moral order.[12] As Emerson noted in an often-quoted passage, "character is moral order seen through the medium of an individual nature."[13]

In the Allport family, building character was not a theoretical ideal; it was an ongoing project, and its development was facilitated in a variety of different ways. The family attended church and religious summer camps regularly, and they frequently entertained visiting missionaries and temperance activists. Nellie was a leading figure in a number of benevolent organizations, including the Women's Christian Temperance Union and the Mother's Club, an organization designed to help mothers cultivate the appropriate moral tone in the home.

As a youth, Allport did not always appreciate the unrelenting earnestness with which his mother preached the language of character. In one of his autobiographical statements, he recalled rebelling against the family faith. "The more I was prodded the more I resisted," he later recalled. By the time he reached early adulthood, Allport had turned away from most of the doctrines and practices of the family faith: Methodist evangelicalism. Allport recalled that even church attendance became rare and then "only [as] a way of appeasing my 'old-fashioned' parents."[14] This break with Methodist practice was a significant departure from family tradition, but for Allport it did not amount to a wholesale repudiation of the values associated with character. Indeed, the records of Allport's undergraduate life at Harvard University reveal a pattern of living straight out of the character-building manuals of the late 19th century.

Allport mapped out an exhaustive program of work for himself that literally stretched from sunrise to sunset. Each half-hour period was dutifully planned and executed, including slots for rest, socializing, and philanthropy.[15] The Victorian themes of balance and order were thus carefully calibrated. Allport's course of study also resonated with the language of character. He developed a particularly strong affinity for what was in effect the scholarly expression of his mother's Christian outreach: social ethics. Harvard's Department of Social Ethics had been founded by theologian Francis Peabody in 1906 in an effort to bring together the 19th century denominational college's traditional concern for religion and ethics with the emerging scientific ideal of pure inductive scholarship.[16] By uniting moral philosophy with the scientific method, Peabody thought that his new department could overcome a debilitating materialism and "summon the young men who have been imbued with the principles of political economy and of philosophy to the practical applications of those studies."[17]

The themes of self-sacrifice, duty, morality, and goodness figured prominently in the discourse of social ethics just as they did in the moral universe that Allport had inhabited since his youth. As an undergraduate, however, Allport became aware that the future of moral endeavor in America was not simply a matter of recapitulating the past. The nation was changing rapidly. The country was becoming increasingly urbanized, industrialized, and ethnically diverse. These developments did not require the re-evaluation of the ideals associated with character; however, they did call for a pointed reassessment of the means by which these ideals were to be promoted. In the past, high-minded Americans had set out to "build character" by exposing wayward citizens to the influence of educated, virtuous, volunteers.[18] Sometimes known as "benevolent" volunteerism, this model of social work enjoyed widespread support in philanthropic circles throughout the late 19th and early 20th centuries. Support for benevolent social work began to wane during the teens, and it rapidly evaporated in the 1920s. Social work theorists such as Richard Cabot, Mary Jarrett, and Mary Richmond argued that industrialization had rendered religiously based philanthropy obsolete. Contemporary social problems overwhelmed the ability of amateurs: Modern circumstances required professional attention. The issue for professional social workers such as Jarrett and Richmond was not simply the amount of time one spent working in the field; the crucial point was the *way* one went about tackling social problems. Professionalism required a new ethic and a new way of conceptualizing the social field.

THE PROFESSIONALIZATION OF BENEVOLENCE

As a Harvard social ethics student, Allport had an opportunity to view the transformation in American social work close up. The principal hallmark of the "new" social work was a commitment to science. Social workers in the past had construed social problems such as illegitimacy and alcoholism as moral problems to be solved by the benevolent understanding and example of an evangelical volunteer. By 1917, social work theorists had begun a wide-ranging campaign to reconfigure the field's language and methods. "Moral problems" were redefined as scientific questions treatable by scientific methods. Part of the professionalizing trend in social work involved establishing a specialized body of knowledge that could be applied to special problems. Between 1915 and 1920, American social workers constructed a specialized knowledge around the concept of casework.[19] It would be difficult to exaggerate the centrality of casework in the thought of the professionally ambitious social workers to whom Allport was exposed. As social work historian Roy Lubove noted, casework "formed the basis of a professional identity."[20] Like many professional code words, *casework* was a broad and generic term. For most of its proponents, however, the term conveyed three ideas that were central to the practice of modern social work.

First, casework involved detailed record keeping. By encoding the lives of their clients in writing, social work theorists believed that they would be better able to accurately diagnose problems and to develop practicable solutions.[21] Second, the proponents of a casework model of social work were also committed to the principle of *differential diagnosis*. Sometimes stated in terms of individual differences, differential diagnosis called attention to what professional social workes believed was one of the principal limitations of the older form of benevolent social work: its inattention to the nuances of each case. For the professional social workers, human diversity was the salient theme of industrial life, and it sustained an ongoing commitment to individualized treatment and diagnosis. "Treat unequal things unequally," counseled Mary Richmond, for "social workers have the great fact of ineradicable individual differences in human beings to face."[22]

The final component of the casework orientation was its reflexive regard for science and sentimentality. Professional social workers were convinced of the necessity and efficacy of scientific thinking. At the same time, however, they were not indifferent to the human element in their craft. Theorists acknowledged that social workers traversed a domain of lived experience and that to approach this realm with the steely detachment of the natural scientist would not be appropriate. Social workers must avoid "cold, sterilized, depersonalized ideas," cautioned sociologist Arthur Todd. In his book *The Scientific Spirit and Social Work*, Todd presented the emerging professional ideal. The modern social worker would "steer between" an extreme form of scientific indifference and the "warm, saccharine, oily, oozy, intoxicating, overpersonalized sentimentalism" long associated with benevolent volunteerism.[23]

From Allport's perspective, one aspect of this ongoing dialogue between science and sentimentality was to assume particular importance. To achieve the necessary balance between science and sentimentality, social workers adopted a new, more scientific language. One of the most consequential developments centered around the concept of character as a designation for an individual's nature. As we have seen, character had been a dominant part of the cultural landscape of Victorian America, and it was precisely this association with the past that made it a liability for the new social work. "Character" smacked of rectitude and prudery; it conjured up images of the benevolent volunteer preaching to the unenlightened. Professional social workers wanted to go beyond the amateurism of this earlier age. Rather than try and purge character of its moral connotations, social workers abandoned the term in favor of the newly emerging category of personality.[24] Indeed, in the late teens and early 1920s, personality became the primary target of social casework. Mary Richmond put the matter succinctly in her authoritative book, *What Is Social Case Work?*

> Let me ... make the broadest generalization about social case work that I can. Its theories, its aims, its best intensive practice all seem to have been converging of late years toward one central idea: namely, toward the *development of personality* [italics added].[25]

What made personality so appealing to social workers such as Richmond was the category's freshness and flexibility. As historian Warren Susman noted, the word *personality* had a decidedly modern resonance, and it enjoyed increasingly wider usage as the century went on.[26] Its popular appeal lay in the lightness of its moral load. In contrast to the Victorian category of character, which carried the full weight of Christian ethics, personality referred largely to the traits of self-presentation. It tended to be associated with adjectives such as *fascination, stunning, magnetic, dominant,* and *masterful*. However, for social workers, personality's attractiveness lay not only in its popularity but also in its ambiguity. For all its modernist charm, *personality* was an extraordinarily broad term. In scientific circles, the term was often used to refer to the "objective" self—a summary statement of the individual when viewed apart from a moral context. In literary and religious circles, commentators frequently used the term in a very different sense. In discussions of ethics and art, *personality* referred to that aspect of human nature that made a person distinctively human. For most religious theorists, this entailed a religiously motivated engagement with the social world.[27]

The footnotes of Richmond's definitive book on casework provide ample testimony to the wide range of interests that personality was able to tie together. Richmond quoted scholars from literary criticism, religion, psychology, pedagogy, biology, and social science, and each theorist used the term in a different way. For the behaviorist psychologist John Watson, *personality* was an objective term that referred to the "'reaction mass' as a whole." In contrast, the literary critic Bliss Perry used *personality* to refer to the distinctively human element within each individual:

> If the revelation of personality unites men, the stress upon mere individuality separates them, and there are countless poets of the day who glory in their eccentric individualism without remembering that it is only through a richly developed personality that poetry gains any universal values.[28]

For a profession struggling to navigate a course between science and sentimentality, the ambiguity of personality was not a liability but a resource to be exploited. The category had a scientific cachet, and it enabled social workers to forge alliances with professional communities in psychiatry and psychology who were interested in personality. At the same time, however, personality was not without its ethical suggestiveness. By orienting their professional project around personality, social workers could be both scientific and ethical.

PERSONALITY: A "BENEVOLENT" PROJECT

Although Allport would later switch out of social work and into psychology, he would remain committed to the language and methods of professionalized benevolence. Indeed, his initial foray into psychology—his 1922 doctoral dissertation—was oriented toward psychology and social work, and it was submitted to Harvard's Department of Philosophy and Psychology and to the Department of Social Ethics. As one might expect, the logic of casework was readily apparent throughout the study. Entitled "An Experimental Study of the Traits of Personality," Allport hoped to provide social workers with something that they had up until this time lacked: the technological means to fulfill the casework ideal.[29] In the late teens and early 1920s, the field of individual measurement was in its infancy. As social ethicist Richard Cabot observed:

> The social worker is liable to disappointment when she tries to find textbooks on personality study. The study of personality does not exist, either as a science or an art, written down. It exists in lives and not in books or lectures. The study of personality is not yet developed.[30]

Allport was among a cohort of newly emerging specialists in psychology, psychiatry, and social work who were enticed by the promise of a science of personality. "To do effective social service," he noted some years later, "one needed a sound conception of human personality."[31] The task as Allport saw it was to render individuality legible. Social workers could not begin to tailor their interventions to the needs of their clients until they had a means of seeing individuality. Like many of his colleagues in the early 1920s, Allport believed that laboratory experiments and intelligence tests brought individuality within a scientific register. By developing measures of what he believed to be the component traits of personality, Allport maintained that individuality could in fact be plotted on a "psychograph."

As we have seen, the social workers to whom Allport looked for inspiration were obliged to walk a delicate line between science and ethics. Excessive moralism was one of the principal failings of the benevolent tradition. To move the field forward, social workers needed to bring to their clients a scientific attitude. However, scientific excess brought its own dangers, especially in a field as deeply immersed in the complexities of the human condition as social work. In his early papers, Allport did not explicitly mention the tensions engendered when science and ethics were brought together. Nevertheless, science and ethics constituted the primary axis around which his psychology of personality revolved.

In attempting to bridge the divide between science and ethics, Allport chose to orient his study around the category that had proved so appealing to social workers: personality. This was a conscious decision on Allport's part, and the scientific and ethical implications of the category of personality did not escape him. He explained the rationale behind his use of the term *personality* in his first publication. Entitled "Personality and Character," this article is thought to have been the first literature review in the field of personality.[32] But while its title suggests linguistic and ethical diversity—character *and* personality—the goal of the article was scientific order. Allport argued that character and personality were distinct entities. Borrowing a distinction from John Watson, Allport maintained that character was a moral category; it referred to the self when viewed from an ethical perspective. Personality, on the other hand, referred to the objective self, the fundamental adjustment patterns that an individual had formed over the course of his or her experience. "Psychologists who accept Watson's view," Allport wrote, "have no right, strictly speaking, to include character study in the province of psychology; it belongs rather to social ethics."[33]

Throughout the 1920s and 1930s, Allport acted as a kind of linguistic policeman on issues of terminology. He renewed his attack on *character* in a 1927 article and again in a lengthy and influential literature review that appeared in 1930.[34] The rationale was always the same: *Character* needed to be expunged from the lexicon of scientific psychology because it was a "moral" term. This critique was clearly informed by the scientism that was spreading throughout American social science in the 1920s.[35] Value-neutrality was a central tenet of this vision, and Allport drew on its logic in suggesting that the value-laden category of character had no place in a scientific discipline such as psychology. But while Allport may have revered the emerging model of value-neutral science, his inspiration was ethical. Moral propriety had been one of the salient themes of his Methodist upbringing, and it remained so throughout his undergraduate education in social ethics. Harvard social ethicists such as Richard Cabot and James Ford argued that rapid industrialization and urbanization had given rise to a growing sense of ethical malaise. There was a clearly felt need to "determine what constitutes goodness" and to then put those ideals forward for Americans to follow.[36] Although Allport attempted to draw a sharp divide between science and ethics, his own program was oriented around the search for "goodness." In a 1923 letter to Ford, Allport remarked that he had "never essentially wavered from my desire to correlate psychology and social ethics. It has merely been a practical question as to how this might be accomplished."[37]

Personality provided Allport with the ideal vehicle for pursuing this correlational end. The category appealed to Allport for the same reason that it appealed to social workers: It had an almost unparalleled versatility and a peculiar resonance to the modern ear. Personality captured both the sublime and basic elements of human nature, and it had both a scientific and a humanistic cachet. "Personality," Allport remarked in 1927, "like Mesopotamia, is a blessed word; it induces in both the writer and in the reader a sweet sense of stability, security, and modernity."[38] The importance of personality's modernist cachet cannot be overstated. During the 1920s, a number of psychologists developed programs of scientific research around the category of character. Although much of this work was published, the psychology of character remained at the margins of scientific respectability. The problem was largely one of connotation. American psychology had embarked on a wide-ranging campaign to purge itself of anything resembling metaphysics. As one of the cultural cornerstones of Victorian ethics, character was an obvious target for objectively minded psychologists. As leading characterologist A. A. Roback remarked in 1927, "the most general use of the word 'character' in everyday life is invariably coloured with moral predicates." In a remark that reflects the positivism of the age, Roback added that the scientific legitimacy of character was "spoilt by [the] ethical atmosphere.... Just because it was born and bred in an ethical milieu, the psychologist would be apt to disown [character] as spurious."[39]

CHARACTER REVISITED, PERSONALITY REMADE

Although Allport was anxious to forge personality into a singular scientific object, as his career unfolded in the 1920s and 1930s he frequently drew on two visions of selfhood. As a purveyor of psychological technologies he displayed an awareness of the kind of self that was coming to dominate the American social landscape. His choice of personality rather than character as his site of scientific investigation is one obvious indication of his investment in the newly emerging self. The personality ideal also was evident in one of Allport's most famous theoretical tenets: uniqueness. Cultural historians have identified qualities of uniqueness, distinctiveness, and standing out from the crowd as recurring motifs in the new language of selfhood.[40] John Burnham characterized this preoccupation with distinctiveness as a "compensatory" response. "In the mass society of the twenties," Burnham wrote, "depersonalization called forth compensatory attitudes from a large proportion of the atoms of the faceless—and presumably lonely—multitude."[41] Allport was among the "multitude" who reacted to the era's sense of unease about the anonymity of life among the masses. Beginning in graduate school, and continuing throughout the 1920s and 1930s, he repeatedly emphasized the "unique" quality of individuals. "The first clue to understanding others," Allport wrote in a characteristic passage, "lies in the perception of their uniqueness."[42]

In his illuminating article on the idea of the "masses" in American popular culture, historian Steven Smith identified distinctiveness as one of the central ironies of John Watson's behaviorism.[43] Watson promised deliverance from the anonymity of the crowd; behaviorism was a technology of uniqueness. Yet, as Smith noted, beneath Watson's rhetoric of distinctiveness lay a remarkably conventional social vision. Allport's psychology of personality harbored a similar incongruity. Despite his celebration of "uniqueness," Allport devised psychometric procedures that implicitly endorsed a certain kind of self. This self did not involve qualities associated with character: duty, honor, self-sacrifice. In his Test of Ascendance–Submission, Allport implicitly valorized those expressive, socially dominant personalities who tended to stand out in a crowd. The logic behind the test was simple enough. "Our current civilization," Allport wrote, "seems to place a premium upon the aggressive person, the 'go-getter'." A technology that could distinguish these individuals from the masses would have an obvious appeal in the newly emerging culture of personality.[44]

Anxious to exploit the possibilities that this practical, observable self offered, Allport simultaneously displayed an ongoing commitment to the morally grounded, self-sacrificing, stable, inner self that was fast disappearing in American culture: the "man of character." This attachment was much more than a nostalgic yearning for that which was lost. The stable inner self was a living reality for Allport, and as a psychologist he drew heavily on its precepts when reflecting on the kind of self he had become. His various autobiographical statements are perhaps the most revealing measure of the depth of his commitment to the character ideal. In these works, the principal theme of the personality ideal—self-realization—was consistently downplayed. Emphasis was instead given to themes central to the Victorian self: service, humility, duty, moral courage, and thrift. For instance, in his autobiography, Allport commented on his dislike of the "aura of arrogance found in presently fashionable dogmas" and of the need for psychologists to view humility as a virtue worthy of cultivation.[45] Moral courage was another aspect of the character ideal central to Allport's autobiographical narratives. He noted on several occasions that he had "crossed swords" with powerful intellectual tendencies in order to stay true to his convictions.[46] "I've never been cowardly," he remarked in one interview. "I'm going to follow [personality research] out the best I can."[47] Allport drew on the language of character again when discussing his remarkable productivity. He linked his professional success to what historian Stefan Collini identified as the "very crown of character": duty.[48] "I wouldn't do [research]," Allport remarked, "unless there were an overwhelming sense of duty and obligation.... It's more than intellectual curiosity," he continued. "I just work because I have to and my sense of duty makes me."[49]

Set in historical context, Allport's autobiographical references to courage, humility, and duty are striking. Their significance is further magnified when considered in relation to Allport's lived experience in the 1920s and 1930s. During this period, and indeed throughout his life, Allport lived in a manner very much in keeping with the character ideal. There was little room for self-indulgence, scandal, or hedonistic excess in this morally disciplined vision. For a man of character, life revolved around morally meaningful work. Allport viewed personality as the site of modern moral endeavor, and as a young faculty member he pursued his research and teaching with the same all-consuming gusto that he brought to his undergraduate studies. "I'm no good at playing," he told an interviewer some years later.[50] Work was the order of the day, but not just any work —like any good man of character, Allport envisioned his own project in relation to a larger moral order. The specific obligations involved in his career as a psychologist were related to a general philosophy of life that he carefully nurtured.[51]

The particular kind of a life philosophy that Allport embraced provides another link between his career as personality psychologist and the kind of self represented by character. In Victorian America, character had a pronounced religious suggestiveness. The man of character was usually a man of Christ. He was a "true Christian gentleman, pure, upright with a strong sense of duty and possessing the 'highest kinship of the soul.'"[52] Although Allport experienced some of the Progressive Era disillusionment with organized religion,[53] he did not emerge from graduate school with what literary critic Joseph Wood Krutch would later describe as a "modern temper."[54] For Allport, unlike most of the moderns described by Krutch, God was not dead. Christianity lived on, and indeed Allport regarded the faith as a robust bulwark against the alienation and drift so characteristic of modern life. He went "heart and soul into ... the good old Church of England" in 1923, and he remained a devoted Episcopalian for the rest of his life. In a letter to a friend, Allport explained that the "ritual and sacrament" of Anglicanism provided him with an "indescribable release for my spirit."[55]

Allport's ongoing personal commitment to the ideals if not the actual category of character invested his scientific psychology with a peculiar duality. As we have seen, aspects of his work can be readily assimilated into the personality ideal. At the same time, however, and in some cases in the same publications, the hallmarks of character are clearly visible. In his Test of Ascendance–Submission, for example, Allport suggested that the qualities typically associated with personality—ascendance, expressiveness, and being a "go-getter"—were not the only way of successfully adjusting to modern life. There were other traits that one could cultivate, traits which in hindsight look very much like the virtues that Nellie Allport had endeavored to instill in her character-building project: "expansion, insight, sociality, unselfishness, . . . [and] social intelligence."[56]

Scientific ambitions prevented Allport from acknowledging any link between these "other traits" and the character ideal that he so assiduously cultivated. Nevertheless, as his career developed, the human image represented by character was to assume increasing prominence despite his unrelenting commitment to the scientificity of personality. The influence of character is evident in Allport's work as early as 1924 in an article entitled "The Study of Undivided Personality."[57] Like many of his later publications, the article was informed by a logic of defense. At stake, as far as Allport was concerned, was human nature itself. Psychology had launched a frontal assault on the human subject. Armed with a behavioristic language and a set of psychometric procedures, psychologists had constructed a human image that reflected the moral uncertainties of the age. This was a self without a core; it was a plastic behavioral shell readily susceptible to external manipulation.

In "The Study of Undivided Personality," and in a series of later articles, Allport endeavored to use psychology for a rather different cultural purpose. Instead of celebrating the veneer, as many of his colleagues in personality psychology were doing, Allport argued that there was a stable core at the heart of every person. This was the basic message of one of Allport's better-known works from the 1920s: trait theory. In his influential article "What Is a Trait of Personality?", Allport took issue with the environmentalism of many of his colleagues. Instead of viewing the individual as a shell passively mirroring the environment, Allport argued that personality consisted of a powerful bundle of neurologically grounded qualities or "traits." A "trait is dynamic, or at least determinative," he wrote. "The stimulus is not the crucial determinant that expresses personality; the trait is itself decisive."[58]

In putting psychology at the service of a self of depth and substance, Allport subtly reintroduced many of the themes of the character ideal. Like character, the self of Allport's trait theory possessed qualities of tangibility and inner directedness. There was something deep and enduring about traits; like character they had a groundedness that transcended social circumstance. For Allport, these qualities of depth and stability all served to underscore the importance of one of Victorian America's central truths: namely, that individual conduct was largely determined by a relatively stable core of inner attributes. The Victorians identified this core with character and morals. In the scientifically minded, morally fluid world of the 1920s, Allport translated this same construction into the language of personality and traits.

Allport's commitment to the character ideal reached its apogee in what is undoubtedly his most famous publication from this period: *Personality: A Psychological Interpretation*.[59] The book was Allport's attempt to bring a measure of discipline to the fractious field of personality psychology. Hailed as an instant classic, *Personality* is widely celebrated as the book that launched personality studies into the psychological mainstream. Although professional recognition of this sort was important to Allport, the ethical ambitions that had first inspired him to enter psychology featured prominently in the book's construction. The book can in fact be read as an exercise in re-enchantment. By mobilizing science and exploiting the ambiguities of personality, Allport attempted to breathe new life into that model of human nature that had formally been associated with character. The nostalgic thrust of this project is apparent throughout the book. Allport accused psychologists of "drawing the blood and peeling the flesh from human personality leaving only ... a skeleton framework of mind." Psychologists were more concerned with methodological precision and scientific respectability. In the rush to professionalize they had not done "justice to the richness and dignity of human personality."[60]

Personality was thus conceived as a work of restoration. Allport wanted to bring "richness and dignity" back to human nature. Not surprisingly, his vision of a rich and dignified human nature bore a striking resemblance to the character ideal of his youth. Nowhere is this clearer than in Allport's discussion of the "mature personality." As was his practice in discussions of personality, Allport began his consideration of maturity by insisting on the scientificity of his program. He suggested that there were three "universal and indispensable" ways to "distinguish a fully developed personality from one that is still unripe." However, when Allport began developing his maturity criterion his universalistic ambitions led him straight back to the moral world of character. In keeping with the character ideal, the mature personality was an active citizen, deeply concerned with social and religious causes. Unlike the "garrulous Bohemian, egotistical, self-pitying, and prating of self-expression," the mature personality was a "man of confident dignity" who could "lose himself in work, in contemplation ... and in loyalty to others."[61] Like character, Allport's model also reflected a reverence of the golden mean and a religiously derived seriousness of purpose. The mature personality had a well-developed "sense of proportion" and a "sensitive and intricate balance."[62] He could "pursue his course diligently" in the knowledge that he "has a place in the scheme of things according to the dispensations of a Divine Intelligence."[63]

Although the mature personality was suffused with the values of character, like most nostalgic invocations it contained a number of modern themes.[64] To begin, Allport encouraged an exploratory attitude to one's individuality and an openness to experience. The mature personality would live a "creative pattern of life" rather than a "static and stupid conventionality."[65] In another departure from character, Allport encouraged people to monitor their conduct not strictly in relation to a higher moral code but in relation to a set of psychologically derived norms. Termed *insight*, Allport defined this property as the "relation of what a man thinks he is to what others (especially the psychologist) think he is."[66] To be high in insight was to move ever closer to the ideal of maturity. A final point of difference concerns Allport's characterlike directive to embrace a higher moral code. Social historians have observed that 19th-century discussions of the self "presupposed an agreed moral code." The ideals to which one should surrender were thus not in dispute; for the proponents of character, the issue was not "moral relativism but weakness of will."[67] For Allport, however, moral relativism was a presupposition. While insisting on the necessity of self-sacrifice to higher ideals, Allport left the exact content of these ideals unspecified.

DISCUSSION

Informed by the values of both character and personality, and by a spirit of nostalgia and innovation, Allport's psychology of personality is a telling illustration of the elasticity and ambiguity of interwar American psychology. By putting science at the service of higher ideals, Allport's psychology was clearly part of a wider movement to stem the tide of moral relativism and religious decline in interwar America. Yet, as we have seen, Allport was no ordinary cultural conservative. Far from holding dogmatically to a religiously based "language of character," Allport led the charge against it. He repudiated the category of character and replaced it with the ideal of a devaluated individual: an objective essence that existed independently of any ethical frame of reference.

Consolidating personality as a research category in psychology was Allport's consuming passion in the interwar period. However, his professional efforts in this regard harbored a paradoxical moral intent. By banishing existing evaluative frameworks from scientific discussions of personality, Allport's goal was not to destroy the traditional ethical foundations of America but to revitalize them. He wanted to celebrate the "man of confident dignity" and to scientifically affirm the values that that self represented: honor, duty, humility, stability, religiosity, and self-sacrifice. This tactic was not entirely unsuccessful; however, it came with an ironic price. By promoting the idea of a devaluated self—a self that exists independently of moral frameworks—Allport unintentionally reinforced a tendency that lay at the heart of the new culture of personality: a detachment of the self from social and cultural contexts.[68]

The personality ideal made the individual self "the ultimate locus of salvation."[69] Personal fulfillment involved an efficient mobilization of the self's own resources; social and ethical considerations were of secondary importance. Although Allport occasionally warned his readers about the dangers of "self-seeking and vanity," most of his scholarly time was spent celebrating the capabilities and prowess of the individual self.[70] To "study [a person] most fully is to take him as an individual," he wrote.[71] In Allport's hands, this position implied that selfhood could, and perhaps should, be considered in relation to its own internal properties rather than a broader cultural or moral milieu. By 1937 Allport thus found himself advocating a position that was largely identical to the emerging personality ideal. In both cases, the isolated individual was the proper object of scrutiny and the source of fulfillment.

Although Allport's participation in the culture of personality may have been unwitting, the moral thrust of his psychology was by no means idiosyncratic. Despite their century-long valorization of objectivity, American psychologists have frequently traversed the divide between scientific description and moral prescription. Indeed, a number of historians have persuasively argued that morality is one of the discipline's driving concerns.[72] According to Graham Richards, American psychology has been animated by an "enduring moral project" for most of its history.[73] Its mandate has been to provide a "culturally authoritative foundation for conventional morality in a society which is constitutionally pluralistic in terms of religion and ideology."[74]

Allport's 20-year engagement with personality represents an illuminating illustration of American psychology's moral project at work. Like many of his colleagues in the 1920s, he was convinced that the solution to America's ethical dilemmas lay not in history, culture, or religion but in science, in particular, psychology. Psychometric methods, experiments, and case studies could cut through the layers of prejudice and distortion that had long governed matters of conduct. The appeal of this program lay in psychology's ability to shift the basis of ethical authority from society to human nature itself. Instead of haggling over arbitrarily defined social creeds, psychologists could use their methods to scrutinize the "actual nature of personality."[75] An objective understanding of human nature would serve as the foundation for a new moral code. Such a code would be ethical, as historian Nikolas Rose explained, "because it has a basis not on an external truth—be it divine right or collective good—but one essential to the person over whom it is exercised."[76]

Although representative of psychology's "enduring moral project," Allport's early engagement with personality provides an important historical insight of its own. Historians of personality psychology have frequently portrayed the field in modernist terms. The field is thought to have grown as a result of the confluence of bureaucratic need and methodological convention; Victorian notions of selfhood were largely absent from personality psychology. According to Danziger, "'personality' [psychology] ... never had anything in common with traditional concepts of the person as a social agent." Although there is much to recommend this position, Allport's experience suggests that it is somewhat overdrawn. Victorian notions of selfhood continued to inform some of the most important discussions of personality in psychology long after the category of character had been formally abandoned. What is particularly important to note at this juncture is the mediating role that personality sometimes played in American moral discourse of the 1920s and 1930s. In Allport's hands, the category served as a conceptual link between the values of character and those of the newly emerging industrial order.

NOTES

1. See Warren Susman, "'Personality' and the Making of Twentieth-Century Culture," in *New Directions in American Intellectual History*, eds. J. Higham & P. Conkin (Baltimore: Johns Hopkins University Press, 1979), pp. 212–226; Burton Bledstein, *The Culture of Professionalism: The Middle Class and the Development of Higher Education in America* (New York: W. W. Norton, 1978), pp. 129–158; see also Stanley Coben, *Rebellion Against Victorianism: The Impetus for Cultural Change in 1920s America* (New York: Oxford University Press, 1991), especially chap. 1, "Victorian Character," pp. 3–35.

2. Kurt Danziger, *Constructing the Subject: Historical Origins of Psychological Research* (Cambridge, England: Cambridge University Press, 1990); James Parker, "In Search of the Person: The Historical Development of American Personality Psychology" (PhD diss., York University, 1991).

3. Danziger, *Constructing the Subject*, 1990.

4. Ibid., 163.

5. Ian Nicholson, "Moral Projects and Disciplinary Practices: Gordon Allport and the Development of American Personality Psychology" (PhD diss., York University, 1996); Franz Samelson, "The APA Between the World Wars: 1918 to 1941," in *The American Psychological Association: A Historical Perspective*, eds. Rand Evans, Virginia Sexton, and Thomas Cadwallader (Washington, DC: American Psychological Association, 1992), pp. 119–147.

6. Nellie Wise Allport, diary entry, 1896, quoted in Allport, *The Quest*, 1944, p. 14.

7. Gordon Allport, "Gordon Allport," in *A History of Psychology in Auto-*

biography, Vol. 6, eds. Edwin Boring & Gardner Lindzey (New York: Appleton Century), pp. 3–25.

8. For a detailed discussion of John and Nellie Allport, see Nicholson, "Moral Projects and Disciplinary Practices," 1996.

9. See Whitney Cross, *The Burned-Over District: The Social and Intellectual History of Enthusiastic Religion in Western New York, 1800–1850* (Ithaca, NY: Cornell University Press, 1950).

10. Nellie Wise Allport to Gordon Allport(?), June 1, 1922. Letter courtesy of Robert and Ardys Allport. In this letter, Nellie recalled an example of the religious dedication of her youth: "The other girls in the class suggested that I wave [sic] my convictions and wear a stylish dress for once; and I remember my stand, *if it be right at all, it is right for always*" (emphasis added).

11. Susman, "'Personality' and the Making of Twentieth-Century Culture," 214.

12. Ibid.

13. Cited in Samuel Smiles, *Character* (London: John Murray, 1875), p. 1.

14. Gordon Allport, "The Appeal of Anglican Catholicism to an Average Man," *The Advent Papers* (n.d.): 1–19. This article may be viewed as the religious counterpart to the "professional" autobiography Allport published in *The History of Psychology in Autobiography*. On the first page Allport describes the book as the "story of my religious development." It was published anonymously by the Boston-based Church of the Advent.

15. A record of Allport's course of study and extracurricular activities can be found in his undergraduate scrapbook in the Allport Papers, Harvard University Archives.

16. For an insightful history of social ethics at Harvard see David Potts, "Social Ethics at Harvard, 1881–1931: A Study in Academic Activism," in *Social Sciences at Harvard, 1860–1920*, ed. Paul Buck (Cambridge, MA: Harvard University Press, 1965), pp. 91–128. See also James Ford, "Social ethics, 1905–1929," in *Development of Harvard University, 1869–1929*, ed. S. Morison (Cambridge, MA: Harvard University Press, 1930), pp. 223–230.

17. Potts, "Social Ethics," 97.

18. Regina Kunzel, "The Professionalization of Benevolence: Evangelicals and Social Workers in the Florence Crittenton Homes, 1915–1945," *Journal of Social History* 22 (1988): 20–43.

19. Roy Lubove, *The Professional Altruist: The Emergence of Social Work as a Career, 1890–1930* (Cambridge, MA: Harvard University Press, 1965), p. 20.

20. Ibid.

21. According to the prominent social theorist Mary Richmond, casework provided the social worker with a "clearer understanding of the numberless ways in which bad social conditions affect the lives of individuals." Record keeping also served as an "indispensable guide to future action in (sic) behalf of the person recorded." See Mary Richmond, *What Is Social Case Work?* (New York: Russell Sage, 1922).

22. Ibid., 151, 149.

23. Arthur Todd, *The Scientific Spirit and Social Work* (New York: Macmillan, 1920).

24. Susman, "'Personality' and the Making of Twentieth-Century Culture."

25. Richmond, *What Is Social Case Work?*, 90.

26. Susman, "'Personality' and the Making of Twentieth-Century Culture."

27. For a good discussion of the place of personality in Protestant theology see William King, "An Enthusiasm for Humanity: The Social Emphasis in Religion and Its Accommodation in Protestant Theology," in *Religion and Twentieth-Century American Intellectual Life*, ed. Michael Lacey (New York: Cambridge University Press, 1989), pp. 49–77.

28. Cited in ibid., 93–94.

29. Gordon Allport, "An Experimental Study of the Traits of Personality With Application to the Problems of Social Diagnosis" (PhD diss., Harvard University, 1922).

30. Cabot's remarks appear in the "Informal Discussion" section of Mary Jarrett, "The Psychiatric Thread Running Through All Social Case Work," *Proceedings of the Conference of Social Work* 46 (1919), 587–593, p. 593.

31. Allport, "Gordon Allport," 7.

32. Gordon Allport, "Personality and Character," *Psychological Bulletin* 18 (1921): 441–455.

33. Ibid., 443.

34. Gordon Allport, "Concepts of Trait and Personality," *Psychological Bulletin* 24 (1927): 284–293; Gordon Allport and Philip Vernon, "The Field of Personality," *Psychological Bulletin* 27 (1930): 677–730.

35. Dorothy Ross, *The Origins of American Social Science* (Cambridge, England: Cambridge University Press, 1991).

36. James Ford, "Introduction," in *Social Problems and Social Policy*, ed. James Ford (Boston: Ginn & Company, 1923), 1–7, p. 1.

37. Allport to Ford, November 20, 1923, Department of Social Ethics Papers, Harvard University Archives.

38. Gordon Allport, "Review of Social Psychology," *Psychological Bulletin* 27 (1930): 731–733, p. 731.

39. A. A. Roback, *The Psychology of Character* (New York: Harcourt, 1927), pp. 6, 7. Allport read *The Psychology of Character* before it went to press. In the preface, Roback expressed his "indebtedness to Dr. G. W. Allport of Dartmouth College" for his "numerous critical suggestions" (p. xi). The difficulties Roback experienced in trying to constitute character as an object of scientific study may have underscored Allport's earlier conviction that character needed to be expunged from psychological lexicon.

40. Susman, "Personality and the Making of American Culture," 220.

41. John Burnham, *Paths Into American Culture: Psychology, Medicine and Morals* (Philadelphia: Temple University Press, 1988), 77.

42. Gordon Allport, "Some Guiding Principles in Understanding Personality," *The Family* (1930): 124–128, p. 125.

43. Steven Smith, "Personalities in the Crowd: The Idea of the 'Masses' in American Popular Culture," *Prospects* 19 (1994): 225–287, p. 274.

44. J. Herman Randall, *The Culture of Personality* (New York: H. M. Caldwell, 1912).

45. Allport, "Gordon Allport," 23.

46. Ibid., 22.

47. Anne Roe, interview by Gordon Allport, March 1952, Anne Roe Papers, American Philosophical Society Library.

48. Stefan Collini, "The idea of 'character' in Victorian political thought," *Transactions of the Royal Historical Society* 35 (1985): 29–50, p. 36.

49. Anne Roe, interview by Gordon Allport, November 1962, Anne Roe Papers, American Philosophical Society Library.

50. Ibid.

51. Ibid.

52. Susman, "'Personality' and the Making of Twentieth-Century Culture," 219.

53. See Ian Nicholson, "Gordon Allport and His Religion" (paper presented at annual meeting of the Cheiron Society, Montreal, Quebec, Canada, 1994).

54. Joseph Krutch, *The Modern Temper* (New York: Harcourt Brace, 1927). For a good discussion of Krutch's work see Peter Slater, "The Negative Secularism of *The Modern Temper*: Joseph Wood Krutch," *American Quarterly* 33, no. 2 (1981): 185–205.

55. Gordon Allport to Edwin Powers, March 20, 1923. Letter courtesy of Ardys Allport.

56. Gordon Allport, "A Test of Ascendance–Submission," *Journal of Abnormal and Social Psychology*, 23 (1928): 118–136, p. 134.

57. Gordon Allport, "The Study of Undivided Personality," *Journal of Abnormal and Social Psychology* 19 (1924): 132–141.

58. Gordon Allport, "What is a trait of personality," in *Personality & Social Encounter*, ed. Gordon Allport (Boston: Beacon Press, 1960), p. 132. This article was read at the 1929 International Congress of Psychology and published in the *Journal of Abnormal and Social Psychology*, 25 (1931): 368–372.

59. Gordon Allport, *Personality: A Psychological Interpretation* (New York: Henry Holt, 1937).

60. Ibid., vii.

61. Ibid., 213.

62. Ibid., 224, 223.

63. Ibid., 226.

64. For an intelligent discussion of nostalgia see David Lowenthall, *The Past Is a Foreign Country* (New York: Cambridge University Press, 1985).

65. Allport, *Personality: A Psychological Interpretation*, 218.

66. Ibid., 221.

67. Collini, "The Idea of 'Character,'" 37.

68. Robert Bellah et al., *Habits of the Heart: Individualism and Commitment in American Life* (Berkeley: University of California Press, 1985).

69. Philip Cushman, "Why the Self Is Empty: Toward a Historically Situated Psychology," *American Psychologist* 45 (1990): 599–611.

70. Allport, *Personality: A Psychological Interpretation*, 213.

71. Ibid., 566.

72. See Geoffrey Bunn, "The Lie Detector, Wonder Woman, and Liberty: The Life and Work of William Moulton Marston," *History of the Human Sciences* 10 (1997): 91–119.

73. Graham Richards, "'To Know Our Fellow Men to Do Them Good': American Psychology's Enduring Moral Project," *History of the Human Sciences* 8 (1995): 1–24.

74. Ibid.

75. Allport and Vernon, "The Field of Personality," 716.

76. Nikolas Rose, "Engineering the human soul: Analyzing psychological expertise," *Science in Context* 5 (1992): 351–369, p. 361.

V

PSYCHOLOGY BETWEEN THE WORLD WARS

INTRODUCTION: PSYCHOLOGY BETWEEN THE WORLD WARS

The heterogeneity of American psychology between the world wars is often underappreciated. Many textbook histories focus on the dominance of neo-behaviorism in this period. However, psychologists faced a number of challenges in the workplace and in society. Their responses helped to shape the discipline in unforeseen ways.

The Great Depression that began in October 1929 had an enduring influence on the further development of psychology. In ways both obvious and subtle, the changes in American life that flowed from the Depression affected psychology and psychologists like few other events before or after it. The Depression figures in some way in each of the chapters in this section, with the possible exception of chapter 20.

Chapter 17, "Unemployment, Politics, and the History of Organized Psychology" (1976), by Lorenz J. Finison, discusses Depression-era unemployment among psychologists, a little-studied aspect of the history of American psychology. During the Depression, a large number of younger psychologists, both applied and academic, were either underemployed or unemployed. However, the American Psychological Association (APA), which was led by psychologists who were already well-established in their careers, paid insufficient attention to the dire circumstances of their colleagues. When it became obvious that the APA was not going to work actively to increase employment, some who were involved in politically leftist or socialist groups, such as New America, formed two major groups to work for improving psychologists' career opportunities. The Psychologists' League, centered in New York City, organized to work for full employment of psychologists, especially in such government programs as the Works Progress Administration. The Society for Psychological Study of Social Issues (SPSSI) was centered in the Midwest. Both groups worked to force the APA to become more actively involved in expanding employment opportunities for psychologists. The Psychologists' League eventually disbanded at the time of World War II. Members of the SPSSI worked on a greater range of social issues, including industrial conflict and, after the war, race relations (Finison, 1986). The SPSSI thrives today as APA's Division 9.

In chapter 18, "Organized Industrial Psychology Before Division 14: The ACP and the AAAP" (1997), Ludy T. Benjamin, Jr., describes an important extension of psychological practice into new areas in the 1930s. The number of psychologists increased steadily throughout the 1920s and 1930s, with the most significant growth in the applied and professional fields. During this period, the number of psychologists engaged in various professional practices dramatically increased. Among APA members alone, the percentage grew from 9.3% in 1916 to 39% in 1940 (Finch & Odoroff, 1939, 1941). Four semidistinct areas of practice emerged: clinical, consulting, educational, and industrial/business. The employment settings for applied psychologists included schools, clinics (of various kinds), homes for people with mental retardation, courts, prisons, police departments, psychiatric hospitals, guidance offices in educational settings, psychotherapy offices, social agencies, state and federal agencies, film and radio studios, personnel offices, advertising and marketing firms, life insurance companies, and private consulting firms (Napoli, 1981).

In an analogous fashion to the social activism of the Psychologists' League and the SPSSI, applied psychologists had to go outside of APA to form more sympathetic organizations. (It should be kept in mind that many applied psychologists were not members of APA in this period.) Many of them did not meet the standards for full membership in the APA. When the organization needed to increase its revenue stream to pay for the purchase of several psychological journals, a new, non-voting class of associate member was established in 1926. It was this second-tier membership that applied or professional psychologists could obtain.

Perhaps because of this second-class status, the APA did little on behalf of these psychologists. Frustrated, they formed their own organization in 1930, the Association of Consulting Psychologists (ACP). Benjamin describes how the ACP evolved into the American Association of Applied Psychologists (AAAP). The AAAP, like the ACP before it, was concerned with professional issues of education, training, internships, licensing, standards of practice, and employment of its members. By the time that World War II began, the AAAP was beginning to make substantial progress. During the war, the initiative to reform the APA to make it more inclusive and more responsive to both scientific and professional concerns began. The AAAP gave up its independent identity to the APA on behalf of this goal.

The rise of national socialism in Germany, with the attendant ostracism and eventual persecution of Jews, led a number of Jewish scientists, including psychologists, to immigrate to the United States. After arriving, the immigrants were forced to compete with American psychologists in a very tight job market. Those fortunate enough to find suitable employment often worked in intellectual and cultural settings very different from what they were accustomed to in their native country. The influence of particular social and cultural contexts on research is a much-debated topic.

In chapter 19, "Cultural Contexts and Scientific Change in Psychology: Kurt Lewin in Iowa" (1992), Mitchell G. Ash delineates how the changing cultural contexts of Kurt Lewin's (1890–1947) career influenced his work. Ash shows how Lewin's research changed after he moved to the United States from Berlin. The conditions that Lewin found at Iowa in terms of funding, students, and institutional support were markedly different from those he was accustomed to in Germany. However, in the nine years that Lewin was at Iowa, he was remarkably successful in forging a workable blend of the approaches he had used in Berlin with new approaches made possible and necessary by having an almost entirely new staff. The institutional setting at Iowa and the willingness of private foundations to provide financial support were also critical to Lewin's success. Ash also examines the enduring influence of Lewin's work and why it may not have had the lasting impact that might have been predicted by his success while still alive. The chapter makes clear the interaction of social and cultural factors with the microcultures of science.

Controversial research presents journal editors with tough choices about publication. Mainstream journals in psychology, as in other sciences, often avoid publishing research articles whose results fall outside the mainstream of psychological science and practice. In the 1930s and 1940s, S-R psychology (learning theory) dominated the pages of the most prestigious psychological journals. The use of animal models to study abnormal behavior in humans emerged as a viable, although minor, research area during this period. Norman R. F. Maier's (1900–1977) research on induced seizures in experimental rats was a fine example of this body of research. Other psychologists, especially younger ones, at such well-known institutions as Harvard, Yale, and Brown also published research in this area, some of it specifically designed to test psychoanalytic concepts (Sears, 1943). However, it was not the primary research program of those who were the leaders of the discipline, nor were the results typically published in the best experimental journals of the day. Controversy erupted when Maier won the

American Association for the Advancement of Science Thousand Dollar Prize in 1939 for his work on the induction of neurotic behavior in rats in an experimental situation. (Maier is one of only three psychologists to ever win the prize.)

In chapter 20, "On Publishing Controversy: Norman R. F. Maier and the Genesis of Seizures" (1993), Donald A. Dewsbury illustrates how those who have influence within the psychological power structures can use their position to diminish results with which they do not agree. The controversy that developed after the prize was awarded to Maier eventuated in favor of his chief critic, Clifford Morgan (1915–1976), and made it difficult for Maier to publish in the mainstream journals. Even though Morgan later acknowledged that he was wrong, he sought to avoid public acknowledgment of his error. The chapter shows the importance of social factors, in this case, social status, on the reception and dissemination of psychological research.

The diversity of psychological interests and issues during the period between the world wars is represented in these four chapters. Together they provide rich support for the notion that psychological science and practice are inextricably embedded in the society of which they are a part.

REFERENCES

Finch, F. H., & Odoroff, M. E. (1939). Employment trends in applied psychology. *Journal of Consulting Psychology, 3*, 118–122.

Finch, F. H., & Odoroff, M. E. (1941). Employment trends in applied psychology, II. *Journal of Consulting Psychology, 5*, 275–278.

Finison, L. J. (1986). The psychological insurgency, 1936–1945. *Journal of Social Issues, 42*, 21–33.

Napoli, D. S. (1981). *Architects of adjustment: The history of the psychological profession in the United States.* Port Washington, NY: Kennikat Press.

Sears, R. R. (1943). *Survey of objective studies of psychoanalytic concepts.* New York: Social Science Research Council.

17

UNEMPLOYMENT, POLITICS, AND THE HISTORY OF ORGANIZED PSYCHOLOGY

LORENZ J. FINISON

The last crisis of employment in academic psychology occurred during the Great Depression, 40 years ago:

> The Depression robbed campuses of present hope for multiplying either buildings or faculty. Holding the line was enough. As gifts fell off, interest from investments shriveled and tax support declined, capital expenditures dropped.... Appropriations for libraries and laboratories had to be reduced, salaries pared, and though the number of professors remained virtually unchanged, instructors' ranks were thinned. Numerous young M.A.'s and Ph.D's, ... hatched by alma mater in expectancy of limitless demand, now joined the unemployed, which by 1933 included some two hundred thousand certified teachers. (Wecter, 1948, p. 190)

During the 1930s, two opposing positions emerged within organized psychology on what should be done about the unemployment of academic

---

Reprinted from *American Psychologist, 31,* 747–755 (1976). Copyright © 1976 by the American Psychological Association. Reprinted with permission of the author.

psychologists. I will call the two positions restrictivist and expansionist. Very simply, psychologists of the restrictivist persuasion favored lowering the number of psychologists produced, while the expansionists favored increasing the number of opportunities for employment. In this article I discuss the ideological roots of these two positions and their contention during the middle 1930s.

One of the dominant ideologies of the psychological establishment during the 1920s and early 1930s was that of social darwinism. Social darwinism had several aspects, the most important being the notion that social inequities were a "natural" result of the "survival of the fittest." A corollary was the notion that since social inequities were natural (with natural often taken to mean biologically or genetically determined), the process should not be interfered with. Thus, social darwinists believed in a laissez-faire economic policy (Hofstadter, 1955). They feared that educational, social, and charitable programs would be dysgenic, that is, would lead to the survival of the unfit and lower the quality of the "national genetic stock."

But social darwinism need not imply passivity in the face of social ill. An elaboration of social darwinist ideology provided the basis for eugenic activism, which became popular in the United States just prior to World War I. Eugenics provided an active approach to the solution of social problems based on the notion that their etiology lay in the internal characteristics of given populations, rather than in their social and economic interrelationships. The eugenical solution to social problems observed in a given population lay in the improvement of the internal characteristics of the population. Eugenicists favored reproductive controls, such as sterilization, to ensure that poorer types would not endure.

Both social darwinism and eugenics can be characterized as "restrictivist" ideologies in that they portray the world as made up of the "fit" and "unfit" and favor restricting the production of the unfit. The politics of a part of the leadership of American psychology during the 1920s and early 1930s was social darwinist and eugenicist. Several of the officers and council members of APA who will concern us in this history had an active interest in eugenics and were in the leadership of the principal eugenics organizations of the day, the Eugenics Research Association and the American Eugenics Society. As we will see, restrictivist ideas dominated the early attempts of psychologists to respond to the employment situation in psychology.

The notion that the APA should respond to the employment situation in psychology was initially presented by Walter S. Hunter, chairman of the Psychology Department at Clark University. In a letter to L. L. Thurstone, then president of APA, Hunter (Note 1) urged the formation of a committee to study the problem.

> I wish to suggest that the Council of the APA consider the establishment of a committee ... for the study of the relationship between supply and demand in the case of Ph.D.'s in psychology. The problem for study seems to me exceedingly important, not only for the welfare of the young men and women who contemplate entering professional work in psychology but for the general welfare of our science. The evident present tendency is toward gross over-production of psychologists, a tendency also present in other disciplines. This tendency was bad enough in days of prosperity and of rapidly expanding college faculties, *but it is inexcusable now if some reasonable checking device can be obtained.* (Italics added)

Some initial opposition to the Hunter proposal came from E. A. Bott (Note 2), a Canadian psychologist who, while voting as a council member *for* the proposal, appended the suggestion that psychologists consider training students for "public service," as was often the case in Canada: "I would favour a broader commission which would include future supply and demand and the prospects of other avenues of demand than merely that of college teaching."

With the concurrence of the rest of the APA Council, Thurstone appointed the Committee on Standard Requirements for the Ph.D. in Psychology.[1] The initial membership of the committee was clearly of the "psychological establishment." Three of the five members (Hunter, L. M. Terman, and H. A. Carr) were former APA presidents. One member (E. G. Boring) was a former APA secretary, and the last member (A. T. Poffenberger) was concurrently an APA council member. Four of the five (Terman, Boring, Hunter, and Poffenberger) had been officers together 15 years before in the famous Army testing program of World War I (Yerkes, 1921). This program influenced large numbers of psychologists to adopt an "individual differences" model of psychology (Boring, 1950) and seems to have encouraged restrictivist thinking in the field. At least two of the five (Terman and Poffenberger) were prominent in the eugenics movement. Of the five, only Carr seems to have been uninfluenced by the restrictivist viewpoint.[2]

The first report of the committee was a compilation of data on the supply of and demand for psychologists. In it the committee indicated that while the production of new psychologists was increasing, the number of placements was falling. The conclusions of the committee were that

---

[1]The interest of psychologists in defining formal standards for professionals in the field was already in evidence several years previous to the appointment of the committee. A 1929 survey sent out by the Program Committee of the APA elicited a large number of responses indicating that psychologists were interested in the topic "requirements for the Ph.D. degree" (Fernberger, 1929).

[2]It is interesting to note that Carr's papers show no evidence of concern with problems of individual or racial differences, except as they relate to habit formation. Carr had no contact, apparently, with the Army aptitude testing program, working instead for the Committee on Problems of Vision Which Have Military Significance.

the trend is certainly for the supply of both Ph.D.'s and M.A.'s to exceed the demand. The remedy must be either to decrease the supply or to increase the demand, or both. *It is easier to decrease the supply than to increase the demand.* But this remedy must be applied with great caution. (APA, 1933, p. 653; italics added)

The next report, "Standards for the Ph.D. Degree in Psychology," contained only formal requirements for the PhD at various graduate schools of psychology, without obvious interpretative comment. But while the report itself gives no direct statement of the thinking of committee members, an examination of the correspondence among them gives some insight. In an exchange between Boring and Hunter, Boring (Note 3) reported some dissatisfaction with the Standards questionnaire on the part of the Harvard University faculty:

> Our staff felt that the questionnaire was prejudiced in the direction of suggesting that psychologists ought to have special training in biological or in natural sciences and in not making comparable suggestions about other fields.[3]

Later, in response to a draft of the committee report, Boring (Note 4) was more specific about the source of the problem:

> But I face this ... problem concretely when I face my responsibility toward the work that now goes on with us under Gordon Allport or even Harry Murray. Both of them, mind you, stick to our requirements at present and urge their students into more experimental psychology and biology than the law requires, but my point is: should they? or should they after social psychology is further developed toward a scholarly attack. [See Footnote 3.]

But near the end of this letter, Boring withdraws his objection: "I have just stopped to read through your draft of the report again. My judgment is that you should not change a word of it" (see Footnote 3).

Hunter (Note 5) answered this letter with the defense that

> such courses [as physics and chemistry] will serve as a filter to *strain out weak brothers and sisters* who would prefer to study English and Sociology and then turn to Psychology. ... [Furthermore] a man going to Kansas or Illinois is sized up by the other scientists at once. If he has never heard of chemistry or physics or physiology, if he is not even a master of experimental work, his road—and the road of psychology—is very much harder than if he can fit into the general picture of what constitutes a scientist. (Italics added)

Thus, in Hunter's letter we have both the concern with a scientific image for psychology and the suggestion of a restrictivist response to this concern.

---
[3]Quoted with permission of the Harvard University Archives.

The following year, A. T. Poffenberger, as the new chairman of the committee, reported that it had been continued with instructions:

> To prepare the facts for presentation to prospective graduate students in psychology who are thinking of teaching in psychology as a career, and furthermore to consider the problem of redirecting graduate training in psychology in such a way that professional psychological service can make increasing contributions to community life, and finally, to serve as a clearing house of information regarding such matters as standards of training for various types of psychological service.
>
> One member of the Committee, Dr. Boring, considered the program of the Committee futile and resigned. The Chairman of the Committee, Dr. Hunter, also resigned, although consenting to serve as a member. The present Chairman [Poffenberger] accepted that responsibility with misgivings. (APA, 1934, p. 663)

The committee finally decided that there wasn't much they could or wanted to do other than study the situation. Poffenberger reported that

> the ... task of "redirecting psychological training so that professional psychological service can make increasing contributions to community life," together with the *apparent need for raising standards of training*, has been left untouched. [Furthermore] it is the opinion of the Chairman that *to tamper too much with the laws of supply and demand even in psychology may be a precarious business*, with consequences as little forseen as the limitation of crops on the eve of a widespread drought. (APA, 1934, p. 664; italics added)

Thus, the committee held to the "natural" laws of supply and demand in their application to psychology as a profession. However, in the internal correspondence on the Standards report, and explicitly stated in the final report, is the restrictivist solution to the social problem of unemployment among psychologists, that of actively reducing their supply by raising standards. Though many established psychologists of the time adhered to the restrictivist notions of the leadership of APA, opposition movements began to develop. These movements were composed mainly of younger and unemployed psychologists. Two principal bases of opposition formed, differentiated politically and geographically. The greatest concentration of unemployed and underemployed professionals during the 1930s was in New York City. At the same time, union and political organizing was going on at many of the public institutions in the New York City area. At Bellevue Psychiatric Hospital, for example, both psychiatric interns and psychologists were meeting to discuss *hospital* issues.[4] Their activity led to the formation of a group that began to bring together both unemployed and employed psychologists to discuss matters of common concern. The first

---

[4]There was "no formal open organization" at this point (Bressler, Note 6).

citywide public meeting was announced for January 1935, at Bellevue Psychiatric Hospital, and included the following call:

> In analyzing the conditions of unemployment and precariousness in the psychological profession, we must come to the only honest conclusion, and that is, that there is no more overproduction of psychologists than there is of food. The community can use as many well trained and competent psychologists as the university can produce. ... The question is then resolved into whether there is an overproduction of psychologists or an underconsumption of them when judged in terms of community needs. Stated this way, the decision is that the fault is underconsumption—underconsumption due to the general social and economic conditions affecting all professionals. (Anonymous, 1935, p. 188)

By mid-1935, the "small nucleus" of psychologists who put together this statement had grown considerably and called itself the Psychologists League.[5]

If the psychologist establishment of the early 1930s had a social darwinist and restrictivist outlook, the opposition, those I have called the "psychological insurgents," had a socialist and expansionist outlook.[6]

The League took as its principal mission and organizing tool the securing of employment opportunities for psychologists. The League agitated for federal support for unemployed psychologists through the Works Progress Administration (WPA). Psychologists who could meet the stringent means test were put to work on various projects in the schools and hospitals of New York City.[7] The data collection for the Wechsler-Bellevue Scale, for example, was carried out by WPA psychologists. Attempts to cut back on WPA funding were met by petition and telegram drives and at times by street demonstrations involving Psychologists League members (Horelick, Note 8).

The WPA projects also helped the Psychologists League to grow because psychologists and psychology graduate students from different city universities might well end up on the same WPA job. Thus, traditional

---

[5] The growth of the Psychologists League was attributable in part to the concentration of unemployed and underemployed psychologists in the New York City area and in part to the Popular Front politics of the period. The history of the League will be recounted in a forthcoming paper.

[6] In this article, the term *socialist* is used to denote adherents of any of the parties and movements listed in Goldwater's (1966) genealogy of radical parties, and any groups in the network of John Dewey's League for Independent Political Action. This definition obviously puts together groups that deserve separate treatment. Such a treatment would require much more space than is available here.

[7] "This statement about the means test was valid at the start of the program, but later regulations were altered, so that between the administrative hierarchy and the WPA beneficiaries came an 'exempt' category of persons hired for their professional skills, working at a somewhat higher rate but at shorter hours so that they did not earn more than subsistence wages" (Diamond, Note 7).

university lines were cross-cut, and the organizational task was made much easier.

The viewpoint of the Psychologists League on unemployment is given in the pages of an early League *News Bulletin.*

> The leaders of the psychological profession and the organizations of psychologists have been distressingly slow to recognize their responsibility to strive for productive utilization of psychological resources. . . . By a curious inversion of logic, they have generally concluded that the solution lies in raising standards, so that the experienced would find it even more difficult to secure jobs. . . .
>
> What then? There is a direction. The direction lies in seeking for the coordination of the premises and the practice of psychology with the forces in society which are striving, not for personal or sectarian gain at whatever cost, but for the progress of mankind generally. It lies in recognizing that the problems of psychologists are not peculiar to them; that only by concerted action of a united profession in collaboration with other professionals and workers generally can the concessions from the present social set-up be won which will permit at least the partial realization of minimal aims. (Psychologists League, Note 9)

In the above passage we have the articulation of several traditional socialist notions: expansionism rather than restrictivism; action based on general rather than individual or sectarian advance; and reform as limited and incomplete within the framework of capitalist society (i.e., the "present social setup").

Throughout the 1930s, the Psychologists League carried on active agitation for the retention and expansion of WPA employment for psychologists. The Psychologists League Committee on Unemployment formed a joint committee with the Unemployed Teachers Association to "add mutual strength and effectiveness in their contact with the WPA" (Psychologists League, Note 10). Also, "the committee cooperated with the WPA Teachers Union in warding off dismissals of both psychologists and teachers from the projects" (Psychologists League, Note 11). Letters of protest as well as telegrams were sent by the League to the WPA authorities in New York and Washington, protesting against WPA dismissals and investigations.

The League drew up and published, in mimeographed form, a series of proposals for expanding the employment of psychologists. They proposed the employment of 4,000 psychologists in the New York City schools (one for every 250 children), one psychologist for every 400 new court cases per year, and one psychologist to every 300 new neighborhood clinic cases per year (with one clinic to every 20,000 of the population). They further proposed the employment of 10 or more psychologists to work in cooperation with teachers on developing new curriculum for educationally maladjusted school children; five psychologists per institution of 2,000 inmates; one full-time psychology instructor for every 200 enrolled students in adult education; and finally,

> establishment of a "Psychological Advisory Board" for the writing of pamphlets to be printed by the government printing office on parenthood, child training, discipline, marriage problems, mental hygiene and family and group relationships, etc., and for creating a question-and-answer service of nationwide scope.[8] (Psychologists League, Note 12)

Alternative methods had been suggested for increasing employment of psychologists. One such method was proposed in the Reynolds–Starnes immigration bill then before the Congress. A provision in the bill provided that all members of a family desiring to immigrate to the United States be given IQ tests. All members would be denied entry if *any* members "fail to pass an intelligence test equivalent to, or higher than, a normal rating of an average sampling of native-born American white stock. . . ." This legislation had been supported by several psychologists in testimony before congressional committees, but drew a protest from the Psychologists League.[9]

> Some psychologists see in the proposed bill vast opportunities for the employment of psychological talent and services. To anticipate them with approval would be opportunistic. Psychologists have far more significant, more useful functions which they are being prevented from serving in the schools, hospitals, clinics, community centers, research laboratories, etc. (Machover, Note 14)

The psychological insurgency in New York, to summarize, was developed through the efforts of members and "friends" of various left-wing political groups and political liberals in the context of the general insurgency of the 1930s. The organizational manifestation of the insurgency, the Psychologists League, had a membership consisting

> mostly of the younger members of the profession, many of whom were unemployed. . . . The League succeeded in drawing attention both to the need for serious consideration of the economic problems of the profession (the evil of "volunteer" work, unemployment, lack of adequate psychological service in the schools and elsewhere, etc.), and to the need for more social orientation of research. (Gley, 1939, p. 554)

I would like to turn now to another source of support for an expansionist program. This group of psychologists was principally active in the

---

[8] A slightly different version of this proposal was published in an article in the *Psychological Exchange* (Diamond, 1935).
[9] A letter of protest was also sent by Gordon Allport (Note 13), ending with the paragraph: "The Act as a whole strikes me as intemperate and bigoted to an extreme degree. Possibly Congressman Starnes' ancestors, as well as yours [Reynolds] and mine would never have arrived in this country if this act were in force."

Midwest, rather than in New York City. It also had a quite different, though radical, political base.

In Chicago, a young psychologist named Isadore Krechevsky (David Krech), was working on an NRC postdoctoral fellowship. He remembered years later that

> immersed though I was in my rats, I was becoming increasingly aware that things outside were not getting better and that my failure to get an academic job was not only a reflection of bad economic times, but also of a bad society. I was becoming disaffected.
> About that time I joined New America. (Krech, 1974, p. 235)

New America had been founded in 1934 by Harry F. Ward, a radical Methodist from Union Theological Seminary; Selden Rodman, an activist in John Dewey's League for Independent Political Action; and a psychologist, Goodwin Watson, who had been a student of both Dewey and Ward (Watson, Note 15, Note 16). Watson (Note 15) remembers going back to Teachers College in 1933 after a trip to Germany where he had witnessed Hitler's rise to power.

> I felt that America was in a very real danger; that some such Nazi movement would grow up in this country, because we were still very deep down in the depression, producing only about half of the goods and services that our economic capacity would have made possible.

Watson began an organization called Forward America, which soon merged with Selden Rodman's Young America to become New America.

> New America [according to Krech], with headquarters in Chicago and the bulk of its (small) membership in the Midwest, was an avowed Marxist revolutionary organization. It was self-consciously indigenous, taking its style from the American scene, and wearing its Marxism lightly. While it assiduously avoided Communist-baiting, most of its members took an exceedingly dim view of the Communist Party and of the USSR. It was completely and compulsively democratic in its public ideology and in its internal activities. New America attracted a number of intellectuals, scientists, students, and writers; scattering of labor, educational, and religious leaders; and even some steel and automobile workers (of whom we were inordinately proud). (Krech, 1974, p. 235)

New America seems to have combined elements of Marxist rhetoric and Deweyite pragmatism. The movement of the organizational headquarters from New York to Chicago was apparently a self-conscious attempt to Americanize the organization, to develop, as Dewey had suggested, a radical *American* ideology.

New America was successful in recruiting to its ranks a number of psychologists and graduate students in psychology. In particular, a nucleus from the University of Chicago, including Krech, joined between 1934 and 1936.

Also in Chicago was Ross Stagner, a Wisconsin PhD who, after receiving his doctorate, had run on the Socialist Party ticket for the Madison Board of Education. In 1934–1935, Stagner was teaching at Peoples Junior College, a barely solvent and short-lived institution at which the faculty pooled and shared equally in the meager tuition payments. He had also been unable to find regular employment.

In early May 1935, the issue of unemployment was discussed informally at the Midwestern Psychological Association (MPA) meetings. Even before that, Stagner, Krech, and others had begun to circulate a petition asking the APA to respond to the unemployment situation.[10] As Stagner (Note 17) remembers the development of events, "we had raised the question with the board of directors of APA in the summer of '34. We were complaining that APA wasn't doing anything about helping unemployed psychologists." "Krech and I got together after the 1934 APA meeting and formulated a petition which was mailed in [about] January, 1935" (Stagner, Note 18).

Subsequent to the May Midwestern meetings, more signatures and resolutions of support were collected and presented at the 1935 APA meetings. The petition requested that the following resolution be adopted: "That a committee be appointed to approach the Federal government immediately with a request that money be made available from the works-relief fund for the employment of the large number of psychologists at present unemployed. . . ." (APA, 1935, p. 648). The resolution was apparently hotly debated. Stagner (Note 17) remembers that at one meeting

> old Dean Carl Seashore was sounding off about the survival of the fittest and the fact that you shouldn't help young psychologists get established because if they're good they'll get jobs for themselves and if they aren't good they'll go by the wayside.

After extended discussion, Poffenberger was appointed as chairman of a new committee of APA, the Committee on the Social Utilization of Unemployed Psychologists. He added three other established psychologists to the committee, two of whom were officers of the Personnel Research

---

[10] The actual original authorship of the petition remains uncertain, since inquiries have elicited different responses from the individuals involved. Also, some of the petitions were sent out after the MPA meeting in May 1935. A fascinating question is whether there was any connection between the New York group and the Chicago group. I am inclined to believe that there was not, even though both got going on the issue of unemployment at approximately the same time, and despite similarities in proposals from the two groups. For one thing, the petitions sent to the APA by the Chicago group contain names of psychologists from all over the country *except* New York City. In addition, important differences existed in political perspective and affiliation, which would have made for uneasy relations between the two groups. Another interesting possibility is that one group operated in indirect *response* to the efforts of the other. There is no evidence to clarify this point either.

Federation (Paul S. Achilles and Lawrence J. O'Rourke) and one of whom was a fellow member of the Eugenics Research Association (Marion R. Trabue). Over the course of the next year, the committee found 214 cases of unemployed psychologists (which would be comparable to about 3,500 today). In its final report, presented at the 1936 APA Convention, the committee stated:

> 1. That the unemployment of psychologists is only in part a product of the depression. Other factors are the approach-saturation point in the academic field and the trend to non-academic pursuits.
> 2. That this trend be recognized by the development of adequate training for these non-academic pursuits, and by a *more rigid selection of psychological personnel for personality as well as for intellect.*
> 3. That the American Psychological Association accept the responsibility for cultivating new fields for practical psychological service.
> ... (APA, 1936b, p. 702; italics added)

While the conclusion "more rigid selection of psychological personnel for personality as well as for intellect" reflects the restrictivist notions of the psychological establishment, there were countervailing elements also present, for example, the suggestion that the APA "accept the responsibility for cultivating new fields for practical psychological service."

The inclusion of this last suggestion in all probability results from the continued agitation of the Psychologists League (many of whose members were students or former students from Poffenberger's own university, Columbia). Notwithstanding the evident increasing sympathy of Poffenberger for the situation faced by many of his students, the committee finally requested its discharge as "not an appropriate body for proceeding with the larger and more extended duties which the problem involves."[11] The Psy-

---

[11] Over this period, Poffenberger seems to have become increasingly expansionist. By the time of his 1935 APA presidential address, he was freely using both restrictivist and expansionist language:

> The principal function here is the hallmarking of the fit rather than the fighting of the unfit. And before the fit can be hallmarked, the condition of fitness must be established. (Poffenberger, 1936, p. 16)

> The survey by your Committee on the Ph.D. in Psychology showed too many qualified psychologists in the ranks of the unemployed, and the number increasing at an alarming rate. Radical contraceptive measures have been proposed and are being employed in some institutions. A counter proposal which deserves equal consideration is that the field for psychological service should be extended. The ... Psychologist's [sic] League has drawn up a series of proposals covering work projects for psychologists which it intends to submit to governmental agencies. It includes, among other activities, a psychological service in the schools, in the courts, in neighborhood clinics, in industrial training, in institutions for the criminal and the maladjusted. This is a commendable effort and shows what might be done if an extensive and painstaking survey were conducted. Why should an organization of the type of the Psychologist's [sic] League have to be set up unless these very pressing problems were being neglected by existing agencies? Our association cannot long hold itself aloof from such practical considerations and still maintain its prestige while other more aggressive groups solve our members' problems. (Poffenberger, 1936, pp. 18–19)

chologists League evidently had in mind the APA taking on just such "larger and more extended duties." At this same convention, it pressed a proposal for the commissioning of a joint committee composed of representatives of the League, the APA, and the Association of Consulting Psychologists. After a good deal of debate, a resolution was finally passed formally commissioning a joint committee of the three organizations involved "to consider the feasibility of working out ways and means of increasing the opportunities for psychological service in education, government, social service and business and industry" (APA, 1936a, p. 687). By the 1936 Convention, then, the APA was committed (on paper at least) to a definitely expansionist program.

The evidence presented thus far suggests that while the original unemployment petition was circulated in early 1935 by New America psychologists aided by others, post-1935 activity on the issue of unemployment was due mainly to the efforts of the Psychologists League. However, beginning with the experience of the unemployment petition, the New America group began to build a broader organization of psychologists.

With Stagner gone to the University of Akron to a regular teaching job, Krechevsky and two other New America psychologists at the University of Chicago placed an ad in a newspaper called the *American Guardian*, also affiliated with Dewey's League for Independent Political Action. The advertisement, published in a free mailing of the *Guardian* to the entire under-forty membership of the APA, called for psychologists to respond who were interested "in the important contemporary problems of social and economic change" (Krechevsky, Note 20). A National Organizing Committee of 18 psychologists was soon formed to carry on organizational work.[12] In an initial letter from the Committee (Note 21), the following reference was made to the employment situation:

The quotation above demonstrates Poffenberger's increasing acceptance of the position of the Psychologists League. On the other hand, it also illustrates support for the expansionist program being expressed in survival-of-the-fittest terminology. In any case, Poffenberger appears to have become more aggressive in defending the positions of psychologists. One former student of his and a founder of the Psychologists League remembers Poffenberger accompanying several League members on a protest trip to the local WPA administrator (Bressler, Note 19).

[12] The Committee (Note 21): J. F. Brown (Kansas); L. W. Doob (Yale); J. H. Elder (Yale); Franklin Fearing (Northwestern); W. C. Halstead (Chicago); I. Krechevsky (D. Krech) (Chicago); W. A. Lurie (Chicago); N. R. F. Maier (Michigan); Lorenz Meyer (Chicago); K. F. Muenzinger (Colorado); T. M. Newcomb (Bennington); M. W. Richardson (Chicago); T. C. Schneirla (New York); J. F. Shepard (Michigan); R. Stagner (Akron); H. C. Steinmetz (San Diego); L. L. Thurstone (Chicago); E. C. Tolman (Berkeley); G. B. Vetter (New York); G. Watson (Columbia). In a later list of the Committee, the names of Elder, Newcomb, Shepard, Thurstone, and Vetter were dropped, and the names of G. Allport, G. W. Hartmann, and F. L. Ruch were added. An interesting coincidence in this is that Thurstone's name is mentioned in an earlier letter from Boring (Note 22) to Hunter, explaining his (Boring's) resignation from the Standards Committee (apparently in objection to the relatively activist charge added by the APA Convention): "I don't understand the APA vote, but so far as I can understand it I applaud your decision in resigning the chairmanship. See also the enclosed carbon with my resignation from the Committee. That motion sounds to me like Thurstone" (see Footnote 3).

> We do not believe it at all necessary to belabor the fact that an economic depression exists in these United States and in the world around us. That other spheres than the purely economic have been affected is also obvious to most of us. Psychology and our other sciences are no less affected. We need but appeal to your own experiences to obtain instances of the senseless fate our present society has assigned to the many capable psychologists we have been turning out with so much hope.

At the 1936 APA Convention in Hanover, New Hampshire, Ross Stagner chaired a meeting at which SPSSI (The Society for the Psychological Study of Social Issues) was founded. Krech was elected Secretary-Treasurer and his fellow New American Goodwin Watson was elected President. Within a year of its founding, SPSSI could claim that one of every six members of APA was also a member of SPSSI. Thus, by 1937, an important political change had occurred in American psychology. Two independent organizations—the Psychologists League and SPSSI—had been set up by socialist insurgents.[13] Both organizations had their roots in the employment and unemployment problems of psychologists themselves and in support of the idea that psychology and psychological research could be used to solve social problems. APA had been pushed into an active stance on the employment problem: into formal cooperation with one insurgent organization—the Psychologists League—and into affiliation with another —SPSSI. To further illustrate the shift from the dominance of the restrictivists, in 1936, E. C. Tolman, one of the liberals on the first SPSSI council (and the only one who had previously been in the APA leadership) was elected President of APA.

Finally, in 1939, the expansionist program was accepted into the APA structure in a single committee, the Committee on Personnel, Promotion, and Public Relations (APA, 1939).

I have several speculative comments to make on this history. The speculations center around the following question: What might have led psychologists during the 1930s to reject restrictivism and embrace, however reluctantly for some, an expansionist program? The easiest answer is, of course, group interest; all psychologists would benefit from an expansionist program. The socialist and New America psychologists, then, merely organized that group interest as APA had failed to do. There was, however, another development in psychology during the 1930s that may have been an equally important factor.

The 1930s, it seems to me, could be called the decade of learning theory. The models of Hull and Tolman are examples of a positive faith

---

[13] The Psychologists League and SPSSI were not the only organizations of psychologists founded during the period. Correspondence relating to the founding of the American Association of Applied Psychologists, for example, exists in the APA Archives at the Library of Congress. This topic has been explored fully by Napoli (1975).

that elaborate learning theory could become the basis for a science of man. And the development of learning theory, it seems to me, occurred at the expense of the individual-differences brand of psychology, which had been associated with hereditarian and social darwinist ideology.

Learning theorists emphasized *general* laws of learning. For them, it was necessary to consider mankind as a unified and mutable *whole*. Thus, it is symbolic of the change in American psychology that by 1935 the President of APA was a learning theorist (Hull) and that in 1936 he gave way to another (Tolman), who was also a founder of SPSSI.

It is perhaps no accident that Krech, the New American, was Tolman's student. What the socialist insurgents and the liberal learning theorists shared was a positive faith in social action. The socialist insurgents believed that society could be scientifically understood and altered for the better. Learning theorists believed that people learn according to scientific laws and that, accordingly, the ways and things they learned could be scientifically understood and altered.

In summary, there appears to have been an ideological shift in the leadership of American psychology in the mid-1930s. The shift had to do most fundamentally with the dominant view of the field on the question of social action. The shift also altered the response of organized psychology to the unemployment of psychologists. Just as the social darwinists believed in the immutability of the social order, and the wisdom of noninterference in it, so they believed that psychologists should rise through their own efforts or "fall by the wayside." Just as the socialist insurgents believed in the *mutability* of the social order, so they believed that organizations of psychologists and others could and *should* attempt to alter the employment situation *for* psychologists.

I have attempted to show that American psychologists have previously dealt with the problem of unemployment in their own ranks and that their viewpoints and actions have altered the organizational landscape of American psychology.

REFERENCE NOTES

1. Hunter, W. S. Personal communication to L. L. Thurstone, October 11, 1932. (Copy in Terman Archive, Stanford University)
2. Bott, E. A. Personal communication to D. G. Paterson, APA Secretary, December 21, 1932. (Copy in Terman Archive, Stanford University)
3. Boring, E. G. Personal communication to W. S. Hunter, June 6, 1933. (Copy in Harvard University Archives, Boring Collection)
4. Boring, E. G. Personal communication to W. S. Hunter, August 9, 1933. (Copy in Harvard University Archives, Boring Collection)

5. Hunter, W. S. Personal communication to E. G. Boring, August 14, 1933. (In Harvard University Archives, Boring Collection)
6. Bressler, M. (now Wolman, M. B.). Response to L. J. Finison draft, April 1976.
7. Diamond, S. Response to L. J. Finison draft, April 1975.
8. Horelick, R. S. Memo to Psychologists League members, January 24, 1939. (Personal copy of L. J. Finison)
9. Psychologists League. Little psychologist, what now. *Psychologists League News Bulletin*, May 1936, p. 1.
10. Psychologists League. Other W.P.A. news. *Psychologists League News Bulletin*, May 1936, p. 2.
11. Psychologists League. W.P.A. *Psychologists League Journal*, 1937, *1*(1), 12.
12. Psychologists League. *Work projects for psychologists*. Undated (1935)? mimeo. (Personal copy of L. J. Finison)
13. Allport, G. W. Personal communication to Senator Robert R. Reynolds, March 6, 1936. (Personal copy of L. J. Finison)
14. Machover, S. The Reynolds-Starnes Bill of the Alien Registration Act. *Psychologists League News Bulletin*, May 1936, pp. 8–10.
15. Watson, G. Oral history, 1963. (Columbia University Oral History Collection)
16. Watson, G. Personal interview, December 1973.
17. Stagner, R. Personal interview, July 1974.
18. Stagner, R. Response to L. J. Finison draft, April 1975.
19. Bressler, M. (now Wolman, M. B.). Personal interview, January 1975.
20. Krechevsky, I. Personal communication to Siegfrid Ameringer, January 17, 1936. (Personal copy)
21. The Committee. Mimeographed statement, undated (1936?).
22. Boring, E. G. Personal communication to W. S. Hunter, October 3, 1933. (Copy in Harvard University Archives, Boring Collection)

REFERENCES

American Psychological Association. Report on supply and demand for psychologists presented by the Committee on the Ph.D. in Psychology. *Psychological Bulletin*, 1933, *30*, 648–654.

American Psychological Association. Report of the Committee on the Ph.D. in Psychology. *Psychological Bulletin*, 1934, *31*, 663–664.

American Psychological Association. Proceedings of the forty-third annual meeting of the American Psychological Association, Inc. *Psychological Bulletin*, 1935, *32*, 637–652.

American Psychological Association. Proceedings of the forty-fourth annual meeting of the American Psychological Association, Inc. *Psychological Bulletin*, 1936, *33*, 677–690. (a)

American Psychological Association. Report of the Committee on Social Utilization of Unemployed Psychologists. *Psychological Bulletin*, 1936, *33*, 701–703. (b)

American Psychological Association. Proceedings of the forty-seventh annual meeting of the American Psychological Association, Inc. *Psychological Bulletin*, 1939, *36*, 740–755.

Anonymous. The economic and social position of the psychologist. *The Psychological Exchange*, 1935, *3*, 188–189.

Boring, E. G. *A history of experimental psychology*. New York: Appleton-Century-Crofts, 1950.

Diamond, S. The economic position of the psychologist. *The Psychological Exchange*, 1935, *4*, 5–8.

Fernberger, S. W. Research interests of American psychologists. *American Journal of Psychology*, 1929, *41*, 163–164.

Gley, R. L. Current trends in American psychology. *The Communist*, 1939, *18*, 553–562.

Goldwater, W. *Radical periodicals in America, 1890–1950: A bibliography with brief notes*. New Haven, Conn.: Yale University Library, 1966.

Hofstadter, R. *Social darwinism in American thought*. Boston, Mass.: Beacon Press, 1955.

Krech, D. David Krech. In *History of psychology in autobiography* (Vol. 6). New York: Prentice-Hall, 1974.

Napoli, D. S. *Architects of adjustment: The practice and professionalism of American psychology 1920–1945*. Unpublished doctoral dissertation, University of California, Davis, 1975.

Poffenberger, A. T. Psychology and life. *Psychological Review*, 1936, *43*, 9–31.

Wecter, D. *The age of the great depression, 1929–1941*. New York: Macmillan, 1948.

Yerkes, R. M. Psychological examining in the United States army. *Memoirs of the National Academy of Sciences*, 1921, *15*, 1–890.

18

ORGANIZED INDUSTRIAL PSYCHOLOGY BEFORE DIVISION 14: THE ACP AND THE AAAP (1930–1945)

LUDY T. BENJAMIN, JR.

In 1894, in its third year of existence, the American Psychological Association (APA) adopted its first constitution. Its single stated objective was "the advancement of Psychology as a science" (Cattell, 1895, cited in Sokal, 1992, p. 115). As the profession of psychology developed—and it began to do so in short order—the mission statement on science would be used again and again by APA's leadership to explain why it was inappropriate, even unconstitutional, for APA to be involved in promoting psychology's use outside of the laboratory. It required more than 50 years

---

Editor's Note. The first five articles in this issue examine the history of applied psychology, with a particular focus on the early history of Division 14 of the American Psychological Association (Society for Industrial and Organizational Psychology—SIOP). SIOP represents one of the original divisions, and APA's celebration of the 50th Anniversary of these divisions has stimulated a renewed interest in the early history of industrial and organizational psychology.—KRM

The archival research for this article was supported in part by an award from the Texas A&M University Mini-Grant Program.

Reprinted from *Journal of Applied Psychology, 82,* 459–466 (1997). Copyright © 1997 by the American Psychological Association. Reprinted with permission of the author.

and the emergency of World War II before APA embraced the profession of psychology. Even then, it did so half heartedly.

Although APA may have considered itself pure with respect to its scientific goal, U.S. psychologists embraced no such narrowness of purpose. Ventures into the world of application began while the ink was still drying on the APA constitution. APA's founder, G. Stanley Hall, who founded the *Journal of Applied Psychology*, was already involved in applying psychology to educational goals with the nationwide Child Study Movement that he began in the 1880s (see Davidson & Benjamin, 1987; and Ross, 1972), and by 1896, Lightner Witmer had opened his psychological clinic at the University of Pennsylvania (McReynolds, 1996). Fresh from successes in treating his early cases of students with learning difficulties, Witmer called on his colleagues at the 1896 APA annual meeting to use their science "to throw light upon the problems that confront humanity" (Witmer, 1987, p. 116).

The late 19th century United States was home to many problems confronting humanity, such as those brought on by immigration, growth of cities, mandatory schooling, and especially industrialization, that created "new management problems and a growing preoccupation with efficiency" (Napoli, 1981, p. 28). The possibilities for application of the new science of psychology seemed endless.

Pioneer applied psychologist Harry Hollingworth (1938) wrote that applied psychology was a career for those with "no sanctity to preserve" (p. 308). Yet, he and others risked their academic reputations in taking psychology to the business world. Harlow Gale conducted experiments on the psychology of advertising as early as 1896 (Kuna, 1976). Walter Dill Scott worked with advertising executives in Chicago as early as 1901 to apply psychology to their concerns, and he published his first book, *The Theory of Advertising*, in 1903. Hugo Münsterberg began his work in business psychology in 1909, which led to the publication of his classic book, *Psychology and Industrial Efficiency*, in 1913. Two years later, Walter VanDyke Bingham founded the Applied Psychology Division at the Carnegie Institute of Technology, a center for applied research that was funded partially by the Pittsburgh, PA, business community and one that researched questions germane to those business interests (see Hale, 1980; and Landy, 1992, 1993). These early industrial–organizational psychologists referred to their field as "business psychology" or, less commonly, "economic psychology." Following World War I, the term *industrial psychology* became the popular label, but it had been used in print at least as early as 1920 (Frost, 1920).

After World War I, the potential for applied careers was obvious to many psychologists. Industrial psychologists in particular had considerable opportunities in employee selection work because many U.S. businesses sought to develop personnel departments. Yet, APA continued to resist the recognition of these colleagues in applied work. In 1919, APA reluctantly established the Section on Clinical Psychology, and 2 years later formed the Committee on the Certification of Consulting Psychologists. That committee urged APA to create two more sections, one on educational psychology and another on industrial psychology. Both sections were rejected by APA, despite that the industrial psychologists polled were generally in favor of such a section (Napoli, 1981). Consequently, industrial psychology enjoyed no organizational structure until the 1930s when such a structure began to emerge with the Association of Consulting Psychologists (ACP).

THE ACP

Applied psychologists, particularly those in clinically related jobs, had sought to organize within APA on numerous occasions. Although they were sometimes given recognition by APA, they were not given the kind of organizational support to further their profession. Pleas for a licensing program and a code of ethics for psychological practice were mostly ignored (although an APA certification program did exist for a few years in the 1920s before it was abandoned). When it was clear that APA would not expand its goals beyond advancing psychology as a science, the applied psychologists realized that another organization was their only answer.

In the 1920s, nearly a dozen applied psychology organizations emerged, mostly defined by state boundaries. The largest of these was the New York State Association of Consulting Psychologists, formed in 1921. The leadership of this group was dominated by academic psychologists, most of whom did applied research. The consulting psychologist members were principally clinical and educational psychologists, many with master's degrees, but a core of industrial psychologists—a number of whom were already working full time in industry—held membership as well.

Industrial psychologists and the other applied psychologists enjoyed considerable opportunity in the 1920s due to the euphoria and prosperity sweeping the United States. In truth, because of the excessive public demand in the 1920s, many individuals who had no training whatsoever in psychology found ample opportunities to promote their services as psychologists (see Brotemarkle, 1940). Legitimate psychologists were concerned with these charlatans; but without legal protection for the label *psychology*, there was little they could do. When the stock market crashed in 1929, job opportunities declined significantly. Consequently, it became even more important to define legitimate psychologists for the public. Many believed that a national organization was needed to develop nationwide standards (Paynter, 1933).

The most visible of the state associations was the New York group, but it had never really developed as a force for consulting psychologists. That would change in 1930 with the result of a reorganization led by New York University psychologist Douglas Fryer. Arguably, the reorganization was the first step in making the New York association a national body. The name of the organization was officially changed to the Association of Consulting Psychologists, thus eliminating any regional reference. Two years later, ACP incorporated, defining its territory in its Articles of Incorporation as "the State of New York, the United States of America, and foreign countries" (Symonds, 1946, p. 339). Its purpose, as stated in its initial yearbook, was to "become an effective force in the professional practice of psychology in the fields of medicine, education, industry, law, social work and guidance" (ACP, 1931, p. 1).

Industrial psychologists were involved in the founding of ACP and its precursor, and they participated each year in the ACP meeting by offering programming for psychologists working in industry. There is no evidence from the surviving reports of meetings of any other special activities by the industrial psychologist members until 1936, when Gertrude Hildreth, then president of ACP, suggested that a committee of industrial psychologists be formed to "work for the improvement of status among industrial psychologists, and possibly develop a set of standards and code of ethics" (*Report of the Committee on Psychology in Industry*, 1936, p. 1). The seven-member committee chaired by R. S. Uhrbrock (Procter & Gamble Company, Ivorydale, OH) included Marion Bills (Aetna Life Insurance Company, Hartford, CT), Rensis Likert (Life Insurance Sales Research Bureau, Hartford, CT), Henry Link (The Psychological Corporation, New York), Millicent Pond (Scovill Manufacturing Company, Waterbury, CT), Sadie Shellow (Department of Police, Milwaukee, WI), and Morris Viteles (University of Pennsylvania). The committee's make-up reveals two aspects of the ACP membership: Many members were employed outside of academia, and many were women.

Uhrbrock's committee began its work by constructing a 12-item questionnaire that was sent to 27 psychologists who were identified as working chiefly in industrial psychology. The committee received 16 replies from Bingham, Harold Burtt, Bruce Moore, Pond, Carroll Shartle, Shellow, Daniel Starch, E. K. Strong, Jr., et al.). The respondents were asked about personal qualities essential for success in an industrial position contrasted with an academic position, relevant undergraduate and graduate courses, leading centers for training in industrial psychology, statistical and other technical skills needed for industry work, the type of thesis an industrial psychologist should complete, opportunities for women in industrial psychology, internships and other training opportunities, and the status that psychologists should enjoy within industry.

The results were communicated to the ACP Executive Committee at the May 1936 annual meeting in Vineland, New Jersey. The report offered little in the way of a summary and no recommendations; instead, it included every response received in a very lengthy report (*Opinions of Sixteen Psychologists*, 1936). One wonders whether anyone outside of the industrial community read the report because there was no further mention of it in the ACP minutes and no apparent action was taken as a follow-up. Of course, there were no recommendations to pursue. Uhrbrock (1938) later published the report in virtually the same format that he had presented to the ACP Executive Committee.

Several months after the ACP meeting, APA held its annual meeting in Hanover, NH. Part of the program was a round table session called *Qualifications of Industrial Psychologists*. The round table was chaired by Uhrbrock, and others participating included Burtt, Likert, Link, Lorin Thompson, Jr., and Viteles. More than likely, the discussion was based on the feedback from the ACP questionnaire, although that cannot be established from the archival record. The outcome of the round table was a recommendation for an APA committee; the recommendation even named the three psychologists who should serve on the committee. Burtt made the formal request at the APA business meeting, and the following motion was passed unanimously:

> That a Committee [the Committee on Qualifications for Industrial Psychology] consisting of Richard S. Uhrbrock, Chairman, Rensis Likert, and Lorin A. Thompson, Jr., as members be appointed to study the qualifications for training and internships for the guidance of persons contemplating a career in this field. (Paterson, 1936)

A few months later, as the committee was beginning its work, Uhrbrock noticed what he believed to be a discrepancy in the charge to the committee as defined in the memorandum from APA Secretary, Donald Paterson, and another version printed in the minutes of the APA business meeting. Uhrbrock noted that the memorandum from Paterson had called for "a study of the qualifications for training" but that the published proceedings of the meeting indicated the charge of the committee to be "the study of the qualifications of industrial psychologists and [the formulation of] specifications for training" (Uhrbrock, 1937, March 24). After correspondence with Uhrbrock and Thompson, Paterson told them that, because the committee was their idea, they should do whatever they had in mind when they recommended the committee in the first place (Paterson, 1937a). So, the committee chose to focus on qualifications for training.

The report of the committee was presented at the 1937 APA meeting. Uhrbrock was asked to read the report but declined because the meeting was running late. The report was then formally accepted, and the committee was discharged (Paterson, 1937b). When the proceedings of the meeting were published, Uhrbrock's report was not included. He protested its omission, claiming that the decision to publish it had been made at the time it was accepted at the 1937 meeting. But the minutes show no such recommendation. Uhrbrock persisted for 5 years in his attempts to get APA to publish the report, ending with an ultimatum he gave APA in 1942 either to publish the report or accept his resignation (Uhrbrock, 1942). The report was not published, but Uhrbrock did not resign.

It is not known why the report was not published by APA. It is certainly possible that some (perhaps much) of APA's leadership would have found parts of the report objectionable. The report called for psychology departments to encourage their best students to enter industry, suggested that academic training emphasizing individualism was not good preparation for functioning in a company setting, and chided departments for not employing psychology professors with industrial experience. Finally, the report called for APA to establish the National Institute of Industrial Psychology "to demonstrate to industry, business, and government that psychology has a contribution to make" (Likert, Thompson, & Uhrbrock, 1937, p. 13). There is no evidence that any of the report's recommendations were acted on. Thus, Uhrbrock proved unsuccessful in his efforts for both ACP and APA.

At the time Uhrbrock's report was delivered to ACP (1937), that association was concerned with two pressing issues. The first was the founding and promoting of a national journal for professional psychologists, the *Journal of Consulting Psychology*, which appeared in 1937. The second was the planning of a new national organization for applied psychologists, one that would create a federation of the existing state associations, ACP, and the Clinical Section of APA.

THE AMERICAN ASSOCIATION FOR APPLIED PSYCHOLOGY

By the mid-1930s, there was considerable dissension among psychologists regarding APA's failure to embrace the changes in psychology and the world of which it was a part. Emotions ran high at the 1936 APA annual meeting. One group of psychologists met to discuss psychology's role in solving social problems, and the following year they founded the Society for the Psychological Study of Social Issues (SPSSI). Another group met to discuss the need for a new national organization to promote the interests of professional psychologists. For that task, Fryer was nominated once more to lead the organizational effort (see National Committee, 1937). Within a year, he had worked out a constitution for the new organization that would be called the American Association for Applied Psychology (AAAP)—an organization that would achieve much in its brief 8 years of existence. The AAAP constitution was approved at a meeting held in conjunction with the 1937 APA meeting in Minneapolis, MN, and plans were made for the first independent AAAP meeting in 1938 (which would be labeled "the second annual meeting," 1938). In approving the AAAP constitution, which called for a new national association and not a federation of existing associations, both ACP and the Clinical Section of APA voted themselves out of existence.

The AAAP constitution divided the membership of the association into four sections: clinical, consulting, educational, and industrial and business. Then it formed a committee titled the Joint Sections Committee on Differentiation Between Clinical, Consulting, and Educational Psychologists, whose purpose was to "establish standards of differentiation between [the] above sections" ("Reports of the AAAP," 1938, p. 81). Apparently, only the industrial psychologists had a distinct identity.

Planning for the Industrial and Business Section of AAAP (Section D) was begun by Burtt, who was appointed by Fryer to chair a committee to decide the membership requirements for Section D (English, 1938). Burtt also appointed two committees: one (chaired by Viteles) to draft a constitution for the section and another (chaired by Shartle) to draft a code of ethical standards for industrial psychologists. The Section D constitution, which included the section on membership requirements, was adopted in 1939. Membership was limited to psychologists

> who are actively engaged in the application of psychology in business, industry, public service, or allied fields ... who have a Ph.D. in psychology or equivalent degree from an accredited university and who have had, in addition, at least two years experience in the application of psychology in business, industry, ... under their own guidance, or who have been responsible for highly significant research contributions of direct value in the application of psychology in business, [and] industry. (*Constitution of Section D*, 1939, pp. 1–2)

The doctoral degree requirement could be waived for "exceptional" persons who had 5 years of industry experience; but from a look at the membership rosters of Section D, this was rarely done.

The AAAP members could belong to more than one section, and many did. But it is likely that multiple memberships were more common among the members of Sections A, B, and C, in conjunction with the identity confusion cited earlier. Even so, Section D was always the smallest of the four original sections (military psychology was added later as a fifth section). At its peak (in 1945), the Industrial and Business Section had around 80 members compared with 410 in clinical, 225 in educational, and 180 in consulting. See Table 1 for a listing of the 52 members of Section D in 1939—the earliest known tabulation of these members.

The purposes of Section D, as defined in its bylaws, illustrate its commitment not only to the profession of industrial psychology but also to the research base of the profession. The section was founded

> (a) to promote high standards of practice in the application of psychology to business, industry, public service, and allied vocational

TABLE 1
Members of the Industrial and Business Section of AAAP (as of 1939)

Paul S. Achilles	Harry M. Johnson	P. Vernon Scheidt
Roger M. Bellows	Forrest A. Kingsbury	Morton A. Seidenfeld
Marion A. Bills	Arthur W. Kornhauser	Agnes A. Sharp
Walter V. Bingham	Paul F. Lazarsfeld	Carroll L. Shartle
Homer G. Bishop	Rensis Likert	Kinsley R. Smith
Harold W. Burtt	Henry C. Link	Frank N. Stanton
Harry R. DeSilva	Howard P. Longstaff	Daniel Starch
Henry N. DeWick	Lillien J. Martin	Edward K. Strong, Jr.
Beatrice J. Dvorak	Robert N. McMurry	Lorin A. Thompson, Jr.
Harold A. Edgerton	Bruce V. Moore	Herbert A. Toops
Theodore W. Forbes	Lawrence J. O'Rourke	Marion R. Trabue
Douglas H. Fryer	Jay L. Otis	Morris S. Viteles
Harold V. Gaskill	Richard H. Paynter	Albert Walton
Edward B. Greene	Albert T. Poffenberger	Frederic R. Wickert
C. Frederick Hansen	Millicent Pond	Louise R. Witmer
Harry W. Hepner	Hermann H. Remmers	Joseph U. Yarborough
Robert Hoppock	Marion W. Richardson	
John G. Jenkins	Elmer B. Royer	

Note. AAAP = American Association for Applied Psychology.

fields; (b) to promote research and publications in these fields; (c) to facilitate the exchange of information and experience among its members; (d) to promote the development of new professional opportunities, and (e) to contribute in general to the advancement of applied psychology. (AAAP, 1940, p. 1)

To promote the development of professional opportunities for psychologists in industry and business, the section identified eight problem areas in which members were "prepared to render professional services" (*Reports of the AAAP*, 1938, p. 80). These can be summarized in such modern jargon as job analysis, personnel selection, and organizational design, but it is more interesting (and instructive) to read the eight problem areas as formulated nearly 60 years ago by Burtt and his committee (see Table 2). Most, if not all, of these areas are part of contemporary industrial–organizational psychology.

The bylaws of Section D call for a number of elected officers: president, secretary, representative to the AAAP Board of Governors (each section had one representative), representative to the AAAP Board of Affiliates (one per section for the group that represents the state affiliate societies), four members to the Board of Editors of the *Journal of Consulting Psychology* (acquired by AAAP from ACP), and three members to serve with the first four officers as members of the section's Executive Council. Burtt was elected the first president of the section and Bills, the first secretary. The individuals to hold those two offices throughout the history of Section D are shown in Table 3.

The committee structure of Section D provides one measure of the

TABLE 2
Areas in Which Industrial and Business Section Members Were Willing to Render Professional Services

Area	Professional Service
1.	Study of the requirements of occupations
2.	Development and use of tests and other scientific techniques in the scientific placement of workers
3.	Formulation of the best methods of applying human energy at work
4.	Organization and systematization of training programs to insure the most complete development and most efficient use of individual ability
5.	Determination of the optimal conditions of work
6.	Analysis of characteristics of industrial organization for the determination of types best adapted to serve both the economic and social, and broadly, human objectives of industrial organization
7.	Examination and control of motivating forces in the case of both workers and management, which influence production and harmonious relationships in the industrial situation
8.	Analysis of human factors influencing the demand for and sale of commodities through the application of scientific techniques of market research

Note. Reprinted from "Reports of the AAAP," 1938, *Journal of Consulting Psychology, 2,* p. 80. In the public domain.

principal activities and concerns of these early industrial psychologists. The initial bylaws identify only three standing committees: membership, elections, and program. Yet, several others were added. One of the earliest to form was the Committee on Training Programs for Industrial Psychology. Moore chaired the initial committee that sought to recommend a graduate curriculum for educating industrial psychologists and for identifying appro-

TABLE 3
Presidents and Secretaries of the Industrial and Business Section of AAAP

Year	President	Secretary
1938	Harold E. Burtt	Marion A. Bills
1939	Walter V. Bingham	Marion A. Bills
1940	Morris S. Viteles	Marion A. Bills
1941	Arthur W. Kornhauser	Millicent Pond
1942	Arthur W. Kornhauser	Kinsley R. Smith
1943	Arthur W. Kornhauser	George K. Bennett
1944	Paul S. Achilles	George K. Bennett
1945	Carroll L. Shartle	Rensis Likert[a]
		Beatrice Dvorak[a]
		Floyd L. Ruch

Note. AAAP = American Association for Applied Psychology.
[a]Resigned due to wartime assignment.

priate course work and internship opportunities for industrial psychologists. Moore's committee report was approved in 1940 and distributed widely to graduate programs in psychology.

Shartle chaired the Committee on Ethical Standards. Although AAAP was working on its own code of ethics (based on the version that ACP had approved in 1933), the industrial psychologists wanted a code that was specific to the nature of their work. A draft of the ethics code was presented to the section's Executive Council in September 1938, with a recommendation from the committee that adoption be delayed until AAAP approved its own code (*Suggestions for a Code*, 1938). The drafted code dealt with relations to the public, employers, employees, and colleagues. It also included a section on research integrity and a penalty section for violators, which simply said that they would be expelled from membership in the section.

In 1940, when the AAAP committee had not been able to develop a code of ethics, Section D members offered their draft as a model. The AAAP, however, was never able to reach an agreement on a suitable document. Section D continued its committee under the leadership of Shellow and later Roy Dorcus, who worked on subsequent drafts of the document until AAAP merged with APA in 1945. Thus, neither AAAP nor Section D ever adopted a formalized ethical code, and APA would not approve such a document until 1953.

Another important committee, headed by Paul Horst, was the Committee on Public and Professional Relations. In the 1920s, many businesses had enlisted the help of pseudopsychologists who offered character analysis, often using physiognomic methods, and a host of other unscientific procedures to assist with such decisions as hiring, promotion, job assignment, and vocational counseling. Especially popular among many managers in the 1920s was a physiognomic system proposed by Blackford and Newcomb (1914) that urged the hiring of employees, especially salespeople, who were blonds because, they argued, blonds were more likely to have convex facial profiles indicating persons "possessing positive, dynamic, driving, aggressive, domineering, impatient, active, quick, hopeful, speculative, changeable, and variety loving characteristics ... [making] this type distinctly the type of action" (p. 141). Psychologists, such as Paterson, used their science to refute such characterological claims, but the practices persisted (Paterson & Ludgate, 1922); when the results proved disastrous, it was the field of psychology that got the blame.

By the late 1920s, U.S. businesses had lost a good deal of their trust in psychology—a situation that worsened considerably with the onset of the Great Depression. The job of Horst's committee was to generate ideas that would restore public confidence in psychology and to expand professional opportunities for industrial psychologists. Uhrbrock's idea of the National Institute of Industrial Psychology—perhaps similar to already existing institutes in England and Germany (see Viteles, 1932)—was resurrected as a clearinghouse for information to businesses about what industrial psychologists could do. The task of organizing this institute was given to Paul Achilles in 1943, but what happened after that is not known.

The most visible accomplishment of Section D was the annual program on industrial psychology prepared for each of the AAAP meetings. One of the features of the first few AAAP meetings was a series of public lectures, given in the evenings and designed to attract the potential clientele of applied psychologists. At the 1938 meeting in Columbus, OH, for example, there were two public lectures from two industrial psychologists: Link on public opinion and buying habits and Burtt on the status of industrial psychology. Over the years, some Section D program events focused on training issues, such as internships in industry; others addressed communication between psychologists and employer, such as an address by Moore on interpreting psychological data for industry and another by Viteles on what management and labor expect from psychologists. Some addresses dealt with specific audiences, such as government workers, college personnel, and employment services. Most, however, focused on research on topics such as advertising, employment tests, public opinion selection, sales effectiveness, and personality traits in workers (*Program of the Fifth*, 1941; *Program of the Fourth*, 1940; *Program of the Third*, 1939; "Second Annual Meeting," 1938).

After the United States became directly involved in World War II, the programs dramatically decreased in size. The U.S. Office of Defense Transportation asked associations to restrict travel of members to meetings, which affected the attendance of some AAAP members. Yet, many of those who did not attend the wartime meetings were involved in military work. Only one of the AAAP wartime meetings (in 1942) was canceled.

AAAP AND WORLD WAR II

U.S. psychology was well prepared for the roles psychologists might play in World War II. Both APA and AAAP had formed committees in 1939 on the pending "national emergency" and, by the following year, had generated extensive plans for the mobilization of psychologists (Capshew & Hilgard, 1992). Not surprisingly, industrial psychologists, both those in academia and industry, found their services greatly needed in the war effort. That topic is beyond the scope of this article but is covered in other sources (Capshew, 1986; Capshew & Hilgard, 1992; Katzell & Austin, 1992). Suffice it to say that the success of psychology in the war proved to be the most important force in the explosive growth of applied psychology after the war, particularly for clinical psychology but also for industrial and organizational psychology.

In 1941, when AAAP was just beginning to stretch its wings as a successful national organization independent of APA, a request came from the National Research Council, urging APA, AAAP, SPSSI, and other psychology groups to organize for the benefit of the national welfare. The result of that request was the formation of an intersociety committee chaired by Robert Yerkes that met for the first time in June 1942 at the Training School in Vineland, New Jersey. Two years later, the various groups had agreed on bylaws for a newly organized APA that would be made up of a number of divisions, each of them operating with a great deal of autonomy. The various parties, principally the original APA and AAAP, approved the new bylaws in 1945; as a result, AAAP disappeared as a separate organization and was reborn in 5 of the 18 charter divisions of the new APA. One of those was the Division of Industrial and Business Psychology (Division 14).

Shartle chaired the organizing committee that would form the new division. He set up a committee to draft bylaws for the division and conducted the first elections. Moore was elected the first president of Division 14. In the next 8 years, he was followed by eight more presidents who also had been active members of Section D: John Jenkins, George Bennett, Floyd Ruch, Shartle, Jack Dunlap, Bills, Jay Otis, and Harold Edgerton.

CONCLUSION

The initial opportunity for industrial psychologists to organize was provided within the ACP. Although there were special committee work and annual program events, including paper sessions, smokers, and banquets for the industrial psychologists at the ACP meetings, it is not clear that there ever was a group with a formal identity. That situation changed with the formation of the AAAP. From 1938 until 1945, industrial psychologists had their organizational home in AAAP as Section D. The membership was inclusive of the most visible individuals in the field. Although dominated by university-based psychologists, Section D also included many psychologists who were employed full time in industry.

The influence of AAAP's Section D on the new APA Division 14 was considerable, which is not surprising given that the membership was virtually the same between the two organizations. The statement of purposes for the division was lifted directly from the bylaws for Section D, the membership requirements were essentially the same, and the leadership of the section became the leadership of the division (see Benjamin, 1997).

In reviewing the considerable record of success for U.S. psychologists in World War II, there is no denying that the mobilization of applied psychologists was due largely to the work of ACP and particularly to the successful organization that AAAP had built by 1939. It seems unlikely that APA would ever have fostered an organization of applied psychologists prior to World War II. In the case of industrial psychology, the organizational impetus cannot be overestimated. Regarding the rapid growth of industrial psychology after World War II, historian Donald Napoli (1981) wrote that

> the military had given psychologists a chance to prove the effectiveness of selection, classification, and aptitude testing, and psychologists met the challenge successfully. Civilian employers also offered new opportunities, which grew largely from the labor shortage produced by wartime mobilization. Business managers, beset by high rates of absenteeism and job turnover, took unprecedented interest in hiring the right worker and keeping him contented on the job. Management turned to psychologists and other behavioral scientists for help, and the amount of psychological testing quickly increased. Surveys showed that in 1939 only 14 percent of businesses were using such tests; in 1947 the proportion rose to 50 percent, and in 1952, 75 percent. (p. 138)

Today, industrial–organizational psychology enjoys considerable success as one of psychology's oldest applied specialties. The contributions of the early researchers, consultants, and practitioners who organized the ACP and AAAP should not be forgotten. Their organization fostered the growth of industrial psychology through the 1930s and readied the applied specialty for the war work that involved industrial psychologists and for the successes that followed. As such, their work bears a very direct link to the vitality of today's newest version of Division 14, the Society for Industrial and Organizational Psychology, and to the strength of the field of industrial–organizational psychology.

REFERENCES

American Association for Applied Psychology. (1940, January). Walter Van Dyke Bingham Papers (Bulletin No. 3). Pittsburgh, PA: Carnegie Mellon University Library.

Association of Consulting Psychologists. (1931). *Yearbook*. Washington, DC: American Psychological Association Archives, Library of Congress, Manuscript Division.

Benjamin, L. T., Jr. (1997). A history of the Society for Industrial and Organizational Psychology. In D. A. Dewsbury (Ed.), *Unification through division: A history of the divisions of the American Psychological Association* (Vol. 2, pp. 101–126). Washington, DC: American Psychological Association.

Blackford, K., & Newcomb, A. (1914). *The job, the man, the boss*. New York: Doubleday, Page.

Brotemarkle, R. A. (1940). The challenge to consulting psychology: The psychological consultant and the psychological charlatan. *Journal of Applied Psychology, 24,* 10–19.

Capshew, J. H. (1986). *Psychology on the march: American psychologists and World War II.* Doctoral dissertation, Department of History, University of Pennsylvania, Philadelphia.

Capshew, J. H., & Hilgard, E. R. (1992). The power of service: World War II and professional reform in the American Psychological Association. In R. B. Evans, V. S. Sexton, & T. C. Cadwallader (Eds.), *The American Psychological Association: A historical perspective* (pp. 149–175). Washington, DC: American Psychological Association.

Constitution of Section D, Industrial and Business Section of the AAAP. (1939, November 23). Washington, DC: American Psychological Association Archives, Library of Congress, Manuscript Division.

Davidson, E. S., & Benjamin, L. T., Jr. (1987). A history of the Child Study Movement in America. In J. A. Glover & R. R. Ronning (Eds.), *Historical foundations of educational psychology* (pp. 41–60). New York: Plenum Press.

English, H. B. (1938). Organization of the American Association of Applied Psychologists. *Journal of Consulting Psychology, 2,* 7–16.

Frost, E. (1920). What industry wants and does not want from the psychologist. *Journal of Applied Psychology, 4,* 18–24.

Hale, M., Jr. (1980). *Human science and social order: Hugo Münsterberg and the origins of applied psychology.* Philadelphia: Temple University Press.

Hollingworth, H. L. (1938). Memories of the early development of the psychology of advertising suggested by Burtt's *Psychology of advertising. Psychological Bulletin, 35,* 307–312.

Katzell, R. A., & Austin, J. T. (1992). From then to now: The development of industrial–organizational psychology in the United States. *Journal of Applied Psychology, 77,* 803–835.

Kuna, D. P. (1976). The concept of suggestion in the early history of advertising. *Journal of the History of the Behavioral Sciences, 12,* 347–353.

Landy, F. J. (1992). Hugo Münsterberg: Victim or visionary? *Journal of Applied Psychology, 77,* 787–802.

Landy, F. J. (1993). Early influences on the development of industrial/organizational psychology. In T. K. Fan & G. R. VandenBos (Eds.), *Exploring applied psychology: Origins and critical analyses* (pp. 83–118). Washington, DC: American Psychological Association.

Likert, R., Thompson, L. A., Jr., & Uhrbrock, R. S. (1937). *Report of the Committee to Study the Qualifications of Industrial Psychologists.* Washington, DC: American Psychological Association Archives, Library of Congress, Manuscript Division.

McReynolds, P. (1996). Lightner Witmer: A centennial tribute. *American Psychologist, 51,* 237–240.

Münsterberg, H. (1913). *Psychology and industrial efficiency.* Boston: Houghton Mifflin.

Napoli, D. S. (1981). *Architects of adjustment: The history of the psychological profession in the United States.* Port Washington, NY: Kennikat Press.

National Committee for Affiliation and Association of Applied and Professional Psychology. (1937). The proposed American Association for Applied and Professional Psychologists. *Journal of Consulting Psychology, 1,* 14–16.

Opinions of sixteen psychologists regarding questions relating to industrial psychology as a career. (1936). Washington, DC: American Psychological Association Archives, Library of Congress, Manuscript Division.

Paterson, D. G. (1936, September 15). [Memorandum to R. Likert, L. A. Thompson, Jr., & R. S. Uhrbrock]. Washington, DC: American Psychological Association Archives, Library of Congress, Manuscript Division.

Paterson, D. G. (1937a, March 29). [Letters to L. A. Thompson, Jr., & R. S. Uhrbrock]. Washington, DC: American Psychological Association Archives, Library of Congress, Manuscript Division.

Paterson, D. G. (1937b). Proceedings of the forty-fifth annual meeting of the American Psychological Association. *Psychological Bulletin, 34,* 639–800.

Paterson, D. G., & Ludgate, K. (1922). Blond and brunette traits. *Journal of Personnel Research, 1,* 122–127.

Paynter, R. H. (1933). The work and aims of our association. *The Psychological Exchange, 2,* 121–135.

Program of the fifth annual professional conference and business meeting of the American Association for Applied Psychology. (1941). *Journal of Consulting Psychology, 5,* 197–204.

Program of the fourth annual professional conference and business meeting of the American Association for Applied Psychology. (1940). *Journal of Consulting Psychology, 4,* 151–160.

Program of the third annual professional conference and business meeting of the American Association for Applied Psychology. (1939). *Journal of Consulting Psychology, 3,* 182–190.

Report of the Committee on Psychology in Industry. (1936, May 9). Washington, DC: American Psychological Association Archives, Library of Congress, Manuscript Division.

Reports of the AAAP. (1938). *Journal of Consulting Psychology, 2,* 77–82.

Ross, D. (1972). *G. Stanley Hall: The psychologist as prophet.* Chicago, IL: University of Chicago Press.

Scott, W. D. (1903). *The theory of advertising.* Boston: Small, Maynard.

Second annual meeting of the American Association of Applied Psychologists. (1938). *Journal of Consulting Psychology, 2,* 128–136.

Sokal, M. M. (1992). Origins and early years of the American Psychological Association, 1890–1906. *American Psychologist, 47,* 111–122.

Suggestions for a code of professional ethics for the Industrial and Business Section. (1938). Walter Van Dyke Bingham Papers, Pittsburgh, PA: Carnegie Mellon University Library.

Symonds, J. P. (1946). Ten years of journalism in psychology, 1937–1946. *Journal of Consulting Psychology, 10,* 335–374.

Uhrbrock, R. S. (1937, March 24). [Letter to Donald G. Paterson]. Washington, DC: American Psychological Association Archives, Library of Congress, Manuscript Division.

Uhrbrock, R. S. (1938). Industrial psychology as a career: Report of the A.C.P. Committee on Psychology in Industry. *Journal of Social Psychology, 9,* 251–286.

Uhrbrock, R. S. (1942, August 5 and 14). [Letters to C. P. Stone]. Washington, DC: American Psychological Association Archives, Library of Congress, Manuscript Division.

Viteles, M. S. (1932). *Industrial psychology.* New York: Norton.

Witmer, L. (1897). The organization of practical work in psychology. *Psychological Review, 4,* 116–117.

19

CULTURAL CONTEXTS AND SCIENTIFIC CHANGE IN PSYCHOLOGY: KURT LEWIN IN IOWA

MITCHELL G. ASH

Before his 1933 emigration from Nazi Germany, Kurt Lewin had already published the formula, B = f(P, E), according to which behavior (B) is regarded as a product of a functional interaction of person (P) and environment (E). In this article, that formula is applied to its creator by examining continuity and change in Kurt Lewin's scientific biography at the State University of Iowa between 1935 and 1944. For a variety of reasons, the context in which he found himself there was considerably different from that of the University of Berlin, where he had been trained and had worked until 1933. In part on the basis of archival sources, it is

---

The central ideas in this article were first presented at a joint meeting of the History of Science Society and the American Historical Association in Cincinnati, Ohio, December 28, 1988. The article in its current form is revised and expanded from a presentation to a symposium on Kurt Lewin at the 37th Congress of the German Society for Psychology in Kiel, Germany, September 26, 1990. Facilities for research and writing were provided by the Center for Advanced Studies, the University of Iowa, and the Wissenschaftskolleg/Institute for Advanced Study, Berlin.
Reprinted from *American Psychologist, 47,* 198–207 (1992). Copyright © 1992 by the American Psychological Association. Reprinted with permission of the author.

asked whether and how Lewin's research interests, his methods, and his theorizing changed after his move to new institutional and cultural surroundings.

This topic has wider relevance beyond that of a biographical episode. Recently, much has been said in science studies about "local knowledge." This concept, originally used in a broader sense by cultural anthropologist Clifford Geertz (1985), now encompasses everything belonging to the microculture of science at the level of a working laboratory or research institute, including the apparatus, prescribed research goals and styles, as well as the working modi, interaction, and communication of research teams. Researchers who try to understand the social construction of science with the help of this concept, however, tend to underemphasize the broader social and cultural contexts within which these practices and relationships are situated, such as funding sources and the relations of particular research topics, goals, and methods to larger society pressures or issues. The case of Kurt Lewin and his coworkers in Iowa shows how wider society and cultural contexts and scientific microcultures can interact.

Closely related to this issue is the possibility that there are culturally formed national research styles in psychology, as Harwood (1987) claims for genetics. Recent research suggests that the different conditions of academic and professional life in the United States and in German-speaking Europe led to important differences in the institutionalization and professionalization of psychology (Ash, 1990; Danziger, 1987, 1990; Morawski, 1988). In German-speaking Europe, limited opportunities for new disciplines in the established system of higher education made it opportune for psychologists to compete for professorships in philosophy, which in turn influenced their research priorities toward the study of human cognition. In the 1920s, this philosophically oriented experimental psychology lived in uneasy balance with varied attempts to transform the field into a science-based profession and to expand its subject matter and methodological options accordingly. In the United States, by contrast, a growing university network and the rise of private research foundations (Geiger, 1986; Kohler, 1991) offered greater opportunities for institutional independence in psychology by the 1920s, but at the cost of implicit and at times explicit demands—willingly met—that academic psychologists present their work as both a quantitative and a socially relevant science. In terms of the organization and ultimate aims of research, the transformation of the field into a science-based profession was farther along in America than in German-speaking Europe.

According to Kurt Danziger (1987, 1990), two features of this development were most important. From 1910 to 1930, there was a growing preference for "group data"—studies addressing variation among or across individuals rather than the behavior or cognition of individuals—a trend that began in intelligence testing and educational psychology and was oriented to the needs of education administrators for classification instruments but which soon spread to basic research in learning and cognition. Corresponding to this was a shift in the relation of experimenter and subject from a situation of nearly equal status and potentially exchangeable roles, as in the German tradition, to one in which the experimenter was clearly in control, and the subjects would more accurately be called "objects" responding to variables manipulated by the experimenter.

Foundational to both of these features was a widespread technocratic orientation that was by no means confined to applied psychologists. Even Clark Hull's American Psychological Association (APA) presidential address, in which he first set out his hypothetico-deductive model of learning theory with the hope of placing psychology on a scientific footing comparable with that of classical physics, included the claim that such work would eventually encompass moral behavior (Hull, 1937) and thus (as he put it in a letter to a Rockefeller Foundation official) help to build "a more rational society" (Hull, 1934).

Applied to the case at hand, three questions thus arise. First, could an important theoretician and researcher like Kurt Lewin, who had developed something like a scientific microculture (or minischool) around himself at the Psychological Institute of the University of Berlin in the 1920s and early 1930s, continue to develop his scientific and professional projects in a scientific world structured differently at both the macro- and microlevels? Second, what processes of scientific change resulted as Lewin adapted to his new setting while simultaneously influencing at least some of his colleagues? Third, what selection did American psychologists ultimately make from the resulting products and why? Framed in this way, a study of a single émigré psychologist could illuminate the impact of society and culture on scientific thought and practice in a way that could be applicable to other cases in psychology and to other disciplines as well.

THE LEWIN GROUP IN BERLIN

Like the Gestalt psychologists, with whom he worked closely in Berlin, Kurt Lewin accepted the double identity of philosopher and experimenting psychologist then prevalent in German-speaking Europe. Recently published early writings show that he worked from the beginning on metatheoretical issues, such as the status of psychological and physical concepts, along with his empirical research on will (K. Lewin, 1981a). A central, and still appealing feature of Lewin's empirical work was the attempt to study ordinary life situations, such as a waiter's sudden inability to remember restaurant orders after the bill has been paid, in a laboratory setting. However, that attempt rested on metatheoretical foundations, specifically on Lewin's modification of certain aspects of Gestalt theory and on his original conception of experimentation.

Lewin shared the commitment of his colleagues, the Gestalt theorists Max Wertheimer and Wolfgang Köhler, to holism; he referred specifically to "action wholes" as the units of study in his research program on the psychology of action and emotion. In the 1920s, however, he elaborated what he called a comparative theory of science that loosened to some extent the monism of the Gestalt theorists (K. Lewin, 1925/1981b). Differing from Köhler's physicalism, Lewin used physical concepts such as "field" as analogies only and left open the question of whether phenomenal structures and brain events were isomorphic. In this analogous sense, Lewin and his Berlin students used concepts from mechanics, such as "tension system," as explanatory constructs in their research on the psychology of action and emotion.

With respect to method, Lewin criticized American-style statistical or group data methods as early as 1931, saying they yielded not general laws but only statements to the effect that one-year-olds in New York City tend to behave one way, whereas one-year-olds in Vienna produce different results (K. Lewin, 1931a). He tried instead to recreate what he called "Galilean" situations, in which the structures of ideal–typical person–environment interactions could be made to appear in the laboratory as it were phenomenologically. This he envisioned as a necessary basis for deriving formal, ultimately mathematical, descriptions of their dynamics with the help of topology. He understood this procedure to be analogous to the way in which Galileo had deduced the laws of free fall and projectile motion from mathematically derived "pure cases." The Lewin group thus created a practice-oriented program of basic research by going beyond Gestalt theory's cognition-centered approach while retaining the holistic assumptions, natural–scientific orientation, and theoretical rigor of Gestalt theory.

Another early work entitled *The Socialization of the Taylor System* (K. Lewin, 1920), written just after the abortive German revolution and published in a series edited by his friend, independent Marxist thinker Karl Korsch, reveals both Lewin's sympathy with independent socialist thinking and an underlying practical aim of even his academic research: to find a basis on which scientists and workers could work together to humanize the factory system. Lewin and his Berlin students acted on this intention in research on the psychology of will and affect (summarized in K. Lewin, 1935a; cf. De Rivera, 1976). Many of the studies produced by Lewin and his co-workers reflected this practical aim in their choice of topic, such as the "satiation" effect of repetitive tasks, memory for completed and uncompleted tasks, the effect of success and failure on level of aspiration, or the dynamics of anger, and by including examples from assembly-line or other real-world situations (see, e.g., Karsten, 1928/1976, p. 152). Lewin himself noted practical implications of his thinking for industrial psychology, pedagogy, and even psychotherapy (e.g., K. Lewin, 1928). The Lewin group's work was thus an attempt to unify philosophically oriented basic research in the German tradition with the requirements of an emerging psychotechnology.

LEWIN'S EARLY RECEPTION IN AND EMIGRATION TO THE UNITED STATES

Lewin was perceived and received first in the United States not as a theoretician or even as an experimental psychologist of action and emotion but as a specialist in child development with an approach alternative to that of behaviorism. The spectacular start of this reception was his film presentation entitled "The Effect of Environmental Forces" at the International Congress of Psychology in New Haven, Connecticut, in 1929 (K. Lewin, 1929). One scene depicted a child trying to sit on a block while keeping eye contact with it. The child solved the problem amusingly and effectively by putting his head between his legs and backing up to the block. Gordon Allport, who was present at the showing, later wrote that "to some American psychologists this ingenious film was decisive in forcing a revision of their own theories of the nature of intellectual behavior and of learning" (Allport, 1968, p. 368).

Lewin was soon invited to publish in the United States. Indeed, the conceptual formula that would be a key to his later success—that behavior is a function of both the person and the environment, or $B = f(P, E)$—first appeared in a chapter he wrote for an American handbook of child psychology in 1931 (K. Lewin, 1931b; cf. K. Lewin, 1935a, p. 75). In the same year, Lewis Terman invited him to accept a visiting professorship at Stanford University. Although Terman cautiously inquired with Edwin Boring at Harvard University whether Lewin was Jewish, Boring's positive answer did not deter him; he reported later that he was very satisfied with his guest's work and his "genial and friendly" manner (cited in Sokal, 1984, p. 1250). Thus, Lewin overcame anti-Semitism and other obstacles with his winning personality and the potential social policy relevance of his ideas. His work had already attracted the attention of the Rockefeller Foundation. Lawrence K. Frank, who helped establish a well-funded research program in child development under the auspices of the Laura Spelman Rockefeller Memorial (LSRM) in 1925 (Samelson, 1985), met Lewin on a trip to Berlin in 1928 (Frank, 1966). This foundation contact proved decisive for Lewin's later career.

As early as May 1933, Lewin received an offer of a research fellowship at Cornell University, funded by the Emergency Committee in Aid of Displaced Foreign Scholars and the Rockefeller Foundation and arranged by

Robert M. Ogden, who had been instrumental in bringing Gestalt psychologist Kurt Koffka to the United States 10 years earlier (Henle, 1984). This he accepted even though he was formally exempted as a decorated World War I veteran from the Nazi civil service law, which mandated the removal of Jewish and socialist state officials. Köhler, his nominal superior in Berlin, wanted to keep him on (Ash, 1985a); but even then he recognized the dangers for Jews who stayed in Germany. As he wrote to Köhler in May 1933, "The actual deprivation of Jews' rights has not decreased, but is extended daily and will doubtless be carried through to the end in the schematically thorough manner of the Germans, whether in the current quiet manner or in further waves" (K. Lewin, 1986, p. 44, translation altered slightly).

For two years, Lewin worked on children's eating habits and other topics at the School of Home Economics at Cornell until he was offered a position at the Iowa Child Welfare Research Station (ICWRS) in 1935. There he remained until 1944, when he became founder and director of the Research Center for Group Dynamics at Massachusetts Institute of Technology (MIT). The Cornell and Iowa positions have been seen as evidence of discrimination against Lewin because they were not located in psychology departments (Coser, 1984; Mandler & Mandler, 1969). However, the writers in question fail to note that these institutions were generously funded by the Rockefeller Foundation's research program in child development. They thus offered Lewin far better funding, contact with socially relevant research issues, access to facilities such as laboratory schools, and support from doctoral students and co-workers than he might have had at many university departments.

Indeed, Lawrence Frank helped to arrange these positions with just that thought in mind. In January 1935, he organized a small conference on the topic "Personality Development in Terms of Gestalt Psychology" at Princeton University. Among those present were Lewin, Köhler, Koffka, and Wertheimer as well as American psychologists such as Gordon Allport, Gardner and Lois Murphy, Barbara Burks, Norman Maier, and George Stoddard, head of the ICWRS. According to Frank's conference notes, a debate occurred between Lewin and the founders of Gestalt theory, which cannot be discussed here. However, Lewin clearly made a strong impression on Stoddard; only one month later, Frank wrote to Ogden that Stoddard wanted to invite Lewin to Iowa for one year and commented as follows:

> I think it would be a very desirable arrangement, since the Iowa station could provide Lewin with exceptional facilities, equipment and personnel and a body of graduate students. I personally hope that he can stay in this country longer because of the value of his work for child research. (Frank, 1935)

Clearly, Frank still identified Lewin as a child psychologist. The remarks about keeping Lewin in the United States referred to an offer from the Hebrew University in Jerusalem that had been made the previous year. A convinced Zionist, Lewin was attracted by the offer, but research facilities were lacking there (K. Lewin, 1935b). As Lewin tried to raise funds to finance a laboratory, Stoddard countered by applying to Frank for a second year of funding in Iowa as well as for stipends for his assistant, Tamara Dembo, and for additional assistantships.

WORKING CONDITIONS IN IOWA

The institutional situation Lewin encountered in Iowa was in many respects well suited both for his style of working and for his research aims. The ICWRS was created by the Iowa state legislature in 1917 with an initial appropriation of $25,000. Its official task was to investigate and ensure the development of normal children as well as to publish research results and train researchers in the field (Stoddard, 1938). The restriction to normal children suggests an attempt to avoid conflicts with physicians, especially psychiatrists and directors of state and private institutions for the mentally handicapped. Equally important was that the ICWRS received the right to publish its results and to train doctoral students independently of the university's psychology department. The extended versions of the Lewin group's research subsequently appeared in the ICWRS's series, *University of Iowa Studies in Child Welfare*. Although Psychology Department head and Graduate College dean Carl Seashore had initially opposed the project, he soon gave the ICWRS a prominent position in his efforts to make Iowa one of the nation's leading public research universities by combining graduate teaching, advanced research, and social service (Persons, 1990).

In the 1920s and 1930s, the ICWRS became nationally known through the work of its first director, Bird T. Baldwin, and his staff on the physical development of children as determined by anthropometric measurements. At least as significant was research under Baldwin's successor, George Stoddard, by his co-workers Beth Wellman, Harold Skeels, Ruth Updegraff, and others on the impact of altered environmental conditions on the intelligence test results of supposedly handicapped children (e.g., Wellman, 1933–1934; Skeels, Updegraff, Wellman, & Williams, 1938). Their claim that removing such children from orphanages and giving them more direct attention in special institutions improved their IQ scores by more than 20 points led to considerable academic and public controversy (Minton, 1984; for the broader cultural context, see Cravens, 1978).

The ICWRS's researchers took neither a hereditarian nor a rigidly environmentalist position but rather an interactionist position on the heritability of intelligence; but Stoddard emphasized the possibility of improving children's development by altering their living conditions at every opportunity. In a 1938 report, for example, he wrote that the ICWRS was primarily oriented to basic research independent of the immediate needs of state institutions but that applied research was by no means excluded: "For the purpose of implementing various procedures believed to be helpful in child development, we undertake projects that are engineering in type" (Stoddard, 1938, 17 f.). With these words, he expressed a commitment to an ideology of social change using basic research that had long been propounded by the progressive movement. The conscious separation of basic research from the immediate needs of welfare institutions served not to protect the purity of basic research but to legitimate its application under the rubric of "objective" science.

As an embodiment of such ideals, the ICWRS began receiving generous funding from the LSRM in 1928 and from the General Education Boards of the Rockefeller Foundation in 1930: on average, $90,000 per year. This amount was two to three times more than it received from the state and far more than comparable European institutes could dream of receiving. (These and the following figures were obtained from ICWRS records, Special Collections and University Archives, University of Iowa.) However, the annual amount was reduced from $75,000 to $39,000 in 1935, the year Lewin came to Iowa. Thus, recruiting Lewin and two assistants with funds from other Rockefeller programs could be seen as one of several efforts by Stoddard to make up for the planned cuts.

Over time, however, it appears that the relationship between Lewin and Stoddard developed beyond one of short-term mutual usefulness. When Lewin's Rockefeller funding expired in 1939 and Harvard University appeared to be recruiting him with the offer of a visiting professorship, Stoddard, who had in the meantime succeeded Seashore as dean of the Graduate College, replied by appointing Lewin to the permanent staff of the ICWRS with the rank of full professor and arranging fellowships for Tamara Dembo and two additional co-workers: "For we want you here" (Stoddard, 1939). This came at a time when university President Eugene A. Gilmore saw the need to reply to an attack on "Jews from the East at the University" published in the *Mason City Gazette*, a regional newspaper (Gilmore, 1939). Thus, even though anti-Semitism was a fact of life in Iowa as elsewhere, every effort was made to retain Lewin at the university.

THE LEWIN GROUP IN IOWA: RECONSTRUCTION OF A MICROCULTURE?

Did Lewin manage to establish a replica of his Berlin research group and thus something like a scientific microculture in Iowa? When Lewin corresponded with Stoddard about coming to Iowa, he inquired whether he could or should bring with him the films and photographic and projection equipment that he had managed to assemble in Berlin and had used at Cornell University in his studies of children's eating habits. Stoddard assured him that the ICWRS was well equipped for film studies, and indeed Lewin was able to use film techniques to impressive effect in his studies of authoritarian and democratic play groups, which are discussed in more detail later. Still more important for the question of continuity and change in Lewin's research style is the aspect of that style symbolized by the term *the chatter line (die Quasselstrippe)*. This designated the constantly changing discussion group that met regularly in the Schwedensche Café directly opposite the Berlin Psychological Institute to talk intensively about all sorts of daily and scientific problems. As one of the first students in this group, Anitra Karsten, reported in an interview, working with Lewin in Berlin was "one long discussion" (Karsten, 1978; cf. Karsten, 1979). The fact that the joking term *Quasselstrippe* constantly reappears in the reminiscences of Lewin's American students already indicates that at least an effort was made to reconstruct or continue this mode of brainstorming in America.

Tamara Dembo summarizes the special quality of this style:

> The intense scientific involvement of Lewin and his followers in the beauty of the subject matter typically overrode personal competitive feelings.... The founder and his followers were on [an] equal footing during their scientific discussions. Lewin was not the domineering "founder" in the sense of a "leader," but Kurt, who always had excellent ideas, and readily accepted ideas from coworkers. (Dembo, 1986, p. 4)

Other co-workers reported less idealistically that it was sometimes their task to record the results of conversations with Lewin, which he would then correct or reformulate (Patnoe, 1988, p. 16). Clearly there was no doubt who was the most important person in this otherwise democratically led group. As Roger Barker (1979, p. 2145) put it, "Lewin established the program of the setting ... but the details of the procedure were worked out in group consultation, where he was first among equals." It should also be noted that Lewin worked with women at Cornell University and at the State University of Iowa as he had in Berlin. However, they were not so much in the majority as they had been before; Lewin even wrote to Frank in connection with a second assistant's position alongside Tamara Dembo that he would prefer to have a man (K. Lewin, 1934).

Nonetheless, Lewin was clearly open to the ideas of other group members especially in the Iowa years. Dorwin Cartwright even suggests that the idea of experimenting with authoritarian and democratic groups came from conversations Lewin had with Ronald Lippitt in Iowa in 1936. According to Cartwright, when Lippitt enrolled at the ICWRS he did not know of

Lewin's presence. They soon met and Lewin learned that Lippitt had had experience with groups during his earlier studies in social work. As Cartwright recalls,

> Lippitt started talking about how kids and teachers interacted and so on, and out of this they cooked up the idea of doing some kind of experiment in which kids would be led in different ways. One way was essentially the German autocrat and the other was American democrat. I think that is about as sophisticated as it started out to be. (cited in Patnoe, 1988, p. 30)

Only later, after further interactions between Lewin, Lippitt, and Robert White, did the idea of setting up a so-called laissez-faire group emerge, one with practically no leadership (K. Lewin, Lippitt, & White, 1939). In Cartwright's view, "the impact of Lippitt cannot be overemphasized. His role was very important. Lippitt had a tremendous influence on Lewin to get him interested in groups specifically" (Patnoe, 1988, p. 31).

Already in 1931 Lewin recognized the significance of the social atmosphere of a school while comparing Montessori with more conventional methods in education (K. Lewin, 1931/1982). In the same year, he emphasized the importance of what he called "systems of ideology," or shared social values, in parent–child or teacher–child relationships for the psychology of reward and punishment (K. Lewin, 1931/1935c, p. 127). As Danziger (1990) shows, the experimental style of the Berlin group was characterized from the beginning by attention to the interaction of experimenter and subject as well as the principle that the psychological experiment should attempt to capture the dynamics of real-life situations. Before 1933, however, the preferred social unit in Lewinian experiments was usually a dyad, a group consisting of two rather than more people. Only in Iowa did Lewin begin to work experimentally with larger groups as units. Thus, it appears that a fundamental change in at least one significant aspect of Lewin's research style was a result of his emigration.

This statement requires two qualifications. First, another central aspect of Lewinian research—the emergence of theory and research ideas from a "continuous discussion" with co-workers discussed previously here—appears to have persisted quite continuously from the Berlin years. Second, the Lewin group was only one small section alongside other generally larger departments in the ICWRS. Dorwin Cartwright reported that the Lewin group members occasionally felt somewhat isolated (Patnoe, 1988). Thus, although the Iowa researchers were certainly willing to cite Lewinian work that was relevant to their own, such as the Berlin studies by Sara Fajans (1933) on reactions of small children to success and failure (cf. Keister, 1943; Updegraff, Keister, & Heiliger, 1937), the particular research style of the Lewin group appears to have had little impact on that of the other groups at the ICWRS.

LEWINIAN THEORY AND RESEARCH IN IOWA

This research activity and Lewin's increasingly rapid shift to applied social psychology went hand in hand with significant changes in his thinking. Lewin's topological psychology appeared during the Iowa years, in 1936, but he himself described the book as the result of "a very long gestation period" (K. Lewin, 1936, p. vii). Discussed here instead are three other themes around which the Lewin group's research work centered in Iowa: national cultural and educational differences, which of course was closely connected with the work on groups already mentioned; frustration and regression, a topic developed from Berlin research on action and emotion but which saw certain important methodological changes in Iowa; and the psychosocial problems of minorities, Lewin's first explicitly social psychological work. (For a list of Iowa studies, see Marrow, 1969, pp. 262–266.)

In 1936—precisely the time of his talk with Ronald Lippitt—Lewin addressed for the first time the topic of national cultural differences in education in an essay entitled "Some Psycho-Sociological Differences Between the United States and Germany" (reprinted in K. Lewin, 1948). The biographical reasons for taking up this topic seem obvious. It was only three years after his emigration, and his children were entering school. However, his engagement in a research center for child study in which the other workers were continually concerned with educational issues clearly played its part as well.

The theoretical approach, however, characterized as stated previously by the flexible use of analogies from the natural sciences, was one Lewin had already developed in Berlin. In this case, he attempted, with the aid of an analogy from perceptual research, to present the "general cultural atmosphere" of a country as a ground against which the characteristic educational styles appear as figures. From this perspective, he saw "the range of free movement," analogous to the physical concept of degrees of freedom, as "the fundamental characteristic" of educational systems (K. Lewin, 1948, pp. 4, 6). Such considerations made it possible for him to recognize hierarchical differentiation even in the so-called democratic educational style of the United States and also to note how much American teachers depended on prescribed lesson plans and teaching techniques. Paradoxically, according to Lewin, just such structures made it possible to prepare American children for independent action in a heterogeneous social system, whereas rigidity and obedience were demanded in Germany's more homogeneous social system.

From these and similar ideas—and, as mentioned, from conversations with Ronald Lippitt—came the studies of democratic and authoritarian groups that finally established Lewin's reputation in America (K. Lewin et al., 1939). As reported in a preliminary note, the methodological aim was to get away from studying group–individual relationships and construct experimental situations "where group life can proceed freely" to consider "the total group behavior, its structure and development" (K. Lewin & Lippitt, 1938, p. 292). This is reminiscent of the distinction Lewin made before his emigration between Aristotelian and Galilean modes of thought and research in psychology mentioned previously here.

From Lewin's metatheoretical perspective, the aim was to transfer the method he had called Galilean from the study of person–environment interactions to group behavior using what he called the "transposition" principle, borrowing a term from Gestalt theory (K. Lewin, 1939, pp. 889–890). The implicit assumption was that in both kinds of subject matter a procedure that retained the essential structural relations of everyday life situations would yield a more believable experimental picture than the manipulation of isolated independent and dependent variables. Thus, a dimension of continuity is evident. However, the contemporary ideological resonances of this work and of the categories chosen could hardly be overlooked even though Lewin denied that these ideal types were intended to correspond to any historical reality. Indeed, George Stoddard (1981, p. 45) later wrote that "the authoritarian classroom resembled many an American classroom in the United States, teacher centered, disciplined and efficient."

It was in vocabulary and in research practice that farther reaching changes were noticeable. Already in their initial report, K. Lewin and Lippitt (1938) used a vocabulary that was only then becoming fashionable in America by speaking of "operational" definitions of the behavioral styles to be investigated. In the authoritarian group, not only the task—making theatrical masks—but its execution was defined by the leader at every stage one step at a time; the leader remained aloof from the group, intervening only to criticize. In the democratic group, the leader acted as a member of the group, facilitating decisions on how and with what materials to proceed; he or she provided technical advice but only when asked and only in the form of alternatives from which the group chose. (For a more complete listing of group characteristics including those of the so-called laissez-faire group studied later, see Lippitt & White, 1943, p. 487.)

In addition, Lewin and Lippitt used both quantitative and qualitative data from the beginning. Complete running records of the groups' activities were analyzed quantitatively, for example, for the level of hostility and scapegoating (30 times higher in the authoritarian group) or cooperation (higher in the democratic group). They were also examined qualitatively for observations of tension level and egocentric behavior (higher in the authoritarian group) or "we-ness" (higher in the democratic group). In Berlin too, Lewin group researchers combined qualitative and quantitative observations. Nonetheless, in the specific combination of the two, one can see here the beginnings of a change in the Lewin group's procedure resulting at least in part from collaboration with Americans.

The studies of frustration and regression (summarized in Barker, Dembo, & Lewin, 1943) continued the Berlin research program in the field of action and emotion and combined it with developmental issues. In her monograph on anger as a dynamic problem. Dembo (1931/1976) mentioned flight into childish fantasies as one possible response to frustrating situations in adults. Lewin himself raised the issue at least indirectly in his writings on children's behavior, for example, when he described how small children in hopeless conflict situations try to become still "smaller" and roll themselves up into fetus-like balls (K. Lewin, 1935a, p. 94). The concept of regression itself was familiar to Lewin from his reading of Freud and Adler before 1933.

However, when the Lewin group in Iowa began to investigate the topic systematically, the change in both physical location and culture of experimentation became noticeable. Thus, the test speaks not of the psychology of action and emotion but of behavior theory. More important still than such terminological adaptations was the instrument used as a sort of diagnostic ruler to establish and measure regression. In this, the impact of Lewin's assistant Roger Barker, who had learned the use of intelligence testing and related measurement techniques at Stanford University (Barker, 1979), was evident. A two-dimensional coordinate system was constructed in which the children's mental ages were correlated with the results of a seven-point constructivity scale that had been created for this study. The scale consisted of ratings of observed play units according to their richness and originality. If the constructiveness ratings for play in test situations were not as high as those for children of the same mental age in free play, then one spoke of regression (Barker et al., 1943, pp. 452–453).

Contrary to widespread beliefs, Lewin's Berlin group had no allergies to quantitative inference. In Zeigarnik's (1927) classic study of the retention of uncompleted tasks, for example, the existence of the effect named after her was shown quantitatively. However, in the frustration and regression studies, just the sort of statistical inference Lewin criticized as "Aristotelian" only a few years before became the chief support for the reliability and validity of the results. Important as it was, however, the quantitative argument was confined to a single section of the study. This was framed by other sections giving a carefully developed phenomenology of the behavior to be measured supported by "topological" sketches. Thus, it could be contended that the statistical inference occurred within the framework of a basically Galilean method. In any case, it appears clear that in this study, not only in the general research style but also in the methods and even in the argumentation, a complex melding of scientific cultures developed in Germany and in the United States had taken place.

However, the earliest indication of changes in Lewin's thinking after his emigration came in his work on the psychosocial problems of minority groups. In a 1935 article entitled "Socio-Psychological Problems of a Minority Group," Lewin extended the concept of the "life space," which he already used to describe the field of individual–environment interaction, to include other people under the rubric "social space." This was also the first of his publications expressly designated as a work of social psychology. His example was the situation of the Jewish population. Using a metaphor from cellular biology, he described the situation of a minority as depending on the relative permeability of the boundary between in- and out-groups. For ghetto Jews before nominal emancipation, he suggested, rigid social boundaries were confining, but strong "we-feelings" provided compensation. For the emancipated and assimilating Jewish people of the 19th and 20th centuries, alternatively, it was difficult to develop a feeling of belongingness to either group. At that time, Lewin still saw Zionism as the solution to this dilemma; when he wrote this article he was considering the offer from the Hebrew University in Jerusalem, as has already been mentioned.

By 1939, in view of the approaching war and the increasing persecution of "half" and "quarter" Jews and of members of his own family in Nazi Germany, Lewin analyzed the issue for the first time from a societal rather than an individual standpoint. In an essay indicatively entitled "When Facing Danger," he wrote: "The Jewish problem is a social problem" (K. Lewin, 1948, p. 162). In a series of popular essays in the 1940s with titles like "Bringing Up the Jewish Child" (reprinted in K. Lewin, 1948, pp. 169–185), he proposed to strengthen the "we-feeling" of American Jews through more active Jewish—although not necessarily religious—education. Lewin could only believe that such proposals would not weaken the bonds of Jews to American society because he had already decided that democratic education in the United States was education for a heterogeneous society.

From all this, it appears clear that reflection on his situation as a German Jew in exile was an important basis for a significant change both in Lewin's theorizing and in his research practices. Carl-Friedrich Graumann (1982) claims that Lewin's turn to social psychology was a logical consequence of his work before 1933. Lewin's early article on "The Socialization of the Taylor System" (K. Lewin, 1920) supports this view. However, the preceding account helps us to understand how and perhaps also why a development that may have been inherent in Lewin's approach took on the dimensions and led in the research directions that it did when it did.

CONCLUSIONS

Nearly alone among the leading émigré psychologists, Kurt Lewin succeeded in creating both a successful career for himself and a "school" of followers in America through his skillful use of the growing network of private, semiprivate, and public funding agencies that formed the infrastructure of psychology's transition from an academic discipline to a science-based profession. His field-theoretical ideas on the problems of minority groups played an important part in the shift in American social psychology "from 'race psychology' to 'studies in prejudice'" (Samelson, 1978, p. 265). Already at Cornell University, Lewin began to organize the "topology group," the first of several alternative discussion groups outside the established psychological organizations to develop and propagate his ideas. Most prominent of these was the Society for the Psychological Study of Social Issues, which Lewin helped found and of which he served as president in 1941. This group united the liberal grouping in the APA, which sought to expand psychological research beyond academic borders.

Quickly Lewin expanded his research activities to national venues. Beginning with the research on authoritarian versus democratic leadership in Iowa and work on conflict resolution in a factory in New York in the late 1930s, he proceeded to morale research for the military in World War II, to community research work for the American Jewish Committee, and finally to the founding of the Research Center for Group Dynamics at MIT in 1944 (for a detailed account, see Marrow, 1969). Like the Gestalt psychologists, Lewin was sharply attacked by proponents of operationalist and neobehaviorist learning theory. Indeed, he experienced tension and conflict in Iowa after the appointment of neobehaviorist Kenneth Spence as chair in 1942, and his growing collaboration with logical positivist Gustav Bergmann, whom Lewin himself had brought to Iowa in 1939 (Kendler, 1989). However, because he had built up a network of institutional as well as financial support and a loyal following of younger researchers, he could react calmly, even in an outwardly friendly way, to such attacks. In a 1944 letter, for example, Lewin proposed to join with his erstwhile opponents in a section for theoretical psychology in the then reorganizing APA and assured neobehaviorists Clark Hull and Edward Tolman that "I am really against schools" (K. Lewin, 1944).

In achieving all this, he built on the interaction of his Berlin work and the techniques contributed by his American co-workers in Iowa. He quickly transferred the model of theory and experimentation first developed for the study of children's play groups to studies of leadership and conflict resolution in adults, for example, in factories and offices. The most interesting aspect of this work in this context is the optimism that Lewin expressed in this and later studies with Alex Bavelas on "Training in Democratic Leadership" (Bavelas & Lewin, 1942). The idea that it is possible not only to select people for democratic leadership by their behavior or personality characteristics, however determined, but to make such leaders even out of people who had not already been recognized as such fit well into the progressivist conception and aims of the ICWRS.

Lewin's pedagogical optimism and his obvious support for democratic education and leadership style fit well indeed with the thinking at least of the liberal, socially activist wing of American psychology at the time. This is true as well for his interest in the involvement of psychologists in conflict resolution at the workplace. Recently historians have argued that Lewin's approach is best described as technocratic rather than as truly democratic; for in that model the experimenter and not the subjects decide what situations to investigate and how, just as managers and not workers determine the organization of production (Graebner, 1986, 1987; van Elteren, 1990b; for replies to Graebner, see Lippitt, 1986; M. Lewin, 1987). Van Elteren (1990a) makes the additional claim that after his emigration Lewin deemphasized the societal dimension in his social psychological writings or reduced them to individual behavior.

The problem with such criticisms is that it is not good historical method to judge past approaches by present standards of participatory democracy. Instead, it would be appropriate to ask whether contemporary participants in these debates made similar claims and to consider as well whether Lewin's position in the context of the bitter battle then underway to ensure union representation for industrial workers was a practically minded effort to mediate between antagonistic forces. The criticisms say less about Lewin's attitudes than they do about a fundamental ambivalence in American society: the combined allegiance to democracy and technological efficiency. In this context, and with a view to the political position Lewin adopted in Germany, perhaps it would be most accurate to call his position in America a liberal technocratic one.

When Lewin died suddenly in 1947 at the age of 57, he was at the height of his career and influence. However, as many writers point out, Lewin's field theory is neither a social psychology nor a theory of personality but rather a metatheory. Such a comprehensive viewpoint did not fit in with the splintering of American psychology in the postwar years into competing specialties. Little more than a decade after Lewin's death, his student Dorwin Cartwright (1959) spoke of a division of labor in which the Hull-Spence learning theory dominated research on behavior that can be subjected to statistical scaling, whereas Lewin's approach and various Americanized variants of psychoanalysis became dominant in the fields in which concepts and methods were necessarily less precise to be effective, such as social psychology and personality research. In the process, Lewin's attempt to develop a mathematical foundation for his own approach with the help of topology was ignored. Thus, some of Lewin's ideas and a changed version of his methods found places in the disciplinary structure of American psychology; but as in the case of Gestalt theory, that integration was ambivalent (on the reception of Gestalt psychology, see Ash, 1985b; Sokal, 1984).

A parallel analysis appears to hold even for work by Lewin's students in experimental social psychology. According to a recent study by Danziger (in press), the philosophy of science on the basis of which Lewin constructed and justified his work in Iowa was either ignored or met with complete incomprehension. His experiments with groups were admired as effective manipulations, and Lewin himself was elevated to iconic status as the founder of experimental social psychology. However, some of his most prominent students rejected his model of procedure; instead, they reconstructed what they took to be Lewinian research on the basis of by-then standard American experimental methodology, which prescribed the parceling out of independent and dependent variables and thus presupposed the very elementarism he criticized (for examples, see Festinger, Back, Schachter, Kelley, & Thibaut, 1950). Other students and former coworkers, however, tried to continue the research style that had evolved in Iowa and thus contributed to the development of ecological psychology (Barker, 1968; Barker & Wright, 1955).

Kurt Lewin not only adapted to the intellectual and institutional situation of American psychology in the 1930s and 1940s, he helped to shape that situation. However, the sequel to that success story is indicative of the complex interaction between his biographical processing of the emigration experience and the selection his erstwhile hosts made from the results of that process. Nonetheless, it is fair to say that the working conditions and the institutional commitments of the ICWRS gave Lewin what George Stoddard (1936) called his "big chance," an opportunity that he clearly grasped to show how he could combine basic and applied or applications-oriented basic research to answer some of the burning questions of the day.

The case presented here could be located on a continuum from basic research with its changing institutional structures, themes, and styles to applied or applications-oriented basic research to professional and especially clinical practice. Gestalt psychology would thus exemplify the reception of émigrés' thinking in basic research, although theirs is clearly not the whole story. Lewinian field theory would represent the section of the continuum from basic to applied research. In no case, however, is it possible to fully separate internal and external histories or pure from applied research, because societal demands for specific kinds of psychological discourse and practices feed back on basic research in complex ways. Such interactions are not limited to psychology or even to social science. Cases in which émigré German-speaking scientists were deeply involved include the rise of "big science" in physics and the interweaving of scientific, technological, economic, and military priorities in the postwar development of computer science and technology (see, e.g., Forman, 1987; Heims, 1981; Kevles, 1977). The kind of analysis presented here will help illuminate the role of émigrés and the issues of science and technology transfer in these fields as well.

REFERENCES

Allport, G. (1968). The genius of Kurt Lewin. In G. Allport (Ed.), *The person in psychology: Selected essays* (pp. 360–370). Boston: Beacon Press.

Ash, M. G. (1985a). Ein Institut und eine Zeitschrift. Zur Geschichte des Berliner Psychologischen Instituts und der Zeitschrift 'Psychologische Forschung' vor und nach 1933 [An institute and a journal: On the history of the Berlin Psychological Institute and the journal *Psychological Research* before and after 1933]. In C.-F. Graumann (Ed.), *Psychologie im Nationalsozialismus* (pp. 113–138). West Berlin, Federal Republic of Germany, Springer-Verlag.

Ash, M. G. (1985b). Gestalt psychology: Origins in Germany and reception in the United States. In C. Buxton (Ed.), *Points of view in the modern history of psychology* (pp. 295–344). San Diego, CA: Academic Press.

Ash, M. G. (1990). Psychology in twentieth-century Germany: Science and profession. In G. Cocks & K. Jarausch (Eds.), *German professions 1800–1950* (pp. 289–307). New York: Oxford University Press.

Barker, R. G. (1968). *Ecological psychology: Concepts and methods for studying the environment of human behavior*: Stanford, CA: Stanford University Press.

Barker, R. G. (1979). Settings of a professional lifetime. *Journal of Personality and Social Psychology, 37,* 2137–2157.

Barker, R. G., Dembo, T., & Lewin, K. (1943). Frustration and regression. In R. G. Barker, J. S. Kounin, & H. F. Wright (Eds.), *Child behavior and development: A course of representative studies* (pp. 441–458). New York: McGraw-Hill.

Barker, R. G., & Wright, H. F. (1955). *Midwest and its children.* New York: Harper & Row.

Bavelas, A., & Lewin, K. (1942). Training in democratic leadership. *Journal of Abnormal Psychology, 37,* 115–119.

Cartwright, D. (1959). Lewinian theory as a contemporary systematic framework. In S. Koch (Ed.), *Psychology: A study of a science, Vol. 4. General Systematic formulations* (pp. 7–91). New York: McGraw-Hill.

Coser, L. A. (1984). *Refugee scholars in America: Their impact and their experiences.* New Haven, CT: Yale University Press.

Cravens, H. (1978). *The triumph of evolution: American scientists and the heredity–environment controversy, 1900–1941.* Philadelphia: University of Pennsylvania Press.

Danziger, K. (1987). Social context and research practice in early twentieth-century psychology. In M. G. Ash & W. R. Woodward (Eds.), *Psychology in twentieth-century thought and society* (pp. 13–34). New York: Cambridge University Press.

Danziger, K. (1990). *Constructing the subject: Historical origins of psychological research.* New York: Cambridge University Press.

Danziger, K. (in press). The project of an experimental social psychology: Historical perspectives. *Science in Context.*

Dembo, T. (1976). The dynamics of anger (H. Korsch, Trans.). In J. De Rivera

(Compiler), *Field theory as human science: Contributions of Lewin's Berlin group* (pp. 324–422). New York: Gardner Press. (Original work published 1931)

Dembo, T. (1986). Approach as a description of the nature of scientific activity: Some reflections and suggestions. In E. Stivers & S. Wheelan (Eds.), *The Lewin legacy: Field theory in current practice* (pp. 3–11). West Berlin, Federal Republic of Germany: Springer-Verlag.

De Rivera, J. (Ed.). (1976). *Field theory as human science: Contributions of Lewin's Berlin group.* New York: Gardner Press.

Fajans, S. (1933). Erfolg, Ausdauer und Aktivität beim Säugling und beim Kleinkind [Success, perseverance, and activity in babies and small children]. *Psychologische Forschung, 17,* 268–305.

Festinger, L., Back, K., Schachter, S., Kelley, H. H., & Thibaut, J. (1950). *Theory and experiment in social communication.* Ann Arbor: University of Michigan, Research Center for Group Dynamics.

Forman, P. (1987). Behind quantum electronics: National security as basis for physical research in the United States, 1940–1960. *Historical Studies in the Physical and Biological Sciences, 18,* 149–229.

Frank, L. K. (1935, February 4). *Letter to Robert M. Ogden.* In Rockefeller Archive Center (GEB Series 1.3, Box 371, Folder 3877), North Tarrytown, NY.

Frank, L. K. (1966). [Kurt Lewin]. Unpublished statement. In Lawrence K. Frank papers, National Library of Medicine, Bethesda, MD.

Geertz, C. (1985). *Local knowledge: Further essays in interpretive anthropology.* New York: Basic Books.

Geiger, R. (1986). *To advance knowledge: The growth of American research universities, 1900–1940.* New York: Oxford University Press.

Gilmore, E. A. (1939, May 15). *Letter to W. Earl Hall.* In President's papers, Special Collections and University Archives, University of Iowa, Iowa City.

Graebner, W. (1986). The small group and democratic social engineering, 1900–1950. *Journal of Social Issues, 42*(1), 137–154.

Graebner, W. (1987). Confronting the democratic paradox: The ambivalent vision of Kurt Lewin. *Journal of Social Issues, 43*(3), 141–146.

Graumann, C.-F. (1982). Zur Einführung in diesen Band [Introduction to this volume]. In C.-F. Graumann (Ed.), *Kurt-Lewin-Werkausgabe, Bnd. 4. Feldtheorie* (pp. 11–37). Bern, Switzerland: Huber & Stuttgart, Federal Republic of Germany: Klett.

Harwood, J. (1987). National styles in science: Genetics in Germany and the United States between the world wars. *Isis, 78,* 390–414.

Heims, S. (1981). *John von Neumann and Norbert Wiener: From mathematics to the technologies of life and death.* Cambridge, MA: MIT Press.

Henle, M. (1984). Robert M. Ogden and Gestalt psychology in America. *Journal of the History of the Behavioral Sciences, 20,* 9–19.

Hull, C. L. (1934, March 3). *Letter to W. A. Weaver.* In Rockefeller Archive Center (RG 3, Series 915, Box 4, Folder 37), North Tarrytown, NY.

Hull, C. L. (1937). Mind, mechanism and adaptive behavior. *Psychological Review*, 44, 1-32.

Karsten, A. (1976). Mental satiation. In J. De Rivera (Compiler), *Field theory as human science: Contributions of Lewin's Berlin group* (pp. 151-207). New York: Gardner Press. (Original work published 1928)

Karsten, A. (1978, February 22). [Interview with M. G. Ash, Frankfurt am Main].

Karsten, A. (1979). Anitra Karsten. In L. Pongratz, W. Traxel, & E. Wehner (Eds.), *Psychologie in Selbstdarstellungen* [Psychology in Autobiographies] (Vol. 2, pp. 77-109). Bern, Switzerland: Huber.

Keister, M. E. (1943). The behavior of young children in failure. In R. G. Barker, J. S. Kounin, & H. F. Wright (Eds.), *Child behavior and development: A course of representative studies* (pp. 429-440). New York: McGraw-Hill.

Kendler, H. H. (1989). The Iowa tradition. *American Psychologist*, 44, 1124-1132.

Kevles, D. (1978). *The physicists: The history of a scientific community in modern America*. New York: Knopf.

Kohler, R. E. (1991). *Partners in science: Foundation and natural scientists, 1900-1945*. Chicago: University of Chicago Press.

Lewin, K. (1920). *Die Sozialisierung des Taylorsystems. Eine grund-sätzliche Untersuchung zur Arbeits- und Berufs-Psychologie* (Praktischer Sozialismus, Heft 4) [The socialization of the Taylor System: A fundamental investigation in industrial and occupational psychology (Practical socialism, Pt. 4)]. Berlin-Fichtenau: Verlag Gesellschaft und Erziehung.

Lewin, K. (1928). Die Bedeutung der 'psychischen Sättigung' fur einige Probleme der Psychotechnik [The significance of "mental satiation" for some problems in psychotechnics]. *Psychotechnische Zeitschrift*, 3, 182-188.

Lewin, K. (1930). Die Auswirkung von Umweltkräften [The impact of environmental forces]. In *9th International Congress of Psychology: Proceedings and papers* (pp. 286-288). Princeton, NJ: The Psychological Review Company.

Lewin, K. (1931a). The conflict between Aristotelian and Galileian modes of thought in contemporary psychology. *Journal of General Psychology*, 5, 141-177.

Lewin, K. (1931b). Environmental forces in child behavior and development. In C. Murchison (Ed.), *Handbook of child psychology* (pp. 94-127). Worcester, MA: Clark University Press.

Lewin, K. (1934, September 25). *Letter to L. K. Frank*. In Rockefeller Archive Center (GEB Series 1.3, Box 371, Folder 3877), North Tarrytown, NY.

Lewin, K. (1935a). *A dynamic theory of personality* (D. K. Adams, Trans.). New York: McGraw-Hill.

Lewin, K. (1935b, April 13). *Letter to R. A. Lambert*. In Rockefeller Archive Center (RG 1.1, Series 200, Box 82, Folder 981), North Tarrytown, NY.

Lewin, K. (1935c). The psychological situation in reward and punishment. In K. Lewin (Ed.) & D. K. Adams (Trans.), *A dynamic theory of personality* (pp. 114-170). New York: McGraw-Hill. (Original work published 1931)

Lewin, K. (1936). *Principles of topological psychology*. New York: McGraw-Hill.

Lewin, K. (1939). Field theory and experiment in social psychology: Concepts and methods. *American Journal of Sociology, 44*, 868–896.

Lewin, K. (1944, March 13). *Letter to C. L. Hull and E. Tolman*. In Kenneth Spence papers (Box M937), Archives of the History of American Psychology, Akron, OH.

Lewin, K. (1948). *Resolving social conflicts: Selected papers on group dynamics*. New York: Harper & Row.

Lewin, K. (1981a). Erhaltung, Identität und Veränderung in Physik und Psychologie [Conservation, identity and change in physics and psychology]. In A. Métraux (Ed.), *Kurt-Lewin-Werkausgabe: Vol. 1. Wissenschaftstheorie I* (pp. 87–110). Bern, Switzerland: Huber & Stuttgart, Federal Republic of Germany: Klett.

Lewin, K. (1981b). Über Idee under Aufgabe einer vergleichenden Wissenschaftslehre [On the idea and the task of a comparative theory of science]. In A. Métraux (Ed.), *Kurt-Lewin-Werkausgabe: Vol. 1. Wissenschaftstheorie I* (pp. 49–80). Bern, Switzerland: Huber & Stuttgart, Federal Republic of Germany: Klett. (Original work published 1925)

Lewin, K. (1982). Sachlichkeit und Zwang in der Erziehung zur Realität [Objectivity and coercion in education for reality]. In F. E. Weinert & H. Gundlach (Eds.), *Kurt-Lewin-Werkausgabe: Vol. 6. Psychologie der Entwicklung und Erziehung* (pp. 215–224). Bern, Switzerland: Huber & Stuttgart, Federal Republic of Germany: Klett. (Original work published 1931)

Lewin, K. (1986). "Everything within me rebels." A letter to Wolfgang Köhler, 1933. *Journal of Social Issues, 42*(4), 39–47.

Lewin, K., & Lippitt, R. (1938). An experimental approach to the study of autocracy and democracy: A preliminary note. *Sociometry, 1*, 292–300.

Lewin, K., Lippitt, R., & White, R. K. (1939). Patterns of aggressive behavior in experimentally created 'social clmates.' *Journal of Social Psychology, 10*, 271–299.

Lewin, M. (1987). Kurt Lewin and the invisible bird on the flagpole: A reply to Graebner. *Journal of Social Issues, 43*(3), 123–139.

Lippitt, R. (1986). The small group and participatory democracy: Comment on Graebner. *Journal of Social Issues, 42*(1), 155–156.

Lippitt, R., & White, R. K. (1943). The "social climate" of children's groups. In R. G. Barker, J. S. Kounin, & H. F. Wright (Eds.), *Child behavior and development: A course of representative studies* (pp. 484–508). New York: McGraw-Hill.

Mandler, J. M., & Mandler, G. (1969). The diaspora of experimental psychology: The gestaltists and others. In D. Fleming & B. Bailyn (Eds.), *The intellectual migration: Europe and America, 1930–1960* (pp. 371–419). Cambridge, MA: Harvard University Press.

Marrow, A. J. (1969). *The practical theorist: The life and work of Kurt Lewin*. New York: Basic Books.

Minton, H. L. (1984). The Iowa Child Welfare Research Station and the 1940 debate on intelligence. *Journal of the History of the Behavioral Sciences, 20,* 160–176.

Morawski, J. G. (Ed.). (1988). *The rise of experimentation in American psychology:* New Haven, CT: Yale University Press.

Patnoe, S. (1988). *A narrative history of social psychology: The Lewin tradition.* Berlin: Springer-Verlag.

Persons, S. (1990). *The University of Iowa: An institutional history.* Iowa City: University of Iowa Press.

Samelson, F. (1978). From "race psychology" to "studies in prejudice": Observations on the thematic reversal in social psychology. *Journal of the History of the Behavioral Sciences, 14,* 265–278.

Samelson, F. (1985). Organizing for the kingdom of behavior: Academic battles and organizational policies in the twenties. *Journal of the History of the Behavioral sciences, 21,* 33–47.

Skeels, H. M., Updegraff, R., Wellman, B. L., & Williams, H. L. (1938). A study of environmental stimulation: An orphanage preschool project. *University of Iowa Studies in Child Welfare, 15*(4), 151–191.

Sokal, M. M. (1984). The Gestalt psychologists in behaviorist America. *American Historical Reviews, 89,* 1240–1263.

Stoddard, G. (1936, March 16). *Letter to E. A. Gilmore.* In ICWRS records, Special Collections and University Archives, University of Iowa, Iowa City, IA.

Stoddard, G. (1938). The second decade: A review of the activities of the Iowa Child Welfare Research Station, 1928–1938. *University of Iowa Studies in Child Welfare, 15,* 1–18.

Stoddard, G. (1939, May 4). *Letter to Kurt Lewin.* In ICWRS records, Special Collections and University Archives. University of Iowa, Iowa City, IA.

Stoddard, G. (1981). *The pursuit of education: An autobiography.* New York: Vantage Press.

Updegraff, R., Keister, M. E., & Heiliger, L. (1937). Studies in preschool education, I. *University of Iowa Studies in Child Welfare, 14*(1), 29–82.

van Elteren, M. (1990a). Die Sozialpsychologie Lewins, marxistische Soziologie und Geschichte [Lewin's social psychology, Marxist sociology and history]. *Psychologie und Geschichte, 2,* 1–18.

van Elteren, M. (1990b, September). *From emancipating to domesticating the workers: Lewinian social psychology and the study of the work process till 1947.* Paper presented at the 9th Annual Conference of Cheiron-Europe, Weimar, Germany.

Wellman, B. L. (1933–1934). Growth in intelligence under differing school environments. *Journal of Experimental Education, 3,* 59–83.

Zeigarnik, B. (1927). Über das Behalten erledigter und unerledigter Handlungen [On the retention of completed and uncompleted tasks]. *Psychologische Forschung, 9,* 1–85.

20

ON PUBLISHING CONTROVERSY: NORMAN R. F. MAIER AND THE GENESIS OF SEIZURES

DONALD A. DEWSBURY

Psychological journals are pressed for space as an increasing flow of submissions exerts pressure on editors both to limit the kinds of articles they publish and to be increasingly selective within those ranges. One issue of concern is the utility of publishing critical comments—exchanges of views concerning an experiment, approach, or theory without new data—within a journal otherwise limited to reports of empirical research. The controversy between Norman R. F. Maier and Clifford T. Morgan over the

---

Ludy T. Benjamin, Jr., served as action editor for this article.

Work on this problem was suggested to me by John A. Popplestone of the Archives of the History of American Psychology in Akron, Ohio. He discussed some aspects of this conflict in a paper at the New York Academy of Sciences, March 28, 1979.

I wish to express my appreciation to M. E. Bitterman, Jane Colburn, Frank Finger, Nathan Glaser, Mary Henle, Roger Heyns, Jane D. Hildreth, L. Richard Hoffman, James Klee, Marion White McPherson, Ayesha Maier, Richard Maier, Jean Morgan, Alfred Raphelson, Allen Solem, Eliot Stellar, Edward L. Walker, Seymour Wapner, Wilse B. Webb, and two anonymous reviewers for their correspondence, interviews, reading of drafts, and other help in the preparation of this article.

Reprinted from *American Psychologist*, 48, 869–877 (1993). Copyright © 1993 by the American Psychological Association. Reprinted with permission of the author.

genesis of seizures in rats provides a case study that suggests such articles can play an important role in the development of psychological science. Although rarely discussed today, Maier's research received extensive publicity in its day.

There has been much controversy about the utility of controversy in science (e.g., Vanderplas, 1966; Wenner & Wells, 1990). Many scientists believe that the facts will speak for themselves and that therefore controversy can be counterproductive. However, with increased appreciation of the role of extrascientific factors in shaping the discipline, there has been increased tolerance for such disagreements. Henle (1973) viewed them as playing a useful and necessary role in the development of the science. Ziman (1968) saw a well-fought controversy as a form of cooperation, analogous to two contesting barristers dedicated to the common cause of seeing justice done. Although Boring (1929) found the conclusion abhorrent, he too held that "scientific truth, like juristic truth, must come about by controversy" (p. 99).

The situation is complicated when one combatant works outside of the in-group or the prevailing paradigm of the discipline (see Bennett, 1968; Keller, 1983; Wenner & Wells, 1990). Both the creative innovator and the crackpot work at the fringes of the prevailing paradigm, and it often is difficult to distinguish one from the other in the early stages of development. The scientific establishment, therefore, must develop a commitment to scientific orthodoxy that makes it hostile to challenges to that orthodoxy. Limiting access to the publication outlets controlled by the scientific establishment is one way in which those who are part of a scientific in-group or who are working within the dominant perspective can help defend that perspective (see Bennett, 1968; Mahoney, 1976). The themes of the importance of publishing controversy and the reaction of the establishment to the outsider are intertwined in the Maier–Morgan story.

THE PHENOMENON

The research of Normal R. F. Maier and his associates followed in the tradition of Ivan Pavlov, Howard S. Liddell, and others in using animal models for the study of abnormal behavior in humans. The apparatus used was a Lashley Jumping Stand (Lashley, 1930). In this apparatus a rat is placed on a small stand facing two small windows, from which it is separated by a gap. It must jump from the stand toward one of the two windows, in each of which is a card. In a typical learning experiment, when a rat makes a correct choice, the card blocking the window falls over and the rat goes though the window to a food reward. The incorrect card, in the other window, is latched closed, so that if the rat jumps at the wrong card, the animal bumps its nose and falls into a net at the bottom of the apparatus. The choice designated as correct can be based on either location (left vs. right) or the pattern printed on the cards. Rats generally learn such discriminations readily. Under some conditions, however, rats resist jumping, preferring to remain on the small platform. Such resistance is overcome by introducing electric shock or a blast of air.

In the typical experiments in Maier's work, rats first were trained to jump to a card bearing a white circle on a black background and not to jump to a card bearing a black circle on a white background. After the discrimination was learned well, the conditions were changed in one of several ways so that the original solution no longer was appropriate and the problem became insoluble. Different procedures were used with different animals. According to Maier (1939), "The essential condition seems to be the necessity of reacting in a situation in which all ordinary modes of behavior have been removed" (p. 79).

Maier and his associates studied two major phenomena. One, which was their primary interest, was the fixation of response when rats were presented with two choices in insoluble problems. Often the rats became fixated on one response, generally a position habit, and it was difficult to change their behavior (see Maier, 1949). The other was the phenomenon of the convulsive seizures, the focus for the present discussion.

The convulsive seizures often occurred as the animal leapt from the apparatus. They were characterized by three stages, the first of which lasted approximately 20 seconds and entailed a bout of violent, undirected running. The second, or convulsive, phase, generally lasting from one to three minutes, involved clonic activity of the legs, biting, salivation, urination, defecation, and sometimes ejaculation. The third phase was one of passivity. Righting reflexes were absent, and the animal could be molded into almost any position. Heart rate could drop to 50% of normal.

From the beginning, Maier (1939) recognized that auditory stimulation was a factor in producing the seizures. Convulsive seizures did not occur when electric shock was used to break resistance; the air blast was required. Indeed, one rat convulsed in response to air blasts given outside of the training situation. Maier (1939) observed seizures in some rats tested outside of the training situation either by placing them on a shelf approximately eight feet from the air blast or by jingling keys. However, Maier pointed out that air blasts had been used when testing animals in difficult discrimination tasks for many years without the elicitation of convulsive seizures; seizures occurred primarily with insoluble problems. Thus, he concluded that "the essential condition seems to be the necessity of reacting in a situation in which all ordinary modes of behavior have been removed. In these experiments compressed air was used to furnish the necessity of reacting" (Maier, 1939, p. 79).

NORMAN R. F. MAIER

Norman R. F. Maier (1900–1977) received his BA degree from the University of Michigan in 1923. After a year of graduate work, he studied at the University of Berlin during 1925 and 1926 and completed his PhD at Michigan in 1928. He was a National Research Council Fellow with Karl Lashley at the University of Chicago 1929–1931 and joined the faculty at Michigan in 1931. The influences on Maier included John Shepard at Michigan; Wolfgang Köhler, Max Wertheimer, and Kurt Lewin in Berlin; and Lashley and Heinrich Kluver at Chicago (see Solem & McKeachie, 1979). Together with Theodore C. Schneirla, Maier authored the classic textbook, *Principles of Animal Psychology* (Maier & Schneirla, 1935). Maier was out of the then-prevalent Eastern corridors of power in psychology (see, e.g., Benjamin, 1977). His Gestalt background and early work on reasoning in problem solving in rats and humans left him out of the mainstream of the psychology of the time, especially Hullian approaches. He was thus subject to criticism from its proponents (e.g., Wolfe & Spragg, 1934). In the words of Hilgard (1950), "Where others might point out continuities, Maier prefers to point out discontinuities" (pp. 129–130). Furthermore, Maier was rather probing and direct in interpersonal contracts, and he developed a reputation for being a difficult man with whom to get along. The notion that a psychological process, such as conflict, could produce so dramatic a response as seizures appeared heretical to the devotees of the very hard-nosed experimental psychology of the day. They preferred to view the response as more reflexive—especially when the reports came from the likes of Maier.

THE PRIZE AND THE MEDIA

What catapulted this research from the level of being just another rat study into the eye of the media was the awarding of a prize by the American Association for the Advancement of Science (AAAS). The AAAS Newcomb Cleveland Prize, originated in 1923 and formerly called the AAAS Thousand Dollar Prize, is the oldest award given by the AAAS, the leading scientific organization in the United States. Before 1977 the award was given for the best paper presented at the annual meeting; more recently it has been awarded for an article published in *Science*. Only twice in its history have psychologists received the prize: Neal E. Miller and James Olds shared it in 1956, and Norman R. F. Maier received it for a paper on "Experimentally Produced Neurotic Behavior in the Rat," presented at the 1938 AAAS meeting (AAAS, 1980, 1989/1990; Wolfle, 1989).

The awarding of the AAAS prize was an important event within psychology and outside of it. In summarizing the activities of the Psychology Section of the AAAS, Leonard Carmichael (1939) reported that "American psychologists as a whole are especially proud of the fact that this year for the first time in history the American Association Prize of $1,000 was awarded to a psychologist" (p. 107).

The response in the media was widespread. The work was written up in the *New York Times*, under the headline "'Neurosis of Rats' Wins Science Prize" ("Neurosis," 1939). The *Washington Post* gave the prize front-page treatment with the more sensationalistic headline "Scientist Who Double-Crossed Rats Into Lunacy Wins $1,000" ("Scientist Who Double-Crossed," 1939).

An article in *Life* magazine, appearing the following March, was entitled "Rats Are Driven Crazy by Insoluble Problems" and included 13 photographs ("Rats," 1939). According to *Life*, "From these experiments Professor Maier concludes that many human beings suffer nervous breakdowns when forced to solve problems which have no apparent solutions" ("Rats," 1939). Two authors of published letters to *Life* were generally sympathetic and found generalizations to human behavior quite easy (Phelan, 1939; Wattles, 1939).

Several years later, *Time* magazine covered Maier's attempts to apply his frustration theory to questions concerning the treatment of Nazis after World War II. The article opened, "Norman Raymond Frederick Maier is a man who has made his name and fame by driving rats crazy" ("Cure for Germans?" 1944).

Noted author E. B. White (1939) also saw parallels between Maier's rats and the human situation. He wrote a short story, "The Door," based on an application of Maier's work to urban life in humans. The story entails a man's musings on the changing situations one encounters in life and the frequency with which a "door" that formerly yielded reward becomes fastened shut; life is full of changing reward situations and insoluble problems.

In 1939, after Maier received the AAAS award, the University of Michigan conferred on him its prestigious Henry Russel Award, granted annually to its most promising junior faculty member.

Few attended to the warnings of caution, suggesting some hesitancy on the part of the AAAS committee that made the award. Its citation included qualifications with its praise:

> He has produced in rats behavior, the neurotic character of which seems to the committee, and the critical audience which heard his paper, to be beyond doubt.... The committee does not feel that the author's analysis of the phenomena is complete, nor does it believe that the small number of rats in which neurotic behavior was experimentally induced is sufficient for generalization or sweeping conclusions, and it gives credit to Dr. Maier for the conservatism he exhibited and for the scrupulous avoidance of applying his discoveries prema-

turely to the field in which they ultimately will be vastly significant —namely, neurotic behavior in human beings. (Moulton, 1939, p. 93)

THE DECLINE

Maier's work on convulsive seizures is largely forgotten, rarely mentioned in recent reviews. What led to this virtual disappearance? The initial journal reviews of Maier's monograph were considerably less favorable than those in the media. One issue concerned the appropriateness of calling the behavior *neurotic*. Maier later conceded that it was the abnormal fixations, rather than the convulsive seizures, that should be labeled neurotic (Maier, 1943, p. 141). The more troubling criticism concerned the possibility that the seizures were caused by the auditory stimulus from the air blast, with no role played by the conflict situation (see, e.g., Cook, 1940; Karn, 1940).

The most stringent critic was Clifford T. Morgan (1915–1976). Morgan completed his PhD at the University of Rochester in 1939, working with Leonard Carmichael and Elmer Culler. Morgan then accepted a position at Harvard University, where he became a colleague of Karl Lashley and worked in Lashley's laboratory early in his (Morgan's) Harvard career. He then made a war-complicated move to Johns Hopkins University, assuming duties there in 1946.

Morgan and Morgan (1939) reported that convulsive seizures, identical to those reported by Maier, were elicited in rats exposed to the sound of air blasts but without the training regime used by Maier. Later, Morgan (1940) was critical of "the sketchy and unquantitative character of the experimental work" (p. 227). Morgan concluded that "the validity of Maier's interpretations is open to serious question on both logical and experimental grounds" (p. 233).

This led to a long series of articles by a variety of authors during the 1940s. The reader is referred to the reviews of Finger (1947) and Munn (1950) for complete treatments. Maier conducted an active research program during this period, publishing 24 numbered articles in a series on "Studies of Abnormal Behavior in the Rat." Much of this work involved exploration of the determinants of the fixated responses that occurred in situations with insoluble problems (e.g., Maier & Klee, 1941). Other studies were devoted to an exploration of the parameters affecting seizures triggered by auditory stimuli (e.g., Maier & Glaser, 1940). During this period, Maier made only minor modifications of his original views, extended his interpretations to a wider range of situations, and developed a frustration theory to deal with his results (see Maier, 1949).

Meanwhile, much of Morgan's work entailed a systematic exploration of the auditory stimuli that could trigger seizures (e.g., Morgan, 1941; Morgan & Gould, 1941; Morgan & Waldman, 1941). Morgan and his associates held that because the auditory stimuli appeared critical for the occurrence of convulsive seizures, they should be called *audiogenic seizures*, a term that Maier never accepted.

Various other investigators entered the field (e.g., Griffiths, 1942; Humphrey & Marcuse, 1944). A skirmish broke out between M. E. Bitterman and Frank W. Finger, with Bitterman generally supporting Maier and Finger supporting Morgan (e.g., Bitterman, 1944, 1946; Finger, 1945).

The end result of this research and publishing activity was the perception of a resolution in favor of Morgan's position regarding the primacy of auditory stimuli in the genesis of convulsive seizures. Finger (1944) wrote that "the conclusion has gradually evolved that the pattern occurs as a relatively reflex reaction to direct sensory stimulation (primarily of an auditory nature), and has little immediate significance to the study of 'conflict'" (pp. 414–415) and of "the banishment of the phenomenon from the realm of the neuroses" (p. 416). Elsewhere, Finger (1947) concluded that "the majority of investigators now prefer to regard the behavior as something other than conflict-induced experimental neurosis" (p. 204). Later, Bevan (1955) noted that "the widespread appeal of the Morgan interpretation of audiogenic seizures has resulted in little consideration, except by Maier and his students, of the possible significance of psychologically specified variables in the etiology of these convulsions" (p. 190). Although purporting to avoid the ensuing controversy, Marx and Hillix (1973) discussed Maier's work as "an interesting and important illustration of the necessity for the combination of analytic thinking and control as a basis for interpretation" (p. 13). In the view of Garner (1976), Morgan "demonstrated, in a series of papers, that the effect was not due to a neurotic conflict, but rather to high auditory frequencies, inaudible to man, in the blast of air" (p. 410).

SUBSEQUENT CAREERS OF MORGAN AND MAIER

Before the controversy, Maier had been viewed as the senior, successful, although controversial, psychologist—the coauthor of *Principles of Animal Psychology* and numerous other publications. Morgan and Finger were recent PhDs (F. Finger, personal communication, September 11, 1990). The careers of Maier and Morgan took very different routes after the controversy. Morgan became an extremely successful experimental psychologist, administrator, and publisher. He was at the heart of the power structure in experimental psychology. In Maier's surely overstated view, "He built his reputation on his refutation of Maier" (Maier, 1967b).

Morgan served as chair of the psychology department at Johns Hopkins and was credited with building the department in its modern form.

After leaving Johns Hopkins, Morgan served on the faculties of the University of Wisconsin; the University of California, Santa Barbara; and the University of Texas. Morgan became a part of the establishment in experimental psychology; he was elected to the Society of Experimental Psychologists before his 31st birthday. Later, he became the leader of the Psychonomic Society, serving as its first chair and building its stable of journals. Morgan became a highly successful writer of textbooks, beginning with his *Physiological Psychology* (Morgan, 1943), published, like Maier's early books, by McGraw-Hill. His *Introduction to Psychology* was so successful that it made him independently wealthy and caused him eventually to drop other commitments and essentially become a professional writer (Garner, 1976).

Maier, by contrast, left the field of animal psychology to find success in industrial psychology. Maier appears to have been positively attracted to work in industrial psychology and to the opportunity for work in a new "laboratory" (R. Heyns, personal communication, February 27, 1990; A. Solem, personal communication, February 9, 1990). Thus, it would appear unfair to conclude that the rejection of his animal research was the only factor in Maier's change in research focus. However, it is clear that Maier believed that he had been forced to change research areas (Maier, 1966b).

Maier's perception of his treatment by psychologists was charged with the controversy-related emotion of which Boring (1929) wrote (A. Solem, personal communication, February 9, 1990; S. Wapner, personal communication, August 10, 1989). Maier noted that before he had received the AAAS prize, he had been on various committees and had been runner-up in an election for president of the Midwestern Psychological Association. After that, he never was even a runner-up, and his committee invitations declined. He opined, "Of course all this naturally is maneuvering behind your back but I think there must have been a lot of hostility toward it" (Popplestone, 1967, p. 15).

Maier was told that he had been nominated as a member of the Society of Experimental Psychologists on many occasions and had more votes than others but that he was kept out by a blackball system that enabled a single member to veto a membership (Popplestone, 1967, pp. 15–16). Maier recalled various other occasions on which negative comments or actions affecting him had been relayed by friends (Popplestone, p. 15). He experienced difficulty in placing his graduate students (Popplestone, p. 16).

Maier reported difficulties in getting his papers published in journals of the American Psychological Association (APA). He did note that the frustration papers had been published, but he reported many editorial hassles and "nasty letters that I would get from the editors" (Popplestone, 1967, p. 16). Maier recalled that he eventually had to resort to the less competitive and less prestigious journals published by Carl Murchison. He recalled, "It was this type of control over the journals that forced me to change research areas" (Maier, 1966b).

The awarding of a prize should provide a moment of glory and a sense of accomplishment for a hardworking scientist. Such was not the case for Norman Maier. He reflected in an interview, "I think nationally it did me harm" (Maier, 1967b). Elsewhere in the interview, he opined, "The winning of the AAAS prize was probably the worst thing that happened to me." As summarized by his former student, Allen Solem (personal communication, February 9, 1990):

> Maier was disillusioned, I know by the rejection of the dominant S-R school of thought of Gestalt theory and more specifically the pervasive jealousy and envy incurred by the Cleveland AAAS and the subsequent Russel awards. . . . He said little about it; however on one or two occasions he said the AAAS award was the worst thing that could have happened to him because of the ill feeling it generated.

DISCOVERY OF THE ROLE OF AUDITORY STIMULI

There is an interesting twist beneath the surface of the story of the initial discovery that some rats displayed convulsive seizures in response to the air blast alone. Maier's first monograph appeared in 1939. In it, and in his work in progress at the time (e.g., Maier & Glaser, 1940), Maier used jingling keys to elicit convulsions in some experiments. Morgan and Morgan's article claiming an auditory basis for the seizures appeared in the June 1939 issue of the *Journal of Comparative Psychology*. According to Maier (1966b), he received a letter from Morgan in March 1939 asking for details concerning the production of convulsions. Maier told Morgan of his subsequent studies and stated that one could produce convulsions in some rats simply by jingling keys. Morgan and Morgan's article on audiogenic seizures, with air blasts as the stimuli, was received in the editorial office on April 26, 1939. Maier continued,

> By paying for publication he beat my completed work to print. The tests he ran could have been in a day. He had more than two weeks to make his tests and to write the four-page paper after receiving my letter. Immediate publication in those days was rare. Why did he perform such a limited experiment and hurry to publication? Naturally, when his paper appeared I reacted to his failure to mention my letter in which I had shared a year's research.

In an oral interview, Maier indicated, "It was a very good way of discrediting me" (Popplestone, 1967, p. 15). In another interview, Maier (1967b) stated, "The thing that I think was very unethical was when he paid for publication to beat mine to press. Because I sent him parts of it."

A different perspective on this story is presented by Morgan's coauthor, Jane Hildreth (formerly Jane Morgan). She recalled an experiment she did as a senior honors student at Rochester that required delivering powdered food through a glass tube in a Skinner box. She cleaned the tubes by washing them and drying them with compressed air. One night, when there were rats in the room as she cleaned the tubes, she noted that three of the four rats displayed seizures. She rushed upstairs to her husband "and burst into the room, announcing with some trepidation that we had 'Maier' seizures 'with no frustration'" (J. Hildreth, personal communication, November 25, 1990).

According to a variation on this part of the story, Maier gave a colloquium at Rochester as his work was in progress during the 1938–1939 academic year. His work generated immediate skepticism from the Rochester psychologists. Morgan triggered seizures by running compressed air through a glass tube and confirmed the finding the night of the colloquium (E. Stellar, personal communications, October 9, 1990, and January 4, 1991). Finger has recalled Morgan informing him that it was he (Morgan) who wrote to inform Maier of his finding of seizures in rats outside of the conflict situation (F. Finger, personal communication, September 11, 1990).

It is difficult to reconcile or decide among these alternatives. A check of the submission dates of articles in the 1939 *Journal of Comparative Psychology* suggests that Morgan's article did receive early publication. The Morgan and Morgan article does appear more preliminary than Morgan's later, detailed investigations; it is brief and does not even include a complete description of the stimulus used.

It seems likely that Morgan wrote to Maier. It is possible that Morgan wrote after his wife found and he confirmed the occurrence of audiogenic seizures, but perhaps without mentioning the finding directly. Maier might have informed Morgan of the methods to produce audiogenic seizures and might have perceived Morgan as having published the idea Maier had given him when, in fact, Morgan had discovered it independently. This scenario has the advantage of reconciling the apparently conflicting versions from generally reliable sources and suggests that this aspect of the controversy stemmed from a failure of communication. This, however, is only speculation.

A RESOLUTION KEPT PRIVATE

A more probing analysis of the controversy relies on archival materials but begins with an article by Maier and Longhurst (1947) designed to refute the conclusion of Morgan and Waldman (1941) that the seizures should be viewed as audiogenic. Maier and Longhurst, who provided a fairly detailed breakdown of their results, found seizures on 20.3% of the tests in the experimental group, which had been trained in a soluble problem and tested in an insoluble problem, compared with 7.6% in the control group, which had had no training in a soluble problem. Four times as many individual rats in the experimental as in the control group proved susceptible. However, on average, the control animals received longer exposure to air blasts. Maier and Longhurst concluded that their findings were "definitely contrary to the view which makes auditory stimulation the sole cause of the seizure" (Maier & Longhurst, 1947, p. 409).

Morgan (1948a) wrote a critique of the Maier and Longhurst article and submitted it to the *Journal of Comparative and Physiological Psychology*, the journal in which the Maier and Longhurst article had been published. The manuscript was forwarded to Maier by editor Calvin P. Stone (1948a), with a cover letter dated February 5, 1948. In the letter, Stone appeared favorably disposed toward Morgan and skeptical of Maier, noting that Maier's paper had been "carefully studied" by Morgan. Stone suggested that a joint early publication of Morgan's paper and Maier's reply could be arranged. Stone noted of Morgan, "He would like to have you read it with a view to preparing a short paper that would comment on and answer it, *so far as is possible* [italics added], in light of your work and available data." Stone hoped that such publication would "illuminate the problem, *to show the limitations of the studies already done* [italics added], and to highlight for other researchers the intricacies of crucial experiments in this field."

Although Morgan (1948a) was conciliatory in his article, he offered criticisms of the Maier and Longhurst article that he believed "raise doubts whether their experiment does, in fact, prove or support the hypothesis" (p. 2). Morgan first offered some technical criticisms of Maier's handling of his data. He then raised issues concerning the equivalence of the intensity and duration of exposure to air blasts in the two groups. Next, he turned to an issue concerning the relation between the latencies to seizure and the number of previous seizures. Morgan noted that if five or more rats had their first seizure after 35 seconds, he could account for the results in terms of the greater length of exposure in the experimental group.

Maier (1948b) replied quickly; his cover letter is dated just five days after Stone's. He agreed to the joint publication "since the questions raised are the type of reactions that will continue if they are not expressed." Maier added, "I see no point in communicating with Morgan personally. His position is perfectly clear and since many others share his views it seems best to reply in print." In his succinct three-page reply, Maier (1948a) addressed the issues raised by Morgan. Maier presented a further analysis of his data to show that not even one, let alone five, of his rats could be eliminated on the basis of Morgan's argument concerning the latency to seizure. He pointed out that the orientation of the animals in the jumping box was such that it took the experimental animals further from, rather than nearer to, the air blast. Maier concluded, "I am glad to grant Dr. Morgan a contrary bias and I hope it gives him equal comfort. The unbiased new generations can react to the findings without 'losing face', [sic] and I hope they will find that each point of view contributed to the final solution of the problem" (p. 3).

Morgan's replies provide the focal points of the story. The following are exerpts from Morgan's (1948c) letter to Stone:

> As you no doubt realized, I seem to be clearly off the beam on the principal point of my criticism of the Maier–Longhurst paper.... The long and short of it is that I have had the wind taken from my sails.... So, as you might guess, I am not now particularly anxious to have the two papers published.... I do not believe the publication of these papers would particularly enlighten journal readers.
>
> On the other hand, it is my error which makes me want to withdraw the paper, and it is only fair, I think, to leave the decision with Dr. Maier and yourself.

Morgan sent Maier a copy of his letter to Stone. He wrote to Maier:

> I was quite wrong on the matters of fact in which I attempted to criticize you. I am now convinced that you have done the nearest thing to a crucial experiment, and I am almost convinced that there is no other explanation than "conflict" for the differences which you report. It was a shame, however, that I had to put you to so much trouble, and I am very grateful for your kindness and effort.
>
> As you can see, I feel that the original plan of publishing the "discussion" and "reply" is not particularly good—since I was wrong in my premises. (Morgan, 1948b)

Stone (1948b) wrote to Maier asking "Would you object to our following his suggestion in respect to dropping the plan for publication of his discussion and your reply to his discussion?" Stone added, "I, however, am willing to go ahead with the publication if in the opinion of *both of you* [italics added] this will make a useful contribution to our readers."

Maier (1948d) replied to Stone that he was "willing to let the issue rest." Maier suggested that Morgan might write a paper stating that Morgan had raised certain questions and Maier had supplied him with relevant information. Maier indicated that he would want to see such a paper before publication and raised the possibility that it might be signed jointly. On the same date, Maier (1948c) forwarded a copy to Morgan noting that "the paragraph on the alternative that you write a paper incorporating your questions and our data is merely a suggestion and is not meant to make you feel obligated."

On April 5, Stone (1948c) returned the manuscripts to their authors. Morgan wrote to Maier, "The suggestion in the second paragraph of your letter appeals to me: writing one paper for joint signature." Morgan (1948d) suggested that it "might have a healthy effect on our public to show some substantial agreement." He noted that "I cannot do it right now, however, for I have some other pressing commitments, but I will try to get a draft to you within, say, about a month." That paper never was written.

Maier (1949) did, however, include a footnote in his book, *Frustration: The Study of Behavior Without a Goal*, noting, "Morgan, whose views are reflected by Finger, has informed the author that he wishes to withdraw from the controversy in the light of the Maier–Longhurst study" (p. 136). However, it appears that Morgan resisted public acknowledgment of his revised position. According to Finger (personal communication, September 11, 1990), "When I later asked Cliff if he had abandoned ship, he said that he had not, but that life was short and that Maier's interpretation was unworthy of continued attention. His silence, he assured me, was not to be interpreted as an assent." Sometime later, Maier (1966a) reflected,

> I feel the suppression of these papers was unfortunate because Morgan terminated his interest in the subject but the literature is left with the impression that giving the seizures the name "audiogenic" explains them. The problem of investigating the causes and nature of the conflict therefore has been dropped as an interesting area of investigation.

ON THE PUBLICATION OF CONTROVERSY IN PSYCHOLOGICAL JOURNALS

There can be little doubt that the development of understanding of the genesis of seizures would have been better advanced if the Maier–Morgan exchange had been published. A very dramatic and powerful phenomenon has virtually disappeared from recent literature. It would be difficult to argue that the failure to publish the Maier–Morgan exchange was the only factor leading to the disappearance of the phenomenon from the literature or to the problems later experienced by Norman Maier. However, it is likely that additional research would have been conducted and the public and private resolutions of the controversy might have been brought to accord. The case suggests that the publication of controversy can be important.

The issue of the publication of comments on recently published articles is covered in the new *Editor's Handbook: Operating Procedures and Policies for APA Publications* (APA, 1992). According to that manual, the editor is under no obligation to publish such material. Should the editor decide to publish such a comment, however, he or she should inform the original author so that a reply can be prepared. All comments should be refereed. The exchange should end after a comment and a reply.

In order to determine the actual policies in force, I wrote to the editors of the APA journals that publish primarily empirical contributions. I received 15 replies. Of these, 11 reported that they did publish such material; several editors referred me to particular instances within their journals. None reported a policy that would absolutely prohibit such publication. In 4 cases, the editors reported that there was no policy against such contributions but that no such articles had been published.

The journal in question, the *Journal of Comparative Psychology*, has published a few commentaries at various times (e.g., Hirsch, 1957; LaFleur, 1943, 1944; Schneirla, 1942, 1943; Tinbergen, 1957). However, such articles appear to have disappeared from the journal. I perused the last 30 years of the *Journal of Comparative Psychology* and the *Journal of Comparative and Physiological Psychology* (*JCPP*) and located no such articles. According to the current editor, Gordon G. Gallup, Jr., the journal "does not normally publish such material," although there is no set policy against it. During Gallup's tenure as editor, only one such article was submitted, and it was rejected for substantive reasons (G. G. Gallup, Jr., personal communication, July 13, 1992). Of the journals closest in content to the *Journal of Comparative Psychology*, *Animal Behaviour* regularly publishes such comments, and *Behavioral Neuroscience* includes a "Technical Comments" section (e.g., Dworkin & Dworkin, 1991; Roberts, 1991).

The comments of Stone's successor as editor, Harry F. Harlow (1961), provide an interesting perspective:

> When I took over as editor of *JCPP*, Dr. Calvin Stone gave me some detailed fatherly advice, suggesting that I would do well not to publish apparatus articles which were not backed by an experiment and not to publish controversies. In both cases, in eleven years of editing, I deviated once and I regret both deviations. I am convinced that Stone was right.... I have consistently denied many requests to publish rebuttals and corrections, other than corrections of a mechanical error type (p. 1).

CONTROVERSY AND THE MAVERICK SCIENTIST

It seems clear that Maier was regarded as a maverick, outside of the mainstream psychology of his time. This perception may have been started with his Berlin experience working with Gestalt psychologists and further developed with his view that problem-solving behavior was qualitatively different from normal learning. The seizure and fixation work, which Maier also interpreted as suggesting a discontinuity, surely exacerbated this perception.

It is difficult for the objective student to confirm or disconfirm Maier's perceptions of prejudice against him. In his own view, "No one came out and attacked me, it was always done by the students" (Popplestone, 1967,

p. 14). The majority of psychologists have papers rejected, are not appointed to major committees, are not elected to major office, and fail to get elected to the Society of Experimental Psychologists. Many of Maier's papers on convulsive seizures and fixations were published in APA journals.

On the other hand, Maier was an internationally recognized scientist who produced over 200 articles and over a dozen books. His work was creative and original. Research trends since Maier's departure from the field have been away from the stimulus–response (S-R) reflexology he opposed toward a cognitive emphasis compatible with his views. No longer does it seem heretical to suggest that learning and problem solving may reflect the action of different processes. Clearly, Maier was out of step with his time —ahead of it in many respects. However, perusal of his 1967 Faculty Biographical Data Sheet (Maier, 1967a), *New York Times* obituary ("Norman Maier," 1977), and *American Psychologist* obituary (Solem & McKeachie, 1979) reveals none of the fellow elections, honorary degrees, or national and regional offices one would expect of a scientist of Maier's stature. It is difficult to explain these lacunae if Maier's perceptions were pure paranoia. There appears to be at least some validity to his perceptions of prejudicial treatment.

Eliot Stellar recalled that Morgan regarded those outside of the Eastern establishment as being in the bush leagues. "Maier was in the bush leagues, not only because he was at Michigan, but also because his concept of conflict leading to seizures was thought to be on the border of real science" (E. Stellar, personal communication, June 23, 1992). In his unpublished textbook, another member of the Eastern group, Frank Beach, dismissed the seizures as due to auditory stimuli and used the case as an example of the misidentification of the effective stimulus for behavior (see Dewsbury, 1990).

Maier (1960) summarized his perception of the operation and machinations of behavioristic psychologists in an article entitled "Maier's Law," which appeared in the *American Psychologist*. According to Maier's law, "*If facts do not conform to the theory, they must be disposed of*" (p. 208). Maier delineated several ways in which psychologists dispose of unwanted facts, providing graphic examples of each. The first was to give the phenomenon a new name, which thereby recasts the observations in a form compatible with the theory. Another way of disposing of facts is to omit them from reference books. Still another is to fail to report disturbing facts, such as the number of rats failing to learn discrimination problems.

At one level, Maier's law is a rather bitter presentation of a scientist disillusioned with the treatment of his and others' findings. At another level, however, it can be read as an insightful treatment of the first defense of establishment scientists against anomalies promulgated by maverick scientists (see Kuhn, 1970). Maier was exploring the dynamics of the resistance of mainstream scientists to outsiders and their novel approaches. His own case may provide insight into the operation of these dynamics.

REFERENCES

American Association for the Advancement of Science. (1980). *Handbook*. Washington, DC: Author.

American Association for the Advancement of Science. (1989/1990). *Handbook*. Washington, DC: Author.

American Psychological Association. (1992). *Editor's handbook: Operating procedures and policies for APA publications* (Draft revision May 22, 1992). Washington, DC: Author.

Benjamin, L. T., Jr. (1977). The psychological round table: Revolution of 1936. *American Psychologist, 32*, 542–549.

Bennett, A. M. (1968). Science: The antithesis of creativity. *Perspectives in Biology and Medicine, 11*, 233–245.

Bevan, W. (1955). Sound-precipitated convulsions: 1947 to 1954. *Psychological Bulletin, 52*, 473–504.

Bitterman, M. E. (1944). Behavior disorder as a function of the relative strength of antagonistic response–tendencies. *Psychological Review, 51*, 375–378.

Bitterman, M. E. (1946). A reply to Dr. Finger. *Psychological Review, 53*, 116–118.

Boring, E. G. (1929). The psychology of controversy. *Psychological Review, 36*, 97–121.

Carmichael, L. (1939). Section on psychology (I). *Science, 89*, 107.

Cook, S. W. (1940). [Review of *Studies of abnormal behavior in the rat*]. *Journal of Abnormal and Social Psychology, 35*, 591–593.

Cure for Germans? (1944, June 26). *Time*, pp. 58–59.

Dewsbury, D. A. (1990). Frank Beach's unpublished textbook on comparative psychology. *Journal of Comparative Psychology, 104*, 219–226.

Dworkin, B. R., & Dworkin, S. (1991). Verification of skeletal activity in tibial nerve recordings: A reply to Roberts (1991). *Behavioral Neuroscience, 105*, 773–779.

Finger, F. W. (1944). Experimental behavior disorders in the rat. In J. McV. Hunt (Ed.), *Personality and the behavior disorders: A handbook based on experimental and clinical research* (Vol. 1, pp. 413–430). New York: Ronald.

Finger, F. W. (1945). Abnormal animal behavior and conflict. *Psychological Review, 52*, 230–233.

Finger, F. W. (1947). Convulsive behavior in the rat. *Psychological Bulletin, 44*, 201–248.

Garner, W. R. (1976). Clifford Thomas Morgan: Psychonomic Society's first chairman. *Bulletin of the Psychonomic Society, 8*, 409–415.

Griffiths, W. J. (1942). The production of convulsions in the white rat. *Comparative Psychology Monographs, 17*(8, Serial No. 92).

Harlow, H. F. (1961, December 8). [Letter to D. O. Hebb]. Donald O. Hebb Papers, McGill University, Montreal, Quebec, Canada.

Henle, M. (1973). On controversy and its resolution. In J. Jaynes & J. J. Sullivan (Eds.), *Historical conceptions of psychology* (pp. 47–59). New York: Springer.

Hilgard, E. R. (1950). Review of N. R. F. Maier's *Frustration: The study of behavior without a goal. American Journal of Psychology, 63,* 128–130.

Hirsch, J. (1957). Careful reporting and experimental analysis—A comment. *Journal of Comparative and Physiological Psychology, 50,* 415.

Humphrey, G., & Marcuse, F. (1944). Factors influencing the susceptibility of albino rats to convulsive attacks under intense auditory stimulation. *Journal of Comparative Psychology, 32,* 285–306.

Karn, H. W. (1940). [Review of *Studies of abnormal behavior in the rat*]. *Journal of General Psychology, 23,* 235–238.

Keller, E. F. (1983). *A feeling for the organism: The life and work of Barbara McClintock.* New York: Freeman.

Kuhn, T. S. (1970). *The structure of scientific revolutions* (2nd ed.). Chicago: University of Chicago Press.

LeFleur, L. J. (1943). A reply. *Journal of Comparative Psychology, 35,* 97–99.

LaFleur, L. J. (1944). Ants and hypotheses. *Journal of Comparative Psychology, 37,* 17–22.

Lashley, K. S. (1930). The mechanisms of vision: 1. A method for rapid analysis of pattern-vision in the rat. *Journal of Genetic Psychology, 37,* 461–480.

Mahoney, M. J. (1976). *Scientist as subject: The psychological imperative.* Cambridge, MA: Ballinger.

Maier, N. R. F. (1939). *Studies of abnormal behaivor in the rat.* New York: Harper.

Maier, N. R. F. (1943). Two types of behavior abnormality in the rat. *Bulletin of the Menninger Clinic, 7,* 141–147.

Maier, N. R. F. (1948a). *Reply to Dr. Morgan.* Unpublished manuscript, Archives of the History of American Psychology, Akron, OH.

Maier, N. R. F. (1948b, February 10). [Letter to Calvin P. Stone]. Archives of the History of American Psychology, Akron, OH.

Maier, N. R. F. (1948c, March 30). [Letter to Clifford T. Morgan]. Archives of the History of American Psychology, Akron, OH.

Maier, N. R. F. (1948d, March 30). [Letter to Calvin P. Stone]. Archives of the History of American Psychology, Akron, OH.

Maier, N. R. F. (1949). *Frustration: The study of behaivor without a goal.* New York: McGraw-Hill.

Maier, N. R. F. (1960). Maier's law. *American Psychologist, 15,* 208–212.

Maier, N. R. F. (1966a, September 19). [Letter to John A. Popplestone]. Archives of the History of American Psychology, Akron, OH.

Maier, N. R. F. (1966b, October 25). [Letter to John A. Popplestone]. Archives of the History of American Psychology, Akron, OH.

Maier, N. R. F. (1967a, January 13). *Faculty biographical data, University of Michigan.* Archives of the History of American Psychology, Akron, OH.

Maier, N. R. F. (1967b, October 3). Oral history interview with Alfred C. Raphelson [Cassette recording].

Maier, N. R. F., & Glaser, N. M. (1938). *Experimentally produced neurotic behavior in the rat* [Film]. Bethlehem, PA: A. Ford.

Maier, N. R. F., & Glaser, N. M. (1940). Studies of abnormal behavior in the rat: 2. A comparison of some convulsion-producing situations. *Comparative Psychology Monographs, 16*(80), 1–30.

Maier, N. R. F., & Klee, J. B. (1941). Studies of abnormal behavior in the rat: 7. The permanent nature of abnormal fixations and their relation to convulsive tendencies. *Journal of Comparative Psychology, 29,* 380–389.

Maier, N. R. F., & Longhurst, J. U. (1947). Studies of abnormal behavior in the rat: 21. Conflict and audiogenic seizures. *Journal of Comparative and Physiological Psychology, 40,* 397–412.

Maier, N. R. F., & Schneirla, T. C. (1935). *Principles of animal psychology.* New York: McGraw-Hill.

Marx, M. H., & Hillix, W. A. (1973). *Systems and theories in psychology* (2nd ed.). New York: McGraw-Hill.

Morgan, C. T. (1940). [Review of *Studies of abnormal behavior in the rat*]. *Journal of General Psychology, 23,* 227–233.

Morgan, C. T. (1941). The latency of audiogenic seizures. *Journal of Comparative Psychology, 32,* 267–284.

Morgan, C. T. (1943). *Physiological psychology.* New York: McGraw-Hill.

Morgan, C. T. (1948a). *A discussion of conflict and audiogenic seizures.* Unpublished manuscript, Maier papers, Archives of the History of American Psychology, Akron, OH.

Morgan, C. T. (1948b, March 10). [Letter to Norman R. F. Maier]. Archives of the History of American Psychology, Akron, OH.

Morgan, C. T. (1948c, March 10). [Letter to Calvin P. Stone]. Archives of the History of American Psychology, Akron, OH.

Morgan, C. T. (1948d, April 14). [Letter to N. R. F. Maier]. Archives of the History of American Psychology, Akron, OH.

Morgan, C. T., & Gould, J. (1941). Acoustical determinants of the 'neurotic pattern' in rats. *Psychological Record, 4,* 258–268.

Morgan, C. T., & Morgan, J. D. (1939). Auditory induction of an abnormal pattern of behavior in rats. *Journal of Comparative Psychology, 27,* 505–508.

Morgan, C. T., & Waldman, H. (1941). Conflict and audiogenic seizures. *Journal of Comparative Psychology, 31,* 1–11.

Moulton, F. R. (1939). The Richmond meeting of the American Association for the Advancement of Science and Associated Societies. *Science, 89,* 89–112.

Munn, N. L. (1950). *Handbook of psychological research on the rat: An introduction to animal psychology.* Boston: Houghton Mifflin.

"Neurosis of rats" wins science prize. (1939, January 1). *New York Times,* p. 21.

Norman Maier, 76; Noted psychologist at U. of Michigan. (1977, September 27). *New York Times,* p. 42.

Phelan, E. (1939, March 27). [Letter]. *Life,* p. 5.

Popplestone, J. A. (1967, January 25–26). *Oral history of Norman R. F. Maier,* Ann Arbor, MI. Archives of the History of American Psychology, Akron, OH.

Rats are driven crazy by insoluble problems. (1939, March 6). *Life,* pp. 66–68.

Roberts, L. E. (1991). Evidence for autonomic–autonomic dissociation: An alternative to Dworkin and Dworkin (1990). *Behavioral Neuroscience, 105,* 767–772.

Schneirla, T. C. (1942). "Cruel" ants—and Occam's razor. *Journal of Comparative Psychology, 34,* 79–83.

Schneirla, T. C. (1943). Postscript to "Cruel" ants. *Journal of Comparative Psychology, 35,* 233–235.

Scientist who double-crossed rats into lunacy wins $1,000. (1939, January 1). *Washington Post,* pp. 1, 4,

Solem, A., & McKeachie, W. J. (1979). Norman R. F. Maier (1900–1977). *American Psychologist, 34,* 266–267.

Stone, C. P. (1948a, February 5). [Letter to Norman R. F. Maier]. Maier papers, Archives of the History of American Psychology, Akron, OH.

Stone, C. P. (1948b, March 26). [Letter to Norman R. F. Maier]. Archives of the History of American Psychology, Akron, OH.

Stone, C. P. (1948c, April 5). [Letter to N. R. F. Maier and C. T. Morgan]. Archives of the History of American Psychology, Akron, OH.

Tinbergen, N. (1957). On anti-predator responses in certain birds—A reply. *Journal of Comparative and Physiological Psychology, 50,* 412–414.

Vanderplas, J. M. (Ed.). (1966). *Controversial issues in psychology.* Boston: Houghton Mifflin.

Wattles, M. G. (1939, March 27). [Letter]. *Life,* p. 5.

Wenner, A. M., & Wells, P. H. (1990). *Anatomy of a controversy: The question of a "language" among bees.* New York: Columbia University Press.

White, E. B. (1939, March 25). The door. *New Yorker,* pp. 19–20.

Wolfe, J. B., & Spragg, S. D. S. (1934). Some experimental tests of "reasoning" in white rats. *Journal of Comparative Psychology, 18,* 455–469.

Wolfle, D. (1989). *Renewing a scientific society: The American Association for the Advancement of Science from World War II to 1970.* Washington, DC: American Association for the Advancement of Science.

Ziman, J. M. (1968). *Public knowledge: An essay concerning the social dimension of science.* Cambridge, England: Cambridge University Press.

VI

THE PRACTICES OF PSYCHOLOGY

INTRODUCTION: THE PRACTICES OF PSYCHOLOGY

The transformation of American psychology since World War II is a complex story of scientific, professional, and cultural change. In an evident reversal of the status of psychological science and practice prior to 1940, psychology's identity has been transformed from that of academics practicing science to that of professionals involved in science-based practices. This transformation in the disciplinary and professional boundaries of psychology had its origin in the two decades before World War II.

Despite the rhetoric of experimentalism, American psychologists have been interested in applying psychological science from the first days of organized American psychology. By the end of World War I, there were enough psychologists interested in professional practice to form a new professional organization, the American Association of Clinical Psychologists. Apparently threatened by this move, the American Psychological Association (APA) co-opted the new organization by forming a clinical section in 1919 (Routh, 1994; Samelson, 1992).

The dramatic growth of applied and professional work between the world wars included significant growth in the number of psychologists engaged in mental health work (Finch & Odoroff, 1939, 1941; Napoli, 1981). The major psychological organization for applied or professional work in this period, the American Association of Applied Psychologists, began the process of developing training standards for clinical psychologists (Shakow,

1938, 1942). There were even calls made for a new professional degree, the PsD, that would provide appropriate training for professional psychologists (Poffenberger, 1938; Rogers, 1939).

By the beginning of World War II, applied professional psychology represented the greatest growth in psychology. World War II only exacerbated this trend. Psychologists were asked to apply their knowledge in new ways to assist the military in the war effort. Interdisciplinary work became the norm as psychologists were thrown together with psychiatrists, social scientists, and other professionals to work toward the solution of urgent problems. The APA was reorganized during the war to accommodate both scientific and professional interests, and a national headquarters was established in Washington, DC (Capshew, 1999).

Training issues for the four major practice areas of psychology, Clinical, Counseling, School, Industrial–Organizational, were a focus of discussion among the leaders of the reorganized APA. The need for effective training of clinical psychologists was made clear by the events of the war, which brought recognition of the prevalence of mental disorders. Almost 2 million men were rejected by the U.S. Selective Service for military service because of psychiatric problems or mental deficiencies, while more than half a million men were discharged from service because of mental disorders. The lack of mental health personnel weakened the war effort and frightened policymakers after the war. The shortage of trained mental health workers in the Veterans Administration (VA) alone was critical. Veterans with psychiatric disorders occupied 60% of VA hospital beds in 1946. It was also clear that the nation as a whole did not have enough adequately trained personnel and that the nation's medical schools were not prepared to produce enough psychiatrists to meet the need. The government turned to the professions of clinical psychology, psychiatric nursing, and social work for help. For the first time, the federal government became involved in the large-scale support of training, research, and service in the mental health field.

In 1946, the VA appealed to psychologists in leading universities to become partners with the VA in developing a clinical psychology program. The VA and university representatives agreed to make the doctorate the acceptable credential for work as a clinical psychologist in the VA. The VA, with the support of the U.S. Public Health Service's National Institute of Mental Health (NIMH), also insisted that the APA take on the role of evaluating and accrediting doctoral programs. To do so effectively required training standards that would ensure competencies across the relevant areas of clinical science and practice.

David Shakow (1901–1981) took the lead in developing training standards for clinical psychology. Chapter 21, "Clinical Psychology Seen Some 50 Years Later" (1978), is an important participant history of the development of modern clinical psychology. Shakow's training and background included work with Frederic Wells (1884–1964) and Grace Kent (1875–1973), two pioneers of the application of psychology to problems of mental disorder. Shakow served as chief psychologist for many years at Worcester State Hospital, where he developed a model of clinical training that was influential in setting guidelines for training and internships in the rapid expansion of clinical psychology after World War II. (After the war, Shakow held an appointment at the University of Illinois–Chicago from 1946 to 1954 and then he became the chief of the Laboratory of Psychology at the NIMH.) Shakow's account of these developments is informative of how the dominant "Boulder model" of scientist–practitioner training was created. In this model, clinicians are trained as both research scientists and health care providers.

Seymour B. Sarason attended the Boulder Conference as the young director of Yale University's fledgling clinical psychology program. Chapter 22, "An Asocial Psychology and a Misdirected Clinical Psychology" (1981), offers a sharp critique of the Shakow model and suggests alternative paths a useful clinical psychology might have taken. In particular, Sarason laments the adoption of the medical model of theory and practice that he asserts was embedded in the Shakow model. Together these two chapters provide an opportunity to rethink a critical time in the history of modern psychology and to possibly stimulate a reimagining of what clinical psychology can be.

Psychologists' responses to psychoanalysis have varied widely. The first peak of psychologists' exploration of psychoanalysis occurred during the 1930s. The context for this was public criticism of psychology by intellectuals in the popular press and the perception by younger psychologists of the sterility of many of their experimental research programs. During the Depression there was significant movement among younger psychologists toward applying their science to real-life problems, including problems of mental illness. An example is psychologists' attempts to incorporate psychoanalysis into their experimental work and application.

Psychoanalysis reached the peak of its popularity and cultural influence in the immediate years after World War II. Popular culture was saturated with psychoanalytic ideas in movies, magazines, and literature. Talking about one's problems to a professional became glamorous and, perhaps more importantly, accessible to the reinvigorated American middle class. This public did not necessarily differentiate psychoanalysis and psychology, with the result that new professions were able to take advantage of the public's eagerness for psychological expertise. The cultural opening for therapeutic experiences was exploited by psychologists, trained in the new clinical psychology with new psychotherapies, who were able to move into public prominence as science-based mental health professionals (Cook, 1958). Chapter 23, "The Return of the Repressed: Psychology's Problematic Relations With Psychoanalysis, 1909–1960" (1992), by Gail A. Hornstein, analyzes the problematic relationship of psychology and psychoanalysis during the first 60 years of the 20th century. In her view, psychologists sought to both demonize and domesticate psychoanalysis. She argues that for many psychologists the very meaning of psychological science was at stake. However, psychoanalysis also provided rich resources for conceptualizing psychological disorders and their treatment.

The three chapters included in this section reflect key developments in the clinical practice of psychology. The other major practice areas of psychology—counseling, school, and industrial/organizational—all followed unique developmental tracks and deserve histories of their own.

REFERENCES

Capshew, J. H. (1999). *Psychologists on the march: Science, practice, and professional identity in America, 1929–1969*. New York: Cambridge University Press.

Cook, S. W. (1958). The psychologist of the future: Scientist, professional, or both. *American Psychologist, 13*, 635–644.

Finch, F. H., & Odoroff, M. E. (1939). Employment trends in applied psychology. *Journal of Consulting Psychology, 3*, 118–122.

Finch, F. H., & Odoroff, M. E. (1941). Employment trends in applied psychology, II. *Journal of Consulting Psychology, 5*, 275–278.

Napoli, D. S. (1981). *Architects of adjustment: The history of the psychological profession in the United States*. Port Washington, NY: Kennikat Press.

Poffenberger, A. T. (1938). The training of a clinical psychologist. *Journal of Consulting Psychology, 2*, 1–6.

Rogers, C. R. (1939). Needed emphases in the training of clinical psychologists. *Journal of Consulting Psychology, 3*, 141–143.

Routh, D. K. (1994). *Clinical psychology since 1917: Science, practice, and organization*. New York: Plenum Press.

Samelson, F. (1992). The APA between the world wars: 1918–1941. In R. B. Evans, V. S. Sexton, & T. C. Cadwallader (Eds.), *The American Psychological Association: A historical perspective* (pp. 119–147). Washington, DC: American Psychological Association.

Shakow, D. (1938). An internship for psychologists (with special reference to psychiatric hospitals). *Journal of Consulting Psychology, 2*, 73–76.

Shakow, D. (1942). The training of the clinical psychologist. *Journal of Consulting Psychology, 6*, 277–288.

21

CLINICAL PSYCHOLOGY SEEN SOME 50 YEARS LATER

DAVID SHAKOW

In this article I plan to talk about some aspects of the history and development of clinical psychology over the past 50 years, particularly my views of the field's desirable development over this period. Just a little over 30 years ago, in 1946, a symposium was held at the annual meeting of the APA with the title of "Fifty Years of Clinical Psychology" (Brotemarkle, 1947). It was convened to celebrate the founding of the first clinic at the University of Pennsylvania by Lightner Witmer. I was invited to participate, but because of a change in employment, I was unable to accept. However, the participants—Shaffer (1947), Doll (1947), and Hawley (1946)—dealt with (some of) the issues effectively. The symposium title has clear affinities with the title of the present article—still some 50 years later, although it includes only 30 overlapping years. However, whereas the

---

This article was presented as a Distinguished Professional Contribution Award Address at the meeting of the American Psychological Association, San Francisco, August 28, 1977.

Preparation of this article was in part aided by a grant from the Benevolent Foundation of Scottish Rite Freemasonry, Northern Jurisdiction, United States of America.

Reprinted from *American Psychologist*, 33, 148–158 (1978). Copyright © 1978 by the American Psychological Association.

title 30 years ago was based on an event of considerable consequence, today's title commemorates a personal event.

You will have to bear with whatever narcissism may be revealed in my account, but I'll try to make the burden not too intolerable! Although there is a certain immodesty in regarding that with which one has been associated as important, it so happened that my own career was intertwined with earlier developments of clinical psychology. My involvement of over six decades in the history of this field dates from early adolescence. It was about 1915 when my curiosity was intrigued by a reference to *Yungenfroid* by the headworker of a settlement house in New York. (I have recounted the event elsewhere: Shakow, 1969, pp. 281–287.)

I realize that in dealing with this span of time I am in a sense taking unfair advantage of you, for there are few or no readers who can make similar claims to longevity. But there are advantages as well as disadvantages to having seen and participated in the movement of a field over this long time. I thought at first of making my topic 30 years, since the 1947 report of the Committee on Training in Clinical Psychology was written just 30 years ago, an event which turned out to be a major turning point in the development of clinical psychology. But in the end I decided that I would deal with the earlier 20 years as well, for it was during this period that major developments, insofar as I was concerned, had their roots.

Earlier, in "Reflections on a Do-It-Yourself Training Program in Clinical Psychology" (Shakow, 1976a), I described the outline of my own growth. When I went up to Harvard in 1921, I was buttressed by William James's notion (and Freud's also, to some extent) of *psychology being one*. Because of my own high regard for James, I expected to have a fairly easy time of it in this respect. Harvard *was* James to my way of thinking, and psychology and particularly its abnormal expressions, as he held, were essentially unified.

What did I find? A few thought as I did, but this thinking was far from universal. McDougall, who had recently come to Harvard, had general views which were sympathetic. He had been glad to leave Oxford, where he had had a hard time because psychology there was still considered a branch of philosophy. Like myself, he had come to Harvard because of James. But McDougall did not have much impact on Harvard students, perhaps because of his instinct theory, his views on the inheritance of intelligence, and his concern with extrasensory perception. Although I learned a great deal from him, he did not generally sway Harvard students or faculty. On the other hand, other associates at Harvard, notably Lundholm at McLean and Wells at the Psychopathic, were both sympathetic and influential in their spheres. The program was grand in many ways, especially the individualistic views of the professors and the diverse points of view represented in their teaching. But the major features which I thought so clear (which came from my absorption with James), that psychology was one and that abnormal psychology was part of psychology, were far from accepted. The continuous spectrum of personality that was so obvious to me was not obvious to others at all! (I know that Nevitt Sanford [1976, pp. 243–258], in his discussion of his Harvard days, believed that more of an integration of the psychologies existed than I do. However, this opinion may have arisen from Sanford's close relationships within the Psychology Clinic group on Plympton Street, which by that time had been established under Murray. This association served as a sort of "protected universe" [enhanced by the "antagonism" they encountered from Emerson Hall], and its members experienced much mutual support. I, on the other hand, had my contacts, admittedly during a slightly earlier period, with the group at Emerson Hall, which consisted almost entirely of experimentalists). Perhaps I was naive. Who knows?

Although this was made fairly obvious to me during my undergraduate days, I realized it most poignantly in the 1st year of my graduate work while living at the Psychopathic and attending Harvard. Among my other activities at that time, I took part in a seminar by Boring which I have described elsewhere in detail (Shakow, 1976a, p. 25). This seminar was on the "Nature of Control in the Psychological Experiment." Aside from the many benefits I gained from the seminar, I was left with the impression that no matter how much good will was expressed toward me personally, the principles I held to were not accepted everywhere in psychology. In fact, the dominant voice in psychology, that of the experimental psychologists, did not accept the notion of the unity of psychology at all. For them, experimental psychology was quite a different field from clinical psychology, and now some 50 years later, it still seems to be for some. (See the report of the Committee on the Scientific and Professional Aims of Psychology, 1967.)

Another point of view is indicated by the following episode with David Krech. It was just such a fission that David Krech, whose very recent passing we must mourn and whose death psychology could ill afford, had in mind. I ran across a short article of his written in 1946, from Swarthmore, on this topic. He started off, "The spectre of fission is haunting academic psychology" (p. 402), and continued with a statement of the problem of the presumed basic differences between academic and experimental psychologists. The article ended with, "But some of our important 'pure' experimental work can be done with *material* that is 'practically' important. It will be difficult, but it can be done and is very much worth doing" (p. 404). I wrote him congratulating him on his perspicacity and received a letter back reiterating this point even more vehemently.

Hilgard (Note 1) gives some contrary evidence from a review of the Presidential addresses of the Wundtian students of the early period and other psychologists of the pre-World War II period. But at least I am describing the situation as I saw it in the late 1920s at Harvard.

In addition to my belief in this fundamental principle of the oneness of psychology, I became convinced that it was necessary for psychologists to have contact with persons on the outside, in the field, as well as in the laboratory. I could not see how psychologists could be satisfied solely with carrying out laboratory studies of subjects, which was at that time virtually the exclusive practice of psychologists or so it seemed. It seemed obvious to me that it might be necessary to develop a combined "correlation and manipulative" psychology, as these two forms of psychology were later to be called (Cronbach, 1975). I had anticipatory visions that if I were ever in a position to influence students, I would direct their attention and efforts to the field outside the laboratory.

In 1928, my first dissertation on the effects of subliminal stimuli on the psychometric function yielded equivocal results. But, being married, with a child on the way, I could not refuse the offer I had from the Worcester State Hospital to direct the psychological aspects of a program on research in schizophrenia and to take charge of the psychological program as a whole. Fourteen years later I returned to Cambridge with a dissertation on schizophrenia (Shakow, 1946).

The next 18 years were utterly full and, to say the least, most profitable (Shakow, 1972). My major activity was with research in schizophrenia, but the training of clinical psychologists was a close second. I did not write anything on training this early in my career except a short essay on the "Psychologist in the State Hospital" (Shakow, 1930). It was about 10 years before I published "An Internship Year for Psychologists" (Shakow, 1938) and "The Functions of the Psychologist in the State Hospital" (Shakow, 1939).

In the first paper, the purposes of internships were formulated. I outlined these as follows: (a) to give the student facility in the use of already acquired techniques, (b) to saturate the student with experience in the practical aspects of psychology, (c) to develop in the student the objective attitude that the psychologist should have, and (d) to acquaint the student with the types of thinking and the attitudes of colleagues in other disciplines.

This was the program that was adopted and carried out by the psychology staff at Worcester, where it was constantly being revised and improved. In its final stages, this program was essentially the one described in the report by the Subcommittee on Graduate Internship Training to the Committees on Graduate and Professional Training of the American Psychological Association and the American Association for Applied Psychology (1945). The Subcommittee consisted of Brotemarkle, Doll, Kinder, B. V. Moore, Stevenson Smith, and myself. Although there was considerable discussion on aspects of the report by the Committee, the program was adopted essentially as drawn, with allowances being made for different settings. We presented this program to the two organizations and recommended that the Association appoint a committee on professional training in clinical psychology to represent the universities and the internship centers.

In rough outline, this report began with an introduction on the opportunities for professional practice in psychology. This was followed by a consideration of the general aspects of the problem of preparation and a separate section discussing the qualifications, both personal and academic, required for training in clinical psychology. These were treated for the junior (the bachelor's degree), the senior (the PhD), and the postgraduate (postdoctoral) levels of training. The major part of the report was on experimental qualifications for the internship, the content of the experience, the work with institution populations, and work with the administrative aspects. The section on the manner of instruction primarily discussed supervision. Internships and externships were considered, but the main section emphasized particularly the value of a 3rd-year internship with a 4th year spent at the university. I will come back to this point very shortly because it is important. A section was then devoted to the noneducational aspects of the internship dealing with such issues as remuneration and the kinds of institutions that should be involved. A further section concerned the integration of the academic and internship programs, the methods of selection and appointment of students, and issues of content and supervision. A final section was devoted to accrediting and certification of the individual, the university, and internship centers. In conclusion, there was a set of recommendations to the APA and to the AAAP.

I have devoted this much time to the report of this Subcommittee on Graduate Internship Training because it was the basis for the 1947 report, "Recommended Graduate Training Program in Clinical Psychology" by the Committee on Training in Clinical Psychology of the APA. This report was submitted at the Detroit meeting of the APA during September 9–13, 1947. I consider it the most important of the APA activities in which I participated in relation to training programs in clinical psychology.

But here a caveat must be entered. I am working on the assumption that these committees and activities were deliberate and well-thought-out efforts of groups who saw a need and acted upon it. The situation was not, in fact, that simple. What had been merely dabs here and there of developments in clinical psychology, leftovers from World War I, were accelerated immensely by World War II. This factor established itself as a true *Zeitgeist*—and was to become the major influence.

The 1947 report was the result of serious and intense discussions from different points of view on the part of the members of the committee. It might be worthwhile to examine the chronological development of the report. The U.S. Public Health Service addressed a request for advice on clinical psychology to a meeting of the Board of Directors of the APA, March 28–30, 1947, and indicated that it would be able to give financial support to such studies. The Executive Secretary indicated other related problems, such as accrediting schools for such training, which had already been raised by the Veterans Administration.

Realizing the importance of these questions, the President of the Association was empowered to appoint a chairperson of the Committee with the consent of the Board of Directors. It was expected that a preliminary report would be forthcoming for the September 1947 meeting of the APA, and an evaluation of training institutions, by February 1948. Rogers, then President, called on me early in April 1947, and I accepted the chairpersonship. The rest of the Committee was appointed by June 25th.

In July 1947, the Committee had a meeting lasting a few days in which we drew up the preliminary work on the details of the report. A first draft of the report went to the Committee members on August 12th, with a call for "instant" response. The Committee members cooperated effectively and the reports came back promptly. The final report was accepted by general and unanimous agreement on the principles as drawn up. Primary emphasis was on principles that would make clinical psychologists more competent substantively. Issues of certification, licensing, and recognition, although discussed, were considered of secondary importance. The final report was sent out to the Council of the APA on August 21st and accepted at the September 9–13 meeting.

The report was much more extensive than the ones preceding it. After an introduction, preprofessional requirements (which propose the personal characteristics required of the qualified person in pursuit of a career in clinical work), as well as recruitment and selection, were considered. This was followed by a discussion of the preprofessional program in college.

The general principles for the graduate professional program were described as follows: (1) A clinical psychologist must be first and foremost a psychologist. (2) The program for doctoral education in clinical psychology should be as rigorous and as extensive as that for the traditional doctorate. (3) Preparation should be broad; it should be directed toward research and professional goals. (4) In order to meet the above requirements, a core program calls for the study of six major areas: general psychology, psychodynamics of behavior, diagnostic methods, research methods, related disciplines, and therapy. (5) Programs should consist mainly of basic courses in principles, rather than the multiplication of courses in technique. The specific program of instruction should be organized around a careful integration of theory and practice, of academic and field work, by persons representing both aspects. (6) Through all 4 years of graduate work, the student should have contact, both direct and indirect, with clinical material. (8) The atmosphere should encourage maturity, particularly since a weakness in the training of psychologists, when compared with that of physicians and social workers, is the lack of a sufficient feeling of responsibility for patients and clients. Further, responsibilities should be associated with the day-to-day activities of the psychologist. (9) A systematic plan should be outlined to use representatives of related disciplines for teaching the trainee in clinical psychology, and opportunities for joint study with students in these disciplines should be provided. (10) Throughout the course of training there should be an emphasis on the research implications of phenomena as well as their evaluation. (11) Finally, trainees should become sensitive to the social implications of their work as well; they must acquire the ability to see beyond the responsibilities they owe the individual patient, to those they owe society. (This last point becomes increasingly valid when one considers the last Presidential address to the Division of Clinical Psychology [Siegel, Note 2]. Siegel argues for an absolute devotion of the therapist to the cause of the patient. The point of view here was decidedly not so absolute. It depends on the circumstances.)

A program of graduate training was then outlined. The schedule of courses presented was to serve merely as an example. We emphasized particularly that this program was to be an illustration of a plan, which might be met in various ways. There were six major instructional areas: General Psychology, Dynamics of Human Behavior, Related Disciplines, Diagnostic Methods, Therapy, and Research Methods. The 3rd year consisted of an internship whose content was discussed in more detail in a later section. The reasons for the 3rd-year internship were that the student could come from his or her experience with live cases and present before the more academically oriented psychologist the problem that he or she had found, so that together they might consider possible solutions. The goal was to enhance communication between the separate disciplines of psychology. Since communication includes "listening" as well as expounding, this communication was considered invaluable. Further, it was necessary to intrigue the academic psychologist with whether an internship might not offer *him* an unusual opportunity as well! (As it was for Thurstone, who once told me in an introspective moment that a period he had spent in a state hospital was his most valuable single experience. In fact, in his autobiography, [Thurstone, 1952, p. 314], he states that he became convinced that "no one should ever receive a doctorate in psychology without such an experience, no matter what his major field might be.")

For the 4th year, which was to be spent at the university, there was the final work on the dissertation, cross-discipline seminars, a seminar on professional problems, additional courses in psychology as needed to round out the individual student's program, additional courses from related fields as needed, therapeutic work if indicated, and a program of self-evaluation if that was called for, and it *was* called for with few exceptions (Shakow, 1976b, p. 556).

The next section was given over to the detailed discussion of the internship which took place in the 3rd year; it roughly followed a previous paper (Subcommittee on Graduate Internship Training, 1945). A further program was outlined on the dissertation, which was preferably to be done on a topic from the field. Again, this was followed by an integration of academic and field programs. An outline of a program of self-evaluation was included. The importance of student relationships and the significant part that these play in the student's learning were discussed and emphasized. In conclusion, the evaluation of accomplishment was considered. This section examined the doctoral degree, membership in the special division of the professional association, state certification after 1 year of postdoctoral experience, and finally, qualification for the American Board of Examiners in Professional Psychology after 5 years of postdoctoral experience.

The Committee on Training in Clinical Psychology (CTCP) consisted of Ernest Hilgard, Lowell Kelly, Bertha Luckey, Nevitt Sanford, Laurance Shaffer, and myself. The recommendations of the Committee were that (a) the report be endorsed, (b) the program be presented to the universities as a recommended program, and (c) the report be recommended for publication in the *American Psychologist*. These were acted upon favorably at the September meeting of the APA Council of Representatives. The CTCP's 1947 report was followed by a short, first progress report entitled, "Clinical Training Facilities: 1948" (Committee on Training in Clinical Psychology, 1948). It recommended that the first evaluation of schools by the Sears committee (which had preceded CTCP) should be honored until the next report came out. The second report, "Doctoral Training Programs in Clinical Psychology: 1949" (Committee on Training in Clinical Psychology, 1949), was longer and dealt with the problem of evaluation in detail. The work was financed by a grant of $12,000 from the APA. Karl Heiser was appointed as administrative officer of the Committee.

The 1949 report considered the criteria for evaluation of schools for clinical psychology and presented the methods of the committee in the evaluation procedure. It was to be sent to the Board of Directors of the APA, the Veterans Administration, and the U.S. Public Health Service, Mental Hygiene Division. In regard to the latter two, the evaluations were to serve as guides for the approval of grants. (Sitting on the Committee of Psychology in the U.S. Public Health Service, I can tell you that the recommendations of the Evaluations Committee were given extremely high consideration.)

The problem of evaluation was discussed with the schools on the methods used in selection and evaluation. The topics considered were (a) the selection and evaluation of students, (b) student load and staff size, (c) planning and integration of work, (d) breadth of curriculum, (e) clinical courses and techniques, (f) field work, and (g) physical equipment and general departmental facilities. This was followed by a summary of the current state of doctoral education in clinical psychology in the universities. Tables presented the estimated number of regular graduate students by degree in major areas and objectives, predictions of degrees (PhD) in clinical and other areas of psychology from 42 graduate departments, the student/staff ratios of university departments for clinical and other areas of psychology, and the distribution of graduate students by departments.

The next section followed with generalizations. In the first place, acknowledgement was made of the excellent job being done in the schools we had visited, through conscientious, highly motivated instruction in psychology. Nevertheless, we pointed out that there were serious shortcomings which needed attention. These were listed and considered. A serious problem arose in connection with the selection and evaluation of students. A rough classification seemed to be developing in the predominant motivations among students, which might be termed *scientific, economic,* and *human welfare*. The committee thought that a combination of the best aspects of all of them should be sought in the selection and training of students in clinical psychology. There seemed to be an overemphasis on training in clinical techniques at the expense of education in psychological theory and research methodology. In some respects, there was a narrow orientation as to the scope of clinical psychology as well. There was a recognition that psychiatric hospitals and clinics, the area which at the time offered the most complete field training, were predominant but that efforts should be made to go beyond these. There was a widespread concern about research (which included evaluation), training, and motivation, but there were difficulties in determining just how modifications were to be effected. The question on psychotherapy came particularly to the fore. Further, there was a concern about the problem of the extent to which students would go into the private practice of clinical psychology. The Committee, although taking no stand, felt that in our present state of knowledge, private practice by the single independent psychologist offered much less of value either to the client or the psychologist than did the team or group approach.

The subsequent series of conferences from Boulder in 1949 to Vail in 1973 should now be considered briefly. There have been five major conferences, and several minor ones. The five major conferences were held in Boulder (1949), Stanford (1955), Miami (1958), Chicago (1965), and Vail (1973).[1]

The CTCP of the APA would have been the logical group to organize the Boulder Conference, as this group had already prepared a report which was to serve as a basis for the Conference and was in the process of evaluating universities essentially according to the report. But it was deemed expedient to have another committee for this vital function. We recommended therefore that the APA Board of Directors set up a somewhat different plan. Since training programs for clinical psychology had been developed within the framework of academic departments of psychology,

---

[1] I am indebted to Pottharst (see Korman, 1976) for some of the features of this summary.

the departments themselves bore a large share of the responsibility for professional training and therefore should be heavily represented. For the Conference on Training in Clinical Psychology, two representatives were to be elected by university departments themselves on the basis of a mail ballot, and one person was to represent the Committee of University Departmental Chairmen.

As finally constituted, the Executive Committee included E. Lowell Kelly and Ann Magaret as representatives of the CTCP; William A. Hunt and James G. Miller as departmental representatives; and Wayne Dennis as representative of the APA Committee of University Departmental Chairmen. John C. Eberhart and Karl F. Heiser, representing the U.S. Public Health Service and the American Psychological Association, respectively, served as ex officio members of the Executive Committee. Victor Raimy of the University of Colorado served as administrative officer. Lowell Kelly became Chairman of the Executive Committee and later served as general chairman of the Conference.

Let me examine the stages of development of clinical psychology in the context of the Conferences. Before 1949, in the pre-Boulder stage, the responsibility for any kind of professional training in clinical psychology was placed on the student. It consisted essentially of "do-it-yourself" programs. The second stage, the Boulder model (see Raimy, 1950), set up university and practicum programs to implement the scientist/professional concept in courses but placed responsibility for acquiring professional competence, beyond bare entry-level skills, on the student in his or her postdoctoral years. It did, however, give considerable attention to the professional model of training in the context of the scientist/professional. The Stanford (Strother, 1957) and the Miami (Roe et al., 1959) Conferences held essentially the same point of view. The third stage, the Chicago Conference (Hoch, Ross, & Winder, 1966), opened and broadened the scientist/professional model with mandates for diversification and innovation within the programs. The fourth stage was promulgated at the Vail Conference (Korman, 1976), which was an action-oriented conference emphasizing the roles of minorities and women. It called for needed changes in standards of accreditation, in line with professional and professional/scientist models as alternatives to the scientist/professional model of Boulder.

In summary then, we seem to have developed a more catholic and comprehensive view of clinical psychologists. Not only do they practice within medical settings, which was predominant in the original view, but now they practice in all kinds of social settings and in private practice. They are in tune with developments in other fields, as can be seen in the growth of professional schools, are more in touch with the needs of minority groups (race and sex), both as clients and practitioners, and may practice in a limited way with bachelor's and master's level degrees. In practice, there is a tendency toward a preoccupation with helping people rather than with research and evaluation. Part of this is due to the greater number of persons recruited to the field and the demand for service, but part may be due to a change in the structure and goals of training.

Having given you a broad view of the development of certain phases of clinical psychology, I would next like to consider what changes I would like to see implemented. It is my private view developed over half a century. In this respect I can point to three minor events and one major event which had certain effects on the development of clinical training programs and on my views of such training. The first minor event grew out of the fact that I was a consultant for the Committee on Clinical Psychology of the Group for the Advancement of Psychiatry (GAP), from its beginning as an official organization in 1947. At the first meeting in Minneapolis, the Committee developed a statement on clinical psychology. During the course of this meeting I stated that, from the viewpoint of psychology, it was "only plain common sense for psychologists, who were competent, to participate in psychotherapy." Word of this got out to the Committee on Therapy who were meeting in an adjoining room. (It was then the practice in GAP, which consisted at the time of some 15 committees, to meet separately in committees and then meet in a plenary session.) In the midst of our meeting, they, as a total Committee, swarmed into our room and complained bitterly about such a statement being incorporated in our report. The "plain common sense" got to be something of a battle cry with which thereafter my psychiatrist friends kidded me.

Shortly afterwards another minor event occurred. Two leading clinical psychologists came to visit me at Illinois (where I had recently come) and remonstrated with me, claiming that I had sold psychology short. They did this on the basis of what they had heard as rumors, now somewhat distorted, from the GAP meeting. I explained as best I could, but I'm afraid that perhaps I did not quite allay their anxieties.

Against this background, a third minor event happened. A short time after this confrontation I was called on personally by Dr. Carl Rogers, then president of the APA, who urged me to undertake the chairpersonship of a Committee on Training in Clinical Psychology. This Committee would be responsible for a comprehensive report on clinical psychology and subsequently supervise the evaluations of universities and internship centers. I accepted the Committee appointment and the other members of the Committee were selected. The report that I have already discussed was one of its results. As I have indicated, the 1947 program was followed by the short report in 1948, and a second, longer report in 1949.

But now let us follow another path from that which we took a short time ago in tracing the succession of Conferences at Boulder and elsewhere. Shortly after our 1949 report, the *major* event to which I have alluded took place. It was Fill Sanford's Annual Report of the Executive Secretary of the APA for 1951 (Sanford, 1951). In this report, Fill Sanford presented an unusual document, one in which he developed a series of statements about psychology as a profession. Fill Sanford was an unusual human being —a grand personality, a grand secretary, and the most socially minded of our executive secretaries. Any tribute to him would have to take more time than I can devote. The document he prepared was as unusual as the man. These thoughts of Sanford's were considered at the next (August) meeting of the APA Ad hoc Committee on Relations between Psychology and the Medical Profession (1952). A slightly revised form of the statement, including the 13 aspirations of psychology as a profession and the basic principles to guide the relationship between psychology and the other professions, was drawn up. This was a report that psychology could very well be proud of, and it remains a monument to social–ethical thinking in the profession. (These 13 aspirations remind me a great deal, at its level, of Maimonides' 13 principles of faith, [the Ani Maimons (I Believes)] of the Jewish creed which is recited daily as part of the morning prayers.) These aspirations served concurrently as a declaration of independence and a code of ethics. The members of the committee were Joseph Bobbitt, Arthur Combs, J. McV. Hunt, Carlyle Jacobsen, Rensis Likert, Fill Sanford, and myself, with Lowell Kelly as chairman.

Because of their importance, I am here outlining the characteristics that were included in these aspirations for the profession. A good profession: (1) guides its practices and policies by a sense of social responsibility; (2) will devote relatively little of its energy to "guild" functions, to the building of its own ingroup strength, and relatively much of its energy to the serving of its social functions; (3) will not represent itself as able to render services beyond its demonstrable competence; (4) has a code of ethics designed primarily to protect the client and only secondarily to protect the members of the profession; (5) will find its unique pattern of competence and focus its efforts on carrying out these functions for which it is best equipped; (6) will engage in rational and cooperative relations with other professions having related or overlapping competences and common purposes; (7) will be characterized by an adaptive balance among efforts devoted to research, teaching, and to application; (8) will maintain good channels of communication among the "discoverers," the teachers, and the appliers of knowledge; (9) is free of nonfunctional entrance requirements; (10) is one in which preparatory training is validly related to the ultimate functions of the members of the profession; (11) will guard against adopting any technique or theory as the final solution to its problems and is continually concerned with the validity of its techniques and procedures; (12) is one whose members are socially and financially accessible to the public; and finally, (13) is a free profession.

As an outgrowth of these aspirations, certain basic principles were seen to guide the relationship between psychology and other professions. The APA accepts full responsibility for coordinating the development and furthering of the profession of psychology. It accepts, first of all, (a) the responsibility for advancing basic knowledge concerning human behavior, (b) the responsibility for training qualified aspirants to professional competence, (c) the responsibility for establishing and maintaining standards of professional competence, and (d) the responsibility for serving society in accordance with the code of ethics designed to protect both the individuals and the society which it serves.

Second, psychology is concerned with the application of the methods of science to the problems of human behavior. The profession assumes responsibility for encouraging research and facilitating the communication of research findings.

Third, as teachers, psychologists accept and share the ethics and ideals of the teaching profession.

Fourth, as administrators of the professional activities of psychologists and/or other professional persons, psychologists accept and share the responsibilities and ethics of persons serving in an administrative capacity.

Fifth, as appliers of their knowledge, skills, and techniques, psychologists accept and share the responsibilities and ethics of the group of professions which deal with human advancement and welfare.

Sixth, as an autonomous profession, psychology cannot accept limitations upon the freedom of thought and actions of its members other than limitations imposed by its social responsibility and considerations of public welfare. The professions must resist moves from any source to establish nonfunctional restraints on the behavior of psychologists, whether in the role of teacher, researcher, administrator, or practitioner.

Encompassed in these aspirations I see the eight principles that I have identified with, explicitly and implicitly, over these years: (1) Psychology is one, and the clinical psychologist is primarily a psychologist; (2) psychology must be studied in the field as well as in the laboratory; (3) the preparation of the psychologist should take place with due attention to scientific background, although the psychologist may practice a professional skill afterwards; (4) in practice, the psychologist may be a scientist, a scientist/professional (and it is a task much more combinable than is often thought to be [Albee, 1970]), a professional/scientist, or a professional, but the important thing is that he or she be *prepared* with the viewpoint of the researcher and evaluator of results; (5) the psychologist is humble and modest, making relatively few claims for his or her knowledge; (6) the psychologist is identified with the client but in those rare instances where there is a conflict must take a social point of view; (7) the clinical psychologist and the experimental psychologist work harmoniously toward a common overriding goal; and (8) the ultimate aim of psychologists is to achieve the maturity to treat conflicts among disciplines or professions objectively.

All in all I tend to think that to accomplish these goals, the persons involved, though having diverse interests in psychology, must have essential goodwill and a desire to work for the good of the whole. Thus I have emphasized, among other things, (a) the use of good universities as initial training centers for doctoral programs, rather than professional schools, because of the university's greater flexibility, scope, and standards; (b) a third-year internship, in hopes of getting academic and clinical psychology working closer together, and (c) a self-evaluation program.

I can of course, be accused of being for motherhood and all the other celebrated virtues! (Although the first of these is an increasing doubtful value in some circles!) Or you can attribute it, at best, to a certain type of conservatism, the aspiration for values which seem essentially outdated and out of style. At worst, you can blame my stubbornness. But in line with a relatively recent article by Fairlie in *The New Republic* (November 13, 1976), I say that, at one level, the clinical psychologist is the analogue of the political journalist who should "go out on a limb, commit not only his judgment but his faith." Judgment, taken as far as it can possibly go, and then, faith—this is what I am doing now.

What psychology needs at this point is to define clinical psychology within itself and in its relations with the experimental group, and then to clarify relationships with related professions. It need not deal with the issues as extremely as, for instance, either a Derner (1977) or as Albee (1977) does in relation to health insurance. For Derner, "Psychology *is* a health profession" (p. 3), and should be covered by national health insurance. Since the field is behavioral, the psychologists can challenge the psychiatrists in many areas for its control. Albee, on the other hand, maintains that the field of the medical is much restricted and that problems of living are not medical: Problems in living are not sicknesses; psychotherapy should not be covered under national health insurance. The behavioral model is quite different from the medical model, so he leaves the former field to the psychologists. However, life, and even models, are not so simple. The lines of distinction between the medical and the behavioral are not so easy to determine. They overlap considerably, and competent practitioners of each will have to live in harmony with each other and define the fields of their operation amicably; otherwise, the patient or client, the person for whom we are doing all of this, will suffer, especially the poor and indigent, who deserve our particular attention (Meltzer, 1975).

I must say that I lose my "cool" temporarily when I hear of violations of the sensible borders of mutual practice by psychiatrists. I react in a similar way when psychologists are to blame, although I hold them less responsible, for they are relatively fresh in this field and bound to be "pushy." As I said in 1948,

> Psychologists work from the normal end of the distribution toward the middle, and psychiatrists work from the pathological end toward the

middle. There is bound to be a very considerable area of overlap where definition *is* not, and *cannot* be, clear. Is not our major concern with the development of adequately prepared professional people who have a care for the needs of the person studied, who are sensitive to the range of problems in their own field and to the problems of colleagues in other fields, who are appreciative of social needs, and who above all possess essential good will? Under such circumstances, couldn't we depend on specific problems being taken care of satisfactorily as they arise? (Shakow, 1949, pp. 381–382)

A clarification of the issues within clinical psychology and between the different fields of psychology is needed. An experience of my own in conflict with a leading experimental psychologist highlights this relationship. When I wrote that the academic psychologists "ought to come off it" and pay attention to the objective aspects of clinical psychology rather than to the activities of a few (Shakow, 1965), this psychologist raised questions, and a lively epistolary interchange ensued. I maintained that the experimentalists had not given the clinical psychologists a chance, had not supported clinical training, and had been ready to think the worst of clinical psychologists. He reluctantly came to the same conclusion, although he felt that the clinical psychologists had placed too much emphasis on therapy in the process and had therefore prejudiced their case.

On the other hand, clinical psychologists have to be certain of their own development and cause. Clinical psychology is in the unique position, both as a social discipline and as a profession, to recognize the dangers in too early professionalization and an abandonment of the researcher's prerogatives. These pertain more to the clinical psychologists than they do to other professions. This is true at least historically speaking. Just as in the World War II days the matter was taken out of our hands with the rapid development of events, so great social pressures take the present development out of our hands: health insurance, Medicare and Medicaid, and the urge to practice. It would indeed be too bad to give way to these trends altogether. For in the long run, it is the task-oriented psychologist, the one who maintains standards, the one who makes good work rather than devout wishes his or her goal, who will come out ahead.

I support Atkinson (1977) in his "Reflections on Psychology's Past and Concerns about Its Future," and in another sense, I accept the pleas that Engel (1977) makes, for psychiatrists, for the need for a bio/psycho/social model. This need for psychology is equally urgent and the major means to its fulfillment is still through research and evaluation.

There are many remaining problems, as there should be in any viable field. One of the outstanding items is that of a decision on the relative emphasis on therapy or research as the nature of the major practice by the clinical psychologist. Such patterns as that of McCullough (Note 3) of Virginia Commonwealth University and several others that I am sure I am not aware of seem worthwhile. Another problem has to do with the length of the program. At the time of the CTCP there was a strong suspicion that the 4-year program would not be sufficient. But for the purpose of expediency, it was decided (assuming that PhD programs were ideally 3 years in length) to make it 4 years. It has in fact turned out to be insufficient. Therefore, a 5-year program seems advisable. In addition, there seems to be a need for more flexibility in the placement of the internship. It might be determined in large part on the basis of situation, such as the location of the graduate school and the internship center. This (either the 3rd-year placement in a 4-year program, or a 4th-year placement in a 5-year program) remains the ideal.

Closely related to this is the matter of program financing. A financial scheme should be worked out with the National Institute of Mental Health (and other agencies) which permits the support of the program throughout. There are, of course, political issues that become heated because of the implications of the money problems related to national health insurance, and there are the remaining issues which are as old as this field—the questions about the goals and principles of the program, the personality requirements, the best organization of academic and field experiences, etc.

I might conclude with a series of pleas to departments of psychology, to divisions of clinical psychology, and to other disciplines in the field of mental health. I would plead with the departments of psychology to view the training of clinical psychologists as equally worthy as the training of experimental or research psychologists. I would plead with the divisions of clinical psychology to make their programs equally valid for their purposes, as is the training of experimental psychologists for their purposes, and to make field training as valid as the laboratory experience. To the students in clinical psychology, I would plead to make *standards* in whatever they do their criterion. I would plead with other disciplines to see psychology as having its place in the diagnostic, preventive, therapeutic, and research aspects of mental health in relation to the competences of these psychologists to carry out these functions. (In other words, to judge the person, as well as the profession.) The pleas are ultimately not directed *at* the professions or at the disciplines, but *for* the patient. If the patient or client is to be considered in the end central, then what may be viewed as variations in conduct and trespasses on each other's fields will indeed become secondary.

REFERENCE NOTES

1. Hilgard, E. R. How broad was psychology before and after World War II? In D. L. Krantz (Chair), *Psychology, pre and post World War II*. Symposium pre-

sented at the meeting of the American Psychological Association, San Francisco, 1977.
2. Siegel, M. *Privacy, ethics, and confidentiality.* Division 12 Presidential Address presented at the meeting of the American Psychological Association, San Francisco, August 1977.
3. McCullough, J. P. *The coming of age of clinical psychology.* Unpublished manuscript, Virginia Commonwealth University, 1977.

REFERENCES

Ad hoc Committee on Relations between Psychology and the Medical Profession. Psychology and its relationships with other professions. *American Psychologist,* 1952, *7,* 145–152.

Albee, G. W. The uncertain future of clinical psychology. *American Psychologist,* 1970, *25,* 1071–1080.

Albee, G. W. Problems in living are not sicknesses. *Clinical Psychologist,* 1977, *30,* 3–6.

Atkinson, R. C. Reflections on psychology's past and concerns about its future. *American Psychologist,* 1977, *32,* 205–210.

Brotemarkle, R. A. Fifty years of clinical psychology—1896–1946. *Journal of Consulting Psychology,* 1947, *11,* 1–4.

Committee on Scientific and Professional Aims of Psychology. The scientific and professional aims of psychology. *American Psychologist,* 1967, *22,* 49–76.

Committee on Training in Clinical Psychology. Recommended graduate training program in clinical psychology. *American Psychologist,* 1947, *2,* 539–558.

Committee on Training in Clinical Psychology. Clinical training facilities: 1948. *American Psychologist,* 1948, *3,* 317–318.

Committee on Training in Clinical Psychology. Doctoral training programs in clinical psychology: 1949. *American Psychologist,* 1949, *4,* 331–341.

Cronbach, L. J. Beyond the two disciplines of scientific psychology. *American Psychologist,* 1975, *30,* 116–127.

Derner, G. F. Psychology—a health profession or a settled issue, so why the question. *Clinical Psychologist,* 1977, *30,* 3–8.

Doll, E. A. Psychometric pitfalls in clinical practice. *Journal of Consulting Psychology,* 1947, *11,* 12–21.

Engel, G. L. The need for a new medical model: A challenge for biomedicine. *Science,* 1977, *196,* 129–136.

Hawley, P. R. The importance of clinical psychology in a complete medical program. *Journal of Consulting Psychology,* 1946, *10,* 292–300.

Hoch, E. L., Ross, A. O., & Winder, C. L. (Eds.). *Professional preparation of clinical psychologists: Proceedings of the Conference on the Professional Preparation of Clinical Psychologists meeting at the Center for Continuing Education, Chicago, Illinois,*

August 27–September 1, 1965. Washington, D.C.: American Psychological Association, 1966.

Korman, M. (Ed.). *Levels and patterns of professional training in psychology: Conference Proceedings, Vail, Colorado, July 25–30, 1973.* Washington, D.C. American Psychological Association, 1976.

Krech, D. A note on fission. *American Psychologist,* 1946, *1,* 402–404.

Meltzer, M. L. Insurance reimbursement—A mixed blessing. *American Psychologist,* 1975, *30,* 1150–1164.

Raimy, V. (Ed.). *Training in clinical psychology* (by the staff of the Conference on Graduate Education in Clinical Psychology held at Boulder, Colorado in August of 1949). New York: Prentice-Hall, 1950.

Roe, A., Gustad, J. W., Moore, B. V., Ross, S., & Skodak, M. (Eds.). *Graduate education in psychology: Report of the Conference on Graduate Education in Psychology* (sponsored by the Education and Training Board of the APA and held at Miami Beach, Florida, November 29 to December 7, 1958). Washington, D.C.: American Psychological Association, 1959.

Sanford, F. H. Annual report of the executive secretary: 1951. *American Psychologist,* 1951, *6,* 664–670.

Sanford, N. Graduate education, then and now. In J. Katz & R. T. Harnett (Eds.), *Scholars in the making: The development of graduate and professional students.* Cambridge, Mass.: Ballinger, 1976.

Shaffer, L. F. Clinical psychology and psychiatry. *Journal of Consulting Psychology,* 1947, *11,* 5–11.

Shakow, D. The psychological department in a state hospital. *Bulletin of the Massachusetts Department of Mental Diseases,* 1930, *14,* 7–9.

Shakow, D. An internship year for psychologists (with special reference to psychiatric hospitals). *Journal of Consulting Psychology,* 1938, *2,* 73–76.

Shakow, D. The functions of the psychologist in the state hospital. *Journal of Consulting Psychology,* 1939, *3,* 20–23.

Shakow, D. The nature of deterioration in schizophrenic conditions. *Nervous Mental Disease Monographs,* 1946, No. 70, 1–88.

Shakow, D. Psychology and psychiatry: A dialogue (Parts I and II). *American Journal of Orthopsychiatry,* 1949, *19,* 191–258; 381–396.

Shakow, D. Seventeen years later: Clinical psychology in the light of the 1947 CTCP report. *American Psychologist,* 1965, *20,* 353–362.

Shakow, D. *Clinical psychology as science and profession: A forty year odyssey.* Chicago: Aldine Press, 1969.

Shakow, D. The Worcester State Hospital research on schizophrenia (1927–1946). *Journal of Abnormal Psychology,* 1972, *80,* 67–110.

Shakow, D. Reflections on a do-it-yourself program in clinical psychology. *Journal of the History of the Behavioral Sciences,* 1976, *12,* 14–30. (a)

Shakow, D. What is clinical psychology? *American Psychologist,* 1976, *31,* 553–560. (b)

Strother, C. R. (Ed.). *Psychology and mental health: A report of the Institute on Education and Training for Psychological Contributions to Mental Health, held at Stanford University in August, 1955.* Washington, D.C.: American Psychological Association, 1957.

Subcommittee on Graduate Internship Training to the Committees on Graduate and Professional Training of the APA and AAAP. Graduate internship training in psychology. *Journal of Consulting Psychology,* 1945, 9, 243–266.

Thurstone, L. L. *A history of psychology in autobiography* (Vol. 4). In E. G. Boring, H. S. Langfeld, H. Werner, & R. M. Yerkes (Eds.), Worcester, Mass.: Clark University Press, 1952.

22

AN ASOCIAL PSYCHOLOGY AND A MISDIRECTED CLINICAL PSYCHOLOGY

SEYMOUR B. SARASON

In what social-historical context did the major features of modern clinical psychology initially gain expression? How did this context affect the universe of policy alternatives modern clinical psychology could have considered in its early phase? Why did clinical psychology so readily accommodate to a public policy that not only defined what the "mental health problem" was in our society but also outlined how that problem was to be approached? And why did the basis of that approach in an individual psychology go unexamined? It is the last question that interests me the most because I have come to believe that from its inception a hundred years ago, American psychology has been quintessentially a psychology of the individual organism, a characteristic that however it may have been

---

This article was originally the presidential address to Division 12 (Clinical Psychology), presented at the meeting of the American Psychological Association, Montreal, September 1980. The author gratefully acknowledges the help provided by Michael Klaber during the writing of this article.
Reprinted from *American Psychologist*, 36, 827–836 (1981). Copyright © 1981 by the American Psychological Association. Reprinted with permission of the author.

and is productive has severely and adversely affected psychology's contribution to human welfare. I elaborate later on this point, but those who may want to delve more deeply into this question I urge to read the APA publication edited by Hilgard (1978), which contains addresses of presidents of the association, beginning with William James. With one notable exception one would hardly know that psychology existed in a particular society having a distinctive social order deriving from a very distinctive past, that psychologists did not (and do not) represent a random assortment of people, and that by virtue of their socialization into their society, and their social–professional niche in it, the *substance* of their theories had to reflect these factors. Instead, one finds a riveting on the individual organism. The one notable exception, and it is a dramatically instructive exception, is a presidential address given in 1899 in New Haven with the title "Psychology and Social Practice." If psychology (then and now) had been able to understand this address, which was quite critical of the directions psychology was taking, American psychology would not now be suffering the malaise it is.

I have recently completed a book, *Psychology Misdirected* (Sarason, 1981), that is dedicated to the APA president who gave that address: John Dewey. Psychologists think of John Dewey, when they think of him at all, as an educator and philosopher who *once* was a psychologist. But Dewey saw clearly what psychology still is blind to: The substance of psychology cannot be independent of the social order. It is not that it *should not* be independent but that it *cannot* be. But American psychology has never felt comfortable pursuing the nature and consequences of the social order. Let the other social sciences wrestle with such matters! Besides, a true understanding of the social order, as well as efforts to change and improve it, could only come after psychology illuminated human nature, individual human nature. Psychology had it backwards, a fact to which it cannot be sensitive as long as theories are about individuals—as single individuals, as individuals in a dyad or small group, or as individuals in a family. For all practical purposes, social history and the social order were ignored. And this explains why when psychology really entered the "real world" and the arena of public policy in the post-World War II period, it was, from my standpoint, the beginning of a disaster. I must now turn to elaborating on these points by reflecting on the history of modern clinical psychology. This introduction has been necessary if only to underline the point that the limitations of clinical psychology inhered in American psychology.

CONSEQUENCES OF WORLD WAR II

Modern clinical psychology was a direct outgrowth of World War II. At all levels of federal government during the war, there was recognition that the government would have responsibility for a staggering number of veterans who in one way or another would be physical or mental casualties. That the government "owed" these casualties the best kind of care was clear, and the best kind of care would have to be quite different from that provided veterans in the decades after World War I. To provide this care would require a policy that would facilitate the placement of facilities and services in or near medical centers. That policy was intended to create a partnership between the Veterans Administration (VA) and the medical centers, the bulk of which would be university based. The VA wanted the quality services the medical centers could provide, and the medical centers needed the new facilities for training and research. No one raised the possibility that given the traditions of medical centers, especially their professional preciousness and imperialistic ambience, partnership would, in practice, mean domination by the medical centers. It was a policy that assumed that self-serving professionalism would not be a problem. It was not a policy rooted in the sociology of professions in general and the medical profession in particular. Indeed (as I discuss later in relation to clinical psychology), one of the characteristics of the policymaking process is the absence of sensitivity to social history. But there was an even more fateful, implicit assumption to the policy: Veterans would get "better" in the hospitals and clinics and then return to their homes and communities. That assumption contains a kernel of truth in relation to physical illness, but if I had the time I would have no difficulty demonstrating that from the standpoint of prevention of personal, family, and work problems, this kernel of truth is not all that impressive. In relation to psychological problems there is no kernel of truth. By their very nature these problems are individual–family–work–community related. In fact, as the VA learned in subsequent decades, hospitalization and clinic visits that focused on the intrapsychic dynamics of the individual were frequently counterproductive or simply ineffective.

Another important stimulus to the formulation of a policy for casualties of the war was an economic one, not only in terms of money for facilities and personnel but in terms of payments to veterans depending on their degree of war-incurred handicap. I am not attributing unworthy motivations to the policymakers when I say they were quite concerned that many veterans would seek to obtain payments from the government disproportionate to their handicaps and that some would manufacture symptoms to be eligible for payments. In short, there was the potential for an adversary relationship between the veterans and the professionals in the medical centers who would have to render judgments about degree of disability. This, of course, raised the question, Whom did the professionals represent? The potential for conflicts of interests, as well as for self-serving actions, was obvious on all sides. If what was obvious was not taken seriously, it was in part because everyone assumed that money would not be a problem, that the VA budget would increase to meet needs. So what if some veterans were getting benefits they did not merit? It may be somewhat unfair to say that the policymakers envisioned an endless gravy train. It is not unfair to say that they were naively ahistorical in the extreme in adopting such a stance toward the future. It took less than a decade for the professionals to learn that they were enmeshed in a system which put serious obstacles in the way of their therapeutic efforts and raised ethical-moral questions the professionals did not know how to deal with, except by getting out, which many began to do.

Unless one lived through those early post-World War II days, it is hard to appreciate the role of money as an incentive to medical center departments to enter the partnership. In the case of psychiatry, which up to World War II was not a strong or prestigeful part of medical schools and medical centers, the VA presented a fairyland of delights: new facilities, additional personnel, residencies paid for by the government, consulting fees for faculty, research budgets, and all else that makes for gracious living. There are no grounds for questioning the sincerity of departments of psychiatry insofar as helping veterans was concerned. There are grounds for saying that the VA medical center tie presented psychiatry with the opportunity to become more influential vis-à-vis other specialties. And it is also true that departments of psychiatry did not see this tie as an end in itself but as a means whereby other non-VA activities were made possible. Noblesse oblige characterized psychiatry's stance, which in practice meant, as it does in some legal partnerships, that there was a general partner and a limited partner. Guess who was the limited partner? The economics of the VA medical center tie reinforced the imperialistic traditions of American medicine, resulting in battles among medical departments and in "foreign" wars with "allied" health fields centering around resources, status, and prerogatives.

One could ask me, "Assuming you are even partially correct—about not getting 'better' in a hospital or clinic; about the consequences of personal troubles for family, community, and work; about the self-serving actions that money (a lot of it!) as an incentive played into—why didn't the policymakers know these things? Did they know them but in examining alternative policies find none that had fewer pitfalls?" To answer these questions requires that one ask and answer the question, Who were the policymakers? In a formal, flow chart, descriptive sense this is not an easy question to answer, but in terms of informal process and power the answer is clear: The "official," legislatively sanctioned policymakers were mightily influenced by representatives of university medical centers who were in high positions in the armed forces during World War II or who were called in as consultants. Their sincerity was as unquestioned as their ability to dispassionately consider alternatives was lacking. On the surface it might seem that their support for a VA–medical center relationship was blatantly self-serving; after all, they were advocating a policy that would pour millions of dollars into their institutions. The self-serving feature was there, but it should not obscure the fact that academic psychiatry saw itself at the threshold of a new era, as leaving behind the aridities, superficialities, and sterile biologisms of prewar psychiatry for a new psychiatry that was "dynamic," "deep," and effective. Psychoanalysis became legitimated by academic psychiatry, which meant that the analytic-training institutes—religious in attitude and ritual, desperate to become a recognized medical specialty, uncomfortable and silent about Freud's position on lay analysis, and disdainful of those who did not accept Freud's truths as interpreted by institute-anointed ayatollahs—added an ingredient quite compatible with the medical profession's attitudes of preciousness, exclusiveness, special social status, and tradition-conferred leadership role.

All that I have said so far can be summarized as follows: Health policy for veterans, formulated in terms of medical concepts, practices, and traditions, sought to interrelate two organizational curltures—the university medical center and a large, complex federal bureau. Neither of the organizations had experience with such a formal interrelationship, and neither attempted to understand the other's culture and what that presaged for their future relationships. It was a policy that stemmed from a process amazingly devoid of serious consideration of alternative approaches; it was a medical policy in terms of who would be responsible for implementation and what the nature (and language) and where the site of diagnosis and treatment would be.

Concern and responsibility for veterans was only one of the ingredients that helped usher in the new Age of Mental Health (Sarason, 1977). World War II was truly a world war, and it was a long one. No one in this country was unaffected by the war. For millions of people family life was disrupted as one or more of a family's members (sons, fathers, close relatives) were gone for months or years, died, or came back a casualty or stranger. And many who remained at home also changed and were as strangers to the returning veterans. It was a mammoth upheaval that accelerated the pace of prewar, socially centrifugal forces of change. In films, novels, plays, and radio dramas there was a common message: As a result of the war, the world, and everyone in it, would never be the same. That was "good" because it meant that the opportunity to build a better world was at hand, but it also raised the question of whether people were appropriately prepared for the coming changes. Although the end of the war was greeted with ecstatic relief, it was also accompanied by anxiety about another economic depression, the readjustment of veterans to civilian life, and whether the government could move quickly enough to mount programs that would head off social unrest.

By saying that World War II ushered in the Age of Mental Health, I am trying to reflect several facts. One was the influential role of mental health professionals in the corridors of power and policy, roles undreamed of in the prewar period. If they gained such roles, it was in large part because there was in the larger society an inchoate consensus that the frequency of personal problems had escalated and would continue to do so. If the incidence of personal breakdowns among veterans during the war was disturbingly high, if the incidence would increase with war's end as veterans returned to civilian life, it followed that a large segment of the civilian population would be subjected to disabling stress. A health policy for veterans alone would not be adequate to deal with the nonveteran population. Viewed in this way, it was obvious that a crash program to train more mental health professionals would be needed. But, the mental health professionals said, there was not only a shortage of personnel but a shortage of scientific knowledge about the causes and treatment of personal disorders. What the government had to do, they said, was to support basic research. If the atomic scientists had contributed so much to the successful prosecution of the war, it was because they were able to exploit the findings of basic research. What the government had to recognize was that in the coming decades the frequency of disabling personal problems would emerge near or at the top of society's problems and unless more basic knowledge about human behavior was obtained, there was no telling what the consequences would be. These were the considerations that led to the annual increases in the budget of the National Institute of Mental Health (NIMH). The mental health professionals promised a lot, wanted a lot, and got a lot. I need not elaborate on the fact that psychiatry dominated in the formulation of NIMH policy and obtained the largest fraction of financial support. The social sciences were deemed important but in terms of expenditures, not all that important. In the case of NIMH training grants for clinical psychology, they were dispensed by criteria which required that clinical psychologists obtain their field training in medical–psychiatric settings.

The Age of Psychotherapy is another way to label the post-World War II years. From the standpoint of psychology as a field, it really began with the publication of Rogers's (1942) *Counseling and Psychotherapy*, a book that had quite an impact in and beyond psychology. This book was truly a pioneer effort, and I in no way intend to devalue it when I say that from my standpoint its consequences for clinical psychology and public policy were unfortunate. For one thing it defined (and made extraordinarily interesting) the problems of people in terms of an individual psychology: Problems were personal or narrowly interpersonal and for all practical purposes independent of the nature and structure of the social order. The mode of treatment was an individual one, which started a lively controversy about the comparative efficacy of different modes of individual treatment. Psychotherapy became the mental aspirin and people flocked to get the credentials to dispense it. The problem for public policy was how to train enough psychotherapists to deal with the people who needed them. But that problem ran headlong into another policy issue: Who owned psychotherapy? This issue is implied in the title of Rogers's book because if counseling and psychotherapy were basically the same, medicine and psychiatry could not claim, as they did, that these were only in their domain.

Anyone who lived through those days will testify to the vehemence and resources with which organized medicine and psychiatry fought to keep others from their turf. Organized psychiatry was faced with a problem in large measure of its own making. It had helped formulate and promote a public policy that recognized the need for clinical psychologists in the psychiatric setting, albeit in a subordinate role. But in terms of the overwhelming need for psychologists in these settings, on what basis could one deny clinical psychologists a therapeutic function? And even if one wanted to restrict psychologists to a diagnostic and research role, how could one deny them a function that would make those roles more cogent and effective? The battle was waged on legal, professional, and social grounds. It was also waged on financial and status grounds because about the only thing that was clear in the smoke of battle was that in the psychiatric setting there was a near perfect correlation between salary and status, on the one hand, and who did how much psychotherapy, on the other hand. But one thing was clear: Psychiatric–medical settings were not created by and administered for nonmedical personnel.

One would be very wrong if one interpreted all that I have said as a diatribe against medicine and psychiatry. But one would be right in interpreting what I have said, albeit too briefly and oversimplified, as a way of describing characteristics of the culture of American medicine in our society. It is a culture that socializes its members to view themselves and others in isolating ways; it cannot countenance challenges to its conceptions of leadership; it is quintessentially clinically oriented in contrast to a preventive orientation; it operates on the principle that what is good for medicine is good for the society; and it is almost totally lacking in the sense of social history that makes one humble before the fact that as individuals and collectivities we are inevitably prisoners of time and place, that self-interest and public interest should not be assumed to be identical, that how self-interest is defined depends on where one is in the social order and that to transcend time and place, even in small part, requires that one put into words what the socialization process, because it was so effective, made it unnecessary to verbalize. I could, of course, say many positive things about American medicine, but to understand public policy in regards to illness—which means how, as a professional culture, it tries to influence the use and direction of society's resources—one has to look at American medicine in terms of its traditions, institutional structures, rites of passage, and economic base and interests. It is trivializing the issue to discuss it in terms of the "good guys and the bad guys," a Manichean view derived from an individual psychology that leads to premature moralizing.

THE NARROW DIRECTION OF CLINICAL PSYCHOLOGY

Now let me turn to clinical psychology and why it took the directions it did. What factors led it, unfortunately from my standpoint, to become embroiled in the culture of American medicine and psychiatry? To do justice to this question would require writing a book. Here I briefly discuss only a few of the major facets of my answer. To begin, the clinical tradition had a very flimsy base in prewar American psychology. At best psychology was aclinical in orientation; at worst, it was anticlinical. That is to say, psychology had no experience with what was involved in training clinical psychologists, with the creation of settings for clinical practice, and with the culture of existing settings devoted to clinical service. It was a Johnny-come-lately to the clinical scene. When, as a direct result of the experience of leading psychologists during the war, as well as of the stimulus provided by an emerging federal policy, psychology sought (and was sought) formally to enter the clinical scene, it self-consciously had and proclaimed two assets, one major and one minor. The major asset was its research traditions and sophistication. The minor asset was embedded in psychology's role in the testing movement. I call it a minor asset because the area of testing was never in the mainstream of American psychology, but was a tributary, and also because so much of what went on in testing was either nonclinical in goal or very superficially clinical. (It could be argued that, major or minor, psychology's contribution to the testing movement has had negative consequences for society.) These two assets were also highly regarded by psychiatry, which, in propagandizing (used here nonpejoratively) for a new public mental health policy, emphasized the need for research on diagnosis and treatment. Psychology may have come late to the scene, but it was cordially welcomed. It presented no challenge, conceptually and institutionally, to psychiatry. Psychology would be part of the team. There was no question about who would captain the team and where the game would be played.

I must digress here to mention another asset, far more subtle than the first two, that was fateful for the future. It was an asset (more in the nature of a mixed blessing) that was as overlooked as it was obvious, but it had the kind of obviousness the significance of which could only be appreciated if one looked at psychology in terms of its institutional placement and culture. I refer to the fact that psychology was an arts and science discipline, not a professional one, in the university. It had successfully fought for and obtained an independent status in the university, which is another way of saying that it was constituted of fiercely independent individuals encouraged to do and used to doing things their way. The socialization process in graduate education inculcated the values of autonomy and no-holds-barred pursuit of knowledge. The spirit of accommodation, let alone subordination, was not in the picture. Of course, this spirit was not in the picture of psychiatry and medicine either. Two subcultures were on a collision course, but like in so many partnerships and marriages, the characteristics that can produce collisions are rarely confronted despite their obviousness.

From the standpoint of psychology, the tie that was being forged between clinical psychology and the psychiatric setting was a socially responsible one. Psychology saw itself as meeting social needs in ways consistent with and enriching of its own traditions and knowledge. What was also attractive about this tie was that it would be financially underwritten by the federal government, meaning that students would be supported, faculties enlarged, and consultantships arranged. Were it not for federal policy and funds, would clinical psychology have forged the tie that it did? And if this question had been clearly raised, the truly important policy question for psychology would have to come to the fore: What was the universe of alternatives that psychology, in general, and clinical psychology, in particular, should consider in deciding how they could best contribute to what was defined as a staggering mental health problem? This was the question psychology had to ask in arriving at a policy. But the question was never seriously raised for several reasons. One is that psychology had no conceptual and research tradition in regard to policy formulation. Psychology had a long tradition of research on problem solving, but the significance of this tradition for the process of policy formulation was not seen. Another reason is that psychology, no less than psychiatry and medicine, was a babe-in-the-woods when it came to understanding the history and nature of government. This is but another way of saying that social psychology had never come to grips with the history, culture, and organization of American society. Social psychology was social in the sense that it was riveted on individuals and interactions among them: the attitudes individuals brought with them and the ways attitudes changed as a consequence of the interactions. It was social in the sense of having an interpersonal or a small-group focus. It was not social in the sense of placing these interactions in the context of a highly differentiated society with a distinctive culture and ideology that were reflected in and reinforced by governmental, political, educational, religious, and financial (profit-making) systems of institutions. This is the point that John Dewey made in his presidential address to the American Psychological Association in 1899 (see Hilgard, 1978). It is a point also made by Brown (1936) in his book *Psychology and the Social Order*, a heroically systematic effort to conceptually integrate Marx, Freud, and Lewin and a massive indictment of academic social psychology as well. Brown's book was the only social psychology text of the time to deal with the significance of the Great Depression. And more than passing mention must be made of Dollard's (1935) *Criteria for the Life History*, a title that unfortunately does not reflect what Dollard was about, which was to examine case descriptions of major theorists to see how seriously they took the concepts of culture and social order in relation to socialization and development. Dollard (1935) wrote,

> A life historian, sophisticated in the above sense, can see his life history subject as a link in a chain of social transmission; there were links before him from which he acquired his present culture; other links will follow him to which he will pass on the current of tradition. The life history attempts to describe a unit in that process; it is a study of one of the strands of a complicated collective life which has historical continuity. The fact that an individual believes his culture to be "his" in some powerful personal sense, as though he had thought out for himself how to do the things which he actually does by traditional prescription, will not impress the observer who has the cultural view. He will regard this conviction as unimportant and will stress the point of uniformity of the subject's behavior with that of persons who have lived before him and who now live in the same group. In such a "march" of a culture through time the individual is seen as less than a phantom; in point of fact, the individual only appears in times of crisis when the mores are not adequate to meet some real life situation which the group faces.
>
> *We are stressing at this point the fact that the scientific student of a human life must adequately acknowledge the enormous background mass of the culture; and not as a mere mass either, but rather as a configurated whole.* Before any individual appears his society has had a specific social life organized and systematized, and the existence of this life will exercise a tyrannical compulsion on him. Seen from this point of view the problem of the life history is a statement of how the new organism becomes the victim or the resultant of this form structure of the culture. Each life history that is gathered will be a record of how a new person is added to the group. It will be a case of seeing "the group plus a person." To state the point in an extreme manner we can think of the organic man as the mere toy of culture, providing it with a standardized base, investing its forms with affect but creating very little that is new alone or at any one time.
>
> If our life historian is not equipped with the above criterion he will certainly fall into error by referring to accident, whims of individuals, or organic propulsion, much that is properly seen only as a part of the society into which the individual comes. These errors seem so chronic and immortal in social science thinking that it is hard to overdo the necessity of a very schematic statement of the cultural view. *Many individuals who are quite able to state the point, after one fashion or another, are persistently unable to work it through into their manner of dealing with problems.* One of the marks of an effective grasping of this point is the stated or implied "in our culture" whenever one makes any point in connection with individual behavior; it is a good thing to get into the habit, for example, of saying "men are more able than women to exhibit aggressive behavior in our culture." One might venture that to the social psychologist the three most

indispensable letters in the alphabet are I.O.C. (in our culture). (pp. 15–17, italics added)

Although Dollard found the clinical case descriptions inadequate by the criteria he employed, it would be a mistake to see his book only as a contribution to the clinical area. A close reading would convince the reader that Dollard—a sociologist, psychoanalyst, anthropologist, and psychologist—was indicting an asocial and acultural psychology.

It is hard to overestimate the consequences for clinical psychology of the lack of a foundation in a social psychology oriented, at least in part, to the nature of American society. There was nothing in American psychology that would have put on clinical psychology's agenda the role of women, the social class bias of the mental health movement, a similar bias in connection with all health services, the history of racial, religious, and ethnic discrimination, and perhaps most bothersome of all, the lack of a self-consciousness among psychologists that they were largely male, white, economically secure, and urbanized. One would be hard put to find evidence that in those days psychology knew that millions of people still lived in rural areas; one would be pardoned if one concluded from this that rural people were psychologically more hardy than their urban counterparts.

I said earlier that in serving as a matchmaker between clinical psychology and the psychiatric–medical setting, psychology was trying to meet the needs of society in ways that would be mutually beneficial. If this is true, how then can one explain that so many departments favored the tie with the VA even though their students would not see children or women? From the standpoint of theory and practice, as well as of the generality of research findings, how could psychology benefit from such parochialism? There are two parts to the answer: Psychology did not explore the universe of alternatives available to it, and few things rival money on the table in its capacity to short-circuit imagination. A fettered imagination impoverishes awareness of the universe of alternatives. Psychology was so focused on the money behind the proposed programs—in part because it served both narrow and socially desirable goals—that it totally failed to ask *the* question, If there was no money powering the invitation for clinical psychology to become part of the medical–psychiatric team, would psychology have moved in that direction? I submit that the failure to ask and examine this question was the hallmark of psychology's naiveté about itself and the social world in which it was embedded. The fact is that clinical psychology could have taken directions different from those it did. I am not saying that these directions were equally desirable and practical but, rather, that they were options that could have been considered. I could argue that from the standpoint of tradition and expertise, it would have made little difference which direction (or combination of directions) psychology took; it would in any event learn as it went along. It could, of course, have done nothing, as was the case in Canada, where after World War II psychiatry helped form a public policy that had no need of clinical psychology.

I would not be stressing the concept of the universe of alternatives if I did not believe that tying clinical psychology to the psychiatric setting was a major mistake from which clinical psychology continues to suffer. Clinical psychology became part of a medically dominated mental health movement that was narrow in terms of theory and settings, blind to the nature of the social order, and as imperialistic as it was vigorous. At least three generations of clinical psychology students became veterans of the war with psychiatry. Many had service-connected disabilities, but rather than ask for benefits, they preferred to leave and stay away from the battleground. There were more local battles and more Versailles-like peace conferences than some of us care to remember. And, of course, the superpowers—the American Psychological Association and the American Psychiatric Association—took over and the local skirmishes were eclipsed in importance by superpower collisions in the courts, the legislatures, and the executive branches of state and federal government. Wars rarely, if ever, have the consequences the combatants envision. Clinical psychology did not fight the war to become like psychiatry (as it is now tending to be), that is, exclusive, money oriented, a lobbying force, supersensitive and superpious about upholding standards and monitoring credentials, and tolerant but not respectful of the research endeavor. It is a classic case, if I may momentarily resort to an individual psychology, of identification with the aggressor, a process as revealing as it is unconscious. I do not say this sneeringly but, rather, despairingly. By tying clinical psychology to the psychiatric setting, both sides put themselves on a collision course with each other. Clinical psychology—the young David to the big Goliath—needed more than a slingshot. It had to show that it was more protective of the public welfare, more concerned with quality, more concerned with credentialing and standards. The war was fought on psychiatry's grounds around issues primarily determined by the medical and psychiatric traditions.

THE SIGNIFICANCE OF THE BOULDER CONFERENCE

And now I must turn to the 1950 Boulder Conference (see Raimy, 1950) that was so fateful in determining the directions clinical psychology would take. Boulder was fateful not because it moved clinical psychology in new directions, but because it legitimated an orientation that had already been established during and immediately after the war. Boulder was sponsored by the Veterans Administration and the National Institute of Mental Health, a not unimportant fact because it indicates what outcomes were expected, if not in detail then in broad outline. As conferences go, and they rarely really *go*, Boulder was exceptional in terms of length, seriousness, level of intellectual discussion, and pursuit of goals. There was an unusual self-consciousness about the fact that a new field was being shaped which would impact on society and psychology as a field. The outcome was not surprising in terms of tying clinical psychology to medical–psychiatric settings, but this was not because the conference discussion did not permit challenges to its main thrust. It was as open a conference as has ever been held. Every criticism and reservation I voiced earlier about tying clinical psychology to the psychiatric setting was explicitly brought up at the conference.

I was at the conference as a young, upstart, nontenured associate professor who was inevitably in awe of the well-known influential psychologists who were there. During graduate school at Clark University, I had had an externship at Worcester State Hospital, which was one of the few places (in my opinion, the only place) where there was real intellectual substance to what was then clinical psychology. But I also learned at Worcester State Hospital what it meant to be a second-class citizen in a psychiatric setting. If I had any doubts on this score, they evaporated after I took my first job at a new educationally oriented institution that had no psychiatrists and the superintendent of which, an educator, had been appointed over the most strenuous objections of the medical community. So coming from these experiences to Yale, and representing Yale at Boulder, I had strong convictions about tying clinical psychology to the medical–psychiatric setting. We were, I believed, not only asking for trouble but walking into a fight with chin out, hands down, and blurred vision. Why must the internship be in a psychiatric setting? Would psychology be capitalizing on its research traditions if clinical students were unsophisticated in psychotherapy? How could one justify the clinical emphasis at the expense of a preventive orientation? Would not psychology be more responsive to societal needs if it made a commitment to the public schools? Why should clinical psychology be tied to a setting that would not expose its members to such areas as mental retardation, criminality, physical handicap, and vocational planning and adjustment? Why was the curriculum that was being outlined weighted in favor of such elective courses as neurophysiology, pharmacology, and neuroanatomy? These issues were raised and joined, and the outcome was predictable. Only a handful of people at Boulder took the position I did. I do not think I ever expressed it at Boulder, but I know the following thought crossed my mind: If the funding for the development of clinical psychology was coming from other sources with no strings attached, would clinical psychology move in the direction it was going? In some vague way I knew that the conference was not confronting the age-old maxim that the hand that feeds you is the hand that can starve you, that money as an incentive is almost always powerful and frequently and unwittingly corrupting. And by corrupting I mean that dependence, in whole or in part, on a funding source facilitates rationalizations that constrict one's thinking about alternatives more congruent with one's initial values, expectations, and capabilities. The problem is made more difficult when one is part of a professional field, the internal policies of which reinforce the tie with the external funding source.

By virtue of the nature and details of the origins of modern clinical psychology, it is not surprising that one of the characteristics of its development has been concern with achieving independence from and a kind of parity with psychiatry. This concern catapulted the field into the arenas of politics, legislation, lobbying, and public policy. It was a move to gain and preserve independence, not to change the conceptual substance of mental health policy. It was a move to be considered as good as and as financially deserving as "them." It was not a move that challenged the underlying conceptions of public policy, for example, its focus on the individual organism deriving from an asocial psychology. Nor was it a move that stemmed from an attempt to identify past conceptual mistakes but rather, one that recognizes past organizational mistakes. Self-scrutiny has never been a notable characteristic of professional organizations. I should amend this statement, however, by saying that professional organizations do scrutinize their political–organizational mistakes, but only when their status is threatened. The recognition that a field may have based itself on faulty conceptions of the nature of its subject matter always reflects sea-swell changes in the society, impacting on the field along a time dimension quite different from our usual experience of time.

Now to an instructive anecdote that illustrates how we can be unfortunate prisoners of time and place unless our education builds into us schemata that aid us in taking distance from our time and place. One not only has always to say "in our culture" (Dollard, 1935) but to add "at this time and place." This anecdote relates to a future condition that already existed in the present but to which no one was paying heed. If the cast of characters had had the conceptual tools to help them divorce themselves from the compelling quality of their concrete present, clinical psychology might not have made the kinds of commitments it did. The anecdote is about a meeting that took place either shortly before or shortly after the Boulder Conference. I do not remember the point of the occasion or the names of most of the dozen or so people who were there. I do know that there were representatives of university clinical training programs and staff from the regional and central VA offices. At one point a VA staff person said, "Do you realize that the young veterans we are talking about will someday be old veterans, and we have a lot of those now from World War I, and we will not have the appropriate knowledge or facilities?" Nobody, including myself, responded to his comments and the meeting went on, probably to rehash the problems of training clinical psychologists. But it is as if his words were seared on my brain. I knew that what he said was important, but it took years for me to appreciate the wisdom of his words.

I would like to believe that he understood, like no one else at the meeting, the difference between preventive and clinical thinking. His totally uninfluential comments were, of course, confirmed in subsequent years: The VA is now responsible for more geriatric cases than any other societal agency—responsible but unprepared.

The point of the anecdote, thus, is that after World War II a health policy was being forged that was narrow in scope, not grounded in an attempt to conceptualize the nature of society and its social order, amazingly ahistorical, and resting on the belief that the future would be a carbon copy of the present. It was a policy forged by professionals who had no way of asking, How are the ways we are defining problems and modes of attack a function of where *we* are in the social order? How should awareness of our place in the social order serve as a warning that we are subject to certain biases and distortions in regard to our society and its needs? How does our place in its social order—the result of a host of selective factors which interact with a distinctive, prolonged education that emphasizes how different we are from the rest of society—prevent us from recognizing that, like it or not, we are part of the problem because we are in the stream of social history? One cannot ask these kinds of questions without being realistically humble. Humbleness is not a word that easily comes to mind when one reviews the mental health movement after World War II. Personal, intellectual, and professional arrogance comes more quickly to mind. The roots that clinical psychology had in American psychology were shallow, but they at least contained the fertilizing ingredient of skepticism. But that ingredient came only from an individual psychology, and it was (and still is) inadequately sustaining when psychology, in general, and clinical psychology, in particular, entered the arena of social reality and public policy. In those arenas an individual psychology is a mammoth distraction.

The therapeutic endeavor needs no justification, but when that endeavor becomes nearly all-encompassing in focus and policy, one must suspect not only the crippling role of parochial thinking but also the failure to examine and confront the nature of the society itself. A clinical psychology not rooted in a realistic social psychology—that is, a social psychology which sees itself as a cultural and social-historical product and agent, which sees itself by virtue of time, place, and social and institutional status as both a cultural cause and a cultural effect—is a misdirected clinical psychology. This point has been recognized by others of my generation who grew up in clinical psychology and none has said it better than Cowen (1980) in his recent stimulating article on primary prevention. Cowen is too realistic to be other than humble about our knowledge of how to approach primary prevention. As a clinician he knows how a part of us, as individuals, needs and treasures our symptoms, and as a community psychologist he knows how refractory our communities have been and will be to the efforts at primary prevention. He also knows that going the route of primary prevention will illuminate not only important features of the social order but also how those features will be obstacles to mounting effective programs in primary prevention. And he also knows that psychology will vigorously resist changing its dependence on an individual psychology.

I sense a breeze of change in psychology's air. The October 1979 issue of the *American Psychologist*, a special issue, was devoted to "Psychology and Children: Current Research and Practice." One of the articles is as incisive as it is brief. It was written by an eminent child developmentalist, William Kessen. Kessen's (1979) comments about what is wrong in child psychology are similar to what Cowen and I have said. American psychology, invented in and by American society, went on to invent its subject matter: the self-contained individual. The necessity for reinvention is at hand. Necessity may be the mother of invention, but let us never forget that inventions are rarely unmixed blessings.

Nothing in what I have said, and nothing in what Cowen and Kessen have said, denies that individual psychologies have contributed to our knowledge of human behavior and development. And, it should go without saying, nothing in what I have said in this article should in any way be interpreted as subordinating one approach (e.g., biological) to another. It is precisely the subordination of one approach to another that I have argued against. Anyone who is familiar with the past and current status of departments of public health in medical schools—or the sad fate of departments of community medicine—will be familiar with the adverse institutional and social consequences of subordinating one approach to another in the health area. Human illness and misery have diverse sources within and without the individual. If only because of this glimpse of the obvious, we must radically reexamine how we conceptualize the individual organism. This reexamination is crucial if we are to deepen our understanding and direct more effectively our capacities to prevent and repair.

The shortcomings of extant psychologies would not have been exposed in the way they have if psychology had remained a narrow, university-based, and encapsulated discipline. But the world—our entire, globe-straddling social world—changed and psychology was drawn into it as never before. To understand individuals for the purpose of influencing or helping them is one thing. To understand and influence social orders for the purpose of influencing parts of them is another thing, even if what one seeks to influence is a particular service to individuals. Ultimately, both types of understanding and the actions derived from them have to be conceptually interrelated because in the real world they are interrelated. The shortcomings of clinical psychology were inherent in those of American psychology. By emphasizing the shortcomings of clinical psychology, I have run the risk of blaming the victim. My aim has not been to blame victim or aggressor because to do so would be to trivialize the matter by resort to what Mills (1959) called unwarranted and misleading "psychologisms" deriving from an individual psychology. There is a creeping sense of malaise in psychology about psychology. But that malaise is not peculiar to psychology. It is suffusing the atmosphere in all the social sciences. Indeed, in some of the social sciences, like economics, there are those who not only believe that the emperor is naked but also that he has a terminal disease. But this kind of medical metaphor, however apt it may seem, is but another example of how our thinking is imprisoned in an individual psychology.

REFERENCES

Brown, J. F. *Psychology and the social order.* New York: McGraw-Hill, 1936.

Cowen, E. L. The wooing of primary prevention. *American Journal of Community Psychology,* 1980, 8, 258–284.

Dollard, J. *Criteria for the life history.* New Haven, Conn.: Yale University Press, 1935.

Hilgard, E. (Ed.). *American psychology in historical perspective.* Washington, D.C.: American Psychological Association, 1978.

Kessen, W. The American child and other cultural inventions. *American Psychologist,* 1979, 34, 815–820.

Mills, C. W. *The sociological imagination.* New York: Oxford University Press, 1959.

Raimy, V. C. (Ed.). *Training in clinical psychology.* Englewood Cliffs, N.J.: Prentice-Hall, 1950.

Rogers, C. R. *Counseling and psychotherapy.* Boston: Houghton Mifflin, 1942.

Sarason, S. B. *Work, aging, and social change. Professionals and the one life–one career imperative.* New York: Free Press, 1977.

Sarason, S. B. *Psychology misdirected.* New York: Free Press, 1981.

23

THE RETURN OF THE REPRESSED: PSYCHOLOGY'S PROBLEMATIC RELATIONS WITH PSYCHOANALYSIS, 1909–1960

GAIL A. HORNSTEIN

Freud and Jung were having dinner in Bremen. It was the evening before they set sail for the Clark conference, the occasion of Freud's only visit to America. Jung started talking about certain mummies in the lead cellars of the city. Freud became visibly disturbed. "Why are you so concerned with these corpses?" he asked several times. Jung went on talking. Suddenly, without warning, Freud fell to the floor in a faint. When he recovered, he accused Jung of harboring death wishes against him. But it was not Jung who wanted Freud dead. Had Freud only known what Amer-

---

I gratefully acknowledge Winifred Connerton's excellent research assistance and Verlyn Klinkenborg's incisive comments on earlier drafts. I also thank several groups of colleagues at Mount Holyoke for their encouragement and suggestions, and John Burnham for his careful reading of a later draft. Preparation of this article was supported by a fellowship from the Mary Ingraham Bunting Institute of Radcliffe College.
Reprinted from *American Psychologist*, 47, 254–263 (1992). Copyright © 1992 by the American Psychological Association. Reprinted with permission of the author.

ican psychologists were about to do to psychoanalysis, he might never have gotten up off the floor.

There is no easy way to talk about psychology's relations with psychoanalysis.[1] It is a story dense with disillusionment and the shapeless anger of rejection. Each side behaved badly, and then compounded its insensitivity with disdain. Their fates bound together like Romulus and Remus, psychology and psychoanalysis struggled to find their separate spheres, only to end up pitted against one another at every turn. Too much was at stake —property lines, areas of influence, and a deeper question: Which field would ultimately dictate the ground rules for a science of the mind?

In the 1890s, when this struggle began, there was little sign that it would become another Hundred Years' War. Psychologists had just begun to apply experimental methods to some of the classic problems of metaphysics, with the hope of answering questions that had bedeviled philosophers for centuries. By systematically organizing the psychological world into a set of discrete variables, these methods brought the unruly phenomena of mind within the purview of science. It was a heady time, a time of possibility and change and the reckless felicity of the new. American psychologists raced around founding laboratories at every college that would let them, in closets, basements or wherever they could snatch a little space, setting up apparatus in their own homes if necessary. They invented new forms of measurement, odd devices, tests of all sorts. Reports of their findings poured into the journals that sprang up suddenly to fill the need. The *new psychology*, as they liked to call it, seemed destined even in its infancy to do what had been declared since Kant to be impossible—to create a truly scientific approach to mind.

Psychoanalysts thrust themselves directly into the middle of this scene, brazenly trying to supplant the new psychology at the moment of its greatest promise. At first psychologists stood aside, astonished, as the analysts, bursting with self-importance and an almost frightening zealotry, pronounced themselves the real scientists of the mind. By the time psychologists began to take this threat seriously, psychoanalysis had so captured the public imagination that even its pretensions could not be ignored.[2]

The question was how to define science. To the analysts, science had nothing to do with method, with controlling variables or counting things.

---

[1] The standard reference on this whole topic is Shakow and Rapaport (1964). Their study remains invaluable as a thoughtful, systematic review of much of what psychologists have had to say about psychoanalysis. However, because their goal was to document Freud's influence on American psychology, they focused more on positive effects than on negative ones. My goal is to characterize psychologists' attitudes toward psychoanalysis. Many psychologists saw psychoanalysis as a threat and not as a positive influence, and thus my version of the story is inevitably more conflicted than Shakow and Rapaport's.

[2] A discussion of the popular reception of psychoanalysis in America is beyond the scope of this article. See Hale (1971, 1978) and Burnham (1968, 1978, 1979, 1987) for detailed treatments of this issue.

What made something scientific was that it was true. Constructing a science of the mind could mean only one thing—finding some way to peer through the watery murk of consciousness to the subaquean reality that lay beyond. The efforts of psychologists, with their bulky equipment and piles of charts and graphs, seemed superficial and largely irrelevant to this goal.[3]

For their part, psychologists initially saw psychoanalysis as just another of the "mind cures" that flashed across the American landscape in the 1890s—like Christian Science or the Emmanual movement—a popular craze that had nothing to do with the scientific study of mind. Most psychologists who attended Freud's Clark lectures in 1909 saw his speculations about dreams and sex as a pleasant diversion, about as relevant to their work as Mrs. Eddy's epistles. The occasional articles about psychoanalysis that appeared in psychology journals before 1910 (e.g., Putnam, 1906; Scott, 1908) made it seem mildly interesting, but not essentially different from related methods like suggestion.

By 1915, readers of a publication like *The Journal of Abnormal Psychology* had an opportunity for more varied exposure to psychoanalytic ideas.[4] Books by Freud, Jung, and A. A. Brill were regularly reviewed. Articles demonstrating the therapeutic effectiveness of psychoanalytic techniques began to appear, along with some discussion of the theory itself (see, e.g., Coriat, 1910; Emerson, 1912–1913; Gordon, 1917; MacCurdy, 1913; Maeder, 1910; Putnam, 1909–1910). Criticisms, when made, were fair-minded and well within the spirit of scientific repartee. Donley (1911), for example, suggested that anxiety neurosis might have other causes beyond those considered by Freud. Bellamy (1915a) argued that dreams fulfill fears or states of anger just as often as they represent wishes. Taylor (1911) noted that there were cases of neurosis in which patients recovered without having had their childhood or sexual life dissected. Even critics with a broader focus expressed little ire. Wells (1913) was concerned about "looseness in the formulation of psychoanalytic theories" (p. 227). Solomon (1916) argued that the term *sexual* was used inconsistently by analytic writers. The psychiatrist Morton Prince (1910) expressed the common view that psychoanalysts "fit the facts to the universal concepts which dominate the school" (p. 349).

There were occasional writers who became exasperated and called psychoanalysis "weird" (Donley, 1911), "esoteric" (Carrington, 1914), or

---

[3] Psychologists were not alone in having to struggle with competing definitions of science. Kuklick's (1980) analysis of boundary maintenance in sociology offers a general model for understanding how each of the social sciences resolved this dilemma.

[4] Of all major psychology journals of the period, the *Journal of Abnormal Psychology* was the one with the greatest number of articles relevant to psychoanalysis (both pro and con). Not all were written by psychologists, but they were clearly intended for this audience. G. Stanley Hall published the text of Freud's, Jung's, and Ferenczi's Clark lectures in his *American Journal of Psychology* in 1910, but from then on that journal concentrated primarily on reviews of the psychoanalytic literature (both German and English) and carried very few original articles by psychologists.

"grotesque" (Bellamy, 1915a), its assumptions "fantastic" or "sheer nonsense" (Humphrey, 1920b), but these imprecations were unusual in the early years. The sexual nature of psychoanalytic interpretation was a problem for some; Bellamy (1915b), for example, in reviewing a book by Coriat, made plain his relief that "there is not a word or sentence in this book that a precise maiden lady need hesitate to read to her Sunday school class or at a pink tea" (p. 434). On the whole, however, psychologists were initially so supportive of psychoanalysis that when Roback reviewed Dunlap's (1920) *Mysticism, Freudianism and Scientific Psychology*, he felt he had to defend its critical tone on grounds of balance: "Freud has had so many warm advocates of his views in this country and so few systematic critics among the psychologists that Dunlap's discussion is both timely and important" (Roback, 1921, p. 406).

These positive attitudes might well have resulted from more than psychologists' open-mindedness. Analysts, ever worried about their public image, left little to chance. Soon after the Clark conference they embarked on a systematic campaign to win Americans to their cause. A. A. Brill, the founder of the New York Psychoanalytic Society, was charged with disseminating information about psychoanalysis in that city; Ernest Jones, Freud's scrappy lieutenant, took the rest of the country for himself (Burnham, 1967, pp. 134–137). Psychologists were among the major recipients of Jones's educational largess; by 1916, they had been treated to 20 of his articles, abstracts, reviews, and comments in the *Journal of Abnormal Psychology* alone. Most of these pieces were patient expositions of psychoanalytic concepts, designed to lead the uninitiated to a correct understanding of the theory. But Jones also maintained a vigilant watch over what psychologists were writing about psychoanalysis, and shot back a tart riposte whenever he encountered an "erroneous" statement (see also Tannenbaum, 1916, 1917).

Neither Jones nor his colleagues gave serious attention to the careful criticisms that psychologists leveled against psychoanalysis in the early years. Acutely aware of the tenuous status of their own new field, psychologists found this highly disconcerting. After all, they were constantly obliged to defend their science against attacks from philosophy and biology; what gave analysts the right not only to ignore legitimate criticism but to patronize their opponents? Who knows what might have happened had analysts been more responsive; what did happen was that psychologists sharpened their pencils and began to fight.

The first skirmish actually occurred as early as 1916, when the Princeton philosopher Warner Fite reviewed Jung's *Psychology of the Unconscious* for *The Nation* (Fite, 1916). His surprisingly nasty tone incited a riot of response from psychologists. In her letter to the editor, Christine Ladd-Franklin, the eminent experimentalist, characterized psychoanalysis as a product of the "undeveloped ... German mind" (hardly a compliment in

1916), and concluded ominously that "unless means can speedily be found to prevent its spread ... the prognosis for civilization is unfavorable" (Ladd-Franklin, 1916, p. 374). R. S. Woodworth of Columbia (1916), a bit more circumspect, called psychoanalysis an "uncanny religion" (probably not the psychologist's highest accolade) that led "even apparently sane individuals" to absurd associations and nonsensical conclusions. In a telling illustration, he showed how the words *Freudian principles* led to a train of thought that revealed his own "deep-seated wish ... for a career of unbridled lust" (p. 396).

Woodworth went on to publish an extensive critique of "Freudism" in the 1917 volume of the *Journal of Abnormal Psychology*. Adopting the peevish tone that soon became commonplace in these sorts of articles, he complained that analysts disregarded psychological research, contemptuously dismissed it as superficial, and treated psychologists "shabbily" (Woodworth, 1917, p. 175). What most annoyed Woodworth was the analysts' slippery dodge, their way of attributing any criticism of psychoanalysis to unconscious resistance on the part of the critic.

Other writers echoed these complaints, often with less poignancy and considerably more pique than Woodworth. But what soon emerged as the real irritant for psychologists was the analysts' insistence, at times moralistic, at times snide, that only those who had themselves undergone a personal psychoanalysis were qualified to evaluate the theory. To an experimental psychology whose raison d'etre was to differentiate itself from religion, this talk of initiation rites and secret knowledge was anathema. Such a rule also conveniently disenfranchised just about every psychologist from serving as a potential critic; even those Americans who sought analysis had a hard time finding it in this country before 1920. Of course the real issue here was not who had been analyzed and who had not (a good thing, since Freud and his closest colleagues would have had to disqualify themselves); what was at stake was the fundamental question of subjectivity in science.

For experimental psychologists, being scientific meant creating distance. It meant opening up a space, a "no man's land," between themselves and the things they studied, a place whose boundary could be patrolled so that needs or desires or feelings could never infiltrate the work itself. Every aspect of the experimental situation was bent toward this goal—the "blind subjects," the mechanized recording devices, the quantified measures, and statistically represented results (Danziger, 1990; Hornstein, 1988; Morawski, 1988). What united experimental psychologists more than anything else was a distrust of personal experience, a sense that feelings in particular were dangerous and had to be held carefully in check lest they flood in and destroy the very foundations of the work. They were willing to make a number of sacrifices to protect psychology from this threat, including a radical narrowing of the field to include only phenomena that could be studied "objectively."

Having gone to these lengths, psychologists found it profoundly disquieting to have analysts claim that being psychoanalyzed was what made someone a credible scientist. This implied that science was subjective, that it was ultimately about personal experience rather than rigorous method. Even worse, it suggested that the unconscious was so powerful a part of mind that its force had to be experienced directly, in one's own life, in order to understand the psychology of others.

Such a view could not go unchallenged. "Voodooism," Watson (1927, p. 502) called it. "A delusion," echoed Jastrow (1932, p. 285). The very idea of an unconscious conjured up the chaos and irrationality that psychologists had banded together to escape. If analysts wanted to plunge into that nightmare world and call it science, so be it, but they could not be allowed to drag everyone else down with them.

The technique of free association came in for particular scorn (Heidbreder, 1933). It struck psychologists as an elaborate subterfuge, a way for analysts to appear not to influence patients when of course they did. Interpretation, they argued, was nothing but a new name for suggestion; that patients were gullible enough to mistake it for truth was hardly proof of its scientific status. Analysts were "free," all right—free to define as evidence whatever would meet their needs, free to label any challenge "resistance," free to pretend that they were doing nothing of the sort.

Heidbreder (1933), in her typically fair-minded way, struggled to make these practices sound reasonable. But even she could muster only this faint defense: Just because "psychoanalysts offer a different kind of evidence from that accepted by science ... does not mean that they offer *no evidence*" (p. 402). To most psychologists, calling an analyst's retrospective musings about events that occurred in the secrecy of the consulting room evidence was an insult to science. Even first-year students knew that the cardinal rule of scientific proof was publicly verifiable data. Knight Dunlap (1920, p. 8) put it bluntly: "psychoanalysis attempts to creep in wearing the uniform of science, and to strangle it from the inside."[5]

By the mid-1920s, psychologists seem to have decided that the best way to defend science was simply to do it. Critiques of psychoanalysis began to be displaced in the literature by enthusiastic works like *Great Experiments in Psychology* (Garrett, 1930). Any remaining aggressive tendencies were easily absorbed by the interminable debates over behaviorism and Gestalt

---

[5]With characteristic irony, Dunlap (1920) concluded that psychoanalysis might ultimately prove beneficial to psychology: "Just as Christian Science has tremendously accelerated the progress of Scientific Medicine, so Psychoanalysis, by compelling psychology to put its house in order, will eventually help in the development of the Scientific Psychology it aims to thrust aside" (p. 9).

psychology.[6] Psychologists did not need psychoanalysis, and it surely did not need them.

Or so it seemed, until one day in the fall of 1934 when the rumor got out that Edwin Garrigues Boring, the self-acknowledged dean of experimental psychology, had entered analytic treatment. To preserve his reputation, he told colleagues that he was studying the relation between the two fields; actually, he was depressed, frightened, and unable to work. The strange saga of Boring's analysis gives a glimpse into psychologists' continuing ambivalence about psychoanalysis.

Boring chose as his analyst the emigré Berliner, Hanns Sachs, who had been a member of Freud's inner circle and was therefore above reproach. Despite his depression, Boring embarked on the analysis with customary gusto, quickly absorbing the daily analytic sessions into the swirl of his 80-hour work week.

Boring struggled to make the analysis a success. He missed no sessions. He wept. He threw things. He made enough of a financial sacrifice to demonstrate the seriousness of his commitment. He discussed his childhood, explored his dreams, and scrutinized the motivations for his actions. Then, at the end of 10 months, he ran out of money, time, and desire. He had completed 168 sessions, for which he had paid $1,680, more than a fifth of his yearly salary. But his efforts brought little relief:

> [A]ll that happened was that the analysis petered out in an uneventful session on June 21st and my analyst went abroad! . . . I was distraught. I had tried a last resource, and it had failed. Yet, unwilling to accept so bitter a conclusion, I found myself seizing on the analyst's casual statement that I ought to wait a month. I waited anxiously, hoping for a new personality by July 21st. None came. Finally I sought out my psychologist-friends who believe in psychoanalysis, and we sat in conference discussing this sad immutability of my personality—on August 21st, as I suddenly realized. Their advice was patience, the less haste the more speed; wait at least until December 21st, they urged. So I waited. . . . And finally I ceased to expect a miracle. (Boring, 1940, pp. 9–10)[7]

How could a man like Boring, whose name was practically synonymous with hard-nosed experimentation, have such childlike faith in psychoanalysis? He actually seemed to expect that he would wake up a new

---

[6]See, for example, a classic work like *Psychologies of 1925* (Murchison, 1926), which allots four chapters to behaviorism, three to Gestalt, and even three to the dying gasps of structuralism, but none to psychoanalysis.

[7]Among those Boring consulted was his colleague Henry Murray, who advised him to let Sachs have it "right between his eyes. . . . give him the works—don't omit a single grievance, not one." (H. Murray to E. G. Boring [n. d., August 1935?], Box 43, Folder 919, E. G. Boring Papers, Harvard University Archives quoted by permission.) There is no evidence that Boring took this advice: He and Sachs maintained a cordial relationship for some time thereafter, dining together at the Harvard Club and exchanging papers and letters on professional topics.

man, that "a light from heaven" would change him "from Saul to Paul" (p. 9). There are certainly no hints of these hopes in his published writings. In the first edition of his classic *History of Experimental Psychology* (Boring, 1929), published just five years before the analysis, there were only four brief mentions of Freud in almost 700 pages. Psychoanalysis did not even appear in the index of *Psychology: A Factual Textbook*, the text Boring published with Langfeld and Weld in 1935, the same year he saw Sachs.

Yet in his own life, Boring kept searching for some sign that the analysis might have worked. Five years passed. Still no light. In 1940, he tried a new strategy. He proposed to the *Journal of Abnormal and Social Psychology* that it locate other well-known psychologists who had been analyzed, solicit reports of their experiences, and publish them in a special issue. Perhaps they would reveal something that he had missed. Leaving nothing to chance, Boring even persuaded Sachs to write a companion piece to his own account, evaluating the analysis from the analyst's perspective.

Psychologists turned out to be surprisingly excited by the prospect of reading about their colleagues' adventures on the couch. The American Psychological Association even reprinted the articles and sold them as a set, exhausting the entire edition within a few months. Boring, ever hopeful, titled his piece "Was This Analysis a Success?" Sachs (1940) replied with a tactful "no." Wistful and perplexed by the whole experience, Boring struggled to come to terms with his sense of loss: "There is so much about this personality of mine that would be better if different, so much that analysis might have done and did not!" (Boring, 1940, p. 10). Yet he refrained from attacking psychoanalysis directly. His colleagues, however, knew where to lay the blame for their own failed attempts. Carney Landis of Columbia parodied his experience with a statistical analysis of how much time he had allocated to each of eight topics during free association. To Landis, analysts were scientific illiterates who did little but mouth received dogma in order to make themselves rich. Hinting that his "neurosis" was created by the analysis itself, Landis (1940) concluded his tirade by warning that psychoanalysis was safe only when used by experimental psychologists to produce psychopathic phenomena in the laboratory.

The editor of the *Journal of Abnormal and Social Psychology*, apparently concerned about the lack of balance in these articles, invited the eminent analyst Franz Alexander to contribute a rejoinder. Instead of critiquing the other papers, Alexander (1940) made a parable of his own life. Like his readers, he had spent his youth as a devotee of laboratory science. When he first tried to read Freud's work, he found its "vague and ambiguous mental excursions ... equal almost to physical pain" (p. 312). He turned to psychoanalysis only when the evidence in support of it became undeniable. This meant sacrificing his promising academic career, enduring the opprobrium of his colleagues, and being forced from home by his irate philosopher father, who considered psychoanalysis a "spiritual gutter." But for Alexander, there was no choice—having committed himself to empiricism, he had to adopt whatever view had the most evidence, regardless of how distasteful it might be on other grounds. Of course, in the end, his quest for truth was vindicated when his father, near death, gave up his own lifelong belief in the superiority of natural science to express the fervent wish that "psychoanalysis will enthrone again real understanding in place of fumbling—the rule of thought in place of that of the gadget" (p. 314).

Alexander's inspiring tale fell on closed ears. Distrusting subjectivity in all its forms, psychologists put little stock in personal testimony, even that of fellow scientists. This series of articles clearly had less to do with evaluating psychoanalysis than it did with assuaging the anxiety of its contributors, many of whom were worried, like Boring, that their analyses had failed. What they needed was reassurance. But the tangible benefits of this kind of therapy are always elusive. Recall Janet Malcolm's (1984) sardonic comment: "The crowning paradox of psychoanalysis is the near-uselessness of its insights. To 'make the unconscious conscious' ... is to pour water into a sieve. The moisture that remains on the surface of the mesh is the benefit of analysis" (p. 25). Ultimately, these articles were exercises in self-persuasion, attempts by the contributors to convince themselves that psychoanalysis was too ridiculous or too ineffectual to be taken seriously. If they managed in the process to warn off colleagues who might have been tempted to try the thing themselves, so much the better.

By the early 1940s, the situation had reached a critical stage. Psychoanalysis was becoming so popular that it threatened to eclipse psychology entirely. Journalists seemed oblivious to the differences between the two fields, and exasperated psychologists often found their discipline being portrayed as if it were nothing but a branch of psychoanalytic inquiry. This was especially galling because most psychologists assumed that psychoanalytic claims were not even true. But how could they prove this? The critiques of the early years had not worked. Attacking psychoanalysis from the couch had simply allowed Alexander to make psychologists look foolish. There had to be a better way.

The solution turned out to be so obvious that it is hard to believe it took until the mid-1940s to appear. Psychologists would set themselves the job of determining through carefully controlled experiments which, if any, psychoanalytic concepts were valid. This reinstated psychologists as arbiters of the mental world, able to make the final judgment about what would and would not count as psychological knowledge. It allowed them to evaluate psychoanalysis, rather than be overshadowed or absorbed by it. Most important, it restored the objective criterion of the experiment as the basis for making claims and settling disputes, undermining the analysts' attempts to substitute a new, subjective standard for psychological truth.

Psychologists took to their new role with a vengeance. Every conceivable psychoanalytic concept was put to the test, in hundreds of studies whose creativity was matched only by the uselessness of their findings. Mowrer (1940) demonstrated that regression and reaction formation could be produced in rats. Blum and Miller (1952) found that children who were categorized as having an "oral character" ate significantly more ice cream than did other children. Scodel (1957) showed that "high-dependency" men did not manifest the predicted preference for women with large breasts. Schwartz (1956) found more castration anxiety among men than women, with homosexual men scoring the highest of all. Sarnoff and Corwin (1959) reported that "high castration anxious" men showed a greater increase in fear of death than did "low anxious" men after being exposed to photographs of nude women. And Friedman (1952) found that when children were shown a picture of a father and a child near some stairs, more girls than boys fantasized that the father would mount the stairs and enter the room.

Topics like oedipal relations and anal personality had their aficionados, but it was *perceptual defense* that really captured the imagination of psychological researchers. Their hypothesis was a simple one: If the mind did defend against forbidden material, then words with disturbing or salacious associations should be recalled less easily than more neutral stimuli. Fresh-faced graduate students spent hours making certain that items like *whore* and *bugger* were matched in length and salience with their sexless counterparts. Controversies erupted left and right: Were taboo words difficult to recognize just because they were not used very frequently? Wiener's (1955) famous "pussy–balls" study dispatched that idea by demonstrating that the context, not the words themselves, made certain stimuli threatening. But was exposure to a list of scatological words really analogous to the sort of trauma that necessitated repression? Blum (1954) addressed that problem with a new methodology based on the Blacky Pictures, a set of cartoon images of a dog depicted in various psychoanalytically relevant poses (licking his genitals, observing his parents having sex, defecating outside their kennel). When studies with Blacky were found to support the earlier word-item findings, repression gained the sort of empirical reality that only psychologists could give it.

By the 1950s, research on psychoanalysis had become so popular that psychologists were drowning in it. No one could possibly read all the studies that were being published, much less keep track of their results.[8] A new cottage industry was born of this need, with workers who did nothing but summarize and evaluate these studies. Robert Sears had been the first such laborer, commissioned in 1943 by the Social Science Research Council to

---

[8]Fisher and Greenberg's (1977) review includes more than 400 studies from the 1940s and 1950s alone. By the mid-1970s, there were at least 1,000 more.

write an objective review of the scientific literature on psychoanalytic theory. Sears's approach, used by all subsequent evaluators, was straightforward: Having first divided the literature into topic categories (fixation, sexuality, object choice), he then counted how many studies in each area supported Freud's claims. The larger the number, the more scientific the claim. Taken together, these individual scores were supposed to provide an answer to the overall question of whether psychoanalytic theory was valid.

Sears (1943) hedged, saying that some of it was, and some of it was not. Such caution soon vanished. The self-appointed judges whose reports appeared up through the early 1970s placed themselves squarely on one side of the debate or the other. Evaluation studies quickly became as difficult to sort out as research on psychoanalysis itself, and much less fun to read (see, for example, Fisher & Greenberg, 1977; Kline, 1972). Each report took a tone yet more strident than the last, and the original goal of providing an objective review was lost entirely. This was nowhere more evident than in Eysenck and Wilson's (1973) polemic. Every shred of evidence seeming to support psychoanalysis was scrutinized for methodological flaws, whereas studies opposing the theory were flaunted as examples of good science.

No one especially cared that the evaluation literature was becoming debased. It made little difference what the findings were; as long as psychoanalytic phenomena were made subservient to empirical test, empiricism was vindicated.[9] That much of this research supported Freud's theory was an irony appreciated by few. It was the act of doing these studies, of piling them up and sorting them out and arguing about them that was important, not what they revealed about psychoanalysis. Some psychologists found these activities so salubrious that they recommended them even to analysts. As Albert Ellis (1950) cheerfully noted, "sociologists, who but a decade or two ago were mostly concerned with pure theory, now frequently design and execute crucial experiments which enable them to support or discredit hypotheses. There is no basic reason why psychoanalysts cannot do likewise" (p. 190).

Analysts were in no position to point out that the content of these psychological studies had only the dimmest relation to Freud's theory. "Every country creates the psychoanalysis it [unconsciously] needs," said Kurzweil (1989, p. 1), and disciplines surely do the same. Research on psychoanalysis was invigorating because it gave psychologists a sense of mastery: They had ventured onto the battlefield of the unconscious and

---

[9]Hilgard (1952) was the only evaluator who seemed willing to grant this point. He chastised psychologists for doing experiments that "give merely trivial illustrations of what psychoanalysts have demonstrated ... in clinical work," and argued that although "such illustrations may be useful as propaganda," they "do not really do much for science." In his view, psychoanalytic research "ought to *advance* our understanding, not merely *confirm* or *deny* the theories that someone [else] has stated" (p. 43).

returned, triumphant, with a set of dependent variables. Some psychologists even managed to convince themselves that the danger had been exaggerated all along, that they had really been in control. They scoffed that psychoanalysis had never been much more than an inflated way of talking about conditioning, one of psychology's oldest topics. By the time Dollard and Miller (1950) actually began translating every psychoanalytic concept into its learning theory equivalent, their efforts were almost redundant.

These behaviorist reworkings of Freud, although often clumsy, did signal a new strategy in dealing with psychoanalysis—co-optation. More satisfying than silence, with none of the pitfalls of criticism, the appropriation of psychoanalytic concepts into mainstream psychology seemed an ideal compromise. Like the Christianizing of paganism, the dangerous parts were still there somewhere, but in such diluted form as to pose no real threat.[10]

Watson had tried to move in this direction as early as the 1920s. By relabeling the *unconscious* as the *unverbalized*, he could sweep most psychoanalytic phenomena into the neat piles of behaviorist theory. Emotions became sets of habits; neurosis was conditioning; therapy, unconditioning. Watson never denied the reality of Freud's findings; he simply cast them in his own terms (e.g., when he warned [1928, p. 80] that sexual frustration made mothers want to kiss rather than shake hands with their children). At times, Watson even took to calling himself an analyst, as if, like some ancient warrior, he could magically disarm his enemy by assuming his name.[11]

Other behaviorists continued where Watson left off. Humphrey (1920a), following Holt's (1915) earlier lead, dissolved wishes into conditioned reflexes. Keller and Schoenfeld (1950) laid claim to such psychoanalytic staples as the slip of the tongue (yet another reflex) and the oedipal complex (a consequence of early conditioning). But it was Skinner who took the task of appropriating Freud most seriously. In *Science and Human Behavior* (1953), he systematically redefined each of the defense mechanisms in operant terms (*repression*: a "response which is successful in avoiding the conditioned aversive stimulation generated by punishment,"

---

[10]Precisely the same thing was done with Gestalt psychology. At first, the philosophic assumptions of the theory were seen as a challenge to American (behaviorist) psychology, and Gestalt was explicitly opposed. Then the dangerous aspects were simply stripped away, making it appear as if the principles of organization were empirical observations that had arisen out of nowhere. A contemporary student of perceptual psychology would have no idea that these principles were originally formulated in opposition to behaviorist thought.

[11]"I venture to predict that 20 years from now an analyst using Freudian concepts and Freudian terminology will be placed upon the same plane as a phrenologist. *And yet analysis based upon behavioristic principles is here to stay and is a necessary profession in society—to be placed upon a par with internal medicine and surgery*" (Watson, 1925, p. 243). The comparison of psychoanalysis to phrenology was a favorite among psychologists; Dallenbach (1955) later wrote an entire article on this theme.

p. 292; *reaction formation*: "an extension of a technique of self-control in which the environment is altered so that it becomes less likely to generate punished behavior," p. 365). By the end of the book, even symbols and dreams had taken on the veneer of conditioned responses. Artful as these efforts were, they did not really solve the problem. Freud was still there. His new operant outfit gave him a natty American look, but there was no mistaking that sardonic smile. As long as psychoanalytic concepts remained identifiable as such, they were potential rivals to psychology's own constructs.

Help with this problem came from an unlikely source—introductory textbook writers. Typically dismissed as nothing but purveyors of pabulum for college students, these authors, many of them prominent psychologists, played a major role in advancing the co-optation of psychoanalytic theory. This is not so surprising. As Morawski (1992, this issue) shows, introductory texts exist in a liminal space, neither popular nor professional, yet somehow both. They function simultaneously as translators of standard doctrine and contributors to it. Because new texts constantly supplant older ones, they become disciplinary artifacts, frozen moments of taken-for-granted knowledge, X rays of the uncontroversial.

Textbook writers took advantage of their role by assimilating psychoanalytic concepts into mainstream psychology without mentioning their origins. An early example was Walter Hunter's 1923 text, *General Psychology*, in which the various defense mechanisms were stripped of any connection to the unconscious, much the way bagels now appear in the frozen-food sections of Peoria supermarkets. Other writers soon adopted this practice, sometimes using the term *adjustment mechanisms* to expunge any remaining whiff of psychodynamics (Guthrie & Edwards, 1949; Kimble, 1956).

These appropriations took place amidst a general silence in these texts about psychoanalytic theory itself. Many writers ignored the topic entirely: Robinson and Robinson's 665-page *Readings in General Psychology* (1923) included the contributions of every conceivable psychologist, even Helen Keller and the Lord Archbishop of York, but had nothing by Freud or any other psychoanalyst (the section titled "Dreams as a Vehicle of Wish Fulfillment" was written by Watson). Readers of well-known texts like Seashore's (1923) *Introduction to Psychology* or Warren and Carmichael's (1930) *Elements of Human Psychology* would never have known that psychoanalysis existed. Even as late as 1958, a classic like Hebb's *Textbook of Psychology* barely mentioned the topic. When Freud did make an appearance, it was more likely to be in the section on punishment or motivation—topics dear to the heart of experimentalists—than in expected places like the chapter on abnormality.

Of course some textbook writers did discuss psychoanalysis in more depth, but few besides Hilgard (1953) did so sympathetically.[12] Kimble (1956) went to the trouble of including a special section in his introduction warning readers not to make the common error of confusing psychology with psychoanalysis. It was not that Freud had no value: Kimble called his work "one of the great milestones in the history of human thought" with "insights [that] have never been equaled" (pp. 369–370). Psychoanalysis just happened to be "entirely literary and not worth discussion" in a scientific text (p. 370).

In 1956, Gardner Murphy was asked to determine the extent of Freud's impact on the various subfields of psychology. He likened the overall effect to the erosion of the rocky coastline in Maine, but admitted that some areas had remained untouched by the psychoanalytic current. His results, on a numerical scale, of course, constitute what one might call an *index of introgression*, ranging from 0, Freud never had a chance, to 6, he made it all the way in. Here are Murphy's ratings: intelligence and physiological = 0; comparative, learning, thinking, perception, and vocational = 1; memory, drive and emotion, child and adolescent = 2; social and industrial = 3; imagination = 4; abnormal = 5; personality and clinical = 6.

What is surprising about these results is that there are any high scores at all. How could a discipline that had spent 50 years protecting its chastity end up seduced by a ladykiller like Freud? Of course the problem was really only with the clinicians, but there were thousands of them, and more every year (Gilgen, 1982; Kelly, 1947). When the American Psychological Association surveyed a sample of its members in 1954, asking who had influenced them to enter the field, Freud, of all people, got the greatest number of mentions (Clark, 1957, pp. 17–18). True, by that time, 37% of APA members were clinicians (p. 116), but how had that happened? Why were so many psychologists fleeing the laboratory?

Perhaps it was just the money. Or the effects of the war. But what if this exodus had a more ominous meaning?

Repression is a perverse process. It appears to efface the offending material, but this is an illusion—the contents of the unconscious are indestructible. Repressed material, like radioactive waste, lies there in leaky canisters, never losing potency, eternally dangerous. What is worse, it actively presses for expression, constantly threatening to erupt into consciousness. No one can control these forces; the best we can do is try to deflect them. It is a sign of health if we can accomplish this with a few

---

[12]Buys (1976) has argued that it was only in the 1970s that positive portrayals of psychoanalysis became common in introductory texts. See also Herma, Kris, & Shor (1943), whose study focused on how Freud's theory of dreams was presented in such texts. They found such a high degree of criticism that they were forced to make separate tallies for *ridicule*, *rejection on moral grounds*, and *sheer denial*.

judiciously used defenses. We know we're in trouble when we have to resort to the rigidity of symptoms.

Experimentalists took a calculated risk in trying to create a psychology in which subjective phenomena were banned from study. They knew that this would be difficult, that it would require erecting a set of defenses (the experimental method and all its appurtenances) and being vigilant about their use. But subjectivity creeps through every crevice and finds its way around even the strongest barricade. In the early years, this threat was manageable and psychology was willing to tolerate some narrowing of its operations in exchange for the reduction of anxiety its defenses allowed. Psychoanalysis tore this fragile equilibrium to pieces. By embracing subjectivity—sometimes even reveling in it—while still proclaiming itself a science, psychoanalysis forced psychology to define itself in ever more positivist terms. This was no ordinary battle over intellectual turf. It was more like a nightmare, in which psychologists watched, horrified, as the very phenomena they had sought to banish now returned to haunt them. They did what they could to contain the threat, but each new tactic only made things worse. Co-opting analytic concepts proved to be especially disastrous because it let the banned phenomena inside psychology itself. Even in scientific disguise, they were still dangerous, like a well-dressed hitchhiker who pulls a knife after getting into the car. With the threat now internal as well as external, experimental psychology was forced to harden itself still further. What had once been science became scientism, the neurotic symptom of a frightened discipline.

In retrospect, we might say that this was all to the good. The psychology that emerged from these wrenching experiences was stronger and more resilient, able to tolerate a degree of diversity among its members that would once have been unthinkable. The past 30 years have been a time of exponential growth, as older areas like learning have reorganized and newer ones like clinical have matured. The "cognitive revolution" that brought the mind back to psychology transformed even the most hard-core behaviorist, and terms like *self-perception* are now bandied about the laboratory as if they had been there all along. The rigid experimentalism of the 1940s now seems vaguely embarrassing, one of those righteous crusades of adolescence that pales before the complex realities of middle age.

There were many reasons for these changes, and certainly the threat from psychoanalysis was only one of a host of factors pushing psychology toward greater flexibility. But, as Burnham (1978) has argued, psychoanalysis did represent an extreme position against which more conservative disciplines like psychology and psychiatry had to define themselves. The willingness of analysts to occupy the radical frontiers of subjectivity gave psychologists room to maneuver, to create a middle ground in which previously excluded phenomena could enter without threatening the scientific standards psychologists had fought so hard to establish.

Equally important were the changes in psychoanalysis itself. During the period from 1940 to 1960, internecine warfare reached new heights among American analysts. The purges in the New York Psychoanalytic Institute were only the most visible sign that the field had become increasingly intolerant of dissent, and the huge influx of candidates after the war accelerated this slide toward conformity and conservatism (Hale, 1978; Jacoby, 1983). Psychoanalysis in 1950 was fundamentally different from what it had been in 1920, and its new mainstream mentality made it far easier for psychologists to accept.

The Second World War also played a significant role in these dynamics. Psychologists made substantive contributions to the diagnosis and treatment of war-related disturbances, as well as to myriad other problems from personnel selection to instrument design. These efforts enhanced the reputation of professional psychology and stimulated a massive increase in funding for psychological research. The war also brought to America European refugee psychologists, many of whom saw psychoanalytic ideas as part of the psychological canon. Psychologists began to spend less time worrying about whether analysts were eroding the fragile boundary between legitimate and popular psychology (Morawski & Hornstein, 1991) and took advantage of opportunities to get some favorable press of their own.[13]

American psychology has always been distinguished by an uncanny ability to adapt itself to cultural trends as quickly as they emerge. Once it became clear that the public found psychoanalysis irresistible, psychologists found ways of accommodating to it. Instead of concentrating all their efforts on criticism, they identified those parts of the theory that were potentially useful to their own ends and incorporated them. As psychoanalysis became less threatening, psychologists were able to notice that the two fields actually shared many of the same basic assumptions: a commitment to psychic determinism, a belief in the cardinal importance of childhood experience, and an optimistic outlook about the possibility of change.

It has been only 70 years since James McKeen Cattell rose from his seat at the annual meeting of the American Psychological Association to castigate a colleague for having mentioned Freud's name at a gathering of scientists (Dallenbach, 1955, p. 523). Today that same APA celebrates the success of its lawsuit against the psychoanalytic establishment, a suit which gave psychologists the right to become bona fide candidates at the analytic institute of their choice (Buie, 1988). As the moribund institutes prepare to be enlivened by a rush of eager psychologists, perhaps it is not too much to suggest that psychology itself has benefited from having had the psychoanalytic wolf at its door.

---

[13]See, for example, Gengerelli's (1957) rhetorical romp in the *Saturday Review*, which painted psychologists as tireless laborers in the "scientific vineyard" and analysts as "muddle-headed, sob-sisters" (p. 11) who are the cause of every social ill from delinquency to early marriage.

REFERENCES

Alexander, F. (1940). A jury trial of psychoanalysis. *Journal of Abnormal and Social Psychology, 35,* 305–323.

Bellamy, R. (1915a). An act of everyday life treated as a pretended dream and reinterpreted by psychoanalysis. *Journal of Abnormal Psychology, 10,* 32–45.

Bellamy, R. (1915b). Review of Coriat's *The meaning of dreams. Journal of Abnormal Psychology, 10,* 433–434.

Blum, G. S. (1954). An experimental reunion of psychoanalytic theory with perceptual vigilance and defense. *Journal of Abnormal and Social Psychology, 49,* 94–98.

Blum, G. S., & Miller, D. R. (1952). Exploring the psychoanalytic theory of the "oral character." *Journal of Personality, 20,* 287–304.

Boring, E. G. (1929). *A history of experimental psychology.* New York: Century.

Boring, E. G. (1940). Was this analysis a success? *Journal of Abnormal and Social Psychology, 35,* 4–10.

Boring, E. G., Langfeld, H. S., & Weld, H. P. (1935). *Psychology: A factual textbook.* New York: Wiley.

Buie, J. (1988). Psychoanalytic group bolstered by legal win. *APA Monitor, 19,* 21.

Burnham, J. C. (1967). *Psychoanalysis and American medicine, 1894–1918.* New York: International Universities Press.

Burnham, J. C. (1968). The new psychology: From narcissism to social control. In J. Braeman, R. H. Bremmer, & D. Brody (Eds.), *Change and continuity in twentieth-century America: The 1920s* (pp. 351–398). Columbus: Ohio State University Press.

Burnham, J. C. (1978). The influence of psychoanalysis upon American culture. In J. M. Quen & E. T. Carlson (Eds.), *American psychoanalysis: Origins and development* (pp. 52–72). New York: Brunner/Mazel.

Burnham, J. C. (1979). From avant-garde to specialism: Psychoanalysis in America. *Journal of the History of the Behavioral Sciences, 15,* 128–134.

Burnham, J. C. (1987). *How superstition won and science lost: Popularizing science and health in the United States.* New Brunswick, NJ: Rutgers University Press.

Buys, C. J. (1976). Freud in introductory psychology texts. *Teaching of Psychology, 3,* 160–167.

Carrington, H. (1914). Freudian psychology and psychical research. *Journal of Abnormal Psychology, 9,* 411–416.

Clark, K. E. (1957). *America's psychologists: A survey of a growing profession.* Washington, DC: American Psychological Association.

Coriat, I. H. (1910). The psycho-analysis of a case of sensory automatism. *Journal of Abnormal Psychology, 5,* 93–99.

Dallenbach, K. M. (1955). Phrenology versus psychoanalysis. *American Journal of Psychology, 68,* 511–525.

Danziger, K. (1990). *Constructing the subject: Historical origins of psychological research.* New York: Cambridge University Press.

Dollard, J., & Miller, N. E. (1950). *Personality and psychotherapy.* New York: McGraw-Hill.

Donley, J. E. (1911). Freud's anxiety neurosis. *Journal of Abnormal Psychology, 6,* 126–134.

Dunlap, K. (1920). *Mysticism, Freudianism and scientific psychology.* St. Louis, MO: Mosby.

Ellis, A. (1950). An introduction to the principles of scientific psychoanalysis. *Genetic Psychology Monographs, 41,* 147–212.

Emerson, L. E. (1912–1913). A psychoanalytic study of a severe case of hysteria. *Journal of Abnormal Psychology, 7,* 385–406; *8,* 44–56, 180–207.

Eysenck, H. J., & Wilson, G. D. (1973). *The experimental study of Freudian theories.* London: Methuen.

Fisher, S., & Greenberg, R. P. (1977). *The scientific credibility of Freud's theories and therapy.* New York: Basic Books.

Fite, W. (1916). Psycho-analysis and sex-psychology. *The Nation, 103,* 127–129.

Friedman, S. M. (1952). An empirical study of the castration and Oedipus complexes. *Genetic Psychology Monographs, 46,* 61–130.

Garrett, H. E. (1930). *Great experiments in psychology.* New York: Century.

Gengerelli, J. A. (1957, March 23). The limitations of psychoanalysis: Dogma or discipline? *The Saturday Review,* pp. 9–11, 40.

Gilgen, A. R. (1982). *American psychology since World War II: A profile of the discipline.* Westport, CT: Greenwood Press.

Gordon, A. (1917). Obsessive hallucinations and psychoanalysis. *Journal of Abnormal Psychology, 12,* 423–430.

Guthrie, E. R., & Edwards, A. L. (1949). *Psychology: A first course in human behavior.* New York: Harper.

Hale, N. G. (1971). *Freud and the Americans: The beginnings of psychoanalysis in the United States, 1876–1917.* New York: Oxford University Press.

Hale, N. G. (1978). From Bergasse XIX to Central Park West: The Americanization of psychoanalysis, 1919–1940. *Journal of the History of the Behavioral Sciences, 14,* 299–315.

Heidbreder, E. (1933). *Seven psychologies.* Englewood Cliffs, NJ: Prentice-Hall.

Hebb, D. O. (1958). *A textbook of psychology.* Philadelphia: W. B. Saunders.

Herma, H., Kris, E., & Shor, J. (1943). Freud's theory of the dream in American textbooks. *Journal of Abnormal and Social Psychology, 38,* 319–334.

Hilgard, E. R. (1952). Experimental approaches to psychoanalysis. In E. Pumpian-Mindlin (Ed.), *Psychoanalysis as science* (pp. 3–45). New York: Basic Books.

Hilgard, E. R. (1953). *Introduction to psychology.* New York: Harcourt, Brace.

Holt, E. B. (1915). *The Freudian wish and its place in ethics.* New York: Holt.

Hornstein, G. A. (1988). Quantifying psychological phenomena: Debates, dilemmas, and implications. In J. G. Morawski (Ed.), *The rise of experimental psychology* (pp. 1–34). New Haven, CT: Yale University Press.

Humphrey, G. (1920a). The conditioned reflex and the Freudian wish. *Journal of Abnormal Psychology, 14,* 388–392.

Humphrey, G. (1920b). Education and Freudianism. *Journal of Abnormal Psychology, 15,* 350–386.

Hunter, W. (1923). *General psychology.* (Rev. ed.). Chicago: University of Chicago Press.

Jacoby, R. (1983). *The repression of psychoanalysis: Otto Fenichel and the political Freudians.* New York: Basic Books.

Jastrow, J. (1932). *The house that Freud built.* New York: Chilton.

Keller, F., & Schoenfeld, W. (1950). *Principles of psychology: A systematic text in the science of behavior.* New York: Appleton-Century-Crofts.

Kelly, E. L. (1947). Clinical psychology. In W. Dennis et al. (Eds.), *Current trends in psychology* (pp. 75–108). Pittsburgh, PA: University of Pittsburgh Press.

Kimble, G. A. (1956). *Principles of general psychology.* New York: Ronald Press.

Kline, P. (1972). *Fact and fantasy in Freudian theory.* London: Methuen.

Kuklick, H. (1980). Boundary maintenance in American sociology: Limitations to academic "professionalization." *Journal of the History of the Behavioral Sciences, 16,* 201–219.

Kurzweil, E. (1989). *The Freudians: A comparative perspective.* New Haven, CT: Yale University Press.

Ladd-Franklin, C. (1916). Letter to the editor: *The Nation, 103,* 373–374.

Landis, C. (1940). Psychoanalytic phenomena. *Journal of Abnormal and Social Psychology, 35,* 17–28.

MacCurdy, J. T. (1913). The productions in a manic-like state illustrating Freudian mechanisms. *Journal of Abnormal Psychology, 8,* 361–375.

Maeder, A. (1910). Psycho-analysis in a case of melancholic depression. *Journal of Abnormal Psychology, 5,* 130–131.

Malcolm, J. (1984). *In the Freud archives.* New York: Knopf.

Morawski, J. G. (1988). Introduction. In J. G. Morawski (Ed.), *The rise of experimentation in American psychology* (pp. vii–xvii). New Haven, CT: Yale University Press.

Morawski, J. G. (1992). There is more to our history of giving: The place of introductory textbooks in American psychology. *American Psychologist, 47,* 161–169.

Morawski, J. G., & Hornstein, G. A. (1991). Quandary of the quacks: The struggle for expert knowledge in American psychology, 1890–1940. In D. van Keuren & J. Brown (Eds.), *The estate of social knowledge* (pp. 106–133). Baltimore: Johns Hopkins University Press.

Mowrer, O. H. (1940). An experimental analogue of "regression" with incidental observations on "reaction-formation." *Journal of Abnormal and Social Psychology, 35,* 56–87.

Murchison, C. (1926). *Psychologies of 1925*. Worcester, MA: Clark University Press.

Murphy, G. (1956). The current impact of Freud upon psychology. *American Psychologist, 11*, 663–672.

Prince, M. (1910). The mechanism and interpretation of dreams—A reply to Dr. Jones. *Journal of Abnormal Psychology, 5*, 337–353.

Putnam, J. J. (1906). Recent experiences in the study and treatment of hysteria at the Massachusetts General Hospital with remarks on Freud's method of treatment by "psycho-analysis." *Journal of Abnormal Psychology, 1*, 26–41.

Putnam, J. J. (1909–1910). Personal impressions of Sigmund Freud and his work, with special reference to his recent lectures at Clark University. *Journal of Abnormal Psychology, 4*, 293–310, 372–379.

Roback, A. A. (1921). Review of Dunlap's *Mysticism, Freudianism and scientific psychology*. *Journal of Abnormal and Social Psychology, 16*, 406–408.

Robinson, E. S., & Robinson, F. R. (1923). *Readings in general psychology*. Chicago: University of Chicago Press.

Sachs, H. (1940). Was this analysis a success?: Comment. *Journal of Abnormal and Social Psychology, 35*, 11–16.

Sarnoff, I., & Corwin, S. M. (1959). Castration anxiety and the fear of death. *Journal of Personality, 27*, 374–385.

Schwartz, B. J. (1956). An empirical test of two Freudian hypotheses concerning castration anxiety. *Journal of Personality, 24*, 318–327.

Scodel, A. (1957). Heterosexual somatic preference and fantasy dependency. *Journal of Consulting Psychology, 21*, 371–374.

Scott, W. D. (1908). An interpretation of the psycho-analytic method in psychotherapy with a report of a case so treated. *Journal of Abnormal Psychology, 3*, 371–379.

Sears, R. R. (1943). *Survey of objective studies of psychoanalytic concepts*. New York: Social Science Research Council.

Seashore, C. E. (1923). *Introduction to psychology*. New York: Macmillan.

Shakow, D., & Rapaport, D. (1964). *The influence of Freud on American psychology*. New York: International Universities Press.

Skinner, B. F. (1953). *Science and human behavior*. New York: Macmillan.

Solomon, M. (1916). Critical review of the conception of sexuality assumed by the Freudian school. *Journal of Abnormal Psychology, 11*, 59–60.

Tannenbaum, S. A. (1916). Letter to the editor. *The Nation, 103*, 218–219.

Tannenbaum, S. A. (1917). Some current misconceptions of psychoanalysis. *Journal of Abnormal Psychology, 12*, 390–422.

Taylor, E. W. (1911). Possibilities of a modified psychoanalysis. *Journal of Abnormal Psychology, 6*, 449–455.

Warren, H. C., & Carmichael, L. (1930). *Elements of human psychology* (Rev. ed.). Boston: Houghton Mifflin.

Watson, J. B. (1925). *Behaviorism*. New York: Norton.

Watson, J. B. (1927). The myth of the unconscious. *Harpers, 155,* 502–508.

Watson, J. B. (1928). *Psychological care of the infant and child.* New York: Norton.

Wells, F. L. (1913). On formulation in psychoanalysis. *Journal of Abnormal Psychology, 8,* 217–227.

Wiener, M. (1955). Word frequency or motivation in perceptual defense. *Journal of Abnormal and Social Psychology, 51,* 214–218.

Woodworth, R. S. (1916). Letter to the editor. *The Nation, 103,* 396.

Woodworth, R. S. (1917). Some criticisms of the Freudian psychology. *Journal of Abnormal Psychology, 12,* 174–194.

VII

PSYCHOLOGY IN THE PUBLIC INTEREST

INTRODUCTION: PSYCHOLOGY IN THE PUBLIC INTEREST

The American Psychological Association (APA) added the aim of "advancing human welfare" to its mission statement during its World War II reorganization. Yet, psychologists before and after that time were involved in social issues and were working on behalf of the perceived public interest. The four chapters in this section provide the reader with a broader perspective on psychology in its real-world context.

British scholar Graham Richards (1995) has argued persuasively that American psychology has retained a strong moral interest over the course of its development. One aspect of this moral project can be found in psychologists' views of an ideal world. In chapter 24, "Assessing Psychology's Moral Heritage Through Our Neglected Utopias" (1982), which historicizes and humanizes psychological science, Jill G. Morawski examines the utopias proposed by four prominent psychologists, G. Stanley Hall (1844–1924), Hugo Münsterberg (1863–1916), William McDougall (1871–1938), and John B. Watson (1878–1958). Each man dreamed of a world made better by the intervention and leadership of psychologists. Morawski also addresses several of the historiographical issues raised in Part I of this book, thus providing readers with a clear example of critical history.

One of the first examples of serious scholarship in the history of women in psychology is chapter 25, "Placing Women in the History of Psychology: The First American Women Psychologists" (1986), by Laurel

Furumoto and Elizabeth Scarborough. Since its original publication, numerous scholarly articles on women psychologists have appeared, and the field has moved from compensatory history to full inclusion (see, for example, Furumoto, 1992; Milar, 1999; O'Connell & Russo, 1990; Scarborough & Furumoto, 1987; Wentworth, 1999). Case studies are presented of 22 women who were distinguished psychologists in the first generation of the new psychology in America. The chapter is a clear example of the new, critical history of psychology that relies on primary materials and places the subject within the context of its time.

As Furumoto and Scarborough show, women were faced with many obstacles to training and career. Prior to 1900, few American graduate programs existed that would accept women as doctoral students. Some programs that did permit women to study at the doctoral level, such as Harvard or Johns Hopkins universities, would not award the degree to a woman after she successfully completed her work. Those who did receive graduate training usually had to make a choice between career and marriage, as most colleges would not allow married women to serve on their faculties. The authors track the careers of several women to illustrate these obstacles and how the women dealt with them. The article serves as a solid introduction to the study of the role of women in American psychology.

The integration of Jews into post–World War II American psychology has been so successful and complete that it is difficult to imagine that it was ever otherwise. However, recent scholarship has revealed that it was common practice to discriminate against Jews, because of their Jewish identity, until the postwar period. Chapter 26, "'The Defects of His Race': E. G. Boring and Antisemitism in American Psychology, 1923–1953" (1998), by Andrew S. Winston, examines the practices of noted psychologist–historian E. G. Boring (1886–1968) in regard to Jews both before and after the war. Rather than reducing the issue to one of simple racism, Winston shows the delicate balance that Boring sought to bring to the problem of helping Jews find academic jobs in the period between the world wars and how his views appeared to change after the war.

Indirectly, such practices contributed to the development of applied and professional psychology, especially in clinical practice. As was the case with women, when traditional academic positions were not available in the years between the world wars, Jewish psychologists took positions where they could find them, often in state mental hospitals or other clinical settings. Two individuals whose chapters are included in Part VI, David Shakow and Seymour B. Sarason, both began their careers at Worcester State Hospital in Massachusetts. Both men were able to utilize their experiences after the war, when they became influential leaders of the development of modern clinical psychology. Shakow was at one time a graduate student with Boring. The chapter illustrates the complex interplay between sociocultural factors and the practice of psychological science in a specific time period. It also is an excellent example of the importance of primary source materials, in this case the correspondence of Boring, in the writing of fine-grained, critical history that tells us so much more than traditional celebratory histories.

To date, only one African American has served as president of the APA: Kenneth B. Clark (1914–) in 1971. Despite his high name recognition, Clark's life and history are not well-known to many American psychologists. Clark and his wife, Mamie Phipps Clark (1917–1983), conducted research in the 1930s and 1940s that proved crucial in the 1954 U.S. Supreme Court decision that banned segregation in American public schools, *Brown v. the Board of Education*. Essentially, they concluded that the experience of racial segregation was psychologically harmful to Black children. In chapter 27, "Recontextualizing Kenneth B. Clark: An Afrocentric Perspective on the Paradoxical Legacy of a Model Psychologist–Activist" (2000), Layli Phillips offers readers an opportunity to understand the richness of the life and work of Clark by placing him in an Afrocentric perspective, a perspective that places the premium on the value of human relationships. Clark, according to Phillips, was guided by such principles in his personal and professional lives.

Clark's reputation declined in the late 1960s and 1970s as younger Black activists emerged in the academic community. Clark was accused of pathologizing the Black experience in America because he focused on the role of African Americans as an oppressed people. His work that was used by the National Association for the Advancement of Colored People (NAACP) to support their arguments before the Supreme Court was denigrated and found suspect. It is curious that some of the Black activists' arguments against Clark's work accorded with the views of the segregationists who fought the NAACP. A result of the criticism was that by the 1990s, the received historical view by both Black and White Americans was that Clark's work was seriously flawed. Recent historical scholarship, however, has pointed out that such judgments are themselves seriously flawed and presentist. That is, Clark's research and support for desegregation has been judged not in its own historical context, but in the context of developments after the success of the Civil Rights movement of the 1960s (Jackson, 2000). This is a point that is also well made by Phillips.

The portrait of Clark that emerges from Phillips's chapter is of a serious scholar who has been deeply concerned about race issues for most of his life. That he is also a flawed human being is a part of the portrait. Phillips uses an Afrocentric and what she terms a "womanist" perspective to challenge readers to rethink the importance of worldview in the writing of history.

Together, these four chapters offer historical insight into the attempts to develop a psychology that will advance human welfare and serve the public interest.

REFERENCES

Furumoto, L. (1992). Joining separate spheres—Christine Ladd-Franklin, Woman-Scientist (1847–1930). *American Psychologist, 47,* 175–182.

Jackson, J. P., Jr. (2000). The triumph of the segregationists? A historiographical inquiry into psychology and the *Brown* litigation. *History of Psychology, 3,* 239–261.

Milar, K. S. (1999). "A coarse and clumsy tool": Helen Thompson Woolley and the Cincinnati Vocational Bureau. *History of Psychology, 2,* 219–235.

O'Connell, A. N., & Russo, N. F. (1990). *Women in psychology: A bio-bibliographic sourcebook.* New York: Greenwood Press.

Richards, G. (1995). "To know our fellow men to do them good": American psychology's enduring moral project. *History of the Human Sciences, 8,* 1–24.

Scarborough, E., & Furumoto, L. (1987). *Untold lives: The first generation of American women psychologists.* New York: Columbia University Press.

Wentworth, P. A. (1999). The moral of her story: Exploring the philosophical and religious commitments in Mary Whiton Calkins' self-psychology. *History of Psychology, 2,* 119–131.

24

ASSESSING PSYCHOLOGY'S MORAL HERITAGE THROUGH OUR NEGLECTED UTOPIAS

JILL G. MORAWSKI

The centennial of experimental psychology in 1979 heightened interest in the discipline's history by offering the psychologist lore about precursors, innovations, controversies, and great achievements. Paralleling these centennial events has been a growing concern with the state of scholarship in the history of psychology, particularly with histories that primarily document or celebrate intellectual milestones. Such ceremonial histories typically acknowledge the purported antecedents of currently dominant positions within psychology. Whether spawned by purely intellectual or partisan interests, these "presentist" or "conventional" histories have yielded an insular conception of psychology, one that lacks meaning in the broader context of historical events (Stocking, 1965; Young, 1966). However unintentionally, they have also contributed to psychologists' relative ignorance about the social, political, and moral background of their science. The all but forgotten utopias of G. Stanley Hall, William McDougall,

---

Reprinted from *American Psychologist, 37*, 1082–1095 (1982). Copyright © 1982 by the American Psychological Association. Reprinted with permission of the author.

Hugo Münsterberg, and John B. Watson comprise part of this neglected past. Reappraisal of such works contributes to a more complete story of psychology's past and enriches the context for understanding current theoretical, social, and ethical issues.

TOWARD MORE CRITICAL HISTORIES

Recently historians have begun to reevaluate the conventional history of psychology. For the most part, they have assessed various historical "myths" perpetuated in our histories as well as the inordinate concern with psychology's intellectual heritage and consequent neglect of its social and political context. For instance, Samelson (1974) investigated the "origin myths" that date social psychology's birth with Comte's positive social philosophy. Harris (1979) has shown how the conventional interpretations of John B. Watson's experiment with little Albert relate more to the interpreter's particular theoretical interests than to the actual Albert study. Others have investigated how the expansion and activities of American psychology have been shaped by economic and political events (Camfield, 1969; Finison, 1976; Sokal, 1980). Such studies suggest both the inaccuracy of conventional histories and the incompleteness of the more accurate intellectual histories that represent psychology as an isolated corpus of ideas or an accumulation of scientific discoveries.

Similar reexaminations have been undertaken in the history of science (see Agassi, 1963; Brush, 1974; Teich & Young, 1973). A contribution of these studies that has yet to be appreciated in psychology is an understanding of the broader social relations and moral heritage of science. As one historian of science has noted, abeyance of this heritage "deprives scientists of the present time of a historical perspective on their moral problems, with the result that their illusion of suddenly lost innocence makes their dilemmas seem unprecedented and hence worse than they really are" (Ravetz, 1973, p. 210). Conventional or purely intellectual histories of psychology obscure some fundamental issues of the past: the role of psychology and the psychologist in society, the confrontation with ethical problems, the relation of psychology to the humanities and other sciences, and the dissemination of psychological knowledge to the public. Thus, the contemporary psychologist may miss both substantive knowledge about the historical precedence of current social issues and, consequently, the opportunity to assess how these issues have developed relative to theory and epistemology. Furthermore, because more comprehensive and critical studies require scrutiny not merely of dusty texts and journals but also of personal papers, institutional records, unpublished manuscripts, and forgotten publications, they attend to the "human" context in which psychological knowledge is created. Rediscovery of these historical materials may have sobering effects—as with the cases of Cyril Burt and J. B. Watson (Samelson, 1980)—yet there is no reason why such excursions cannot have positive consequences as well.

There are several reasons why the conventional histories of psychology have charted a practically unidimensional course of psychology's advance. Psychology, after all, is a relatively new discipline seeking recognition as a natural science. Histories detailing the discovery of theories and refinement of methods have confirmed its scientific image (Hagstrom, 1965; O'Donnell, 1979). They reified the hopes to establish a true science of the mind, sometimes nearly succumbing to what has been called "physics envy." There is perhaps a more specific reason why conventional histories have not directly addressed social, moral, or political issues of the past. Scientists have long subscribed to discordant moral attitudes. These have been described by Toulmin (1975) as a "Baconian" morality, where science serves as an instrument committed to human improvement, and a "Newtonian" morality, where science serves the rational pursuit of a true understanding of nature. Scientists have adhered to the Baconian image principally in the external affairs of science and have done so to secure the societal support necessary to pursue intellectual interests. For instance, after World War I, the National Academy of Sciences adopted such Baconian arguments in order to retain public support for scientific research (Tobey, 1971). The Newtonian image has guided the internal workings of science, its organization and operations. It also has predominated in psychological textbooks and various other mandates affirming that psychologists "can be most useful to society by staying in their laboratories and libraries, there to remain until they can come forth with reliable predictions and well-tested applications" (Pratt, 1939, p. 179). It is with this attitude that conventional or intellectual histories of social psychology would cite F. H. Allport's (1924) *Social Psychology* as a seminal contribution to the field but would make no mention of his substantial proposals about applying social psychology to ensure a democratic, egalitarian, and controlled society.

This article addresses one unexplored event in psychology's heritage. It treats several victims of a historical perspective that is imbued with a Newtonian image of the science: four utopias published between 1915 and 1930 by the hardly obscure psychologists G. Stanley Hall, William McDougall, Hugo Münsterberg, and John B. Watson. These utopias clearly reflect Baconian thinking, not in a simple resemblance to *New Atlantis*, but in their dedication to explaining how psychology, as a science, is instrumental to human welfare. For this reason alone, the utopias would have no place in conventional histories. However, the utopias and other writings of the four psychologists also belie a clear distinction between the Baconian and Newtonian moralities in psychology. In their epistemological thinking, the four psychologists essentially attempted a unification of psychology as a knowledge system *and* as a social instrument. Their utopias served to illustrate this unity and, hence, to show the imperative for advancing psychology. The correspondence between their utopian and professional writings affirms their dedication to these ideas. When viewed in the broader context of the period 1915 to 1930, these writings cannot be interpreted simply as anomalies, as peculiar pastimes of professionals, but must be seen as plausible answers to perceived crises both in academic psychology and in American society. When viewed in relation to contemporary psychology, the writings intimate a continued reluctance to confront such dual moralities.

G. STANLEY HALL AND THE IDEAL COMMUNITY

G. Stanley Hall generally has been applauded for his strategic role in American experimental psychology: He organized the first psychological journal, the first American psychological association, the first Wundtian laboratory in America, and the first and only American visit of Freud. In addition to enumerating these accomplishments, most histories acknowledge that Hall also was a versatile psychologist who promoted genetic psychology and related evolutionary concepts, an interest in psychoanalysis, and the design of questionnaires (e.g., Boring, 1950; R. I. Watson, 1971). Except for a biography (Ross, 1972), these histories do not examine Hall's comprehensive view of evolution, the philosophical assumptions of his theories, and his prescriptions for resolving social problems.

Written late in Hall's career, "The Fall of Atlantis" (1920a) tells of a utopian civilization. The story purportedly is narrated by a cultural anthropologist who visited Atlantis' remains in 2000 A.D. and learned that it had at one time governed the civilized world with a culture that far exceeded any contemporary vision of progress. Atlantis represented human evolution toward perfection in every detail: its language was the most flexible expression of the human psyche, medicine had excelled to the point of becoming a philosophic science, the political structure integrated all known codes of justice, and education permeated all stages of life.

Atlantis exemplifies the evolution of a society that eventually becomes unified and recognizes a social consciousness or "Man-soul." Atlantean citizens subordinated individual to social desires and celebrated a perception of being "uniquely one with all Nature, the consummate product of her creative evolution" (p. 72). They understood the nuances of evolution and recapitulation and were devoted to preserving those processes. The fall of Atlantis was not cataclysmic, but rather a gradual degeneration initiated by forces of individualism and by physical changes in the environment. Social institutions such as medicine decayed as citizens and physicians violated communal health regulations for personal profit; law, religion, education, science, and the family faltered similarly. At the same time

Atlantis began to sink into the sea, and its citizens either drowned or embarked on sea journeys in search of new land.

Although not the sole focus of the story, science was lauded as foremost among the achievements of Atlantis. Scientific discoveries had yielded means for the chemical synthesis of diamonds and gold, generation of life from crystals, accumulation of data on Martians, and the development of new vegetation. But these and other advances were not the reason for the elevated status of research. In Atlantis research was the ultimate expression of the belief in human improvement. And of all scientific endeavors, psychology represented the most valuable task. After a speculative period, the field had emancipated itself from metaphysics and physiology and "had become a culminating academic theme, the only one which all desired and which it was felt needful to know. It was genetic, comparative, clinical, and strove chiefly to give self-knowledge and self-control" (pp. 57–58). Researchers of this synthetic psychology were exonerated from many social duties, supported for their work, and "regarded as the light and hope of the state" (p. 56). Psychology was instrumental to the attainment of the perfect social order, and the psychologist occupied a social role consistent with the special obligations of the field.

The elevated position of psychology was apparent throughout the Atlantean civilization. Jurisprudence was designed through research on human nature and operated with two rules: the pleasure and pain principles and the assessment of the social value of individual actions. Education was structured according to human development research, and in the universities "the nature of man was the culminating study" (p. 34). Even teachers of religion, the "heartformers," practiced a "higher psychology of the folk-soul" (p. 80).

The tragedy of Atlantis was not a finality because there were survivors who potentially could transmit the Atlantean heritage and strive for some future utopia. The fall had resulted partly from the psychological flaws of individualism and selfishness, and the revered field of psychology did not escape these faults. In the midst of Atlantis' degeneration, psychology was employed "to fit men to be cogs in preexisting machinery" rather than to "develop ever higher powers in man himself which impel him to create ever newer and higher institutions as progress demands" (p. 66). The commercial preoccupations of scientists signaled the eventual demise of the scientific spirit and the collapse of research centers.

Hall's utopian conception of psychology is reflected in many of his psychological writings. In his psychology as well as in his administrative and educational efforts, Hall lauded research as the "greatest achievement of man" and the researcher as a "superman" who deserved extensive freedom and support (Hall, 1908, p. 104). His later writings emphasized not only the privileges of researchers but their leadership responsibilities: "Henceforth, as never before, progress is committed to the hands of the intellectuals and they must think harder, realizing to the full the responsibilities of their new leadership.... In everything it is the expert who must say the final word" (1921, pp. 112–113). If scientific researchers had such responsibilities, then psychologists, who studied what Hall called the queen of the sciences, certainly held a substantial share of the duties. The special responsibilities of psychologists included the discovery of desirable human attributes and methods for readjusting the environment to human needs (Hall, 1917, 1919a, 1919b, 1923). As "queen of the sciences" psychology would promote the unity of knowledge, would bridge pure and practical research, and would embrace a pluralism of systems (Hall, 1906, 1908, 1919b, 1920b, 1923). Accordingly, he called the psychologist "a sort of high priest of souls" who "is not content merely to fit men for existing institutions as they are to-day" but would "develop even higher powers, which gradually molt old and evolve new and better institutions or improve old ones" (1923, p. 436). Here he also commented on the degradation of American science, particularly psychology; he compared intelligence testing to the fads of phrenology and palmistry and described it as a product solely of psychologists' economic interests.

The correspondence between Hall's utopian ideals and his psychological writings is represented through four basic assumptions about human nature. He held (1899, 1904) that human evolution is the growth of consciousness (individual and radical) and is progressive (upward). Further, evolution of the race is repeated in the individual; that is, it involves recapitulation (1904) and occurs in all human aggregates from the family to knowledge systems (1907, 1913). Finally, as the highest life form, humans are responsible for guarding and guiding evolution, and those in leadership positions have the greatest responsibility (1907, 1908, 1917, 1919a, 1919b, 1921, 1923). Because evolution is of consciousness, occurs throughout all human institutions, and requires guidance, psychology is a priority science and the logical source of coordination. With these responsibilities the psychologist, or psychological pedagogue, becomes the "engineer in the domain of nature" (Hall, 1919b, p. 99). Thus, Hall's assumptions about human nature justify the unique moral responsibilities associated with psychology.

WILLIAM MCDOUGAL AND EUGENICS FOR SOCIAL IMPROVEMENT

William McDougall was British by birth, but his career as a psychologist was spent equally in Britain and the United States. Although critical of McDougall's teleological thinking and interest in psychical research, histories of psychology present his scientific work as both innovative and influential. He has been credited with anticipating the behaviorist trend later promulgated by Watson, and his research in purposive psychology and instincts has earned him recognition as the progenitor of the hormic school of psychology. Yet, these accounts pay little attention to his social psychology, evolutionary theory, and psychology of politics and social ethics (see, e.g., Murphy, 1949; Peters, 1962; R. I. Watson, 1971).

One of his neglected publications, "The Island of Eugenia," is a proposal for a utopian society founded on eugenic principles (McDougall, 1921). Eugenia is presented as the plan of an academic scientist who, after 30 years of study, shared his ideas with an old college friend who since had become an affluent philanthropist. The plan is laid out in a dialogue between scientist and philanthropist, between the "Seer" and the "Practical Man." Eugenia would be devoted to propagating "superior strains," which are recruited worldwide on the basis of family history, intellectual abilities, and moral qualifications. Candidates for citizenship would be selected for superb phenotypic characteristics that supposedly represent exceptional genotypic traits, and some preference would be accorded to preserve the "disappearing" race of Nordics.

The story resembles the typical utopia in the sense that Eugenia would have an ideal geography and stable organization. However, only the measures for world improvement, for the social environment, and for the role of scientific institutions are presented in any detail. The program for human improvement is twofold. The selected breeders of Eugenia may reenter the general society to raise genetic fitness by intermarriage or to apply their superior talents to improve social and political conditions. Or Eugenians may marry within the utopia and contribute to genetic refinement. Thus, Eugenia would not be a utopia for everyone, but would admit a select group who aim to advance the lives of all. The scenic physical environment would comprise a conducive atmosphere for optimal work productivity, monogamous marriages, traditional family life, and education.

Just as the design of Eugenia required the knowledge of the scientific "Seer," so the maintenance of the island depended on science. The protagonist, a scientist of nature and society, drafted plans consistent with his belief in the validity and efficacy of science and accordingly with a conviction that other reform measures (those endorsed by Carnegie and Rockefeller) were merely "social plasters" (pp. 5–6). The primary institutions in Eugenia would be the universities and professional schools—places where research would flourish. Scientific studies would center on the science of Eugenia's initial founding—psychology—particularly in its relations to eugenics. The extensive concern with *human* conditions and not social structure followed from the claim that "forms of organization matter little; the all important thing is the quality of the matter to be organized, the quality of the human beings that are the stuff of our nations and societies" (p. 7). Psychology, especially as it pertains to genetic issues, would have precedence: "The science of man will for the first time receive adequate recognition, that is to say, it will dominate the scene. To it all other sciences will be duly subordinated" (pp. 24–25).

McDougall's plan for utopia parallels both his philosophy of knowledge and psychology. He had formulated a model of science in which

> the sole test of criterion of science, or true knowledge of Nature, is that it shall bring us such understanding of the course of natural events as will enable us effectively to intervene and modify the course of such events for our own purposes, direct the course of events teleologically, control them in some degree (however slight) in accordance with our desires and needs. (1934a, p. 15)

Science is an enactment of certain characteristics of human nature, specifically those of purposiveness. But McDougall also insisted that science is empirical and positive (1905, 1912, 1923) and can be distinguished from philosophy, which is criticism and evaluation (1929, 1934a). Of all the sciences, psychology is "the science of the most urgent importance in the present age, when, for lack of sufficient knowledge of human nature, our civilization threatens to fall into chaos and decay" (1930a, p. 221).

After rejecting mechanism and determinism, McDougall developed a purposive psychology with the underlying assumption that organisms have a "disposition" or latent tendency to strive toward some end (1908). He stipulated that the primary focus for psychology should be the study of particular dispositions or "instincts" and innate mental processes (1908, 1910, 1912) such as the hereditary basis of will (1912). He tentatively adopted a Lamarckian theory because it coincided with the premises of purposiveness, holism, and indeterminism (1925, 1929, 1930b, 1934a, 1934b, 1936). Because Lamarckianism stressed the salience of environmental and genetic influences on development, McDougall came to advocate both environmental and eugenic reforms (1921, 1931, 1933, 1934b).

As exemplified in his psychology, McDougall's epistemology contains three root assumptions: mind evolves in a purposive manner toward some ideal end, science is a product of the evolution of mind, and the veracity of scientific knowledge is determined by its successful application (1905, 1923, 1934a, 1938). These assumptions imply that the ultimate purpose of science is the acquisition of knowledge for bettering humanity. They also assert the priority of psychology: If science results from purposive striving of mind, then scientists obviously would benefit from knowledge of purposiveness as investigated in psychology. Psychology is unique in its relevance to all facets of life and in its instrumental role in applying scientific knowledge to human affairs (1908, 1931, 1934b, 1937). McDougall consequently realized the need for better psychologists to "make themselves the saviors of our collapsing civilization" (1927, 1931, 1936). Psychology is essential to humankind's continued progress and to the realization of higher ideals (1923, 1924, 1926, 1934a). Any contradiction between philosophical ideals and scientific facts was resolved by positing a special relation between philosophy and the social sciences. Under appropriate conditions social scientists should implement philosophers' specifications for desirable ends or ultimate values. However, since the right conditions had not yet arrived and philosophical progress still required scientific support, there must be a different relation between the two fields. McDougall suggested that "It is, then, right and well nigh inevitable that the social scientist shall be also a philosopher, or, at least, interested in social philosophy and its problems" (1937, p. 342). Under such conditions the social scientist is responsible for promoting the progress and ideals of humankind; McDougall broached these responsibilities through his research and fiction.

HUGO MÜNSTERBERG AND AN IDEAL TOMORROW

Hugo Münsterberg has been most commonly identified as William James' chosen successor as head of the Harvard psychological laboratories. Although conventional histories acknowledge his early psychological theory and diversified interests, recognition of these contributions is tempered with expressed disappointment concerning Münsterberg's performance as an experimental psychologist. With the exception of a recent biography (Hale, 1980), these studies tend to ignore Münsterberg's contributions to American philosophy and the relation of his political activities to his psychological endeavors (e.g., Boring, 1950; Flugel & West, 1964; Peters, 1962).

One of Münsterberg's attempts to unite political convictions, scientific beliefs, and metaphysics appears in a book-length utopian program published in the last year of his life. *Tomorrow: Letters to a Friend in Germany* (1916) proposes social perfection through attainment of postwar internationalism. The program is delineated in a series of letters from a German-American psychologist to a friend and historian in Germany who has requested the scientist's expertise. At the outset, the psychologist acknowledged the circumstances that permitted him to comment on the future: "You turn to me because one whose lifework is psychology may best foresee the days which wait for us, and one who lives in a neutral country may look with clearer eyes toward the tomorrow than those in belligerent lands" (p. 2). The utopian future, or tomorrow, is the ultimate consequence of the social advances from nationalism and internationalism to pacifism. These social changes require organized and efficient procedures implemented through acceptance of certain eternal and absolute values—through idealism. The nationalism of European countries, particularly Germany, and of America comprised the first signs of a new philosophy and ultimately, of a new world order. This nationalism fosters unity, which in turn would negate selfish individualism and engender the recognition of other absolute values. *Tomorrow* outlines the stages accompanying the realization of idealism. The supraindividual and future-oriented obligations eventually would serve not a single nation, but the entire world; all nations would "repress" memories of earlier animosities, would organize programs for exchange, cooperation, and other common purposes, and would constitute the beginnings of "supernational organizations" (pp. 224–242). The book concludes with a prospectus on postwar reconstruction oriented toward absolute ideals. "If the people of a group, or finally of the globe, are bound by an organization, it demands in the same way that each subordinate its selfish desires to the progress of the whole, to the aims of western culture, to the ideals of mankind" (pp. 267–268).

According to the plan of *Tomorrow*, science would serve these universal ideals. Science, particularly psychology, would contribute directly to these ends: "Movements for vocational guidance and vocational education have spread over the land. . . . The scientific expert is more and more often called into the service of public affairs" (pp. 153–154). Although *Tomorrow* contains numerous references to such psychological expertise, it is primarily an idealist scheme. It is written from the position that current scientific knowledge is faulty and that proper science requires a certain philosophical understanding. The narrator rejects contemporary speculations of a future based solely on scientific advances and argues that science is ancillary to absolute knowledge.

Münsterberg's other writings both correspond to the utopia and further explicate his ideals for science, specifically psychology. Münsterberg referred to experimental psychology as "causal" because it is "a science which aims at description and explanation of inner life" through study of the causal connections of its physical correlates (1910b, p. 26; 1914). But experimental psychology had limited potential and required another type of research (1898, 1899a, 1899b, 1914). "Purposive" psychology studies the same inner experiences as experimental psychology but from the "different standpoint" of understanding the meaning or purposes of inner experiences (1914, p. 297). Beginning where causal psychology terminates, purposive psychology alone can study the absolute ideals of life. Despite this dichotomous model, Münsterberg believed that both psychologies shared an ultimate end since "The whole elaboration of causal psychology, and that is after all the form of psychology which is traditionally accepted as the science of the mind, has significance only if it is ultimately to serve our practical ends" (1914, pp. 345–346). Münsterberg held that observable social degeneration and the demands made by other professionals for psychological expertise demonstrated "the duty of the practical psychologist systematically to examine how far other purposes of modern society can be advanced by the new methods of experimental psychology" (1913, p. 15). Psychology was imperative to successful social control and an ideal social order, and Münsterberg made numerous efforts to realize this potential through both his applied and experimental psychology. Finally, the application of psychology was essential to his idealist stance because the coupling of theory and practice represented a move toward a higher unity, "an ultimate view of pulsating reality" (1914, p. 17). Thus the process of application requires awareness of certain ultimate ends or values—of purposive psychology—and a synthesis of theory and these socially desired ends (1909, 1910a).

The claims that psychology is essential to the success of modern life and that psychologists have unique obligations in serving society are consistent with Münsterberg's theory of knowledge. He held that there exists an absolute knowledge which transcends individual knowledge. The values of truth, beauty, harmony, progress, morality, and unity are subject to "the ultimate demand that all the values become one, that the world remain absolutely itself; and the satisfaction of this demand brings us the values of religion and philosophy" (1906, p. 40; see also 1899b, 1912). The classification and analysis of knowledge are determined on metaphysical and not physical grounds, through philosophical understanding and not experiences in the physical world. From this position it becomes evident that even the causal sciences are purposive and value-laden because they contribute to constructing an ideal system of the world (1911). The ultimate goal of knowledge seeking is the culmination of a "*Weltanschauung*, a unified view of the whole of reality" (1905, p. 95). Both purposive and causal psychology are essential to the study of absolute values and ends; the melding of these two approaches into applied psychology serves the striving for a harmonious social order and a unified system of knowledge.

JOHN B. WATSON AND THE HOPES OF BEHAVIORISM

John B. Watson is noted for his zealous commitment to psychology and his role as a proponent of what was to become for a time its foremost theoretical orientation. He also is credited with persuasively arguing against the validity of consciousness and introspection as psychological concepts, and for the study of behavior, the use of objective methods, the recognition of environmental influences on behavior, and the practical application of psychological research. Of these kudos, conventional histories mention little about his dedication to practical psychology (e.g., Boring, 1950; R. I. Watson, 1971).

Among the products of Watson's interest in the practical applications of psychology that have not received attention is a utopian vision based on behaviorist principles. Originally titled "The Behaviorist's Utopia," the manuscript was published in 1929 as a magazine article titled "Should a Child Have More Than One Mother?" Watson envisioned a thoroughly behavioristic country with "units" of 260 husbands and wives (and a few extras to serve as "spare" husbands and wives). Each husband and wife pair, aided by a "scientifically trained assistant," cares for three children, although they never know the identity of their biological children. Offspring rotate among the parent pairs, spending four weeks at each home, and at the age of 20, "his 260th mother and father pat him on the head and send him out to earn his living unaided" (p. 33). Eschewing religion, politics, philosophy, history, and tradition, Utopia's citizens seek only "behaviorist happiness," and do so "by experimentation." Utopia contains both accepted social traditions and innovations. Watson decreed that the country would be monogamous or "at any rate, I want to see monogamy tried" (p. 32). The social structure is unique in the absence of a "state," judicial system, and clergy. Because social rules are developed through experimentation and misbehavior is corrected by retraining, the behaviorist's utopia has no need for political structures or "that abstract entity we call the State" (p. 35). Citizens contribute to society because they are trained to be independent and absorbed in activities such that in the factories "men work harder if anything because they are trained to be absorbingly active all during the waking hours" (p. 32).

Instead of the usual professionals, Utopia has specialists called "behaviorist physicians" who are trained in the methods of behaviorism to "guard the community on the psychological side just as they guard it on the medical side. There is a preventive psychology in Utopia just as there is a preventive medicine" (p. 34). Among their responsibilities, behaviorist physicians correct behavior disorders, make decisions regarding euthanasia, and treat insanity. In a society where the rearing of children is paramount, the behaviorist physician "takes charge" and assists the mother during the early years of the children's lives. The educational environment is designed for conditioning "emotional and dispositional habits" and is equipped with such unobtrusive observational devices as periscopes. Children begin vocational and professional training at the age of 16 when, segregated by sex, males learn vocations such as medicine, science, and manufacturing while females learn to manage homes, handle men, perfect sex techniques, and rear children. Behavioral scientists apparently do not alter the social and moral standards precisely because such standards are identical with those of behavioral science. Both are behavioristic and without complications inherent in religious, philosophical, or political traditions; both embrace the Utopian morals of "behavioristic happiness."

Watson's utopian stance on the necessity of psychology appears in other nonfictional writings. Before elucidating his "principles for the control of human action," and even before issuing his behaviorist decree of 1913, Watson expounded on the practical value of experimentation (1910, 1912). He subsequently described the goal of research to be the discovery of adjustments to stimuli, adding that "My final reason for this is to learn general and particular methods by which I may control behavior" (1913, p. 168). The control of behavior to "aid organized society in its endeavors to prevent failures" was just as much a function of psychology as the formulation of laws of behavior (1917a, p. 329). He argued that society's leaders had attempted environmental adjustment through "roundabout, hit-and-miss methods," whereas behavior psychology would do so by scientific methods (1917a, p. 330). Watson reiterated claims about the superiority of experimental methods for attaining social control and the need for trained behavior specialists (1919, 1920, 1924, 1928a, 1928b, 1928c).

In addition to the "essential contention," that psychology was a science (1913, p. 427), Watson held several basic assumptions that framed his aspirations for psychology. First, he refrained from compiling a taxonomy of simple and complex behaviors (which would have been a logical extension of his earlier work) in favor of classifying innate and acquired behaviors. This decision fit with his goals for psychology such that

> when we are confronted with the practical and scientific needs of life we are ready to admit that after all what we seek to have psychology busy herself with is just this matter of environmental adjustment; what can man do apart from his training; what can he be trained to do, and what are the best methods for training; and finally, how, when the varied systems of instincts and habits have sufficiently developed, can we arrange the conditions for calling out appropriate action on demand?" (1917a, p. 336)

The consequent research, however limited, led Watson to identify three innate emotions (1919, 1920) and to dismiss the study of inheritance as unnecessary (1924). Watson similarly declared that the study of human behavior involved the reduction of all complex behavior to simple actions (1928d) and that learning occurred in a critical period during the first two or three years of life (1928a, Watson & Watson, 1921).

Watson did not confirm these assumptions with experimental methods, although he believed confirmation was imminent (1921, 1925). Nevertheless, they were used to support a fundamental aim of his psychology: the control of human behavior. Watson's advocacy of a scientific method of social control had important and, as he occasionally recognized, troublesome limitations. He cautioned that psychology should refrain from framing moral rules or social values because "psychology at present has little to do with the setting of social standards of action and nothing to do with moral standards" (1917a, p. 329). Yet, on several occasions Watson acknowledged that if society established social standards by the same hit-and-miss methods that it implemented social control, then successful social standards would be developed only after an indeterminable time, if at all (1919, 1924). His attempts to resolve this problem included occasional abandonment of the prescribed neutral stance by discussing "behaviorist morals" (1927) and proposing that the scientific knowledge of behaviorists replace the legal system (1925). When Watson did maintain his conviction that psychology refrain from value judgments, he anticipated such judgments in a future "functional" or "experimental" ethics that would establish mores by scientific methods, by psychological experimentation (1917b, 1924, 1925). A final solution to the problem of the behaviorist's role in establishing moral standards was the creation of a society according to experimental findings. This solution was essentially an extension of Watson's famous statement, "Give me a dozen healthy infants, well-informed, and my own specified world to bring them up in and I'll guarantee to take anyone at random and train him to become any type of specialist I might select" (1928d, p. 10). He speculated on the feasibility of his "own specified world" with its potential contributions to social betterment and proposed several social experiments, including an "infant farm" for behavioral research (1920, 1928c; Watson & Watson, 1921) and a behaviorist's utopia.

ON UTOPIA AND PSYCHOLOGY

Hall, McDougall, Münsterberg, and Watson devised similar programs for psychology and psychologists in a utopian society. However, these similarities as well as their relation to comparable prescriptions made by other psychologists first should be placed within a broader context of the evolving interplay between utopias and psychology.

Since More's design of the island of King Utopus, the utopian format has been used to describe a variety of extraordinary societies. Since the scientific revolution, most utopias have incorporated what has been called a "scientific imperative," a belief that utopia cannot carry on without science (Dubos, 1961; Eurich, 1967; Golffing & Golffing, 1971). A liberal form of the scientific method appeared when the 17th-century utopists rejected traditional knowledge of church and state and adopted a new epistemology. They held that knowledge could be acquired by humans through empirical methods using sensate experience to observe, record, and analyze human conditions. Just as the 18th- and 19th-century utopists continued this fascination by exploiting ideas from the physical sciences, so late 19- and early 20th-century utopists contemplated the sciences of humankind (R. P. Adams, 1949; Manuel, 1965; Passmore, 1970; Roemer, 1976; Walsh, 1962).

Concepts and technical terminology borrowed from the burgeoning science of psychology supplied a means for making utopian fiction appear authentic and plausible. Notions of hypnotism, trance states, and brain surgery could explain how the narrator was transported to the new world (Bellamy, 1888; Merrill, 1899), and concepts of telepathy, clairvoyance, group mind effects, mind-controlling drugs, prenatal education, and eugenic breeding could account for the protean powers of the utopian citizen (Bulwer-Lytton, 1871; Gregory, 1918; Hudson, 1906; Lloyd, 1895; Taylor, 1901–1902). The continuing reliance on psychology for designing superlative societies and extraordinary beings prompted a historian of utopias to call recent utopian formulas "eupsychias" (Manuel, 1965).

The utopias of Hall, McDougall, Münsterberg, and Watson require analysis beyond a place in the development of eupsychias. These men were psychologists themselves, and in addition to joining the ranks with other psychological thinkers who prepared utopian speculations, such as Leibnitz, Turgot, Comte, Galton, Tarde, and Haldane, they were unique in their tendentious belief that their own profession was absolutely essential to improving society. The seriousness of this belief is evidenced in the correspondence between their utopian visions and many of their scientific and professional writings.

What has no obvious place in histories of utopias and is absent from conventional histories of psychology is an examination of these four utopias and similar convictions about psychology that were not presented in the utopian genre. Consequently, conventional histories of psychology omit psychologists' speculations on psychology's potential power in the reconstruction of American society. Admittedly, Bacon's elaborate plans for Solomon's House show that prescribing a structured role for science is not new to utopian thinking. But the human sciences, psychology in particular, had never before received such attention in utopias; the resemblance between the ideas of the four psychologist–utopists and many of their contemporaries intimates several distinct reasons for this new concern.

REFORM, SOCIAL CONTROL, AND AMERICAN PSYCHOLOGY

The American progressive era spanned the years from 1900 to 1917, a period when it had become increasingly evident to many Americans that the nation's growth had not always been equitable, moral, or without adverse costs. The realization ushered in a series of reforms, often organized by citizens and marked by beliefs in efficient and orderly social progress, equality, national unity, and citizen participation (Gould, 1974; Hofstadter, 1955, 1963; Wiebe, 1967). The perceived decline in enthusiasm for reform during World War I typically is interpreted as a marker for the end of the progressive era. However, interpreting postwar disillusionment as the terminus of these social reforms obscures half of what Morton White (1957) has labeled the "double effect" of the war: a renewed optimism regarding reform. In fact, of all the histories of the 1920s none give interpretations as optimistic as those accounts written in the decade itself (May, 1956).

Nevertheless, the war had brought a shift in reform involvement when the new specialties and techniques anticipated by prewar progressives were actually tested. The progressives had asserted the eventual necessity for scientific guidance in social and political life (Furner, 1975; Haber, 1964; McCraw, 1974; Wiebe, 1967), but the war propelled scientific research and eventually corroborated the idea, held by scientists and laypersons, that specialists had a fundamental role in the future of America (Dupree, 1957; Kaplan, 1956; Tobey, 1971; Yerkes, 1920).

The assertion that scientific techniques implemented and administered by scientific experts were essential to realizing social reforms is evident in many of the writings of Hall, McDougall, Münsterberg, and Watson. Especially in their utopias, these four psychologists advocated social change according to the wisdom of their science and the guidance of its experts. Their speculations were shared by other intellectuals, by trained psychologists, and by the average citizen, all of whom appeared to be captivated by the dazzle of the new scientific psychology. Even acrimonious commentators such as Floyd Dell (1926) lauded the new scientific professionals who "undertake therapeutically the tasks of bringing harmony, order and happiness into inharmonious, disorderly and futile lives" (p. 248). Other social critics and intellectuals also believed that scientists, notably from the human sciences, would provide what Walter Lippmann (1922) described as leadership by "interposing some form of expertness between the private citizen and the vast environment in which he is entangled" (p. 368). And John Dewey (1922) concurrently announced that bettering of democracy and social relations depended on the growth of a "scientific social psychology" (p. 323). Like many natural scientists of the period (Tobey, 1971), American intellectuals thought that society would move toward efficiency, order, and unity. Science, guided by expert minds, would enable the control of social phenomena, primarily by adjusting people to their changing environment. They shared with philosopher F. C. S. Schiller (1924) the hope that "a pragmatically efficient psychology might actually invert the miracle of Circe, and really transform the Yahoo into a man" (p. 64).

Concurrent with these more or less enlightened mandates grew a keen interest in psychology among the populace. Articles on personality, mental tests, psychoanalysis, hormonal processes (gland psychology), and behaviorism were consumed with such fervor by the lay public (G. Adams, 1934; Hart, 1933) that one historian called the preoccupation a "national mania" (Leuchtenburg, 1955, p. 164). Along with all its novelties and promises, the new psychology also captivated those Americans of the 1920s who were enraptured by the personal, by the "cult of the self" (Baritz, 1960; Burnham, 1968).

Psychologists were not excluded from such discussions on the prospects for psychology and social improvement. Although traditional histories view the period as one of theoretical fermentation and the accumulation of scientific techniques, other historical studies suggest that at least some of these conventional images of psychology as an experimental science often served personal and political interests (Danziger, 1979; O'Donnell, 1979). More recent studies have found that, at least after the war, psychologists were as concerned with applied issues as with experimentalism (Camfield, 1969, 1973; O'Donnell, 1979; Samelson, 1978) and were enmeshed in economic, occupational, and political realities of their discipline (Danziger, 1979; Samelson, 1975, 1978, 1979; Sokal, 1980, 1981).

These activities within the psychological community reveal a commitment to an ordered and efficient society and a belief in the possibility of developing scientific measures of control, specifically through the appropriate psychological adjustment of individuals to the environment. This conviction implied that psychologists could and should contribute by extending their scientific expertise to the management of society. In the words of James McKeen Cattell (1926), "Scientific men should take the place that is theirs as masters of the modern world" (p. 8). Applied psychology textbooks published between 1925 and 1938 give ample evidence of these appeals for a well-adjusted society, the development of personalities suited to the social order, and public recognition of the essential participation of psychologists in such efforts (Napoli, 1980).

Psychologists with reputations as experimentalists were not exempted from making these appeals for reform. For example, Knight Dunlap (1928) endorsed the development of social psychology primarily in terms of its potential contribution to understanding social problems (p. 355). Floyd Allport (1924) devoted a major portion of his text, *Social Psychology*, to the study of social control, which he thought corresponded with the "basic requirements for a truly democratic social order" (p. 415). Because psychology was seen as integral to implementing reform measures, many psychologists acknowledged the social responsibility of members of their science: "It is the outstanding feature of our reconstructed psychology that it realized and accepted the obligation to apply . . . the conclusions arising from the study of the mental side of man" (Jastrow, 1927, p. 170). Joseph Jastrow (1928) accordingly argued that the psychologist "should join the small remnant of creative and progressive thinkers who can see even this bewildering world soundly and see it whole. Such is part of the psychologist's responsibility" (p. 436). When writing on social reform in the 1920s and psychologists' fundamental part in it, Jastrow conceded that he was "not optimistic enough to indulge in Utopias" (p. 436), so his proposals were prepared in the format of professional commentary. Just as clinicians and applied psychologists contemplated the future social adjustments and the reconstruction of society, so experimental psychologists made comparable propositions despite the fact that they may not have been directly involved in such applications. To this list must be added the names of Hall, McDougall, Münsterberg, and Watson: Their utopias comprise entertaining pronouncements on psychology's ultimate contribution to a better society and the techniques that should be implemented by psychological experts.

A DUAL MORALITY AND THE FUNCTION OF MORE CRITICAL THINKING

Utopias become excellent vehicles for exploring the utility of scientific knowledge because they implicitly demand the "application" of knowledge to improving society. The fictions of Hall, McDougall, Münsterberg, and Watson expose Baconian thinking about a science in the service of society. Analysis of these Baconian statements has revealed that, despite disparate psychological theories, the four psychologists shared a vision for an ordered, harmonious, and unified society in which psychology is a special science and in which psychologists provide expert leadership and implement scientific measures of social control. Without embarking on fiction, other psychologists suggested similar measures. These findings stand in contrast to the conventional accounts of psychology's scientific achievements and striving toward an objective and experimental enterprise, and they contribute to a largely untold story about American psychology in the decade following World War I. The utopias and the nonutopian proposals for reconstructing American society both affirm the existence of a dichotomy between Baconian and Newtonian thinking and exemplify the dangers of such a dichotomy. The social ideals of these psychologists mirrored popular notions of reform. It is interesting and alarming to discover that, regardless of grossly different assumptions about human nature and the appropriate form for psychological inquiry, psychologists essentially concurred about the social ends that psychology should serve. There existed implicit agreement that psychology was a technique in the service of particular ends. Such a Baconian and Newtonian dichotomy of values suggests two dangers. It perpetuates the utilization of psychology in ways relatively outside the province of psychologists' activities and thus augments their unsophisticated and perhaps credulous acceptance of such utilization. It also heightens the probability that novel or creative ideas succumb to the expediency of other objectives. Not the least of neglected ideas are the attempts to confront psychology's moral dualism in the utopias presented above. Although not a subject of the present study, even a cursory examination of Münsterberg's proposal for both an objective and purposive psychology, Hall's genetic epistemology, and McDougall's model relating psychology and social philosophy illustrates how potential innovations can be buried by externally- or pre-determined objectives.

This study has not attempted to trace the persistence of a dual morality in thinking about psychology nor has it sought to formulate alternatives to the dualism. Anyone familiar with the subtleties of psychology's most noted utopia (Skinner, 1948) and the author's later expositions of its premises (Skinner, 1971, 1981) can appreciate the complexities inherent in such tasks. However, on another front an increasing number of researchers are exploring this duality and its consequences. They are examining how psychology's moral heritage has been obscured by 20th-century attempts to devise an objective science (Leary, 1980), the extrascientific determinants of research (Cowan, 1977; Gorman, 1981; Morawski, 1979; Samelson, 1979, 1980; Steiner, 1974; Steininger, 1979), and the manners in which psychological questions have been pretermitted or disregarded (Apfelbaum & Lubek, 1976; Buss, 1975, 1977; Lubek, 1979). Such historical awareness has enabled other researchers to systematically examine how models of human nature and its potential have been constricted by a tacit striving for relevance and agreement with prevalent social morality (Argyris, 1975; Gadlin & Ingle, 1975; Gergen, 1978; Gilligan, 1977; Hogan & Emler, 1978; Moscovici, 1972; Sampson, 1977, 1978; Sarason, 1981; Shotter, 1975).

The continuation of such critical thinking, both historical and interpretive, is imperative to the health and integrity of psychological knowledge (Samelson, 1980). It not only informs us about the social context of our research activities (Buss, 1975, 1979) but also can contribute to advances in research programs (Harré & Secord, 1972) and in metatheories (Gergen & Morawski, 1980; Israel, 1972; Morawski, in press; Rommetveit, 1976; Rosnow, 1981; Sampson, 1978, 1981; Scheibe, 1979). Overall, more critical thinking can remind us of a persisting relation between utopias and science. In the words of a contemporary social critic, "A vision of a human future cannot do without the indispensable support of scientific expertise, but it encompasses more than the realm of science. The utopia without science is empty, but science without utopia is blind" (Plattel, 1972, p. 97).

REFERENCES

Adams, G. The rise and fall of psychology. *Atlantic Monthly*, 1934, *153*, 82–92.

Adams, R. P. The social responsibility of science in *Utopia, New Atlantis*, and after. *Journal of the History of Ideas*, 1949, *10*, 374–398.

Agassi, J. Towards an historiography of science. *History and Theory*, 1963, *2*, 1–117.

Allport, F. H. *Social psychology*. Boston: Houghton Mifflin, 1924.

Apfelbaum, E., & Lubek, I. Resolution versus revolution: The theory of conflicts in question. In L. H. Strickland, F. E. Aboud, & K. J. Gergen (Eds.), *Social psychology in transition*. New York: Plenum Press, 1976.

Argyris, C. Dangers in applying results from experimental psychology. *American Psychologist*, 1975, *30*, 469–485.

Baritz, L. *The servants of power.* Middletown, Conn.: Wesleyan University Press, 1960.

Bellamy, E. *Looking backward, 2000-1887.* Boston: Ticknor, 1888.

Boring, E. G. *A history of experimental psychology* (2nd ed.). New York: Appleton-Century-Crofts, 1950.

Brush, S. G. Should the history of science be rated X? *Science,* 1974, *183,* 1164-1172.

Bulwer-Lytton, E. *The coming race.* London: Routledge, 1871.

Burnham, J. C. The new psychology from narcissism to social control. In J. Braeman, R. H. Bremmer, & D. Brody (Eds.), *Change and continuity in twentieth century America: The nineteen twenties.* Columbus: Ohio State University Press, 1968.

Buss, A. R. The emerging field of the sociology of psychological knowledge. *American Psychologist,* 1975, *30,* 988-1002.

Buss, A. R. In defense of a critical-presentist historiography: The fact-theory relationship and Marx's epistemology. *Journal of the History of the Behavioral Sciences,* 1977, *13,* 252-266.

Buss, A. R. (Ed.). *Psychology in social context.* New York: Irvington, 1979.

Camfield, T. M. *Psychologists at war: The history of American psychology and the first world war.* Unpublished doctoral dissertation, University of Texas at Austin, 1969.

Camfield, T. M. The professionalization of American psychology. *Journal of the History of the Behavioral Sciences,* 1973, *9,* 66-75.

Cattell, J. M. Some psychological experiments. *Science,* 1926, *63,* 1-8; 29-35.

Cowan, R. Nature and nurture: The interplay of biology and politics in the work of Francis Galton. In W. Coleman & C. Limoges (Eds.), *Studies in history of biology.* Baltimore, Md: Johns Hopkins University Press, 1977.

Danziger, K. The social origins of modern psychology. In A. R. Russ (Ed.), *Psychology in social context.* New York: Irvington, 1979.

Dell, F. *Intellectual vagabondage, an apology for the intelligentsia.* New York: Doran, 1926.

Dewey, J. *Human nature and conduct.* New York: Holt, 1922.

Dubos, R. *The dream of reason, science and utopias.* New York: Columbia University Press, 1961.

Dunlap, K. The applications of psychology to social problems. In C. Murchison (Ed.), *Psychologies of 1925.* Worcester, Mass.: Clark University Press, 1928.

Dupree, A. H. *Science in the federal government, a history of policies and activities to 1940.* Cambridge, Mass.: Harvard University Press, 1957.

Eurich, N. *Science in utopia, a mighty design.* Cambridge, Mass.: Harvard University Press, 1967.

Finison, L. J. Unemployment, politics, and the history of organized psychology. *American Psychologist,* 1976, *31,* 747-755.

Flugel, J. C., & West, D. J. *A hundred years of psychology, 1833–1933*. London: Duckworth, 1964.

Furner, M. O. *Advocacy and objectivity: A crisis in the professionalization of American social science 1865–1905*. Lexington, Ky.: University Press, 1975.

Gadlin, H., & Ingle, G. Through a one-way mirror: The limits of experimental self-reflection. *American Psychologist*, 1975, *30*, 1003–1009.

Gergen, K. J. Toward generative theory. *Journal of Personality and Social Psychology*, 1978, *36*, 1344–1360.

Gergen, K. J., & Morawski, J. G. An alternative metatheory for social psychology. *Review of Personality and Social Psychology*, 1980, *1*, 326–352.

Gilligan, C. In a different voice: Woman's conception of the self and of morality. *Harvard Educational Review*, 1977, *4*, 481–517.

Golffing, F., & Golffing, B. Towards more vivid utopias. In G. Kateb (Ed.), *Utopia*. New York: Atherton, 1971.

Gorman, M. E. Prewar conformity research in social psychology: The approaches of Floyd H. Allport and Muzafer Sherif. *Journal of the History of the Behavioral Sciences*, 1981, *17*, 3–14.

Gould, L. L. *The progressive era*. Syracuse, N.Y.: Syracuse University Press, 1974.

Gregory, O. *Meccania, the super state*. London: Methuen, 1918.

Haber, S. *Efficiency and uplift: Scientific management in the progressive era, 1890–1920*. Chicago: University of Chicago Press, 1964.

Hagstrom, W. O. *The scientific community*. New York: Basic Books, 1965.

Hale, M., Jr. *Human science and social order: Hugo Münsterberg and the origins of applied psychology*. Philadelphia: Temple University Press, 1980.

Hall, G. S. Philosophy. In *Decennial celebration: Clark University*. Worcester, Mass.: Clark University Press, 1899.

Hall, G. S. *Adolescence: Its psychology and its relations to physiology, anthropology, sociology, sex, crime, religion and education*. New York: Appleton, 1904.

Hall, G. S. The affiliation of psychology with philosophy and with the natural sciences. *Science*, 1906, *23*, 297–301.

Hall, G. S. Some dangers in our educational system and how to meet them. *New England Magazine*, 1907, *41*, 667–675.

Hall, G. S. The university idea. *Pedagogical Seminary*, 1908, *15*, 92–116.

Hall, G. S. Social phases of psychology. *American Journal of Sociology*, 1913, *18*, 613–621.

Hall, G. S. Practical relations between psychology and the war. *Journal of Applied Psychology*, 1917, *1*, 9–16.

Hall, G. S. Practical applications of psychology as developed by the war. *Pedagogical Seminary*, 1919, *26*, 76–89. (a)

Hall, G. S. The viewpoint of the psychologist as to courses of study which will meet the future demands of a democracy. *Pedagogical Seminary*, 1919, *26*, 90–99. (b)

Hall, G. S. The fall of Atlantis. In *Recreations of a psychologist*. New York: Appleton, 1920. (a)

Hall, G. S. Psychology and industry. *Pedagogical Seminary*, 1920, *27*, 281–293. (b)

Hall, G. S. The message of the zeitgeist. *Scientific Monthly*, 1921, *13*, 105–116.

Hall, G. S. *Life and confessions of a psychologist*. New York: Appleton, 1923.

Harré, R., & Secord, P. F. *The explanation of social behaviour*. Oxford, England: Blackwell, 1972.

Harris, B. What ever happened to little Albert? *American Psychologist*, 1979, *34*, 151–160.

Hart, H. Changing social attitudes and interests. In *Recent social trends: Report of the President's Research Committee on Social Trends*. New York: McGraw-Hill, 1933.

Hofstadter, R. *Social Darwinism in American thought*. Boston: Beacon Press, 1955.

Hofstadter, R. *The progressive movement, 1900–1915*. Englewood Cliffs, N.J.: Prentice-Hall, 1963.

Hogan, R. T., & Emler, N. P. The biases in contemporary social psychology. *Social Research*, 1978, *45*, 478–534.

Hudson, W. H. *A crystal age*. London: Unwin, 1906.

Israel, J. Stipulations and construction in the social sciences. In J. Israel & H. Tajfel (Eds.), *The context of social psychology: A critical assessment*. London: Academic Press, 1972.

Jastrow, J. The reconstruction of psychology. *Psychological Review*, 1927, *34*, 169–195.

Jastrow, J. Lo, the psychologist! In M. L. Reymert (Ed.), *Feelings and emotions: The Wittenburg symposium*. Worcester, Mass.: Clark University Press, 1928.

Kaplan, S. Social engineers as saviors: Effects of World War I on some American liberals. *Journal of the History of Ideas*, 1956, *17*, 347–369.

Leary, D. L. The intentions and heritage of Descartes and Locke: Toward a recognition of the moral basis of modern psychology. *Journal of General Psychology*, 1980, *102*, 283–310.

Leuchtenburg, W. E. *The perils of prosperity, 1914–1932*. Chicago: University of Chicago Press, 1955.

Lippmann, W. *Public opinion*. New York: Macmillan, 1922.

Lloyd, J. U. *Etidorphy (or the end of the earth): The strange history of a mysterious being* (6th ed.). Cincinnati, Ohio: Robert Clarke, 1895.

Lubek, I. A brief social psychological analysis of research on aggression in social psychology. In A. R. Buss (Ed.), *Psychology in social context*. New York: Irvington, 1979.

Manuel, F. E. Toward a psychological history of utopias. *Daedalus*, 1965, *94*, 293–322.

May, H. Shifting perspectives on the 1920's. *Mississippi Valley Historical Review*, 1956, *43*, 405–427.

McCraw, T. K. The progressive legacy. In L. L. Gould (Ed.), *The progressive era.* Syracuse, N.Y.: Syracuse University Press, 1974.

McDougall, W. *Primer of physiological psychology.* New York: Macmillan, 1905.

McDougall, W. *Introduction to social psychology.* London: Methuen, 1908.

McDougall, W. Instinct and intelligence. *British Journal of Psychology,* 1910, *3,* 250–266.

McDougall, W. *Psychology: The study of behavior.* London: Oxford University Press, 1912.

McDougall, W. *National welfare and national decay.* London: Methuen, 1921.

McDougall, W. *Outline of psychology.* New York: Scribner's, 1923.

McDougall, W. Psychology, disarmament and peace. *The North American Review,* 1924, *219,* 577–591.

McDougall, W. Mental evolution. In *Evolution in the light of modern knowledge: A collective work.* London: Blackie, 1925.

McDougall, W. *The American nation: Its problems and psychology.* London: Allen & Unwin, 1926.

McDougall, W. Our neglect of psychology. *The Edinburgh Review,* 1927, *245,* 299–312.

McDougall, W. *Modern materialism and emergent evolution.* New York: Van Nostrand, 1929.

McDougall, W. Autobiography. In C. Murchison (Ed.), *A history of psychology in autobiography* (Vol. 1). Worcester, Mass.: Clark University Press, 1930. (a)

McDougall, W. The present chaos in psychology and the way out. *Journal of Philosophical Studies,* 1930, *5,* 353–363. (b)

McDougall, W. *World chaos: The responsibility of science.* London: Kegan Paul, Trench, Trubner, 1931.

McDougall, W. Family allowances as a eugenic measure. *Character and Personality,* 1933, *2,* 99–116.

McDougall, W. *The frontiers of psychology.* Cambridge, England: Cambridge University Press, 1934. (a)

McDougall, W. *Religion and the sciences of life, with other essays on allied topics.* London: Methuen, 1934. (b)

McDougall, W. *Psycho-analysis and social psychology.* London: Methuen, 1936.

McDougall, W. Philosophy and the social science. In R. B. Cattell, J. Cohen, & R. M. W. Travers (Eds.), *Human affairs.* London: Macmillan, 1937.

McDougall, W. *The riddle of life: A survey of theories.* London: Methuen, 1938.

Merrill, A. A. *The great awakening: The story of the twenty-second century.* Boston: George, 1899.

Morawski, J. G. The structure of social psychological communities: A framework for examining the sociology of social psychology. In L. H. Strickland (Ed.), *Soviet and Western perspectives on social psychology.* Oxford, England: Pergamon Press, 1979.

Morawski, J. G. Historiography as metatheoretical text for social psychology. In K. Gergen & M. Gergen (Eds.), *Historical social psychology*. Hillside, N.J.: Erlbaum, in press.

Moscovici, S. Society and theory in social psychology. In J. Israel & H. Tajfel (Eds.), *The context of social psychology: A critical assessment*. New York: Academic Press, 1972.

Münsterberg, H. Psychology and the real life. *Atlantic Monthly*, 1898, *81*, 602–643.

Münsterberg, H. Psychology and history. *Psychological Review*, 1899, *6*, 1–31. (a)

Münsterberg, H. *Psychology and life*. Boston: Houghton Mifflin, 1899. (b)

Münsterberg, H. The scientific plan of the Congress. In H. Rogers (Ed.), *(International) Congress of the Arts and Science, Universal Exposition, St. Louis, 1904* (Vol. 1). Boston: Houghton Mifflin, 1905.

Münsterberg, H. *Science and idealism*. New York: Houghton Mifflin, 1906.

Münsterberg, H. *Psychotherapy*. New York: Moffat, Yard, 1909.

Münsterberg, H. *American problems from the point of view of a psychologist*. New York: Moffat, Yard, 1910. (a)

Münsterberg, H. The subconscious. In H. Münsterberg, T. Ribot, P. Janet, J. Jastrow, B. Hart, & M. Prince (Eds.), *Subconscious phenomena*. Boston: Badger, 1910. (b)

Münsterberg, H.. *The eternal values*. London: Constable, 1911.

Münsterberg, H. *Vocation and learning*. St. Louis, Mo.: Servis, 1912.

Münsterberg, H. *Psychology and industrial efficiency*. Boston: Houghton Mifflin, 1913.

Münsterberg, H. *Psychology: General and applied*. New York: Appleton, 1914.

Münsterberg, H. *Tomorrow: Letters to a friend in Germany*. New York: Appleton, 1916.

Murphy, G. *Historical introduction to modern psychology* (Rev. ed.). New York: Harcourt, Brace & World, 1949.

Napoli, D. S. *The architects of adjustment: The history of the psychological profession in the United States*. Port Washington, N.Y.: National University Publications, 1980.

O'Donnell, J. M. The crisis of experimentalism in the twenties: E. G. Boring and his uses of historiography. *American Psychologist*, 1979, *34*, 289–295.

Passmore, J. *The perfectibility of man*. London: Duckworth, 1970.

Peters, R. S. (Ed.). *Brett's history of psychology*. Cambridge, Mass.: MIT Press, 1962.

Plattel, M. G. *Utopian and critical thinking*. Pittsburgh, Pa.: Duquesne University Press, 1972.

Pratt, C. C. *The logic of modern psychology*. New York: Macmillan, 1939.

Ravetz, J. R. Tragedy in the history of science. In M. Teich & R. Young (Eds.), *Changing perspectives in the history of science*. London: Heinemann, 1973.

Roemer, K. M. *The obsolete necessity, America in Utopian writings, 1888–1900.* Kent, Ohio: Kent State University Press, 1976.

Rommetveit, R. On emancipatory social psychology. In L. H. Strickland, F. E. Aboud, & K. J. Gergen (Eds.), *Social psychology in transition.* New York: Plenum Press, 1976.

Rosnow, R. L. *Paradigms in transition: The methodology of social inquiry.* New York: Oxford University Press, 1981.

Ross, D. G. *Stanley Hall: The psychologist as a prophet.* Chicago: University of Chicago Press, 1972.

Samelson, F. History, origin, myth, and ideology: Comte's 'discovery' of social psychology. *Journal for the Theory of Social Behavior,* 1974, *4*, 217–231.

Samelson, F. On the science and politics of the IQ. *Social Research,* 1975, *42*, 467–488.

Samelson, F. From "Race Psychology" to "Studies in Prejudice." Some observations on the thematic reversal in (social) psychology. *Journal of the History of the Behavioral Sciences,* 1978, *14*, 265–278.

Samelson, F. Putting psychology on the map: Ideology and intelligence testing. In A. R. Buss (Ed.), *Psychology in social context.* New York: Irvington, 1979.

Samelson, F. J. B. Watson's little Albert, Cyril Burt's twins, and the need for a critical science. *American Psychologist,* 1980, *35*, 619–625.

Sampson, E. E. Psychology and the American ideal. *Journal of Personality and Social Psychology,* 1977, *35*, 767–782.

Sampson, E. E. Scientific paradigms and social values: Wanted—A scientific revolution. *Journal of Personality and Social Psychology,* 1978, *36*, 1332–1343.

Sampson, E. E. Cognitive psychology as ideology. *American Psychologist,* 1981, *36*, 730–743.

Sarason, S. B. *Psychology misdirected.* New York: Free Press, 1981.

Scheibe, K. E. *Mirrors, masks, lies, and secrets: The limits of human predictability.* New York: Praeger, 1979.

Schiller, F. C. S. *Tantalus, or the future of man.* London: Kegan Paul, Trench, Trubner, 1924.

Shotter, J. *Images of man in psychological research.* London: Methuen, 1975.

Skinner, B. F. *Walden two.* New York: Macmillan, 1948.

Skinner, B. F. *Beyond freedom and dignity.* New York: Knopf, 1971.

Skinner, B. F. Selection by consequences. *Science,* 1981, *213*, 501–504.

Sokal, M. M. James McKeen Cattell and American psychology in the 1920's. In J. Brozek (Ed.), *Explorations in the history of American psychology.* Lewisburg, Pa.: Bucknell University Press, 1980.

Sokal, M. M. The origins of the psychological corporation. *Journal of the History of the Behavioral Sciences,* 1981, *17*, 54–67.

Steiner, I. D. Whatever happened to the group in social psychology? *Journal of Experimental Social Psychology,* 1974, *10*, 94–108.

Steininger, M. Objectivity and value judgments in the psychology of E. L. Thorndike and W. McDougall. *Journal of the History of the Behavioral Sciences*, 1979, *15*, 263–281.

Stocking, G. On the limits of "presentism" and "historicism" in the history of the behavioral sciences. *Journal of the History of the Behavioral Sciences*, 1965, *1*, 211–219.

Taylor, W. A. *Intermere*. Columbus, Ohio: Twentieth Century Publishing, 1901–1902.

Teich, M., & Young, R. M. (Eds.). *Changing perspectives in the history of science*. London: Heinemann, 1973.

Tobey, R. C. *The American ideology of national sciences, 1919–1930*. Pittsburgh, Pa.: University of Pittsburgh Press, 1971.

Toulmin, S. E. The twin moralities of science. In N. H. Steneck (Ed.), *Science and society: Past, present, and future*. Ann Arbor: University of Michigan Press, 1975.

Walsh, C. *From utopia to nightmare*. London: Geoffrey Bles, 1962.

Watson, J. B. The new science of animal behavior. *Harper's*, 1910, *120*, 346–353.

Watson, J. B. Instinctive activity in animals. *Harper's*, 1912, *124*, 376–382.

Watson, J. B. Psychology as the behaviorist views it. *Psychological Review*, 1913, *10*, 158–177.

Watson, J. B. An attempted formulation of the scope of behavior psychology. *Psychological Review*, 1917, *24*, 329–352. (a)

Watson, J. B. Does Holt follow Freud? *Journal of Philosophy, Psychology, and Scientific Method*, 1917, *14*, 85–93. (b)

Watson, J. B. *Psychology from the standpoint of a behaviorist* (3rd ed.). Philadelphia: Lippincott, 1919.

Watson, J. B. Practical and theoretical problems in instinct and habits. In H. S. Jennings, J. B. Watson, A. Meyer, & W. I. Thomas (Eds.), *Suggestions of modern science concerning education*. New York: Macmillan, 1920.

Watson, J. B. *Behaviorism*. New York: Norton, 1924.

Watson, J. B. Recent experiments on how we lose and change our emotional equipment. *Pedagogical Seminary*, 1925, *32*, 349–371.

Watson, J. B. The weakness of women. *Nation*, 1927, *125*, 9–10.

Watson, J. B. (with Watson, R. R.). *Psychological care of the infant and child*. New York: Norton, 1928. (a)

Watson, J. B. The unconscious of the behaviorist. In E. S. Drummer (Ed.), *The unconscious: A symposium*. New York: Knopf, 1928. (b)

Watson, J. B. *The ways of behaviorism*. New York: Harper, 1928. (c)

Watson, J. B. What the nursery has to say about instincts. In C. Murchison (Ed.), *Psychologies of 1925*. Worcester, Mass.: Clark University Press, 1928. (d)

Watson, J. B. Should a child have more than one mother? *Liberty Magazine*, 1929, pp. 31–35.

Watson, J. B., & Watson, R. R. Studies in infant psychology. *Scientific Monthly*, 1921, *13*, 493–515.

Watson, R. I. *The great psychologists* (3rd ed.). Philadelphia: Lippincott, 1971.

White, M. *Social thought in America: The revolt against formalism*. Boston: Beacon Press, 1957.

Wiebe, R. *The search for order, 1877–1920*. New York: Hill & Wang, 1967.

Yerkes, R. M. (Ed.). *The new world of science, its development during the war*. New York: Century, 1920.

Young, R. M. Scholarship and the history of the behavioral sciences. *History of Science*, 1966, *5*, 1–51.

25

PLACING WOMEN IN THE HISTORY OF PSYCHOLOGY: THE FIRST AMERICAN WOMEN PSYCHOLOGISTS

LAUREL FURUMOTO AND E. SCARBOROUGH

Women psychologists have been largely overlooked in histories of the discipline. This is so despite the early participation and contributions of women to American psychology from its beginnings as a science. Here we offer a preliminary account of the first American women psychologists, describing them and the manner in which gender shaped their experiences.[1]

As early as 1960, the history of psychology was identified as a "neglected area" (Watson, 1960). Watson's call for attention was followed by

---

The authors contributed equally; listing is in alphabetical order. We thank Michael M. Sokal especially for his extensive comments on a draft of the article.

This research was supported in part by grants from the Research Foundation of State University of New York and State College at Fredonia to Elizabeth Scarborough (Goodman) and from the Brachman-Hoffman Small Grant Program of Wellesley College to Laurel Furumoto.

[1] A comprehensive study of the lives, contributions, and experience of early women psychologists will be published by Columbia University Press under the title *Untold Lives: The First Generation of American Women Psychologists*.

Reprinted from *American Psychologist*, 41, 35–42 (1986). Copyright © 1986 by the American Psychological Association. Reprinted with permission of the first author.

a dramatic surge of interest in historical scholarship (Watson, 1975). In subsequent years, history of psychology has developed as a vigorous specialty field. However, new scholarship has paid scant attention to women in the discipline. To date, work that has been done on women, whether presented in published sources or in delivered papers, has been limited in scope and descriptive rather than interpretive. It consists generally of efforts to identify some prominent women in previous generations and to provide information about their achievements (see Bernstein & Russo, 1974; O'Connell, 1983; O'Connell & Russo, 1980; Russo, 1983; Stevens & Gardner, 1982). Furthermore, the number of women mentioned in even the most recently published history of psychology textbooks is astonishingly small (see Goodman, 1983).

Omission of women from history is not unique to psychology. As Gerda Lerner (1979), an American historian well known for her work in women's history, pointed out,

> Traditional history has been written and interpreted by men in an androcentric frame of reference; it might quite properly be described as the history of men. The very term "Women's History" calls attention to the fact that something is missing from historical scholarship. (p. xiv)

Beyond calling attention to what is missing from the history of psychology, this article begins to fill the gap by sketching an overview of the lives and experiences of those women who participated in the development of the discipline in the United States around the turn of the century. First, we identify early women psychologists. Second, we describe the women and note some comparisons between them and men psychologists. And last, we discuss women's experiences, focusing on how gender influenced their careers.

IDENTIFYING EARLY PSYCHOLOGISTS

In 1906 James McKeen Cattell published the first edition of *American Men of Science* (Cattell, 1906), a biographical directory containing more than 4,000 entries. This ambitious project provided for the first time a comprehensive listing of all individuals in North America who had "carried on research work in the natural and exact sciences" (p. v). Inclusion in the directory required that a person must have done "work that has contributed to the advancement of pure science" or be "found in the membership lists of certain national societies" (p. v). Cattell himself was a highly visible and influential member of the psychological establishment, centrally involved in founding and controlling the early direction of the American Psychological Association (APA). Not surprisingly then, among the national societies he surveyed was the APA, which in 1906 was 14 years old and had about 175 members.

Although neither the title nor Cattell's preface suggests it, his directory of "men of science" did, in fact, include some women (see Rossiter, 1974). Among these women scientists, a group of 22 identified themselves as psychologists either by field or by subject of research (see Table 1). Our analysis is based on biographical information on these women, who constituted 12% of the 186 psychologists listed in the directory. It should be noted that omitted from the directory were five women who held APA membership in 1906: Elizabeth Kemper Adams, Margaret S. Prichard, Frances H. Rousmaniere, Eleanor Harris Rowland, and Ellen Bliss Talbot. Conversely, nine women were listed who did *not* belong to the APA: Bagley, Case, Gulliver, V. F. Moore, Parrish, Shinn, and Squire, plus McKeag and Williams (who joined after 1906). Presumably those who did not belong to the APA were included because they had made research contributions to the field. The group we are considering therefore omits a few women who clearly qualified for inclusion in *American Men of Science* (AMS) and includes some who never identified themselves with professional psychology. By focusing on the 22, however, we have designated a fairly complete group of early American women psychologists for whom basic biographical information is available. This makes it possible to analyze certain aspects of their lives and compare them with their male cohort.

These women shared with men psychologists the experience of being pioneers in what Cattell called "the newest of the sciences" (Cattell, 1903a, p. 562). Women participated from the beginning in the evolution of the new discipline. They began joining the national professional association soon after it was formed in 1892 and presented papers at annual meetings. They published regularly in the fledgling journals, contributing original research, reviews, and commentaries. The group included several who were prominent and influential (e.g., Mary Calkins, Christine Ladd-Franklin,[2] Lillien Martin, and Margaret Washburn) and others who were recognized by their peers as notable contributors (e.g., Kate Gordon, Milicent Shinn, and Helen Thompson). Included also, however, were women whose careers were short lived, ending with publication of their graduate research, as was true for Florence Winger Bagley and Alice Hamlin Hinman.

Besides being among the first psychologists, these women were also pioneers in another sense. They were in the vanguard of women seeking collegiate and even graduate education in the decades following the Civil War (see Solomon, 1985). The skepticism about women's mental fitness to undertake a rigorous course of studies at the college level had been

---

[2] At some point after her marriage, Christine Ladd began identifying herself as Ladd-Franklin. In Table 1 in this article she is listed as Franklin.

TABLE 1
Characteristics of Women Psychologists Listed in American Men of Science, 1906

Name	Birth year	Subject of research[a]	Baccalaureate degree	Doctoral degree
Bagley, Mrs. W. C. (Florence Winger)	1874	Fechner's color rings	Nebraska 1895	Cornell 1901[c]
Calkins, Prof. Mary Whiton	1863	Association of ideas	Smith 1885	Harvard 1895[d]
Case, Prof. Mary S(ophia)	1854	None given	Michigan 1884	No graduate study
Franklin, Mrs. Christine Ladd	1847	Logic, color vision	Vassar 1869	Hopkins 1882[d]
Gamble, Prof. E(leanor) A(cheson) McC(ullough)	1868	Smell intensities	Wellesley 1889	Cornell 1898
Gordon, Dr. Kate	1878	Memory and attention	Chicago 1900	Chicago 1903
Gulliver, Pres. Julia H(enrietta)	1856	Dreams, subconscious self	Smith 1879	Smith 1888
Hinman, Dr. Alice H(amlin)	1869	Attention and distraction	Wellesley 1893	Cornell 1897
Martin, Prof. Lillien J(ane)	1851	Psychophysics	Vassar 1880	Gottingen 1898[c]
McKeag, Prof. Anna J(ane)	1864	Pain sensation	Wilson 1895	Pennsylvania 1900
Moore, Mrs. J. Percy (Kathleen Carter)	1866	Mental development	Pennsylvania 1890[e]	Pennsylvania 1896
Moore, Prof. Vida F(rank)	1867	Metaphysics	Wesleyan 1893	Cornell 1900
Norsworthy, Dr. Naomi	1877	Abilities of the child	Columbia 1901	Columbia 1904
Parrish, Miss C(elestia) S(usannah)	1853	Cutaneous sensation	Cornell 1896	No graduate study
Puffer, Dr. Ethel D(ench)	1872	Esthetics	Smith 1891	Radcliffe 1902
Shinn, Dr. M(ilicent) W(ashburn)	1858	Development of the child	California 1880	California 1898
Smith, Dr. Margaret K(eiver)	1856	Rhythm and work	Oswego Normal 1883[e]	Zurich 1900
Smith, Dr. Theodate (Louise)	1860	Muscular memory	Smith 1882	Yale 1896
Squire, Mrs. C(arrie) R(anson)	1869	Rhythm	Hamline 1889	Cornell 1901
Thompson, Dr. Helen B(radford)	1874	Mental traits of sex	Chicago 1897	Chicago 1900
Washburn, Prof. Margaret F(loy)	1871	Space perception of skin	Vassar 1891	Cornell 1894
Williams, Dr. Mabel Clare	1878	Visual illusions	Iowa 1899	Iowa 1903

Note. Names are given as they appeared in the directory.
[a] Major topics through 1906. [b] Positions listed in American Men of Science, first and third editions.

quickly challenged by their academic successes. However, there were still those who argued against advanced education for women on the grounds that scholarly work would ruin their health or atrophy their reproductive organs, or both (see Walsh, 1977). Women who undertook higher education in the 19th century did so despite the widespread belief that it would make them unfit to fulfill the obligations prescribed by the widely accepted notion of women's sphere: piety, purity, submissiveness, and domesticity (see Welter, 1966).

The phrase "women's sphere," with its connotation of boundaries that

Date of Marriage	Husband	Children	Professional positions[b] 1906	1921
1901	William C. Bagley	2 sons, 2 daughters	Unemployed	Not listed
1882	Fabian Franklin	1 son, 1 daughter	Professor, Wellesley Associate Professor, Wellesley Lecturer, Hopkins Associate Professor, Wellesley	Professor, Wellesley Not listed Lecturer, Columbia Professor, Wellesley
1943	Ernest C. Moore	0	Associate Professor, Mt. Holyoke President, Rockford	Associate Professor, Carnegie Tech. Not listed
1897	Edgar L. Hinman	1 daughter	Lecturer, Nebraska	Lecturer, Nebraska
1892	J. Percy Moore	1 son, 2 daughters	Assistant Professor, Stanford Associate Professor, Wellesley Head, Bardwell School	Private practice Professor, Wellesley (deceased 1920)
			Professor, Elmira Instructor, Columbia Teachers College Teacher, Georgia Normal	(deceased 1915) (deceased 1916) (deceased 1918)
1908	Benjamin A. Howes	1 daughter, 1 son	Instructor, Radcliffe, Wellesley, Simmons Unemployed	Unemployed Unemployed
1891	William N. Squire	Unknown	Director, New Paltz Normal Research Assistant, Clark Professor, Montana Normal	New Paltz Normal (deceased 1914) Not listed
1905	Paul G. Woolley	2 daughters	Professor, Mt. Holyoke Associate Professor, Vassar	Director Cincinnati Schools Professor, Vassar
1924	T. W. Kemmerer	0	Unemployed	Assistant Professor, Iowa

[c] Doctoral study, no degree granted. [d] Doctoral program completed, no degree granted due to prohibition against women. [e] Program of study less than 4-year course.

limited a woman's activity, could result in personal anguish for those who challenged it. Kate Gordon (1905), one of the first psychologists, spoke of this in discussing women's education:

> The question of woman's education is seductively close to the question of woman's "sphere." I hold it to be almost a transgression even to mention woman's sphere—the word recalls so many painful and impertinent deliveries, so much of futile discussion about it—and yet the willingness to dogmatize about woman in general is so common an infirmity that I am emboldened to err. (p. 789)

To pursue higher education was, for a woman, to risk serious social sanctions; to attempt this in a coeducational situation, which implied competition with men, was commonly considered to be personally disastrous (Thomas, 1908). And yet just this was necessary to gain the graduate training required for entry into the field of psychology.

DESCRIPTION OF EARLY PSYCHOLOGISTS

Each scientist listed in AMS had filled out and returned to Cattell a form that requested the following: name, title, and address; field; place and date of birth; education and degrees; current and previous positions held; honorary degrees and other scientific honors; memberships in scientific and learned societies; and chief subjects of research. Thus, working from the entries alone, it is possible to examine comparative data on pertinent variables.

Women psychologists in 1906 can be described generally as Anglo-Saxon Protestants of privileged middle-class backgrounds. They were similar to men psychologists on most of the variables reported in AMS. Most were born in the Northeastern or Middle-Western United States, though some were Canadians and a few of the men were European born; several were born abroad as children of missionaries. The range of birth years was 1847 to 1878 for women (see Table 1) and 1830 to 1878 for men. The median age of the women in 1906 was 39.5, and the median age for men was 39. The median age at completion of the undergraduate degree for the women was 22.5, for the men 22. In their undergraduate study, the women followed a pattern similar to what Cattell identified for the entire group of psychologists he surveyed in 1903: dispersion across a wide variety of types and locations of undergraduate institutions (Cattell, 1903b). Ten of them had earned their degrees in four women's colleges (Smith, Vassar, Wellesley, and Wilson); the remaining 12 had studied at 11 coeducational institutions, both public and private (see Table 1).

All but two of the women (Case and Parrish) reported graduate work. Approximately one third had traveled to Europe to study at some time, and 18 had completed the requirements for the PhD by 1906 (see Table 1). Cornell University, unusual in that it was founded as a coeducational *private* institution in 1865, was the most hospitable and accessible graduate site for early women psychologists. Six of the group undertook their advanced study there. Cornell was a noted exception to the norm during this period because it not only admitted women as fully recognized students but also considered them eligible for fellowship support. Indeed, four of the women in this sample held the prestigious Susan Linn Sage Fellowship in Philosophy and Ethics: Washburn in 1893–1894, Hinman in 1895–1896, Gamble in 1896–1897, and Bagley in 1900–1901. The other two women who studied at Cornell received graduate scholarships: V. F. Moore in 1897–1898 and Squire in 1900–1901. (Three other women, omitted from the 1906 AMS, had also received PhDs in psychology from Cornell during this period: Ellen Bliss Talbot and Margaret Everitt Schallenberger were Sage Fellows in 1897–1898 and 1899–1900, respectively, and Stella Sharp held a graduate scholarship in 1897–1898.) For the men psychologists, however, Cornell placed a poor fifth as an institution for advanced study, running behind Clark, Columbia, Leipzig, and Harvard—each of which, however, denied women access to graduate degrees in psychology in the 1890s. The remaining 14 women who reported advanced work were spread across 11 different institutions.

The women were somewhat older than the men by the time they completed their graduate studies, with a median age for the women of 31 compared to 29 for the men. The difference is not great, but given the close similarity to men on the other variables, it merits some attention. The two-year gap was not due to the women's prolonging their advanced degree programs. Once they began graduate study, they generally completed their course in good time. A notable exception is Julia Gulliver, who stated that in the time between her 1879 baccalaureate and 1888 doctorate (both from Smith College) she was "at home studying for my degree, in addition to many other occupations." She explained her reason for undertaking study at home: "It was the best I could do, as I could not afford to go elsewhere" (Gulliver, 1938). Gulliver was exceptional also in that she was the only woman in the group to hold a long-term appointment as a college president.

Seven women (Bagley, Gordon, Hinman, Norsworthy, Thompson, Washburn, and Williams) went directly to graduate study after college. Thirteen, however, reported delays ranging from 5 to 18 years between receiving the baccalaureate and the doctorate. During the hiatus, which averaged 11 years, all but three of the women (Gulliver, Shinn, and Squire) were engaged in teaching—primarily in women's colleges and public schools. Squire, who was married a year after her college graduation and widowed the following year, reported no occupational positions before her doctoral study.

The seven women who progressed without interruption from college to graduate study were a later-born cohort, with birth dates ranging from 1869 to 1878. Several factors may have been important in guiding their academic course and delaying the progress of the older women. Prior to the early 1890s, very few graduate programs in any field were open to women, and none of the institutions granting doctoral degrees in psychology admitted women as degree candidates. Thus, the older women had to wait for access, whereas the younger ones were able to move directly into a few available graduate study programs. Furthermore, the older women were not exposed to psychology as a scientific discipline during their college days. As the "new" psychology gained attention in the 1890s, however, it is possible that they learned of it through their teaching activities and saw advanced study as a way of satisfying their continuing intellectual interests or as a means of career enhancement. For some of the women, financial difficulties delayed their academic pursuits. Several taught before attending college as well as afterward to finance their education.

Despite the similarities they shared in several areas, the professional attainments of the women were diverse. Three patterns may be identified. Two of the 22 (Bagley and Shinn) reported no employment following advanced study. Twelve found a permanent place in higher education—seven held teaching or administrative positions at women's colleges, four at co-educational universities, and one at a normal school—and their careers show advancement through the academic ranks. The remaining eight found employment in a variety of positions, academic and applied, full and part-time. Their career paths were marked by frequent job changes, discontinuities in type of work, gaps in employment records, and little or no evidence of professional advancement. This pattern is associated, not coincidentally we believe, with marital status. Six of the eight women whose careers are characterized by discontinuity and lack of advancement were married. (Nine of the 22 did marry; all of those produced children, except the one who was widowed early and the two who married late in life. See Table 1.)

In considering the relation of gender to professional advancement, a comparison of the women with their male counterparts is relevant. Rates of employment within academia were tabulated for both groups. (Comparison is limited to academic institutions, because employment opportunities for psychologists during this period were restricted almost exclusively to that setting.) Counting each psychologist who was a college or university president or a full, associate, or assistant professor in the 1906 AMS, it was found that whereas 65% of the men occupied one of these ranks, this was true for only 50% of the women. A comparison of the two groups 15 years later, when most of the individuals were in their mid-50s, based on the third edition of AMS (Cattell & Brimhall, 1921), revealed a continuing gap. At that time 68% of the men and 46% of the women held a presidency or professorial rank. (See Table 1 for positions held by women in 1906 and 1921.)

All of the women who attained an academic rank of assistant professor or higher were unmarried. (Squire was a widow, and Thompson, listed in AMS 1906 as professor at Mt. Holyoke, had actually left that position when she married in 1905.) Furthermore, the institutions in which they found employment were predominantly women's colleges; and, finally, all but one of the women who held the position of college president or full professor did so within institutions for women. (Lillien J. Martin, who was listed as professor emeritus in the 1921 AMS, had held the rank of full professor at a coeducational university, Stanford, from 1911 until her retirement at age 65 in 1916.)

Concerning employment, then, there was a definite "women's place" for women psychologists: teaching at undergraduate institutions for women. However, there is no indication that these women were restricted to what has been labeled "women's work," as was the case for women in other sciences (see Rossiter, 1982, Ch. 3). An article assessing the status of American psychology in 1904 noted that the field had become differentiated into a host of subfields including—besides experimental psychology—educational, comparative, and a wide variety of other specialty areas (Miner, 1904). The women were active in virtually all areas. Furthermore, the women's research interests spread across the breadth of the discipline in a pattern not discernibly different from that of the men. (See Table 1 for major research interests of the women through 1906.)

To summarize, the first women psychologists were similar in age and training to their more numerous male colleagues. However, when we evaluate the professional development of these women over a 15-year span, it is clear that they were less likely to achieve professional status equivalent to that of the men. When high professional status was attained, it was held exclusively by unmarried women who were employed for the most part in colleges for women.

WOMEN'S EXPERIENCE

Although the women psychologists as a group fared less well professionally than the men, three did receive stars in the first edition of AMS, placing them among the 1,000 scientists whom Cattell had identified in 1903 as the most meritorious in the country (Cattell, 1903a). They were Mary Whiton Calkins (1863–1930), Christine Ladd-Franklin (1847–1930), and Margaret Floy Washburn (1871–1939), who ranked 12th, 19th, and 42nd among 50 starred psychologists. Three other women among the unstarred psychologists in 1906 received stars in subsequent editions of AMS: Ethel Dench Puffer (Howes), Lillien Jane Martin, and Helen Bradford Thompson (Woolley). Here we focus primarily on the three who were most prominent, showing how gender influenced their lives. As they are the best known women of the period, there are a few secondary sources that provide additional biographical information for them (e.g., Boring, 1971; Furumoto, 1979, 1980; Goodman, 1980; Hurvich, 1971; Onderdonk, 1971).

The first three of psychology's eminent women shared several common experiences and in these ways may be considered prototypes for those who, by entering a male-dominated profession, challenged the cultural stereotype that defined women's sphere. Each encountered institutional discrimination in pursuing the PhD. Each experienced limited employment opportunities. Each had to confront the marriage-versus-career dilemma. And each wrestled with family obligations that conflicted strongly with career advancement.

Ladd-Franklin, Calkins, and Washburn began their graduate studies as "special students" at Johns Hopkins, Harvard, and Columbia, respectively. Their "special" status reflected the female-exclusionary policies of these institutions, policies that were waived only partially for them. Ladd-Franklin was admitted because a prominent Johns Hopkins mathematics professor, having been impressed by professional work she had already published, interceded for her. Calkins secured the privilege of attending seminars at Harvard on a petition from her father, accompanied by a letter from the president of Wellesley College (where she was a faculty member). Though both Ladd-Franklin and Calkins completed all requirements, each was denied the doctorate. Washburn would probably have met the same fate had she remained at Columbia. She was advised, however, to transfer to Cornell, where she was eligible for both a degree and a fellowship. There she studied under E. B. Titchener and in 1894 became the first woman to receive a PhD in psychology. Ladd-Franklin was granted the degree in 1926 (44 years after earning it), when Hopkins celebrated its 50th anniversary. Calkins was offered the PhD under the auspices of Radcliffe College in 1902 for work she completed in 1895, but she declined the dubious honor of that arrangement worked out for women who had studied at Harvard.

Employment for women in psychology was almost totally limited to the women's colleges and normal schools. Thus, Calkins spent her entire career at Wellesley College, and Washburn taught first at Wells College and then at Vassar for 34 years. Exclusion from the research universities, then the centers of professional activity, necessarily limited the women's research activities as well as their interaction with the leading figures in the emerging field of psychology. There were, however, personal advantages for faculty at the women's colleges. Recently completed research on the Wellesley College professoriat provides a richly illustrated portrayal of faculty life that concurs with material we have collected on the women psychologists.

Patricia Palmieri's (1983) study is a collective portrait of the women at Wellesley College who had been on the faculty there for more than five years and held the rank of associate or full professor by 1910. These women came mainly from closeknit New England families notable for the love and support given to their bright daughters. Among that group, described as "strikingly homogeneous in terms of social and geographic origins, upbringing, and socio-cultural worldview" (p. 197), were five of the 22 psychologists, including Mary Calkins.

Palmieri emphasized *community* as a central theme that "illuminates the history of academe as it was writ by women scholars, outside the research universities so commonly thought to be the only citadels of genuine intellectual creativity" (1983, p. 196). She drew a sharp contrast between the experience of the academic women at Wellesley and that of men at the research universities. She characterized the male academic of the period as an isolated specialist, whereas the female academic lived within a network of relationships:

> These academic women did not shift their life-courses away from the communal mentality as did many male professionals; nor did they singlemindedly adhere to scientific rationalism, specialization, social science objectivity, or hierarchical association in which vertical mobility took precedence over sisterhood. (Palmieri, 1983, pp. 209–210)

There were, as Palmieri noted, costs as well as benefits associated with the creation and maintenance of a community such as the one she described. For example, there were tensions surrounding the question of commitment to social activism versus institutional loyalty. In one instance, when a prominent faculty member was terminated by Wellesley College because of her pacifist views during World War I, Mary Calkins felt compelled to offer the trustees her resignation because she herself held the same views; her request, however, was refused (Trustees Minutes, 1919). Finally, to remain a member of the Wellesley community, a woman had to forego marriage and motherhood, for Wellesley, like other institutions of higher education in that era, did not consider it acceptable to include married women on its faculty.

Personal relationships were particularly important for each of psychology's first three eminent women; gender and marital status were crucial in determining how these relationships interacted with career. For Ladd-Franklin, marriage and motherhood precluded professional employment. The accepted view in the late 19th and early 20th century was that, for a man, the potential for professional accomplishment was enhanced by marriage. For a woman, however, marriage and career were incompatible. Thus, an educated woman was faced with what was then termed the "cruel choice." A friend of Ladd-Franklin, with whom she had discussed the marriage-versus-career dilemma plaguing women, expressed the sentiment of the time:

> As human nature stands and with woman's physical organization to consider, . . . she ought to be taught that she cannot serve two masters, that if she chooses the higher path of learning and wants to do herself and her sex justice, she must forego matrimony. (Ridgely, 1897)

Whether or not Ladd-Franklin herself agreed with this verdict, she nevertheless was subject to the strong social sanctions against women's combining of marriage and career. She never held a regular faculty appointment.

For Calkins and Washburn, the "family claim"—an unmarried daughter's obligations to her parents—was paramount. Calkins maintained very close ties with her family, living with her mother and father in the family home near Wellesley College for her entire adult life. In 1905 she was offered a unique career opportunity, which she confided to her brother Raymond:

> We go on a walk and she tells me of her brilliant offer from Barnard and Columbia, to be Professor of Psychology with graduate classes from both colleges. A very perplexing decision, involving as it would, the breaking up of her Newton home, hard for mother and father. (R. Calkins, 1905)

As Calkins later explained in a letter to her graduate school mentor, Hugo Munsterberg, her reason for refusing to consider the offer hinged on what she perceived to be her family's best interests. She wrote:

> The deciding consideration was a practical one. I was unwilling to leave my home, both because I find in it my deepest happiness and because I feel that I add to the happiness of my mother's and father's lives. They would have considered transferring the home to New York, but I became convinced that it would be distinctly hurtful to them to do so. (M. W. Calkins, 1905)

Like Calkins, Washburn was particularly close to her parents and felt a strong sense of responsibility for them. Her situation is another example of how the obligations of a daughter might impede professional advancement. As an only child, Washburn clearly acknowledged the demands that the family claim held for her. In 1913 she wrote to Robert Yerkes, to resign responsibility as review editor for the *Journal of Animal Behavior*:

> I doubt if anyone else on the board is teaching eighteen hours a week, as I am. I simply must cut down my work somewhere. If I am ever to accomplish anything in psychology, it must be done in the next five years, for as my parents get older, I shall have less and less command of my time. (Washburn, 1913)

Significantly, the work that she considered her most important contribution was published not long after, as *Movement and Mental Imagery* (Washburn, 1916).

The early women psychologists who remained unmarried and both developed their scholarly careers and lived their lives within the context of the women's colleges shared a common set of experiences. Those who chose to marry, however, as did Ladd-Franklin, constituted another group, whose experiences were similar to each other but different from the unmarried women. None of the married women had regular or permanent academic affiliations. Their career patterns tended to be erratic and without signs of advancement. Even if an individual was able to reconcile the duties and obligations of the domestic and professional roles, her status as a married woman rendered her ineligible for consideration as a candidate for an academic position. Christine Ladd-Franklin, married and without a regular academic appointment, nevertheless managed to continue some scientific work and to earn a star in AMS; most who chose to marry were not as fortunate.

Another one of those who married was Ethel Puffer. We use her experience to illustrate the keenly felt conflict between marriage and career that bedeviled this group. It is worth noting that Puffer and Calkins had several things in common. Besides their Protestant New England heritage, their first-born status in their families, and their undergraduate education at Smith College, they both did their doctoral work in the Harvard Philosophy Department with Hugo Munsterberg as thesis advisor. We suggest that the choice for marriage by Puffer and for career by Calkins contributed to their quite different professional attainments.

After completing her doctoral study in 1898, Puffer held concurrent positions in psychology at Radcliffe and Simmons College in Boston and also taught at Wellesley. Her book *The Psychology of Beauty* was published in 1905. In August 1908 she married an engineer, Benjamin Howes, at which point her career in psychology halted. A letter dated April 29, 1908, from the president of Smith College highlights the negative impact that choosing to marry had on a woman's academic career:

> Dear Miss Puffer: If you really are disposed to think seriously of the position at Barnard I am sure it would be well for your friends in Cambridge to recommend you to President Butler, although I fear the rumor which reached me concerning your engagement may have also affected the recommendation which I myself sent, and that a candidate has already been selected to present to the trustees of Columbia at their next commencement. (Seelye, 1908)

A few years after their marriage, Ethel and Benjamin Howes settled in Scarsdale, New York, where in 1915 and 1917 (when Ethel was in her 40s) two children were born: Ellen and Benjamin, Jr. During this decade, she also found time to do organizational work for the suffrage movement and the war effort.

In 1922, Ethel Howes turned 50. World War I was over, the vote was won, and her two children were of school age. In that year, she publicly addressed the inherent contradiction facing women who attempted to combine a career and marriage. Her typed notes for two articles that appeared in the *Atlantic Monthly* (Howes, 1922a, 1922b) highlighted her own struggle and conflict. In the excerpts presented here, we retain the capital letters Howes used for emphasis. The notes begin: "The basic inhibition still operating to suppress the powers of women is the persistent vicious alternative—MARRIAGE OR CAREER—full personal life vs. the way of achievement" (Howes, undated). Howes reasoned that even if every woman were granted the right to marry and go on with her job, a major problem remained. It was how to reconcile the demands of a career with those of being a mother, for most women who married would have children. Success in a career demanded concentration, and this meant "long sustained intensive application ... [and] freedom from irrelevant cares and interruptions" (Howes, undated). Such concentration, she maintained, was precisely what was unavailable to a woman who was a mother.

The incompatibility between having a successful career and being a successful mother led Howes to advise married women "EXPLICITLY *TO FOREGO THE CAREER.*" She regarded aspirations to a full-fledged career as unrealistic and advised married women to "TRANSCEND THE WHOLE NOTION OF A CAREER, WITH ITS CONNOTATIONS OF COMPETITION, SUCCESS, REWARDS, HONORS, TITLES" (Howes, undated). In her view, this could be done by contracting the scope or modifying the type of professional work: finding opportunities in "borderline subjects," in a "fringe of special research," or in consulting, criticizing, and reviewing. The accommodation to marriage and parenthood that Howes envisioned as necessary for educated women, then, called for an adjustment of professional activity and goals that men have not, until very recently, even had to consider—much less adopt.

CONCLUSIONS

What do we conclude concerning the first American women psychologists and how gender shaped their personal and professional experiences? First, they were similar to American men psychologists on basic demographic variables such as family and geographic origins, age, and social class membership. They were similar to the men in some aspects of their educational experience. They held equivalent degrees but were restricted in the number and types of institutions where both baccalaureate and graduate studies might be undertaken. The women diverged from the men most obviously in the area of career advancement.

Second, these women demonstrated three career patterns: no career beyond the doctorate, continuous careers restricted mainly to teaching in women's colleges and normal schools, and interrupted or disjointed careers with lapses in employment or shifts in employment setting and type of work. Of those women who pursued careers, the unmarried group followed the continuous pattern, whereas the married women displayed the interrupted pattern.

Third, certain gender-specific factors profoundly affected the women's experience: exclusion from important educational and employment opportunities, the responsibility of daughters to their families, and the marriage-versus-career dilemma. These factors are illustrated in the lives of the women discussed here—Calkins, Washburn, Ladd-Franklin, and Puffer.

Acknowledging the early women's presence and their experience is a first step toward placing women in the history of psychology. Integrating women into that history is necessary if we are to achieve a more complete understanding of psychology's past.

REFERENCES

Bernstein, M. D., & Russo, N. F. (1974). The history of psychology revisited: Or, up with our foremothers. *American Psychologist, 29,* 130–134.

Boring, E. G. (1971). Washburn, Margaret Floy. In E. T. James (Ed.), *Notable American women, 1607–1950: A biographical dictionary* (Vol. 3, pp. 546–548). Cambridge, MA: Belknap Press.

Calkins, M. W. (1905, June 18). Letter to H. Munsterberg. (From the Hugo Munsterberg Papers, Boston Public Library, Boston, MA)

Calkins, R. (1905, May 28). Entry in log. (From papers held by the Calkins family)

Cattell, J. M. (1903a). *Homo scientificus Americanus:* Address of the president of the American Society of Naturalists. *Science, 17,* 561–570.

Cattell, J. M. (1903b). Statistics of American psychologists. *American Journal of Psychology, 14,* 310–328.

Cattell, J. M. (Ed.). (1906). *American men of science: A biographical directory.* New York: Science Press.

Cattell, J. M., & Brimhall, D. R. (Eds.). (1921). *American men of science: A biographical directory* (3rd ed.). Garrison, NY: Science Press.

Furumoto, L. (1979). Mary Whiton Calkins (1863–1930): Fourteenth president of the American Psychological Association. *Journal of the History of the Behavioral Sciences, 15,* 346–356.

Furumoto, L. (1980). Mary Whiton Calkins (1863–1930). *Psychology of Women Quarterly, 5,* 55–67.

Goodman, E. S. (1980). Margaret F. Washburn (1871–1939): First woman Ph.D. in psychology. *Psychology of Women Quarterly, 5,* 69–80.

Goodman, E. S. (1983). History's choices [Review of *History and systems of psychology* and *A history of western psychology*]. *Contemporary Psychology, 28,* 667–669.

Gordon, K. (1905). Wherein should the education of a woman differ from that of a man. *School Review, 13,* 789–794.

Gulliver, J. H. (1938, March 1). Letter to E. N. Hill (From the Smith College Archives, Northampton, MA)

Howes, E. P. (undated). Notes for "Accepting the universe" and "Continuity for women." (From the Faculty Papers, Smith College Archives, Northampton, MA)

Howes, E. P. (1922a). Accepting the universe. *Atlantic Monthly, 129,* 444–453.

Howes, E. P. (1922b). Continuity for women. *Atlantic Monthly, 130,* 731–739.

Hurvich, D. J. (1971). Ladd-Franklin, Christine. In E. T. James, J. W. James, & P. S. Boyer (Eds.), *Notable American women, 1607–1950: A biographical dictionary* (Vol. 2, pp. 354–356). Cambridge, MA: Belknap Press.

Lerner, G. (1979). *The majority finds its past: Placing women in history.* New York: Oxford University Press.

Miner, B. G. (1904). The changing attitude of American universities toward psychology. *Science, 20,* 299–307.

O'Connell, A. N. (1983). Synthesis: Profiles and patterns of achievement. In A. N. O'Connell & N. F. Russo (Eds.), *Models of achievement: Reflections of eminent women in psychology* (pp. 297–326). New York: Columbia University Press.

O'Connell, A. N., & Russo, N. F. (Eds.). (1980). Eminent women in psychology: Models of achievement [special issue]. *Psychology of Women Quarterly, 5*(1).

Onderdonk, V. (1971). Calkins, Mary Whiton. In E. T. James, J. W. James, & P. W. Boyer (Eds.), *Notable American women, 1607–1950: A biographical dictionary* (Vol. 1, pp. 278–290). Cambridge, MA: Belknap Press.

Palmieri, P. A. (1983). Here was fellowship: A social portrait of academic women at Wellesley College, 1895–1920. *History of Education Quarterly, 23,* 195–214.

Puffer, E. D. (1905). *The psychology of beauty.* Boston: Houghton Mifflin.

Ridgely, H. W. (1897, February 15). Letter to Mrs. Franklin. (From the Franklin Papers, Columbia University Library, New York, NY)

Rossiter, M. W. (1974). Women scientists in America before 1920. *American Scientist, 62,* 312–323.

Rossiter, M. W. (1982). *Women scientists in America: Struggles and strategies to 1940.* Baltimore, MD: Johns Hopkins University Press.

Russo, N. F. (1983). Psychology's foremothers: Their achievements in context. In A. N. O'Connell & N. F. Russo (Eds.), *Models of achievement: Reflections of eminent women in psychology* (pp. 9–24). New York: Columbia University Press.

Seelye, L. C. (1908, April 29). Letter to Ethel D. Puffer. (From the Morgan-Howes Papers, Schlesinger Library, Cambridge, MA)

Solomon, B. M. (1985). *In the company of educated women.* New Haven, CT: Yale University Press.

Stevens, G., & Gardner, S. (1982). *The women of psychology.* (Vols. 1–2). Cambridge, MA: Schenkman.

Thomas, M. C. (1908). Present tendencies in women's college and university education. *Educational Review, 35,* 64–85.

Trustees minutes. (1919, May 9). Minutes of the Trustees meeting. (From the Wellesley College Archives, Wellesley, MA)

Walsh, M. R. (1977). *Doctors wanted: No women need apply.* New Haven, CT: Yale University Press.

Washburn, M. F. (1913, October 24). Letter to R. M. Yerkes. (From R. M. Yerkes papers, Manuscripts and Archives, Yale University Library, Hartford, CT)

Washburn, M. F. (1916). *Movement and mental imagery: Outlines of a motor theory of the complexer mental processes*. Boston: Houghton Mifflin.

Watson, R. I., Sr. (1960). The history of psychology: A neglected area. *American Psychologist, 15,* 251–255.

Watson, R. I., Sr. (1975). The history of psychology as a specialty: A personal view of its first fifteen years. *Journal of the History of the Behavioral Sciences, 11,* 5–14.

Welter, B. (1966). The cult of true womanhood, 1820–1860. *American Quarterly, 18,* 151–174.

26

"THE DEFECTS OF HIS RACE": E. G. BORING AND ANTISEMITISM IN AMERICAN PSYCHOLOGY, 1923–1953

ANDREW S. WINSTON

> History amply shows that "good behavior" on the part of the Jew is by no means an insurance against anti-Semitism.—Kurt Lewin (1940/1948, p. 182)

By 1925, Edwin G. Boring (1886–1968) was well established at Harvard as the "director of the Laboratory *de jure* and chairman of a nonexistent department *de facto*" (Boring, 1961, p. 46).[1] He worked grueling 80-hour weeks to fulfill his administrative and teaching obligations. Boring

---

Portions of this article were presented at the annual meeting of Cheiron, the International Society for the History of Behavioral and Social Sciences, Earlham College, Richmond, Indiana, June 1996, and at the 104th Annual Convention of the American Psychological Association, Toronto, Ontario, Canada, August 1996. I thank Jacob Levine, Saul Rosenzweig, Leo Hurvich, Lawrence Marks, Didi Stone, and Miriam Lewin for personal communications. I also thank Eugene Taylor, Richard von Mayrhauser, Don Dewsbury, Nicole Barenbaum, and many others for their assistance and Judith Winston for comments on earlier versions of this article.

All Boring correspondence, except for Boring (1933a), is from the Correspondence Files, HUG 4229.5, E. G. Boring Papers, Harvard University Archives, and is quoted by permission of the Harvard University Archives.

[1] For a discussion of Boring at Harvard during the 1920s, see O'Donnell (1979). For biographical information on Boring, see Boring (1961), Jaynes (1969), and Rosenzweig (1970). For Boring's influence, especially as a historian, see Cerullo (1988) and Kelly (1981).

Reprinted from *History of Psychology*, 1, 27–51 (1998). Copyright © 1998 by the American Psychological Association. Reprinted with permission of the author.

felt a special responsibility for placing graduate students, and his letters of reference were careful and detailed. A Harvard degree and a fine recommendation from Boring opened many doors, but in some cases it was not enough. When the William L. Fletcher employment agency asked about Jacob Kelson's suitability for employment in business, Boring (1925b) replied:

> He is a Jew, and on this account we have not found it so far easy to place him in a college teaching position in psychology, because of the personal prejudice that exists against Jews in many academic circles and possibly especially in psychology.[2]

Boring's view of the possible role of antisemitism raises a neglected issue in the standard historiography of psychology. The widespread antisemitism in the United States between the world wars is well documented (e.g., Dinnerstein, 1994; Higham, 1975) as are the discriminatory practices of universities in admissions and hiring (Klingenstein, 1991; Wechsler, 1977). However, the role of antisemitic practices in the history of American psychology has been discussed only briefly in the context of other issues (see Blumenthal, 1991; Sarason, 1988; Sarbin, 1994; Sokal, 1984a, 1984b) and has never been analyzed in detail. Antisemitism has been treated as a European evil, as the persecution from which Kurt Lewin and others escaped, rather than as a problem for them in America (e.g., Mandler & Mandler, 1969; Wellek, 1968).

In a previous article (Winston, 1996), I discussed the identification of Jewish psychologists in the letters of reference written by Robert S. Woodworth of Columbia University. These letters reveal commonly held conceptions of "Jewish traits" that were used to separate Jews into socially acceptable and unacceptable categories, an important distinction in the 1920s through the 1940s. As a matter of academic obligation, it was necessary to state whether the candidate was, or might be, a Jew and whether he or she had the "objectionable traits" commonly expected in Jews. These "traits" were often unspecified or were described with vague terms such as "personal unpleasantness," and these practices suggest a shared understanding of the dangers in admitting Jews to the socioculturally homogeneous professoriate. The concern over these perceived dangers increased as children of the many Jewish immigrants of the 1880s and 1890s made their way into the universities, where some ultimately sought academic careers (see Klingenstein, 1991).

In the present article I discuss how Boring tried to assist Jewish students and colleagues while observing the discursive practices of the times. Boring's uncertainties and inconsistencies in the identification of Jews, and the concealable nature of Jewish identity, allowed for social processes that

---

[2]Jacob Kelson received a PhD from Harvard in 1928. His subsequent employment history is unknown.

shaped the career trajectories of many psychologists.[3] This discussion will focus on Abraham A. Roback and Kurt Lewin, in whom Jewish identity and presumed "Jewish traits" played different roles. In addition, correspondence regarding Leo Hurvich (1910–) will be used to illustrate the barriers to placing Jewish students. Finally, I discuss how the place of Jews in academic psychology remained a concern for Boring in the 1950s, primarily as a problem of historiography. These issues are by no means unique to Boring, nor are the discursive practices regarding Jews unique to psychology, but given Boring's extraordinary contributions and influence, his letters provide an important window on the role of antisemitism in the hiring of psychologists during the interwar years.

BORING AND COMPLETE DISCLOSURE

Boring traced his descent on his father's side from a Maryland settler who arrived in America from England in 1670, and on his mother's side from 17th century Huguenots who fled the Edict of Nantes and eventually landed in Philadelphia (Boring, 1961; see also Jaynes, 1969; Rosenzweig, 1970). His mother's family was a mixture of liberal Hicksite and strict Orthodox Quakers. According to Boring, the family was matriarchal, but he attended the Moravian Protestant church of his father's background while attending an Orthodox Quaker school. Apparently Boring did not attend Quaker meeting, but it is likely that he was exposed to Quaker tolerance for other groups.[4]

Boring was a man of "ferocious convictions" (Bruner, 1983). Slight infractions of proper behavior, such as missing a lecture or removing a book from the reading room, were met with immediate written reproaches (see Boring, 1939; Bruner, 1983; Jacob Levine, personal communication, February 22, 1995).[5] "You knew immediately where you stood with Boring," Bruner recalled (1983, p. 37). Boring's letters of recommendation from the

---

[3] The concealable aspect of Jewish identity is one of the features that distinguishes the history of the exclusion of Jews from that of women and African Americans.

[4] The tradition of tolerance among the Society of Friends was no guarantee against antisemitism. See Pauly (1987) for an account of discrimination against Jacques Loeb by the Founders of Bryn Mawr, then a Quaker school, in the 1890s.

[5] Jacob Levine distinctly remembered receiving such a note, which I subsequently retrieved from the Harvard archives (Boring, 1939). It begins: "Dear Levine, I notice that you have some books withdrawn from the Robbins Library. Will you please return them since the privilege of withdrawing books from the Robbins Library does not extend to you?" Boring then inquired whether Levine has a key to the library, and asks for it back, closing with "I hope this does not cause you too much inconvenience, but we have to have the same rule for everybody." This concern with fairness and "the same rule for everybody" are hallmarks of Boring's discourse. According to Jaynes (1969), a graduate student once handed in his thesis a few days late because his wife had been ill, and Boring refused to accept it on the grounds that it would not be fair to others.

1920s and 1930s show the same straightforward style.[6] He often recommended a number of possible candidates and outlined the strengths and weaknesses of each. For example, Boring (1923) recommended 10 candidates to Lewis Terman, each described with a paragraph. Ranked last was Gilbert Joseph Rich (1893–?), who received his PhD under E. B. Titchener at Cornell University in 1918:

> You would get a good and enthusiastic worker cheap in Dr. G. J. Rich at the University of Pittsburgh, but I most emphatically do not recommend him, because he has some of the personal unpleasantnesses that are usually associated with Jews.

Boring was somewhat milder regarding Rich when he gave evaluations of 10 possible candidates to Stevenson Smith of the University of Washington. He stated that Rich had not received a permanent post at the University of Pittsburgh "because of his race" and was therefore studying medicine (Boring, 1925c).[7] Boring suggested that Rich had "many good points, and if race is not final with you, there is time for me to write you fully about him." The problem was not a lack of openings: In the same letter, Boring noted that "The market for psychologists has been unusually active this spring."

Boring sometimes assigned letter grades to the candidates. He referred to the files that he kept as his "employment agency" (Boring, 1926a) and used forms that candidates could fill out.

> This sheet is just my confidential record. It puts the relevant information right at my hand and keeps me from forgetting any names when an emergency call comes in. I have full professors and first year graduates and all sorts of people in between in this file now. (Boring, 1930)

In the Boring correspondence files, there are materials labeled "employment agency" dating up to 1946.[8] For efficiency, he sometimes sent the candidate's information sheet to the prospective employer.

Boring's recommendations stressed a balance of research skill, dedication, and personal characteristics. Personality was of particular concern in that it had clear implications for collegiality. The intersection between issues of antisemitism and issues of collegiality is critical and is illuminated by examining two contrasting cases: those of Roback and Lewin. These cases help us understand how the personal characteristics of the "bad Jew" were seen as bound up with and stemming from Jewish identity, which was loosely conceived as racial. The "good Jew," through some combination of heredity, background, and experience, had somehow escaped the "defect"

---

[6]For a different, potentially conflicting view of Boring's way of dealing with colleagues, see Stout and Stuart (1990). Those subjected to his critiques did not necessarily see him as "fair."
[7]Rich earned an MD in 1928 and later joined the staff of the Boston Psychopathic Hospital.
[8]See Finison (1976) for a discussion of Boring's role on the APA committee investigating supply and demand of psychologists during the 1930s.

of Jewishness. The former was to be guarded against, whereas the latter might, in some departments, be an acceptable colleague. It may seem that this distinction has nothing to do with antisemitism, given that religion is not the central issue and defects of "character" may occur in members of any group. Although the issues of "character" and Jewishness may be separable from a contemporary perspective, they were certainly conjoined in antisemitic discourse for centuries, during which Jews were described as wicked, perverse, false, aggressive, disloyal, traitorous, sinister, cowardly, unpatriotic, greedy, materialistic, clannish, ostentatious, unclean, and ill-mannered, or worse (see Dinnerstein, 1994; Poliakov, 1965–1985).

ROBACK AND "DEFENSIVE AGGRESSIVENESS"

On April 22, 1925, Boring answered a request from J. H. White at Pittsburgh to recommend candidates for an opening. Boring described 12 candidates. The fifth was Roback (1895–1965), a 1917 Harvard PhD who had been Hugo Münsterberg's last student: "Dr. A. A. Roback ... is a Jew with some of the defects of his race, although much better than Rich. He certainly ought to place somewhere" (Boring, 1925a). To R. H. Wheeler of the University of Kansas, he ranked Roback fifth of eight and noted that he "has not placed because he is a Jew, and his inferiority sometimes expresses itself in aggression" (Boring, 1926c). In the same letter, Boring implied that there were important distinctions among Jews. He placed Nathaniel Hirsch (1897–1984) above Roback, noting that Hirsch "is a Jew but doesn't show it much."[9]

When Madison Bentley asked Boring to recommend someone for a 1-year appointment, he specified that the candidate "should fit without friction of adjustment into the work of the department" (Bentley, 1926). Boring (1926a) recommended Caroll Pratt, Karl Dallenbach, John Beebe-Center, and Frank Pattie, and added:

> If you did not specify an anti-friction surface, I should suggest the eminent Roback, who remains perpetually unplaced. Why not? He knows psychology. What matter if he knows more than you, and tells you so every day?

Thus Roback was perceived as aggressive and likely to disrupt collegial harmony. Boring (1925c) noted that Roback had "some of the defensive aggressiveness that one so often finds in Jews," and his repeated use of the term *aggressiveness* suggests that it had general importance for him. Boring

---

[9]Hirsch, a student of McDougall, is remembered primarily for his work on heredity and racial differences (e.g., Hirsch, 1930). After 2 years as an assistant professor at Duke University, a position probably obtained with McDougall's assistance, he held a variety of clinical positions and in 1945 went into private practice in New York City.

discussed his theory of Jewish "character" in the letter to an employment agency regarding Jacob Kelson mentioned earlier. Although Boring (1925b) used the term *race* for Jews, as was the common practice, he did not support a hereditary interpretation of their "problem":

> As a psychologist I do not myself believe that there is any inherited Jewish temperament. It seems rather that the basis for the common prejudice against the race is a psychological result of the prejudice: Jews find themselves discriminated against and seek to combat what they feel to be an unjust social inferiority by an aggressiveness which increases rather than diminishes the prejudice. Mr. Kelson has this aggressive defensiveness less than many Jews, but he is not entirely without it.

This "vicious cycle" interpretation of antisemitism was certainly less harsh than widespread notions of inherited Jewish defects (see Dinnerstein, 1994; Winston, 1996). Nevertheless, Boring participated fully in the discursive conventions of the times. When describing E. G. Wever and Karl Zener for a position at Pittsburgh, he noted that "they are both good 100% Nordics, and in discussing them one discusses merits rather than defects (which is perhaps a bit unusual)" (Boring, 1926b). He was certainly no supporter of Nordic "theorist" Madison Grant, author of *The Passing of the Great Race* (1916), but Boring's letters illustrate just how widespread these linguistic conventions were. What is most important is the way in which Nordic character could be contrasted with the presumed defects of Jews: In parallel letters to William J. Robbins of the National Research Council, sent 3 weeks apart, Boring recommended two candidates for biological science fellowships. One was presented as a "pleasant agreeable 'Nordic'" with "no eccentricities or defects of personality" (Boring, 1931e), and the other was described as "a Jew. He is a fairly tactful Jew, with a personality which stresses intellectual enthusiasm to such an extent that one is likely to forget the little deferential mannerisms" (Boring, 1931f).[10] The phrase "fairly tactful Jew" indicates what was usually expected. Boring was concerned with possible personality defects in all candidates. But Jewishness might be counted as a special defect and served as the explanation of one's other defects. For a nonacademic research position with Carney Landis, Boring described a brilliant young woman as "having certain obvious defects for the normal academic job.... She is a Jewess. She is not beautiful. Her voice is very bad" (Boring, 1935). Landis judged her "overqualified" and did not hire her. Thus Jewish women, having at least two "defects," were certainly at the bottom of any list.

As in the case of Woodworth's letters, it is clear that information

---

[10]The fact that Boring placed "Nordic" in quotes in 1931 but not in 1926 is likely to be significant. It suggests either that by 1931 Boring no longer thought of "Nordic" as a biological category or that he wanted to slightly distance himself from the more extreme uses of the term.

regarding possible Jewish identity was expected even if the candidate was highly recommended. So strong was the obligation to disclose this information that it might override other obligations or principles. Thus Dallenbach (1934) wrote to Boring regarding a fellowship candidate that "I suppose it is un-American to report that he is of Jewish extraction, but since this is a personal letter I think I should in fairness to you and to him mention the fact." Although it might be thought that the practices regarding Jews were universally accepted as fully correct and appropriate, Dallenbach's candid admission suggests otherwise.

Like Woodworth, Boring used the contrastive conjunction "He is a Jew, *but* . . ." followed by a description of how the personality traits expected in Jews were absent in this particular case (see Winston, 1996). Other psychologists used very similar constructions: Regarding Abraham Maslow, Hulsey Cason (1932) wrote to Robert Yerkes that "Although he is a Jew, I can assure you that he does not have *any* of the objectionable characteristics for which the race is famous." Clark Hull (1932) was initially less positive about Maslow: "He is definitely Jewish, with the characteristic Jewish eagerness," but he softened this assessment a few sentences later by noting that "his personality is rather attractive." Nearly identical phrases were used in other disciplines (e.g., see Dinnerstein, 1994, p. 88; Kuklick, 1977, p. 456). If any sign of the "objectionable traits" was present, it was important to note that the person might *not* be a Jew.[11] Boring repeatedly denied that H. E. Israel (not to be confused with H. F. Israel, i.e., Harry Harlow) was a Jew and offered his observations of Israel's interpersonal behavior in support (e.g., Boring, 1926a, 1926b). Israel obtained a permanent post at Smith College, shortly after Boring's assurances. Similar assurances were required for Harry Helson, whose personal characteristics, such as talkativeness, raised suspicions (Boring, 1925d). For uncertain cases, Boring erred on the side of caution: For W. H. Stavsky, he wrote: "He is probably a Jew, although I do not know" (Boring, 1934).

Even when Boring did not identify a candidate as a Jew, antisemitism was sufficiently strong in some departments that suspicion of Jewishness might override Boring's recommendations. J. S. Moore (1928) wrote to Boring to complain that his department at Western Reserve had missed the opportunity to hire Harry DeSilva because:

> the K.K.K.'s in our Faculty feared he might be a Jew (!), or even a Catholic (!!), though pretty sure he was not a negro (!!!), so we lost him. My good colleagues are excellent and lovable persons, but sometimes a little trying! They do not care what kind of a Protestant a man

---

[11]See Kuklick (1977, p. 456) for similar assurances given by Harvard philosopher C. I. Lewis in 1930.

is, or if he has no religion at all (as is the case with most of them), but a Jew or a Catholic are [sic] anathema.[12]

Boring never suggested that DeSilva was a Jew; on the contrary, his description 3 years earlier was that DeSilva "has a dark complexion and looks just a little bit Spanish. There is probably some Spanish blood. But I do not think that anyone would characterize him as foreign looking" (Boring, 1925c). Thus the barriers for placing even "suspected" Jews were formidable by the late 1920s.

Given this context, the case of Roback was particularly problematic. Roback was widely known to be a very difficult person to both family and colleagues. His correspondence with Boring from the 1920s involves protracted arguments over Roback's keys to Emerson Hall, his use of Harvard facilities, and other issues. Yet Boring continued to respect Roback's prodigious intellect ("He has really an excellent head") and wide-ranging knowledge (Boring, 1925c). He suggested Roback for book reviewing and for contract work, such as testing students at Radcliffe College with the tests that Roback developed. Despite an enormous scholarly output, Roback did not obtain a permanent academic appointment until he joined the faculty at Emerson College in the late 1940s.[13] Although Boring expressed the wish that "we could find a place where his brains counted for more than his personality" (Boring, 1925c), he could not have realistically thought this possible, especially after the onset of the Depression. Roback's personality, seen as a result of and inextricably bound with his Jewishness, was too much of a risk.

The perceived risk was accentuated by the rising antisemitism and nativism of the 1920s (see Dinnerstein, 1994). At the turn of the century, some Jews were clearly acceptable to the founding members of the discipline. The seventh and ninth presidents of the American Psychological Association (APA), Münsterberg and Joseph Jastrow, where known to be of Jewish origin (see Blumenthal, 1991; Hale, 1980). Jewish graduate students at Harvard, such as Boris Sidis and Morris Cohen, were well treated by William James. G. Stanley Hall was encouraging to his Jewish graduate students at Clark University and hired at least three Jewish faculty members (see Sokal, 1990).[14] Although some leading psychologists were liberal in their views, the general societal climate changed considerably by the mid-1920s. Fueled by popular accounts of the mental, moral, and social

---

[12]Although this is the only letter I have seen mentioning discrimination against Catholics in academic psychology, this topic is certainly worthy of further investigation.

[13]According to his *New York Times* obituary (June 8, 1965), Roback had 1,700 published articles and texts, a figure that undoubtedly included his many magazine articles. Many of these works were on Jewish culture. Thus Roback's Jewish identity was never and could never be concealed or in doubt.

[14]Although the reasons for Hall's tolerance are undoubtedly complex, it is likely that his feelings toward Jews were influenced by the very positive experiences he had as a young tutor to the children of the Seligman family of New York (see Ross, 1972).

deficiencies of the Eastern European Jews, descriptions linking Jews to Bolshevism, increased popularity of racial theory, and the spread of international Jewish conspiracy theories by Henry Ford and others, open discrimination against Jews for employment in all realms became a common feature of American life. As Jewish university and college enrollment rose, particularly in the eastern United States, quotas or other measures to reduce Jewish presence were instituted at most schools (Synnott, 1979, 1986). At Harvard, President Lowell was unable to institute a quota but by 1925 he was able to change the selection criteria to emphasize "character and fitness." Harvard Jewish enrollment had risen from 4.4% in 1908–1909 to 27.6% in 1920–1930, but fell to 16.05% by 1934–1935. Similar measures halved Jewish enrollment at Columbia University (Synnott, 1986, p. 241). Jewish faculty were rare and generally unwelcome; according to Dinnerstein (1994), total Jewish liberal arts and sciences faculty in American universities numbered fewer than 100 during the mid-1920s. In such a climate, Roback's chances were indeed slim.

KURT LEWIN AND THE MITIGATION OF THE "DEFECT"

In terms of the social perception of character, the case of Roback contrasts sharply with that of Kurt Lewin. By the late 1920s Boring already knew of Lewin's research in Germany. He first met Lewin at the 1929 International Congress and invited him to Cambridge after the conference. The Borings showed Lewin around Boston (Boring, 1931b), although this visit is not mentioned in Marrow's (1969) biography. His favorable early impression, and favorable reports from Germany, encouraged Boring to recommend Lewin to Lewis Terman as a replacement for Walter Miles:

> Just at present I should say that Lewin is the best young foreigner. . . . at Berlin, Lewin has come into prominence and everyone is excited about him. . . . If you could move him it would be a distinguished appointment. (Boring, 1931a)

He continued 2 months later: "Lewin is anything but self-important after the German manner; he seems like a youngster, a pleasant youngster who wants you to like him." According to Caroll Pratt, who had met Lewin in Germany, Lewin "was on the most friendly terms with everyone" (Boring, 1931b).

The subsequent correspondence between Boring and Terman contains the often-discussed question from Terman, "Is Lewin a Jew?", which I have briefly described elsewhere (Winston, 1996; see also Minton, 1988; Samelson, 1978; Sokal, 1984a, 1984b). Boring consulted his wife but remained uncertain until further information arrived from Pratt in Germany, confirming that Lewin was indeed a Jew (Boring, 1931c, 1931d). Terman

(1931) made it clear that he had no difficulties with Jews who did not show any of the "objectionable traits usually ascribed to Jews." His observation that if Lewin was a Jew, it would not necessarily be "fatal" for hiring him suggests both the gravity of the problem and the possibility of exemption for a Jew with acceptable characteristics. What is most important here is the general assessment of Lewin's personality and interpersonal style, which Boring described as "jolly and gay" (Boring, 1931c). Whatever reservations Terman may have had about Lewin were apparently dispelled after Lewin spent the summer and fall of 1932 at Stanford University.

By 1933, when it was clear that he should not stay in Germany after the dismissal of Jewish faculty (see Geuter, 1992), Lewin was able to enlist the help of both Boring and Terman in hopes of finding a position in America. In response to Lewin's request, Boring sent out 26 letters to prominent psychologists, asking about temporary employment:

> I have had this week two cablegrams from Lewin in Japan on his way back toward Germany. The purport of them is that he has had a telegram from Berlin which makes it appear extremely doubtful that his position will be open to him under the present political conditions, and one can see that there must also be some doubt as to the advisability of his returning to Berlin at all. The implication of his telegram is that he is wondering if there would be any way in which he could find temporary employment in America.
>
> Of course Lewin knows the situation in America fairly well since he has just left Stanford. Doubtless it will be the impression of all American psychologists that America can do nothing for Lewin at the present time. On the other hand, many of us have great admiration for his work and will be emotionally stirred by his present plight. I am therefore addressing this note to a score of American psychologists in order that they should know about Lewin's situation. There is always the chance that something may turn up that can be done for him, and there is never any harm in passing information of this sort around. (Boring, 1933a)

In reply, Terman reported to Boring that 60% of the salary for Miles had been lost to budget cuts, and Stanford could no longer consider hiring Lewin. Terman described his feelings about Lewin:

> I wish I could do something for him.... I have been intending to write you particularly to tell you how highly we appreciated Lewin. ... His work commanded the respect of our students, both graduate and undergraduate, and of our department faculty. Personally he is exactly the type of man you described; faculty and students became so fond of him that it was hard to let him go. I have known few people who were so alive to everything about them, or so genial and friendly. (Terman, 1933)

Boring did not expect much help, and the response bore out his fears, as he reported to Terman:

> From my twenty-six letters I have had thirteen replies and no immediate suggestions. There are vague things, like Tolman's suggestion that I find a rich Jew in Boston to pay him a salary, presumably while at Harvard. Nafe says Wheeler might help him, but Wheeler says Nothing. There is this bare possibility that if Hilgard gets a fellowship you could give Lewin his salary which would be better than nothing. I think if you did write some letters about Lewin, you would create a strong case because you speak accurately on the ground of immediate past experience; but no amount of pressure will create something out of nothing. Well, we must just let each other know if anything turns up. (Boring, 1933b)

This interchange illustrates how Lewin's extraordinary personal qualities seemed to mitigate the "defect" of Jewishness (see also Ash, 1992). So engaging and persuasive was Lewin that he convinced Boring, Terman, E. L. Thorndike, and William McDougall to serve on the 1935 Sponsors Committee of his proposed Psychological Institute of the Hebrew University of Jerusalem (Marrow, 1969, p. 83). Deutsch (1992) described him as "brilliant, enthusiastic, cheerful, effervescent ... both endearing and charming" (p. 36, see also Marrow, 1969). But even Lewin's charm was insufficient to produce an offer of a permanent academic appointment in a psychology department.[15]

Although Lewin was extraordinarily well liked, it should not be thought that he had all of the qualities desired in a colleague. Terman (1934) noted to Boring that "Lewin is more like a mid-western American in personality and lacks the poise and dignity that distinguish Köhler and Koffka." Lewin's informal, enthusiastic and expressive manner was not the repertoire of stern formality of a proper German Herr Professor, a persona developed to near-comic proportions by Münsterberg (see Hale, 1980). As described in Marrow (1969), Eric Trist recalled Lewin "gesticulating and

---

[15] According to Ash (1992), the fact that Lewin's appointments were not in psychology should not be taken as evidence of discrimination. Ash argued that Lewin's positions at Cornell and the University of Iowa offered "far better funding, contact with socially relevant research issues, access to facilities, such as laboratory schools, and support from doctoral students and co-workers than he might have had at many university departments" (p. 200). But the School of Home Economics at Cornell was a "radical change" in intellectual environment (Dembo, quoted in Marrow, 1969, p. 75) and hardly the expected place for an *Ausserordentlicher Professor* from the Faculty of Philosophy at Berlin. The positions at Cornell and Iowa, which Miriam Lewin described as "somewhat marginal" (1992, p. 17), can provide no evidence for or against discrimination in other departments. I have been unable to find evidence that Lewin ever received an offer of permanent, tenure-stream employment from a psychology department. Miriam Lewin (personal communication, September 16, 1996) cannot recall any such offers. The invitations to host the Research Center for Group Dynamics at MIT or the University of California, Berkeley (see Deutsch, 1992), cannot be counted as such positions. Given the correspondence and general climate outlined in Winston (1996) and in the present article, it remains likely that antisemitism played some role in Lewin's career options (see also Sokal [1984b] for a discussion of Lewin's appointments and related correspondence).

talking excitedly" to Frederic Bartlett in a visit to Cambridge in August 1933. Five months earlier, in response to Boring's request for help for Lewin, Bartlett (1933) had written:

> I greatly fear that nothing can be done for him on this side. I would like nothing better than to have Lewin here for a year or two or even permanently.... Unfortunately also his is only one of numerous similar cases that are coming along owing to the present deplorable German situation. *From a social point of view* I think I can understand a little of what lies behind the persecution, but I think they are making a terrible mistake which may cause them very great regret before many years go by. (italics added)

There is no evidence that Bartlett thought ill of Lewin. But to Bartlett, "gesticulating excitedly" might not have been the demeanor of an ideal colleague and would have been consistent with common stereotypes of Jews. Even in the informality of America, Lewin's style might not have been entirely proper to potential colleagues at Harvard, Yale, Princeton, or many other schools.[16]

Yet Boring's efforts to help Lewin were undoubtedly sincere. He was equally sincere in his attempts to help Saul Rosenzweig (PhD Harvard, 1932) and Jerome D. Frank (PhD Harvard, 1934) while identifying both as Jews for some positions but not for others.[17] As the Depression worsened, Boring despaired of helping anyone find a job through the "employment agency," a situation that did not change until the postwar boom in psychology. In 1936–1937, Heinz Werner had a visiting professorship at Harvard, but in April 1937 Boring wrote to Lewin:

> I am distressed and worried about Werner.... What in the world am I to do about Werner, since there is no other job for him here when Allport shall have come back and resumed his entire salary? (Boring, 1937)[18]

Thus Boring lent his influence and effort for individual Jewish psychologists while *usually* satisfying his obligation for full disclosure. In the case of émigrés such as Lewin and Werner, the task of finding employment was doubly difficult. Space precludes extended discussion of the émigré psychologists (but see Ash, 1996; Mandler & Mandler, 1969; Sokal, 1984a, 1984b; Wellek, 1968). Their success in finding suitable academic employ-

---

[16] For a useful discussion of the role of politeness and decorum in the history of Christian–Jewish relations, see Cuddihy (1974).

[17] For a variety of reasons, Frank left psychology, earned an MD, and began a distinguished career in psychiatry (Frank, 1935; Jerome D. Frank, personal communication, June 20, 1995). Rosenzweig, a distinguished clinical psychologist, remained on cordial terms with Boring until Boring's death (Saul Rosenzweig, personal communication, July 30, 1995).

[18] See Franklin (1990) for a discussion of Werner's career. Her careful analysis makes no mention of the potential role of antisemitism in Werner's career difficulties. For mention of Werner's Jewish identity by Woodworth, see Winston (1996).

ment was highly variable. In cases such as that of Werner, who did not receive a regular faculty appointment until the 1947 invitation to Clark, it is not possible to assess the relative contributions of the Depression, foreignness, and Jewishness. However, it is clear that APA did not make the assistance of the émigrés a high priority; only $50 was budgeted for the Committee on Displaced Foreign Psychologists during its first year, and the committee spent less than $1,000 from 1938 to 1943 (see Mandler & Mandler, 1969; Samelson, 1992). The successes of the committee are generally attributed to the hard work of Barbara Burks and the other members: Gordon Allport, William A. Hunt, David B. Klein, Gardner Murphy, Saul Rosenzweig, Edward C. Tolman, and Max Wertheimer. Their position, given the substantial number of "domestic" unemployed psychologists, was a difficult one, and their request for adequate funding apparently went unheeded (see Burks, 1940). Boring summed up the situation in response to a request to help a Dr. Eliasberg, "I don't know what in the world we are going to do about the European exiles. The need is so much greater than there are ways of meeting it." He suggested contacting Burks and closed with: "Beyond this there is nothing I can say. My hands are tied" (Boring, 1938).

"IT SIMPLY CANNOT BE HELPED"

Boring also felt his "hands tied" in the case of his own Jewish graduate students. Leo Hurvich, who received his PhD in 1936, was repeatedly rejected for academic positions.[19] The extent of the problem is indicated by a letter Boring received from Samuel Fernberger, who was on the faculty at Clark when Boring arrived there in 1919. Fernberger, known by all to be Jewish, served as APA secretary and treasurer and maintained a cordial relationship with Boring. On May 4, Boring (1940a) wrote to Fernberger recommending Hurvich for a 1-year position and noted: "Of course he is a Jew. I do not think that we have a trace of anti-semitism here in the Department anywhere, except as against the great problem of placing Jews." But Fernberger (1940) replied on May 20:

> Both Twitmyer and I are convinced that he is the best person available for this particular job and that he has better qualifications and interests than we could have hoped for. But I am extremely sorry to say that we cannot ask him to come.... We cannot ask him simply and solely because of his Jewish background. And you will realize the situation when you remember that Viteles and I are both in the Department. We simply, as a department cannot afford to take on another

---

[19]I am indebted to an anonymous reviewer who brought the archival material on Hurvich and additional letters to my attention. I am also indebted to Leo Hurvich for his comments on all the material.

even for an annual appointment ... it simply cannot be helped no matter how much we all regret the situation.[20]

Thus Fernberger and Viteles, both Jewish, could "not afford" another Jew in the department. Given the commonly held stereotype that Jews would "stick together" and hire other Jews, it is likely that they feared such accusations from both colleagues and administrators.[21]

The case of Hurvich upset Gordon Allport, who also was trying to find him a place, and he immediately sent a note to Boring stating that he would "struggle against the suspicion of anti-Semitism creeping into this Department" (Allport, 1940). He argued that he could not turn away qualified Jewish graduate students because of the problem of placing them but agreed with Boring that students should be informed of the employment difficulties they would face. Boring (1940b) wrote back the next day, in a rather curt tone:

> There is no great divergence between us on the matter of what should be done about Jews in American Psychology, but I do think that you use the phrase *anti-Semitism* a little too readily. (And you a psychologist interested especially in language!) Is it anti-Semitism if we give a Jew only the degree of support that we give a Gentile? Is it anti-Semitism if we give a Jew only twice as much support that we give a Gentile? ... There are situations in which all pro-Semitism is anti-Gentilism, and they happen when there is only so much to go around.

Thus Boring felt constrained not only by his obligation to identify Jews but also by his intense sense of fairness. Special efforts to find fellowships and financial support for Jews while continuing the search for a position would in his view be unfair, despite the particular barriers Jews faced. He continued the discussion of Hurvich's case in a letter to Calvin S. Hall at Western Reserve the next year, when he defended himself and his department against charges of bias. The issue arose when Boring placed Hurvich at the bottom of his list of candidates, mindful of Western Reserve's previous rejection of Jewish candidates. He noted that "You get to a stage where you hesitate to recommend him again because you feel sure that people will refuse him and you might as well spend your time on a more potentially acceptable man" (Boring, 1941). He offered the following explanations for the rejection of Jews, continuing a theme he had expressed regarding Jacob Kelson in 1925:

---

[20] Although he was rejected by the University of Pennsylvania in 1940, Hurvich was hired there as a Full Professor in 1962.

[21] Refusal of Jews to hire Jews, although not common, did occur in a wide range of employment settings during the 1920s and 1930s, generally out of fear that the hiring would provoke an antisemitic reaction. Some Jews even supported immigration restrictions and college quotas in hopes of reducing antisemitism and encouraging rapid integration. Jews were advised to "remain circumspect in their public behavior, to draw no attention to themselves as Jews" (Dinnerstein, 1994, p. 123).

(1) They do not appoint Jews because they are Jews. Word magic. (2) They do not appoint difficult personalities, and that includes competent bright men who, because of frustration, are too aggressive. The incidence of that personality is higher among bright competent Jews than among burght [sic] competent Gentiles because (1) and (2) constitute a vicious circle, the two working by mutual catalysis in the world at large. (3) They do not appoint Jews or encourage them into graduate work because they are afraid of the difficulty of placement after the present job is done. (Boring, 1941)

Boring implied that only (1) was genuine antisemitism and argued that some faculty members at Harvard fell into this category, whereas other faculty members, such as R. B. Perry, "like Jews per se and lean over in favor of them" (Boring, 1941).[22] He did not require any systematic evidence that bright Jews were more likely to be aggressive. There is little doubt that Boring was upset that bright Jewish students were not placed, "though all of us laid awake nights trying to invent new ways to place them" (Boring, 1941).

Boring's policy, as mentioned by Allport, was that incoming graduate students must be warned, a practice widely followed (Winston, 1996). Although Boring was discouraging, there is no evidence that he rejected Jewish applicants for graduate study. Jacob Levine (personal communication, February 22, 1995) recalled a cautionary letter that arrived after his interview for admission to graduate school and encouraged him to come anyway for the "intellectual stimulation," but there is no evidence that Boring ever discussed these aspects of the search for employment once the student had been admitted to graduate work. Leo Hurvich (personal communication, May 22, 1997) recalled no discussions with Boring regarding antisemitism and his job prospects. In the 1940s, Michael Zigler showed Hurvich a letter written by Boring, describing Hurvich as a "likeable Jew," and he was at least pleased that Boring viewed him positively, which was not discernable from Boring's restrained interactions (see Hurvich & Jameson, 1989). Hurvich was not a member of the "aggressive group," such as Roback and Rich, and Boring viewed Hurvich's treatment as completely unfair, resulting from Category 1 in Boring's (1941) division of causes.

Despite these difficulties, the faculty at Harvard did help Hurvich, and took the unusual step of continuing his appointment as an instructor and tutor for at least 3 additional years. Eventually, Western Reserve University did offer Hurvich a position which he did not take, but the chairman at the University of Vermont rejected him as someone who "wouldn't

---

[22]Despite Boring's assessment, Perry had been known to write exactly the same kind of letters as described here, stating that the candidate had "none of the unpleasant characteristics which are supposed to be characteristic of the race" (Perry, 1911, cited in Kuklick, 1977, p. 456). Boring repeated this characterization of Perry in a letter to Roback in 1953, suggesting that Perry thought Jews were a "bit better than Gentiles."

fit into the community" (Hurvich & Jameson, 1989, p. 171). Thus the barriers to entry were formidable but not universal. Richard L. Schanck, a close friend of Hurvich during this period, suggested that he change his name to the English-sounding "Harwich" to improve his chances (Leo Hurvich, personal communication, Oct. 29, 1997).

It might be thought that by 1941 Hurvich and others would not have faced the barriers of the previous two decades. But general antisemitism in America continued to increase during the 1930s and during World War II. Opinion polls during this period suggested that two thirds of Americans believed Jews to be "mercenary, clannish, pushy, crude, and domineering" (Shapiro, 1992, p. 5). Although one might think that the Nazis would have created some sympathy, the proportion of survey respondents who believed that Jews "had too much power" or "are a menace to Americans" increased substantially during the war (see Dinnerstein, 1994). In academic psychology during the 1930s and 1940s, the study of "race psychology" had declined, while the study of the sources of prejudice grew, as outlined by Samelson (1978). However, it is unlikely that psychology departments remained immune to the general societal misgivings over Jews when it came to hiring for the few available positions. For many, Jews remained associated not only with "objectionable traits" but with political radicalism, a most unwelcome attribute to university administrators who scrutinized new faculty appointments (e.g., see Krech, 1974).

BORING AND THE POSTWAR SHIFT

The general climate for hiring Jews changed substantially in the late 1940s, and general antisemitism continued to decline (but not disappear) in the 1950s and 1960s (e.g., see Dinnerstein, 1994; Shapiro, 1992). It is often thought that collective guilt over the Holocaust made discrimination in hiring unfashionable (e.g., Hollinger, 1996), but supply and demand also played a significant role. In academia, the situation changed quite suddenly, and Boring (1947) could now write to C. A. Dickinson of the University of Maine:

> We have no one at all to recommend for any job. The situation is so tight, the demand so heavy, the man-power so few. If I had anyone who would qualify as a second-rate person for your job I would have had six offers for him within two weeks after the moment he made up his mind to be an available candidate.

In this postwar climate, so many Jews were hired and achieved prominence in psychology that the history of earlier discrimination could easily be forgotten. This relaxation of barriers was general in academia and occurred even for the teaching of English literature and American history, two areas for which an Anglo-Saxon background was previously thought to be an absolute necessity (see Shapiro, 1992). However, Boring continued to identify Jews in letters of recommendation in the 1940s and early 1950s. When recommending Silvan Tomkins for a job at the University of California, Los Angeles, Boring (1946) wrote,

> Tomkins is a Jew. I am sure of that, although I never think about it except when I am writing letters of this sort. He has been a delightful person to have in the laboratory, a keen well-informed man with a good sense of humor. He has recently been married, not to a Jewess. I think he has some outside means.

By the early 1950s, the statement "... is a Jew" had become much less acceptable. In some circles, Jewish identity was flagged in a less direct way. Letters sometimes included a discussion about the candidate's need to take time off for religious holidays, a practice experienced by Daniel Berlyne in England and which the author of the letters thought might have eliminated Berlyne from consideration (Myers, 1973). Such an approach permitted the writer and recipient to treat the problem as a practical barrier to employment rather than an issue of hiring Jews per se. In 1953, Boring recommended a student for graduate study who "did excellent work against certain handicaps, that is to say, he missed all of the Saturday discussions in the course because of religious scruples about working on Saturday" (Boring, 1953b). The words *Jew* or *Jewish* do not appear in the letter. Boring's reasons for including the Sabbath issue are difficult to assess and do not necessarily represent a continuation of earlier practices by different means; the fact that such practices were used for exclusion does not mean that Boring did so in this case. Other sources must be used to gauge whether Boring continued to be interested in Jewish identity during the 1950s.

In the Boring archives, two documents from 1953 seem to bear on Boring's approach to Jews: a questionnaire entitled "How Jewish Are You?", with data from an introductory class filled in (Figure 1) and a list of "Marriages of Jewish 'Harvard Psychologists'" (Figure 2). Both are from January 1953 and are in a file labeled "Jews in Psychology" that contains no other information or cross-references to other documents. In view of the preceding discussion and Boring's earlier letters, these documents might be read as an increasing concern over the number of Jewish students and faculty. Fortunately, careful examination of the correspondence with Roback illuminates these puzzling items and adds to the understanding of Boring's interest in Jews and Jewishness.

There was a break in correspondence between Boring and Roback during the 1930s, but the letters resumed in the 1950s. In Roback's (1952a) *History of American Psychology* he tried to do what he had done in his 1929 work, *Jewish Influence in Modern Thought*, and argued that the contributions

<u>How Jewish Are You?</u>   7 Jan. 1953

Dr. Boring wants anonymous answers to this question from the students of Psychology 1.
Please check below the proportion of your ancestors that were Jews (to the best of your knowledge and belief), fold the paper (do not sign it), and turn it in.
Dr. Boring will explain why he wants to know.

I believe that: All of my ancestors were Jews 26½

Most of them were Jews, more than 3/4 . . 1½

Three quarters of them were Jews. 0

Half of them were Jews. 0

A quarter of them were Jews 0

Only a few were Jews, less than 1/4 . . . 1

None of my ancestors was a Jew. 34

January 1953   63

Figure 1. Boring's Introductory Psychology class survey results. (E. G. Boring Papers, Harvard University Archives.) Courtesy of the Harvard University Archives.

of Jews to psychology had not been identified. In particular, Roback argued that histories such as that of Boring identified the nationalities of psychology's founders but did not identify those who were Jews. This omission was particularly egregious in the case of the Gestalt psychologists, according to Roback. M. E. Bitterman (1952), book review editor for the *American Journal of Psychology*, asked Boring to review the book and noted that "A brief look suggests that you could have quite a field day." Boring was reluctant, but agreed and wrote a very long, negative review, which was greatly shortened in the final version (Boring, 1953d). He particularly criticized Roback's notion that Jews should be identified as such and argued that Gestalt psychology was not clearly a Jewish movement. Boring granted that Gestalt psychology might have an overrepresentation of Jews, but he argued in his published review that this might be because "Jews trust one another and are more easily influenced by one another" (Boring, 1953d, p. 653).

Boring sent the original review to Roback, and they corresponded at length. Boring (1952) complained that the ads for Roback's book, in quoting from Boring's review, mistakenly identified Boring as the "head" of the Department of Psychology at Harvard, which he technically was not. Roback (1952b) countered that "It is curious that you acted as if you were head about thirty years ago when you were not, and now when you are

Marriages of Jewish "Harvard Psychologists."

J = Jew.　j = non-Jew.　Husband first, wife second.　　　January 1953.

Alpers	J-J	Gerstmans	J-j	Rogerses	j-J
Fensters	J-J	Hirshes	J-j		
Helds	J-J	Rosenbliths	J-j		
		Rosenzweigs	J-j		
		Saffords	J-j		
		Schneidemans	J-j		
		Wertheimers	J-j		
Heinemanns	J/4-J	Bruners	J?-j		
		Galamboses	J?-j		
		Solomons	J?-j?		

Figure 2. Boring's summary of intermarriage in the Harvard Psychology Department. (E. G. Boring Papers, Harvard University Archives.) Reproduced by permission of the Harvard University Archives.

getting ready to retire as emeritus, you will not admit that you are the head. Whether Harvard has official headships or not is not the point." Thus Boring and Roback began another round of argument very much like that of 30 years earlier.

Boring (1952) commented on a study Roback had conducted in 1935 using the students in Gordon Allport's Social Relations class, and he questioned Roback on how he knew which subjects were Jews, which were non-Jews, and which were "mixed bloods," to use Boring's term. Roback (1952b) wrote back that "You seem to think that every other Jew is a Miscegenatee [sic]. In all my contacts with Jews, many thousands of them, I have come across so few of mixed unions, that I treat them as curios." Boring (1953a) replied:

> Your statement that mixed marriages between a Jew and a non-Jew were so rare as to be curios was so astonishing that I took time to think about it and talk about it especially to Jewish friends. The first thing I did was to try out a little questionnaire on the members of Psychology 1, and I enclose a copy of that with the results for the 63 persons who were in attendance that day. You will see that this is in accord with your statement.
>
> There still remained a question as to why most of us here in the Laboratory, including the Jews, thought that mixed marriages were common. In this matter I have been talking especially with Walter Rosen-

blith and with Didi Stone, both Jews and both interested in the problem.... We undertook to tabulate a very loosely determined category we called "Harvard Psychologists," putting into it psychologists on the staff of our Department and of Social Relations at the present time and recently as well as graduate students in our own Department whom we know well.[23]

Thus the two documents arose from Roback's claim that Jewish intermarriage was rare. The question was important to both men—to Roback because it was his project to emphasize the distinctiveness of the Jews. For failing to recognize the distinctiveness, Roback had chastised Boring. Always the empiricist, Boring came to his own defense with these two small investigations: the classroom survey, which supported Roback's claim, and the faculty survey, which did not.

Boring did not pursue this research further, but later in 1953 he did write to Howard Jones, who had asked about Roback's book:

> My last shock with Roback is his explicit exposition of Gestalt psychology as a Jewish movement and his many complaints about me for not telling in my book when a man is a Jew, thus robbing the Jews of their rightful glory. Well I don't know how to find out whether a man is a Jew, the concept is not always as clear cut as he implies, and I never thought I was doing society a service by trying to find out until Roback put this idea into my head. (Boring, 1953c)

Thus Boring maintained in 1953 that he was completely uninterested in questions of Jewish identity and character. Certainly this disinterest was evident in his historiography, but his statement seems to assert that he was unable to identify Jews or was uninterested in doing so in all aspects of his professional life. Read this way, Boring's justification conflicts with his actions in writing letters of recommendation for the previous 30 years, practices widely shared in academic psychology. To repeat: It was an obligation to identify whether a job candidate was or might be a Jew, and whether he or she had the "defects of the race" that were expected in Jews. In general, Boring carried out this obligation, and he did try to "find out" when job placement was at issue. That he would undertake the surveys in 1953 on the strength of a sentence from Roback suggests that the "problem" of the Jews, at least in the historiographic context, remained a troubling one for Boring. So stung was Boring by Roback's charge that he had been unfair to the Jews in his *History of Experimental Psychology* that he was still discussing the issue a decade later in the Harvard graduate proseminar (Lawrence Marks, personal communication, August 16, 1996).

---

[23] I interviewed Didi Stone, the widow of S. S. Stevens, on August 17, 1995, and showed her the list of "Marriages of Jewish 'Harvard Psychologists,'" but she could not recall the discussions with Boring 43 years previously. In her experience, Boring had never shown signs of antisemitism or group prejudice.

Boring's 1953 list of Jews at Harvard (Figure 2) and his discussions with Roback illustrate the uncertainties of identifying Jews: Even with help, Boring listed Bruner, Galambos, and Solomon as "?". The importance of Boring's list and his survey goes beyond Boring's need to defend himself. These documents speak to the shifting constructions of Jewish identity during the postwar period. With increasing assimilation and a decline in racial conceptions of Jews, the multiple definitions and layers of Jewish identity in terms of parentage, religious practice, ethnicity, and culture made the identification of Jewish job candidates an even more uncertain task.

CONCLUSIONS

Given the prestige of Boring and Harvard, there can be little doubt that Boring's "employment agency" was highly influential from the 1920s to the 1950s. The widespread practice by which Jewish job candidates were scrutinized for the expected "objectionable traits" meant there was a powerful disincentive for any display of Jewish identity or any interpersonal habits that non-Jews thought marked one as a Jew. With "good behavior" and some luck, the issue might never come up. Thus Boring could report to Roback that "I have never known whether Langfeld is Jewish or not, although he is one of my best friends" (Boring, 1953a).[24] The selection processes from graduate school on would have favored those assimilated Jews with no involvement in Jewish observance or Jewish community life. As Bruner (1983) noted in his autobiography:

> To the idealistic young Jew who 'makes it' at Harvard, another symptom may be added to the Harvard disease. If he does not have a good immune system, he turns into a simulated Wasp: Wasp wife, Wasp tastes, even Wasp sports. (p. 244)

The personal cost of concealing Jewish identity, a very common feature of life through the 1950s, can only be guessed at. For many who had been reared in secularized American families, there was little to conceal (see Rubin, 1995). For others, the difficulties in making one's way in a hostile environment may have contributed to the pattern of "Jewish self-hatred" which K. Lewin (1941/1948) described so cogently.

Recently, Hollinger (1996) argued that it was the influx of secularized Jews into postwar academia that transformed so many disciplines. For Hol-

---

[24]The case of Langfeld illustrates just how uncertain the identification of Jews could be. Roback (1953) insisted that Langfeld was from an old Jewish family in Philadelphia. However, Richard von Mayrhauser (personal communication, September 14, 1996) discovered a June 3, 1922 letter from Langfeld to Boring in the Harvard Archives in which it appears that Langfeld makes a mildly antisemitic remark to Boring. Whether Langfeld gave up, was unaware of, was thereby concealing, or had no Jewish origins remains uncertain.

linger, this process was part of the "de-Christianization" and secularization of American intellectual life and the decline of the Protestant hegemony. But in psychology, some features of this change had already taken place. The prominent psychologists of the early 20th century were already highly secularized; many had abandoned plans to enter the ministry or abandoned religion altogether. These psychologists sought a universalistic description of human life that transcended cultural and historical particulars. In contrast, Roback, with his deep commitment to Yiddish culture and Jewish organizations, represented the kind of "parochial Jew" who could not be suitable for the new science of behavior. Although even secularized Jews were denied entry in the 1930s, their "cosmopolitanism" would be an asset for their acceptance in the 1950s.

For some historians, particularly Higham (1955, 1975), the increasing resistance to Jewish entry into academia during the 1920s and 1930s and diminished resistance after the war are part of the more general history of competition among immigrant groups arriving at different times and under different economic climates, advancing in status at different rates.[25] Higham (1955) located the problem of antisemitism as a theme within American nativism, that is, militantly defensive nationalism aroused by the belief that alien elements were intruding and threatening the life of the nation. Nativism, he argued, would surge and recede according to the social and economic crises facing society, and racial nativism was a variation of this theme. From this perspective, the increasing interest of many psychologists in "race psychology" from the early 1900s to the early 1930s was a part of this general trend. Thus many psychologists were by the mid-1920s particularly likely to see Jews in racial terms and thus to think of their "objectionable traits" within that framework.

Although he was attuned to these "objectionable traits," Boring was never a bigot or a racist. He was a sponsor of the 1938 Harvard Committee to Aid German Student Refugees, whose pamphlet was subtitled *Harvard's Book for Religious, Racial, and Political Tolerance: Expressing Opposition to Nazi Persecution*. He was a critic of racial theories, racial difference research, and the misuse of intelligence tests. So completely was Boring devoted to the principle of fairness that any serious prejudice was impossible. There is no evidence that he rejected Jewish graduate students or that he would have opposed the appointment of Jews at Harvard. A person of Boring's character, convictions, and Quaker background could never think of himself as antisemitic. He described "love of tolerance and paradoxical intolerance of intolerance" as the "attitudinal constant" that ran through his entire life (Boring, 1961, p. 82). Like Woodworth, Boring shared some of the prevailing stereotypes and antisemitic discursive practices of the times.

---

[25]For a valuable set of critiques and comments on Higham's (1955) *Strangers in the Land*, see the December 1986 issue of *American Jewish History* edited by Raphael.

To use Kuklick's (1977) measured characterization of the Harvard philosophers in the early 20th century, "they participated in, and therefore in some measure reinforced, a vicious system of prejudice" (pp. 456–457).[26] Such a characterization does not imply personal animosity toward Jews, nor is such participation incompatible with helping individual Jews or having Jewish friends.

Given that Boring was one of the most influential psychologists of the interwar period, both in terms of formal, institutional power and the informal power conferred by professional status, it might be argued that he could have protested vigorously against practices he clearly perceived to be unjust.[27] With access to so many professional groups and journals, it is difficult to see Boring, a man who helped shape the discipline, as a prisoner of a system in which "his hands were tied." Several factors may provide some understanding of Boring's actions and inactions in this arena. First, he did not believe that the failure to hire Jews with "difficult personalities" constituted a form of antisemitism, even though he believed that antisemitism helped produce "difficult personalities" in Jews. Second, given Boring's (1941) belief that bright Jews were particularly likely to be "too aggressive," the failure of a bright Jew to find employment could be explained away as a result of such aggressiveness, and in Boring's view there would be no grounds for protest. Third, he believed that the practice of discouraging Jews from pursuing academic careers was a practice of realism, not antisemitism. Boring's failure to place many Jewish students despite his influence and his efforts led to a decidedly pessimistic outlook. Boring's pessimism should be seen in the context of his own general insecurities and depression, which reached crisis proportions during the 1930s and led him to seek psychoanalysis (see Boring, 1940c). Thus Boring, with his "self-effacing humility" (Rosenzweig, 1970, p. 69), lacked the more optimistic idealism of Edward Chace Tolman, who was much more likely than Boring to engage in outspoken protest.[28] Instead, Boring adopted the strategy of explicitly warning incoming Jewish graduate students and then never discussing the issue with them again. He does not seem to have recognized how this approach might be both realistic and at the same time serve to perpetuate the existing order. Nor did he sense the terrible bind created

---

[26]Kuklick (1977) was referring specifically to Ralph Barton Perry, James Woods, Ernest Hocking, and C. I. Lewis, and their letters regarding Jewish students.

[27]Such pursuit of historic counterfactuals is, for good reason, highly unfashionable (but see Turner, 1997, for a recent example). It is not my intention to assert Boring's omnipotence or revivify a moribund "Great Person History." Nevertheless, the meaning of "what might have been done" is quite different for those who were in powerful positions versus those who were not. I have found no indication that Boring considered the possibility of a general refusal to identify Jewish students as Jews.

[28]When Tolman refused to sign the California loyalty oath and suffered the consequences, Boring (1950) wrote to friends that "I cannot get over feeling—and Ruth Tolman does not like this in me—the oath business in California was a case of hysteria being fought with a little hysteria, and that Edward Tolman let his idealism run away with his wisdom."

by his assumption of a correlation between talent and aggressiveness in Jews: Those who most deserved an academic appointment on intellectual grounds were, by implication, most likely to deserve exclusion on personal grounds. Given the importance of achieving a favorable ranking in Boring's letters, it would have required extraordinary social skills for a Jewish graduate student to demonstrate intellectual superiority over other students while at the same time appearing sufficiently modest and unaggressive.[29] But "good behavior" still provided no insurance against antisemitism (K. Lewin, 1940/1948).

The consequences of these practices extended beyond the social history of the discipline. Whereas some promising careers were undoubtedly ended by the exclusion from academic positions, others were deflected. A number of Harvard's Jewish students moved to clinical work, often for a complex interplay of reasons, a pattern that was repeated at Columbia and elsewhere (see Winston, 1996). At Worcester State Hospital, David Shakow, Saul Rosenzweig, and others brought to bear their rigorous experimental training and deep interest in psychoanalytic theory to develop new research strategies, diagnostic methods, and training programs. In the interwar period, the direction and shape of clinical psychology and other areas may have been influenced by the experimental commitments and training of those who could not pursue these commitments in the university. Some émigré psychologists, such as Werner, who held academic positions in Europe now found themselves in applied settings, and their subsequent contributions to the discipline were certainly altered by these experiences.[30] The amalgam of respectable academic background, experimental outlook, and extensive clinical experience placed Shakow, Rosenzweig, and others in a unique position to provide leadership in the great postwar expansion of clinical psychology and to lay the foundations for much experimental research in psychopathology. The coincidence of the general decline in antisemitism with the sudden expansion of clinical psychology produced an ironic turn: By the late 1940s, some of those who had been forced to migrate out of academia were now welcomed back in, despite the alleged "defects of their race."

REFERENCES

A. A. Roback, Educator, Dead; Psychologist and Prolific Writer. (1965, June 8). *The New York Times*, p. 41.

Allport, G. (1940, May 22). Letter to E. G. Boring. E. G. Boring Papers, courtesy of Harvard University Archives.

---

[29] Women faced an analogous dilemma somewhat later in both academic and corporate realms.
[30] See Ash (1996) for a useful analysis of émigré career dynamics.

Ash, M. (1992). Cultural contexts and scientific change in psychology: Kurt Lewin in Iowa. *American Psychologist, 47*, 198–207.

Ash, M. G. (1996). Emigré psychologists after 1933: The cultural coding of scientific and professional practices. In M. G. Ash & A. Söllner (Eds.), *Forced migration and scientific change: Emigre German-speaking scientists and scholars after 1933* (pp. 117–138). Cambridge, England: Cambridge University Press.

Bartlett, F. C. (1933, April 25). Letter to E. G. Boring. E. G. Boring Papers, Harvard University Archives.

Bentley, M. (1926, March 26). Letter to E. G. Boring. E. G. Boring Papers, Harvard University Archives.

Bitterman, M. E. (1952, July 15). Letter to E. G. Boring. E. G. Boring Papers, Harvard University Archives.

Blumenthal, A. (1991). The intrepid Joseph Jastrow. In G. Kimble, M. Wertheimer, & C. White (Eds.), *Portraits of pioneers in psychology* (pp. 75–87). Washington, DC: American Psychological Association.

Boring, E. G. (1923, February 1). Letter to Louis Terman. E. G. Boring Papers, Harvard University Archives.

Boring, E. G. (1925a, April 22). Letter to J. H. White. E. G. Boring Papers, Harvard University Archives.

Boring, E. G. (1925b, May 5). Letter to Erving Betts. E. G. Boring Papers, Harvard University Archives.

Boring, E. G. (1925c, May 7). Letter to Stevenson Smith. E. G. Boring Papers, Harvard University Archives.

Boring, E. G. (1925d, July 27). Letter to Madison Bentley. E. G. Boring Papers, Harvard University Archives.

Boring, E. G. (1926a, March 29). Letter to Madison Bentley. E. G. Boring Papers, Harvard University Archives.

Boring, E. G. (1926b, April 24). Letter to J. H. White. E. G. Boring Papers, Harvard University Archives.

Boring, E. G. (1926c, December 18). Letter to R. H. Wheeler. E. G. Boring Papers, Harvard University Archives.

Boring, E. G. (1930, January 7). Letter to H. E. Israel. E. G. Boring Papers, Harvard University Archives.

Boring, E. G. (1931a, May 18). Letter to Lewis Terman. E. G. Boring Papers, Harvard University Archives.

Boring, E. G. (1931b, July 31). Letter to Lewis Terman. E. G. Boring Papers, Harvard University Archives.

Boring, E. G. (1931c, August 18). Letter to Lewis Terman. E. G. Boring Papers, Harvard University Archives.

Boring, E. G. (1931d, October 6). Letter to Lewis Terman. E. G. Boring Papers, Harvard University Archives.

Boring, E. G. (1931e, November 27). Letter to William J. Robbins. E. G. Boring Papers, Harvard University Archives.

Boring, E. G. (1931f, December 19). Letter to William J. Robbins. E. G. Boring Papers, Harvard University Archives.

Boring, E. G. (1933a, April 7). Letter to Robert S. Woodworth. Robert S. Woodworth Papers, Columbia University Archives.

Boring, E. G. (1933b, April 17). Letter to Lewis Terman. E. G. Boring Papers, Harvard University Archives.

Boring, E. G. (1934, June 29). Letter to C. A. Dickinson. E. G. Boring Papers, Harvard University Archives.

Boring, E. G. (1935, October 5). Letter to Carney Landis. E. G. Boring Papers, Harvard University Archives.

Boring, E. G. (1937, April 20). Letter to Kurt Lewin. E. G. Boring Papers, Harvard University Archives.

Boring, E. G. (1938, December 5). Letter to Ellis Levy. E. G. Boring Papers, Harvard University Archives.

Boring, E. G. (1939, October 4). Letter to Jacob Levine. E. G. Boring Papers, Harvard University Archives.

Boring, E. G. (1940a, May 4). Letter to Samuel Fernberger. E. G. Boring Papers, Harvard University Archives.

Boring, E. G. (1940b, May 23). Letter to Gordon Allport. E. G. Boring Papers, Harvard University Archives.

Boring, E. G. (1940c). Was this analysis a success? *Journal of Abnormal and Social Psychology, 35,* 4–16.

Boring, E. G. (1941, July 4). Letter to Calvin S. Hall. E. G. Boring Papers, Harvard University Archives.

Boring, E. G. (1946, March 12). Letter to Roy Dorcus. E. G. Boring Papers, Harvard University Archives.

Boring, E. G. (1947, May 2). Letter to C. A. Dickinson. E. G. Boring Papers, Harvard University Archives.

Boring, E. G. (1950, October 17). Letter to Karl and Beth de Schweinitz. E. G. Boring Papers, Harvard University Archives.

Boring, E. G. (1952, December 9). Letter to A. A. Roback. E. G. Boring Papers, Harvard University Archives.

Boring, E. G. (1953a, January 20). Letter to A. A. Roback. E. G. Boring Papers, Harvard University Archives.

Boring, E. G. (1953b, April 17). Letter to Boston University Graduate School. E. G. Boring Papers, Harvard University Archives.

Boring, E. G. (1953c, May 14). Letter to Howard M. Jones. E. G. Boring Papers, Harvard University Archives.

Boring, E. G. (1953d). Review of *History of American Psychology*, by A. A. Roback. *American Journal of Psychology, 66,* 651–654.

Boring, E. G. (1961). *Psychologist at large: An autobiography and selected essays.* New York: Basic Books.

Bruner, J. (1983). *In search of mind: Essays in autobiography*. New York: Harper & Row.

Burks, B. S. (1940). Report of the Committee on Displaced Foreign Psychologists. *Psychological Bulletin, 37*, 715–718.

Cason, H. (1932, March 7). Letter to Robert M. Yerkes. Robert M. Yerkes Papers, Manuscripts and Archives, Yale University Library.

Cerullo, J. J. (1988). E. G. Boring: Reflections on a disciplinary builder. *American Journal of Psychology, 101*, 561–575.

Cuddihy, J. M. (1974). *The ordeal of civility: Freud, Marx, Lévi-Strauss and the Jewish struggle with modernity*. New York: Basic Books.

Dallenbach, K. (1934, March 12). Letter to E. G. Boring. E. G. Boring Papers, Harvard University Archives.

Deutsch, M. (1992). Kurt Lewin: The tough-minded and tender-hearted scientist. *Journal of Social Issues, 48*, 31–43.

Dinnerstein, L. (1994). *Antisemitism in America*. New York: Oxford University Press.

Fernberger, S. W. (1940, May 20). Letter to E. G. Boring. E. G. Boring Papers, Harvard University Archives.

Finison, L. J. (1976). Unemployment, politics, and the history of organized psychology. *American Psychologist, 31*, 747–755.

Frank, J. D. (1935, February 27). Letter to E. G. Boring. E. G. Boring Papers, Harvard University Archives.

Franklin, M. (1990). Reshaping psychology at Clark: The Werner era. *Journal of the History of the Behavioral Sciences, 26*, 176–189.

Geuter, U. (1992). *The professionalization of psychology in Nazi Germany* (R. J. Holmes, Trans.). New York: Cambridge University Press.

Grant, M. (1916). *The passing of the great race, or the racial basis of European history*. New York: Scribner.

Hale, M. (1980). *Human science and social order: Hugo Münsterberg and the origins of applied psychology*. Philadelphia: Temple University Press.

Higham, J. (1955). *Strangers in the land: Patterns of American nativism, 1860–1925*. New Brunswick, NJ: Rutgers University Press.

Higham, J. (1975). *Send these to me: Jews and other immigrants in urban America*. New York: Atheneum.

Hirsch, N. D. (1930). *Twins: Heredity and environment*. Cambridge, MA: Harvard University Press.

Hollinger, D. (1996). *Scicence, Jews, and secular culture: Studies in mid-twentieth century American intellectual history*. Princeton, NJ: Princeton University Press.

Hull, C. (1932, February 25). Letter to Robert M. Yerkes. Robert M. Yerkes Papers, Manuscripts, and Archives, Yale University Library.

Hurvich, L. M., & Jameson, D. (1989). Leo M. Hurvich and Dorothea Jameson. In G. Lindzey (Ed.), *A history of psychology* (Vol. 8, pp. 157–208). Stanford, CA: Stanford University Press.

Jaynes, J. (1969). Edwin Garrigues Boring: 1889–1968. *Journal of the History of the Behavioral Sciences, 5,* 99–112.

Kelly, B. (1981). Inventing psychology's past: E. G. Boring's historiography in relation to the psychology of his time. *Journal of Mind and Behavior, 2,* 229–241.

Klingenstein, S. (1991). *Jews in the American academy 1900–1940: The dynamics of intellectual assimilation.* New Haven, CT: Yale University Press.

Krech, D. (1974). David Krech. In G. Lindzey (Ed.), A history of psychology in autobiography (Vol. 6, pp. 219–250). Englewood Cliffs, NJ: Prentice Hall.

Kuklick, B. (1977). *The rise of American philosophy, Cambridge, Massachusetts 1869–1930.* New Haven, CT: Yale University Press.

Lewin, K. (1948). Bringing up the Jewish child. In G. W. Lewin (Ed.), *Resolving social conflicts: Selected papers on group dynamics* (pp. 169–185). New York: Harper & Brothers. (Original work published 1940)

Lewin, K. (1948). Self-hatred among Jews. In G. W. Lewin (Ed.), *Resolving social conflicts: Selected papers on group dynamics* (pp. 186–200). New York: Harper & Brothers. (Original work published 1941)

Lewin, M. (1992). The impact of Kurt Lewin's life on the place of social issues in his work. *Journal of Social Issues, 48,* 15–29.

Mandler, J., & Mandler, G. (1969). The diaspora of experimental psychology: The Gestaltists and others. In D. Fleming & B. Bailyn (Eds.), *The intellectual migration: Europe and America, 1930–1960* (pp. 371–419). Cambridge, MA: Harvard University Press.

Marrow, A. (1969). *The practical theorist: The life and work of Kurt Lewin.* New York: Basic Books.

Minton, H. (1988). *Lewis M. Terman: Pioneer in psychological testing.* New York: New York University Press.

Moore, J. S. (1928, May 26). Letter to E. G. Boring. E. G. Boring Papers, Harvard University Archives.

Myers, C. R. (1973). *Interviews with eminent psychologists: Daniel E. Berlyne.* (Transcript provided by Dr. Gerald C. Cupchik, University of Toronto)

O'Donnell, J. M. (1979). The crisis of experimentalism in the 1920s: E. G. Boring and his uses of history. *American Psychologist, 34,* 289–295.

Pauly, P. J. (1987). *Controlling life: Jacques Loeb and the engineering ideal in biology.* New York: Oxford University Press.

Poliakov, L. (1965–1985). *History of anti-semitism, Vols. 1–4* (R. Howard, Trans.). New York: Vanguard Press.

Raphael, M. L. (Ed.). (1986). A reexamination of a classic work in American Jewish history: John Higham. Stranger in the land. *American Jewish History, 76,* 107–226.

Roback, A. A. (1929). *Jewish influence in modern thought.* Cambridge, MA: Sci-Art.

Roback, A. A. (1952a). *History of American psychology.* New York: Library.

Roback, A. A. (1952b, December 15). Letter to E. G. Boring. E. G. Boring Papers, Harvard University Archives.

Roback, A. A. (1953, January 24). Letter to E. G. Boring. E. G. Boring Papers, Harvard University Archives.

Rosenzweig, S. (1970). E. G. Boring and the Zeitgeist: Eduditione gesta beavit. *Journal of Psychology, 75,* 59–71.

Ross, D. (1972). *G. Stanley Hall: The psychologist as prophet.* Chicago: University of Chicago Press.

Rubin, B. (1995). *Assimilation and its discontents.* New York: Random House.

Samelson, F. (1978). From "race psychology" to "studies in prejudice": Some observations on the thematic reversal in social psychology. *Journal of the History of the Behavioral Sciences, 14,* 265–278.

Samelson, F. (1992). The APA between the world wars: 1918 to 1941. In R. Evans, V. Sexton, & T. Cadwallader (Eds.), *The American Psychological Association: A historical perspective* (pp. 119–147). Washington, DC: American Psychological Association.

Sarason, S. B. (1988). *The making of a psychologist: An autobiography.* San Francisco: Jossey-Bass.

Sarbin, T. R. (1994). Steps to the narratory principle: An autobiographical essay. In D. J. Lee (Ed.), *Life and story: Autobiographies for a narrative psychology* (pp. 7–38). Westport, CT: Praeger.

Shapiro, E. S. (1992). *A time for healing: American Jewry since World War II.* Baltimore: Johns Hopkins University Press.

Sokal, M. M. (1984a). The Gestalt psychologists in behaviorist America. *American History Review, 89,* 1240–1263.

Sokal, M. M. (1984b). James McKeen Cattell and American psychology in the 1920s. In J. Brozek (Ed.), *Explorations in the history of psychology in the United States* (pp. 273–323). Cranbury, NJ: Associated University Presses.

Sokal, M. M. (1990). G. Stanley Hall and the institutional character of psychology at Clark, 1889–1920. *Journal of the History of the Behavioral Sciences, 26,* 114–124.

Stout, D., & Stuart, S. (1990, June). *E. G. Boring's review of Brigham's A study of American intelligence: A case study in the politics of reviews.* Paper presented at the 22nd annual meeting of Cheiron, the International Society for the History of Behavioral and Social Sciences, Westfield State College, Westfield, MA.

Synnott, M. G. (1979). *The half-opened door: Discrimination and admissions at Yale, Harvard, and Princeton, 1900–1970.* Westport, CT: Greenwood Press.

Synnott, M. G. (1986). Anti-semitism and American universities: Did quotas follow the Jews? In D. A. Gerber (Ed.), *Anti-semitism in American history* (pp. 233–171). Urbana: University of Illinois Press.

Terman, L. (1931, August 13). Letter to E. G. Boring. E. G. Boring Papers, Harvard University Archives.

Terman, L. (1933, April 11). Letter to E. G. Boring. E. G. Boring Papers, Harvard University Archives.

Terman, L. (1934, November 25). Letter to E. G. Boring. E. G. Boring Papers, Harvard University Archives.

Turner, H. A. (1997). *Hitler's thirty days to power: January, 1933*. Reading, MA: Addison Wesley Longman.

Wechsler, H. (1977). *The qualified student: A history of selective college admission in America*. New York: Wiley.

Wellek, A. (1968). The impact of the German immigration on the development of American psychology. *Journal of the History of the Behavioral Sciences, 4,* 207–229.

Winston, A. S. (1996). "As his name indicates": R. S. Woodworth's letters of reference and employment for Jewish psychologists in the 1930s. *Journal of the History of the Behavioral Sciences, 32,* 30–43.

27

RECONTEXTUALIZING KENNETH B. CLARK: AN AFROCENTRIC PERSPECTIVE ON THE PARADOXICAL LEGACY OF A MODEL PSYCHOLOGIST–ACTIVIST

LAYLI PHILLIPS

I look back and I shudder at how naive we all were in our belief in the steady progress racial minorities would make through programs of litigation and education, and while I very much hope for the emergence of a revived civil rights movement with innovative programs and dedicated leaders, I am forced to recognize that my life has, in fact, been a series of glorious defeats. (K. B. Clark, 1989, p. 18)

Much earlier versions of this article were presented at the annual meetings of the Association for the Study of Afro-American Life and History, Atlanta, Georgia, and in the Department of Psychology, University of Georgia, both in October 1994. I thank Lee D. Baker and Roger K. Thomas for extremely helpful comments on prepublication drafts of this article, Josh C. Haskell for transcribing the interview I conducted with Kenneth B. Clark in October 1994, and Russia Hughes for her role in arranging the interview. I offer much thanks, of course, to Kenneth B. Clark for participating in the interview, which allowed me to fill in some of the gaps in the historical record and to obtain a first-person view of my biographical subject. Reprinted from *History of Psychology, 3,* 142–167 (2000). Copyright © 2000 by the American Psychological Association. Reprinted with permission of the author.

Kenneth B. Clark is a scientist with whose role in history I have long been fascinated.[1] Best known for his research on racial self-concept in Black children and also for his important contributions to the National Association for the Advancement of Colored People Legal Defense Fund's (NAACP–LDF) battle for an end to legalized racial segregation in the United States in *Brown v. Board of Education* (1954), Clark was also the first and only Black president of the American Psychological Association (APA) and has been the author of numerous books on race-related topics.[2] He is considered one of the most important early figures in both social psychology and Black psychology (Guthrie, 1998; see photograph).

Although Clark has been regarded as a hero of the civil rights movement for his role in *Brown v. Board of Education*, his reputation declined, particularly among Black social scientists, with the rise of the Black Power movement, and it has continued to be controversial ever since (Martin, 1992). There appear to be five reasons for this: (a) His overtly expressed devotion to "integration"; (b) the relationship between his book *Dark Ghetto* and Sen. Daniel Patrick Moynihan's report *The Negro Family: A Case for National Action* (1965); (c) his direct criticism of the Black Power movement; (d) his failure to join the "Black strengths" bandwagon within the social sciences, as exemplified by books such as Andrew Billingsley's *Black Families in White America* (1968) and Robert Staples's *The Black Family* (1971), and his insistence on instead maintaining a within-race critical stance; and (d) his perceived progenitorship of and association with notable Black conservatives, such as William Julius Wilson and Michael Mayer. All in all, these points of contention add up to an often-unstated perception that Clark has failed to live up to the promise of the early stance he demonstrated in *Brown*; there are disappointment and chagrin that he has failed to identify or align himself with later incarnations of the very same struggle that he was fighting in 1954—the struggle to obtain quality, and equality of, education for Black children and youths and, by extension, to overcome all vestiges of the inequalities generated by 350 years of slavery and a half century of legally sanctioned segregation for all Black Americans.

My purpose in this article is to present Kenneth B. Clark, now 85, as an exemplary Afrocentric scientist–activist through a recontextualiza-

---

[1]In keeping with the womanist scientific principle of locating oneself and one's perspective at the center of inquiry and acknowledging and highlighting one's own biases, I use the first-person voice in this article. Furthermore, in keeping with the womanist principle that people should be allowed to speak for themselves, Clark will be quoted rather than paraphrased whenever possible in this article.

[2]It is important to note that many of Clark's professional activities, such as the racial self-concept studies and the founding of the Northside Center for Child Development in New York City, were carried out with his fellow psychologist and wife, Mamie Phipps Clark. Indeed, it was Mamie who devised the well-known doll technique used by the Clarks (Kluger, 1976). Although Mamie Clark is not the topic of this article, her contributions to psychology and U.S. society strongly warrant their own historiographic examination.

tion and rehistoricization of his actions and statements across 65 years of public and scholarly life. I argue that close inspection of Clark's life, including careful consideration of its patterned complexities and curious inconsistencies, yields important insights about the effects of personal background on the conduct of science and the effects of historical and political contingencies on the extrapolation of scientific findings to other contexts.

WHAT DEFINES AN AFROCENTRIC SCHOLAR?

I take my insights about what defines an Afrocentric[3] scholar primarily from the writings of two contemporary social scientists with influential writings on the philosophy of science from an Afrocentric view: Linda James Myers and Patricia Hill Collins. Although I agree with Mama (1995) that "there is no single set of principles that can be defined as the essential African philosophy" (p. 57), I do believe it is useful to imagine alternate epistemological bases for social scientific praxis, as Myers (1991) and Hill Collins (1991) have skillfully and provocatively done.

According to Myers (1991), the Afrocentric worldview places the highest value on positive interpersonal relations between individuals as well as groups. Thus, all scientific praxis ideally contributes toward this aim. The scientist begins her or his approach to discovery or knowledge production from a place of self-knowledge that is rooted in personal experience, collective consciousness, or both. Such a scientist enters into scientific activity with an openness to the interconnection between material and spiritual planes of existence and their reciprocal causality with regard to events of interest. Furthermore, according to Myers (1991; but also see C. Clark, 1972), the Afrocentrically inclined scientist is more interested in "understanding and unification" than in "prediction and control" (p. 23). Borrowing from Cruse (1967), she ultimately argues that, within the traditional Western, positivist scientific context, Afrocentric scientists have a special responsibility to redeem humanity—particularly Blacks and other oppressed peoples of the world—from the inhumanities levied by the scientific community's endorsement of prediction and control of humans by other humans. Thus, an Afrocentric scientist is, by default, a scientist–activist.

Hill Collins (1991) rejected the dichotomy between scholarship and activism, thinking and doing, for Afrocentric[4] researchers. In addition, she

---

[3]*Afrocentric* is used in this article as a general term that refers to people of African descent who have retained psychocultural remnants of their African heritage, in this case, as modified by their passage through the Caribbean and America. The term is not being used to reference or connect to any specific individual or position within what has been referred to as the Afrocentricity Movement.

[4]Although Hill Collins (1991) focused on Black feminist epistemology, it is my position that the specific points being discussed herein apply equally well to Afrocentric male and female scholars.

Kenneth Bancroft Clark and Mamie Phipps Clark, circa 1960 (photo by Ken Heyman). Courtesy of the Library of Congress.

has included empowerment as a step in the scientific process; that is, she claimed that an Afrocentric scientist cannot rest on her or his scientific production but rather must somehow apply it toward the betterment of humankind before the scientific process can be considered complete or one's role as a scientist can be considered fulfilled. The notions of scientific objectivity and subject–object distance lose validity for Afrocentric scholars precisely because of their contributions to oppression and exploitation of Black people and others (see also Phillips, 1994a). Afrocentric science demands the explication of each researcher's own assumptions, biases, and objectives, particularly as they pertain to such essentialized categories as race, class, and gender, and also requires that scholarly productions be historicized.[5]

Although neither Myers (1991) nor Hill Collins (1991) argued that all people of African descent identify with or operate within Afrocentric frames, both offered Afrocentric perspectives as culturally situated alternatives to traditional scientific positivism. It must be acknowledged, however, that the idea of an Afrocentric perspective has been challenged on the grounds that it essentializes Blackness or, alternatively, Africanness, and that it oversimplifies and, in some respects, mocks Black subjectivity (e.g., see Gilroy, 1993; Richards, 1997; and Mama, 1995). I argue that Afrocentric perspectives, however problematic and imperfectly devised they may appear from certain angles, offer a succinct yet comprehensive counterpoint to traditional positivist social scientific perspectives. These Afrocentric perspectives are important not only because they represent the phenomenology of a segment of people whose experience has been summarily dismissed or selectively distorted within social science but also because they challenge the cultural exclusivity of social science as an endeavor altogether. Without forcefully stated alternatives to the meta-theoretical status quo, one cannot step outside or beyond the lenses that currently frame and constrain his or her vision. Nevertheless, one must remain cognizant that there are Afrocentricities within Afrocentricities, so to speak—that is, many ways to relate to Blackness as a Black person. Perhaps nowhere else in psychology is there a better illustration of these complexities than in the person of Kenneth B. Clark.

KENNETH B. CLARK: AFROCENTRIC SCHOLAR

Given the basic tenets of Afrocentric science, it can be argued that Clark did in fact conduct science from an Afrocentric standpoint, although he did so before a language of Afrocentric science had been explicitly developed. A rehistoricizing of Clark's scholarly and activist productions suggests that a large part of his personal struggle, and a major cause of the inconsistencies associated with some of his statements and actions, can be linked to an attempt to conduct science without an articulated Afrocentric scientific position from which to draw. The fact that Clark still surfaced as

---

[5]These insights were further confirmed by cross-cultural psychologist Robert Serpell (1994), who reported his discovery from research in Zaire on intelligence that "[t]he ideal endpoint of personal development in [indigenous African cultures] is construed as someone who can preside effectively over the settlement of a dispute, whose judgement can be trusted in questions of character, [and] who can and will take on social responsibility" (p. 160).

a pioneer, both in terms of his science and his activism, can be considered a major credit to his legacy.

Perhaps most emblematic of Clark's Afrocentric scholarship was his participation in *Brown v. Board of Education* (1954). In 1951, while an assistant professor at the City College of New York (CCNY), he was approached by NAACP lawyer Robert Carter about helping the NAACP–LDF team, headed by Thurgood Marshall, prove to the federal courts that segregation caused psychological harm to children. Kluger (1976) recounted:

> Robert Carter read Dr. Kenneth Clark's White House Conference monograph [Clark, 1950] and saw in it an Aladdin's lamp. [He came back to Clark and said,] "It's just what we're looking for. It's almost as if it were written for us." (p. 321)

Clark, quoted in Kluger (1976), stated:

> Within a few days, he came to my office with a blueprint of what they wanted me to do—and he was clear as a bell about it: (a) be a witness in the *Briggs* case, (2) enlist other social scientists, as prestigious as possible, to testify, and (3) work directly with the NAACP lawyers in going over the briefs as they dealt with the social-science material. And he wanted me to get started yesterday. (p. 321)

Quoting Kluger (1976) again:

> Clark did not hesitate. He had met Thurgood Marshall socially and occasionally visited the NAACP offices. "I both admired their work and was critical of it, much as the young people today may feel about the establishment people," Clark recounted twenty years later. "I had some doubts about the effectiveness of the legal approach in curing the basic problems, but I guess I was envious that they were actually doing something to improve things while I was off in the scholarly area, vaguely wishing to be a part of what they were doing." When the chance came, he took it. (p. 321)

Shortly after the *Brown* decision was handed down by the Supreme Court in 1954, Clark's participation in the entire process was criticized by a number of legal scholars and social scientists (Cahn, 1955; Schwartz, 1959; van den Haag, 1960). Cahn, a law professor, suggested that Clark had exaggerated his scientific findings (Cahn, 1955). He argued that Clark had failed to sample enough children; although more than 300 were sampled, only 16 were reported on directly in the South Carolina legal testimony. Perhaps more significant, Cahn argued that Clark had failed to investigate "abnormal or eccentric backgrounds" (p. 163) in the children he studied—implying that the children's putative negative reactions to segregation might be attributable to personal idiosyncracies. Regarding the amicus brief submitted to the Supreme Court by Clark and others (Clark,

Cook, & Chein, 1952[6]), Cahn wrote that he found the scientific evidence presented, Clark's in particular, to represent no innovation over "literary psychology' (by which I mean such psychological insights as one finds continually in the works of poets, novelists, essayists, journalists, and religious prophets)" (p. 161). Schwartz, a professor of sociology and law, argued that, on close inspection, Clark's racial preference studies (Clark & Clark, 1939a, 1939b, 1940, 1947, 1950) revealed less positive outcomes for children in Northern, mixed-race schools than for children in Southern, segregated schools—the opposite of what the courts seemed to be promoting (Schwartz, 1959). Van den Haag, then adjunct professor of social philosophy at New York University, echoed similar concerns; he questioned how Clark could advance the notion that segregation hurt Black children when the children in the segregated schools showed "better" outcomes than the children in the integrated schools. In what was perhaps the most scathing remark of all, van den Haag asserted that "From the Clarks' experiments, his testimony and, finally, the essay to which I am replying, the best conclusion that can be drawn is that he did not know what he was doing; and the worst, that he did" (p. 79).[7]

---

[6]Unless otherwise noted, all Clark references are to be K. B. Clark.

[7]Indeed, the "science" of the Clarks's studies (Clark & Clark 1939a, 1939b, 1940, 1947, 1950) was criticized much later during a period of resurgence in racial self-concept studies (Baldwin, Brown, & Hopkins, 1991; Banks, 1976; Brand, Ruiz, & Padilla, 1974). Several features of the studies were argued to be problematic: (a) the Clarks's choice of materials—line drawings in the first three studies and dolls that were identical in all respects except skin and hair color in the last two—which, in all probability, were not physiognomically realistic; (b) the Clarks's use of projective, rather than objective, methodology, because it assumed that young children's feelings about themselves could be inferred from stimuli that were not literal depictions (e.g., photos) of them; (c) failure to vary the order of questions during the doll study interview protocol, producing a higher likelihood of a situation in which a child might feel ambivalent about self-identifying with a doll to which she or he had attributed negative attributes previously; (d) tacit endorsement of the ethnocentric model of racial preference, in which it is considered normal to prefer one's own group over others (as opposed to a no-choice or chance pattern of responding); and (d) failure to consider the possible orthogonality of racial self-identification and racial self-esteem. These criticisms, while valid, were unforgivingly ahistorical, insofar as few realistic Black stimuli were available prior to 1960 (Baldwin et al., 1991), and ethnocentric perspectives on group identification were normalized by the pervasiveness of enforced racial segregation in the United States prior to 1954. Furthermore, it should be noted that, in their use of projective methodology, the Clarks were challenging an earlier study by Horowitz (1939), in which she argued, on the basis of similar projective tests, that young Black children's identification with White stimuli demonstrated "wishful thinking." The charge of possible order effects, however, is more difficult to dismiss. Careful critics, even contemporaneous ones, could have argued that the Clarks likely oversampled children who identified themselves with the White doll by setting up an artificially stressful choice situation and thus increased the probability of Type I error. The Clarks's contention that the fact that a "substantial proportion" of Black children chose the White doll meant that racial segregation hurt children's self-concept was undermined by their failure to present the request "Show me the doll that looks like you" before, during, and after the requests pertaining to racial preference ("Show me the doll that looks bad," "Show me the doll that you would like to play with," etc.), and the racial understanding ("Show me the Negro doll," "Show me the White Doll," etc.). Clark explained that his decision to use the single, unvarying interview protocol during South Carolina court testimony (reprinted in Cahn, 1955, p. 162): "I wanted to get the child's free expression of his opinions and feelings before I had him identified with one of these two dolls."

Clark vociferously defended the scholarly quality of his work as well as the innocence of his participation in the *Brown* proceedings on more than one occasion (Clark, 1955/1963, 1959–1960), in particular insisting that the original studies used as the basis of his court testimony had been conducted "ten years before the authors had any knowledge that these findings could have any specific practical use" (Clark, 1959–1960, p. 239; see also Clark, 1974). I argue, however, not only that Clark knew what he was doing but also that his knowledge and his resultant actions fall squarely within the parameters of Afrocentric science, which rejects a neutral engagement with one's subject matter and places a high value on activity that will advance the welfare of one's fellows. Hermeneutic writers such as Martin Heidegger (1962), Hans-Georg Gadamer (1975), and Charles Taylor (1985) have explained how this historiographic stance is different from the Machiavellian "end justifies the means" credo.

Kluger (1976) reported that even the NAACP–LDF was not aware of the "inconsistencies" in Clark's racial preference studies—in particular the finding that youngsters in Northern schools often showed evidence of less positive psychological outcomes than youngsters in Southern schools. Nevertheless, Kluger also reported that "the [NAACP–LDF] lawyers coached [David Krech], Kenneth Clark, and the other social psychologists on how to respond in the event their competence as experts was challenged by the lawyers for the state" (p. 338). The fact that Clark assented to such coaching is evidence of his feeling of solidarity with the cause that the NAACP-LDF lawyers represented. I argue that Clark's act of assent represented not a crafty act of deception but rather a calculated act of sacrifice. As I have stated elsewhere (Phillips, 1994b, 1994d), Clark had the opportunity to set the stage for the realization of his ideal vision (in this case, of education), but circumstances—in this case, the intersection of his value system with an acute historical situation, that is, the palpable yet limited opportunity presented by *Brown*—caused him to sacrifice the vision itself —at least visibly—that it might re-emerge later in fuller form. In the balance, the Afrocentric value of achieving justice and harmony among people outweighed the unseemliness of distorting an "objective" representation of a fact that he intuitively knew to be true: Racism harms Black children.[8] In fact, to present "just the facts," divorced as they were from lived experience, would itself have been a grosser distortion from an Afrocentric perspective.

---

[8] The fact that this was more clearly illustrated in his Northern than his Southern data did not undermine the basic truth. In fact, it created a paradoxical syllogism: Racism hurts children (as seen, arguably, in the Northern children); segregation is the legal residue of racism; children in the South are segregated; therefore, children in the South are hurt by racism. Between 1939 and 1954, at least in his published writings, Clark elided this paradox, subtly shifting back and forth between a discourse on the effects of segregation on children's self-concept (e.g., Clark & Clark, 1939b, 1940) and a discourse on the effects of racism on children's self-concept (e.g., Clark, 1950, 1955/1963; Clark et al., 1952).

My argument is supported in Clark's book *Pathos of Power* (1974), a collection of various essays and speeches authored by him between 1947 and 1973. In a particularly illuminating essay titled "Social Critic or Social Apologist?" he asserted that "the primary concern and loyalty that social scientists must have [is] in the search for truth *and* [italics added] justice" (p. 131). Later, he noted:

> Even with a methodology which seeks to assure a higher degree of objectivity in arriving at an understanding of social dynamics, social scientists cannot justifiably claim to be immune from class and racial biases which distort their interpretations. . . . Like other human beings, they may be receptive to the same influences—both explicit and subtle—of the groups with which they identify or those groups or individuals whom they perceive as having determinative power. (1974, p. 132)

Finally, he stated,

> Not infrequently a social system confronted with persistent social diagnosticians and dissenters seeks to protect itself from these threats by blaming the diagnosticians for the undeniable symptoms and the increased severity of the illness of the social system. But, despite persistent hostility and even repression, throughout American history there have been dissenters . . . [who] have played a major role in balancing the more pragmatic, realistic, negative symptoms of the American illness. Unlike the majority of their fellow citizens, they do not seem to have lost the capacity for outrage—they do not seem to be easily intimidated and it does not seem to be easy to silence or destroy them. They have contributed to the functional stabilization of the American society and they have *bargained for and obtained the needed time in which progression toward the health of the society could be achieved* [italics added]. (1974, p. 136)

Although one cannot be certain, it is reasonable to assume that Clark was thinking about his own inclusion in this category of individuals, as he has made his general views plain. The Afrocentrisms peal clearly through the fog of his verbiage: The request for truth and justice is inseparable; class and race inform one's "objectivity"; and bargaining for time in the interest of progress toward social welfare is acceptable, if not laudable.

Clark's commitment to Afrocentric scientific principles is more explicit in *Dark Ghetto* (1965/1989), however. In a section titled "Moral Objectivity," he stated:

> Objectivity, without question essential to the scientific perspective when it warns of the dangers of bias and prejudgement in interfering with the search for truth and in contaminating the understanding of truth, too often becomes a kind of a fetish which serves to block the view of truth itself, particularly when painful and difficult moral insights are involved. . . . When carried to its extreme, this type of objectivity could be equated with ignorance. . . . It may be that where

> essential human psychological and moral issues are at stake, noninvolvement and noncommitment and the exclusion of feeling are neither sophisticated nor objective, but naive and violative of the scientific spirit at its best.... Feeling may twist judgement, but the lack of feeling may twist it even more. (pp. 78–80)

In the introduction to the same book, he wrote:

> An important part of my creed as a social scientist is that on the grounds of absolute objectivity or on a posture of scientific detachment and indifference, a truly relative and serious social science cannot ask to be taken seriously by a society desperately in need of moral and empirical guidance in human affairs. (p. xxxv)

On the subject of "truth"—a term that appears frequently in his writings, he stated:

> A few years ago a highly respected friend ... interrupted a humorous but somewhat serious discussion by observing that I would not permit "the facts to interfere with the truth." ... To obtain the truth of Harlem, one must *interpret* the facts.... Fact is empirical while truth is interpretive. (pp. xxxvii–xxxviii)

Clearly, Clark's thinking processes reflected Afrocentric beliefs about science.

Evidence of such Afrocentric beliefs can be found in action as far back as Clark's tenure as an undergraduate at Howard University in the early 1930s. According to his autobiographical essay "Racial Progress and Retreat: A Personal Memoir" (1989), Clark indicated that, as a New York City high school student who had attended overwhelmingly White schools, he became fascinated when introduced to the possibility of attending an all-Black educational institution. He enrolled at Howard University, which at that time was considered the "Black Harvard" and boasted a faculty of such luminaries as Ralph Bunche, Alain Locke, Sterling Brown, Abraham Harris, Allison Davis, Francis Cecil Sumner, Charles Hamilton Houston, and Mordecai Johnson—a concentration that, although in some respects wonderful, was primarily due to segregation (see also Baker, 1998; Guthrie, 1998).

While at Howard, Clark, who was a psychology major, first gained notoriety as the controversial editor of the campus paper, the *Hilltop* (Kluger, 1976). A short time later, greater notoriety came when he orchestrated a demonstration against segregation in the Capitol building. He and his fellow students were arrested and charged with disorderly conduct. Although the municipal charges were eventually dismissed, the story was mentioned in *The New York Times* ("Students to Fight Evils," 1934), compelling Howard University officials to discipline the students, primarily to prevent a reaction in Congress, from whom Howard, the nation's only federal university, received its funds. Thus began Clark's scientist–activist career.

Other incidents demonstrating the inseparability of science and activism for Clark abound. In the 1940s he was the first African American to join, and thus integrate, the faculty of CCNY (Hentoff, 1982). During this same period he worked with Ralph Bunche and Gunnar Myrdal on the study that would eventually become *An American Dilemma* (Myrdal, 1944) and founded, with his wife Mamie, the Northside Center for Child Development, a child guidance center specializing in Black children. In a brief, second junior faculty position at the Hampton Institute in Hampton, Virginia, during 1941, Clark resigned when reproached by the university's White president for trying to "stimulate [his] students by combining social psychology concepts with American racial attitudes and realities" (Clark, 1989, p. 11). Next, he joined the Office of War Information to direct a study on the morale of Black civilians; the fact that he, a Black man, had been placed in charge of a mixed-race, mixed-gender research team, however, caused logistical problems that mortally impeded the research. Clark ultimately resigned from this post and returned to CCNY, where he stated that he was "surprised that [his] racial hostility did not spill over into [his] relationship with [his] colleagues" (p. 13). Clark was also active in the Society for the Psychological Study of Social Issues (SPSSI)—a relatively politically active professional organization composed of such other noted psychologists as Otto Klineberg, Gardner Murphy, and Gordon Allport. The associations and activities of this period culminated first in Clark's paper for the Mid-Century White House Conference (which can be considered activist because it resulted from Clark's being informed by Alain Locke and Otto Klineberg that no minority interests were being represented at the large-scale, federally sponsored event) and second in Clark's production (with Thomas Cook and Isidor Chein) of "The Effects of Segregation and the Consequences of Desegregation: A Social Science Statement" (1952), also known as the famous social science brief submitted to the Supreme Court in *Brown*.

Few people dispute Clark's activism in the period prior to the time the *Brown* (1954) decision was handed down. After *Brown*, Clark published the popular book *Prejudice and Your Child* (1955/1963), loosely based on the Mid-Century Conference report (Clark et al., 1952), then the book *Dark Ghetto* (1965/1989), after which much controversy ensued. Between these years, Clark participated in other activities that fall under the rubric of scientist–activist. Most notably, during the early 1960s he served as chief consultant, chairman of the board of directors, and "informed observer" of the Harlem Youth Opportunities Unlimited Project (HARYOU), on the basis of which *Dark Ghetto* was ultimately written. *Dark Ghetto* represents a turning point in Clark's reputation, particularly with African American social scientists.

As noted by Nicholas Lemann (1988), *Dark Ghetto* was considered a liberal text at the time it came out. This quickly changed, however, when its terminology, in particular the phase *tangle of pathology*, was appropriated by Daniel Patrick Moynihan in his notorious government report, *The Negro Family: A Case for National Action* (1965). In this report, Moynihan, who was once Clark's student, advanced the thesis that the "matriarchal structure" of the Black family was responsible for several of the social and economic problems associated with Blacks in America, including juvenile delinquency, higher rates of joblessness and poverty, poorer performance on mental tests, and the general failure of Blacks to assimilate fully into the American mainstream. The situation was exacerbated by the burgeoning Black Power movement, which spawned both a number of new social science perspectives (e.g., Cross, 1971; White, 1970) and a separatist backlash against the ideal of integration, to which Clark was clearly and explicitly wedded. I argue that it is at this point that a rift of misunderstanding arose between Clark and both the Black and the White general public, as Clark was placed on the defensive with regard to his (a) connection to the Moynihan agenda and the Black conservative positions it spawned and (b) deceptively radical conceptualization of the meaning and proper operationalization of the term *integration*. In the next section I explore Clark's views on integration. Following this, I attempt to locate Clark within the debate that is framed by Black conservatives and Black radicals.

CLARK'S VISION OF INTEGRATION

Clark's vision of integration is clearly discernible from his earliest scholarly productions, and his views on the subject have come into clearer focus over the years. His various statements suggest that the debate over his true views is more emblematic of the consuming public's readiness to react to red flags and red herrings than it is of any shifts of perspective on his part. I would further suggest that Clark has not been unaffected by the public's reaction to him and that the sometimes-cryptic and seemingly ambiguous nature of his various pronouncements has been the result of the interaction among his own background characteristics, traits, and goals; the historical contingencies to which he has been subjected; and the effects of the general public's reaction to him. That Clark has been so extraordinarily human—replete with the contradictions inherent in a life that has comprised both giant steps and missteps—is why his life is particularly worthy of examination.

Perhaps the best early statements giving some indication of Kenneth (and quite possibly Mamie) Clark's views on integration occurred in 1939 and 1950. First, in the article "Segregation as a Factor in the Racial Identification of Negro Pre-School Children: A Preliminary Report" (1939b), the Clarks distinguished between the semisegregated school ("all Negro children, some Negro teachers, one White teacher and a White cook," p. 161) and the mixed school ("both White and Negro children and White personnel," p. 161)—a distinction that indicated they were sensitive to the idea that "not all integration is created equal"—and found that the children in the Northern semisegregated school fared about the same as the children in the Southern segregated school, both sets of which fared better than the children in the Northern mixed school.[9] At the end of the article the Clarks remarked:

> The most obvious factor seemingly responsible for [the Northern children's confusion with regard to racial self-identification] . . . is the presence of white children of their own age in the same nursery school. . . . This suggests the possibility that the racial identifications of children in the mixed group were to a large extent determined by the physical characteristics of those in their immediate environment. It is a question, to be settled by further work, whether this social factor has not gained priority over the factor of their own skin color as a determinant of the racial identifications of Negro children. (p. 163)

At this time, only racial self-identification behavior from drawings and pictures had been studied. By the time of the later study (Clark & Clark, 1950; but see also Clark & Clark, 1947), however, both racial self-identification and racial preference had been studied, and the doll-and-coloring techniques had been added. Although a majority of Black children preferred White dolls and a large (but nonmajority) proportion of Black children identified themselves as White in the later studies that used the doll-and-coloring techniques, the most alarming psychological conditions were witnessed in Northern children rather than Southern children. The Clarks concluded:

> It is clear that the Negro child, by the age of five is aware of the fact that to be colored in contemporary American society is a mark of inferior status. . . . These results seem most significant from the point of view of what is involved in the development of a positive, constructive program for more wholesome education of Negro children in the realities of race in the American culture. They would seem to point strongly to the need for a definite mental hygiene and educational program that would relieve children of the tremendous burden of feelings of inadequacy and inferiority which seem to become integrated into the very structure of the personality as it is developing. (1950, p. 350)

That Clark was concerned and chagrined by his findings is evident in the

---

[9]Because this report is being discussed in its historical context, the Clarks's implied suggestion that in-group racial self-identification behavior constitutes positive adjustment is not being questioned at this time (but see Banks [1976] and Cross [1985] for another perspective).

fact that he waited several years to publish the data (Kluger, 1976). Nevertheless, both passages presage an implementation of integration that cannot be described as color blind or assimilatory.

The first explicit passages reflecting Clark's views on integration appeared in the amicus curiae brief submitted during *Brown* (1954), also known as the social science statement, and in *Prejudice and Your Child* (1955/1963, which, as indicated earlier, derived from the Mid-Century Conference report). In the social science statement one finds, the following passage:

> *Segregation* refers to that restriction of opportunities for different types of associations between the members of one racial, religious, national or geographic origin, or linguistic group and those of other groups, which results from or is supported by the action of any official body or agency representing some branch of government. We are not here concerned with such segregation as arises from the free movements of individuals which are neither enforced nor supported by official bodies. (Clark et al., 1952, p. 2)

I suspect that the lack of concern "here" with "unofficial" segregation was probably a reflection of the very focused, official nature of the social science brief rather than a true reflection of Clark's views because, as I show below, he has never condoned segregation of any kind and has explicitly discussed unofficial segregation elsewhere. Nevertheless, it demonstrates Clark's conviction that the government has a responsibility to moderate, and at times mediate, the relations among the various groups that society comprises. In the social science statement, Clark et al. (1952) went on to imply, and at times explicitly state, that segregation cannot be separated from the social context in which it exists—a context that is characterized by prejudice and discrimination, which themselves have such deplorable sequelae as "high disease and mortality rates, crime and delinquency, poor housing, disrupted family life and general substandard living conditions" (p. 3). These authors later stated that the ill effects of segregation are essentially founded on the facts that "enforced segregation results from the decision of the majority group without the consent of the segregated" and "historically segregation patterns in the United States were developed on the assumption of inferiority of the segregated" (p. 9). These statements underscored the social scientists' concern with inequality of power and representation among different groups in society, that is, with oppression, rather than with social assortation per se. Such themes were later further developed in Clark's writings.

Although the assumption was that the removal of barriers to free association was a necessary precondition for the removal of oppression, Clark et al. (1952) clearly believed that school integration in the absence of other corrective measures would not effect much change. Note their language in the conclusion of the social science statement:

> The available evidence ... suggests the importance of consistent and firm enforcement of the new policy by those in authority. It indicates also the importance of such factors as: the absence of competition for a limited number of facilities or benefits; the possibility of contacts which permit individuals to learn about one another as individuals; and the possibility of equivalence of positions and functions among all of the participants within the unsegregated situation. These conditions can generally be satisfied in a number of situations, as in the armed services, public housing developments, and public schools. (p. 17)

Clark echoed these sentiments in *Prejudice and Your Child* (1955/1963):

> If teachers and administrators recognize their responsibility in the area of racial practices and procedures, including a concern for the control of prejudiced behavior on the part of those in authority; if they are concerned with the constructive role of textbooks and class discussions; if they are sensitive to the many subtle human problems that may be expected in the transitional stages [of desegregation]; if they realize that the over-all atmosphere of the school, including the assignment of personnel, inevitably communicates either democratic or undemocratic racial patterns—then one can expect that in a surprisingly short time Negro and white children will gain a respect for one another based on the intelligence and personality of each individual. Such an atmosphere will produce a setting where it will be possible to provide all children with the foundations of democratic education. (p. 94)

Furthermore, he stated:

> In such a school, there will be no need for the self-conscious and often ineffectual procedure of an isolated "intergroup relations" program, with a specified duration of a day or a week. In such a school, children will not be required to attend an assembly program on a given day of the year when it is emphasized that Negroes too are considered to be Americans—thus implying that on other days they may be considered less "American" than other children. Concern for all children, every day of the school year, means that an "intergroup relations" program is an integral part of the atmosphere. This is the achievement of a truly non-segregated school. (p. 94)

Thus, several key tenets of Clark's view of integration could be discerned by 1955. First, it is clear that Clark viewed integration as a responsibility of the state geared toward the moderation of the interpersonal relations and balance of power among the various groups in a multiracial–multiethnic society. Second, it is clear that he believed that integration is to be neither an assimilatory process nor one that maintains pluralism; rather, it is to be a radical reorganization of American public education that incorporates the life experiences of all American subpopulations. In other words, he envisioned the desegregation of the ideological and symbolic climate and not just the desegregation of bodies. These notions are quite at variance with both the way Clark's views on integration typically have been represented and the way the framers of Brown (1954), the implementers of Brown, and the critics of the framers and implementers of Brown had conceptualized integration.

Clark's explication of his views did not cease in 1955. Many more statements emblematic of his radical conception of integration can be identified in later writings, most notably those collected in Pathos of Power (Clark, 1974). Some examples:

> Initially, the attempt was to use the Brown decision as a form of therapy, to free American whites and Negroes from the depths of the disease. It became apparent, however, that the extent of the metastasis had been underestimated and misunderstood, that the pattern of resistance, evasion, and tokenism that followed Brown could be explained only by a racism that had rotted the roots of American life North and South. (pp. 100–101)

> Racial integration in America must mean more than the right of the Negro to share equally in the moral emptiness, hypocrisy, conformity, and despair that characterize so much of American life. To be truly meaningful, integration must provide the Negro with the opportunity, the right, and the obligation to contribute to our society a resurgence of ethical substance, moral strength, and general integrity. (p. 28)

> Pluralism, if indeed it is desirable, must follow not precede integration, for it is meaningful only in a context of limited voluntary separation under conditions where all share in the necessarily integrated economic and educational system. Therefore, to argue for pluralism—when the status of the Negro is unequal—is to obscure injustice. Pluralism without equality would best be described by the caste model. (p. 109)

> Our colleges must transfer the monies, the brains, and the prestige previously associated with space and war research to research on how man can live in peace and justice with his fellow man, how the urban environment can be transformed into beauty and tranquillity, and how the masses of human beings can come to understand that love and kindness and justice and empathy are the necessary parameters of human intelligence. (p. 48)[10]

In addition to illustrating in greater detail Clark's views on integration, these passages highlight his Afrocentric bearing and demonstrate that he remained Afrocentric in orientation well past the Brown (1954) and Dark Ghetto (1965/1989) periods. His central concern remained with positive relations between people (in this case, Blacks and Whites), and he advocated the application of scientific resources toward the solution of social problems.

---

[10] Cf. Serpell (1994), cited in footnote 5.

EFFECTS OF SEGREGATION ON WHITES: A NEGLECTED ASPECT OF CLARK'S VIEWS ON INTEGRATION

One of the most overlooked aspects of Clark's views on integration is his insistence that White people must also change before any true social or educational progress can be made. This theme is most emphatically stated in the social science statement (Clark et al., 1952):

> Confusion, conflict, moral cynicism, and disrespect for authority may arise in majority group children as a consequence of being taught the moral, religious and democratic principles of the brotherhood of man and the importance of justice and fair play by the same persons and institutions who, in their support of racial segregation and related practices, seem to be acting in a prejudiced and discriminatory manner. Some individuals may attempt to resolve this conflict by intensifying their hostility toward the minority group. Others may react by guilt feelings which are not necessarily reflected in more humane attitudes toward the minority group. Still others react by developing an unwholesome, rigid, and uncritical idealization of all authority figures—their parents, strong political and economic leaders. As described in *The Authoritarian Personality* [Adorno, Frenkel-Brunswik, Levinson, & Sanford, 1950] they despise the weak, while they obsequiously and unquestioningly conform to the demands of the strong whom they also, paradoxically, subconsciously hate. (pp. 6–7)

The Supreme Court, however, ignored this particular aspect of the social science statement (Clark, 1988), choosing instead to focus only on the effects of segregation on minority children:

> We come then to the question presented: Does segregation of children in public schools solely on the basis of race, even though the physical facilities and other "tangible" factors may be equal, deprive the children of the *minority* [italics added] group of equal educational opportunities? We believe that it does. (Warren, 1954, cited in Clark, 1955/1963, p. 158)

> To separate [the colored children] from others of similar age and qualifications solely because of their race generates a feeling of inferiority as to their status in the community that may affect their hearts and minds in a way unlikely ever to be undone.... Segregation of white and colored children in public schools has a detrimental effect upon the colored children. (*Brown v. Board of Education* [1954], cited in Clark, 1965/1989, pp. 76–77)

> Segregation with the sanction of law, therefore, has a tendency to retard the educational and moral development of Negro children. (Warren [1954], citing *Brown v. Board of Education* [1954], cited in Clark, 1955/1963, p. 159)

In *Prejudice and Your Child* (1955/1963), Clark revisited the theme of majority children, titling one of his chapters "The White Child and Race Prejudice." In *Pathos of Power* (1974), he remarked:

> Special programs must be developed to help white students from less privileged backgrounds and from more privileged affluent families grow beyond the constricted racist view of their parents and peers. Colleges and universities must assume the special task of educating these young people so that they will be free of such moral and ethical disadvantage. (p. 47)

One theme that Clark has explored in his revisitations of *Brown* (1954; e.g., 1965/1989, 1979, 1988) is that if the framers and implementers of *Brown* had incorporated the notion that the psychology of White people as a group is not altogether without problems and that Whites, not just Blacks must also be educated differently, the success of school desegregation might have been greater, and the relation between school desegregation and the reduction of prejudice and discrimination in society might have been better accomplished. Although this belief has still been evident in recent years, Clark has changed his emphasis somewhat.

EDUCATION FOR EMPATHY AND RESPECT

The themes of empathy and, later, respect, have surfaced repeatedly in statements and articles by and about Clark. His most recent activities and statements, from the years 1986–1999, graphically illustrate the above themes:

> Teachers—and society in general—should stress that no person can be called educated if he lacks respect for people because of race or ethnicity.... Education in America has been woefully deficient in teaching people mutual respect. Since the Supreme Court's decision forced the integration of public schools, ... there has been some change for the better, but it's minimal. (Browning, 1991, quoting Kenneth Clark)

> I'm now concerned not only with basic education, but also with education in terms of human sensitivity. I think that should start in the elementary grades ... where white children and black children can help each other.... Multicultural education that says ... individuals of this color make a contribution that people of another color can't make; to me, that doesn't make sense. I'm in favor of teaching youngsters that human beings under proper circumstances can help their fellow human beings make contributions across cultural lines. That's how, if I were younger, I would teach multicultural education—education across the stupidity of racial isolation. (Feeney, 1992, quoting Kenneth Clark)

> Unfortunately, in the years since [Brown] we have not significantly modified the structure, function or substance of American education. Beyond the failures to desegregate, we have not yet developed a technique by which reading, writing, mathematics and the arts are seen as skills for fostering cooperation and for identifying with others. We have not yet made education a process whereby students are taught to respect the inalienable dignity of other human beings.... By encouraging and rewarding empathetic behavior in all of our children—both minority and majority youth—we will be protecting them from ignorance and cruelty.... We will be educating them. (Clark, 1993)

Despite this thematic continuity with regard to the teaching of empathy and respect, one of the most controversial events that occurred during the recent period was Clark's outspoken criticism of the Ujamaa and Latino Leadership Schools of the New York City school system under the chancellorship of Joseph A. Fernandez. The Ujamaa and Latino Leadership Schools were originally designed to respond specifically to the educational and psychological needs of African Americans and Latino American males by providing all-male, all-ethnic environments in which ethnically centered curricula were taught by ethnic male teachers. These schools, which were based on accumulated research showing how ethnic male children in particular are subjected to lower expectations and higher rates of academic neglect (e.g., Hare & Castenell, 1985; Kunjufu, 1984, 1988; Rubovitz & Maehr, 1973), were intended to be demonstration projects. Clark, however, was quoted as saying,

> For adults to impose this nonsense on children is academic child abuse.... It's outrageous. It's absurd. It's a continuation of the whole segregation nonsense.... I didn't expect that anybody would come up with anything like this. This is what I was fighting against. (Roberts, 1990, quoting Kenneth Clark)

In a letter to the editor of *The New York Times*, Clark himself wrote:

> To the Editor:
> Your report that the Board of Education of New York City is seriously contemplating the establishment of an experimental high school for minority men ... is shocking.... This proposal and its rationalizations are a flagrant, not even subtle, violation of the *Brown v. Board of Education* decision of 1954.... The Board of Education is shamefully proposing racial and gender segregation of its public schools. If this plan is accepted and put into practice, it would make our public schools important institutions for the perpetuation of racism. The use of public schools for isolating racial and ethnic groups in schools and classes is not only unconstitutional but also results in inescapable stigma and feelings of inferiority on the part of the students who are so rejected.

It is of social and psychological significance that the children of other ethnic groups—for example, Italians, Irish, Jews, Poles and Asians—are not being so isolated. The argument that black and Hispanic males are for the most part responsible for crime and personal and widespread social instability is a perpetuation of the negative stereotypes that permeate our society. In establishing separate public schools and classes for minority males, educators and educational decision makers reinforce these stereotypes. They are also suggesting that these schools become prep schools for correctional institutions—or become indistinguishable from correctional schools and thus block the upward-mobility educational goal for these students. A truly serious social, psychological and educational approach to the children who are now being neglected and rejected in our society is not to turn our public schools into stigmatized correctional institutions. Parallel to a comprehensive and human educational program we must raise the social and educational standards for all children. And we must turn our present correctional institutions into educational institutions, with appropriate methods and goals of high social and educational standards. (1991, p. A18)

With this latest pronouncement Clark's views pose something of a quandary, because a progressive and experimental educational strategy grounded in part in research spawned by his own early research is being rejected by him as reactionary, while he is being rejected as reactionary by its proponents. Perhaps the missing link can be found in the Black Power movement—a movement that Clark criticized vociferously, but a movement that transformed the line of research that he at one time began.

RECONTEXTUALIZING KENNETH CLARK

William E. Cross, Jr. (1991), has stated that Clark "never really advocated collective Negro enterprise or group (cultural) solidarity as a countermeasure and proactive strategy for Negroes living in America" (p. 37). Furthermore, Cross has stated that Clark is at least partially responsible for "producing an image of the Negro dominated by feelings of inferiority" (p. 37) and "help[ing] distort Black history and the social scientific analysis of Black life" (p. 38). How can Clark be redeemed from such criticisms without glossing over and obscuring the very facts that may have produced them? To be fair, Clark has at times made statements that appear to be inconsistent with the level of commitment to the Black race that he showed in *Brown* (1954). Cross's statements, however, seem to imply that Clark was not or is not a "Race man."[11] Before such a judgment can be

---

[11] A "Race man" is an individual whose self-identify is so closely aligned with the welfare of the Black race that he works assiduously for the race's collective uplift and is willing to do

levied, however, two hermeneutical frameworks must be considered: the historical and the developmental.

As Cross (1991) showed, an important period of Black history within Clark's lifetime (i.e., the Black Social movement) can be divided into two distinct periods: the civil rights phase (1954–1968) and the Black Power phase (1968–1975). These two phases were characterized by distinctions in the prevailing Black ethos that could not have failed to affect both Clark the man and interpretations of his work. Clark's lifetime, particularly the 65-year span that has encompassed his professional and public life, can be divided into three distinct historical periods that correspond roughly to the years 1934–1954 (the pre–Black Social movement period), when Clark was 20–40 years old; 1954–1974 (the Black Social movement period), when Clark was 40–60 years old; and 1974–1999 (the post–Black Social movement period), when Clark was 60–85 years old.

I propose that to adequately understand Clark's views on integration and Black solidarity one must place his views, as they appeared at various times and in various places and forms, against the backdrop of these historical periods. Furthermore, one must consider the developmental forces to which Clark may have been subject at various times in his life and the way in which these forces may have affected his views. I contend that such a process will eventuate in a recognition that Clark's views on race and integration have been consistently revolutionary and that his most seemingly incongruous and unpopular actions have merely been the result of the development of his personal identity as a "Negro intellectual" and social critic. I will proceed from a somewhat inside-out position, beginning with the middle historical period.

Examining the Black Social Movement and Kenneth Clark

A crucial point of recontextualizing Kenneth Clark historically is the recognition of the fact that his controversial book *Dark Ghetto* (1965/1989) was positioned at the brink of change between the civil rights and Black Power phases of the Black Social movement. As indicated previously, Lemann (1988) argued that the book was considered progressive at the time it appeared. Nevertheless, its swift appropriation by Moynihan (1965) into a text that proved to be a nemesis of the Black community and its socioeconomic progress, not to mention a springboard for a nascent Black conservative movement, likely alienated Clark with the more radical arm

---

virtually anything to improve the status or well-being of the race as a whole. To quote Drake and Cayton (1945/1993, p. 394), a Race man is "all for The Race" and "fearless in his approach to white people." Thus, a Race man is a type of hero who "beats the white man at his own game and forces the white world to recognize his talent or service or achievement" (Drake & Crayton, 1945/1993, p. 394). Implied is the notion that the Race man retains his loyalty to Blacks and some level of disdain for Whites, despite the latter's recognition of or admiration for him. A Race man achieves without "selling out."

of the Black Social movement, both within the social sciences and outside them. Concurrent with the period during which *Dark Ghetto* appeared, the Student Nonviolent Coordinating Committee (SNCC) was going through changes that would transmute the civil rights movement, as emblematized by the Rev. Martin Luther King, Jr., and the Southern Christian Leadership Council (SCLC), into the Black Power movement, as emblematized by the Black Panthers. Young Black social scientists who were sympathetic with this shift were in the process of redefining the parameters of social science particularly as they pertained to the investigation and explanation of Black people's behavior and experiences (Cross, 1971; Jones, 1972; Nobles 1972; see also Bunzel & Grossman, 1997). Critical models that emphasized Black strengths, even in such stressful environments as "the ghetto," were gaining currency (Billingsley, 1968; Staples, 1971; White, 1970). Black identity, self-concept, and self-esteem became "hot topics" and necessarily precipitated a critical re-examination and re-evaluation of the Clarks's seminal studies.

Clark was taken to task both personally and professionally by proponents of the "new" social science (Wilson, 1989), and he had a great deal to say about the young "radicals" who gave them inspiration. Clark's remarks wax most inflammatory in a section of *Pathos of Power* (1974) titled "Black Nationalism: A Verification of the Negative Consequences of Segregation":

> Under the guise of assuming a positive identity, black nationalism has adopted an imitation of white racism with its deification of race, its attempt to make a virtue out of color, its racist mystique.... Many of its advocates are dominated by deep feelings of racial self-hatred. Part of the pattern of pretense and posturing includes a suicidal eagerness to ascribe all middle-class patterns of speech, grammar, dress, manners, and style of life to whites, while reserving for the exclusive use of Negroes the uncouth and vulgar. This is garden-variety racism at its most obscene.... Whatever the motivation for individuals associated with the black nationalist movement, I consider the movement as a whole to be sick, regressive, and tyrannical. (pp. 112–116)

Clark further stated:

> Given the fact that the realities of racism in America have not changed, ... the cult of blackness must be recognized as what it is—a ritualized denial of anguished despair and resentment of the failure of society to meet its promises.... Black separatism can be seen as a "sour-grapes and sweet-lemon" reaction against the failure of the society to implement and enforce the findings of *Brown*. (pp. 115–117)

Although it might be reasonable to interpret these statements as Clark's personal reaction to criticism lodged against him and his work, we must not overlook that he was also critical of Black leaders of his own and the previous generation. In *The Negro Protest* (Clark, 1962), a transcription of his WGBH-TV interviews with James Baldwin; Malcolm X; and the Rev. Martin Luther King, Jr.; and in *Dark Ghetto* (1965/1989) and *Pathos of Power* (1974), statements indicating his general dissatisfaction with any single strategy for the amelioration of Black–White social inequality abound. Clark consistently demonstrated partial identification and partial sympathy with most Black leaders, causes, and political strategies, but he never endorsed any without reservation. In *The Negro Protest* (1962), Clark's verbal dynamics as well as his concluding remarks suggest that he preferred King's strategy to Baldwin's and Baldwin's to Malcolm X's, although, in a much later interview (Phillips, 1994c), he expressed some identification with Malcolm X's post-Mecca views, which expressed a movement away from racial separatism. In *Dark Ghetto* and *Pathos of Power*, however, he explicitly presented what he perceived to be both strengths and weaknesses of King's and Malcolm X's causes and strategies, and other remarks indicated that he felt something of a kinship with Baldwin, whom he identified as an outspoken, iconoclastic, "Negro intellectual." I make these points to illustrate how strongly Kenneth Clark identified with the role of social critic and "Negro intellectual."

The way that Clark construed this role required him to retain the freedom to critique both Whites and Blacks alike. That he took issue with the notion that there existed a Black "party line" is exemplified in his sarcastic criticism of two "rules of the ghetto":

1. *One basic rule* is to present to the hostile white world a single voice of protest and rebellion. No Negro who is concerned with his acceptance in the ghetto dares to violate this rule.
2. *Another basic rule* is that no issue can take precedence over the basic issue of race and, specifically, of racial oppression. (Clark, 1965/1989, p. 194)

A subtext of much of Clark's writing is discomfort with such confinement. That an individual who made such a dramatic and momentous contribution to civil rights should feel so confined is indeed an ironic twist on the fact that the historical moment called for intense and focused group solidarity. Although the appearance of the lack of group solidarity between Clark at mid-life and those who, in popular consciousness, stood for Black progressiveness during the 1960s and early 1970s could, in fact, be interpreted as a true lack of group solidarity, paradoxically, it could also be interpreted as a manifestation of Clark's fierce intellectual independence —he had already "proven" his group solidarity by collaborating with the NAACP–LDF in *Brown* (1954).

Before the Black Social Movement—The Ethnic Identity Development of Clark

Development, viewed one way, is merely personal history. In the Author's Notes to *Dark Ghetto*, Clark stated that "*Dark Ghetto* is a summation of my personal and lifelong experiences and observations as a prisoner within the ghetto long before I was aware that I was really a prisoner" (1965/1989, p. 252). Born in the Panama Canal Zone in 1914, Clark was brought at the age of 5 by his mother to Harlem at the dawn of the Harlem renaissance (Locke, 1925/1992) and the tail end of the Great Migration, when Black Americans left the rural South in large numbers for the economic opportunities of the industrial Northeast and Midwest (Lawrence, 1941/1993). His mother, a strict and courageous garment worker, took pains to ensure that her son completed his lessons, retained access to the academic track in the New York City public schools, and was able to attend college during the Great Depression (Hentoff, 1982).

Clark (1989) reports that his first exposure to racism was at the age of 6, when he and his mother were refused service at Childs Restaurant in New York City. This incident, which was psychologically structured for him by his mother over the remaining years of his childhood and which left an indelible mark on him, was recapitulated over a decade later when he, then a Howard freshman, was working in the main post office of Washington, DC. His attempt to gain service at the White Tower Restaurant near the Capitol during one of his meal breaks was refused. This event catapulted him into his first act of protest, described in the beginning of this article.

Using Cross's (1971, 1991) nigrescence ("Negro-to-Black shift") model of identity development as a rubric, this latter restaurant incident can be construed as something of an "Encounter" (crisis) for Clark, which thrust him into "Immersion–Emersion" (exploration of his Black identity). At that time, the "Blackest" causes with which an African American youth could align himself were the NAACP's effort to eliminate segregation in public facilities and the Communist-directed Black nationalist movement. Being at Howard, alignment with the NAACP was an easy choice for young Clark. Furthermore, having the opportunity to be mentored by some of the most illustrious Black minds in America surely facilitated his transition out of Immersion–Emersion and into "Internalization" (adoption of a transracial identity anchored in one's Blackness). On leaving graduate school, Clark demonstrated his internalization by seeking to integrate the faculty at CCNY, but his "Internalization–Commitment" (internalization expressed as commitment to a cause) surfaced more clearly when he resigned from the Hampton Institute. This first cycle of his identity development (Parham, 1989) culminated in his participation in *Brown v. Board of Education* (1954), the event that precipitated the Black Social movement.

Identity Development After Brown (1954)

The *Brown* (1954) victory as well as the coincident disintegration of the NAACP–LDF produced another Encounter for Clark and precipitated another cycle of identity development for him. He responded to this in the early 1960s by shifting his attention from desegregation to economics —a shift that anticipated the transition of public concern from desegregation to economics a few years later and which was exemplified by his participation in HARYOU. This cycle culminated in his authorship of *Dark Ghetto* (1965/1989), a text derived from the HARYOU report *Youth of the Ghetto: A Study of the Consequences of Powerlessness and a Blueprint for Change* (1964) that precipitated both controversy and another Encounter.

Clark responded to this Encounter by turning his attention to the gentler, subtler, more "touchy-feely" aspects of integrated education as he envisioned it, namely, empathy and respect. This cycle of developmental change (Parham, 1989) culminated in the publication of *Pathos of Power* (1974), a collection of essays and speeches he had been composing since the late 1940s, and it remains evident in the oral and written statements he has produced since that time. Although it is evident that Clark possessed these views prior to their publication in 1974, it was at this time that he chose to focus on them and place them in the public spotlight. Since 1974 he has remained something of an elder spokesperson who is often sought for commentary when the topics of race and education arise.

After the Black Social Movement—The Elder Spokesman

These newly aroused concerns motivated Clark to place all of the resources at his disposal toward the struggle for justice. He did so primarily by offering his person and his scientific writings to the causes he found credit worthy. During his late 30s he worked for *Brown v. Board of Education* (1954); during his late 40s he worked for HARYOU and produced the volume *Dark Ghetto*. In his elder years, Clark reached the highest pinnacles of his professional life, serving as President of both SPSSI and APA. The introduction to *Pathos of Power* (1974) suggests that during this time he was also confronting and examining his emotions and the more "touchy-feely" aspects of his views on education and social integration in general. Although these thoughts may not have fit the prevailing scientific ethos, he ultimately felt compelled to publish them as a statement that might complete "the record." Mentioning his admiration for such figures as "[Albert] Einstein, ... [Bertrand] Russell, ... [Robert J.] Oppenheimer, [and

Linus] Pauling" (1974, p. 141), he seemed at last to find justification for his own concern with values, morality and, ultimately, emotion. To wit, he wrote, "I have come, at this stage of my life, to the conclusion that the antidotes [to the destructive polarizations among men] are embarrassingly simple—humor, empathy, compassion, and kindness" (Clark, 1974, pp. ix–xiii). After the publication of *Pathos of Power*, Clark felt liberated to embark on a full-scale crusade for these issues, as demonstrated in his most recent statements. For example:

> When Martin Luther King preached non-violence, many of his listeners thought he meant ending just physical violence. But he also meant psychological violence. This part of the civil-rights lesson has not been learned in the post-war period.
>
> Consider the standards for college admissions. For the past half century, we have determined advancement by the grades of students in reading, writing, math and other subjects, and by their performance on standardized tests. Ignorance in any of these areas can hold them back. By contrast, social sensitivity—an awareness of the needs of others—is rarely seen as part of the curriculum. Throughout the system, these social values are generally viewed as subjective interference with more objective indications of being well educated. Ignorance of decency and respect has rarely caused anyone to be flunked or kept out of college.
>
> By encouraging and rewarding empathetic behavior in all of our children—both minority and majority youth—we will be protecting them from ignorance and cruelty. We will be helping them to understand the commonality of being human. We will be educating them. (Clark, 1993, p. 38)
>
> Q. [interviewer Mark Feeney] You keep coming back to the human factor, the individual level. That seems to be your central concern.
>
> A. [Kenneth Clark] Absolutely. At my age, I guess I have nothing else to be concerned about. (Feeney, 1992, p. 74).

Let us suppose, for a moment, that Clark's statements during the third historical period emanate from a core of wisdom based on a "transracial" identity (Cross, 1991) informed by a native Afrocentricity rooted in his experience as a person of African descent. Using his lens, his recent statements, which are often framed as manifestations of "liberalism" or "racelessness," can be reread as simply wise. Taking this a step further, statements such as these can even be characterized as radical (referencing *radix*, or *root*) and revolutionary, because essentially they are suggesting a reorganization of American public education around principles—such as a supreme concern with positive human interrelations—which, though Afrocentric in origin, are relevant to all people. The wisdom in Clark's exhortations is that he recognized the necessity of overhauling the effective American value system as an antidote to its current and interracially shared travails.

Given this framework, can we reconstrue the most controversial and, to some, uncomfortable stands made by Kenneth Clark, such as those pertaining to Black rationalism or the Ujamaa and Latino Leadership Schools? His focus on stigma and the perpetuation of negative stereotypes in both discussions signifies a deeper concern with the tragic fact that static and oppressive power relations that condone and benefit from separatism interact with and negate separatism that is founded on either self-defensive or self-determinative postures. Because a central aspect of Clark's conceptualization of integration is the adjustment of power relations to begin with, one possible argument is that he viewed both Black nationalism and single-race schools as diversionary and palliative. Although other explanations are possible, I prefer this one.

If there has been one flaw in Clark's thinking, it has been the failure to completely articulate an organismic organizational framework for human cultural groups. His various statements collectively have suggested that he has envisioned a world in which each culture retains its identity enough to contribute to a more robust and interesting human collective, yet he has failed to suggest the mechanism by which such cultures might retain their integrity in a fully integrated society. Perhaps the reason why separatist arguments have retained their level of cogency over many generations is that they implicitly reflect the continuing inability of all groups in U.S. society to conceive of a mechanism by which cultures might retain their integrity in a fully integrated society.

CONCLUSION

I have attempted to show that Clark's views on integration have consistently been radical, revolutionary, nonassimilationist, and affirmative of Black people as well as of others. I have attempted to demonstrate this by recontextualizing his actions and statements using both political–historical and personal–historical (developmental) frameworks. I have relied on Clark's published statements as data for my analysis, and I have attempted to synthesize perspectives from psychology, history, and philosophy of science.

To return to my original question, what makes Clark a model Afrocentric psychologist–activist? First, he has maintained a supreme concern with positive human relations across the course of his life, and he has applied his scientific expertise and scholarly capital toward the betterment of human relations, particularly as they pertain to race. In this process he has rejected positivist scholarly detachment and scientific neutrality in favor of a praxis that is rooted in his own experiences as a member of an oppressed racial–cultural group and the collective political consciousness that accompanies that membership. Second, he has demonstrated an unfailing commitment to Black people underneath a rubric of concern which, paradoxically, embraces the entire human race. This commitment and concern have manifested themselves as advocacy for the equalization of power relations among the diverse groups composing pluralistic societies, including but not limited to the United States, through the symbolic as well as the physical integration of educational environments in particular and the increase of social intercourse between people from diverse backgrounds in general. The beauty of Clark's Afrocentric praxis—which should be appreciated particularly by those who are skeptical of Afrocentrism itself—is that, third, he has at all times retained his prerogative to critically engage various Black perspectives, thus respecting the diversity and complexity of Black people themselves and their many possible positions.

Despite Clark's characterization of his own life as a "series of glorious defeats," the weight of historical evidence argues otherwise. At a time when many academic institutions are concerned with the diversification of their faculty, students, and curricula, it becomes ever more important that exemplars of diverse scientific approaches be brought to light. Clark is but one exemplar of Afrocentric scientific principles and praxis. As more are singled out and studied, from Afrocentric as well as other-centric perspectives, architects of multiculturalism will gain not only a firmer understanding of the fact that diversification requires deep and difficult change but also bigger and better blueprints for such change.

REFERENCES

Adorno, T. W., Frenkel-Brunswik, E., Levinson, D. J., & Sanford, R. N. (1950). *The authoritarian personality.* New York: Harper & Row.

Baker, L. D. (1998). *From savage to Negro: Anthropology and the construction of race, 1896–1954.* Berkeley: University of California Press.

Baldwin, J. A., Brown, R., & Hopkins, R. (1991). The Black self-hatred paradigm revisited: An Africentric analysis. In R. L. Jones (Ed.), *Black psychology* (3rd ed.), (pp. 141–166): Berkeley, CA: Cobb & Henry.

Banks, W. C. (1976). White preference in Blacks: A paradigm in search of a phenomenon. *Psychological Bulletin, 83,* 1179–1186.

Billingsley, A. (1968). *Black Families in White America.* Englewood Cliffs, NJ: Prentice Hall.

Brand, E., Ruiz, R., & Padilla, A. (1974). Ethnic identification and preference: A review. *Psychological Bulletin, 81,* 860–890.

Brown v. Board of Educ., 347 U.S. 483 (1954).

Browning, D. R. (1991, April 18). Schools fight racism by stressing respect, psychologist says. *St. Louis Post–Dispatch,* p. 6A.

Bunzel, J. H., & Grossman, A. S. (1997). Black studies revisited. *The Public Interest, 127,* 71.

Cahn, E. (1955). Jurisprudence. *New York University Law Review, 30,* 150–169.

Clark, C. (1972). Black studies or the study of Black people. In R. L. Jones (Ed.), *Black psychology* (pp. 3–17). New York: Harper & Row.

Clark, K. B. (1950). *The effects of prejudice and discrimination on personality development* (Fact-Finding Report, Mid-Century White House Conference on Children and Youth). Washington, DC: Federal Security Agency, Children's Bureau.

Clark, K. B. (1959–1960). The desegregation cases: Criticism of the social scientist's role. *Villanova Law Review, 5,* 224–240.

Clark, K. B. (1963). *Prejudice and your child.* Boston: Beacon Press. (Original work published 1955)

Clark, K. B. (1962). *The Negro protest: James Baldwin, Malcolm X, Martin Luther King talk with Kenneth B. Clark.* Boston: Beacon Press.

Clark, K. B. (1964). *Youth of the ghetto: A study of the consequences of powerlessness and a blueprint for change.* New York: Harlem Youth Opportunities Unlimited.

Clark, K. B. (1974). *Pathos of power.* New York: Harper & Row.

Clark, K. B. (1979). The role of social scientists 25 years after *Brown. Personality and Social Psychology Bulletin, 5,* 477–481.

Clark, K. B. (1988). The *Brown* decision: Racism, education, and human values. *Journal of Negro Education, 57,* 125–132.

Clark, K. B. (1989). *Dark ghetto: Dilemmas of social power.* New York: Harper & Row. (Original work published 1965)

Clark, K. B. (1989). Racial progress and retreat: A personal memoir. In *Dark ghetto: Dilemmas of social power* (2nd ed). Middletown, CT: Wesleyan University Press.

Clark, K. B. (1991, January 15). Schools for minority men violate '54 segregation decision [Letter to the editor]. *New York Times,* p. A18.

Clark, K. B. (1993, January 11). Unfinished business: The toll of psychic violence. *Newsweek,* 38.

Clark, K. B., & Clark, M. P. (1939a). The development of consciousness of self and the emergence of racial identification in Negro preschool children. *Journal of Social Psychology, 10,* 591–599.

Clark, K. B., & Clark, M. P. (1939b). Segregation as a factor in the racial identification of Negro pre-school children: A preliminary report. *Journal of Experimental Education, 11,* 161–163.

Clark, K. B., & Clark, M. P. (1940). Skin color as a factor in racial identification of Negro preschool children. *Journal of Social Psychology, 11,* 159–169.

Clark, K. B., & Clark, M. P. (1947). Racial identification and preference in Negro children. In T. M. Newcomb & E. L. Hartley (Eds.), *Readings in social psychology* (pp. 169–178). New York: Holt.

Clark, K. B., & Clark, M. P. (1950). Emotional factors in racial identification and preference in Negro children. *Journal of Negro Education, 19,* 341–350.

Clark, K. B., Cook, T., & Chein, I. (1952). The effects of segregation and the consequences of desegregation: A social science statement. *Brown v. Board of Education of Topeka, Shawnee County, Kansas: Appendix to Appellant's Briefs.* Washington, DC: Supreme Court of the United States (October Term, 1952).

Cross, W. E., Jr. (1971). Negro-to-Black conversion experience. *Black World, 20,* 13-27.

Cross, W. E., Jr. (1985). Black identity: Rediscovering the distinction between personal identity and reference group orientation. In M. B. Spencer, G. K. Brookins, & W. R. Allen (Eds.), *Beginnings: The social and affective development of Black children* (pp. 155-171). Hillsdale, NJ: Erlbaum.

Cross, W. E., Jr. (1991). *Shades of black: Diversity in African-American identity.* Philadelphia: Temple University Press.

Cruse, H. (1967). *The crisis of the Negro intellectual.* New York: Morrow.

Drake, S. C., & Cayton, H. R. (1993). *Black metropolis: A study of Negro life in a northern city.* Chicago: University of Chicago Press. (Original work published 1945)

Feeney, M. (1992, May 31). A racial justice pioneer on the way we live now. *Boston Globe,* p. 74.

Gadamer, H. G. (1975). *Truth and method.* New York: Continuum.

Gilroy, P. (1993). *The Black Atlantic: Modernity and double consciousness.* Cambridge, MA: Harvard University Press.

Guthrie, R. V. (1998). *Even the rat was white: A historical view of psychology* (2nd ed.). Boston: Allyn & Bacon.

Hare, B., & Castenell, L. (1985). No place to run, no place to hide: Comparative status and future prospects of Black boys. In M. B. Spencer, G. K. Brookins, & W. R. Allen (Eds.), *Beginnings: The social and affective development of Black children* (pp. 201-214). Hillsdale, NJ: Erlbaum.

Heidegger, M. (1962). *Being and time.* Oxford, England: Basil Blackwell.

Hentoff, N. (1982, August 23). Profiles: The integrationist. *The New Yorker,* 37-73.

Hill Collins, P. (1991). *Black feminist thought: Knowledge, consciousness, and the politics of empowerment.* New York: Routledge.

Horowitz, R. (1939). Racial aspects of self-identification in nursery school children. *Journal of Psychology, 7,* 91-99.

Jones, J. M. (1972). *Prejudice and racism.* Reading, MA: Addison-Wesley.

Kluger, R. (1976). *Simple justice.* New York: Knopf.

Kunjufu, J. (1984). *Countering the conspiracy to destroy Black boys.* Chicago: Afro-Am.

Kunjufu, J. (1988). *To be popular or smart: The Black peer group.* Chicago: African American Images.

Lawrence, J. (1993). *Jacob Lawrence: The migration series.* Washington, DC: Rappahannock. (Original work published 1941)

Lemann, N. (1988, December). The unfinished war: A product of the conflicting ambitions of the men who shaped it. *Atlantic Monthly, 262*(6), 37.

Locke, A. (Ed.). (1992). *The new Negro: Voices of the Harlem renaissance*. New York: Atheneum. (Original work published 1925)

Mama, A. (1995). *Beyond the masks; Race, gender, and subjectivity*. London, Routledge.

Martin, J. (1992). Kenneth B. Clark. *Contemporary Black Biography, 5,* 51–55.

Moynihan, D. (1965). *The Negro family: The case for national action*. Washington, DC: U.S. Department of Labor, Office of Policy Planning and Research.

Myers, L. J. (1991). Expanding the psychology of knowledge optimally: The importance of world view revisited. In R. Jones (Ed.), *Black psychology* (3rd ed., pp. 15–28). Berkeley: Cobb & Henry.

Myrdal, G. (1944). *An American dilemma: The Negro problem and modern democracy*. New York: Harper & Row.

Nobles, A. W. (1972). African philosophy: Foundations for Black psychology. In R. Jones (Ed.), *Black psychology* (pp. 18–32). New York: Harper & Row.

Parham, T. A. (1989). Cycles of psychological nigrescence. *Counseling Psychology, 28,* 187–226.

Phillips, L. (1994a). On the variegation of authority: The role of womanism in the reformulation of knowledge production and validation processes. *The Womanist, 1,* 18–20.

Phillips, L. (1994b). A re-examination of the Clark doll studies at the 40th anniversary of the *Brown v. Board of Education* case: Implications for a critique of a landmark decision. In R. A. Pratt (Chair), *Brown v. Board of Education at 40: Reassessing the case*. Symposium conducted at the annual meeting of the Association for the Study of Afro-American Life and History, Atlanta, GA.

Phillips, L. (1994c). [Interview with Kenneth B. Clark].

Phillips, L. (1994d, October). *Kenneth B. Clark: Afrocentric scientist or not? The importance of critical models and questions in psychology*. Departmental colloquium, University of Georgia, Athens.

Richards, G. (1997). *'Race,' racism and psychology*. London: Routledge.

Roberts, S. (1990, November 12). Separate schools for male Blacks igniting debate. *New York Times,* p. B1.

Rubovitz, P. C., & Maehr, M. L. (1973). Pygmalion Black and White. *Journal of Personality and Social Psychology, 25,* 210–218.

Schwartz, R. D. (1959). The law and behavioral science program at Yale: A sociologist's account of some experiences. *Law School Developments, 12,* 91–98.

Serpell, R. (1994). The cultural construction of intelligence. In W. J. Lonner & R. Malpass (Eds.), *Psychology and culture* (pp. 157–163). Boston: Allyn & Bacon.

Staples, R. (Ed.). (1971). *The Black family: Essays and studies*. Belmont, CA: Wadsworth.

Students to fight evils in politics. (1934, April 5). *New York Times,* p. 23.

Taylor, C. (1985). *Philosophy and the social sciences*. Cambridge, England: Cambridge University Press.

van den Haag, E. (1960). Social science testimony in the desegregation cases—A reply to Professor Kenneth Clark. *Villanova Law Review, 6,* 69–79.

White, J. (1970, August). Toward a Black psychology. *Ebony, 25,* 44–45, 48–50, 52.

Wilson, J. W. (1989). Introduction. In K. B. Clark, *Dark ghetto: Dilemmas of social power* (2nd ed., pp. ix–xxii). Middletown, CT: Wesleyan University Press.

INDEX

AAAP. See American Association for Applied Psychology
AAAS. See American Association for the Advancement of Science
AAAS Newcomb Cleveland Prize, 410
AAAS Thousand Dollar Prize (1939), 352, 410, 414, 415
Abnormal psychology, 72, 98n48, 175, 201, 435
Accreditation, 438, 442
Accuracy checking, 307
Achilles, Paul, 363, 379
Acker, Joan, 35
ACP. See Association of Consulting Psychologists
Acute experiments, 220
Adams, Elizabeth Kemper, 529
Adams, Grace, 91
Adolescence, 295–296, 299
Adolescence (G. Stanley Hall), 292–293
Advancement of Learning (Francis Bacon), 257
Advertising, 156, 370
Aesthetics, 113
Affect, Wundt's theory of, 72–73
"Affiliated Societies," 143, 150–151, 160
African Americans, 29–30
Afrocentric scholars, 577–586
Agassiz, Louis, 96n31, 286
"Age of Mental Health," 457
"Age of Psychotherapy," 458
Age scaling, 303, 314–315
Aggressiveness, 549, 550, 559, 567
Air blasts, 409, 412
Albee, G. W., 446
Albert B. study. See Little Albert study
Alexander, Franz, 478–479
Alexander III Charity Home for the Mentally Ill, 223, 225
Allen, Gay Wilson, 108
Allport, Floyd, 501, 515
Allport, Gordon, 276, 325–341, 356, 360, 390, 556
    as APA president, 326
    and Committee on Displaced Foreign Psychologists, 557
    and concept of character, 333–339, 341
    and concept of personality, 332–341
    early life of, 327–328
    as Harvard student, 328–329
    and Leo Hurvich, 558
    on Kurt Lewin's film, 389
    as "linguistic policeman," 333
    mature personality as envisioned by, 338–339
    Personality of, 276, 338
    selfhood as viewed by, 334–335
    and social work, 329–332
    in SPSSI, 585
    trait theory of, 337–338
    uniqueness as tenet of, 335
Allport, Nellie Wise, 327–328
Ambiguity, 331–332
American Association for Applied Psychology (AAAP), 429
    and APA, 142–143, 350–351
    founding of, 365n13
    and industrial psychology, 374–381
    Norman R. F. Maier's receipt of, prize, 410–412, 415
    report on graduate training to, 436, 437
American Association for the Advancement of Science (AAAS)
    and APA, 62, 153–154, 162
    founding of, 142
    Norman Maier and, 352, 410–411, 414, 415
American Association of Anatomists, 143
American Association of Applied Psychologists, 429
American Association of Clinical Psychologists, 429
American Association of Clinical Psychology, 4
American Association of Universities, 312
An American Dilemma (Gunnar Myrdal), 585
American Eugenics Society, 354
American Guardian, 364
American Jewish Committee, 399
American Journal of Psychology
    and APA, 144, 148–150, 155, 156, 158–162
    and Jews, 562

607

and Little Albert study, 240
and *Psychological Review*, 62
and spiritualism, 127, 145
terminology used in, 171
American Journal of Religious Psychology and Education, 298
American Men of Science (Cattell), 528–531
American Morphological Society, 143
American Naturalist, 155
American Philosophical Association, 160–161
American Physiological Society, 143, 146
American Psychiatric Association, 464
American Psychological Association (APA), 141–163
   and AAAS, 142–143
   addresses of presidents of, 454
   Gordon Allport as president of, 276, 326
   as American group, 141–142
   autobiographical reports of psychoanalysis published by, 478
   Edwin Boring and, 50–52
   Boulder Conference organized by, 441–442
   James McKeen Cattells' involvement in, 528–529
   centennial of, 275
   Kenneth Clark as president of, 576, 599
   and clinical psychology, 464
   clinical section of, 429
   Committee on Displaced Foreign Psychologists of, 557
   Committee on Physical and Mental Tests, 151–153, 157
   and definition of psychology, 200, 202
   Depression Era employment issues in, 349
   John Dewey's address to, 454, 461
   diversity of, 5
   dues for, 156–157
   Editor's Handbook of, 419
   educational standards of, 356–357
   and emergence of psychology as discipline, 143–145
   employment issues of, 354–356
   Fifty Years of Clinical Psychology symposium of, 433
   first local branches of, 154, 160–161
   and growth of university psychology departments and institutions in early 20th century, 161–162
   G. Stanley Hall's role in, 62, 145–149
   Clark Hull as president of, 387
   and industrial psychology, 369–371, 373–375, 378, 381
   meetings of, with other organizations in 1890s, 150–151
   membership criteria of, 51, 148–150, 157, 159, 161
   1910 meeting of, 200, 202
   1951 report of the Executive Secretary, 443–444
   1949 report on doctoral training programs, 440
   1947 report on graduate training from, 436–440
   1949 report on training facilities, 440
   number of members in early, 150
   percentage of members of, in professional practices in 1930s, 350
   promotion of philosophy by, 157–161
   and psychoanalysis, 486
   Psychological Review of, 154–156
   publication by, 154–155, 414, 420
   reorganization of, 380, 430
   second-tier membership in, 350
   survey of influences by, 484
   training issues in, 430
   John B. Watson as president of, 239
   Robert M. Yerkes as president of, 306
American Psychological Society, 5
American Psychologist, 421, 440, 468
American psychology, 82, 91, 144
American Psychology Before William James (Jay Wharton Fay), 81
"The American Scholar" (Ralph Waldo Emerson), 106
American Sketches (Thomas C. Upham), 93n9
American Society for Psychical Research (ASPR), 124, 126–127, 130, 133, 144, 145
American Society of Naturalists, 62, 142, 146, 150, 155, 162
American Zoological Society, 143
Amherst College, 80, 82, 83, 286–287
Analogies, use of, 61, 104–105, 109, 113, 115, 395
The Analogy of Religion to the Constitution and Course of Nature (Joseph Butler), 83
Analysis of psychological processes, 176
Anderson, John, 51
Anderson, Margaret, 36
Andover Theological Seminary, 83

Angell, James Rowland
    and APA, 150, 200, 202
    and behavioralism, 203, 209
    E. G. Boring's correspondence to, 48
    and functionalism, 89, 90
    and spiritualism, 129, 134, 136
Animal Behaviour, 420
Animal models, 351
Animal psychology, 201
Annual Review of Psychology, 18
Anomalies, 195, 205
Anonymity, 177
Anthropometric tests, 148, 311
Anti-Semitism, 4–5, 389, 390, 392, 545–552, 557–559
APA. *See* American Psychological Association
Appearance of anomaly stage (of scientific revolution), 195
Apperception, 60, 68
Apperceptive synthesis, 71–73
Appetite, 222
Applied psychology
    after World War I, 46–47, 49, 429–430
    APA members in, 52
    in business, 370–371
    and diversity of intellectual ability, 276
    experimental psychology vs., 46–54
    first American department of, 319
    journal for, 303
    organizations for, 350
Aristotelian tradition, 257, 258
Aristotle, 17, 116n10, 256, 257, 287
"Army alpha," 320–321
Artifacts, facts vs., 258
Artificial intelligence, 209
"Art" (Ralph Waldo Emerson), 106
Ash, M., 351, 555n15
ASPR. *See* American Society for Psychical Research
Associate membership (APA), 51
Associationism, 69, 71, 309, 313
Association of American Anatomists, 143
Association of Black Psychologists, 5
Association of Consulting Psychologists (ACP), 350, 364, 371–374, 376, 378, 380, 381
Astronomy, 192
Atkinson, R. C., 447
Atlantic Monthly, 125, 539
Atlantis, 502–503
Attention, 73–74, 114

Attenuation, 312
Attitude measurement, 33
Audiogenic seizures, 413, 415, 416
Auditory stimuli, 409, 412, 413, 415–416
Authoritarian group studies, 393–396, 399
The Authoritarian Personality (Adorno, Frenkel-Brunswik, Levinson & Sanford), 591
"Authoritative scientism," 130
Authority, 131–132
Authority figures, 591

Baars, B. J., 108, 204–207, 209
Babkin, Boris, 228–230
Bacon, Sir Francis, 22, 189, 256–266, 269, 513
    Advancement of Learning of, 257
    Essays of, 257
    The New Atlantis of, 257, 262, 265
    New Organon of, 257
Baconian tradition, 83–85, 88, 89, 95n22, 257–269, 501, 516
Bagley, Florence Winger, 529–534
Baldwin, Bird T., 391
Baldwin, James, 597
Baldwin, James Mark
    and APA, 154, 155
    and Committee on Physical and Mental Tests, 151–153
    Dictionary of Philosophy and Psychology of, 155
    on English psychology, 90
    Mental Development in the Child and the Race of, 153
    and *Psychological Review*, 149, 155, 156
    and spiritualism, 124
Balzac, Honoré de, 107
Barker, Roger, 393, 397
Bartlett, Frederic, 556
Barzun, Jacques, 102
Baumgardner, S. R., 248
Bavelas, Alex, 399
Bawden, H. Heath, 201
Bayliss, W. M., 226
Beach, Frank, 421
Beard, George M., 131
Beaunis, H., 173
Becker, Howard, 29
Beebe-Center, John, 549
Behavior, 201, 202
Behavioralism, behaviorism vs., 203
Behavioral Neuroscience, 420

Behavioral psychology, 204, 389, 482–483
Behavioral technology, 263
Behaviorism
  aims of, 255–257
  and American culture, 256
  American phenomenon of, 202
  behavioralism vs., 203
  and Little Albert study, 247, 248
  as revolution in psychology, 198–203
  E. B. Titchener on, 46
  John B. Watson and, 239
Behaviorism (John B. Watson), 241
Behaviorist revolution, 187, 198–203
Behaviorists, 191
"The Behaviorist's Utopia" (J. B. Watson), 509
Behavior Research Fund, 49
Behavior theory, 397
Behavior therapists, Little Albert study as seen by, 243–245
Bekhterev, V. M., 223, 225–227, 239–240
Belief, psychology of, 114
Bellamy, R., 473, 474
Bellevue Psychiatric Hospital (NYC), 357–358
"Benevolent" volunteerism, 329
Bennett, George, 380
Bentley, Madison, 51, 53, 549
Berenson, Bernard, 116n10
Bergmann, Gustav, 399
Berlin Physical Society, 75
Berlin style of experimentation, 394
Berlyne, Daniel, 561
Bernard, Claude, 218
Bevan, W., 413
Beyond Freedom and Dignity (B. F. Skinner), 264
Bias, 26–27
Bible, 95n23
Bibliography, 154
Bibliography of Philosophy, Psychology, and Cognate Subjects (Benjamin Rand), 155
Bifurcated consciousness, 28
Billingsley, Andrew, 576
Bills, Marion, 372, 376, 380
Binet, Alfred
  and experimental hypnosis, 173–175
  and memory tests, 153
  and mental testing, 303, 308, 314–318, 320
Binet age scale, 314–315

Bingham, Walter VanDyke, 370, 372
Bitterman, M. E., 413, 562
Bjork, Daniel, 102
Black Families in White America (Andrew Billingsley), 576
The Black Family (Robert Staples), 576
Blackford, K., 378
Black Panthers, 596
Black Power movement, 576, 586, 594, 596
Black psychology, 576
Black rationalism, 601
Blacks, 27–30
Black separatism, 596
Black Social movement, 595–597
Black strengths movement, 576
Blacky Pictures, 480
Blum, G. S., 480
Blumenthal, Arthur L., 60
Boas, Franz, 177
Bobbitt, Joseph, 444
Boghossian, Ghazaros, 94n16
Bohr, Niels, 116n10
Bolton, Thaddeus, 201
Borges, Jorge Luis, 116n10
Boring, Edwin G.
  and antisemitism, 4–5, 545–559
  and APA, 50–52
  on controversy, 408
  on early American psychology, 81
  and experimentalism, 13, 45–54
  family background of, 547
  History of Experimental Psychology of, 18, 45–46, 48, 52–53, 60, 80, 92n5, 478, 564
  and Jews/Judaism, 549–568
  and Kurt Lewin, 389, 553–556
  and Norman Maier, 414
  personal character of, 547–549
  and psychoanalysis, 477–478
  and David Shakow, 435
  and standards, 355–357
  and Wilhelm Wundt, 60, 68, 69
"Boston Society," 144
Botanical Society of America, 143
Bott, E. A., 355
Boulder Conference, 441–442, 464–466
Boulder model, 431, 442
Bowditch, Henry Pickering, 287, 288
Bowdoin College, 82, 94n16, 98n45
Braid, James, 176
Bregman, E. O., 245
Brewer, William F., 207

Bridges, J. W., 247
Brightness and size constancy, 113
Brill, A. A., 473, 474
"Bringing Up the Jewish Child" (Kurt Lewin), 398
British colonization, 91
British psychology, 82, 90
British tradition, 84
Brotemarkle, R. A., 436
Brown, J. F., 461
Brown, Sterling, 584
Brown, Thomas, 79
Browning, Robert, 106, 107
Brown University, 82, 287, 351
Brown v. Board of Education, 3, 576, 580, 582, 585, 588, 590–593, 597–599
Bruner, J., 547, 565
Bryan, William L., 148
Bryn Mawr, 154, 547n4
Buchner, E. F., 200
Buffon, Georges-Louis Leclerc de, 174
Bunche, Ralph, 584, 585
Burks, Barbara, 390, 557
Burnett, Charles T., 98n45
Burnham, J. C., 485
Burnham, John, 335
Burnham, William H., 147
Burt, Sir Cyril, 19, 501
Burtt, Harold, 372, 373, 375, 376, 379
Business psychology, 370
Butler, Joseph, 83
Butler, Nicholas Murray, 149, 150
Butterfield, E., 207

Cabot, Richard, 329, 332, 334
Cahn, E., 580–581
California loyalty oath, 567n28
Calkins, Mary Whiton, 149, 159, 529, 530, 535–538
Cambridge (Massachusetts), 265
Canada, 464
Canadians (in APA), 147
Careers, 311, 316, 320, 350
Caring, 28
Carmichael, Leonard, 411, 412, 483
Carnegie Institute of Technology, 319, 370
Carpenter, William B., 123
Carr, Harvey, 247, 355
Carroll, L., 31
Carson, Rachel, 265
Carter, Robert, 580
Cartwright, Dorwin, 393–394, 400

Case, Mary Sophia, 529, 530
"The Case of John Bunyan" (Josiah Royce), 150
Casework, 330, 332
Cason, Hulsey, 551
Catalogue of psychological literature, 154
Catholic University, 147
Cattell, James McKeen
    American Men of Science of, 528–531
    and APA, 147–157
    as APA secretary, 149, 150, 157
    and Committee on Physical and Mental Tests, 151–153
    on definition of psychology, 88
    as first professor of psychology, 92n3
    and Sigmund Freud, 486
    on management of society, 515
    and mental testing, 311–312, 314, 316
    in National Academy of Sciences, 162
    on new psychology, 87
    and philosophy, 80–81
    and *Psychological Review*, 149, 155, 156
    role structure of experiments by, 172
    and spiritualism, 130
    and survey of psychologists, 532
    terminology used by, 171, 175
    Wilhelm Wundt on, 91
CCNY. *See* City College of New York
Center for Human Learning at University of Minnesota, 206
Central nervous system, 293
Chambers, Robert, 284
Character, 277
    Gordon Allport influenced by, 336–338
    concept of, 328
    of dogs, 220
    personality vs., 325, 331, 333–334
    and social work, 330
The Chatauquan, 129
"Chatter line," 393
Chein, Isidor, 585
Cheiron, the International Society for the History of Behavioral and Social Sciences, 5
Cherryholmes, C. H., 31
Chicago Conference (1966), 442
Chicago World's Fair. *See* World Columbian Exposition (1893)
Child and adolescent development psychology, 292–299
Child development, 27, 288–290, 299, 389–392, 394

activities/feelings of, 290
automatism/instincts/attitudes of, 289–290
and church processes and practices, 292
control of emotion/will in, 290–291
higher faculties in, 291
individual differences in, 291
and school processes and practices, 292
Child psychology, 201, 389
Children's Bureau, 298
Childs Restaurant (NYC), 598
Child studies, 146, 176, 177, 276, 288–292
Child Study Movement, 370
Chomsky, Noam, 72, 205–207, 256
Christianity, 83
Chronic experiments, 220
"Chronoscopic Measurement of Simple Reactins on All Classes of Persons" (Lightner Witmer), 148
Chrysostom, B., 158, 159
Churchland, P. S., 210
Church processes and practices, 292
City College of New York (CCNY), 580, 585, 598
Civil War, 122
Clairvoyance, 126
Clark, J. C. D., 192
Clark, Jonas, 145, 288
Clark, Kenneth B., 3, 7, 575–602
as Afrocentric scholar, 577–586
and Black Social movement, 595–597
criticisms of, 580–581
Dark Ghetto of, 583–586, 590, 595–599
on educating for empathy and respect, 592–594
ethnic identity development of, 598–599
integration as envisioned by, 586–592
The Negro Protest of, 597
Pathos of Power of, 583, 590, 592, 596, 597, 599, 600
photograph of, 578
Prejudice and Your Child of, 585, 588, 589, 592
reputation of, 576, 594
"transracial" identity of, 600–601
Youth of the Ghetto, 599
Clark, Mamie Phipps, 3, 576n2, 578, 585
Clark method, 289
Clark model, 178
Clark University (Worcester, MA), 49, 354, 465, 473, 533, 552, 557

and *American Journal of Psychology*, 144
and APA, 147
G. Stanley Hall at, 145, 178, 275, 276, 287–289, 298
and spiritualism, 128, 133
statistical studies at, 177
Robert M. Yerkes at, 306
Classics, study of the, 312–314
Clinical psychology, 201, 433–448, 453–469
beginnings of, 4
and CTCP, 440–443
and culture of American medicine and psychiatry, 460–464
effect of 1950 Boulder Conference on, 464–466
experimental psychology vs., 435, 446–448
at Harvard, 434–435
1947 APA report on graduate training in, 437–440
number of AAAP members in, 375
as outgrowth of World War II, 454–459
and principles of psychology, 444–445
and psychotherapy, 458–459
and Fill Sanford's report on psychology as a profession, 443–444
stages of development of, 442–443
"Clinical Training Facilities: 1949" (APA), 440
Cognition/cognitive processes, 27, 84, 191–192
Cognitive Psychology (U. Neisser), 206, 207
Cognitive revolution, 187–188, 203–209
Cognitive science, 207
Cohen, Bernard, 196–197, 210
Cohen, Morris, 552
Cohen's criteria for revolution, 196–197
College presidents, 309
College professorships, 83, 86
College students, 177
Collegiality, 548
Colloni, Stefan, 336
Columbia University
advanced study at, 533
James McKeen Cattell at, 92n3
Contributions to Philosophy and Psychology of, 144
Jews at, 546, 553, 568
and *Journal of Philosophy*, 156
mental testing at, 151, 311
women at, 536
Combs, Arthur, 444

Committee on Bibliography (APA), 154
Committee on Classification of Personnel in the Army, 321
Committee on Clinical Psychology (GAP), 443
Committee on Displaced Foreign Psychologists (APA), 557
Committee on Measurements (APA), 153
Committee on Physical and Mental Tests (APA), 151–153, 157
Committee on Problems of Vision Which Have Military Significance, 355n2
Committee on Public and Professional Relations (AAAP), 378–379
Committee on Relations between Psychology and the Medical Profession (APA), 444
Committee on the Certification of Consulting Psychologists (APA), 371
Committee on the Classification of Personnel in the Army, 307
Committee on Training in Clinical Psychology (CTCP), 434, 440–443
Common intellective factor, 312
Common sense, 309
Commonsense realism, 95n22
Communication
    with the dead, 126
    between disciplines, 439
    between living persons, 129
    spiritualistic, 122
Communist Party, 361
Community, 536–537
Comparative psychology, 201
Comparative Psychology of Mental Development (H. Werner), 74
Computer science, 206
Comte, Auguste, 248, 500
Comtemplative ideal, 256
Concensus, 319
Concurrent validities, 307
Conditionality, 282–283
Conditional reflexes, 188, 225, 228–233
Conditioned fear, 248
Conditioned reflex, conditional vs., 228
Conditioned responses, 238–240
Conditioned stimulus, 245
Conditioning, 242, 243, 246
Conflict situations, 412
Congregationalism, 83
Connectionism, 192
Consciousness

bifurcated, 28
false, 36
William James on, 111
motor theory of, 201–202
psychology of, 115n8
study of, 202–204
Wundt's experiments on, 198–199
Consciousness and Society (H. S. Hughes), 75
Conservation of energy, 69
Consistency, 316
Consulting psychology, 375
Contemporary testimony test (of revolution), 196
Continuous discussion, 394
Contributions to Philosophy and Psychology, 144
Control, 260
    of culture, 264–265
    of human behavior, 255, 510–511
    of nature, 256, 262, 263
Controversy
    in APA, 148
    in research, 351–352
    in science, 408, 419–420
Conversion stage (of Cohen model), 196
Convulsive seizures, 412
Cook, Thomas, 585
Coon, Deborah J., 61
Coover, John E., 129
Copernican Revolution, 193
Coriat, I. H., 474
Cornell University
    German model at, 142
    Jews at, 548
    Kurt Lewin at, 389–390, 393, 399, 555n15
    philosophy at, 160
    E. B. Titchener at, 147
    women at, 393, 532–533, 536
Cornwell, D., 242, 247
Correlation, 311
Correlation statistics, 312
Corwin, S. M., 480
Counseling and Psychotherapy (Carl Rogers), 458
Courage, 336
Cowles, Edward, 147, 149, 467
Creative cognition, 105
Credibility, 29
Creighton, J. E., 160
Crisis stage (of scientific revolution), 195
Criteria for the Life History (J. Dollard), 461
Crookes, William, 123, 131

Cross, William E., Jr., 594–595
CTCP. *See* Committee on Training in Clinical Psychology
Culler, Elmer, 412
Cultural approach, 277
Cultural reforms, 267n2
Culture
    of American medicine and psychiatry, 459, 460–464
    behaviorism and American, 256
    control of, 264–265
    differences in, 395, 399
    personality psychology in context of, 326
Cumulative recorder, 260

Dabblers, 11, 12
Dallenbach, Karl, 50, 549, 551
Daniels, George, 46
Danziger, Kurt, 62, 289, 307–308, 326, 341, 401
Dark Ghetto (Kenneth B. Clark), 583–586, 590, 595–599
Dartmouth College, 83
Darwin, Charles, 85–86, 105, 109, 289
Darwinian theories, 90, 96n31, 110, 144, 201, 202, 279, 310, 316
Davidson, Thomas, 123–124
Davis, Allison, 584
Dean, P. R., 318
Deconstruction, 33
Defensive aggressiveness, 549, 550
Degeneracy, 291
Delaboeuf, J., 173
Delacroix, Eugène, 106n1, 107
Dell, Floyd, 514
Dembo, Tamara, 391–393, 397
Democratic educational style, 395
Democratic group studies, 393–396, 399
Dennis, Wayne, 442
Derner, G. F., 446
DeSilva, Harry, 551–552
Development, human, 144
Developmental psychology, 153, 275–276, 289, 299
Dewey, John
    and American ideology, 361
    and APA, 147, 151
    on bettering democracy, 514
    education impacted by, 297
    on William James, 102
    William James' influence on, 116n10
    and laboratory method, 89
    and League for Independent Political Action, 358n6
    Psychology of, 93n16
    and psychology vs. philosophy, 96n31
    and social adjustment, 201
    and social order, 454, 461
The Dial, 136
Dickinson, C. A., 560
Dictionary of Philosophy and Psychology (James M. Baldwin), 155
Differences, individual, 36–37
Differential diagnosis, 330
"Difficult personalities," 567
Digestive physiology, 217–226
Dilthey, Wilhelm, 8
Dinnerstein, L., 553
Disciplinary matrix, 208
Disciplinary societies, 142
Discourse analysis, 33
Distribution of psychological characteristics in populations, 177
Diversification (of scientist/professional model), 442
Diversity, 5, 276, 330
Division 9 (APA), 350
Division 14 (APA), 380–381
Division 26 (APA), 5
Dixon, T. R., 206
Doctoral education, 438
"Doctoral Training Programs in Clinical Psychology" (APA), 440
Doctor–patient relationship, 174
Dogs, 220
Doll, E. A., 433, 436
Doll-and-coloring techniques, 587
Dollard, J., 461–463, 482
Doll technique, 576n2, 581n7, 587
Dominant ideology, 37
Donders, F., 74
Donley, J. E., 473
"The Door" (E. B. White), 411
Dorcus, Roy, 378
"Double effect" of war, 513
DuBois, W. E. B., 116n10
Duke University, 49n6, 549n9
Dunlap, Jack, 380
Dunlap, Knight, 474, 476, 515
Duty, 336
Dyad experiments, 394

Eagley, Alice, 25

Early Forms of Vocal Expression questionnaire, 290
Eastern Psychological Association, 154
Eberhart, John C., 442
Ecological psychology, 401
Economic psychology, 370
Edgerton, Harold, 380
Editor's Handbook (APA), 419
Educated elite, 309
Education
    for empathy and respect, 592–594
    and mental testing, 318
    multicultural, 592
    public, 589
    reform goals for, 315
    studies of groups in, 394
    for women, 530–532
    Yerkes' pland for reform of, 317–318
Educational fitness, 315
Educational Problems (G. Stanley Hall), 298
Educational psychology, 371, 375
Educational systems, 176
"The Effect of Environmental Forces" (Kurt Lewin), 389
"The Effects of Segregation and the Consequences of Desegregation" (Clark, Cook & Chein), 585
Einstein, Albert, 599
Elemental processes, 70–71
Elements of Human Psychology (Warren & Carmichael), 483
Elements of Intellectual Philosophy (Francis Wayland), 93n16
Elements of Intellectual Philosophy (Thomas C. Upham), 91n2, 93n16, 95n26
Elements of Mental Philosophy (Thomas C. Upham), 88, 91n2, 93n16, 96n26
Elements of Moral Science (Francis Wayland), 94n19
Elements of the Philosophy of the Human Mind (Dugald Stewart), 79, 91n2, 97n44
Eliot, Charles, 310
Ellis, Albert, 481
Emergency Committee in Aid of Displaced Foreign Scholars, 389
Emerson, Ralph Waldo, 104, 106, 109, 328
Emerson College, 552
Emotion
    and child development, 290–291
    James–Lange theory of, 201
    theory of, 240
Empathy, 593, 599, 600

Empirical Psychology (Laurens P. Hickok), 93n16, 94n20
Empiricism, feminist, 26–27
Employee selection, 370
Employers, mental testing and, 320
Employment of psychologists
    in early 19th century, 161
    female, 534
    during Great Depression, 349–350, 353–366
    Jewish, 546–568
"Enduring moral project," 340–341
Energy, conservation of, 69
Engel, G. L., 447
English-language studies, 175–176
English philosophy, 91
Enlightenment, 193
Environmentalism, 337
Episcopalianism, 336–337
Epistemologies, feminist standpoint, 27–30, 37–38
Epstein, Cynthia Fuchs, 25
Ericsson, K. A., 208
Essay Concerning Human Understanding (John Locke), 79, 91n1
Essays (Francis Bacon), 257
Estel, V., 171
Ethical malaise, 334
Ethics code (for industrial psychologists), 378
Ethnic identity, 598–599
"Eugenia," 505
Eugenics, 354, 355, 505
Eugenics Research Association, 354, 363
"Eupsychias," 513
Evaluation
    criteria for, 33–34
    of psychoanalysis, 479–481
    of schools for clinical psychology, 440–441, 443
Evans, Rand, 82
Evolution, 85–86, 201, 202, 315, 504
"The Excursion" (William Wordsworth), 106, 109
Executive Council (APA), 50–51
Expansionism, 358–361, 364, 365
Experience, Wundtian view of, 66–67, 71–72
Experimental introspection, 198, 199
Experimentalism. *See* Experimental psychology
Experimentalists, 46, 147, 158
"Experimentalizers," 47

"Experimentally Produced Neurotic Behavior in the Rat" (Norman Maier), 410
Experimental method, 89, 261–262
Experimental psychology, 121, 159. *See also* Psychological experiment
  APA members in, 52
  applied psychology vs., 46–54
  beginnings of, 59, 65
  clinical psychology vs., 435, 446–448
  founding of, 198
  Norman Maier and, 413
  Clifford Morgan and, 414
  in 1920s, 45–54
  promotion of, 263
  and reform movement, 515–516
  and spiritualism, 125–135
  visibility of, 52–53
  Wilhelm Wundt and, 67–68
"Experimental Psychology at the World's Fair" (Joseph Jastrow), 148
Experimental reality, 261
Experimental social psychology, 401
"An Experimental Study of the Traits of Personality" (Gordon Allport), 332
Experimenter (term), 170–173, 175
"Extinction," 225, 226
Eye, study of the, 97n38
Eyelid reflexes, 225–226
"Eye-picture," 113
Eysenck, H. J., 243, 245, 481

Factory system, 388
Facts, artifacts vs., 258
Failure, reactions to, 394
Fairness, 566
Faith, 336, 446
Fajans, Sara, 394
"The Fall of Atlantis" (Hall), 502
False consciousness, 36
"Family claims," 537–538
Farrand, Livingston, 151
Fay, Jay Wharton, 81
Fear, 238–247
Fechner, Gustave Theodor, 123, 125, 289
Federal government, 430
  clinical psychology funded by, 461
  funding proposals for, 362
  research funded by, 458
  and veterans, 454–455
Feeney, Mark, 600
Feinstein, Howard, 102, 106
Fellowship of the New Life, 123

Feminism, 22–38
  alternate research based on, 35–36
  feminist empiricism, 26–27
  feminist method, 35–36
  feminist postmodernism, 30–34
  feminist standpoint epistemologies, 27–30, 37–38
Feminist empiricism, 26–27
Feminist method, 35–36
Feminist postmodernism, 30–34
Feminist standpoint epistemologies, 27–30, 37–38
Feminist (term), 23
Féré, C., 173
Fernandez, Joseph A., 593
Fernberger, Samuel, 50, 51, 557–558
Fichte, Johann, 75
Field theory, Lewinian, 400, 401
"Fifty Years of Clinical Psychology" (APA), 433
Film studies, 240n1, 393
Financial support, 351
Finger, Frank W., 412, 413, 416, 419
Firm rank method, 320
Fite, Warner, 474
Fontenelle, Bernard de, 193, 202
Ford, Henry, 553
Ford, James, 334
Forward America, 361
Founders of Modern Psychology (G. Stanley Hall), 287
Fox, Kate, 122
Fox, Margaret, 122
Frank, Jerome D., 556
Frank, Lawrence K., 389–391, 393
Free association, 476
"The Freedom of Will" (B. Chrysostom), 158, 159
French philosophy, 81
French Revolution, 193
Freud, Sigmund, 23
  behaviorist reworkings of, 482–483
  and E. G. Boring, 478
  and J. F. Brown, 461
  James McKeen Cattell on, 486
  and G. Stanley Hall, 298
  impact of, 484
  studies of theories of, 481–482
  U.S. visit of, 471–474, 502
Freud–Jung word association tests, 134
Friedman, S. M., 480
Frustration (Norman Maier), 419

Frustration studies, 397, 412, 414
Fryer, Douglas, 372, 374, 375
Fuchs, Alfred H., 60–61
Fullerton, George, 124, 147, 151
Functionalism, 47–48, 89–90, 199, 310
Functional uniformity, 313
"The Functions of the Psychologist in the State Hospital" (David Shakow), 436
Fundamental human emotions, 240

g. *See* General intelligence
Gadamer, Hans-Georg, 582
Gale, Harlow, 370
"Galilean" situations, 388, 397
Galileo, 192, 388
Gall, Franz Joseph, 16
Gallup, Gordon G., Jr., 420
Galton, Sir Francis, 62, 152, 311
Galtonian model, 177, 178
Galvanic skin response (GSR) conditioning, 245
Gamble, Eleanor Acheson McCullough, 530, 532
Ganzheit psychology, 71
GAP (Group for the Advancement of Psychiatry), 443
Gardner, H., 204–207
Garfield, James, 282
Garner, W. R., 413
Garrett, H. E., 476
Gavey, Nicola, 33
Geertz, Clifford, 386
Gender, 37, 173
Gender bias, 23
General intelligence (*g*), 312–314, 316–320
General Psychology (W. S. Hunter), 483
Genetic engineering, 265
Geological Society of America, 143
George, Lloyd, 313
Gergen, Mary, 35
Geriatric cases, 467
German education, 287
German Idealism, 143
German laboratory method, 90
German language, 83, 95n21
German model, 144
German philosophy, 81, 91
German psychology, 80, 82, 86
German research ideal, 142
German-speaking Europe, 386–389
German universities, 173

Germany, 52, 351, 390, 395, 507, 554
Gestalt psychology, 52, 71, 387, 388, 401, 562, 564
Ghelpanov, G. I., 223
Gifted students, 316
Gilded Age, 141–142
Gilligan, Carol, 28–29
Gilman, Benjamin I., 147
Gilman, Daniel Coit, 145, 279, 280
Gilmore, Eugene A., 392
Glorius Revolution (1688), 193
Goddard, H. H., 315
Goethe, Johann Wolfgang von, 75, 106
Goldwater, Barry, 358n6
Goodman, Nelson, 116n10
Goodness, search for, 334
"Good physiology," 218, 224, 226, 229, 230, 232
Gordon, Kate, 529–531, 533
Governance, orders of, 284–285
Graduate professional programs, 438, 439, 533–534
Grant, J., 33
Grant, Madison, 550
Grant approval, 440
Graumann, Carl-Friedrich, 398
Great Depression
    applied-science movement during, 431
    employment of psychologists during, 349
    organized psychology during, 353–366
    psychology during, 53
    reputation of psychology during, 378
Great Experiments in Psychology (Garrett), 476
"Great Man" studies, 12
Greek language, 313
Group behavior studies, 393–399
Group-data studies, 386–388
Group for the Advancement of Psychiatry (GAP), 443
Groups, ranked, 29
GSR (galvanic skin response) conditioning, 245
Gulliver, Julia Henrietta, 529, 530, 533

Haggerty, M. E., 202
Hall, Calvin S., 558
Hall, G. Stanley, 279–281, 285–299
    Adolescence of, 292–293
    and *American Journal of Psychology*, 144, 155
    American psychology promoted by, 176, 177

APA role of, 62, 141, 145–149
child and adolescent development psychology of, 292–299
child studies of, 288–292
at Clark University, 178, 288–289, 298
and educational applications of psychology, 370
Educational Problems of, 298
Founders of Modern Psychology of, 287
and Sigmund Freud's American visit, 502
on William James, 101, 131
Jesus, the Christ, in the Light of Psychology of, 298
at Johns Hopkins University, 279–280, 287–288
late life interests of, 297–298
Life and Confessions of, 281, 282, 297–298
personal background of, 281
and psychic phenomena, 127
and recapitulation theory, 315
seminary training of, 86
and spiritualism, 124, 132–134, 145
terminology used by, 171, 175
treatment of Jewish students by, 552
utopianism of, 499, 501–504, 514–516
on war's effect on applied psychology, 46
at Williams College, 275, 281, 285–287
and Robert M. Yerkes, 306
Hamlin, Cyrus, 94n16
Hampton Institute, 585, 598
Hand-writing scale, 319
Harding, Sandra, 13, 22, 26
Hare-Mustin, Rachel, 32
Harlem, 598
Harlem Youth Opportunities Unlimited Project (HARYOU), 585, 599
Harlow, Harry F., 420
Harper, William Rainey, 146, 288
Harper's, 125, 131
Harris, Abraham, 584
Harris, B., 189, 500
Harvard Book for Religious, Racial, and Political Tolerance, 566
Harvard Committee to Aid German Student Refugees (1938), 566
Harvard University, 287, 351
  Gordon Allport at, 328–329, 332
  Edwin Boring at, 47–50, 389, 545
  clinical psychology at, 434–435
  G. Stanley Hall at, 288
  Leo Hurvich and, 559
  William James at, 108
  Kurt Lewin and, 392
  Hugo Münsterberg at, 147, 507, 539
  new pluralistic liberal style at, 310
  philosophy at, 91n2
  and psychic research, 128, 129
  Psychological Studies of, 144
  psychology separate from philosophy at, 92n5
  and standards, 356
  treatment of Jews at, 552, 553, 565, 568
  Unitarian theology of, 83
  and women, 533, 536, 539
Harwood, J., 386
HARYOU. *See* Harlem Youth Opportunities Unlimited Project
Haven, Joseph, 60, 80, 82–85, 92n3, 93n16, 94n19
Haverford College, 287
Hawley, P. R., 433
Hawthorne, Nathaniel, 106, 285
Health insurance, national, 446, 448
Hebb, D. O., 483
Hebrew University, 391, 398
Hegel, G. W. F., 75, 92n8, 287
Heidbreder, E., 476
Heidegger, Martin, 582
Heiser, Karl, 440, 442
Helmholtz, Hermann von, 125
Helson, Harry, 551
Henle, M., 408
Henry Russel Award, 411
Herbart, Johann, 69, 287
Heredity, 4, 549n9
Hickok, Laurens, 60, 82–85, 93n16, 94n19
Higham, J., 566
Hildreth, Gertrude, 372
Hildreth, Jane, 416
Hilgard, Ernest R., 82, 410, 435, 440, 454, 481n9, 484, 555
Hill Collins, Patricia, 577–579
Hillis, Cora Bussey Hillis, 298
Hillix, W. A., 413
Hilltop, 584
Hinman, Alice Hamlin, 529–533
Hiroshima, 265
Hirsch, Nathaniel, 549
Historian's judgment test (of revolution), 196
"Historicists," 12
Historiography, 11

"History and Prospects of Experimental Psychology in America" (G. Stanley Hall), 148
A History of American Psychology (A. A. Roback), 81, 561
History of Experimental Psychology (E. G. Boring), 18, 45–46, 48, 52–53, 60, 80, 92n5, 478, 564
History of psychology, 3–5, 16–20, 499–501
    and applied psychology vs. experimental psychology controversy, 53–54
    and experiments, 169–170
    influence of imported philosophies in American, 91
    mental philosophy neglected in, 80–82
    treatment of Wilhelm Wundt in, 66, 67
    women omitted from, 528
History of Psychology (journal), 5
History of science, 15–16, 500
History of the Human Sciences, 5
Hitler, Adolf, 361
Hixon Symposium on Cerebral Mechanisms in Behavior, 204, 205
Hobbs, S., 242, 247
Hodgson, Richard, 147
Holism, 70–71, 388
Hollinger, D., 565–566
Hollingworth, Harry, 247, 370
Hollingworth, Leta, 4
Holocaust, 560
Holt, E. B., 48, 482
Homo faber, 259
Homo sapiens, 259
Hooks, Bell, 29
Hopkins, Mark, 96n29, 281–286, 297
Hormic school of psychology, 505
Hornstein, Gail A., 431–432
Horowitz, R., 581n7
Horst, Paul, 378
Horton, D. L., 206
Houston, Charles Hamilton, 584
Howard University, 584
Howes, Ethel. *See* Puffer, Ethel Dench
"How Jewish Are You" questionnaire, 561, 562
Hughes, H. Stuart, 75
Hull, Clark, 19, 365, 366, 387, 399, 551
Hull, D., 204, 209
Hull-Spence learning theory, 400
Human cognition, 386
Human development, patterns of, 293–297
The Human Intellect (Noah Porter), 92n2

Humanistic psychology, 198
Humanization (of factory system), 388
Human sensitivity, 592
Human understanding, 104–116
Humboldt, Alexander von, 75
Humility, 335, 336
Humphrey, G., 482
Hunt, J. McV., 444
Hunt, William A., 442, 557
Hunt, William Morris, 102, 106n1, 107, 108n2, 114n6
Hunter, Walter S., 203, 354–357, 483
Hurvich, Leo, 547, 557–560
Huxley, Thomas, 231, 279
Hypnosis, 62, 173–176
Hypnotizer, 129
Hypothetico-deductive model of learning theory, 387
Hyslop, James H., 124, 147
Hysterics, 174

Iconic memory, 199
ICWRS. *See* Iowa Child Welfare Research Station
Identity, multiple status, 30
Imageless thought controversy, 199, 200
Immigration, 360
    and American nativism, 566
    German-speaking, 401
    Jewish, 546, 556–557, 568
Inclusiveness, 98n48
Independent socialist thinking, 388
Indiana University, 148
Individual differences, 36–37, 291, 311
Individuality, personality vs., 332–333
Induced seizures in experimental rats, 351–352
Industrialization, 329, 334
Industrial–organizational psychology, 370, 376, 381
Industrial psychology, 369–381
    AAAP and, 374–381
    ACP and, 371–374
    areas of, 377
    Norman Maier and, 414
    1939 AAAP membership list for, 376
    number of AAAP members in, 375
    presidents and secretaries for, section of AAAP, 377
    as term, 370
    during World War II, 379–380
Infants, 174, 238–241, 243–245, 290

Information processing, 67, 192
Information-processing devices, 209
Information-processing psychology, 207–209
"The Inheritance of Acquired Characteristics" (William James), 151
Innate mentality, 318
"Inquisition of Causes" (Francis Bacon), 259
Insight, 339
Insoluble problems, 409, 412
Institute of Child Welfare, 51
Instrumental-learning paradigms, 245
Integration, 586–592, 601
Intellect, 84
Intellectual philosophy, 79
Intelligence, 4
"Intelligence Quotient" (IQ), 315–316
Intelligence testing, 397
Intelligible perspective, 112
Interest, concept of, 112, 114
"Intergroup relations," 589
"Internalists," 12
International Congress of Physiologists, 228
International Congress of Psychology, 144, 389
International Congress of Psychology, Proceedings and Papers, 92n4
Internships, 439–440, 446
    placement of, 448
    in psychiatric vs. medical settings, 465
    purposes of, 436
"An Internship Year for Psychologists" (Shakow), 436
Interpretive–phenomenological approach, 28
Introduction to Psychology (Carl Seashore), 483
Introduction to Psychology (Clifford T. Morgan), 414
Introspection, 67, 89, 198–200
Iowa, 144, 351
Iowa Child Welfare Research Station (ICWRS), 298, 390–394, 399, 401
IQ. *See* "Intelligence Quotient"
"The Island of Eugenia" (William McDougall), 505
Israel, H. E., 551

Jacklin, Carol, 24
Jackson, John Hughlings, 293
Jacobsen, Carlyle, 444
James, Henry, 106–108, 109n3, 116
James, William, 5, 7, 101–117, 507
    and American psychology, 60
    analogies and metaphors of, 110–115
    and APA, 147, 149
    as APA president, 149, 454
    as artist, 102–103, 106–109, 116
    and Edwin Boring, 80
    and Darwinism, 110
    death of, 47
    at first International Congress of Psychology, 144
    and G. Stanley Hall, 101, 280, 287
    on human understanding, 104–116
    and John La Farge, 107–108
    in National Academy of Sciences, 162
    on new psychology, 87
    on philosophy, 103–104
    Principles of Psychology of, 61, 86, 101, 105, 109–116, 129, 199
    reductive psychology of, 210
    and self-introspection, 199
    and David Shakow, 434
    and A. T. Snarski, 223
    and spiritualism, 61, 123–125, 129–131, 133
    treatment of Jewish students by, 552
James–Lange theory of emotion, 201
Janet, Pierre, 124
Jarrett, Mary, 329
Jastrow, Joseph
    as APA president, 552
    and applied psychology, 47
    on authority, 131–132
    and behaviorism, 202
    and Committee on Physical and Mental Testing, 152
    at first International Congress of Psychology, 144
    on history of psychology, 53
    on psychoanalysis, 476
    and social psychology, 515
    and spiritualism, 124, 127, 128, 134, 135
    and World Columbian Exposition, 146–148, 151
Jaynes, J., 547n5
JCPP. *See* Journal of Comparative and Physiological Psychology
Jefferson, T., 316
Jenkins, John, 380
Jesus, the Christ, in the Light of Psychology (G. Stanley Hall), 298
Jewish immigrants, 351
Jewish Influence in Modern Thought (A. A. Roback), 561

Jewish self-hatred, 565
Jews/Judaism, 147, 398, 545–568
Johns Hopkins University
    James M. Baldwin at, 156
    James McKeen Cattell at, 80
    German research ideal adopted at, 142
    G. Stanley Hall at, 145, 275, 279–280, 287–288
    infant studies at, 240n1, 241
    Clifford T. Morgan at, 412, 413
    terminology used at, 171
    women at, 536
Johnson, Mordecai, 584
Jones, Ernest, 474
Jones, H. E., 245
Jones, Howard, 564
Jones, M. C., 240n1
The Journal. See *American Journal of Psychology*
Journal of Abnormal and Social Psychology, 478
Journal of Abnormal Psychology, 473–475
Journal of Animal Behavior, 538
Journal of Applied Psychology, 52, 305, 306, 320, 370
Journal of Comparative and Physiological Psychology (JCPP), 417, 420
Journal of Comparative Psychology, 415, 416, 420
Journal of Consulting Psychology, 374, 376
Journal of Educational Psychology, 303
Journal of Experimental Psychology, 240n1
Journal of Genetic Psychology, 146, 288
Journal of Philosophy, Psychology and Scientific Methods, 156
Journal of the History of the Behavioral Sciences, 5, 18
Journals, 5
Judd, Charles, 53
Judgment, 446
Jung, Carl, 471–474
Justice, 28–29

Kant, Immanuel, 75, 83
Karier, C. J., 281
Karsten, Anitra, 393
Keller, Evelyn Fox, 27
Keller, F., 482
Keller, Helen, 116n10, 483
Kelly, Lowell, 440, 442, 444
Kelson, Jacob, 546, 550, 558
Kendler, H. H., 205
Kendler, T. S., 205

Kent, Grace, 4, 431
Kent-Rosanoff Test, 4
Kentucky, 29
Kessen, William, 468
Kimble, Gregory A., 16–20, 484
King, Martin Luther, Jr., 596, 597, 600
Kitzinger, Celia, 33
Klein, David B., 557
Klineberg, Otto, 585
Kluger, R., 580, 582
Kluver, Heinrich, 410
Knee reflexes, 225–226
Knowledge, subjugated, 29
Kodama, Seiji, 94n16
Koffka, Kurt, 390
Köhler, Wolfgang, 388, 390, 410
Kohlstedt, S. C., 286
Kollert, J., 171
Korsch, Karl, 388
Koyré, Alexander, 194
Kraepelin, Emil, 72
Krech, David (Isadore Krechevsky), 361, 362, 364–366, 435
Krutch, Joseph Wood, 336
Kuhn, Thomas S., 193–196, 200, 203–208, 210, 248n4
Kuhn's stages of scientific revolution, 194–195
Kuklick, B., 567
Kurzweil, E., 481

Laboratory of Psychology (NIMH), 431
Lachman, J., 207
Lachman, R., 207
Ladd, Christine. See Ladd-Franklin, Christine
Ladd, George Trumbull, 86, 96n31, 147, 149, 151
Ladd, James, 147
Ladd-Franklin, Christine, 124, 149, 474–475, 529–531, 535–539
La Farge, John, 102, 107–108
Lafayette College, 80
Lamarckian theory, 506
Landis, Carney, 478, 550
Langfeld, H. S., 48, 50–51, 478, 565
Language, 30–31
    of technology, 261
    Wundt's analysis of, 72
Lashley, Karl, 49, 205, 239, 410, 412
Lashley Jumping Stand, 408–409
Later documentary history test (of revolution), 196

Lather, P., 36
Latin, study of, 312
Laura Spelman Rockefeller Memorial (LSRM), 389, 392
Lavoisier, Antoine, 193, 202
Law of limitation, 283–284, 297
Lay, W., 318
League for Independent Political Action, 358n6, 361, 364
Leahey, Thomas Hardy, 188, 199
Learning theory, 242, 351, 365–366, 387, 400
Leary, David E., 61
Lectures on Conditioned Reflexes (Ivan Pavlov), 231
Lectures on Moral Science (Mark Hopkins), 282
Lectures on the Work of the Principal Digestive Glands (Ivan Pavlov), 219
Leibniz, Gottfried Willhelm, 116n10
Leipzig model, 62, 170–171, 175, 176
Leipzig University, 144, 533
Lemann, Nicholas, 586, 595
Lerner, Gerda, 528
Leuba, James H., 154
Levine, Jacob, 547n5, 559
Lewin, Kurt, 351, 385–401, 461
  and anti-Semitism, 389, 390, 545, 547
  and Edwin Boring, 553–556
  criticisms of, 400
  emigration of, to United States, 389–390
  frustration and regression, research on, 397
  at Iowa Child Welfare Research Station, 390–394, 399
  on Jewish self-hatred, 565
  and Lewin Group in Berlin, 387–389
  and Norman Maier, 410
  minority groups, research on psychosocial problems of, 397–398
  national cultural differences, research on, 395–396, 399
  The Socialization of the Taylor System of, 388, 398
  students of, 400–401
Lewin, Miriam, 555n15
Lewinian field theory, 400, 401
Liberalized S–R theory, 205, 208
Life and Confessions (G. Stanley Hall), 281, 282, 297–298
Life magazine, 411

"Life space," 398
Life-span development, 298
Likert, Rensis, 372, 373, 444
Limitation, law of, 283–284, 297
Linguistic uniformity, 174
Linguists, 206
Link, Henry, 372, 373, 379
Lippitt, Ronald, 393–396
Lippmann, Walter, 116n10, 316, 514
Little Albert study, 19, 189, 237–249, 500
  behavior therapists' views of, 243–245
  context of, 239–241
  introductory-level textbook versions of, 241–243
  and preparedness theory, 245–247
Local knowledge, 386
Locke, Alain, 584, 585
Locke, John, 19, 79, 83, 91n1
Lodge, Oliver, 123, 131
Loeb, Jacques, 223, 547n4
Logical positivism, 19, 209
Longhurst, J. U., 416–417
Lorde, Audre, 30
Lorenz, G., 172
Lowell, A. L., 48–49, 553
Loyalty oath, California, 567n28
LSRM. *See* Laura Spelman Rockefeller Memorial
Lubove, Roy, 330
Luckey, Bertha, 440
Lyceum of Natural History, 286

MacCorquodale, K., 204
MacDonald, Arthur, 151–153
MacKinnon, Catherine, 31–32
Magaret, Ann, 442
Maher, Brendan, 18
Maher, Winifred, 18
Maier, Norman, 351–352, 390, 407–422
  AAAS prize awarded to, 410–412, 415
  controversy surrounding, 412–413, 416–421
  decline in reputation of, 412–413
  and discovery of role of auditory stimuli, 415–416
  Frustration of, 419
  later career of, 413–415
  and Clifford T. Morgan, 412–419, 421
  personal background of, 410
  Principles of Animal Psychology of, 410, 413
  research of, 408–409

"Maier's Law," 421
Maimonides, 16
Malcolm, Janet, 479
Malcolm X, 597
Mama, A., 577–579
Mandler, George, 209
Manicas, Peter, 37
"Man of character," 335, 336
"Man-soul," 502
Maracek, Jeanne, 32
Marks, I., 246
Marriage(s)
    career vs., 537–540
    Jews in mixed, 561, 563–565
Marrow, A., 553, 555
Marshall, Thurgood, 580
Marshall College, 287
Martin, Joanne, 33
Martin, Lillien, 529, 530, 534–535
Marx, Karl, 461
Marx, M. H., 413
Marxism, 361
Maslow, Abraham, 551
Mason City Gazette, 392
Massachusetts Institute of Technology (MIT), 128, 204–205, 390, 399
Materialism, 280
Matisse, Henri, 106n1
"Matriarchal structure" (of the Black family), 586
Mature personality, 338–339
Mayer, Michael, 576
Mayrhauser, Richard von, 276, 565n24
McCullough, J. P., 447
McDougall, William, 49
    at Harvard, 434
    and Nathaniel Hirsch, 549n9
    and Kurt Lewin, 555
    utopianism of, 499, 501, 504–507, 514–516
McHugh, Maureen, 26
McKeag, Anna Jane, 529, 530
McLean Hospital, 147
Measurement techniques, 397
Mechanistic psychology, 74
Mediational psychology, 204
Mediational S–R behaviorists, 209
Mediational theories, 205
Medical context, 174
Mediums, 133–134
Meehl, P., 204
Mehner, M., 172

Memory tests, 153
Mental Development in the Child and the Race (James Baldwin), 153
Mental disorders, 98n48, 430
Mental energy, 311
Mentalism, 191
Mentality, 310–313, 315
    definition of, 311
    explanation of, 310
Mental philosophy, 79–91
    in early to mid-19th century, 82–84
    and experimental method, 89
    and functionalism, 89–90
    late 19th-centruy rejection of, 84–87
    legacy of, 87–90
    neglect of, in history of psychology, 80–82
    19th-century, 81–82
Mental Philosophy (Joseph Haven), 80, 92n3, 93n16
Mental telepathy, 126, 129, 130
Mental testing, 151, 303–321
    assumptions of, 311
    Alfred Binet and, 303, 308, 314–317, 320
    James McKeen Cattell and, 311–312, 314, 316
    and emergence of ideal of validity, 307–308, 311–321
    first appearance of, in United States, 310–311
    Walter D. Scott and, 305, 307
    Carl E. Seashore and, 304–305
    and social change in late 19th century, 308–310
    Charles Spearman and, 308, 312–318, 320
    Lewis Terman and, 306, 315–318
    Edward L. Thorndike and, 305, 307, 313, 318–319
    Robert M. Yerkes and, 303–307, 316–318, 320–321
Merkel, J., 172
Metaphors, use of, 61, 104–105, 109, 113, 115
Methodist evangelism, 328
Methodology, 11–12, 249
    feminist method, 35–36
    standards of, 62–63
    of Wilhelm Wundt, 66–68
The Metropolitan, 132
Miami Conference (1959), 442

Middle class, 310, 314
Midwestern Psychological Association (MPA), 154, 362, 414
Migration to cities, 200–201
Miles, Walter, 553
Military personnel testing, 4, 306–307, 321
Miller, Beulah, 132–133
Miller, D. R., 480
Miller, George, 207
Miller, James G., 442
Miller, Neal E., 410, 482
Mills, C. W., 468
Mills, J. S., 69, 70
Mind
    powers of the, 284
    and spiritualism, 126
    study of the, 87
    understanding the, 104–105
    unitary, 276
Mind–body dualism, 67
"Mind of the glands," 223, 226
Mind-picture, 113
Mind-reading, 132–133
Ministry, 82–83, 86, 285, 292
Minorities, 29–30, 397–398, 442
Mischel, T., 68
Missionaries, 327
MIT. See Massachusetts Institute of Technology
Mixed schools, 587
Modes of research, 27
Moore, Bruce V., 372, 377–380, 436
Moore, J. S., 551
Moore, V. F., 529–531, 533
Moral code, 339, 340
Moral courage, 335–336
Moral development, 28–29
Moralism, excessive, 333
Morality, 340, 501
Moral philosophy, 94n19, 275, 281, 282
Moral Philosophy (Joseph Haven), 94n19
Moral relativism, 339
Moral science (of Mark Hopkins), 282–285
Moral sentiments, 291
Morawski, J. G., 483
More, Thomas, 262, 512
Morgan, Clifford T., 352, 407, 412–419, 421
Morgan, J. D., 412
Morgan, J. J. B., 240
Morgan, Jane. See Hildreth, Jane
Morris, George Sylvester, 145, 280

Motherhood, career vs., 537–540
Mother's Club, 328
Motor activity, 295
Motor tests, 152
Motor theory of consciousness, 201–202
Movement and Mental Imagery (M. F. Washburn), 538
Mowrer, O. H., 480
Moynihan, Daniel Patrick, 576, 586, 595
MPA. See Midwestern Psychological Association
Mucin, 221
Multicultural education, 592
Multiple status identities, 30
Munn, N. L., 412
Münsterberg, Hugo, 47–48, 370
    and APA, 147
    as APA president, 552
    Mary Calkins/Ethel Puffer mentored by, 538, 539
    as introspectionist, 201
    persona of, 555
    Psychology and Industrial Efficiency of, 370
    and A. A. Roback, 549
    and spiritualism, 126, 128, 132–135
    Tomorrow of, 507–508
    utopianism of, 500, 501, 507–509, 514–516
Murchison, Carl, 414
Murphy, Gardner, 390, 484, 557, 585
Murphy, Lois, 390
Murray, Harry, 356
Myers, F. W. H., 124
Myers, Linda James, 577, 579
Myrdal, Gunnar, 585
Mysticism, Freudianism and Scientific Psychology (K. Dunlap), 474

NAACP. See National Association for the Advancement of Colored People
NAACP–LDF. See National Association for the Advancement of Colored People Legal Defense Fund
Napoli, Donald, 381
Narrative accounts, 299
Nascent stages, 294
Natinal Research Council Fellow, 410
The Nation, 125
National Academy of Sciences, 162, 501
National Association for the Advancement of Colored People Legal Defense

Fund (NAACP–LDF), 576, 580, 582, 597
National Association for the Advancement of Colored People (NAACP), 3, 598
National Educational Association (NEA), 146
National health insurance, 446, 448
National Institute of Industrial Psychology, 378–379
National Institute of Mental Health (NIMH), 430, 431, 448, 458, 464
National Organizing Committee, 364–365
National Psychological Institute, 127
National Research Council, 380, 550
National socialism, 351
Nativism, 566
Natural history societies, 286–287
Natural philosophy, 83
Natural theology, 83
Natural Theology (William Paley), 83
Nature, 256, 258–259, 262, 263
Nature, 125
"Nature of Control in the Psychological Experiment" (E. G. Boring), 435
Nazis, 361, 390, 411
NEA (National Educational Association), 146
The Negro Family (Daniel Patrick Moynihan), 576, 586
The Negro Protest (Kenneth B. Clark), 597
Neisser, U., 206–208
Neobehaviorists, 399
Neo-Kantianism, 75–76
Neo-Platonism, 17
Neurosis, 473
"Neuro–Social Data" (Arthur MacDonald), 151
Neurotic behavior, 412
New America, 350, 361–362, 364
The New Atlantis (Francis Bacon), 257, 262, 265
Newcomb, A., 378
Newcomb, Simon, 123
Newell, A., 205
New England transcendentalism, 92n8
"New history" of psychology, 12
New Organon (Francis Bacon), 257
"New psychology," 59–63, 86–87, 98n45, 125, 472
News Bulletin, 359
Newton, Isaac, 105, 194
"Newtonian" morality, 501, 516

Newton's method, 95n22
New York Academy of Sciences, 154
New York City Board of Education, 593
New York Psychoanalytic Society, 474
New York State Association of Consulting Psychologists, 371
New York Times, 411, 421, 584, 593
Nicholson, Ian A. M., 276–277
Nigrescence, 598
NIMH. *See* National Institute of Mental Health
Nisbett, R. E., 208
Nobel Prize, 217
Nomenclature, 170–171
"Nordic character," 550
Normal cognition, 175
Normal science stage (of scientific revolution), 194–195
Norsworthy, Naomi, 530, 533
North American Review, 125
Northern Congress of Physiologists (Helsinki), 227
Northside Center for Child Development (NYC), 576n2, 585
"A Note on Anaximander" (Nicholas Butler), 150
Noyes, William, 147, 149

"Objectionable traits," 546, 551, 554, 560, 565, 566
Objective Psychology (V. M. Bekhterev), 239
Objective self, 331, 333
Objectivity, 23, 31, 578, 583–584
Objects, 290
Observer (term), 171, 175
O'Donnell, John M., 13, 158
Office of War Information, 585
Ogden, Robert M., 390
Ol'denburgskii, Prince, 227, 228
Olds, James, 410
Oneness of psychology, 434–436
Openness (in APA), 147
Operant conditioning, 190
Operant psychology, 259–261, 267–269
Opinion of working scientists test (of revolution), 196–197
Oppenheimer, Robert J., 599
Orbeli, L. A., 228
Orders
    of governance, 284–285
    of physical matter, 283
    of psychological faculties, 284

INDEX   625

Organismic psychology, 74
Organizational psychology, 379. *See also* Industrial psychology
"Origin myths," 80, 189, 248, 500
Ormond, A. T., 160
O'Rourke, Lawrence J., 363
Osgood, C., 73
Otis, Jay, 380
Ouija board, 129

Pace, Edward A., 147
Palermo, David, 204–207
Paley, William, 83
Palmieri, Patricia, 536–537
Pantheism, 81
Paper and pencil instruments, 177
Paradigm, acceptance of a, 204
Paris model, 62, 175, 176
Parrish, Celestia Susannah, 529, 530
The Passing of the Great Race (Madison Grant), 550
Paterson, Donald, 373, 378
Pathos of Power (Kenneth B. Clark), 583, 590, 592, 596, 597, 599, 600
Pattie, Frank, 549
Pauling, Linus, 600
Pavlov, Ivan, 217–233
    coworkers of, 219
    as cultural icon, 217
    decisions of, to shift investigations from digestion to psyche, 226–230
    departure of, from scientific tradition, 218
    on digestive system, 219–220
    on his transition to research on conditional reflexes, 231–233
    Lectures on Conditioned Reflexes of, 231
    Lectures on the Work of the Principal Digestive Glands of, 219
    as physiologist, 217–218
    on psyche, 221, 222
    and A. T. Snarskii, 223–224
    and I. F. Tolochinov, 225–226
    and S. G. Vul'fson, 221–223
Pavlov, Ivan P., 6, 188
Peabody, Francis, 329
Pearsonian techniques, 177
Pedagogical Seminary, 146, 176, 241, 288
Pedagogists, 147
Peirce, Charles Sanders, 145, 280
Pepper, Stephen, 116n10
Perception, 114, 125, 203, 288

Perceptual defense, 480
Percipient (term), 175
Perry, Bliss, 332
Perry, Ralph Barton, 48, 102, 559
Personality, 276–277
    character vs., 325, 331, 333–334
    development of, 331
    individuality vs., 332–333
    mature, 338–339
"Personality and Character" (Gordon Allport), 333
"Personality Development in Terms of Gestalt Psychology" conference, 390
Personality (Gordon Allport), 276, 338
Personality psychology, 326
Personnel departments, 370
Perspective, 110, 112, 113
Perspectivism, 115n8
Philanthropy, 309
Philosophers, 147, 149, 156
A Philosophical and Practical Treatise on the Will (Thomas C. Upham), 96n27
Philosophical societies, 160–161
Philosophische Studien, 127, 144
Philosophy, 48, 148, 150, 151
    APA promotion of, 157–161
    William James on, 103–104
    at Johns Hopkins University, 280
    psychology emerging from, 143
    psychology separate from, 62, 92n5, 142
Phobias, 243–245
"Phobias and preparedness" (M. E. P. Seligman), 246
Phrenologists, 309
Phrenology, 310
Physical education movement, 152
Physical matter, orders of, 283
Physics, psychology vs., 68–69
Physiognomic system, 378
Physiological age, 316
Physiological psychology, 85, 89, 199
Physiological Psychology (Clifford T. Morgan), 414
Physiology, 143, 218–219, 288
Piaget, Jean, 19, 256
Picasso, Pablo, 106n1
Piper, Leonora, 129, 133–134
"Plain common sense," 443
Plato, 103, 116n10
"The Poet" (Ralph Waldo Emerson), 106
Poffenberger, A. T., 355, 357, 362, 363
Point Scale, 317

A Point Scale for Measuring Mental Ability (Robert M. Yerkes), 303
Political revolution, 192–193
Polybius, 192
Pond, Millicent, 372
Popular Front politics, 358n5
Popular Scientific Monthly, 125
Population of individuals, 176–177
Porter, Noah, 92n2
Porter, R., 197, 207
Porter's model of revolution, 197
Positive interpersonal relations, 577
Positive social philosophy, 500
Positivism, 310
Positivistic science, 130
Positivist scientific context, 577, 579
Postmodernism, feminist, 30–34
Poststructuralism, 30–34
Powers of the mind, 284
Pragmatism, 201
"Pragmatism" (William James), 130
Pratt, Caroll, 549, 553
Precocity, dangers of, 290, 297
"Prediction and control," 189, 577
Prediction of behavior, 255
Predictive validation, 307, 320
Prejudice, studies in, 399
Prejudice and Your Child (Kenneth B. Clark), 585, 588, 589, 592
Preparedness theory, 245–247
"Presentists," 12
Prichard, Margaret S., 529
Prince, Morton, 473
Princeton University, 150, 156, 390
Principia (Isaac Newton), 194
Principles of Animal Psychology (Norman Maier), 410, 413
Principles of Psychology (William James), 61, 86, 101, 105, 109–116, 129, 199
Private commitment stage (of Cohen model), 196
Private foundations, 351, 386
Probable error equation, 312
Proceedings (APA)
"Production of Effects" (Francis Bacon), 259
Professional advancement (of women), 534–535
Professional associations, 4
Professional degrees, 430
Professionalized benevolence, 332
Professional organizations, 5
Professional social workers, 329
Professorships, 83, 86, 92n3, 279
Progressive era, 513–514
Project Pigeon, 264
Prolegomena (E. B. Titchener), 47
Protestantism, 85
Protestant religious views, 81
Pruett, L., 281
Prytula, R. E., 242
PsD professional degree, 430
Pseudopsychologists, 378
Pseudoscience, 122, 124, 126, 128, 129, 132, 135, 310
Psyche, 221–224
Psychiatric hospitals, 161
Psychiatrists, 147, 276, 446–447
Psychiatry, 460–461, 466
Psychical (term), 126–127
"Psychic secretion," 218, 220, 222–228, 232
Psychoanalysis, 471–486
    Franz Alexander's role in, 478–479
    behaviorist reworkings of, 482–483
    Edwin Boring's role in, 477–478
    campaign for, in America, 474
    founding of, 198
    free association in, 476
    initial responses to, 473–476
    integration of, with mainstream psychology, 485
    internecine struggles within, 486
    popularity of, in 1940s, 479
    rejection of, in 1920s, 476–477
    repression in, 484–485
    responses to, 431–432
    and rise of "scientific" psychology, 472–475
    scientific evaluation of, 479–481
    treatment of, in textbooks, 483–484
    and World War II, 486
Psycholinguistics, 72
Psychological, psychical vs., 126–127
Psychological Bulletin, 156, 200
Psychological Care of Infant and Child (John B. Watson), 241, 242
Psychological experiment, 169–180
    absence of uniform nomenclature for identifying participants in early years of, 170–171
    American innovations in, 176–178
    embeddedness of, in historically limited normative framework, 178–179
    experimental hypnosis as alternative to, 173–176

literature of social psychology of, 169–170
role structure of Wundtian, 172–173
and social contextualization of psychology, 179
and theoretical position vs. social practice of investigation, 179–180
Psychological faculties, orders of, 284
Psychological Index, 154, 156
Psychological Institute of the Hebrew University of Jerusalem, 555
Psychological Institute of the University of Berlin, 387, 393
Psychological Monographs, 144
"Psychological Progress in 1906" (E. F. Buchner), 200
Psychological Review, 62, 127, 149, 150, 154–156, 160, 171
Psychological Review Monographs, 156
Psychological Studies, 144
Psychological tests, Kent-Rosanoff, 4
"Psychological Tests in the Schools of Springfield" (William L. Bryan), 148
Psychologische Studien, 127
"Psychologist in the State Hospital" (David Shakow), 436
Psychologists, 276, 446–447. *See also* Women psychologist(s)
Psychologists League, 350, 358–360, 363–365
Psychology. *See also* Experimental psychology; History of psychology
of aesthetics, 112n4
basic premise of, of Wilhelm Wundt, 66
of belief, 114
bias within, in study of women, 23–25
comparative, 201
debates within, 199
developmental, 153
as litmus test for science, 122
mechanistic, 74
modern reconstructions of, of Wilhelm Wundt, 71–74
national research styles in, 386
1920s popularity of, 514
organismic, 74
and philosophy, 62, 92n5
principles of, 444–445
revolutions in, 198–210
schools of, 98n55
and science, 514
as a science, 60
and social order, 454
spiritualism and blurred boundaries of, 126–128
Psychology: A Factual Textbook (Boring, Langfeld & Weld), 478
Psychology and Industrial Efficiency (Hugo Münsterberg), 370
"Psychology and Social Practice" (John Dewey), 454
Psychology and the Social Order (J. F. Brown), 461
Psychology (as discipline), 143–145
Psychology (as profession), 512–513
African Americans in. *See* Clark, Kenneth B.
aspirations of, 444
during Great Depression, 353–366
opportunities in, 437
responsibilities of, 445
Psychology (John Dewey), 93n16
Psychology Misdirected (S. B. Sarason), 454
The Psychology of Beauty (E. D. Puffer), 539
Psychology of deception and belief, 134–136
Psychology of the Unconscious (Carl Jung), 474
Psychology or a View of the Human Soul (Frederick Rauch), 93n15
Psychometrics, 276, 307
Psychonomic Society, 414
Psychopathology, 18
Psychophysics, 288
Psychosocial problems, 397–398
Psychotechnology, 46, 389
Psychotherapy, 458–459
Publication, 162, 351–352
access to, 408
APA eschewing opportunities in, 154–155
controversial, 419–420
Norman Maier's difficulty in getting, 414
and new psychology, 125
Publications of the University of Pennsylvania, 144
Public education, 589
Public relations, 378–379
Puffer, Ethel Dench, 530, 531, 535, 539–540
Punishment, 394
Pure psychology, 13
Pure research, 46–49
Pure science, 276
Purified behaviorism, 205
Putnam, James Jackson, 101

Q-sort methodology, 33
Quakers, 122, 547
Qualifications of Industrial Psychologists (APA session), 373
Qualitative data, 396
Quantitative data, 396
Die Quasselstrippe, 393
Questionnaire methods, 276, 288–292, 299

"Race man," 594–595
Race psychology, 399
Rachman, S., 243
Racial differences, 549n9
Racial identification, 587
Racial preference, 587
Racial preference studies, 581, 582
"Racial Progress and Retreat" (Kenneth B. Clark), 584
Racial self-concept, 576
Racism, 4, 582, 596, 598
Radcliffe College, 48, 539
Radical behaviorism, 204
Raimy, Victor, 442
Rand, Benjamin, 155
Ranked groups, 29
Rank method, firm, 320
"Rating Scale for Selecting Captains," 321
"Rating Scale for Selecting Salesmen," 319
Rational psychology, 94n20
Rational Psychology (Laurens Hickok), 94n20
Rats, seizures in, 408–417
Rauch, Frederick, 93n15
Rayner, Rosalie, 189, 237–244, 246–249
Reaction formation, 483
Reaction-time measurement, 73–74
Readings in General Psychology (Robinson & Robinson), 483
Reagent (term), 171
Reality, perception of, 114
Real-life situations, 394
Recapitulationism, 315
Reciprocal inhibition, 243
"Recommended Graduate Training Program in Clinical Psychology" (APA), 437
Record keeping, detailed, 330
"Reflections on a Do-It-Yourself Training Program in Clinical Psychology" (David Shakow), 434
"Reflections on Psychology's Past and Concerns About Its Future" (R. C. Atkinson), 447
Reflexes, 188, 225–227, 231–233

Reflexes of the Brain (I. M. Sechenov), 231
Reform movement, 513–516
Regression studies, 397
Reid, Thomas, 79
Reinharz, Shulamit, 25
Reliability, 313
Religion, 97n34, 298
Religiously based philanthropy, 329
Religious sentiments, 291
Remembered consciousness, 199
Renaissance, 17
Repression, 480, 482, 484–485
Research Center for Group Dynamics (MIT), 390, 399
Respect, 593, 599
Responsibilities
    for acquiring professional competence, 442
    of psychologist, 438–439
    of the state in multiracial society, 589
Restrictivist ideologies, 354, 355, 363
Retreads, 11–12
Review. See Psychological Review
Revolution on paper stage (of Cohen model), 196
Revolution(s), 188, 191–210
    behaviorist, 198–203
    cognitive, 203–209
    Cohen's criteria for, 196–197
    concept of, 192–193
    Kuhn's stages of scientific, 194–195
    Porter's model of, 197
    in psychology, 198–210
    in science, 193–197
Revolution stage (of Cohen model), 196
Revolution stage (of scientific revolution), 195
Reward, 394
Reynolds–Starnes immigration bill, 360
Rich, Gilbert Joseph, 548, 559
Richards, Graham, 340
Richet, Charles, 124, 173
Richmond, Mary, 329–331
Riger, Stephanie, 13
Roback, Abraham A.
    and antisemitism, 547, 549, 552, 559, 561–566
    on character, 334
    A History of American Psychology of, 81, 561
    Jewish Influence in Modern Thought, 561
    and psychoanalysis, 474

Robbins, William J., 550
Robinson, E. S., 483
Robinson, F. R., 483
Rochester (New York), 122
Rockefeller Foundation, 389, 390, 392
Rodman, Selden, 361
Rogers, Carl, 438, 443, 458
Rose, Nikolas, 340
Rosenblith, Walter, 563–564
Rosenzweig, Saul, 556, 557, 568
Ross, D., 127, 281, 287
Rousmaniere, Frances H., 529
Rowland, Eleanor Harris, 529
Royce, Josiah, 147, 150, 162
Ruch, Floyd, 380
Ruckmich, Christian A., 127
"Rules of the ghetto," 597
Russell, Bertrand, 599
Rutgers University, 287

Sachs, Hans, 477, 478
Sacks, Oliver, 116n10
Sage Fellowship. *See* Susan Linn Sage Fellowship in Philosophy and Ethics
St. Petersburg Military–Medical Academy, 219n2
Salivation, 221–224
Salvation of humankind, 263, 267
Samelson, F., 248, 500, 560
Sanford, Edmund C., 146, 151, 152, 156, 158, 160
Sanford, Fill, 443–444
Sanford, Nevitt, 435, 440
Santayana, George, 102, 115n8
Sarason, Seymour B., 431, 454
Sarnoff, I., 480
Scalar method, 319
Scattershot approach, 314
Schallenberger, Margaret Everitt, 533
Schanck, Richard L., 560
Schiller, F. C. S., 514
Schizophrenia, 72, 436
Schlesinger, Kurt, 16–20
Schlosberg, H., 73
Schoenfeld, W., 482
Schoolchildren, 314
School integration, 588–590
School of Home Economics (Cornell), 390
School processes and practices, 292
Schools, 314–316
School segregation, 3
Schools for the feebleminded, 161

Schools of psychology, 98n55
Schopenhauer, Artur, 75
Schultz, D. P., 169
Schurman, Jacob Gould, 149
Schwartz, B. J., 480
Schwedensche Café, 393
Science
    bias against women in positivist, 22–23
    feminist challenges to "neutrality" of, 26–34
    history of, 500
    Plato on, 103
    and psychology, 514
    psychology as litmus test for, 122
    revolutions in, 193–197
    B. F. Skinner and technological ideal of, 255–269
Science, 125, 130, 155, 410
Science and Human Behavior (B. F. Skinner), 482
Science-based profession, 386
Scientific eras, 194
"Scientific imperative," 512
Scientific methods, 21–23
Scientific Monthly, 242
Scientific naturalism, 135
Scientific positivism, 577, 579
Scientific psychology, 472–473, 475
Scientific revolutions, 194–195
Scientific social psychology, 514
The Scientific Spirit and Social Work (Arthur Todd), 330
Scientific thinking, 330
Scientist–activist, 577, 585
Scientist/professional model, 442
Scientists (as judges of spiritualistic phenomena), 124
Scodel, A., 480
Scott, Walter Dill, 305, 307, 318–320, 370
Scottish philosophy, 89, 91
Scottish realism, 143, 144, 309
Scottish school, 80, 83
Scripture, E. W., 134
Search for goodness, 334
Sears, Robert, 480–481
Seashore, Carl E., 304–305, 362, 391, 483
Sechenov, Ivan Mikhailovich, 223, 231, 232
Secondary education, 309
Secord, Paul, 37
Secretin, 226
Section D (AAAP), 375–380
Section on Clinical Psychology (APA), 371

Seelye, Julius, 93n16
Segregation, 3
    Kenneth Clark and, 576, 580–588
    effects of, on White people, 591–592
    in public facilities, 598
"Segregation as a Factor in the Racial Identification of Negro Pre-School Children" (Clark & Clark), 586
Seizures, in rats, 408–417
Selective attention, 73–74
Self-evaluation programs, 446
Self-help, 315
Selfhood, 325, 328, 334–335, 341
Self-image, 28
Self-introspection, 198, 199
Seligman, M. E. P., 245–247
Seminaries, 83
Semisegregated schools, 587
Senescence (G. Stanley Hall), 298
Sensation, 125, 203, 288
"The sensibilities," 84
"Sensitives," 132–133
Sensory tests, 134, 152
Separatism, 596, 601
"Series of Physical and Mental Tests on the Students of Columbia College" (Livingston Farrand), 151
Serpell, Robert, 579n5
Sex differences research, 23
Sex-of-experimenter effects, 23
Shaffer, L. F., 433
Shaffer, Laurance, 440
Shakespeare, William, 16, 105
Shakow, David, 4, 430–431, 436, 440, 444, 568
Shared exemplar, 208
Sharp, Stella, 533
Shartle, Carroll, 372, 375, 378, 380
Shaw, Robert E., 206
Shellow, Sadie, 372, 378
Shepard, John, 410
Shinn, Millicent, 529, 530, 534
"Should a Child Have More Than One Mother?" (J.B. Watson), 509
Sidgwick, Henry, 124
Sidis, Boris, 552
Siegel, M., 439
Silent Spring (Rachel Carson), 265
Silverman, J., 72
Simmons College, 539
Simon, H. A., 205, 208
Simon, Theodore, 314–318

Skeels, Harold, 391
Skinner, B. F., 6, 188–190, 255–269, 482–483
    on aim of behavioral science, 255
    and Baconian tradition, 257–269
    Beyond Freedom and Dignity of, 264
    and experimental method, 261–262
    operant psychology of, 259–261, 267–269
    Science and Human Behavior of, 482
    and society's growing disillusionment with technology, 265–266
    on technology of behavior, 267–268
    Walden Two of, 257, 263–265, 268–269
Skinner box, 260
Smith, Dorothy, 28
Smith, Laurence D., 189
Smith, Robert Pearsall, 145
Smith, Stevenson, 335, 436, 548
Smith College, 539, 551
Snarskii, A. T., 223–227, 231, 232
SNCC (Student Nonviolent Coordinating committee), 596
Social adjustment, 201
Social–biological conception of childhood, 299
Social change, 308–310
Social class, 309, 310, 314, 316
Social context, 179, 307–308, 588
"Social Critic or Social Apologist" (Kenneth B. Clark), 583
Social darwinism, 354
Social ethics, 329
Socialism, 351
Socialist outlook, 358
Socialist (term), 358n6
Socialist thinking, 388
The Socialization of the Taylor System (Kurt Lewin), 388, 398
Social order, 454
"Social proof structures," 180
Social psychology, 398, 399, 401, 461, 467, 576
Social Psychology (F. H. Allport), 501, 515
Social regeneration, 123
Social relations, 37
Social science, bias against women in, 22–23
Social Science Research Council, 480
"Social space," 398
Social work, 329–332
Society, dominant ideology of, 37

Society for Psychical Research (SPR), 126, 127, 130, 133
Society for the Psychological Study of Social Issues (SPSSI), 350, 365, 366, 374, 380, 399, 585, 599
Society of Experimentalists, 50
Society of Experimental Psychologists, 158, 414
Society of Naturalists of the Eastern United States, 142
Sociocultural factors, 28
"Socio-Psychological Problems of a Minority Group" (Kurt Lewin), 397–398
Sokal, Michael M., 62
Solem, Allen, 415
Solomon, M., 473, 565
"Solomon's House," 262, 513
Some Common Traits and Habits questionnaire, 290
Somnambulists, 174
Spearman, Charles, 308, 312–318, 320
Species mentality, 316
Spence, Kenneth, 399
Sperling, G., 73, 199
Spiritualism, 122–136
    blurred boundaries of psychology and, 126–128
    Thomas Davidson and, 123–124
    enthusiasm for, in 19th century, 122–123
    experimental psychology's response to, 127–135
    G. Stanley Hall and, 124, 132–134, 145
    William James and, 61, 123–125, 129–131
    origins of American, 122
    research on, 128–134
    and rise of experimental psychology, 125–126
    and scientific naturalism, 135
SPR. *See* Society for Psychical Research
SPSSI. *See* Society for the Psychological Study of Social Issues
Squire, Carrie Ransom, 529–531, 533, 534
S–R psychology, 351
S–R theories. *See* Stimulus–response theories
Stagner, Ross, 362, 364, 365
Standards
    in applied psychology, 371
    in clinical psychology, 448
    for graduate schools, 356–357
    in industrial psychology, 372–373
    for professionals, 355n1
Standing Committee on Psychological and Philosophical Terminology, 153
Stanford-Binet. *See* Stanford Revision of the Binet Scale
Stanford Conference (1957), 442
Stanford Revision of the Binet Scale (Stanford-Binet), 306, 317
Stanford University, 128, 129, 142, 389, 397, 535, 554
Staples, Robert, 576
Starch, Daniel, 372
Starling, E. H., 226
State University of Iowa, 385, 393
Statistical studies, 177
"Statistics of the American Psychological Association in 1920" (E. G. Boring), 51
Stavsky, W. H., 551
Stein, Gertrude, 116n10
Stellar, Eliot, 421
Sternberg, S., 74
Sterns, William, 315
Stevens, Wallace, 116n10
Stevenson, Robert Louis, 112n4
Stewart, Dugald, 79, 83, 87, 91n2, 97n44
Stimulus generation, 242
Stimulus–response (S–R) theories, 205, 208, 209
Stoddard, George, 390–392, 396, 401
Stone, Calvin P., 417, 418, 420
Stone, Didi, 564
Straight liners, 12
Strict behaviorism, 204
Strong, E. K., Jr., 372
Structuralism, 89–90
Structural psychology, 48, 199
The Structure of Scientific Revolutions (Thomas Kuhn), 193–195, 206, 210
Student Nonviolent Coordinating committee (SNCC), 596
Students
    responsibilities of, 442
    selection of, 441
Studies in prejudice, 399
Studies in Psychology, 144
"Studies of Abnormal Behavior in the Rat" (Norman Maier), 412
"The Study of Children" (G. Stanley Hall), 146
"The Study of Undivided Personality" (Gordon Allport), 337

Subjectivity, 34, 475–476, 479, 485
Subject (term), 170–177
Subjugated knowledge, 29
Success, reactions to, 394
Sumner, Francis Cecil, 584
Supervision (of training), 437
Surveys, 33
Susan Linn Sage Fellowship in Philosophy and Ethics, 532, 533
Susman, Warren, 328, 331
Symposium on Information Theory at MIT, 204–205
Synthetic fibers, 258n1
Systematic Psychology (E. B. Titchener), 47
A System of Moral Science (Laurens Hickok), 94n19

Tachistoscope, 73
Tachistoscopic method, 199
Talbot, Ellen Bliss, 529, 533
"Tangle of pathology," 586
Tanner, Amy, 128–129, 133–134
"Tasks of parenthood," 317
Taylor, Charles, 582
Taylor, E. W., 473
Teachers, 592
Teaching (as a profession for women), 533, 534
Technocratic approach, 400
Technological ideal, 256, 258, 260, 266
Technology
    large-scale applications of, 268
    problems of, 267
    society's growing disillusionment with, 265–266
Telegraph, 122
Temporal extension of thought, 125
"Tension system," 388
Terman, Lewis M.
    and antisemitism, 548, 553–555
    and Army testing, 307
    on Edwin Boring, 52
    on Harvard's laboratory, 48
    and Kurt Lewin, 389
    and mental testing, 306, 315–318
    and standards, 355
Terminology, 153, 170–171, 175
Testing, 276. *See also* Mental testing
Test of Ascendance–Submission, 335, 337
Textbook of Psychology (D. O. Hebb), 483
Textbooks
    William James' lead followed by writers of, 97n37
    Little Albert study treatment in, 241–243, 247, 248
    pre-Civil War, 93n16
    psychoanalysis treatment in, 483–484
    Wilhelm Wundt's treatment in, 66, 67
Themata, 210
Theologians, 96n31
The Theory of Advertising (W. D. Scott), 370
Thilly, Frank, 160
Thompson, Helen Bradford, 34, 529–531, 533–535
Thompson, Lorin, Jr., 373
Thorndike, Edward L.
    and antisemitism, 555
    education impacted by, 297
    and mental testing, 305, 307, 312, 313, 318–321
    and psychological experiments, 177
Through the Looking Glass (L. Carroll), 31
Thurstone, L. L., 354, 355, 439
Tigerstedt, Robert, 218
Time magazine, 411
Timofeev, A. V., 223
Titchener, Edward B., 19
    and antisemitism, 548
    and APA, 147
    and APA presidential bid, 50
    on bankruptcy of commonsense psychologizing, 53
    on behaviorism, 46
    Edwin Boring on, 52
    and Experimentalists Conference, 306
    and experimental psychology, 46–48, 158, 159
    introspective techniques of, 199, 202
    Prolegomena of, 47
    and spiritualism, 128, 130, 134
    on structuralism, 89–90
    Systematic Psychology of, 47
    and Mary Floy Washburn, 536
    and Wundtian psychology, 68
    and Robert M. Yerkes, 306
Todd, Arthur, 330
Toddlers, 290
Todes, Daniel P., 188
Tolman, Edward Chace, 19
    and antisemitism, 555, 557, 567
    as APA president, 365, 366
    at Harvard, 48
    as neobehaviorist, 399
    and psychology revolutions, 204, 208, 209

Tolochinov, I. F., 225–232
Tolstoy, Leo, 105
Tomkins, Silvan, 561
Tomorrow (Hugo Münsterberg), 507–508
Topics in the History of Psychology (Kimble & Schlesinger), 16–20
Topology groups, 399
Toulmin, S. E., 501
Trabue, Marion R.
The Tragic Muse (Henry James), 116
Training
    APA issues of, 430
    Boulder Conference on, 441–442
    evaluation of, 440–441
    for industrial psychologists, 373, 377, 378
    David Shakow on, 436–448
    standards for, 429–431
    universities' role in, 446
"Training in Democratic Leadership" (Bavelas & Lewin), 399
Trait theory, 337–338
Transcendentalism, 92n8
Transposition principle, 396
"Transracial identity," 598, 600–601
Trinitarian Congregationalism, 83
Trist, Eric, 555
Troland, Leonard Thompson, 129
Truth, 584
Tsitovich, I. S., 227

Uhrbrock, R. S., 372–374, 378
Ujamaa and Latino Leadership Schools (NYC), 593, 601
Understanding, 189, 255–256, 266
"Understanding and unification," 577
Unemployed Teachers Association, 359
Unger, Rhoda, 33, 34
Union College, 82, 83
Union Theological Seminary, 287
Uniqueness, 335
Unitarian theology, 83
United States
    beginnings of psychology in, 60–61
    culture of, 395
    independence of, 92n9
    mental testing in, 310–311
    origins in psychology in, 81–82
    psychological experiment innovations in, 176–178
    university network in, 386
Universities
    classic studies at, 312
    growth of psychology departments in, 161–162
    modern, 309–310
    state, 142
University network, 386
University of Berlin, 385, 387, 393, 410
University of California, Los Angeles, 561
University of California, Santa Barbara, 414
University of Chicago, 129, 142, 146, 288, 362, 364, 410
University of Colorado, 442
University of Illinois, 127, 206
University of Illinois–Chicago, 431
University of Iowa, 555n15
University of Iowa Studies in Child Welfare series, 391
University of Kansas, 549
University of Leipzig, 59
University of Maine, 560
University of Michigan, 410, 411
University of Minnesota, 206
University of Missouri, 160
University of Pennsylvania, 92n3, 144, 148, 152, 370, 433
University of Pittsburgh, 548
University of Rochester, 412
University of Texas, 414
University of Vermont, 559–560
University of Washington, 548
University of Wisconsin, 127, 146, 414
Unlearned human emotions, 240
Updegraff, Ruth, 391
Upham, Thomas C., 60, 82–85, 87–88, 91n2, 96n27
    American Sketches of, 93n9
    case for arts and literature by, 93n9
    Elements of Intellectual Philosophy of, 91n2, 93n16, 95n26
    Elements of Mental Philosophy of, 88, 91n2, 93n16, 96n26
    inclusiveness of, 98n48
    A Philosophical and Practical Treatise on the Will of, 96n27
    study of number 7 in Bible, 95n23
Upper classes, 313
U.S. Army testing program, 248, 355
U.S. Bureau of Education, 151
U.S. Office of Defense Transportation, 379
U.S. Public Health Service, 430, 437, 440, 442
U.S. Selective Service, 430

U.S. Supreme Court, 3–4, 580, 585, 591, 592
Utility theory, 318
Utopianism, 262–265, 499–517
    of G. Stanley Hall, 502–504
    of William McDougall, 504–507
    of Hugo Münsterberg, 507–509
    and psychology, 512–513
    of John B. Watson, 509–512

VA. *See* Veterans Administration
Vagner, V. A., 223
Vail Conference (1976), 442
Valentine, C. W., 245
Validity, 200, 276, 307–308, 311–321
Value-neutrality, 333
Values, 37
Van den Haag, E., 581
Van Elteren, M., 400
Vassar College, 536
Vestiges of the Natural History of Creation (Robert Chambers), 284
Veterans, 454–455
Veterans Administration (VA), 430, 438, 440, 455–456, 463, 464, 466, 467
View of the Evidences of Christianity (William Paley), 83
Viteles, Morris, 372, 373, 375, 379, 557, 558
Volition, 68, 71
Völkerpsychologie (W. Wundt), 60, 74, 75
Vul'fson, S. G, 221–224, 231, 232

Walden Two (B. F. Skinner), 257, 263–265, 268–269
Wallace, Alfred Russell, 123
War, double effect of, 513
Ward, Harry F., 361
Warren, H. C., 483
Warren, Howard C., 150, 156
Washburn, Margaret Floy, 529, 530, 532, 533, 535–538
Washington Post, 411
"Was This Analysis a Success?" (E. G. Boring), 478
Watson, Goodwin, 365
Watson, J. G., 47
Watson, John B., 6, 208, 333, 335, 476, 482, 500, 501
    on aim of behavioral science, 255
    and artificial markets, 269
    and behaviorism, 46
    Behaviorism of, 241
    in behaviorist revolution, 187–189, 198
    conditioning research of, 238
    and Little Albert study, 237–249
    on personality, 331–332
    on psychoanalysis, 202
    Psychological Care of Infant and Child of, 241, 242
    utopianism of, 509–512, 514, 515
Watson, R. I., Sr., 527
Watson, Robert I., 82
Watson, Rosalie Rayner. *See* Rayner, Rosalie
Wayland, Francis, 60, 82–85, 93n16, 94n19
Wechsler-Bellevue Scale, 358
"We-feelings," 398
Weisstein, Naomi, 23
Weld, H. P., 478
Wellesley College, 149, 536–539
Wellman, Beth, 391
Wells, Frederic, 431, 473
Wells College, 536
Weltanschauung, 194, 509
Werner, H., 71, 74, 568
Werner, Heinz, 556, 557
Wertheimer, Max, 388, 390, 410, 557
Wesleyan University, 287
Western Philosophical Association, 160
Western Reserve University, 551, 558, 559
Wever, E. G., 550
"What Is a Trait of Personality?" (Gordon Allport), 337
What Is Social Case Work? (Mary Richmond), 331
Wheeler, R. H., 549, 555
"When Facing Danger" (Kurt Lewin), 398
"Whig" histories, 12
Whigs, 16
White, E. B., 411
White, J. H., 549
White, Morton, 513
White, Robert, 394
White, Sheldon H., 275
Whitehead, Alfred North, 116n10
White House Conference, 298
White House Conference monograph (Clark), 580, 585
White people, effects of segregation on, 591–592
White Tower Restaurant, 598
"Whole child professions," 289
Wiener, M., 480
Will, 84, 96n27, 115n8, 288
    and child development, 290–291
    research on, 387, 388

Williams, K., 202
Williams, Mabel Clare, 529–531, 533
Williams College, 96n29, 275, 281–282, 285–287
Williston Seminary, 281
"The Will to Believe" (William James), 130
Wilson, G. D., 481
Wilson, L. N., 289
Wilson, T. D., 208
Wilson, William Julius, 576
Winston, A. s., 555n15
Wissler, Clark, 311
Witchcraft persecutions, 18
Witmer, Lightner, 148, 152, 159, 370, 433
Wolpe, Joseph, 243, 245
Womanist scientific principle, 576n1
Women, 442
    in APA, 150
    bias within psychology in study of, 23–25
    bias within social science against, 22–23
    Kurt Lewin and, 393
    role of, in experiments, 173
Women psychologist(s), 527–541
    in Cattell's *American Men of Science*, 528–532, 535
    characteristics of early, 532–535
    omission of, from history of psychology, 528
    professional experiences of early, 535–540
Women's Christian Temperance Union, 328
Women's colleges, 534–536
"Women's sphere," 530
Woodworth, Robert S., 88
    and antisemitism, 546, 550–551, 566
    and behaviorism, 202, 203
    and mental testing, 312
    and psychoanalysis, 475
    Psychology of, 248
Woolley, Helen. *See* Thompson, Helen Bradford
Worcester (Massachusetts), 288
Worcester State Hospital (MA), 431, 436, 465, 568
Word association tests, 134
Wordsworth, William, 104, 106, 109
Works Progress Administration (WPA), 350, 358–359
World Columbian Exposition (1893), 146–148, 151

World War I
    applied psychology after, 46–47, 49
    mental testing in, 306, 320–321
    military personnel testing during, 4
    psychologists used during, 276, 306
    psychology after, 370–371
    U.S. Army testing program during, 248
World War II
    applied psychology during/after, 430
    clinical psychology accelerated by, 437, 454–459
    industrial psychology during, 379–380
    popularity of psychoanalysis after, 431
    and psychoanalysis, 486
WPA. *See* Works Progress Administration
WPA Teachers Union, 359
Wundt, Max, 70
Wundt, Wilhelm, 7, 19, 65–76
    and abnormal psychology, 72
    American misinterpretations of, 310
    and associationism, 69
    basic premise of psychology of, 66
    on Cattell's research, 91
    on elemental processes, 70–71
    and experimental psychology, 59, 67–68
    experiment criteria of, 199
    G. Stanley Hall as student of, 275
    historical contexts of, 74–76
    journal of, 127
    methodology of, 66–68
    modern reconstructions of psychology of, 71–74
    Philosophische Studien of, 144
    and psycholinguistics, 72
    psychology of, 81
    and psychology revolutions, 188, 198–199, 202, 203, 210
    research community of, 170
    and selective attention, 73–74
    and A. T. Snarski, 223, 224
    theoretical system of, 68–69
    theory of affect of, 72–73
    treatment of, in psychology texts, 66, 67
    Völkerpsychologie of, 60, 74, 75
Wundtian experiments
    limitations of, 174
    role structure of, 172–173

Yale University, 91n2, 287, 351, 431, 465
Yerkes, Robert M., 4

and John Anderson, 51
　　and antisemitism, 551
　　and APA, 380
　　and Army testing, 46
　　at Harvard, 48
　　and mental testing, 303–307, 316–321
　　A *Point Scale for Measuring Mental Ability* of, 303
　　and Margaret Floy Washburn, 538
Young, Robert, 46

Young America, 361
Youth of the Ghetto (Kenneth B. Clark), 599
Yungenfroid, 434

Zaire, 579n5
Zeigarnik, B., 397
Zener, Karl, 550
Zigler, Michael, 559
Ziman, J. M., 408

ABOUT THE EDITORS

Wade E. Pickren grew up in then-rural central Florida, where he roamed the forests and orange groves. After an early adulthood marked by communal living, hitchhiking around the country, and serving as a Christian minister, he returned to college and completed his BS in psychology at the University of Central Florida. He left the ministry when he entered the University of Florida's Graduate Program in Clinical and Health Psychology, intending to become a clinical psychologist. However, after he completed his MA in clinical psychology, he took a history of psychology course with Donald A. Dewsbury and found his true intellectual interest. He switched programs and earned his PhD in the history of psychology with a minor in the history of science. He now serves as director of archives and library services at the American Psychological Association and is the editor of the section on the history of psychology and obituaries in the *American Psychologist*. His scholarly interests include the history of post-World War II American psychology, psychology and the public, and the history of religion and psychology.

Donald A. Dewsbury was born in Brooklyn, New York; grew up on Long Island; and received an AB degree from Bucknell University in Lewisburg, Pennsylvania. After completing his PhD in psychology at the University of Michigan with Edward L. Walker, he spent a year as a postdoctoral fellow at the University of California at Berkeley with Frank A. Beach. Through much of his career he has been a comparative psychologist with a special interest in the evolution of reproductive and social behavior. He now works primarily in the area of the history of psychology, with an interest in comparative psychology. He is the author or editor of 12 books, including *Comparative Animal Behavior* (1978) and *Comparative Psychology in the Twentieth Century* (1984). He has published more than 300 articles and book chapters. He is a fellow of the American Psychological Association's (APA) Division 1

(Society for General Psychology), 2 (Society for the Teaching of Psychology), 6 (Behavioral Neuroscience and Comparative Psychology), and 26 (History of Psychology); of the American Association for the Advancement of Science; of the American Psychological Society; and of the Animal Behavior Society (ABS). He has served as president of the ABS and of APA's Divisions 6 and 26. He is the historian for Divisions 1, 6, and 26; of the Psychonomic Society; of the ABS; and of the Cheiron Society.